Teaching to Change the World

Teaching to Change the World is an up-to-the-moment, engaging, social justice–oriented introduction to education and teaching, and the challenges and opportunities they present. Both foundational and practical, the chapters are organized around conventional topics but in a way that consistently integrates a coherent story that explains why schools are as they are. Taking the position that a hopeful, democratic future depends on ensuring that all students learn, the text pays particular attention to inequalities associated with race, social class, language, gender, and other social categories and explores teachers' role in addressing them.

This thoroughly revised fifth edition remains a vital introduction to the profession for a new generation of teachers who seek to become purposeful, knowledgeable practitioners in our ever-changing educational landscape—for those teachers who see the potential for education to change the world.

Features and Updates of the New Edition:

- Fully updated Chapter 1, "The U.S. Schooling Dilemma," reflects our current state of education after the 2016 U.S. presidential election.
- First-person observations from teachers, including first-year teachers, continue to offer vivid, authentic pictures of what teaching to change the world means and involves.
- Additional coverage of the ongoing effects of Common Core highlights the heated public discourse around teaching and teachers, and charter schools.
- Attention to diversity and inclusion is treated as integral to all chapters, woven throughout rather than tacked on as separate units.
- "Digging Deeper" resources on the new companion website include concrete resources that current and future teachers can use in their classrooms.
- "Tools for Critique" provides instructors and students questions, prompts, and activities aimed at encouraging classroom discussion and particularly engaging those students least familiar with the central tenets of social justice education.

Jeannie Oakes is Presidential Professor (Emeritus) in Educational Equity at UCLA's Graduate School of Education and Information Studies and founding director of UCLA's Center X: Where Research and Practice Intersect for Urban School Professionals.

Martin Lipton is an education writer and consultant, a communications analyst at UCLA's Institute for Democracy, Education, and Access, and a former public high school teacher.

Lauren Anderson is an associate professor of education at Connecticut College and a former upper-elementary teacher.

Jamy Stillman is an associate professor of educational equity and cultural diversity at the University of Colorado Boulder and a former bilingual elementary teacher.

Teaching to Change the World

Fifth Edition

Jeannie Oakes
Martin Lipton
Lauren Anderson
Jamy Stillman

Routledge
Taylor & Francis Group

NEW YORK AND LONDON

Fifth edition published 2018
by Routledge
711 Third Avenue, New York, NY 10017

and by Routledge
2 Park Square, Milton Park, Abingdon, Oxon, OX14 4RN

Routledge is an imprint of the Taylor & Francis Group, an informa business

First edition published by McGraw Hill 1999
Fourth edition published by Paradigm 2013

Library of Congress Cataloging-in-Publication Data
Names: Oakes, Jeannie, author.
Title: Teaching to change the world / [Jeannie Oakes, Martin Lipton, Lauren
   Anderson, Jamy Stillman].
Description: Fifth edition, revised and updated. | New York : Routledge, 2018. |
   Includes bibliographical references and index.
Identifiers: LCCN 2017037151 | ISBN 9781138569263 (Hardback : alk. paper) |
   ISBN 9781138569362 (Paperback : alk. paper) | ISBN 9781351263443 (eBook)
Subjects: LCSH: Public schools—United States. | Curriculum planning—United States. |
   Classroom management—United States. | Effective teaching—United States. |
   Educational change—United States.
Classification: LCC LA217.2 .O25 2018 | DDC 371.010973—dc23
LC record available at https://lccn.loc.gov/2017037151

ISBN: 978-1-138-56926-3 (hbk)
ISBN: 978-1-138-56936-2 (pbk)
ISBN: 978-1-351-26344-3 (ebk)

Typeset in Galliard
by Apex CoVantage, LLC

Visit the companion website: www.routledge.com/cw/teachingtochangetheworld

Contents

Figures, Concept Tables, and Focal Points

Figures

Concept Tables

Focal Points

Preface

This book provides a comprehensive introduction to teaching in twenty-first-century American schools. Both foundational and practical, the chapters address conventional topics—history, philosophy, curriculum, instruction, classroom management, school culture, policy, and so on.

The book also has a point of view: a hopeful, democratic future needs schools that provide *all* students with a *socially just education* including *rigorous, authentic learning experiences*.

Socially just education requires that teachers look beneath the surface of school structures and practices and

- consider the values and politics that pervade education, along with the technical issues of teaching and organizing schools;
- ask critical questions about how conventional thinking and practice came to be, and who in society benefits from them; and
- pay attention to inequalities associated with race, social class, language, gender, and other social categories, while looking for alternatives to those inequalities.

Rigorous, authentic learning experiences require that teachers, schools, and the larger education system

- use curricula, teaching practices, and assessment approaches that promote intellectual development and prepare students to be knowledgeable citizens, capable workforce participants, contributing members of families and communities, and empowered agents of change in their lives and the lives of others; and
- provide learning opportunities that engage students in *constructing knowledge*—whereby they actively integrate new knowledge with their prior learning and experiences—in contrast to teachers *transmitting knowledge*—whereby students are passive recipients of facts their teachers give to them.

Accordingly, this book does not offer a smorgasbord of educational theories and practices that readers can browse and then choose from as suits their preferences. We have tried to be diligent in faithfully describing prominent theories, philosophies, and practices—historical and current—that comprise education in the United States. But we would be neither honest nor objective if we described schooling in a neutral manner. Just as the world is not a neutral place, teaching is not a neutral profession.

Making choices that advance social justice and promote rigorous, authentic learning requires of teachers certain personal qualities—integrity, decency, the capacity to work very hard, and so on. This book hopes to bolster these personal qualities with professional and scholarly insights drawn from social theory broadly, and educational research in particular. Indeed, grounding teaching in a deeper understanding of the theory and evidence that underlie education practices makes teachers' decisions about their own work credible to others and, just as important, sustainable for themselves.

Overview of the Book and Its Organization

The twelve chapters of this book are grouped into three parts:

1. The *foundations* of education, which provides an overview of the history, philosophy, politics, and policy of schooling in the United States.
2. The *practice* of teaching, which addresses subject matter, instruction, assessment, and classroom management—all important aspects of teachers' day-to-day work.
3. The *contexts* for learning and leading, which explores issues related to school culture and organization, the local community (specifically, the relationship between families and teachers, communities and schools), and the profession.

Each of these parts is preceded by a short introduction that orients the reader, offers more detail about the ensuing chapters, and eases the transition from one part of the book to the next.

Because of the book's integrated, thematic approach, there are no separate chapters here on multicultural education, bilingual education, or special education. Rather, the book treats diversity and inclusion as integral to all aspects of education—curriculum and instruction, classroom management, assessment and testing, grouping, school culture, and so on—and thus integrates attention to them in every chapter.

Similarly, throughout the book we emphasize the sociological, historical, and philosophical foundations of education. The first three chapters foreground these foundations. But because foundations make the most sense when we can see how they support actual practices and concerns, each chapter also includes the history, philosophical positions, and social theories most relevant to that chapter's topic. Some chapters present entirely new foundational material; others offer a new view of material presented earlier.

A Chorus of Teachers' Voices

Throughout the book, we also include the observations of teachers—using their own words. The words of most teachers whom we cite come from their UCLA master's degree portfolios. Most, but not all, of their observations were written during their first year of teaching. Four of these teachers are introduced in some detail in Chapter 1, since they and their students appear in photographs and excerpts scattered throughout the book.

We would expect these teachers, like most new teachers, to experience some struggles related to lesson planning, classroom and time management, paperwork, school bureaucracy, and so on. And, of course, they do. But listen carefully to their voices; what is crucial is not just that they struggle, but the quality of the problems with which they struggle. Their struggles reflect their commitments to rigorous, authentic learning experiences and to the pursuit of social justice. And their comments reveal the profound relevance of educational theory to their teaching practices and their problem-solving efforts.

We recommend that all potential teachers write about their experiences, thoughts, and observations, as the teachers quoted in this book have done. Whether a personal journal or a portfolio that presents a full record of a teacher-candidate's intellectual and professional growth, a written record inevitably provides rich opportunities for reflection and learning.

rces: "Digging Deeper" and "Tools for Critique"

ound *Teaching to Change the World* provocative and challenging, but also
sting to read and learn from. That said, making the most of the book requires
mmarizing the material. It requires that readers furnish what the book itself
...cussion, reflection, and elaboration that press readers to make sense of the
material in light of their own experiences, observations, and prior knowledge.

To help readers get started with that discussion, we offer two online resources located on the book's website at www.routledge.com/cw/teachingtochangetheworld. By placing these resources online, we hope to make them more accessible to readers, who can find them wherever they have Internet access. Web-based tools are also easier to update, which means we can provide pertinent resources as they become available, rather than waiting for publication of the book's next edition.

The first online resource is called "Digging Deeper." It includes chapter-by-chapter lists that readers can consult if they want to dig more deeply into the chapter's content. These lists identify scholars who are studying or working on practical applications of issues we raise, and some of the books and articles that readers might find interesting and useful. When applicable, the lists also include professional organizations and activist groups working to make education policy or school practices more consistent with and supportive of socially just teaching. And, when possible, we include resources that current and future teachers can use in their classrooms.

The second online resource is called "Tools for Critique." It provides a set of prompts and activities meant to provoke thinking about the topics and points of view in the book. Its chapter-specific overviews, and additional resources can serve as a springboard for supporting readers to think critically about and get the most out of the text. Prompts might ask, for example, What memories of your own schooling or other experiences does the book stir up? What, if any, aspects of the text make you angry? What sounds reasonable, but you can't believe it is true? What have you always known, but you didn't know you knew it? What do you imagine your acquaintances would think about the material? What questions are you asking?

Toward Teaching to Change the World

The ultimate goal of this book and its accompanying resources is to help new teachers take the first steps toward "teaching to change the world." Judy Smith, one of the teachers quoted in this book, describes her experience taking these first steps. We wish just such beginnings for all the readers of this book.

> Teaching challenges my every fiber—from lesson design to classroom management. My first year in the classroom showed me the tremendous joy of teaching and the work that must be done to be the best teacher I can be. Through constant self-reflection, student work assessment, and professional development, I am learning the craft to better bridge theory and practice and to better bridge students, parents, and the community. Through academically rigorous and culturally responsive curriculum, my students and I can begin to transform the school and the community. Indeed, the focus of my classroom is on all of our responsibility to make the community and the world a better place.
>
> —Judy Smith
> High school social studies

New to the Fifth Edition

Teaching to Change the World has a new publisher. We are pleased to join Routledge, a leading academic publisher in the humanities and social sciences. A division of the Taylor & Francis

Group, Routledge publishes books and journals each year for scholars, instructors, and professional communities around the world. Changes in the text itself include the following:

- Up-to-date statistics, graphs and figures, and timeline.
- Updated content with special attention to

  - key education policy initiatives like the Every Student Succeeds Act, as well as the shifts in federal education policy preferences following the 2016 presidential election, such as school choice, vouchers, and privatization;
  - the development of, implementation of, and controversies around the Common Core State Standards and aligned assessments;
  - the heated public discourse about teachers and teaching—specifically, debates about teacher quality, teacher education, and teacher evaluation; and
  - the growing influence of education organizing that brings community members and teachers together around the common cause of ensuring that all youth have access to just and equitable schooling experiences.

- A new, more extensive, open-access online supplement that includes chapter-by-chapter "Digging Deeper" lists and "Tools for Critique," both of which incorporate an extended range of suggested readings, resources, and organizations that professors, teachers, and teacher education students can draw on in their work. Available at www.routledge.com/cw/teachingtochangetheworld.

About the Authors

Jeannie Oakes is Presidential Professor (Emeritus) in Educational Equity at UCLA's Graduate School of Education and Information Studies, where she was the founding director of UCLA's Center X: Where Research and Practice Intersect for Urban School Professionals. Her more than 100 scholarly books and articles examine the impact of social policies on the educational opportunities and outcomes of low-income students of color. One book, *Keeping Track: How Schools Structure Inequality*, has been honored as one of the twentieth century's most influential books on education, and a second, *Becoming Good American Schools: The Struggle for Civic Virtue in Education Reform* (with Karen
Hunter Quartz, Steve Ryan, and Martin Lipton), won the American Educational Research Association's Outstanding Book Award. Oakes's many other honors include the Southern Christian Leadership Conference's Ralph David Abernathy Award for Public Service and the World Cultural Council's Jose Vasconcelos World Award in Education. Oakes began her career in education as a middle-school and high school teacher. From 2008 to 2014, she served as the director of Educational Opportunity and Scholarship at the Ford Foundation in New York. She is the former president of the American Educational Research Association and a member of the National Academy of Education.

Martin Lipton, former public high school teacher, has had a parallel career as an education writer and consultant and worked for ten years as a communications analyst at UCLA's Institute for Democracy, Education, and Access. Among his publications are *Learning Power: Organizing for Education and Justice*, with Jeannie Oakes and John Rogers, and *Becoming Good American Schools: The Struggle for Civic Virtue in Education Reform*, with Jeannie Oakes, Karen Hunter Quartz, and Steve Ryan. Lipton's photographs, appearing in this book and elsewhere, portray the possibilities for educational justice in urban communities.

Lauren Anderson is an associate professor of education at Connecticut College. A former upper-elementary teacher and support provider for K–6 public school teachers, Lauren has lived,
worked, and conducted research in the country's three largest
urban school districts: New York City, Chicago, and Los Angeles.
Lauren's research collaborations focus on the preparation and
early-career experiences of equity-minded educators, including
teacher educators. She has written for a number of educational
journals and recently coauthored the book *Teaching for Equity
in Complex Times: Negotiating Standards in a High-Performing
Bilingual School* (with Jamy Stillman).

Jamy Stillman is an associate professor of educational equity and cultural diversity at the University of Colorado Boulder. A former bilingual elementary teacher, she worked as a support provider to public school teachers of Emergent Bilinguals for more
than fifteen years. She has also worked as a teacher educator and
conducted research on teacher education in California, Colorado,
and New York, in both urban and rural settings. Jamy's research
and teaching focus primarily on the preparation of teachers to
serve diverse learners, with an emphasis on how schools and
teachers can effectively meet the needs of Emergent Bilingual
students. She has published several book chapters and a number
of articles in educational journals that explore the relationship
between teacher learning, language and literacy instruction, and
teachers' navigation of educational policies. She recently coauthored the book *Teaching for Equity in Complex Times: Negotiating Standards in a High-Performing Bilingual School* (with
Lauren Anderson).

Acknowledgments

The most immediate inspiration for this book was the courage, passion, and hard work of the UCLA graduates whose words and photographs appear throughout the chapters. We are enormously appreciative of their commitment to students and to making the rhetoric of socially just education real. We are indebted to UCLA's teacher education faculty, notably Megan Franke, Eloise Metcalfe, Jody Priselac, and other Center X faculty who read and commented insightfully on the book, along with the novice and resident teachers at UCLA. Their reflections on teaching provided illuminating direction. Teachers Mauro Bautista, Mark Hill, Kimberly Min, and Judy Smith, who are featured throughout the book, deserve special thanks for welcoming us into their classrooms and answering all our questions so generously and openly. We thank our former editor Dean Birkenkamp, now at Routledge, who remains a thoughtful and energetic champion, as well as our current editor, Catherine Bernard, for her ongoing encouragement, support, and patience. We would also like to thank the many teacher educators across the country who have offered helpful feedback on prior editions of this text—too numerous to name.

We are also grateful to the many scholars who, over the years, have contributed to the ideas and approach we take here. These colleagues' rich ideas and generous conversations have shaped our thinking in subtle and not-so-subtle ways. We have also learned a great deal about schooling and the struggle for social justice from former and current doctoral students and postdoctoral scholars whose academic work has enriched our own. Thanks, too, are due to the many generous funders who have sponsored our research.

Martin and Jeannie's family provides both a solid rock of support and substantive contributions: Lisa Oakes brought her considerable expertise as a developmental psychologist and provided many helpful suggestions and examples of the learning theory that underlies teaching; Tracy Oakes Barnett offered inspiring anecdotes and the constant reminder of how much fun teaching for social justice can be; Lowell Lipton, an aficionado of rhetoric and composition, contributed a fresh look at the postmodern struggle for meaning; and Ethan Lipton, a fellow writer, extended knowing encouragement and good dinner company throughout the writing process. Their spouses, Steve Luck, Ron Barnett, and Rene Huey-Lipton, have been wonderful friends as well as spectacular parents to our grandchildren. Emily and Haley Barnett, Alison and Carter Luck, and Max and Sophia Lipton remind us of why this matters so much. We thank them all.

Finally, a word of thanks to Jamy's and Lauren's respective families, especially Jamy's husband, Charles Framularo and daughter, Sasha Framularo, and Lauren's partner, Chris Barnard; all were (as usual) loving, encouraging, patient, and generous during the production of this most recent edition.

Part I

Democracy, Diversity, and Inequity

In early May 2017, the forty-fifth president of the United States stopped by and cheered a White House event where Secretary of Education Betsy DeVos had gathered a group of local children and parents. Her goal was to persuade Congress to continue funding a program that uses public dollars to pay private school tuition for schoolchildren in the nation's capital. It was a call for support that reflected well the broad suite of education reforms favored by the new administration—public financing of private alternatives to public schools, including corporate-run charter schools, publicly subsidized homeschooling, and voucher plans much like the DC-based one at the center of the day's event.

Meanwhile, halfway across the country in Chicago, Illinois, a coalition of grassroots organizations from twenty-four cities, the Journey for Justice (J4J) Alliance, was advocating for a very different approach to securing high-quality education for the nation's most vulnerable children. In fact, in J4J's view, choice and privatization are a big part of the problem *facing* public education, rather than viable solutions for improving it. J4J's director, Jitu Brown, who has worked for years as an organizer and educator in the Kenwood Oakland neighborhood of Chicago, laid out J4J's perspective in a *Chicago Reporter* opinion piece, published just a few days later and entitled, "School Choice Is a Scam in Segregated Neighborhoods."

"We feel the same urgency to transform struggling schools," Brown wrote about the new administration's proposals. "But we understand that imposing failed, top-down corporate education interventions on communities of color is merely the status quo, amplified." Drawing from the lived experience of thousands of residents of low-income communities of color, J4J's campaign—*#WeChoose: Educational Equity, Not the Illusion of School Choice*—argues that public schools "are being killed by an alliance of misguided, paternalistic 'reformers,' education profiteers, and those who seek to dismantle the institution of public education."[1] What J4J wants for children in Kenwood Oakland and communities like it across the country is not choice and competition (or the unevenness and instability they assure), but what families in more affluent communities can simply count on: well-resourced, stable, sustainable, government-supported, *community* schools.

In short, public education today is caught in the crosshairs of a deep cultural divide. It's a divide that will influence the careers of new teachers for many years to come. Indeed, teachers' work is always shaped, interpreted, inspired, and constrained by the particularities of its historical moment. And while this moment is a particular one, this country has always had its deep disagreements about education. Consider, for example, the blatant evil of lawful segregation that kept our country's children separated by race, the many who battled for and against its de jure dismantling, and the many who are battling for and against its de facto realization still.

This book provides foundational knowledge that explains why public schools are what they are today, and why public education is an institution worth saving and improving, worth fighting for, and worth choosing as a career. In the first section, we introduce the broader demographic, historical, philosophical, and political context. We apply a critical approach meant to provide readers with new insights and useful tools that will support them to make positive contributions to contemporary public schooling.

Chapter 1, "The U.S. Schooling Dilemma: Diversity, Inequity, and Democratic Values," looks at who contemporary U.S. students are and what basic conditions they encounter in their lives, both inside and outside school. We pay attention to the structural inequities and opportunity gaps that students experience in the educational system.

Chapter 2, "History and Culture: How Expanding Expectations and Powerful Ideologies Shape Schooling in the United States," presents an overview of important events in the history of schooling in the United States. The chapter sketches out how expectations for schools have increased over the past 200-plus years. It also discusses two powerful and pervasive ideologies— meritocracy and racial superiority—that have shaped and continue to shape schooling in this country.

Chapter 3, "Politics and Philosophy: The Struggle Over the School Curriculum," explores how people in Western societies think about knowledge and schooling. We review traditional and progressive educational philosophies and the role they have played in struggles over what schools should teach, how they should teach it, and to whom. These philosophies have consequences— explored throughout the book—that show up in every aspect of public education, including school policies, curriculum, teacher preparation, relationships between students and teachers, and so on.

Chapter 4, "Policy and Law: Rules That Schools Live By," unpacks how local, state, and fed- eral governments, including the courts, translate our ever-growing expectations for public edu- cation into education policy and law. This incredibly complex process requires policymakers and judges to juggle the competing social, historical, philosophical, and political forces described in Chapters 1–3. The chapter also identifies how Americans' idealization of economic enterprise exerts a huge influence in the education policymaking process.

Part I introduces big, historical ideas at the heart of American schooling—ideas like diversity, equity, and democracy, as well as meritocracy, racial superiority, and privilege. We don't leave these ideas behind when we move on to Part II. There, our attention to the theory and practice of learning and teaching recalls the tension over the mission and purpose of public schools. Looking at the usual educational divisions such as subject matter, instruction, assessment, class- room management, and so forth, we make the case that equity is essential, in theory *and* in practice—that a social justice perspective does not compromise, but rather drives teachers and schools *toward*, quality.

Part III attends to the teaching profession more broadly; in doing so, however, it profiles specific teachers who describe their philosophies and how they put them into practice as profes- sionals. These profiles give readers a sense of the challenges and inspirations that teachers find in their profession. They also give readers a sense of what's possible—in other words, how real teachers are drawing on and deepening their foundational knowledge about U.S. schooling (Part I) and their knowledge of teaching and learning (Part II) as they navigate conditions in the present, work to transform educational inequities, *and* strive to make schools and the teaching profession what socially just, democratic principles suggest they can and should be.

Note

1 Journey for Justice Alliance, *Death by a Thousand Cuts: Racism, School Closures, and Public School Sabotage*, 2014, www.issuelab.org/resource/death_by_a_thousand_cuts_racism_school_ closures_and_public_school_sabotage.

The U.S. Schooling Dilemma
Diversity, Inequity, and Democratic Values

What does it mean to be a socially just teacher in a socially unjust world? What do all students deserve?

I grew up in a household that discussed these questions. My father, an accountant, and my mother, a professional educator, always led me to believe that education could solve just about any problem in the world. At mealtimes we often talked about the state of education, the gross inequities my mother observed between urban and suburban schools, and the reform efforts. I knew that someday I wanted to be a teacher. . . .

Schooling in our society, though inherently democratic, needs to direct students toward critical consciousness—of their potential, of their freedom, of ongoing injustices, and of the obligation to ensure our democracy and improve upon it for future generations.

—Judy Smith
High school social studies

Teacher Judy Smith grapples every day with one of the most challenging teaching dilemmas of our time: making good on the promise of equal education in a society that is profoundly unequal. Teachers like Judy and the others you'll meet in this book recognize the relationship between the nation's diversity and its inequity; they understand the history of this relationship and know why schooling inequalities persist. They have knowledge, skills, and a sense of possibility that equip them to be agents for educational equity as they support students' social and emotional development, intellectual curiosity, and academic competence. They teach to change the world.

Chapter Overview

This chapter focuses on inequities that shape students' lives. It provides a numerical breakdown that describes today's students and the relationship between students' diverse characteristics and their educational experiences and outcomes. Most people in the United States, and certainly all teachers, have heard about the nation's racial and economic achievement gaps. Those gaps reflect equally important opportunity gaps. As we show in what follows, persistent patterns of unequal conditions, resources, and opportunities in and outside of school underlie the gaps, or disparities, in students' achievement.

Educators like Judy Smith don't just want to understand these inequities; they also want to help remedy them. This activist goal is encompassed in teacher educator and critical scholar Gloria Ladson-Billings's idea of an education debt. "Debt" asks us to understand that a high-quality, equitable education is not something that youth must earn or prove they deserve, but something that society *owes* to them. To *owe* or *repay* means we must first look beyond the classroom, the community, and the nation, and into history itself, to understand long-lived and new inequalities that students face inside and outside of school. "Education debt" also points to "equity" rather than "equality" as the appropriate approach for repayment. Making schooling opportunities equal is a worthy goal, but it's not enough to remedy harms that have accumulated over generations. Equity requires providing what students need to thrive and succeed. That means far more must be provided to the children to whom we owe the debt than to others who have been spared generations of inequality. We marshal every conceivable skill, resource, and commitment within our reach to align learning and teaching with democratic and just aspirations instead of conforming to past habits and injustice. The teachers profiled throughout this book believe that there exists no worthier pursuit than transforming the world of schooling as it is—and re-creating it as it should be.

Starting with a broad, demographic look at students in the United States, in this first chapter we set the national context of students' lives outside of school and the inequalities they experience within the educational system. We conclude the chapter by introducing Judy Smith and three other teachers who recognize and embrace their students' diversity, acknowledge their struggles, and work to bring social justice and academic excellence to their classrooms.

Who Are American Students?

In 2016, an estimated 55 million young people were enrolled in elementary and secondary schools—an increase of about 10 million over the past thirty years. With small increases expected every year, projections are that the school population will grow to 57.9 million children by 2024.[1]

Where Do U.S. Students Live and Go to School?

Much of the nation's population growth over the past thirty years has been in the South, where schools now teach about 39 percent of the country's students. Schools in the West, which enroll about a quarter of the nation's children, have expanded as well. These are also the regions where future growth is expected. Such shifts pose challenges for southern and western states, which tend to have far less wealth in terms of tax revenue than northeastern states, where the fewest schoolchildren reside.

Among the 55 million students in the United States, roughly 50 million are enrolled in public schools. Though charter schools—schools that receive public funding but operate outside the typical school district structure—receive much attention in the media and have grown considerably over the past decade, they still represent a relatively small proportion (2.7 million in 2014, or about 5 percent) of public school enrollment. Slightly more than 5 million, or 10 percent, of school-age children in the United States attend private schools, and 38 percent of them are in Catholic schools. Private school enrollments, in decline since 1989, are projected to diminish further between now and 2024.[2] Despite all of the budget problems and criticism public schools have faced in the past two decades, the proportion of students they serve has increased compared to private schools.

About 3.4 percent of students—a total of 1.8 million in 2012—were homeschooled. These students received instruction under their parents' guidance at home and spent fewer than twenty-five hours a week at a public or private school. Although still a small fraction of all students, homeschooled children increased from 850,000 in 1999, the first time these data were recorded, to 1.3 million in 2015.[3]

How Diverse Are Students in the United States?

Today's U.S. schoolchildren are a diverse group. Long gone are the days when U.S. public school students were overwhelmingly White, native born, and English speaking. Immigration status, religiousness, family composition, sexual orientation, and disability status—all represent important dimensions of student identity and experience. Consider, for example, the diversity reflected in first-year teacher Michelle Calva's description below.

> Most of my students either are recent immigrants from Latin America (most from Mexico) with limited prior academic experience or are low academic achievers for a variety of reasons. Out of twenty-nine students, one is vision impaired, three attend resource specialist classes daily, one attends speech therapy weekly, and two receive special math assistance two days a week. All of my students come from economically disadvantaged homes, every one receives either free or reduced-price lunches at school, and twelve receive free breakfast. Twenty-eight are Mexican Americans, and one is of Puerto Rican descent. Many of my students' parents have limited education; none attended schools in the United States. Two speak English.
>
> What exactly is our obligation to prepare my students for the future? I hope that the everyday lessons of math, language arts, social studies, and science, which require the majority of my attention, are helping to prepare them for the world outside of our classroom. But I believe that becoming bicultural requires more than just readying the individual for the dominant society. It also requires preparing society for the minority members. I can only guide my students in their quest to become individuals. I can help them define valuable assets within their own culture, I can provide them with assistance in achieving personal success, but eventually they will have to face the rest of society without me or other educators at their sides.
>
> —Michelle Calva
> First-year teacher, grades 4, 5, and 6

Classrooms like Michelle's are prevalent in cities like Los Angeles, New York, Chicago, and Miami and increasingly common in small and midsize cities, as well as in rural and suburban areas. For teachers today, multiculturalism cannot be reduced to a lesson, a curriculum, a teaching style, or even a philosophy. Multiculturalism is a fact—a fundamental condition that characterizes our culture.

Race

In 2014, White students made up 50 percent of school-age children in the United States; 25 percent were Hispanic (or Latinx[4]), 16 percent African American, and 5 percent Asian.[5] This amounts to a huge shift since the 1970s. Latinx students have tripled their representation, while White students' proportion of the total has decreased about 30 percent. Although still relatively small proportionally, Asian enrollment has also grown rapidly over the past thirty years, and these trends are projected to continue. (See Figure 1.1.)

In addition, students who identify as biracial or multiracial now account for roughly 3 percent of enrollment.[6] While representing a relatively small chunk of schoolchildren, multiracial babies born in the United States increased from 1 to 10 percent between 1970 and 2013, making multiracial youth the fastest-growing youth subgroup in the country.[7]

Although racial groups are not distributed evenly across the country, every region has experienced growth in students of color. In 2014, White students were the minority in both the West and the South. In the West, White students, at 38 percent, represented a smaller share of the student population than Latinx students, at 42 percent in the same year. In the Northeast, the South, and the West, Latinx students now outnumber their Black peers.[8]

Figure 1.1 **Percentage Distribution of Students Enrolled in Public Elementary and Secondary Schools, by Race/Ethnicity**

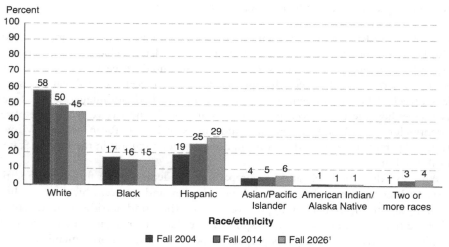

† Not applicable.
1 Data for 2026 are projected.
Note: Race categories exclude persons of Hispanic ethnicity. Prior to 2008, separate data on students of Two or more races were not collected. Although rounded numbers are displayed, the figures are based on unrounded estimates. Detail may not sum to totals because of rounding.

Source: U.S. Department of Education, National Center for Education Statistics, Common Core of Data (CCD), "State Nonfiscal Survey of Public Elementary and Secondary Education," 2004–05 and 2014–15; and National Elementary and Secondary Enrollment by Race/Ethnicity Projection Model, 1972 through 2026. See *Digest of Education Statistics 2016*, table 203.50.

Proportionately more students of color attend public schools than private schools. In 2012, private school students were 72 percent White, about 20 percent "Whiter" than public schools.[9] Homeschooled children are predominantly White as well, 83 percent in 2012.[10]

Immigration

Immigrants are so much a part of U.S. history, with every generation seeking a new beginning— seeking a better quality of life for themselves and their families. Many immigrants are refugees, or people seeking asylum from persecution in their home countries.

Three times as many immigrants entered the United States in the 2000s compared with the number that arrived in the 1960s, and today the United States is home to 43.3 million immigrants. However, the percentage of foreign-born residents is only slightly larger than in the 1950s—about 9 percent then, compared with almost 13.5 percent in 2015. Recent estimates put the undocumented immigrant population in the United States at over 11 million—about one-quarter of the total foreign-born.[11]

Between 1970 and 2000, the proportion of students in K–12 schools who were children of immigrants tripled. In 2015, 17.9 million children lived with at least one immigrant parent. They accounted for 26 percent of children under age 18 in the United States.[12] No longer do most immigrants head for California, New York, Texas, Florida, New Jersey, and Illinois; in the past decade, immigrants have increased their presence in states in the Southeast, Midwest, and Rocky Mountain region as well. In addition, the number of refugee students is on the rise, too, in various regions of the United States. In 2015, top origin countries for immigrants were, in order, India, China, and Mexico. Top origin countries for refugees in the United States currently include Iraq, Somalia, Syria, Afghanistan, and Sudan, among others.[13] Of undocumented immigrants, 71 percent hailed from Mexico and Central America. In 2015, it was reported also that more than 62,000 unaccompanied youths, many escaping violence and/or economic despair, were detained at the Mexico-U.S. border. Many such youth have subsequently been released to sponsors and are now enrolled in schools nationwide. The highest concentrations of such students are in California, Florida, New York, and Texas.[14] Despite the prime place of immigrants in U.S. history, and as we discuss in later chapters, such demographic shifts often bring to the surface some of the more xenophobic tendencies still permeating U.S. culture.

Language

Today's schools include just under 12 million students who speak languages other than English—also called heritage languages—at home.[15] In 2015, this group accounted for 22 percent of school-age children, up from 10 percent in 1980. Approximately three-quarters of these young people come from homes where Spanish is spoken, with the remaining quarter (approximately 3 million) from homes where other languages are spoken, with Arabic, Vietnamese, and Chinese being the next most common.[16]

As Figure 1.2 indicates, states vary enormously in their percentages of students from homes where languages other than English are spoken. For fifteen states in 2015, 20 percent or more of their students were in this category—topped by a high of 45 percent in California.[17] Only four states had fewer than 5 percent of students from homes with languages other than English spoken, and in all states the number of students who speak languages other than English was (and is) increasing rapidly.

When schools determine that a student does not yet speak English proficiently, the label *English Learner* is typically assigned. English Learners are the fastest-growing student group in the United States. In 2012–2013, 4.85 million students, or 10 percent of the K–12 student population, were identified as English Learners.[18] These students attend schools in all fifty states, but, as Figure 1.3 indicates, student enrollments by state vary considerably.

Figure 1.2 K–12 Students Who Speak a Language Other Than English at Home, 2015

State	Number	Percentage
United States	11,931,000	22.2
California	2,954,000	44.7
Texas	1,862,000	35.5
Nevada	157,000	31.9
New York	912,000	30.1
New Jersey	424,000	28.8
Florida	861,000	28.7
Arizona	341,000	28.6
New Mexico	104,000	28.5
Illinois	532,000	24.4
Rhode Island	36,000	23.2
Massachusetts	228,000	22.4
Washington	260,000	22.3
Connecticut	122,000	21.2
Hawaii	45,000	20.8
Oregon	129,000	20.5
Colorado	185,000	20.0
District of Columbia	14,000	18.5
Maryland	181,000	18.5
Georgia	293,000	15.8
Virginia	210,000	15.4
North Carolina	249,000	14.8
Delaware	21,000	14.0
Kansas	73,000	13.9
Minnesota	130,000	13.9
Utah	90,000	13.6
Nebraska	45,000	13.2
Alaska	17,000	13.1
Oklahoma	84,000	12.1
Pennsylvania	221,000	11.2
Wisconsin	107,000	11.2
Michigan	174,000	10.7
Idaho	33,000	10.2
Indiana	114,000	9.9
Arkansas	50,000	9.6
Iowa	51,000	9.6
Wyoming	10,000	9.5
Tennessee	98,000	9.0
South Carolina	64,000	7.9
Ohio	144,000	7.4
Louisiana	56,000	6.9
Missouri	69,000	6.8
New Hampshire	13,000	6.7
Kentucky	49,000	6.6
Alabama	52,000	6.3
South Dakota	9,000	5.7
Maine	10,000	5.2
Vermont	5,000	5.1
Montana	8,000	4.8
North Dakota	5,000	4.4
Mississippi	22,000	4.0
West Virginia	6,000	2.3

Source: Kids Count Data Center, 2015 *American Community Survey,* http://datacenter.kidscount.org/data/tables/81-children-who-speak-a-language-other-than-english-at-home#detailed/1/any/false/573,869,36,868,867/any/396,397.

Figure 1.3 Top Fifteen States With Highest English Language Learner (ELL) Student Enrollment in Public Schools, School Year 2012–2013

State	ELL enrollment	Total K–12 enrollment	Share of ELLs among K–12 students (%)
United States	4,851,527	49,474,030	9.8
California	1,521,772	6,213,194	24.5
Texas	773,732	5,077,507	15.2
Florida	277,802	2,692,143	10.3
New York	237,499	2,708,851	8.8
Illinois	190,172	2,055,502	9.3
Colorado	114,415	863,121	13.3
Washington	107,307	1,051,694	10.2
North Carolina	102,311	1,506,080	6.8
Virginia	99,897	1,163,660	7.9
Georgia	94,034	1,703,332	5.5
Arizona	91,382	1,087,697	8.4
Michigan	80,958	1,513,153	5.4
Nevada	77,559	445,017	17.4
Massachusetts	71,066	954,507	7.4
Minnesota	70,436	845,291	8.3

Source: Migration Policy Institute (2015), *ELL Information Center Fact Sheet Series*, www.migrationpolicy.org/research/states-and-districts-highest-number-and-share-english-language-learners.

Despite the prevalence of the English Learner label, it is increasingly common to refer to this student group as *Emergent Bilinguals* or *Dual Language Learners*. This shift reflects growing understandings about the benefits of supporting students' developing bilingualism; it also challenges monolingual and English-only ideologies that privilege students' acquisition of English over speaking or retaining their heritage languages.[19] The newer terminology also responds to the changing demographics of this student group, 71 percent of whom are native-born U.S. citizens.[20] While many of these students previously entered school as *sequential bilinguals*, meaning they had communicated predominantly in their heritage language and experienced little to no exposure to English before entering school, many enter school today as *simultaneous bilinguals*. These students have been exposed to and have communicated in English *and* their heritage languages since (or nearly since) birth, and enter schools in the United States with varying degrees of proficiency in *both* languages.

As we discuss later in this chapter and others, the paths of Emergent Bilinguals through U.S. schools—much like the paths of immigrants through U.S. society—are often difficult, as evidenced in new teacher Karen Recinos's description of her own experiences and those of her family.

> When I immigrated to this country as a 13-year-old, one of the most difficult hurdles I had to overcome was that of learning a second language. I knew I had to take advantage of the priceless gift my mother had given me by bringing me to this country. From the day my dad died, she worked tirelessly to provide for my two younger brothers and myself. She left us in Guatemala to pursue the American dream, a dream that caused her to shed many tears. . . . For eight years, she worked long days to send dollars so we could have food on the table and receive a good education. She dreamed of one day bringing us to the United States where we would have a better life, a future with more possibilities. It was not easy for her to accomplish that dream, but she did it. Today, eleven years later, I have the privilege of telling my story and what I had to overcome once I got to the "land of opportunities."
>
> —Karen Recinos
> First-year teacher

Students With Disabilities

In 2015, about 13 percent (approximately 6.6 million) of students in kindergarten through grade 12 in U.S. public schools were classified as having disabilities related to learning. Most (about 35 percent) of these students were identified as learning disabled. Another 20 percent were identified as having speech impairments, and another 13 percent as experiencing other health impairments that interfere with learning. Students with disabilities such as autism (autism spectrum disorder), emotional disturbances, intellectual disabilities, and developmental delays each accounted for between 5 and 9 percent of children served under the Individuals With Disabilities Education Act (IDEA).[21]

While terms such as "learning disabled" are in common use, many educators prefer to avoid this general labeling when they can, instead referring to "children with learning (or hearing or developmental) disabilities," thus separating one characteristic of the child from the total individual. This is often referred to as using "people-first" language. In recent years, many also have come to question taken-for-granted, socially constructed understandings of what it means to be "able" or have "ability." As we address in later chapters, classifications related to disability are hotly disputed.

Referral practices have led to disproportionate designations of disability among students from certain groups; boys of color, for example, are among those most likely to be referred for and subsequently diagnosed as having attention-deficit/hyperactivity disorder and/or emotional disturbance.[22] Conversely, they are much less likely—as are low-income children—to be represented among those designated as "gifted." In fact, most students qualified for and placed in gifted programs and advanced classes are White or Asian, while Black students remain significantly underrepresented.[23] Because of long histories of discrimination and their concentration in underfunded school districts—a phenomenon we address later in this chapter—certain groups of children are disproportionately at risk, for various reasons, of having their learning needs significantly (and to their detriment) misdiagnosed.

Religion

Perhaps due to the stated separation of church and state in the United States, religion is often sidelined in conversations about student diversity. And although religion has become somewhat less important (for many people) in recent years, the vast majority of adults in the United States report religious affiliations, and more than half report that religion is very important in their lives.[24] While Christians account for 71 percent of the adult population, religious diversity overall and within the broad category of Christian is on the rise.[25] Increasingly, the media and public discourse find salient social and political differences between what are termed "fundamental" or "evangelical" Christians and "traditional" Christians.

Members of various faiths, including Judaism, Buddhism, Islam, and Hinduism, constitute 6 percent of the population. Those reporting no religious affiliation account for the remaining roughly 23 percent—a 7 percent increase since 2007—with younger people born after 1980 less likely to claim religious affiliation than older generations.[26]

Americans' religious beliefs and practices do not fit neatly into conventional categories. Increasing numbers of families report engaging in multiple and mixed practices, not surprising given that roughly 39 percent of married adults have spouses who affiliate with a religion or denomination different from their own. Even with such shifts, however, exclusionary views of religion's role in public life have increased. In 2014, for example, more than half of people surveyed said Christian faith was an important attribute of being "truly American."[27]

These statistics speak to religious diversity among adults; in doing so, they reveal trends that no doubt influence the beliefs and behaviors children bring to school, perhaps especially so in our current political climate. Organizations such as the Southern Poverty Law Center, for example, have reported spikes in bullying and hate crimes against Muslim students. In fact, in one recent survey, 42 percent of Muslims with children in K–12 schools reported that their children had been bullied because of their faith, compared with 23 percent of Jews, 20 percent of Protestants, and 6 percent of Catholics.[28] Some have argued that, without intentional supports put in place by judicious educators, Muslim youth are at risk of suffering discriminatory treatment given the "perfect storm"[29] of economic downturn, anti-immigrant sentiment, U.S. military action in predominantly Muslim countries, and mainstream conflation of Islam with terrorism.[30]

Family Composition

Families in the United States come in all shapes and sizes. In many ways, the traditional image of a family—a woman and a man of the same race who are married and both biologically related to their children—represents outdated assumptions about who raises children, how, and in what configurations nationwide.[31] In 2014, less than half—46 percent—of children were living with two parents who were both in their first marriage—down from 61 percent in 1980 and 73 percent in 1960.[32] That likely means that more than half of today's young people have experienced shifts in family structure and routines before or during their time in K–12 schools.

In fact, roughly one-fourth (26 percent) of children 18 or under are living with a single parent, and 5 percent are living with neither of their parents. Meanwhile, a substantial percentage of children (16 percent in 2014) are living in blended families that include stepparents, half siblings, and/or stepsiblings. (See Figure 1.4.) In 2009, 1.8 million children lived with adoptive parents, up from 1.1 million in 1991.[33] In 2015, roughly 427,000 children lived in foster care each day, with a total of 671,000 children in the foster care system that year.[34] In 2015, 2.9 million children were being raised by grandparents.[35]

In addition, multiracial families are on the rise; one in eight new marriages occurs between spouses of different races and ethnicities.[36] Growing numbers of children are also being raised by same-sex parents. Although more concentrated in particular metropolitan areas, approximately 600,500 households headed by same-sex couples reside across every state and nearly every county nationwide.[37]

Sexual Orientation and Gender Expression

Characterizing diversity along the lines of sexual orientation remains difficult because of limited national survey data. A 2016 study finds that about 10 million people in the United States identify as lesbian, gay, bisexual, or transgender (LGBT). This conservative estimate translates to about 4.1 percent of adults identifying as LGBT.[38] Interestingly, when polled, U.S. adults estimated in 2011 that a much higher percentage—25 percent—of the population is gay or lesbian.[39] Today, 63 percent of Americans say homosexuality should be accepted by society, and 55 percent say they favor allowing same-sex marriage.[40]

Despite increasing acceptance of homosexuality (particularly among young adults), half of states still do not include sexual orientation or gender expression in the language of nondiscrimination laws that apply to schools.[41] Since terminology shifts and changes, a few definitions are helpful here. *Sexual orientation*, familiar to most Americans, refers to how people think of themselves in terms of who they are attracted to romantically or sexually. *Gender expression* refers to the way individuals perform their gender roles; it may or may not correlate with the gender that individuals claim to have, or with their sexual orientation. Notably, as transgender and gender nonconforming students have become more visible, some states and school districts have taken action to ensure they are protected from discriminatory speech and acts.

Figure 1.4 Children's Family Arrangements: Growing Diversity[42]

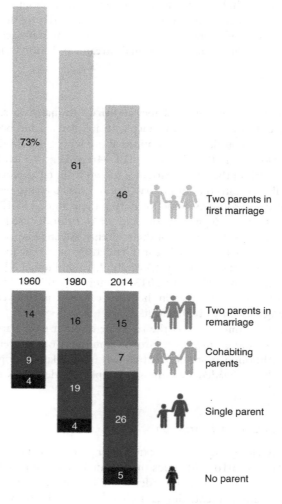

% of children living with ...

73%

61

46 — Two parents in first marriage

1960   1980   2014

14   16   15 — Two parents in remarriage

9   7 — Cohabiting parents

4   19   26 — Single parent

4   5 — No parent

Note: Based on children under 18. Data regarding cohabitation are not available for 1960 and 1980. In those years, children with cohabiting parents are included in "one parent." For 2014, the total share of children living with two married parents is 62 percent after rounding. Figures do not add up to 100 percent due to rounding.

Source: Pew Research Center analysis of 1960 and 1980 decennial census and 2014 American Community Survey (IPUMS).

The absence of such legislation has been a source of growing concern in light of high-profile hate crimes committed against LGBT students. (While statistics have not quite caught up, LGBT has gained some new letters, QIA, in recent years, which we address more fully in Chapter 9.) In 2015, nearly nine out of ten LGBT middle and high school students reported verbal and/or physical harassment at school in the past year, nearly three-quarters felt unsafe because of their sexual orientation, and nearly a third had skipped at least one day of school in the past month because of safety concerns.[43] Bullying on the basis of gender expression is likewise an area of growing concern.[44]

Class

Social and economic class are important aspects of identity, and they structure students' schooling experiences and outcomes. Sometimes social class is treated objectively—such as when people are sorted according to an income and/or wealth scale. Thus, an individual or family becomes "poor" or "upper middle class" on the basis of their income and/or wealth. In such sorting, other objective factors—those that can be measured empirically, like years of schooling—might also be included. But as an aspect of identity and diversity, class has subjective and cultural dimensions that are far more complex than those that can be measured empirically. Social class differences contribute to the different kinds of knowledge, preferences, and tendencies that students bring into the classroom and, therefore, the way students ultimately experience school.

As one example, sociologist Annette Lareau has studied the expectations and parenting practices of parents from different social class backgrounds.[45] Lareau found that upper-middle-income and high-income parents dedicated a certain kind of attention—what she calls "concerted cultivation"—to preparing their children for habits and behaviors that ensured school success. These parents scheduled play dates, enrolled children in (often costly) extracurricular activities, and otherwise fostered children's talents through parent-*organized* activity. Meanwhile, working-class parents tended to grant their children more *unstructured* time and freedom for self-directed activity—what Lareau calls "the accomplishment of natural growth."[46]

Importantly, Lareau shows how these tendencies—actually, child-rearing preferences—are related to the different amounts of money and free or flexible time parents had to structure children's activities. She also shows that while both approaches have benefits and drawbacks for children's development, concerted cultivation prepares children to be a better match with what mainstream schooling looks for in school readiness and success. Thus, the children of advantaged middle-class and affluent parents often find it easier to acclimate to schools' expectations for "good" student behavior. For example, these children might be well practiced in moving from activity to activity under an adult's direction and in interacting with peers according to the highly specialized rules shared by schools. The important takeaway here is that what might look like relative *success* at school is often a function not of students' skills or smarts but of the *synergy* along class lines between their families and their schools.

Recognizing the Complexity of Identity

Of course, the data and statistics just reviewed don't describe real, "whole" people or the complex social dynamics that shape their lives. Data points are reductive by nature. No one person is only a woman or only heterosexual or only a native Spanish speaker or only Asian American or only middle class. Likewise, data can't tell us every salient detail. A child might live in a "single-parent household" with his dad and his dad's unmarried partner, while going to his grandparents' house after school until dinner.

We all identify ourselves—and are identified by others—using multiple "official" demographic categories or labels (e.g., categories related to race, gender, age, education level, language, and income), each of which encompasses enormous variation. Indeed, race, gender identification, language, wealth, and the rest each exist on their own continuum, and the combinations are infinite. Walt Whitman famously wrote, "I am large, I contain multitudes."[47] In fact, we *all* contain multitudes—multiple identities that intersect and interrelate, and that have profound implications for how we experience the world, including schooling.

Social theorists have devised concepts that help educators understand some of these complexities. *Hybridity* and *dynamism* describe how the biological and cultural mixing (hybridity) and constant change (dynamism) that characterize many societies can preserve cultures and enrich them at the same time. For example, Spanglish is now spoken with pride on English-language sitcoms, New York City "fusion" restaurants serve Dominican and Chinese food, and growing numbers of multiracial families are bringing together diverse histories and heritages and creating new traditions.

Intersectionality, meanwhile, describes the connections among oppressive beliefs, habits, and social structures such as racism, sexism, homophobia, religious discrimination, and so on. Intersectionality emphasizes that these -isms do not exist in isolation; rather, they intersect and operate together. In doing so, they contribute to *systems* of privilege and oppression, *layers* of discrimination, and *patterns* of social inequality.

Teacher Mark Hill gives concrete examples of how these concepts of identity, hybridity, and intersectionality manifest in the lives and learning of teachers and students.

> When I think about culture I feel that I sit in a unique space. While it is a given that as individuals we all have a unique upbringing, I have yet to find anyone's quite as singular as my own. My family consists of myself, my twin brother, and my mother and father. When my mother, who is White, married my father, who is Black, her family immediately disowned her. . . .
>
> As a person of color I am assumed to have grown up with all the typical assumptions Americans have for Black people, but I have few memories of any such experiences. I grew up in a poor, racially mixed neighborhood, but I was never allowed out of the house or the walled-up backyard, and we never had any visitors. Thus, my cultural identity was formed almost solely based on my mother, a White Jew. I lit the candles of our menorah on Hanukkah, celebrated Rosh Hashanah, and am sympathetic to Israel in the Middle East conflict. . . .
>
> I have found that this experience helps me to relate with all of my students. I remember as a child wanting others to "see" me the same way I saw myself. Because of this, I make a tremendous effort to "see" students as individuals and accept them on their own terms, regardless of preconceived notions of race, gender, or age.
>
> —Mark Hill
> High school mathematics

Whether diverse voices, perspectives, and languages are heard or ignored in classrooms, they are there; they will not be silenced or assimilated out of existence. Some teachers will view the tremendous diversity of the children in their midst as an asset; others, sadly, will not. Some teachers, like Mark Hill, Michelle Calva, and Judy Smith, will struggle to construct something whole and wonderful that connects individuals and groups across differences; others won't. We hope most do, because we believe that this is the only way to provide a free and equal education to all. That said, the inequalities of American society and schools that disadvantage so many children certainly make the jobs of today's teachers especially challenging; of course, they also make teachers' jobs all the more important.

Inequity Outside of School

"Generations of Americans have been told that they live in the world's richest nation. But the United States today might more accurately be described as the nation with the world's richest rich people," observed the authors of a report on inequality in the United States.[48] You might be wondering: why did they say this? In fact, among the twenty rich, industrialized countries that belong to the Organization for Economic Cooperation and Development (OECD), the United States ranks highest in income per person.[49] Despite its riches, however, the United States is one of the most economically unequal countries in the world, with poverty rates unmatched in other wealthy countries. Children, more than any other group, bear the burden of this inequality.

Economic Inequality

The gap between the wealthy and the poor is enormous. As Figure 1.5 shows, the top 10 percent of U.S. families own 76 percent of the nation's wealth. Meanwhile, the bottom 50 percent of families share the remaining 1 percent of total wealth.[50] Although some in the media feature these and other stark differences, smaller and seemingly less dramatic gaps also profoundly impact Americans' daily lives. For example, the difference between living in poverty and earning a "living wage" can appear trivial in the context of macroeconomic data, but for a family that difference can mean having—or not having—food security and safe shelter. Many families once assumed to be "middle class" now find themselves on the margins of being able to afford college for their children.

The accelerating gap between rich and poor in the United States isn't just a consequence of the wealthy becoming richer, but of the relative income stability of those who have far less. Figure 1.6 shows that in 2012 high-income households in the top 5 percent of the income distribution received almost sixteen times the income of low-income households in the bottom 10 percent.[51] Also, most middle- to low-income families have made only modest income gains over the past thirty years, and the average income in the lowest quintile has barely budged.[52]

Figure 1.5 Distribution of Wealth in the United States

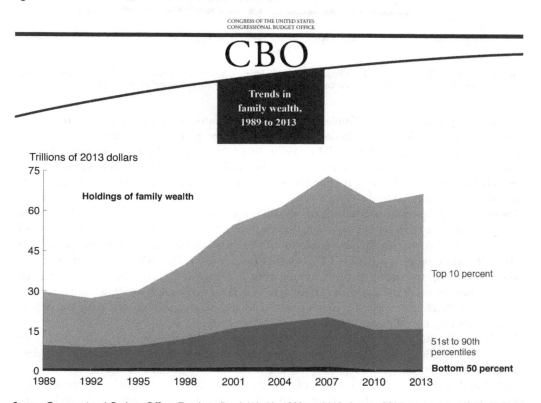

Source: Congressional Budget Office, *Trends in Family Wealth*, 1989 to 2013, August 2016, www.cbo.gov/sites/default/files/114th-congress-2015-2016/reports/51846-familywealth.pdf.

Figure 1.6 Real Family Income by Income Percentile, 1967–2012 (in 2012 dollars)

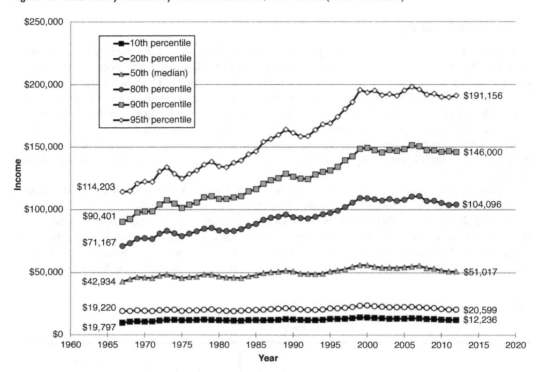

Source: Data from C. DeNavas-Walt, B. D. Proctor, and J. C. Smith, U.S. Census Bureau, Current Population Reports, P60-245, *Income, Poverty, and Health Insurance Coverage in the United States: 2012*, September 2013, Table A-2.

Most income gains result from families working longer hours, often by adding a second wage earner. In 2009, married women in the middle three income groups worked almost eight weeks more a year, on average, than they did in 1979. In addition, it has become increasingly more difficult for parents to afford time off to care for their children in the United States than in most other OECD countries, because the United States is the only one that does not mandate paid maternity or paternity leave.[53]

Increasingly, people who are fully employed do not earn enough to keep their families out of poverty—hence the term *the working poor*. It's not that U.S. workers earn less because they work less. In fact, workers in the United States, on average, work about 1,768 hours per year, more than their counterparts in other OECD countries (except Greece).[54] All told, poverty rates are higher, and living standards are lower, for the poor in the United States than they are for the poorest people in other industrialized countries.[55] Comparatively speaking, those who are poor in the United States also typically remain poor for longer periods of time, and with less opportunity to move up out of poverty, as well.[56]

While statistics indicate some improvements—such as the official poverty rate dropping from 14.8 in 2014 to 13.5 percent the following year—poverty still impacts an enormous and unacceptable number of Americans, especially children. This has long been a concern.

In the mid- and late 1990s, Clinton-era Democrats found common ground with conservative politicians and instituted significant changes to welfare policies. Those changes reduced benefits and established more stringent eligibility requirements for Aid to Families With Dependent

Children, food stamps, and other public assistance for poor children. In the intervening years, the effects of these changes on the overall economy have been hotly debated, but they have done nothing to stem childhood poverty. One in four young children in the United States now lives in poverty. The number of low-income students receiving free or reduced-price lunch at school increased from 18 million in 2006–2007 to 31 million in 2012, and now more than half of students in the United States qualify for the program.[57]

Despite the recovery from the recession of 2008, 4.5 million children under age 18 were living in poverty in 2015, representing 23.1 percent of the total population and 33.6 percent of those living below the poverty line.[58] These poverty rates were more acute for certain children, affecting approximately 12 percent of White children,[59] 36 percent of African American children, 30 percent of Latino children, and 32 percent of American Indian children.[60]

These discrepancies reflect socioeconomic inequality that includes and goes beyond food, shelter, health, and education insecurity for the current generation. The gaps represent cross-generational challenges; some groups have significant wealth and other supports to pass on to their children, while other groups have far less. In 2013, for example, the average wealth for White families was seven times higher than for Black families,[61] and ten times that of Latinx households.[62]

Ease of finding employment likewise differs along racial lines. African Americans with high school diplomas and college degrees are unemployed at nearly twice the rate of their White counterparts.[63] Of course, these and other employment discrepancies have a trickle-down impact on children's lives and livelihoods. In 2015, for example, Black and Latinx children were less likely than White children to have a parent working year-round, full-time. Seventy-seven percent of White children, about 66 percent of Latinx children, and 55 percent of African American children had parents with secure employment.[64]

Wage disparities also contribute to the higher rates of poverty among children of color. For example, in 2015, Black men made 22 percent less in average hourly wages than White men with the *same* education and experience.[65]

In addition, although the gender gap has diminished, women still make lower wages than men, even when they hold the same qualifications and work the same hours. They are also more likely to be heading up single-parent households with dependent children. Given the intersections of race and gender, women of color are, in turn, among those most likely to earn poverty-level wages. In 2013, 36 percent of African American workers and 42 percent of Latinx workers earned poverty-level wages, compared to 23 percent for Whites; in all cases, these rates were higher—while average wages were lower—for women than men within racial subgroups.[66]

Racial disparities in wealth and income, as described above and in what follows, lead to corollary disparities in children's access to the basics of life—food, health care, housing, and safety— as well as access to high-quality schooling.

Inequity in the Basics of Life

On December 10, 1948, the General Assembly of the United Nations adopted and proclaimed the Universal Declaration of Human Rights. Following this historic act, the assembly called on all member countries to publicize the text of the declaration and "to cause it to be disseminated, displayed, read and expounded principally in schools and other educational institutions, without distinction based on the political status of countries or territories."[67] Article 25 of the declaration states:

> Everyone has the right to a standard of living adequate for the health and wellbeing of himself and of his family, including food, clothing, housing and medical care and necessary

social services, and the right to security in the event of unemployment, sickness, disability, widowhood, old age or other lack of livelihood in circumstances beyond his control.[68]

The United States was one of the original signers of the declaration, and yet many Americans would likely disagree with its provisions; others would see it as a worthy statement of principle applying mostly to other countries; and still others would take it as a call to action. All would have to agree that it remains unrealized; access to the most basic social supports in the United States (e.g., adequate food, health care, and housing) depends on wealth and income. As one report on inequality phrased it, "In the U.S., perhaps more than in any other prosperous society, inequality reaches into dimensions of life where most people would prefer to believe that money does not rule."[69]

Food

Interviewed by Bill Moyers in 2013, Joel Berg, as head of the New York City Coalition Against Hunger, explained the web of consequences to children who live with "food insecurity."

Food insecure means families don't have enough money to regularly obtain all the food they need. It means they are rationing food and skipping meals. It means parents are going without food to feed their children. It means kids are missing breakfasts. And, ironically, because healthy food is usually more expensive than junk food, and because healthier options often don't even exist in low-income neighborhoods, it means that food insecurity and obesity are flip sides of the same malnutrition coin, so food insecurity may actually increase a family's chance of facing obesity and diabetes. Fifty million Americans, including nearly 17 million children, now live in food insecure homes.[70]

Given the poverty statistics shared in prior sections, it's not surprising—and yet still shocks the conscience—that in 2015 27 percent of African American and 27 percent of Latinx children were living in households where they could not count on having enough food for an active, healthy life for everyone in their family.[71]

Health

Children's health in the United States is highly related to their families' income status.[72] Asthma and lead exposure—both associated with environmental toxins, including pollution and unsafe building materials—are just two of the health problems that affect lower-income children at higher rates. In one dramatic example, the percentage of children in Flint, Michigan, with elevated levels of lead in their blood—known to lower cognitive functioning and increase learning problems—nearly doubled after the lead started leaching out of the city's old lead water pipes in 2014.[73] More than 40 percent of Flint's residents live below the poverty line.

Key to maintaining children's health and preventing their illness is their access to a health care system. Although local, state, and national health insurance and services are accessible to most, many lack good health care, and this is especially true for the nation's poorest children. We recently saw historically low rates of uninsured children, in part due to the Obama administration policies. The Kaiser Family Foundation reported the following in 2017:

Following decades of steady progress, largely driven by expansions in Medicaid and CHIP [Children's Health Insurance Program], the children's uninsured rate has reached an all-time low of 5. Medicaid and CHIP are key sources of coverage for our nation's children, covering nearly four in ten (39 percent) children overall and over four in ten (44 percent) children with special health care needs. Medicaid serves as the base of coverage for the nation's low-income children and covered 36.8 million children in fiscal year 2015. CHIP, which had 8.4 million children enrolled in fiscal year 2015, complements Medicaid by covering uninsured children above Medicaid eligibility limits.[74]

These gains are in peril in the political backlash against universal health care. Looking ahead, the Kaiser report identified serious concerns growing out of the political landscape, including potential coverage losses for children, more limited benefits and higher out-of-pocket costs for children's coverage, reduced access to care for children, and increased financial pressure on states and providers.[75] There is much to be concerned about.

Housing

In 2013, 40 percent of U.S. households with children had a serious housing problem. These problems included physically inadequate housing, overcrowded housing, or housing that cost more than 30 percent of household income.[76] Approximately 16 percent of households spend more than half of their income on housing,[77] leaving little for other basic necessities, such as food and health care.

African American and Latinx families are far more likely to experience housing problems than are White families, as are immigrant families.[78] In 2017, when nearly 72 percent of Whites owned their homes, less than half of African Americans or Latinx were homeowners.[79] (See Figure 1.7.) In addition, families of color have suffered disproportionately in the recent housing crisis. They have been targeted by predatory lenders and subjected to high-interest adjustable rate mortgages, and they are among those experiencing the highest rates of foreclosure.[80] Children, of course, are not immune to the negative effects of these "adult" issues.

In fact, the homeless population in the United States is increasingly made up of families *with* children, and this will likely continue given the recent economic downturn and housing crisis. As of 2008, families with children accounted for 32 percent of the homeless population, a 9 percent increase since 2007.[81] During 2013, an estimated 138,000 children (2 per 1,000 children) were found to be homeless at a single point in time,[82] and 2.5 percent of elementary and secondary students were identified as homeless in 2015. School-age homeless children face barriers to enrolling and attending school, including transportation problems, residency requirements, inability to obtain previous school records, and lack of clothing and school supplies.

Figure 1.7 Homeownership Rates by Race and Ethnicity of Householder, 2017

| Year | United States | Non-Hispanic white alone | Black alone | All other races | | Hispanic (of any race) |
				Total	Asian, Native Hawaiian, and Pacific Islander alone	
2017	63.6	71.8	42.7	53.6	56.8	46.6

Source: U.S. Census Bureau, *Quarterly Residential Vacancies and Homeownership*, First Quarter 2017, www.census.gov/housing/hvs/files/currenthvspress.pdf.

Clearly then, young people comprise a significant proportion of the U.S. homeless population; among those on their own are significant numbers of LGBT youth. Research suggests that roughly one in four LGBT youth who comes out to his or her parents is told to leave home.[83] For this and other reasons, about 40 percent of all homeless youth identify as LGBT, compared to less than 10 percent of the overall youth population.

Safety

In 2012, one in four (23 percent each) Black and Latinx children lived in neighborhoods reported by their parents to be never or only sometimes safe, compared with only 7 percent of White children. Children living at or below the poverty line were more than three times as likely as better-off children to live in such neighborhoods. It's long been known that unsafe neighborhoods have higher rates of infant mortality and low birth weight, as well as child abuse and neglect; children there watch more television (frequently a safer pastime than going outside), participate less in after-school activities, and have lower school achievement and high school graduation rates. Young people growing up in neighborhoods with high levels of crime and gun violence are themselves much more likely to become victims or perpetrators of violent crime. They are also more likely than children in safer neighborhoods to experience trauma resulting in social and emotional problems.[84]

News reports remind us of another kind of truth—that some young people are also at greater risk, as are their families, of experiencing discriminatory public policies and practices, including policing practices that put them in significant danger.[85] The number of police shootings of young Black men in 2016 (ages 15–34) was nine times greater than for other Americans, and four times the rate for young White men.[86] Tragic instances of unarmed Black teenagers being killed by police in Chicago, Illinois; Ferguson, Missouri; Cleveland, Ohio; Dallas, Texas; and Terrebonne, Louisiana, have been profiled in the media and been the subject of significant activism on the part of community members concerned for the safety of local youngsters. Black Lives Matter, which began as a hashtag on Twitter following the not-guilty verdict in the killing of 17-year-old Trayvon Martin in Florida, became a rallying cry after the police shooting of Michael Brown in Ferguson and evolved into a national movement against both police brutality and a broader set of racial injustices.

Geographic and Economic Isolation

Disparities in children's access to basic life necessities are compounded by the segregation of low-income children and students of color in large urban centers, and increasingly in residentially segregated suburban and rural neighborhoods, too. One particularly well-documented trend has been for middle- and working-class families—minoritized[87] and White—to move away from central cities, leaving the remaining residents to face problems of unemployment, poverty, racial isolation, and crumbling schools. As city smokestack industries continue to be "downsized," go overseas, or disappear entirely, jobs have also moved beyond the urban core.

The jobs remaining in the city tend to be "new economy" jobs in information and high-tech industries that are more difficult to qualify for than jobs in the "old economy" factories. Few inner-city residents—especially the large number of newly arrived, hardworking immigrants—qualify for these jobs. Most settle for irregular, part-time work in services and lack security, benefits, and a *living wage*—a term used to describe the income, calculated for each community, that ensures that a person working full-time will not fall below the poverty line.

These employment constraints, common in inner cities, together with housing policies and the preferences of White families to buy homes in school districts that are predominantly White, mean that, despite increased racial diversity in the United States, most young people live in highly segregated neighborhoods. White children typically live in communities where the vast majority of people are White. African American children, on average, live in neighborhoods where most of the other children are Black or Latinx; Latinx children typically also live in places where they are in the majority.[88]

Schooling Inequities

In 2002, Senator Christopher Dodd and Congressman Chaka Fattah introduced into Congress legislation that would ensure that basic educational opportunities are available to all U.S. students. Their Student Bill of Rights would hold states accountable for providing all students with the "fundamentals of educational opportunity,"[89] including highly qualified teachers and guidance counselors, challenging curricula, up-to-date textbooks and materials, and small classes. These are resources known to have an enormous positive impact on achievement, especially for disadvantaged students. See Focal Point 1.1 to read the text of this legislation.

One might think that such a bill of rights would be unnecessary in the United States, given its wealth and long history of public education, but many of the nation's children do not routinely experience these basic elements of education in their public schools. This declaration of student rights has yet to be passed.

Segregated Schools

Over the past decades, racial segregation has continued to have profound effects on public schools; so too has the continued existence and exacerbation of division between poor cities (and city centers) and surrounding affluent neighborhoods, including outer-urban and suburban communities. As a result, more than sixty years after *Brown v. Board of Education*,[90] many cities' public school systems remain predominantly attended by students of color. Middle-class Whites in those urban centers—often older than other parents of school-going children and more affluent—increasingly choose private education for their own kids. Some seek private schools for the resources, status, and privilege. Others praise the ideal of integration but worry that integration in practice would trigger declining school quality. Still others fear for their children's safety. Whatever the reasons, withdrawal of support by the middle class has left many urban public schools resource-poor and decaying. At the same time, demographic shifts have brought lower-income, more diverse populations into the suburban and sometimes segregated ring around cities—not without some predictable (and deeply problematic) backlash.[91]

Focal Point 1.1
Student Bill of Rights

H.R.236
Student Bill of Rights
In the House of Representatives

To provide for adequate and equitable educational opportunities for students in State public school systems, and for other purposes.

Be it enacted by the Senate and House of Representatives of the United States of America in Congress assembled, SEC. 112. State Educational Adequacy And Equity Requirements.

(a) Fundamentals of Educational Opportunity—A State shall provide for all public schools in the State access, at levels defined by the State under section 113 as ideal or adequate, to each of the following fundamentals of educational opportunity: (1) high-quality classroom teachers and school administrators (2) rigorous academic standards, curricula, and methods of instruction (3) small class sizes (4) quality facilities, textbooks, and instructional materials and supplies (5) up-to-date library resources (6) up-to-date computer technology (7) quality guidance counseling.

Overall, school segregation has increased since the 1980s, especially for Black and Latinx students.[92] Most striking, the percentage of schools with enrollments of 90–100 percent students of color has tripled in that time (see Figure 1.8). In 2013, 38 and 43 percent of Black and Latinx students, respectively, attended schools where the student body was 90 to 100 percent minoritized students. For Gary Orfield and his colleagues at the UCLA Civil Rights Project, these shifts represent a "striking" and consequential rise in segregation by race *and* poverty for African American and Latinx students in schools that "rarely attain the successful outcomes typical of middle class schools with largely White and Asian student populations."[93] This increased racial and socioeconomic separation is followed by unequal access to educational resources, opportunities, and outcomes.

Unequal Spending

In 2014, per-pupil spending ranged from a high of $18,165 in New York to a low of $5,838 in Idaho. In both high- and low-spending states, however, schools typically spend less on low-income children and children of color than they spend on economically advantaged and White students.[94]

Individual states vary greatly; some are much better, and some are much worse. A handful of states—Delaware, Minnesota, New Jersey, and Massachusetts—have generally high funding levels and also provide significantly more funding to districts where student poverty is more prevalent. Twenty-one states, however, provide less funding to school districts with higher

Figure 1.8 Percentage of 90–100 Percent White Schools and 90–100 Percent Non-White Schools in the United States, 1988–2013

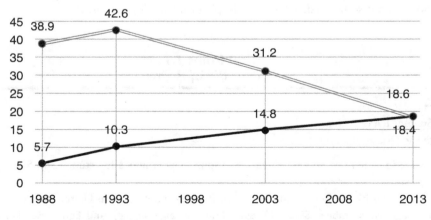

Concept Table 1.1 Per-Student Funding Gaps Add Up

For example, when you consider the cost-adjusted per-student funding gap for low-income students in . . .	Between two typical classrooms of students, that translates into a difference of . . .	Between two typical elementary schools of 400 students, that translates into a difference of . . .	Between two typical high schools of 1,500 students, that translates into a difference of . . .
New York	$57,975	$927,600	$3,478,500
Michigan	$14,325	$229,200	$859,500
North Carolina	$8,600	$137,600	$516,000
Delaware	$5,175	$82,800	$310,500

Source: The Education Trust, *The Funding Gap,* 2006, www.edtrust.org/dc/publication/the-funding-gap-0/.

concentrations of low-income students. In Wyoming, high-poverty districts receive 70 cents for every dollar allotted to low-poverty districts. In Nevada, high-poverty districts receive only 59 cents to that dollar.[95]

The Education Trust, an advocacy and research organization, calculated the impact of the funding gap for individual schools. (See Concept Table 1.1.) It found that in New York, almost $58,000 less per year would be spent on a classroom of twenty-five students in a high-poverty district, almost $1 million less per year would be spent at a high-poverty elementary school of 400 students, and over $3.4 million less per year would be spent at a high-poverty high school of 1,500 students.[96] The Education Trust asks an obvious and important question: "Consider the daily struggle for progress that occurs in many of our poorest schools. What could those schools do with another $1 million per year—resources that their more wealthy peers already enjoy?"[97]

Although this analysis is at least a decade old, the patterns still hold. While postrecession spending has increased overall in many states, as noted above, twenty-one states continue to spend less in high-poverty school districts.

Unequal Opportunities to Learn

The fifth-grade class was relocated into portables in October. The portables are half the size of the regular classroom. There is barely enough room to walk around because all books and supplies are nestled around the perimeter of the room on the floor. There are no cabinets. There are no windows. The district is in such dire financial straits that the teachers can't make photocopies; we don't have overhead projectors, nor do we have enough space for the children.

—Steven Branch
First-year teacher, grade 5

The boys' and girls' bathrooms had been flooded for over two months. After two months of sickening smell and slimy scum (literally, the students were walking in slime), the bathrooms were fixed. For two days . . . all day long, there was a jackhammer going off in the back of my room. Couldn't they have done this work after 2 P.M.? Or during recess and lunchtime? Or given me some advance notice so that I could have made some outdoor plans? I lost two days of learning.

—Jennifer Haymore
First-year teacher, grade 4

Steven Branch's and Jennifer Haymore's experiences in city school systems are not unique. Jonathan Kozol's wrenching account from the early 1990s, *Savage Inequalities,* portrays inequalities that many studies have since documented. Kozol found that Black and Latinx students in Camden, New Jersey, were learning keyboarding without computers, science without laboratories, and other subjects without enough textbooks to go around. Seven minutes away in the White, affluent community of Cherry Hill, students enjoyed well-kept facilities, including a greenhouse for those interested in horticulture, and abundant equipment and supplies. Since the publication of *Savage Inequalities*, journalists and scholars have increased the public's awareness of disparities in school conditions, and activists in many states have pursued legal action to correct them.

In 1997, for example, the *Los Angeles Times* published a humiliating story of textbook shortages in the city's schools. Fremont High School, attended almost entirely by Latinx youth, reported needing 7,200 textbooks simply to comply with state law. For its 1,200 tenth graders, Fremont owned only 210 English textbooks. And Fremont was hardly the only high school in the district wrestling with serious book shortages. It is difficult to imagine that a school or district with mostly affluent White students, anywhere, would ever face such a problem. Within a few weeks of the exposé, the newspaper was filled with reports of school district money, private donations, and action at the state level, along with large photos showing stacks of new books at Fremont.[98] Yet these stopgap measures on behalf of one school did little to address the broader set of inequities facing so many of the city's students.

In 2000, some angry Californians asked the courts to remedy such inequities. A group of young people and their parents filed suit in the name of Eliezer Williams, an African American student at a San Francisco middle school. Nearly all of the forty-eight student plaintiffs named in the case were Black, Latinx, or Asian/Pacific Islander, and they all attended schools filled with fellow students of color from low-income communities. They sued California's governor, the state board of education, and the superintendent of public instruction.

The Williams plaintiffs claimed that they, and many students like them, attended "schools that shock the conscience."[99] They provided evidence that schools across the state lacked "trained teachers, necessary educational supplies, classrooms, even seats in classrooms, and facilities that meet basic health and safety standards." They also showed that these schooling basics were systematically less available to low-income students of color, and that a school experiencing one of the problems was much more likely to experience more or all of them. The Williams students argued that, by permitting such schools, California's educational system failed to meet its constitutional obligation to educate all students and to educate them equally. In 2004, the governor of California agreed to settle the case, allocating $1 billion and developing standards requiring that all students have qualified teachers, instructional materials, and decent and safe school buildings.

Such schooling inequalities were not then and are not now confined to California, nor were they entirely remedied even in California. Across the nation, students at high-poverty schools have fewer well-qualified teachers than their White counterparts in affluent, suburban schools. Their schools also suffer more teaching vacancies, which principals then have a tougher time filling.

In part because of the scope of these issues nationwide, the U.S. Department of Education required in 2015 that each state file an equity report documenting the distribution of teachers across various student populations. Those reports revealed that, across the country, unqualified, inexperienced, or out-of-field teachers were found in disproportionately high numbers in high-poverty schools and/or schools serving students of color. Figure 1.9 shows the numbers of states where access to qualified teachers remains a serious problem.

In total, forty states reported inequitable access to *experienced* teachers for low-income students and students of color. Likewise, twenty-nine states reported that *unqualified* teachers more often teach low-income and/or minoritized students.[100]

Less qualified teachers are a particular problem because study after study shows that, of all the resources schools provide, highly qualified teachers with expertise in their subject areas are the

Figure 1.9 Qualified Teachers: Number of States Where Access Is Problematic

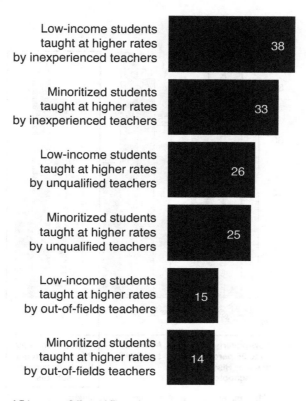

Source: U.S. Department of Education, Office of Elementary and Secondary Education, *State Plans to Ensure Equitable Access to Excellent Educators*, 2015, www2.ed.gov/programs/titleiparta/resources.html.

most important for student learning, and underqualified teachers are particularly damaging for children who also face inequities outside of school.

Moreover, having enough teachers also matters. In fact, children from low-income families have higher rates of achievement, and suffer less of an achievement gap, when their states target staffing increases to their own (highest-needs) schools.[101]

It's not just *who* teachers are, but *how* they teach that matters for student learning. In schools serving low-income communities and communities of color, teachers—who may have less experience and expertise, given staffing issues addressed above—tend to place less emphasis on inquiry and problem-solving skills and offer fewer opportunities for active learning.[102] This, too, puts students in those schools at a disadvantage.

Furthermore, *what* is taught matters, too. Schools attended predominantly by Black and Latinx students often offer fewer critical college "gatekeeping" courses such as advanced mathematics and science. Figure 1.10 shows the disparities among schools with different populations in advanced middle and high school mathematics. Notably, there is a 30 percent gap between low- and high-poverty schools when it comes to seventh and eighth graders' access to algebra.

Advanced placement (AP) courses that enhance students' college-going opportunities are also unevenly distributed. In 1999, Rasheda Daniel, a working-class African American teenager, sued her school district and the state of California because her high school did not offer the advanced

Figure 1.10 Distribution of Math Courses in Middle and High Schools, by Student Race/Ethnicity, 2011–2012

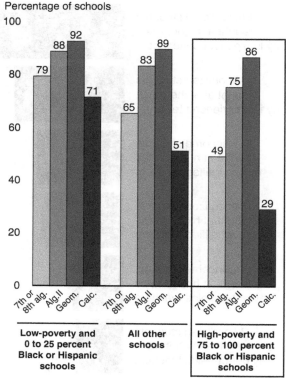

7th or 8th alg. = seventh- or eighth-grade algebra
Alg.II = Algebra II
Geom. = Geometry
Calc. = Calculus

Source: GAO Report to Congressional Requesters, *K–12 Education: Better Use of Information Could Help Agencies Identify Disparities and Address Racial Discrimination,* 2016.

classes that she needed to attend the state's university as a science major. Nobody thought she was wrong, and nobody thought she was an isolated case. Daniel's suit prompted the state legislature to provide new funding to schools like hers so they could begin offering the requisite advanced courses.

However, addressing any single inequity is often a moving target, because proposed solutions rarely address underlying, systemic issues. Even when schools in poor neighborhoods make headway in providing new resources and college-prep classes, the rate at which they improve is typically outpaced by more advantaged schools, which typically don't have myriad other challenges to address, too.

Indeed, as Jonathan Kozol's more recent book, *The Shame of the Nation: The Restoration of Apartheid Schooling in America,* attests, equitable schooling opportunities remain elusive for numerous reasons—many of which we address in detail in subsequent chapters. Published fifteen years after *Savage Inequalities, The Shame of the Nation* shows in unflinching detail how far we have yet to travel on the path to equitable schooling, and also how important the work of equity-focused teachers is in carrying us forward toward that worthy goal.

Gaps in Achievement, School Completion, and College Attendance

Gaps in schooling outcomes inevitably follow gaps in opportunities like those detailed above. From elementary school on, we see this adversely impacting students considered English Learners and African American, Latinx, and low-income children vis-à-vis their White and more well-off peers. They more often end up in lower-level and remedial classes, and less frequently end up in college-preparatory classes. They consistently receive lower scores on measures of student achievement that schools claim are crucial. They drop out—or are pushed out—of school at higher rates. Fewer go on to college; fewer still earn college degrees.

In a 2009 report from the Educational Testing Service, *Parsing the Achievement Gap II*, analysts Paul Barton and Richard Corey identified what they call the "correlates" of achievement. (See Concept Table 1.2.) In all sixteen of the factors related to achievement, Barton and Corey showed gaps between White students and students of color. In twelve of the sixteen, there

Concept Table 1.2 Correlates of Achievement and Gaps

	Are there gaps between racial minority and majority student populations?	Are there gaps between students from low-income families and higher-income families?
In-school correlates		
Rigor of curriculum	Yes	Not available
AP participation	Yes	Not available
Teacher certification	Yes	Yes
Teacher preparation in discipline	Yes	Yes
Teacher experience	Yes	Yes
Teacher absences	Yes	Yes
Teacher turnover	Yes	Yes
Class size	Yes	No*
Internet access	Yes	Yes
Computer-to-student ratio	Yes	Yes
Fear at school	Yes	Not available
Street gangs at school	Yes	Not available
Physical fighting	Yes	Not available
Before and beyond school		
Parent participation	Yes	Yes
Student mobility	Yes	Not available
Birth weight	Yes	Yes
Lead exposure	Yes	Yes
Mercury poisoning	Yes	Yes
Hunger and nutrition	Yes	Yes
Talking and reading to children	Yes	Yes
Television watching	Yes	Yes
Parent-pupil ratio	Yes	Yes
Summer achievement gain/loss	Yes	Yes

* Not all researchers agree that class size is a correlate with achievement for low-income students.

Source: Paul E. Barton and Richard J. Coley, *Parsing the Achievement Gap, II* (Princeton, NJ: Educational Testing Service, 2009).

were gaps between low-income and higher-income students.[103] Three indicators of educational success—academic achievement, high school graduation, and college attendance—continue to reveal the impact of these persistent inequalities.

Academic Achievement

The academic achievement of the nation's schoolchildren is measured every few years by the National Assessment of Educational Progress (NAEP), a paper-and-pencil test in reading, writing, mathematics, science, U.S. history, civics, geography, and the arts. Often called "the Nation's Report Card," NAEP tests a sample of students in grades 4, 8, and 12 in every state. Unlike most standardized tests, NAEP doesn't produce scores for every child, but it does report the results for the nation's 9-, 13-, and 17-year-olds as a whole, and it compares the performance of males and females, racial groups, and poor and not-poor students.

In 2012, NAEP released a study reporting trends in the achievement of U.S. students over the past forty years. There was some promising news: for example, 9- and 13-year-olds today are scoring higher in reading and mathematics than when NAEP began testing students in the early 1970s. African American and Latinx students have shown the most impressive gains, and, as a result, the gaps between their achievement and that of their White peers were smaller than they had ever been. The Black-White gap alone was nearly half the size of the gap measured in 1971. However, these gaps are still meaningful when we compare students across ages and racial groups. For example, by the end of high school, the math and reading score of Latinx and African American students are roughly the same as those of White 13-year-olds.[104]

High School Graduation

Nationwide, approximately 83 percent of those who enter ninth grade graduate from high school with a diploma at the end of the twelfth grade.[105] Graduation rates, however, remain higher for White, wealthier students. In 2015, for example, 75 percent of African American students, 72 percent of Native American students, and 78 percent of Latinx students graduated from high school, compared to 88 percent of their White peers. However, because the U.S. education system provides second chances for those who leave high school without a diploma, about 90 percent of all 25- to 29-year-olds in 2010 held a diploma or some form of equivalency certificate. Even so, White students were more likely (95 percent) than African American students (91 percent) and Latinx students (81 percent) to have eventually attained the status (via diploma or GED) of a high school graduate.[106]

College Attendance

In 2015, more students than ever before from all racial groups were going to college, but the gains among groups were not equal. In particular, Latinx participation rates lagged behind those of African Americans and Whites. Nearly half of all 25- to 29-year-olds, for example, had completed a two-year college degree, with Asian and White students (54 and 72 percent) more likely than African American and Latinx students (31 and 26 percent) to have done so. Thirty-four percent of all 25- to 29-year-olds had at least a bachelor's degree. Although the percentage with a bachelor's degree or higher has increased for all racial/ethnic groups, the gaps between White and both Black and Latinx students have actually widened over time. Figure 1.11 shows the gaps in college attainment.

Figure 1.11 Percentage of Persons 25 to 29 Years Old With an Associate's or Higher Degree, by Race/Ethnicity: 2000 and 2015

| Year | Total | Race/ethnicity | | | |
		White	Black	Hispanic	Asian
2000 ...	37.7	43.7	26.0	15.4	– – –
2015 ...	45.7	54.0	31.1	25.7	71.7

Source: U.S. Department of Commerce, Census Bureau, Current Population Survey (CPS), Annual Social and Economic Supplement, 1992 through 2015. (This table was prepared January 2016.)

The Struggle for Socially Just Teaching

In the remaining chapters of this book, we continue to share the experiences and reflections of teachers who identify themselves as teachers for social justice. Many of them are writing at the conclusion of their first year of teaching. Through their teacher education courses, their work in classrooms, and their own life experiences, they understand the inequalities and inequities we've described in this chapter, and they've begun their careers committed to teaching in ways that will change the world. Their voices are hopeful and optimistic about the possibilities socially just education opens up in a diverse, unpredictable world. These teachers also reveal their struggles to put knowledge and values into practice as they strive to create classrooms and schools where students develop the moral commitment, academic capacities, and sense of agency they'll need to shape their own place in a more socially just future.

Four of these teachers deserve a special introduction, since they and their students appear in photographs throughout the book. These four teachers seek to build community without diminishing difference. They hold fast to the idea that their teaching and their students' learning can help change a world marked by poverty, discrimination, and injustice.

Mauro Bautista

Mauro Bautista is coordinator of bilingual education at his middle school. He teaches—and lives with his wife and three kids—in the same Latinx neighborhood where he grew up. He sees himself in his sixth-, seventh-, and eighth-grade students, and he sees his own parents in their parents. Consequently, he always treats students as he hopes his own children will be treated.

> I define "social justice educator" as someone who identifies inequities in education, builds coalitions with others affected by the inequities, and then takes action to disrupt the reproduction of these inequities. . . . I look at educational practices with critical lenses. Instead of doing certain things longer and stronger, I often take a step back and ask, "How else can we do this?"
>
> There are always questions: "Am I doing justice to my students?" "How do I know that what I am doing is socially just?" "Why do we have to do it this way?" "Can I do it this other way?" "If I can't do it this other way, what does that mean to my students?"

Mauro holds the highest expectations for his students and their parents, and he tries to treat them with the utmost respect.

Kimberly Min

Kimberly Min teaches third grade in South Los Angeles. At the conclusion of her first year working in a neighborhood that is home to some of the city's most acute poverty, Kimberly dedicated her master's degree project to her students. She said that she couldn't have asked for a more endearing, bright, and loving group of children, and she thanked them for being incredibly patient with a first-year teacher.

> Education is viewed by many as an equalizing agent in our society. However, children of color, children of poor working families, and children of immigrants are still marginalized and victims of an unequal society that privileges rich, White, middle- and upper-class values. More than fifty years after *Brown v. Board of Education*, inequity, injustice, and compensatory education continue to be the experiences of our children in inner-city schools. Although the *Brown* decision marked a turning point in history, the struggle for equality in education continues.
>
> So it's been fifty-plus years. Now what? Educators must continue to teach students about their history; have discussions about inequity, race, and privilege; and create a space in which students can express what they are thinking, feeling, and learning, as well as share their opinions and perspectives. . . . As an elementary school teacher in South Los Angeles, I empower, engage, and encourage my students to disrupt cycles of oppression and inequity with a curriculum that requires them to read text (literature, media, art, expression) with a critical eye.

Mark Hill

Mark Hill is a high school math teacher. Mark's students live in a racially diverse, working-class community where more than thirty different languages are spoken. Neither uniformly well-off nor poor, the community's average household earns $47,500 per year. Even so, 18 percent of families live below the poverty line.

Mark's own experience as a biracial person, the son of a White mother and a Black father, has had a profound effect on his teaching. He understands the limits that our culture's struggle with race places on students of color. He also knows how important it is for students to be seen as more than just their race, gender, or age—how important it is for them to be accepted on their own terms. As a first-year teacher, he explained:

> I see social activism relating to my teaching in a very simple way. I am a role model for students of color and low socioeconomic status. It is my goal that every one of my students leaves my classroom believing in themselves and their ability to reach college. I treat each student with respect, and I hope to teach them to respect each other and themselves in the same way.

Judy Smith

Teaching is Judy Smith's second career. Before obtaining her teaching credential, Judy worked in the private sector—in a high-tech industry. The high school where she teaches history and government to eleventh and twelfth graders enrolls more than 3,000 Latinx, African American, Asian, and White students. Two-thirds of the students come from low-income families, and a third are learning English as their second language. When she came to the school, it had just failed to meet its achievement test score targets under state and federal law and thus had been identified by the state as academically "low performing."

Judy loves her job and the challenge of bringing academic rigor and engaging learning opportunities to her students, despite mainstream beliefs that students like hers won't succeed in

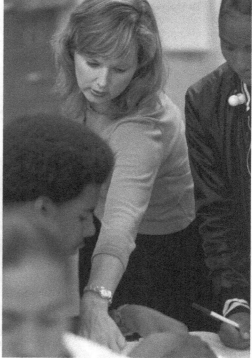

high-level academic work. As her comments at the beginning of this chapter make clear, her determination to make a difference is driven by extraordinarily difficult questions:

> How does a social justice teacher teach in an urban school where very large class sizes, minimal resources, low expectations, and low literacy affect both students and teachers? What does it mean to be a socially just teacher in a socially unjust world? What do all students deserve?

This book seeks to help answer the questions Judy and her colleagues raise about social justice teaching in the twenty-first century. Its goal is to provide aspiring teachers with an understanding of the hopeful struggle that these teachers are engaged in. It also aims to provide a knowledge base and a sense of possibility that will equip new teachers to be effective agents for educational equality—ready to teach to change the world.

Digging Deeper and Tools for Critique

www.routledge.com/cw/teachingtochangetheworld

Notes

1 William J. Hussar and Tabitha M. Bailey, *Projections of Education Statistics to 2024* (NCES 2016-013). U.S. Department of Education, National Center for Education Statistics. Washington, DC: U.S. Government Printing Office, 2016.
2 Ibid.
3 Jeremy Redford, Danielle Battle, and Stacey Bielick, *Homeschooling in the United States: 2012* (NCES 2016-096.REV). National Center for Education Statistics, Institute of Education Sciences, U.S. Department of Education. Washington, DC, 2017.
4 Although the term *Latinx* has been the subject of some debate, we use it throughout the book in addition to *Hispanic* and *Latino/a*. We recognize that some may view *Latinx* as critical of the Spanish language and/or of Latino culture. We do not use the term in the spirit of critique, but rather because it represents the most established gender-neutral and nonbinary option at this time, and it is used widely now in the field of education. However, we also use *Latino* and *Hispanic* whenever it's the language of the statistics being used or when we are quoting others.
5 Joel McFarland, Bill Hussar, Cristobal de Brey, Tom Snyder, Xiaolei Wang, Sidney Wilkinson-Flicker, Semhar Gebrekristos, Jijun Zhang, Amy Rathbun, Amy Barmer, Farrah Bullock Mann, and Serena Hinz, *The Condition of Education 2017* (NCES 2017-144). U.S. Department of Education. Washington, DC: National Center for Education Statistics, 2017, https://nces.ed.gov/pubsearch/pubsinfo.asp?pubid=2017144.
6 Ibid.
7 Pew Research Center, *Multiracial in America: Proud, Diverse and Growing in Numbers*. Washington, DC, June 2015, www.pewsocialtrends.org/2015/06/11/multiracial-in-america/.
8 McFarland, Hussar, de Brey, Snyder, Wang, Wilkinson-Flicker, Gebrekristos, Zhang, Rathbun, Barmer, Bullock Mann, and Hinz, *The Condition of Education 2017*.
9 The Southern Education Foundation, *Race and Ethnicity in a New Era of Public Funding for Private Schools: Private School Enrollment in the South and the Nation*, 2016, www.southerneducation.org/getattachment/be785c57-6ce7-4682-b80d-04d89994a0b6/Race-and-Ethnicity-in-a-New-Era-of-Public-Funding.aspx.
10 Redford, Battle, and Bielick, *Homeschooling in the United States: 2012*.
11 Migration Policy Institute, *Frequently Requested Statistics on Immigrants and Immigration in the United States*, 2017, www.migrationpolicy.org/article/frequently-requested-statistics-immigrants-and-immigration-united-states#Demographic.
12 Ibid.
13 American Immigration Council, *An Overview of U.S. Refugee Law and Policy*, 2015, www.americanimmigrationcouncil.org/sites/default/files/research/an_overview_of_united_states_refugee_law_and_policy.pdf.

14 Offices of Refugee Resettlement, *Unaccompanied Children Released to Sponsors by State*, 2017, www.acf.hhs.gov/orr/programs/ucs/state-by-state-uc-placed-sponsors.

15 Kids Count Data Center, *2015 American Community Survey*, 2015, http://datacenter.kidscount. org/data/tables/81-children-who-speak-a-language-other-than-english-at-home#detailed/1/ any/false/573,869,36,868,867/any/396,397.

16 Ibid.

17 Ibid.

18 Ariel G. Ruiz Soto, Sarah Hooker, and Jeanne Batalova, *ELL Information Center Fact Sheet Series. Migration Policy Institute*, 2015, www.migrationpolicy.org/research/states-and-districts-highest-number-and-share-english-language-learners.

19 Ofelia García, Jo Anne Kleifgen, and Lorraine Falchi, "From English Language Learners to Emergent Bilinguals," *Equity Matters: Research Review No. 1*. New York: A Research Initiative of the Campaign for Educational Equity, 2008.

20 Jie Zong and Jeanne Batalova, *Frequently Requested Statistics on Immigrants and Immigration in the United States*. Washington, DC: Migration Policy Institute, 2017, www.migrationpolicy.org/ article/frequently-requested-statistics-immigrants-and-immigration-united-states.

21 U.S. Department of Education, Office of Special Education Programs, *Individuals With Disabilities Education Act (IDEA) Database*, www2.ed.gov/programs/osepidea/618-data/state-level-data-files/index.html#bcc, retrieved on September 25, 2015.

22 U.S. Commission on Civil Rights, *Minorities in Special Education (2007 Briefing)*, 2009, www. usccr.gov/pubs/MinoritiesinSpecialEducation.pdf; National Education Association, *Truth in Labeling: Disproportionality in Special Education*, 2007, www.nea.org/assets/docs/HE/EW-TruthInLabeling.pdf; U.S. Department of Education, *29th Annual Report to Congress on the Implementation of the Individuals With Disabilities Education Act*, 2007, www2.ed.gov/about/ reports/annual/osep/2007/parts-b-c/29th-vol-2.pdf.

23 Seon-Young Lee, Michael S. Matthews, and Paula Olszewski-Kubilius, "A National Picture of Talent Search and Talent Search Educational Programs," *Gifted Child Quarterly* 52, no. 2 (2008): 55–69; Donna Y. Ford, Terek C. Grantham, and Gilman W. Whiting, "Another Look at the Achievement Gap: Learning From the Experiences of Gifted Black Students," *Urban Education* 43, no. 2 (2008): 216–238; Frank C. Worrell, "Why Are There So Few African Americans in Gifted Programs?" in *Surmounting All Odds: Education, Opportunity, and Society in the New Millennium*, eds. C. C. Yeakey and R. D. Henderson (Greenwich, CT: Information Age, 2003), 423–454.

24 Pew Research Center, *U.S. Public Becoming Less Religious*, November 3, 2015, www.pewforum. org/2015/11/03/chapter-1-importance-of-religion-and-religious-beliefs/.

25 Pew Research Center, *America's Changing Religious Landscape*, May 12, 2015, www.pewforum. org/2015/05/12/americas-changing-religious-landscape/.

26 Ibid.

27 *Pew Research Center's Spring 2016 Global Attitudes Survey*, www.pewglobal.org/.

28 Institute for Social Policy and Understanding, *American Muslim Poll 2017: Muslims at The Crossroads*, www.ispu.org/wp-content/uploads/2017/03/AMP-2017-Key-Findings_Final.pdf.

29 National Education Association, *Muslims in America: When Bullying Meets Religion*, 2012, www. nea.org/home/42528.htm.

30 Reuters, *CAIR Asks DOE to Address Bullying of Muslim Students*, June 9, 2011, www.reuters. com/article/2011/06/09/idUS215018+09-Jun-2011+PRN20110609/; Southern Poverty Law Center, *SPLC Testifies About Increase in Anti-Muslim Bias*, March 29, 2011, www.splcenter. org/get-informed/news/splc-testifies-about-increase-in-anti-muslim-bias/.

31 Forum on Child and Family Statistics, *America's Children: Key National Indicators of Well-Being, 2011, Family Structure and Children's Living Arrangements*, www.childstats.gov/americaschildren/ famsoc1.asp.

32 Pew Research Center, *Parenting in America: Outlook, Worries, Aspirations Are Strongly Linked to Financial Situation*, 2015, www.pewsocialtrends.org/2015/12/17/1-the-american-family-today/.

33 U.S. Census Bureau, *Living Arrangements of Children: 2009*, 2011, www.census.gov/prod/ 2011pubs/p70-126.pdf.

34 U.S. Department of Health and Human Services, Administration for Children and Families, *Trends in Foster Care and Adoption: FY 2006-FY 2015*, 2015, www.acf.hhs.gov/sites/default/ files/cb/trends_fostercare_adoption2015.pdf.

35 Teresa Wiltz, *Why More Grandparents Are Raising Children*. Washington, DC: Pew Charitable Trust, 2016, www.pewtrusts.org/en/research-and-analysis/blogs/stateline/2016/11/02/why-more-grandparents-are-raising-children.

36 Pew Research Center, *Multiracial in America: Proud, Diverse and Growing in Numbers.*

37 Gary J. Gates and Taylor N. T. Brown, *Marriage and Same-Sex Couples After Obergefell.* Los Angeles, CA: Williams Institute, UCLA School of Law, 2015, http://williamsinstitute.law.ucla.edu/wp-content/uploads/Marriage-and-Same-sex-Couples-after-Obergefell-November-2015.pdf.

38 Social Issues, January 11, 2017, In US, More Adults Identifying as LGBT, www.gallup.com/poll/201731/lgbt-identification-rises.aspx.

39 Gallup, *U.S. Adults Estimate that 25% of Americans Are Gay or Lesbian*, May 27, 2011, www.gallup.com/poll/147824/adults-estimate-americans-gay-lesbian.aspx.

40 Hannah Fingerhut, *Support Steady for Same-Sex Marriage and Acceptance of Homosexuality*, 2016, www.pewresearch.org/fact-tank/2016/05/12/support-steady-for-same-sex-marriage-and-acceptance-of-homosexuality.

41 Gay, Lesbian and Straight Education Network, *Safe Schools Laws*, 2017, www.lgbtmap.org/equality-maps/safe_school_laws.

42 Pew Research Center, *Parenting in America: Outlook, Worries, Aspirations Are Strongly Linked to Financial Situation.*

43 Joseph G. Kosciw, Emily A. Greytak, Noreen M. Giga, Christian Villenas, and David J. Danischewski, *The 2015 National School Climate Survey: The Experiences of Lesbian, Gay, Bisexual, Transgender, and Queer Youth in Our Nation's Schools.* New York: GLSEN, 2016, www.glsen.org/sites/default/files/2015%20National%20GLSEN%202015%20National%20School%20Climate%20Survey%20%28NSCS%29%20-%20Full%20Report_0.pdf.

44 Mitch van Geel, Paul Vedder, and Jenny Tanilon, "Bullying and Weapon Carrying a Meta-Analysis," *JAMA Pediatrics* 168, no. 8 (2014): 714–720. doi:10.1001/jamapediatrics.2014.213, http://jamanetwork.com/journals/jamapediatrics/fullarticle/1879724.

45 Annette Lareau, *Unequal Childhoods: Class, Race, and Family Life* (Berkeley and Los Angeles: University of California Press, 2003).

46 Ibid., 1.

47 Walt Whitman, "Song of Myself," in *Leaves of Grass* (New York: Rome Brothers, 1855).

48 Institute for Policy Studies, *How Unequal Are We, Anyway? (A Statistical Briefing Book)*, July 2004, www.psicopolis.com/statistiche/inequality.htm.

49 OECD, *How's Life? 2015: Measuring Well-being*, www.oecd.org/statistics/Better-Life-Initiative-2016-country-notes-data.xlsx.

50 Congressional Budget Office, *Trends in Family Wealth, 1989 to 2013*, August 2016, www.cbo.gov/sites/default/files/114th-congress-2015-2016/reports/51846-familywealth.pdf.

51 *RSF Russell Sage Foundation—Chartbook of Social Inequality*, www.russellsage.org/sites/all/files/chartbook/Income%20and%20Earnings.pdf.

52 Institute for Policy Studies, *Income Inequality*, 2011, http://inequality.org/income-inequality/.

53 Economic Policy Institute, *State of Working America Data Library*, 2017; Economic Policy Institute, *State of Working America, 2011*; National Center for Children in Poverty, *Paid Leave in the States*, 2009, www.paidfamilyleave.org/pdf/PaidLeaveinStates.pdf.

54 Economic Policy Institute, *State of Working America, 2011.*

55 Elise Gould and Hilary Wething, *U.S. Poverty Rates Higher, Safety Net Weaker Than in Peer Countries* (Washington, DC: Economic Policy Institute, 2015), www.epi.org/publication/ib339-us-poverty-higher-safety-net-weaker/.

56 Lawrence Mishel, Jared Bernstein, and Sylvia Allegretto, *State of Working America, 2004–2005* (Washington, DC: Economic Policy Institute, 2005), www.epinet.org.

57 U.S. Department of Education, Office of Planning, Evaluation and Policy Development, Performance Information Management Service, *Free and Reduced-Price Lunch Eligibility Data in EDFacts: A White Paper on Current Status and Potential Changes*, Washington, DC, 2012.

58 U.S. Census Bureau, *Income and Poverty in the United States: 2015*, www.census.gov/content/dam/Census/library/publications/2016/demo/p60-256.pdf.

59 Forum on Child and Family Statistics, *America's Children: Key National Indicators of Children's Well-Being 2011.*

60 McFarland, Hussar, de Brey, Snyder, Wang, Wilkinson-Flicker, Gebrekristos, Zhang, Rathbun, Barmer, Bullock Mann, and Hinz, *The Condition of Education 2017.*

61 Economic Policy Institute, *The Racial Wealth Gap: How African-Americans Have Been Short-changed Out of the Materials to Build Wealth*, 2017, www.epi.org/blog/the-racial-wealth-gap-how-african-americans-have-been-shortchanged-out-of-the-materials-to-build-wealth/.

62 Hispanic Wealth Project, *Annual Report 2016*, http://hispanicwealthproject.org/downloads/2016-HWP-Annual-Report.pdf.

63 United States Department of Labor, Bureau of Labor Statistics, *Labor Force Statistics From the Current Population Survey*, 2017, www.bls.gov/cps/cpsaat07.htm.

64 Population Reference Bureau, analysis of data from the U.S. Census Bureau, *2008–2015 American Community Survey*, http://datacenter.kidscount.org/data/tables/5064-children-living-in-families-where-no-parent-has-full-time-year-round-employment-by-race?loc=1&loct=1#detailed/1/any/false/573,869,36,868,867/10,11,9,12,1,185,13/11486,11487.

65 Valerie Wilson and William M. Rodgers III, *Black-White Wage Gaps Expand With Rising Wage Inequality*, Economic Policy Institute, 2016, www.epi.org/files/pdf/101972.pdf.

66 Economic Policy Institute, *State of Working America Data Library*, 2017, www.stateofworkingamerica.org/chart/swa-wages-figure-4f-share-workers-earning/.

67 UN General Assembly, "Publicity to Be Given to the Universal Declaration of Human Rights," Resolution 217 D (III), 1948, Paris.

68 UN General Assembly, Universal Declaration of Human Rights, Article 25, 10 December 1948, Resolution 217 A (III), available at http://www.refworld.org/docid/3ae6b3712c.html.

69 Institute for Policy Studies, *How Unequal Are We, Anyway? (A Statistical Briefing Book)*.

70 *Going to Bed Hungry*, http://billmoyers.com/2013/04/05/going-to-bed-hungry/.

71 Child Trends Databank, *Food Insecurity*, 2016, www.childtrends.org/?indicators=food-insecurity.

72 University of Wisconsin-Madison, Institute for Research on Poverty, *Reducing Health Disparities by Poverty Status*, 2015, www.irp.wisc.edu/publications/policybriefs/pdfs/PB4-ProvenPoliciesToReduceHealthDisparities.pdf.

73 Center for Disease Control, *CDC Investigation: Blood Lead Levels Higher After Switch to Flint River Water*, 2016, www.cdc.gov/media/releases/2016/p0624-water-lead.html.

74 Samantha Artiga and Petry Ubri, *Key Issues in Children's Health Coverage*, The Henry J. Kaiser Family Foundation, 2017, p. 1, www.kff.org/medicaid/issue-brief/key-issues-in-childrens-health-coverage/.

75 *Key Issues in Children's Health Coverage*, www.kff.org/medicaid/issue-brief/key-issues-in-childrens-health-coverage/.

76 Forum on Child and Family Statistics, *America's Children: Key National Indicators of Children's Well-Being 2015*, www.childstats.gov/pdf/ac2015/ac_15.pdf.

77 Joint Center for Housing Studies of Harvard University, *State of the Nation's Housing 2010*, June 2011, www.jchs.harvard.edu/research/publications/state-nations-housing-2010/.

78 Urban Institute, *Issues in Focus: Immigration*, www.urban.org/content/IssuesInFocus/immigrationstudies/immigration.htm.

79 U.S. Census Bureau, www.census.gov.

80 Urban Institute, *Investor-Owners in the Boom and Bust*, 2011, www.metrotrends.org/commentary/mortgage-lending.cfm.

81 U.S. Department of Housing and Urban Development, *The 2008 Annual Homeless Assessment Report to Congress: A Summary of Findings*, July 2009, www.hmis.info/ClassicAsp/documents/2008AHARSummary.pdf.

82 Forum on Child and Family Statistics, *America's Children: Key National Indicators of Children's Well-Being 2015*.

83 Laura E. Durso and Gary J. Gates, *Serving Our Youth: Findings From a National Survey of Service Providers Working With Lesbian, Gay, Bisexual, and Transgender Youth Who Are Homeless or at Risk of Becoming Homeless* (Los Angeles: The Williams Institute With True Colors Fund and The Palette Fund, 2012), http://williamsinstitute.law.ucla.edu/wp-content/uploads/Durso-Gates-LGBT-Homeless-Youth-Survey-July-2012.pdf.

84 Child Trends Data Bank, *Neighborhood Safety: Indicators of Child and Youth Well Being*, 2013, www.childtrends.org/wp-content/uploads/2012/08/107_Neighborhood_Safety-1.pdf.

85 The "stop-and-frisk" policy of the New York City Police Department, which became a topic of national media coverage and even a subject of debate in the 2016 presidential election, is one example of a controversial formal policing practice that has been shown to disproportionately impact youth of color. Under "stop-and-frisk," officers can detain, question, and even search civilians for weapons, drugs, or other contraband. In 2011 alone, the New York City Police Department stopped and questioned over 684,000 people, only 12 percent of whom were issued summonses. Of those stopped, 92 percent were male, most between the ages of 14 and 24, and 87 percent were African American or Latinx.

86 "Young Black Men Faced Highest Rate of US Police Killings in 2016," *The Guardian*, January 8, 2017, www.theguardian.com/us-news/2017/jan/08/the-counted-police-killings-2016-young-black-men.

87 Throughout the book we often use the term *minoritized* instead of *minority*. The choice reflects our recognition that, because of socially constructed differences in race, religion, national origin, sexuality, and gender, certain groups have less power or representation than members of other groups in society.

88 Richard Rothstein, *The Color of Law: A Forgotten History of How Our Government Segregated America* (New York: Liveright, 2017); Ann Owens, "Racial Residential Segregation of School-Age Children and Adults: The Role of Schooling as a Segregating Force," *RSF: The Russell Sage Foundation Journal of the Social Sciences* 3, no. 2 (2017): 63–80. doi:10.7758/RSF.2017.3.2.03.

89 H.R. 2178, Student Bill of Rights, 109th Congress, 2005–2006.

90 *Brown v. Board of Education of Topeka*, 347 U.S. 483, 1954.

91 Brookings Institute, *The Suburbanization of Poverty: Trends in Metropolitan Areas, 2000–2008*, January 20, 2010, www.brookings.edu/papers/2010/0120_poverty_kneebone.aspx.

92 Gary Orfield, Jongyeon Ee, Erica Frankenberg, and Genevieve Siegel-Hawley, *"Brown" at 62: School Segregation by Race, Poverty and State* (Los Angeles: UCLA Civil Rights Project-Proyecto Derechos Civiles, 2016).

93 Ibid., 1.

94 Bruce Baker, Danielle Farrie, Monete Johnson, Theresa Luhm, and David G. Sciarra, *Is School Funding Fair? A National Report Card*. Newark, NJ: Education Law Center, 2017, www.schoolfundingfairness.org/National_Report_Card.pdf.

95 Ibid.

96 The Education Trust, *The Funding Gap, 2004* (Washington, DC: Education Trust, 2004), www.edtrust.org/sites/edtrust.org/files/publications/files/funding2004.pdf.

97 Ibid.

98 Amy Pyle, "Attacking the Textbook Crisis," *Los Angeles Times*, September 29, 1997, http://articles.latimes.com/1997/sep/29/local/me-37364/.

99 *Williams v. State of California*, Complaint Filed May 17, 2000, www.decentschools.org.

100 U.S. Department of Education, Office of Elementary and Secondary Education (1915), *State Plans to Ensure Equitable Access to Excellent Teachers*, https://www2.ed.gov/programs/titleiparta/equitable/titleiiequityanalysis1031.pdf.

101 Bruce D. Baker, Danielle Farrie, and David G. Sciarra, "Mind the Gap: 20 Years of Progress and Retrenchment in School Funding and Achievement Gaps," *ETS Research Report Series* 2016, no. 1 (2016): 1–37.

102 Jeannie Oakes, *Multiplying Inequalities* (Santa Monica, CA: RAND, 1990).

103 Paul E. Barton and Richard J. Coley, *Parsing the Achievement Gap II* (Princeton, NJ: Educational Testing Service, 2009), www.ets.org/Media/Research/pdf/PICPARSINGII.pdf.

104 National Center for Education Statistics, *The Nation's Report Card: Trends in Academic Progress 2012* (NCES 2013 456), Institute of Education Sciences, U.S. Department of Education, Washington, DC, 2013, https://nces.ed.gov/nationsreportcard/subject/publications/main2012/pdf/2013456.pdf.

105 McFarland, Hussar, de Brey, Snyder, Wang, Wilkinson-Flicker, Gebrekristos, Zhang, Rathbun, Barmer, Bullock Mann, and Hinz, *The Condition of Education 2017*.

106 Ibid.

History and Culture

How Expanding Expectations and Powerful Ideologies Shape Schooling in the United States

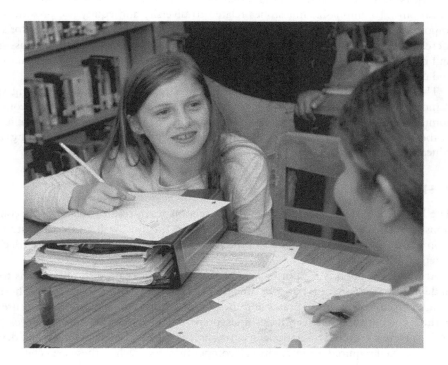

Education is viewed as the equalizing agent in our society, and meritocracy is viewed as the path to achieve that end. According to this belief, anyone who works hard will fare well. However, the ideology of meritocracy has an underlying flaw: It does not take into account the prevalent inequalities in our society.

Inequality, injustice, discrimination, and *racism* are terms we generally do not associate with school. However, they are real. We must face and define these terms for our children and ourselves, as we try to make sense of what school is and can be. . . .

Education and schooling should equip students with tools not only to learn how to participate in this society, but also to challenge the oppressing structures that limit their lives. Theories of social justice can move us toward tolerance, awareness, respect, meaning, and fulfillment. Teaching for social justice can occur at any school site. However, teachers and students alike must cast a critical eye upon schooling, and transform it to mirror their realities and aspirations.

—Kimberly Min
Third-grade teacher

Teacher Kimberly Min wrote these words at the end of her first year of teaching in South Los Angeles, in a neighborhood challenged by many of the inequalities we outlined in Chapter 1. Kimberly's words remind us all that while our nation has been slow to address these inequalities, teachers have a crucial role to play in supporting students to make sense of them and to imagine how we might work together, wherever we are, for justice.

Chapter Overview

In this chapter, we explore why unequal school opportunities and outcomes seem so normal that sometimes we might even fail to recognize them. Informed by history and social theory, we discuss how events and ideologies that shape our national character also shape schools and classrooms. To emphasize milestones related to diversity and equity, we provide a timeline of important events in the history of U.S. schooling. We sketch how expectations for schools have increased over the past 200-plus years; discuss two influential cultural assumptions—meritocracy and racial superiority; and highlight educators who are struggling hopefully against the history and culture that constrain teaching and learning in today's schools.

The history and traditions of the United States reflect sometimes conflicting values: from democratic values to capitalistic ones, from concerns for individual freedoms to concerns for the common good. Teachers like Kimberly Min work to identify the values and conflicts in society, in their schools, and in their own thinking. This helps them focus their teaching and advance educational equity.

A History of Increasing Expectations

The knowledge, skills, and dispositions that schools teach result from society's collective decisions about what adult members need in order to function well and contribute to the common good. We can better understand the present if we understand how these "decisions" have emerged and evolved over time.

At first, U.S. publicly supported schools emphasized preparing future citizens to participate in democratic governance, but over time they have assumed other social roles. These include, in rough chronological order, preserving the predominantly Anglo Protestant culture established in the eighteenth and nineteenth centuries, preparing the nation's workforce, developing the scientific prowess required for national security, ameliorating social inequalities, and developing the human capital required for international competitiveness. Each of these expectations emerged at a critical historical moment.

Public Schools Should Secure Democracy

At the republic's founding, Americans placed their hopes for democracy in public schools. Thomas Jefferson argued that citizens must deliberate publicly and use reason to determine which competing ideas should guide our democracy.[1] Citizens needed to read in order to debate the ideas that a free press circulated; therefore, Jefferson wanted the government to provide children with three years of schooling. He advocated that schools teach basic reading, writing, and mathematics and, beyond that, perhaps the rudiments of Greek, Roman, English, and U.S. history.

Jefferson included slaves in his public schooling plan, though he proposed limiting their education to industrial training to prepare them for their eventual freedom. Furthermore, as historian Carter G. Woodson observed, Jefferson was not confident that Black men "could be made the intellectual equals of white men," nor did he advocate preparing them to participate as full citizens.[2]

In arguing for public schooling (with caveats), Jefferson followed other late-eighteenth-century intellectuals who believed that creative and rational thought must be the foundation of orderly and stable modern societies. Perhaps Jefferson's most enduring ideal is that democratic institutions must ensure individual liberties even as they advance the common good. Perhaps the ugliest idea, one he shared with so many others, is that race provides a meaningful and useful way to distinguish among people's capacities, rights, and opportunities.

In the 1830s, Horace Mann augmented Jefferson's vision of the public school as the cornerstone of democratic life. Mann argued that all youth should be educated in "common" schools that would supplement what families taught at home. Mann defined the essential characteristics of what would become the "public school." These would be *free* and *equal* schools for the sons and daughters of farmers, businessmen, professionals, and all others.[3]

Mann wanted common schools to teach the knowledge, habits, and basic literacy that citizens needed to function in a democracy. He envisioned the common school as the "great equalizer" and the "creator of wealth undreamed of" and hoped it would eliminate poverty and crime and shape the destiny of a wise, productive country. Like other modern thinkers of the day, Mann believed that social improvement would follow from advances in knowledge and that schooling would extend individual rights and liberties to all.

Mann's ideal of the common school has never been fully realized. Prior to the Civil War, laws in most southern states forbade the education of slaves. Schools in the South were opened to freed Blacks during Reconstruction, but in 1896 the U.S. Supreme Court ruled in *Plessy v. Ferguson* that racially separate facilities did not violate the Constitution, so long as those facilities were "equal."[4] The court decided that a Louisiana law requiring separate accommodations for Blacks and Whites did not violate the rights of Homer Plessy, who had purchased a first-class ticket and then was arrested because he refused to move from the first-class car to one designated for "Negro" passengers (which Plessy was considered to be because one of his

The Common School

eight great-grandparents was Black). The new doctrine of "separate, but equal" led to widespread legally required segregation, called "Jim Crow" laws, mandating separate public facilities (including schools) for Whites and Blacks throughout the South. Outside the South, racially segregated neighborhoods were supported by property covenants that restricted housing ownership and tenancy by race. The resulting racial separation was nearly as effective as the Jim Crow laws in creating and maintaining segregated schools.

It was not until the 1954 *Brown v. Board of Education* decision that the court struck down *Plessy*, ruling that segregation and separate public facilities were inherently unequal. *Brown* established the courts' role in protecting education as a right in U.S. society. Much was accomplished through *Brown*, but officially permitted (or even officially promoted) segregation remains today. Writing for a unanimous Supreme Court, Chief Justice Earl Warren argued:

> Today, education is perhaps the most important function of state and local governments. Compulsory school attendance laws and the great expenditures for education both demonstrate our recognition of the importance of education to our democratic society. It is required in the performance of our most basic public responsibilities, even service in the armed forces. It is the very foundation of good citizenship. Today it is a principal instrument in awakening the child to cultural values, in preparing him for later professional training, and in helping him to adjust normally to his environment. In these days, it is doubtful that any child may reasonably be expected to succeed in life if he is denied the opportunity of an education. Such an opportunity, where the state has undertaken to provide it, is a right which must be made available to all on equal terms.[5]

The educational timeline (see pp. 42–46) places these two legal milestones, *Plessy* and *Brown*, among others, in the ongoing struggle for socially just public school systems.

Horace Mann's ideal for the common school, to advance liberty and democracy, persists. Mann would surely smile if he heard first-year teacher Sarine Gureghian discuss her efforts to teach her mostly immigrant first and second graders the key principles of democracy.

> First and second graders can affect the conditions they live in. . . . Throughout the year, voting and classroom meetings provided a medium for conflict resolution. The voting was not simply a hand poll. We visited polling stations, filled out registration cards, set up polls and an ongoing voting station in our classroom; we voted on specific units to study. I did anything possible to make students realize that they have a voice.
>
> —Sarine Gureghian
> First-year teacher, grades 1–2

Public Schools Should Preserve American Culture

The idea that public schools should preserve American culture was established early, with assimilation being the key mechanism for achieving that goal. For example, in the late nineteenth and early twentieth centuries, Indian boarding schools, established by Christian missionaries and funded by the U.S. government, aimed to rapidly assimilate indigenous youth into Euro-American norms and customs. School officials at times forcefully removed Indian youth from their families and homes, while the schools themselves typically restricted students from engaging in native cultural practices, including speaking native languages.[6]

A key objective of early-twentieth-century reformers was to use public schools to establish religious and moral homogeneity. Despite the country's constitutional commitment to the separation of church and state, politically powerful Christian beliefs and puritanical values have long been at the center of U.S. schooling. The content and methods underlying school rules and

Carlisle Indian Industrial School Group Photos (left: November 1886; right: March 1887)

literacy instruction paid little attention to the values or customs practiced in the homes of native youth; working-class youth; youth from long-established Latinx, Asian, and African American families; and immigrants. Often schools sought to extinguish these culturally "different" beliefs and practices altogether.

The twentieth century brought rapid demographic changes and growth. Industrialization, urbanization, and immigration resulted in near-overwhelming new demands on public schools.[7] Not only did new immigrants arrive in unprecedented numbers, but they came from southern and eastern Europe, which made them seem more "foreign" than earlier waves of northern European immigrants. Many, escaping poverty and persecution, had scant possessions or formal education, and politicians pressed schools to "Americanize" these children. In response, schools were asked to go beyond teaching basic computation and literacy, and to emphasize citizenship and patriotism to ensure students acquired the habits, values, and language of the predominantly Anglo-Saxon Protestants, who considered themselves the trustees of American culture.

Both hopes and fears drove Americanization. Many immigrants were hopeful about new opportunities and were eager to adopt the ways of their new country. Their enthusiasms were bolstered by the appealing romantic idea of America as a great "melting pot." Sure enough, there were plenty of examples—in fiction and reality—of individuals who gained wealth and security after arriving in their adopted country. And, of course, schools would be the places to meld peoples and cultures into a new and harmonious composite.[8]

Yet fear and disappointment also prevailed. Schools were caught between an idealistic melting pot vision and a broad social xenophobia—fear and distrust of all people foreign or unfamiliar. Generally (but with abundant exceptions), long-established Americans wanted no part of customs and languages that might contaminate the Anglo Protestant values they thought were the strength and heart of the nation.[9] Race, countries of origin, religion, and social class combined into a messy, overlapping animus. As a result, people from Italy, Ireland, Greece, and other European countries were deemed "non-White," at least for a time.

Tensions were rarely far from the surface. Skin color and accents were the easy identifiers of "others" or "outsiders," but everyday habits like ways of greeting or dressing, or unfamiliar foods and odors, could set off harsh judgments about trustworthiness and character. Many Americans looked for rational and scientific evidence to help them live with both their exclusionary, discriminatory views *and* their cherished views of American justice and equality. Some of the strongest, if illogical, support for navigating these contradictions developed around the belief that certain people had genetic deficiencies—reliably revealed in their skin color, accented English, or many behaviors—that neither they nor schools could overcome.

EDUCATIONAL TIMELINE

1600s	**P**	1600s–1700s	*Enlightenment philosophy* influences the meanings and methods of education.
	H	1647	Massachusetts requires towns of at least fifty families to hire a schoolmaster to teach reading and writing.
1700s	**H**	1779	Thomas Jefferson proposes a system of public schools for the state of Virginia as a way to ensure responsible citizens.
	P	1780s–1880s	Blue-backed spellers, developed by *Noah Webster*, incorporate lessons in reading and writing, all aimed at developing patriotic Americans.
	H	1787	Confederation Congress's Northwest Ordinance requires that a section of land in every township of each new state be reserved for the support of education.
1800–1850	**H**	1821	First public high school, Boston English High School, opens.
	H	1827	Massachusetts requires towns of more than 500 families to have a public high school open to all students.
	LM	1830s	Laws prohibiting slaves from learning to read are passed in several states (Louisiana, Georgia, Virginia, Alabama, South Carolina, North Carolina).
	P	1830s–1840s	*Horace Mann* argues for "common schools" that will teach basic literacy, numeracy, and citizenship.
	P	1836–1920	McGuffey Readers, edited by *Williams Holmes McGuffey*, are introduced and used as textbooks in schools nationwide.
	H	1837	Horace Mann, advocate of free "common schools" as the foundation of democracy, becomes secretary of the Massachusetts State Board of Education.
	L	1839	Ohio is the first state to adopt a bilingual education law, allowing German-English instruction at the parents' request.
	L	1847	Louisiana passes a law similar to Ohio's, allowing French-English instruction.
	L	1848	Mexico and the United States sign the Treaty of Hidalgo, giving Mexicans the right to speak Spanish in the United States. In the second half of the nineteenth century, those who had a language other than English as their primary language were taught in public schools in a monolingual or bilingual setting.
1850–1895	**H**	1852	Massachusetts passes a first mandatory attendance law.
	L	1864	Congress prohibits Native Americans from being taught in their own languages.
	LM	1868	"Compulsory ignorance" laws are deemed illegal.
	L	1870s	William Harris, the school superintendent in St. Louis schools and later the U.S. commissioner of education, argues for bilingual education, stating that "national memories and aspirations, family traditions, customs and habits, moral and religious observances cannot be suddenly removed or changed without disastrously weakening the personality."[10] Harris establishes the first "kindergarten" in America, taught solely in German, to give immigrant students a head start in the St. Louis schools.
	P	1873	The country's first child-centered reforms are instituted in Quincy, Massachusetts.
	H	1879	Carlisle Indian Industrial (Boarding) School is founded as part of the government's effort to assimilate Native American children into mainstream U.S. culture.
	H	1885	Sixteen states have compulsory-attendance laws.
	L	1889–1991	Attempts begin to legislate against German and in favor of English. The 1889 Bennett Act in Wisconsin legislates that children ages 8 to 14 in public or private schools must be instructed in English in the "three R's" and American history. The Illinois legislature passes a similar measure known as the Edwards Act. Both are eventually repealed, not without damage to bilingual education.
	H	1890–1920	The Great Wave of immigration brings southern and eastern Europeans to newly industrialized cities in the United States.
	H	1892	First Pledge of Allegiance, followed by "One Country! One Flag! One Language!"
	P	1893	National Education Association's Committee of Ten recommends that secondary schools offer different, but all academic, curriculum for students.

H	Key Events in the History of U.S. Public Schools
L	Language Policies
LM	Legal Milestones in the Struggle for Socially Just Education
P	People and Movements Shaping Curriculum in the United States

H 1896 — *Plessy v. Ferguson* (U.S. Supreme Court) upholds Louisiana law stating that the Fourteenth Amendment "had not been intended to abolish distinctions based on color."[11]

LM — This makes racially segregated public facilities legal and sets a precedent for the justification of "separate but equal" education.

H 1899 — Jane Addams founds Hull House.

L 1900 — Over 15 million children are enrolled in American public schools. Between 1891 and 1900, 3.7 million new immigrants arrive. Thirty-three states and the District of Columbia have compulsory education laws, heightening the issue of language instruction. At least 600,000 elementary students (about 4 percent) receive some part of their education in German.

P 1900s — *Francis Parker, John Dewey*, and *Jane Addams* advocate and organize on behalf of an experiential, child-centered curriculum that is focused on democracy and solving social problems.

P — *G. Stanley Hall* introduces the idea of child study and curriculum based on scientific study of the stages of child and adolescent development.

L 1906 — Congress passes the first federal language law, requiring that those seeking to become naturalized citizens speak English.

H 1909 — Those seeking to advance African Americans' rights found the NAACP.

H 1910 — Schools enroll 59 percent of the nation's 5- to 19-year-olds, including a majority of Black children; 10 percent of American youth graduate from high school.

H 1917 — Congress passes the Smith-Hughes Act, providing federal funding for vocational education.

L — The United States enters World War I, spurring a wave of language restriction in schools.

H 1918 — All states have compulsory-attendance laws.

P — The *NEA Commission on the Reorganization of Secondary Education*'s Cardinal Principles of Secondary Education state that schools should "track" students into different curricula based on abilities and interests.

L 1919 — Fifteen more states legislate English as the language of instruction. Linguistic uniformity is seen as crucial to rooting out "aliens" and containing the "radical labor movement."[12]

H 1920 — The majority of Mexican, Asian, and Native American children now attend school.

H 1920s — Congress enacts the strictest immigration quotas in U.S. history, which limit entry of Italians, Poles, Jews, and Greeks and totally exclude Asians.

H — Most bilingual education formally eliminated.

H — Introduction of IQ tests

P — *Franklin Bobbitt* and others emphasize scientific efficiency and a curriculum based on a scientific inventory of human life and occupations and formulated as an efficient series of specific objectives and activities.

P 1926 — Prominent African American scholar *Carter G. Woodson* initiates Negro History Week, which eventually becomes Black History Month.

H 1930s — The Great Depression brings reduction in education funding, school closings, teacher layoffs, and lower salaries.

P — *George Counts, Harold Rugg*, and other social reconstructionists advocate that schools strive to solve social and economic problems.

H 1940 — Schools enroll 75 percent of the nation's 5- to 19-year-olds; 50 percent of American youth graduate from high school.

P 1940s — The *Intergroup Education Movement* lays the foundation for later developments in multicultural education.

P 1940s– 1950s — *Ralph Tyler* advocates for an emphasis on "life adjustment" curriculum, which matches education to the life activities of U.S. citizens.

H 1950s — Twelve-year education becomes an important policy objective.

H 1954 — Rights to desegregated education "on equal terms": the *Brown v. Board of Education of Topeka, Kansas* (U.S. Supreme Court) ruling states that "separate educational facilities are inherently unequal"[13] and outlaws legally segregated schools—overturning *Plessy v. Ferguson*.

LM

[Handwritten margin notes: "WEB DuBois"; "1916 teacher unions start"]

H 1958   One year after Sputnik, Congress passes the National Defense Education Act (NDEA), increasing funding for scientific research and science education.

L 1959   A renaissance of bilingual education occurs with the arrival of Cubans flocking to Miami after the revolution. New immigrants start their own private bilingual schools and eventually establish a public bilingual school in the Miami school system.

P 1960s   *Jerome Bruner* publishes *The Process of Education*, in which he argues that children, as active problem solvers, should explore the structure of the academic disciplines; this thinking led to "new" curricula in math and science.

P   *A. S. Neill* argues for "free" schools; specifically, his best-selling book *Summerhill* advocates an "open," child-directed curriculum.

P 1960s–   *B. F. Skinner, Robert Gagne*, and other proponents of behaviorism advocate teaching
1970s   "machines" and programmed instruction, where each lesson must be mastered in order to go on to the next.

P   *Paulo Freire* publishes his influential book *Pedagogy of the Oppressed*, which becomes a foundational text on critical pedagogy.

H 1965   Lyndon Johnson's War on Poverty leads Congress to pass the Elementary and Secondary Education Act (ESEA), providing federal funds for educational programs such as Title I, Head Start, and bilingual education for low-income students.

H 1966   The Equality of Educational Opportunity Study, often called the "Coleman Report," concludes that African American children benefit from attending integrated schools but not from increased resources.

L 1968   Congress passes the Bilingual Act of 1968, which gives federal funding to school districts to try to incorporate native-language instruction. Many states follow suit, enacting their own bilingual laws.

P 1969   Harvard psychologist Arthur Jensen argues that because national antipoverty programs did not appreciably raise children's IQs, children of the poor must be genetically intellectually inferior.

H 1970   Schools enroll 90 percent of the nation's 5- to 19-year-olds; 79 percent of young people are high school graduates.

L   Chicano students in Crystal City, Texas, demand to speak Spanish, study Chicano history, and be taught by Chicano teachers. After the political takeover of the school board, city council, and county offices, the school district inaugurates an unprecedented district-wide policy that calls for bilingual and bicultural education. La Raza Unida (The United People) is born from this struggle.

P 1970s   Some communities and schools (e.g., Black Panther Schools) begin to advocate and implement explicitly "ethnocentric" curricula.

P   *Carl Rogers, Abraham Maslow, Lawrence Kohlberg*, and others emphasize the importance of "humanistic education," a holistic approach to schooling and learning.

P 1970s–   The ideas of cultural psychologist Lev Vygotsky begin gaining prominence among
1980s   those interested in teaching and learning.

LM 1971/   Rights of the disabled to education are established by two U.S. district court cases:
1972   *Pennsylvania Association for Retarded Children (PARC) v. Pennsylvania* and *Mills v. the Board of Education of Washington, D.C. PARC* rules that students with mental retardation are entitled to free public education. *Mills* extends *PARC* to include other disabilities and requires "adequate alternative educational services ... which may include special education ..."[14]

H 1972   *Title IX*, a new amendment to the ESEA, prohibits discrimination based on sex in all aspects of education.

LM 1973   Rights of Latinx students to desegregated schools are established by *Keyes v. Denver School District No. 1* (U.S. Supreme Court), which expands what counts as illegal segregation.

(left margin) 1955–1973

H	Key Events in the History of U.S. Public Schools
L	Language Policies
LM	Legal Milestones in the Struggle for Socially Just Education
P	People and Movements Shaping Curriculum in the United States

H **L** **LM**	1974	In a class action suit on behalf of 1,800 students, 8-year-old Kenny Lau sues the San Francisco School District over English-only instruction in a school where most students speak only Chinese. The U.S. Supreme Court rules in *Lau v. Nichols* that schools without special provisions to educate language-minority students are not providing equal education and violate the Civil Rights Act of 1964. The federal government publishes new materials in nearly seventy languages and allocates $68 million for bilingual education.
LM		Limits to desegregation: *Millikin v. Bradley* (U.S. Supreme Court) blocks interdistrict desegregation remedies, effectively relegating minority school districts to remain segregated.
H	1975	The *Education of All Handicapped Children Act* (PL 94-142) becomes federal law, requiring free and appropriate public education for disabled children (in 1997, this becomes the *Individuals With Disabilities Education Act*).
LM		Rights to equal school funding: *Rodriguez v. San Antonio* (U.S. Supreme Court) rules that education is *not* a right guaranteed by the U.S. Constitution, ending hopes that the Constitution requires equal education spending.
L	1980	The Mariel boatlift brings younger and poorer Cubans to Dade County, Florida, where voters pass an anti-bilingual ordinance prohibiting expenditure "for the purpose of utilizing any language other than English, or promoting any culture other than that of the U.S."[15] The measure is repealed in 1993, but the harsh language of the ordinance exposes growing anti-immigrant sentiment.
P	1980s	*Howard Gardner* introduces the notion of "multiple intelligences."
P		Critical Race Theory emerges, first among legal scholars who focus on the intersections of race, law, and power in U.S. life, past and present.
P	1980s– 1990s	*Allan Bloom's* emphasis on the Western canon, *E. D. Hirsch's* emphasis on cultural literacy, and *Diane Ravitch's* emphasis on standards popularize a call for schools to teach a common, canonical (versus diverse, multicultural) curriculum.
L **MP**	1982	Rights of undocumented immigrants: *Plyler v. Doe* (U.S. Supreme Court) prohibits public schools from denying immigrant students access to public education and grants undocumented children the right to free public education (striking down a school district's attempt to charge undocumented immigrants a $1,000/year tuition fee).
P	1983	The report of the National Commission on Excellence in Education, *A Nation at Risk*, laments "mediocre" schools and calls for sweeping reforms.
L		Creation of *US English*, an anti-immigrant, pro-English-only "citizen's activist group."
P	1990s	*James Banks, Gloria Ladson-Billings, Sonia Nieto, Christine Sleeter*, and others advance multicultural education, culturally relevant pedagogy, and critical analysis of Whiteness and privilege.
P	1991	Secretary of Labor's Commission on Achieving Necessary Skills specifies what graduates need to succeed in the labor market.
LM		Limits to desegregation: *Board of Education of Oklahoma City v. Dowell* (U.S. Supreme Court) establishes a "good faith" test that allows courts to end desegregation once a district has made an effort "to the extent practicable."[16]
P	1994	*The Bell Curve* is published, reasserting theories of racial differences in intelligence.
H		The Educate America Act requires all states to develop academic "standards" that all children will be expected to meet.
L		California passes Proposition 187, making it illegal for the children of undocumented immigrants to attend public schools. The federal courts find this unconstitutional.
LM		Limits to desegregation: *Freeman v. Pitts* (U.S. Supreme Court) allows courts to gradually stop supervising desegregation cases if a school district has complied with the good faith standard from *Dowell*.
LM	1995	Ending desegregation: *Missouri v. Jenkins* (U.S. Supreme Court) allows schools to be released from desegregation, even though they have not satisfied the court's requirement of raising African American students' test scores.
L	1998	California voters overwhelmingly (61 percent to 39 percent) approve Proposition 227, an initiative that eliminates the state's bilingual education programs and requires that all instruction be conducted in English.

EDUCATIONAL TIMELINE *(continued)*

L **2000** Arizona passes its own English-only law, Proposition 203.

LM *Williams v. California*, a landmark civil rights case brought on behalf of California students by Eliezer Williams, challenges the state to ensure quality learning conditions for millions of low-income students of color and is settled by the state in 2004.

P The *standards movement* gains momentum, as do *high-stakes accountability*, the development of *charter schools*, the proliferation of *alternative pathways into teaching*, and so on.

H **2001** The *No Child Left Behind Act* (NCLB), reauthorizing the ESEA, is signed into law by George W. Bush, holding schools accountable for students' scores on standards-based achievement tests.

L **2002** Colorado voters reject English-only laws.

L **2005** Introduced into Congress, the *English Language Unity Act of 2005* proposes that the U.S. government conduct all official business in English only.

L **2007** *Parents Involved in Community Schools v. Seattle School District No. 1* invalidates
MP voluntary school desegregation in Seattle, Washington, and Louisville, Kentucky.

H **2008** Economic recession leads to severe education budget cuts in many states.

H **2009** *Race to the Top*, part of the *American Recovery and Reinvestment Act*, promotes competition among states for federal funding, emphasizing standards, accountability, and teacher evaluation.

H **2010** The *Common Core State Standards* initiative officially begins, establishing national standards in English language arts and mathematics.

H The *Los Angeles Times* publishes individual teachers' names and value-added scores.

LM California passes a "Parent Trigger" law, which allows parents to bring about whole-school reform if they gather signatures from 51 percent of parents at their school site.

LM Arizona bans ethnic studies programs.

H **2011** President Barack Obama signs the America COMPETES Act, which aims to strengthen science, technology, engineering, and mathematics education in the United States.

LM California passes the DREAM Act extending postsecondary educational opportunities to immigrant youth by making them eligible for financial aid if they attended U.S. schools on a regular basis and otherwise meet in-state tuition and GPA requirements.

LM **2012** President Obama issues the *Deferred Action for Childhood Arrivals* (DACA) executive order that allows undocumented immigrants who entered the United States as minors to receive a renewable period of deferred action from deportation, plus eligibility for a work permit. Approximately 65,000 undocumented students graduate from U.S. high schools on a yearly basis.

H **2016** President Obama signs the *Every Student Succeeds Act* (ESSA), easing restrictions on states. A chief feature modifies the previous heavy reliance on standardized testing, while keeping such tests at the forefront of school accountability policies.

L **2016** California voters reinstate bilingual and multilingual education's legality in public
ML schools.

P **2017** President Trump sends chilling law enforcement and rhetorical signals to undocumented immigrants previously seen as "low priority" for deportation, including students protected by DACA.

P **2017** President Trump appoints as Secretary of Education Betsy DeVos, whose conservative, pro-privatization leanings worry many Americans.

H Key Events in the History of U.S. Public Schools
L Language Policies
LM Legal Milestones in the Struggle for Socially Just Education
P People and Movements Shaping Curriculum in the United States

2000—present

This led many to ask: How, then, should these newcomers be educated? The result was an Americanization process that sought to eliminate heritage languages other than English while promoting American cultural norms and values. When schoolchildren first recited the Pledge of Allegiance in 1892, for example, their teachers were told to have them follow the pledge by shouting, "One Country! One Flag! One Language!"[17] Not surprisingly, since many consider language the heart of a culture, Americanization campaigns of the early twentieth century insisted that English be the "official" language of the United States. Controversy over the teaching and acceptance of multiple languages in schools remains today.

Bilingual education in German and French had been a common practice in the nineteenth century. Yet after the arrival of Italians, Slavs, and Jews from southern Europe, President Theodore Roosevelt argued that the United States had room for only one language—English. In 1906, Congress passed the first federal language law, requiring that those seeking to become naturalized citizens speak English. With the U.S. entry into World War I in 1917, language policies tightened further. Worried about German speakers' loyalty, many states enacted English-only instruction laws, and most schools stopped teaching German. In some communities, mobs burned German textbooks. The educational timeline includes references to these and other key language policies that have been enacted throughout U.S. history.

Immigrant Children, 1921

In the Red Scare period following World War I and the Russian Revolution, long-standing xenophobic unease with "foreignness" sharpened into palpable fears of foreign political takeover—particularly communist takeover. Foreign languages were an easy proxy for identifying people who held beliefs deemed threatening and disloyal. Fifteen states adopted English-only instruction laws in 1919. Driving these new laws was the belief that linguistic uniformity would root out alien conspiracies and stem the emerging radical labor movement. This tightened ideological linkages between speaking "good English" and being "good Americans." Across the nation, most bilingual education was eliminated in the 1920s.[18]

In today's schools, intrusive Americanization and kneejerk xenophobia still hold power. In the wake of the September 11 terrorist attack, for example, some public schools discouraged Muslim girls from wearing their headscarves, infringing indefensibly on their freedom of religious expression. And as recently as 2017, parents in New Jersey, South Carolina, Florida, and Texas have complained to the media and local officials about including material about Islam in the curriculum and allowing Muslim students to pray at school.[19]

Additionally, values and perspectives rooted in Christianity still infuse discourse about public life and service (e.g., when political candidates are questioned about their faith and church attendance), as well as debates about what can and should be taught in public classrooms (e.g., when school boards and teachers argue over teaching evolution and sex education).[20] Traditional Christian values and practices tend to be treated as the norm while marginalizing or discriminating against other views.

On the surface, schools' broad pursuit of "Americanization" may seem like a sensible effort to help students adjust, gain acceptance, find school success, and get jobs in the United States. But as the examples above suggest, that underlying motive is often mixed with prejudices related to race, religion, or national origin. Another example is when language policy works to *extinguish* students' home languages while teaching them English. The drive to limit Spanish speaking in the 1960s and 1970s could be taken as a substitute or proxy protest against increased Latinx immigration. At the end of the century, California's Proposition 227 and Arizona's Proposition 203 replaced bilingual education with English-only instruction, and federal education policy replaced many references to "bilingual education" with "English language acquisition."[21] This occurred despite considerable evidence of the benefits to students of bilingual education, especially when it is supported by adequate resources and well-prepared teachers.[22] A third example is the Arizona law passed in 2010 banning ethnic studies programs from the K–12 curriculum. Supporters of the ban argued that such programs exhibit "high treason" and "ethnic chauvinism."[23] Here, too, a growing body of research shows both academic and nonacademic benefits for students of such programs.[24]

These language and curriculum battles are tied to the tensions between narrow views of American culture and more open, inclusive perspectives. Although proponents of restrictive laws claim that the laws are race neutral—that is, that they have no racial intent—contemporary scholarship shows that many school policy measures are part of a broader reaction or backlash against immigrant communities generally. Furthermore, these laws disproportionately disadvantage students and teachers from groups that have less power in society because of their immigrant status or race.[25] As high school history teacher Matthew Eide attests, policies like these—and the beliefs and practices they ultimately support—send powerful, problematic messages about who is welcome (and unwelcome) in our schools and what constitutes valid knowledge and linguistic competence.

Eighty percent of the students at my school are Latino, many of whom are recent immigrants or speak a language other than English at home. The other 20 percent are African Americans whose English is often discriminated against and devalued. There are many teachers here who believe that students should transition completely into Standard English and, in the process, divest themselves of their linguistic and cultural rights. Several students have complained about teachers who permit no talk in any language other than Standard English. One P.E. teacher publicly humiliates any student who speaks Spanish in her presence. Another veteran advised me that the only way to create a positive classroom environment is to only permit English to be spoken, even in informal small-group conversations. Students report that teachers penalize their participation grades. . . . Perhaps the most pernicious aspect of this linguistic repression is that many students have internalized the negative attitudes about their native language. I began teaching aspiring to resist the hegemony of English in my classroom by creating an environment that supported, respected, and valued my students' first language while developing their academic English.

—Matthew Eide
First-year teacher, high school history

As his words also suggest, teachers have an important role to play in countering the influence of these beliefs, attitudes, and policies in our schools.

Public Schools Should Support the Nation's Workforce and Economy

Before the twentieth century, people did not view schools as connected to the nation's economy. Except for a few learned professions that required advanced academic training (law, ministry, etc.), education was not seen as preparation for work. Most job skills were learned through hands-on apprenticeships that were unrelated to children's typical five years of common schooling.

With the manufacturing boom of the early twentieth century, however, public schools took on the role of developing the human capital required by the new industrial economy. Both manufacturers and labor unions asked schools to prepare students by developing in them the competencies required by modern workplaces. Thus, by the 1920s, a major role of schools was to teach both specific job skills and the dispositions required for factory work.

Industrial employers needed workers trained with technical skills and socialized with the work habits and attitudes required to fit in at the factory (e.g., punctuality, proper deportment, willingness to be supervised and managed, and compliance with routines). These needs matched educators' views of appropriate high school education for the children of the nation's new immigrants. These young people seemed so different—less capable, some thought—from those who had enrolled in secondary schools in earlier times, and the traditional academic curriculum seemed not to suit many or most of them.

Responding to these demands and uncertainties, educators departed from the shared or common curriculum and created separate "tracks" that focused on academic work for some and industrial (vocational) preparation for others. The separate tracks prepared students for the different kinds of work that the industrial economy demanded—a great many "blue-collar" factory positions and relatively fewer management or "white-collar" jobs. When it came to deciding which students were capable of which kinds of work—and therefore in which track they belonged—educators often relied on problematic reasoning and fundamental misunderstandings about the intelligence and potential of immigrants' children. Later in this chapter, we discuss some of the ideologies that drove, and still drive, such decisions; in Chapter 10, we return to this practice of "tracking" and describe how it continues to shape students' school experiences and life chances.

Teaching Future Housewives

During the Great Depression, education progressives banded together to advance a curriculum that would support a new social and economic order—one that would reduce income inequalities, free the nation from the threat of economic collapse, and empower students through civic engagement and collective action. Their efforts to align schools with new understandings of pedagogy and progressive politics brought them in direct conflict with educators and policymakers who sought to preserve traditional, fact-bound academic disciplines and skill-based vocational education. For example, they argued that the distinct topics or school subjects of geography, history, and government should be combined into "social studies," which would integrate important concepts from sociology, anthropology, political science, economics, and more, in order to help students make sense of and "reconstruct" contemporary society and the economy.

When a new technology-based economy emerged in the late twentieth century, debates over workforce preparation continued. While expected jobs and skills may have changed (technological innovation and business services rather than industrial jobs), familiar dilemmas remained. As they did in middle of the twentieth century, policymakers and business leaders today continue to lament that there are too few U.S.-born workers who are highly skilled in science, technology, and engineering. They decry the fact that many of those jobs are filled by foreign nationals—on U.S. soil or elsewhere—or by immigrants. At the same time, the demand for skilled and lower-skilled workers has lessened as manufacturing and customer service jobs have sought cheaper labor outside the United States. All of this contributes to a sense of mismatch between the skill-sets of many domestic workers and the jobs available to them here.

As economic conditions and demands shift, and as globalization becomes the norm, U.S. schools remain the primary mechanism for preparing our country's students for the workforce—a workforce that can serve the country's economic interests. With the increasing and changing demand for highly skilled workers, education has become an even more high-stakes affair. President Obama, for example, argued during a 2008 campaign speech that "education is the currency of the Information Age, no longer just a pathway to opportunity and success but a prerequisite."[26] He also estimated that if 16,000 Colorado students had finished high school rather than dropping out, they would have earned an additional $4.1 billion in wages in the state over their lifetimes.[27]

Given the widespread belief that U.S. schools should prepare students for jobs, many people understandably see U.S. schools as failing when students can't get jobs or when available jobs go unfilled. They seem to forget that schools are just one factor in a much larger political economy. To take a single example, secondary schools may face intense criticism for their high dropout rates—in some places graduating as few as a quarter of their incoming students. However, some analysts argue that potential dropouts are influenced by their (not inaccurate) knowledge that even if they did graduate, they still might not qualify for a living-wage job or an affordable college education. Furthermore, budget pressures at local, state, and federal levels do little to raise confidence among schools or students that there will be resources to meet the changing demands of the workforce.[28]

By most accounts, high school graduation is necessary but not sufficient for surviving economically in the United States. Indeed, as predicted at the turn of the twenty-first century, the majority of job openings for long-term careers now require at least some postsecondary education.[29] Politicians, philanthropists, and pundits increasingly call for aligning the demands and opportunities of the new economy with K–12 schooling, postsecondary education, and workforce training.

Public Schools Should Ensure National Security and International Competitiveness

It was not until the 1950s that even a majority of students graduated from high school. By then, twelve years of education for all had become an important public policy goal. Then, in 1957, when Russia launched the first space satellite, Sputnik, the content of those twelve years of school became a target of national concern. The press and politicians, anxious about falling behind the Russians, lambasted so-called flabby academic courses in U.S. high schools and thrust upon teachers the job of developing the nation's capacity in science and mathematics—particularly in developing competitive Cold War space and defense technology. As we describe in Chapters 3 and 5, the 1960s brought significant curriculum reform, including an overhaul of science and mathematics teaching.[30]

Unquestionably, U.S. schools had demanded too little from all their students in the decades before 1957. However, in the crisis of the moment, most critics neglected to see or note that U.S. universities were the envy of the world, and that elite (White and wealthy) high schools were producing the highest-achieving students anywhere. In places where it was willing to concentrate its priorities and resources, the United States had proven perfectly capable of supporting students to become well-educated citizens with world-class science and mathematics skills. In fact, the *least* likely explanation for the United States' lagging in space exploration was its perceived shortage of smart scientists.

Nevertheless, once schools were blamed for the nation's second-place status in the international space race and asked to upgrade the nation's scientific expertise, policymakers and educators swung into action to live up to the new expectations society had for schools. Since the

1960s, schools have been blamed for not being academically rigorous enough, and educators have continued striving to meet higher and higher academic expectations.

One particularly scathing indictment came in the form of a 1983 government-commissioned report. Authored by a panel of government officials, leaders from the private sector, and education experts, *A Nation at Risk* blamed public schools for the faltering U.S. economy and declining national self-esteem. Arguing that the U.S. education system was "being eroded by a rising tide of mediocrity that threatens our very future as a Nation and a people,"[31] *A Nation at Risk* called for increases in academic courses taken by all high school students—four years of English and three years each of social studies, science, and mathematics—and it added computer literacy as a "new basic." In 1991, the Secretary of Labor's Commission on Achieving Necessary Skills specified what graduates needed to succeed in the labor market and to enhance the nation's economic competitiveness on the international stage. These workplace skills closely matched those advanced in *A Nation at Risk*, and policymakers and educators increasingly saw workplace preparation and intellectual development as complementary components of common schooling.

President Clinton elaborated on and extended this definition of a competitive common school. The Clinton-sponsored Goals 2000: Educate America Act, passed by Congress in 1994, specified that all students would leave grade 12 "having demonstrated competency over challenging subject matter including English, mathematics, science, foreign languages, civics and government, economics, the arts, history, and geography." It decreed that every school must ensure that all students learn to use their minds well so that they may be "prepared for responsible citizenship, further learning, and productive employment in our nation's modern economy."[32] With much opposition, the act funded the development of academic standards in a whole range of subject areas that specify what all students need to live and work in the twenty-first century.

The passage of No Child Left Behind (NCLB) in 2001 (i.e., the reauthorization of the 1965 Elementary and Secondary Education Act, or ESEA) involved connections, both rhetorical and logistical, between education reform and national security. Arguing in favor of the legislation, which was presented in its final form to Congress just a few months after the September 11 attacks on the World Trade Center and the Pentagon, then Secretary of Education Rod Paige drew a direct parallel between the nation's schools and its security: "The events of September 11th didn't make an education bill less important, it made it more important. Education is a national security issue. This is not something we can put on the shelf and come back to later."[33]

And indeed, as we address in greater detail in later chapters, NCLB's subsequent bipartisan passage not only served as an opportunity to project a sense of national unity during a time of relative insecurity but also served as logistical security, as it required schools receiving federal funds to provide military recruiters access to students.

In the years since NCLB's passage, national security and international competitiveness have remained central in discourse about U.S. schools, with President Obama lamenting that U.S. students score lower on international math and science assessments than their counterparts in other countries; that, "already, China is graduating eight times as many engineers as we are"; and that "countries who out-educate us today will out-compete us tomorrow."[34]

As we discuss further in later chapters, the most recent reauthorization of the federal ESEA (replacing NCLB with the Every Student Succeeds Act, or ESSA, in 2016) and the implementation in many states of new national standards (the "Common Core") have carried forward an emphasis on standards-based schooling and test-based accountability. Both reflect the enduring expectation that schools will play a critical role in ensuring national security and international competitiveness.

It is too soon, as we write this, to know how much emphasis President Donald Trump and Secretary of Education Betsy DeVos will place on K–12 education as a means for keeping the nation strong and competitive internationally. During his campaign, Trump lamented the low international ranking of U.S. students, but his concern focused more on whether taxpayers' money was being wasted, rather than on any international threats the low ranking posed.[35]

Public Schools Should Solve Social Problems

U.S. society also expects public schools to help solve social problems associated with poverty, racism, inequality, urban decay, and the social unrest those conditions often bring. For example, the initial pressure in the early 1900s for lengthening the number of years of compulsory schooling came, in part, from a need to solve the social problem of youngsters roaming footloose on city streets during parents' long factory hours, as well as from the perception that preparation for adulthood in an industrialized society required more education.

Since then, schools have been asked to solve other social problems. Founded in 1909, the National Association for the Advancement of Colored People (NAACP) viewed public schooling as the institution most likely to undo the Jim Crow segregation laws that had legalized racial segregation following the Civil War. Schools became the focus of lawsuits over teachers' unequal pay in southern states and, eventually, over the constitutionality of racial segregation itself.[36]

In the 1960s and 1970s, expectations for schools to solve social problems increased. The 1960s federal War on Poverty legislation specified funding for "categorical" programs—programs targeted to particular types of students. The intention was to ensure that federal money was spent on equalizing opportunities among all groups of students by increasing resources for students in poverty, specifically. These programs and subsequent legislation also created financial incentives for identifying students in particular ways, thus setting up new categories and creating labels and identities for students. The labels may have been an administrative, equity-minded necessity at the time, but they also had unintended consequences in a country with many racial and ability biases. For example, Title I of the historic ESEA of 1965 created the label "educationally deprived" and promised schools financial assistance to "improve educational opportunities" for any students identified as such.[37] Unfortunately, these labels were often taken up as *explanations* for education gaps; for example, some came to assume that students labeled "deprived" couldn't be expected to learn well, while those labeled "remedial" couldn't progress until they had repeated and mastered the most basic information.

School boycotts and other protests by Latinx students and communities in the 1960s led Congress to pass the Bilingual Education Act in 1968, supporting programs advancing Latinx culture and language for Spanish-speaking students. In 1974 *Lau v. Nichols*—a suit brought on behalf of non-English-speaking Chinese students in San Francisco—required that *all* schools provide special services to students speaking a native language other than English.

By the 1970s, advocacy groups attending to a variety of issues were insisting on legal protections for equal access to education. Women's rights activism, for example, led to the amending of Title IX of the Civil Rights Act to state that no one could, "on the basis of sex, be excluded from participation in, denied the benefits of, or be subjected to discrimination under any education program or activity receiving Federal financial assistance."[38] Title IX had equalizing effects throughout school programs, including girls' and women's opportunities to participate in high school and college athletics. Today Title IX is also used to protect students from discrimination based on sexual orientation, including—until the Trump administration reversed it in 2017—defending the right of transgender students to use school bathrooms of their choice.

Activists also demanded services for students whose learning disabilities were attributable to neurological problems. They argued that these students needed help that was different and separate from students whose troubles were thought to result from other forms of disadvantage. A series of court decisions ruled that students with disabilities have the right to a suitable free education, and in 1975, Congress passed the Education of All Handicapped Children Act

The One-Teacher Negro School in Veazy, Green County, Georgia

(PL 94-142). The act (which became the Individuals With Disabilities Education Act [IDEA] in 1997 and was reauthorized in 2004) requires schools to provide a "free and appropriate" education to students diagnosed with "mental retardation"; learning disabilities; hearing or vision impairments; and/or speech, emotional, or physical difficulties.[39]

Even as the demands on schools grew, politicians and the public had little appetite for addressing the social and economic inequalities beyond school that underlie the problems educators were expected to solve in schools. Many people overlooked that the effectiveness of antipoverty programs hinged on adequate resources reaching schools and communities. As a result, they interpreted the 1960s and 1970s reforms as wrongheaded or as failures. For example, conservative economist Charles Murray argued in his best-selling book *Losing Ground* that spending money on poverty programs created dependence on government assistance, eroded families, and undermined individual effort.

The Reagan and Bush administrations of the 1980s followed Murray's argument and claimed that government money spent to improve social conditions actually *caused* social problems and poor school performance. Conservative ideology called on schools to solve problems with a values-based approach that would restore the moral base to community and family life and enable individuals to solve their own problems. Schools were to emphasize "character education" and certain "traditional" values, such as sexual abstinence outside of marriage, disdain for welfare, exercise of will over the temptation of drugs, hard work, respect for public institutions, traditional definitions of marriage, and so on.

In the early 2000s, the second Bush administration continued this conservative approach of engaging the schools in solving social problems. With the 2001 passage of the federal NCLB Act, poverty and racism were posed as unacceptable excuses for low achievement. The policy's underlying logic assumed that the nation could overcome poverty and racism and the damage they do simply by setting high academic standards and implementing strict behavioral controls (zero-tolerance policies, for example). Whereas the earlier reforms emphasized fair distribution of the resources that all students need in order to learn, the newer reforms emphasized motivation and competitive market-based approaches. Under these newer reforms, if students and schools do not reach expected standards—so the logic goes—they must find ways to try harder and compete better in order to avoid severe consequences.

These shifts in thinking about opportunity and achievement have remained steady across recent political administrations and, to the surprise of many progressives, gained strength under the Obama administration. Taking a different approach, the Trump administration appears inclined to emphasize parental choice as the key variable in the education system's efforts to meet the many expectations placed on schools, including responding to the problems of poverty and inequality.

A Culture of Powerful Ideologies

Today's educational policies and practices embody policymakers' and educators' attempts to satisfy the multiple expectations placed on public schools. However, historians and social theorists argue that policymakers and educators don't select particular policies and practices after a rational, neutral weighing of all the options. Rather, their decisions reflect prevailing ideologies that, over time, shape what people consider to be the best ways to meet those expectations.

Ideologies can be understood as collections of ideas that a society views as common sense. They are like filters that often screen out less compatible facts and interpretations. They represent ideas so familiar and comforting that they seem natural, whereas those that don't fit come to seem unacceptable, countercultural, or radical. Political analysts often use the term *ideological* to convey an interpretation of reality that powerful groups use to make their dominance seem legitimate and to preserve social cohesion.[40]

Much of this book points out evidence and research that contradicts prevailing policies and practices. When one asks, "Why do such policies and practices persist in the face of contradictory evidence?" the answer is partly that the policies and practices that "stick" are often those that fit with the most powerful ideologies. Evidence is often dismissed precisely because it contradicts what prevailing ideologies have established as true or common sense.

As we describe next, contemporary social theorists argue that a mix of ideologies both supports and undermines broad commitment to equitable public schooling in the United States. Taken together, these ideologies help explain why our social structures and practices create the inequalities described in Chapter 1 and why remedying them is so difficult.

Here we explore two related ideologies—meritocracy and racial superiority—that characterize our country's culture and our schools' enactment of that culture. On the one hand, we often hear prideful proclamations about our country's meritocratic nature. On the other hand, we seldom hear about how being White in the United States carries with it privileges that others don't enjoy. As we explore these ideologies, it becomes clear how they constrain society and schools from realizing their democratic possibilities.

The Myth of Merit

Historically, Western societies distributed wealth and privilege according to how close one was to an elite or ruling class. Prior to the surge of democratic thinking in the seventeenth century, societies were organized to concentrate wealth among royalty, church leadership, landowners, and wealthy merchants—not artisans, peasants, and slaves. Not everyone thought this was fair, but few with power apologized or felt they had to justify their relative comfort and prosperity.

Explaining such disparities in wealth and privilege remains a central dilemma of modern and more egalitarian societies.

Since the colonial period, one source of enormous national pride has been the idea that the United States, unlike its more aristocratic European cousins, forged a fair society in which individual ability and determination, rather than wealth or personal connections, hold the key to success and upward mobility. The earliest conception of merit in the United States was based on Calvinist and Puritan religious ideas. According to these views, those favored by God were prosperous, and those not favored had less. Conversely, then, being poor was considered a sign of not being favored by God. Another explanation was that hard work and ambition resulted in wealth and social advantage, and thus people who did not work hard enough were poor. This explanation positioned individuals' limited wealth as the product of their lagging effort and ambition.

Throughout history, the United States has considered itself a "meritocracy"—in other words, a system in which meritoriousness gives moral legitimacy to what might otherwise appear unfair or undemocratic. Merit presents an easy rationale for why some citizens and their children are so well off while others have so little. Merit not only explains how people obtain wealth and power but also explains that the wealthy and powerful *deserve* their wealth and power because of their determination, cleverness, and hard work.[41] And yet an increasingly small percentage of the population now controls most the nation's wealth and sends its children to well-resourced schools. This lopsided distribution of wealth and power cannot be attributed to some groups (women, traditionally underrepresented communities, etc.) lacking cleverness or ambition. The emphasis on meritocracy—and not necessarily equality—is what Swedish economist Gunnar Myrdal, after studying race in the 1940s United States, called the "American Creed."[42]

Understanding the "Achievement Ideology"

Notably, social theorists have cast considerable doubt on the idea of the United States as a meritocracy. Jay MacLeod describes what he considers to be the *myth* of merit in his book *Ain't No Makin' It.* He tells of the hopes and disappointments of young men growing up in a low-income neighborhood. MacLeod describes "the achievement ideology" and explains:

> In this view, success is based on merit, and economic inequality is due to differences in ambition and ability. Individuals do not inherit their social status; they attain it on their own. Since education insures equality of opportunity, the ladder of social mobility is there for all to climb. A favorite Hollywood theme, the rags-to-riches story resonates in the psyche of the American people. We never tire of hearing about Andrew Carnegie, for his experience validates much that we hold dear about America, the land of opportunity. Horatio Alger's accounts of the spectacular mobility achieved by men of humble origins through their own unremitting efforts occupy a treasured place in our folklore. The American Dream is held out as a genuine prospect for anyone with the drive to achieve it.[43]

MacLeod, of course, notes that "for every Andrew Carnegie" there are uncountable hardworking and able others who fare much less well, and that most people in the United States wind up in positions similar to their parents'. In fact, with the exception of the wealthy, there is evidence that those now entering the labor market will do less well than their parents.[44] MacLeod is one of many to identify schools' complicity in inhibiting social class mobility. In general, schools tend toward "social reproduction"—or the perpetuation of class status generation by generation. For example, scholars such as W. E. B. Du Bois, Carter G. Woodson, and a host of others (e.g., indigenous peoples who resisted the schooling the "pioneers" forced on them) have long opposed their people being "trained"—what Woodson called "mis-educated"—for their "proper place" in society.[45]

Ambition and Hard Work Matter, But Inequalities Do, Too

Like most myths, the myth of merit draws its strength from the grain of truth embedded in it. All other things being equal, more ambitious and hardworking people may achieve more success in society than their less ambitious and hardworking peers. As we discuss in later chapters, for example, effort and persistence are hugely important to children's school achievement. The problem with the myth of merit is that it presumes basic equality of opportunity and resources, and assumes that individual merit represents the *only* variable of real consequence.

Yet, as Chapter 1 shows, society is shaped by social *structures* that constrain what is possible for people to achieve. Social structures are firm and stable arrangements of social roles and relationships—for example, school attendance zones drawn by those with relative power, or a ten-month school year and a six-hour school day that poses far more challenges for some families than others (e.g., families helmed by single working parents versus economically stable families who can afford a full-time, stay-at-home caregiver). Such structures might make some administrative sense, even if they don't produce good education for all children. At best, they cause little harm; at worst, they work against equitable school opportunities. When we look closely at social structures in and beyond schooling—including those related to health, housing, transportation, and so forth—to determine whether or how they constrain opportunity, a consistent pattern emerges: children from wealthy, White families are rarely disadvantaged by those structures, while children from poor families and families of color are rarely advantaged by them.

Notably, even the most meritorious schoolchildren have very little control over structural inequalities. The common characteristics of merit (hard work, social awareness, intelligence, etc.) occur with no less frequency in low-income families or among students of color, immigrants, or Emergent Bilinguals. However, inequalities in opportunity and resources limit the degree to which members of those groups can parlay qualities like determination and hard work into school success and enhanced life chances. The myth of merit distracts us (or lets us hide) from confronting those social structures that nearly always exacerbate inequities.[46]

Attempts to Address Inequality: The Civil Rights Movement and the War on Poverty

Inequalities related to race and social class persist in society and in schools despite the civil rights movement in the 1960s and the War on Poverty in the 1970s. These social reforms dented barriers to racial equality and alleviated the worst poverty. Activism and progressive social policies during this period did lead to significant political gains for African Americans and strengthened the social safety net for poor people, but they did not eradicate the structural problems or the ideologies that underlie inequalities in educational and life opportunities. Moreover, many of the gains achieved during the 1960s and 1970s have been rolled back in subsequent years.

After World War II, Americans were extraordinarily confident about the goodness of their democracy. Although these years were filled with unsettling discord, including the start of the Cold War, McCarthy-era political repression, and the Korean War, this was also a time of unprecedented prosperity, growth, and optimism. The nation occupied an undisputed position of political and economic world dominance. The dark days of the Great Depression were over, and many thought that the abject poverty of that period would never be seen again. The G.I. Bill opened college to returning World War II servicemen, and federal housing policies opened the doors to homeownership for enormous numbers of first-time purchasers who were mostly White. This was also a period of optimism for those who believed, along with Gunnar Myrdal, that racism was an aberration that could and should be removed from an otherwise equitable society.[47] The 1954 *Brown v. Board of Education* decision, described earlier, enabled those who saw themselves as fair-minded to feel satisfied by the idea that any residue of racial prejudice was being addressed.

Given the optimism of the 1950s, most people were shocked in 1962 when Michael Harrington's influential book *The Other America: Poverty in the United States* documented a huge underclass of unemployed and working poor.[48] How could it be that such a large segment of society simply did not "earn" better conditions? Harrington argued that this underclass, contrary to popular view, was not an artifact of temporary economic conditions. Rather, increasing numbers of people were locked into lifelong and intergenerational webs of poor education, housing, nutrition and health care, and more. Similar revelations were occurring around race. In reality, by the 1960s the nation had made little progress toward a desegregated society (an elusive goal to this day).[49]

Many who read Harrington's revelations were favorably disposed to social action that would right the obvious wrongs. At this time in U.S. history, civil rights activism was also gaining mainstream support. By the mid-1960s, it had become clear that regardless of their merit, some people could never overcome the inequitable conditions into which they were born. It was as if they were playing on a field tilted in their opponents' favor—they might kick or throw farther and run faster, but their efforts reaped fewer positive results because their work took place on an uphill slope. In the eyes of many, it was time to reject the faulty myth of meritocracy and fix what ailed the country.

Inequalities associated with gender, social class, and age began to shape the social conscience and enrich the climate of social change. Women took stock of their lack of opportunity, silenced perspectives, lower wages, and more. College students reacted to what seemed a hypocritical gap between their lessons in democracy and the limits that college campuses placed on free speech. As student protesters took a stand and refused to back down, they were both confused and energized by the force with which their college administrators and state governors opposed them. Television viewers were horrified when nightly news programs exposed the violence of racism and, later, the carnage of the Vietnam War. Little in the national rhetoric had prepared most people to witness how abusive those in positions of relative power could be. The social fabric in the United States seemed to be disintegrating and, with it, the notion that all Americans get what they deserve.

From the mid-1960s until 1980, the federal government pursued social policies designed to level the playing field. Civil rights activism following the *Brown* decision and War on Poverty legislation sought to remedy hunger, inadequate housing, and discrimination. As already noted, schools were expected to do much of this work.

These actions paid off. The civil rights movement brought political gains, particularly in voting rights. The War on Poverty slowed the widening gap between rich and poor. Programs fed hungry children and provided important learning experiences. However, these advances barely scratched the surface of the problems of racism and poverty. *Brown v. Board of Education* may have overturned the *Plessy* decision, ruling that separate is inherently unequal, and ordered schools to desegregate with "all deliberate speed."[50] However, the initial promise *Brown* held for equal opportunity has never been realized. Today, as we described in Chapter 1, Black students in the United States remain nearly as racially isolated as before *Brown*, and Latinx students' racial isolation steadily increases. Just as good people look back at the pre-*Brown* days and express anger that a society would allow segregated and unequal schools, cause for anger remains today. Indeed, there is evidence that segregation has *increased* and schooling conditions have *worsened* for many students since the *Brown* ruling.[51]

The impact of the ambitious War on Poverty has also proven to be limited. The country lacked experience and expertise in formulating and administering antipoverty programs and equity-minded interventions, and national politics allowed little room for error. When programs faltered or needed reworking, skeptics judged them failures. Most pernicious of all, many of society's most well-off continued to view "the problem" as inherent to poor people themselves rather than as a product of the social and economic conditions that made people poor. The country was not prepared to concede that large social and economic structures, including schools, had to change fundamentally, and that the necessary changes would be costly and difficult, and would sometimes disrupt the relative advantages of wealthier people who may not have realized that they had advantages until they were threatened with losing them.[52] This ideological context laid the groundwork for the systematic dismantling of antipoverty and antidiscrimination policies beginning in the Reagan administration and continuing today.

Enduring Challenges

Today, many look back on this short-lived but significant national effort on behalf of African Americans and the poor and interpret its disappointing results to conclude that if people of color and the poor did not prosper with the aid of new political opportunities and social programs, then the fault lies with them and with their misguided helpers. Others use the ideology of merit to argue that the success achieved by some African American and Latinx individuals, despite burdens of racism and poverty, is evidence that all have the opportunity to achieve, provided they bring sufficient effort.[53]

Thus, a theoretically possible, but statistically rare outcome—hammered home by highly touted examples—obscures what is actually possible and likely for most children. For every President Obama and U.S. Supreme Court Justice Sotomayor there are thousands of men, women, and children of color whose success and achievements have been challenged by racism and the myth of meritocracy. Indeed, it strains credibility to suggest that the few who manage to succeed under unlikely or inequitable, even miserable, conditions are evidence that *all* can succeed, and that if they do not, it is their own fault. Yet that's exactly where the myth of merit leads. It's crucial to note here that the statistics we report throughout this book—however unpleasant—are important to inform public policy and teachers' understandings of how society is structured.

Why does our society support the convoluted logic that failure to overcome poverty or inferior education proves a lack of merit? The answer may be that people prefer believing that their own wealth stands on a moral platform of merit. Also, like many ideologies, the myth of merit depends on *everyone* believing in the myth just as strongly as those who benefit from it. Many poor and minoritized people in the United States also believe schooling benefits are equally accessible to all. In fact, students with dismal schooling experiences often blame their own lack of ability or effort or their failure to take advantage of opportunities. Describing "the Brothers"—the young African Americans he studied—Jay MacLeod put it this way:

> They blame themselves for their mediocre academic performances because they are unaware of the discriminatory influences of tracking, the school's partiality toward the cultural capital of the upper classes, the self-fulfilling consequences of teachers' expectations, and other forms of class-based educational selection. Conditioned by the achievement ideology to think that good jobs require high academic attainment, the Brothers may temper their high aspirations, believing not that the institution of school and the job market have failed them, but that they have failed themselves.[54]

In sum, merit permeates how many people in the United States make sense of schooling—emphasizing the role of the individual and deemphasizing the responsibilities of school or society. And yet, as attention turns to the widening wealth gaps between rich and poor and the corollary extreme concentration of wealth among the top 1 percent of the population, broad-based skepticism is taking hold concerning the degree to which such enormous financial success could ever be explained by individuals' efforts alone. As collusion and corruption among politicians, private interests, and the mega-rich come to light, more and more people are starting to question the degree to which merit could account for such "wealth undreamed of"—to borrow from Horace Mann—and yet only for so few.

Deficit Thinking, Racial Superiority, and White Privilege

> Prior to the first day of school, I had already been told that "these kids are low," and not to worry if the students did not do as well as I hoped because "the entire school is low overall."
> —Rosalinda Perez Silva
> First-year teacher, grade 1

Rosalinda Perez Silva, who teaches a class of twenty 6- and 7-year-olds in a Spanish-speaking immigrant neighborhood, says that her young students are "brilliantly intelligent" but "already struggling." Certainly, a large part of their struggle is to overcome the judgments that some educators have already made about them.

The judgments Rosalinda reports reflect powerful societal assumptions that youth who are not White and middle class come to school with deficits that make their school success difficult, if not impossible. The system of thought that supports such judgment is often referred to as "deficit thinking"—a belief that the source of academic struggle is flawed or undeveloped genetic makeup, cultural background, and/or students' individual experiences.

Deficit thinking, racial superiority, and White privilege are intertwined. In the United States, people who identify with various races might ascribe some superior qualities to their own race or other races, but since White Americans hold the greatest wealth and influence, they have the most capacity to act on and maintain their positions of privilege (their access to power, excellent schooling, etc.). Even though explicit public expression of racial superiority has been totally discredited in the United States—devoid of any scientific backing and nearly intolerable—private and public (or structural) racism remains widespread.

Admitting to deficit thinking is likewise unfashionable—quite like admitting to racism. And yet deficit thinking often creeps into schools when students don't thrive and adults fail to take responsibility for deficits in schools' resources and practices, rather than in students. Such thinking reflects and reinforces ideas of "racial superiority" and assumes that a person's "Whiteness" plays no role and has no consequence in his or her relative success or failure. It also reflects and reinforces privilege—including the privilege of continued blindness to one's own feelings of superiority and deficit thinking. White privilege allows people in positions of relative power to believe that their ways of knowing and being in the world represent intelligence and merit, and, therefore, to believe that they deserve the disproportionate school and life advantages they enjoy. And when it comes to education specifically, the privileges that come with being White in the United States allow children to learn and develop unhampered by the vulnerabilities associated with not being White—for example, the negative judgments against which Rosalinda's students struggle.

As we explain in what follows, deficit thinking and White privilege help explain why U.S. society remains far less meritocratic than we would like to believe.

Deficit Thinking

From the earliest colonial times, many in the United States obtained their prosperity with stolen land and slave labor. The removal and extermination of Indians and the African slave trade were justified (when they were challenged at all) on economic grounds and biblical explanations of

White superiority. After the mid-eighteenth century, a new group of modern natural scientists—craniologists—offered empirical evidence, arguing that White superiority rested on racial differences in skull size, with the larger skulls of Caucasians proving their greater capacities.

Widespread agreement about the moral and intellectual deficiencies of people of color justified denying them citizenship and prohibiting them from passing property on to their heirs. Likewise, many southern communities passed "compulsory ignorance" laws that banned schooling for slaves, motivated partly by fear of their empowerment through literacy. Communities in the North established segregated schools because it was simply unimaginable to many White people that their children could be safe from physical threat and moral corruption if schooled in racially integrated settings. Thus, by the time Horace Mann described his vision for a common public school, the country had already established deep traditions that allowed the government to limit those it would "count" among the collection of persons called the "public."

As the nation expanded westward, new groups were added to the U.S. racial hierarchy, and from time to time groups would be reclassified. Whites migrating to the Southwest judged Mexicans to be "half-civilized" (in comparison to "uncivilized" Indians) but also "White," due to their Spanish language, Catholicism, and the presence of a property-owning elite boasting European as well as Indian heritage. On the other hand, Asian men, imported in the late nineteenth century to build California's railroads and work its mines and farms, joined the ranks of the Black slave laborers brought from the American South and were disdained for their "strange" customs, "pagan" religions, and "incomprehensible" language. It was the mid-nineteenth century when a California court classified the Chinese officially as Indians and, therefore, "non-White."

Social Darwinism

By this time, Charles Darwin's *On the Origin of Species* had established that all races were human; however, it had also spawned a group of less reputable "social Darwinists" who advanced theories that Whites were a more highly evolved, cognitively superior race.[55] Such theories were used, in turn, to support continued segregation. Even after the abolition of slavery, most Whites viewed Blacks as inferior and supported racial segregation.

Although the U.S. government had declared in 1868 that "compulsory ignorance" laws were illegal and that native-born people of color were citizens, the states could—under the principles of states' rights—choose whether to fund schools for children of color. Many opted not to do so, and it was not until 1910 that the majority of Black children attended school, and not until 1920 that the majority of Mexican, Asian, and Indian children attended school.

The misapplication of Darwin's evolutionary theories to cultural as well as racial groups confirmed for many that immigrant students were less socially and morally developed. Consider, for example, the superintendent of Boston schools, who warned in 1889: "Many of these children come from homes of vice and crime. In their blood are generations of iniquity. . . . They hate restraint or obedience to the law."[56] Because immigrants at the turn of the nineteenth century arrived from different parts of Europe than previous waves of immigrants, racial and religious prejudices were typically at the core of such warnings and worries. Writing about recent immigrants in 1909, for example, the prominent educator Ellwood Cubberley explained:

> These southern and eastern Europeans are of a very different type from the north Europeans who preceded them. Illiterate, docile, lacking in self-reliance and initiative, and not possessing the Anglo-Teutonic conceptions of law, order, and government, their coming has served to dilute tremendously our national stock, and to corrupt our civic life.[57]

Sentiments such as these led many to believe that Americanization and assimilation should serve as common schools' principal objectives. Although many considered immigrants' language and culture to be biological, and therefore unchangeable, reformers expressed hopes that schooling could offer immigrant children constructive direction. In Cubberley's words, "Our task is to . . . assimilate and amalgamate these people as a part of our American race and to implant in their children, as far as can be done, the Anglo-Saxon conception of righteousness, law and order."[58]

G. Stanley Hall and Lewis Terman

Psychologist G. Stanley Hall's theories also played a powerful role in shaping deficit thinking about immigrants. Hall thought that children's development followed that of the entire race—that is, infants were like "presavages," and adults were more highly civilized. He also included the argument that environments such as the neighborhood and school profoundly influenced this development. In his view, the unstable and corrupting environments in city neighborhoods pressed individuals toward depravity—especially vulnerable were children and adolescents, whom Hall described as being at the developmental stage of savage, vagrant, and nomadic life. Unless adolescents were in homes where "industry, intelligence and thrift prevail, where books and magazines abound, where the library table forms the center of an interested group, where refinement of thought and life prevail," they would surely fall into delinquency and moral depravity.[59]

As children of color and children from southern and eastern European immigrant families began attending school in larger and larger numbers, a new "science" of intelligence emerged. With it came theories and data with which its proponents argued that mental deficits among these youth would necessarily limit their school achievement. Psychologist Richard Valencia has traced the links between tests, test bias, and widely held beliefs—what he first termed "deficit thinking"—about cultural deficits among students of color.[60]

Among the most well known of those developing the science of intelligence was Stanford University professor Lewis Terman, who developed and promoted intelligence tests for U.S. schoolchildren. Although Terman purported that his IQ tests measured innate abilities, the following items taken from one section of his test make clear that children from educated, culturally mainstream families were more likely to earn high IQs:[61]

4. Most exports go from
    Boston   San Francisco   New Orleans   New York

9. Larceny is a term used in
    Medicine   Theology   Law   Pedagogy

16. A character in *David Copperfield* is
    Sinbad   Uriah Heep   Rebecca   Hamlet

Because children of color and those from poor families scored lower than more socially advantaged ones, Terman used IQ test results to confirm his view that heredity determined intelligence. He also used test results to support his advocacy of low-level schooling for those who tested poorly as well as population control among what he called the "feebleminded." After testing a group of boys who lived in an orphanage, Terman wrote:

> The tests have told the truth. These boys are ineducable beyond the merest rudiments of training. No amount of school instruction will ever make them intelligent voters or capable

citizens. . . . Their dullness seems to be racial, or at least inherent in the family stocks from which they came. . . . [O]ne meets this type with such extraordinary frequency among Indians, Mexicans and Negroes. . . . Children of this group should be segregated in special classes and be given instruction which is concrete and practical. . . . There is no possibility at present of convincing society that they should not be allowed to reproduce, although from a eugenic point of view they constitute a grave problem because of their unusually prolific breeding.[62]

Although IQ tests were periodically modified after the 1920s, their use (and the scores their use generated) was continually marshaled as "evidence" in support of deficit views and assumptions of racial superiority similar to those held by Terman.

The second half of the twentieth century brought significant structural changes that promised to alter deficit thinking. The 1954 *Brown* decision overturned laws that separated children in school by race, and the *Lau v. Nichols* decision in 1974 set forth the constitutional requirement that equal educational opportunity demanded that schools offer help for students unable to understand English.

However, neither these decisions nor considerable ensuing legislation that was meant to make schools more respectful and inclusive eradicated the prevailing ideologies of deficit thinking and racial superiority. These ideologies—and the norms and practices to which they give rise—have kept most neighborhoods and schools segregated and have perpetuated discrimination, disadvantage, and disparity.

Mauro Bautista, one of the teachers portrayed in Chapter 1 and in the rest of this book, is committed to turning his firsthand experience with deficit thinking into teaching that defies it.

> I am living one of my life goals by teaching in the neighborhood where I grew up, went to school, and still live. In 1982, my parents and I immigrated into East Los Angeles from Mexico. Unfortunately, I am only one of a handful of students from urban immigrant communities who have the opportunity to pursue higher education. Many teachers and scholars contend that minorities occupy an inferior economic, social, and political status because of some deficiency within the minority groups themselves. As a social justice educator, I want to challenge deficit thinking. I want to challenge the traditional educational practice of holding low expectations of underrepresented students. I expect my students not only to survive in this country, but also to excel. My students have high career goals, and, therefore, I expect them to at least have the option to attend a higher learning institution in order to pursue those goals. My students' parents also have high expectations of their children and are interested in their education.
>
> —Mauro Bautista
> Middle-school bilingual education coordinator

The Bell Curve

Modern-day deficit thinking is alive and well. Two months after its publication in 1994, *The Bell Curve: Intelligence and Class Structure in American Life* had 400,000 copies in print. Richard Herrnstein and Charles Murray's best-selling book claimed to offer scientific proof that African Americans inherit lower IQs than Whites and that these IQ differences are virtually impossible to change. Put bluntly, Herrnstein and Murray argued that the average African American was less well educated and less wealthy than the average White person because they were not born with the capacity to be as smart. Therefore, the authors also claimed, social programs that attempted to close opportunity gaps—programs such as Head Start, compensatory education, and affirmative action—were both costly and useless. Following this logic, the authors argued that (1) such programs hurt those they intend to help by steering them away from the lower-level aspirations and occupations that suit their abilities, and (2) such programs harm society because they give less intelligent people access to social positions that require greater aptitude. The authors, well-known academics from prestigious universities, bolstered these claims with impressive-looking charts, graphs, and statistics in their 800-plus-page book.

The Bell Curve claimed profound implications for schools and teaching. More likely, the book just emboldened people who already subscribed to ideologies of merit and deficits. *The Bell Curve* argued that Americans need to face the reality that "in a universal education system, many students will not reach the level of education that most people view as basic."[63] Moreover, according to the authors, efforts to teach groups of children with low IQs—disproportionately, disadvantaged children of color—more than the most modest skills will benefit neither those children nor society. Rather, government and educators should shift most of their teaching resources and efforts from the disadvantaged to the intellectually gifted.

Readers of *The Bell Curve* and of the countless magazine and journal reviews that followed its publication, as well as listeners of TV talk shows and radio call-in programs about the book, were frightened and enraged. Those who liked the book were angry because it confirmed their political views about the futility (or worse) of social programs that aimed to improve life chances among people of color. Those who disagreed were furious because they found the book dishonest, unscientific, and morally offensive. And much of this anger endures, as evidenced by heated protests that broke out in 2017 on college campuses where Charles Murray was invited to speak about his scholarship.

A book such as *The Bell Curve* appears every few decades. In 1969, for example, Harvard psychologist Arthur Jensen argued that because national poverty programs did not appreciably raise children's IQs, the children of the poor must be genetically intellectually inferior. Around the same time, physicist William Shockley reemerged years after coinventing the transistor to bring the authority of his scientific credentials to a proposal for reimbursing voluntarily sterilized individuals according to their number of IQ points below 100.

What is notable is the tendency of such views, once expressed, to quickly gain popularity. In each instance, findings from these reports made front-page headlines and gave readers permission to speak aloud otherwise private convictions about racial superiority, merit, and the deservingness of the poor. Respected scholars instantly refuted the books and reports, but they were consigned to smaller pieces on the editorial pages and to magazines and journals with smaller audiences than television or newspapers. Under these conditions, some of the most fair-minded teachers experienced shock in recognizing the extent to which *The Bell Curve*'s old-fashioned, inaccurate (at best), and racist perspectives remained present in the minds and hearts of so many, including among their colleagues at school.

The theories of race and intelligence embedded in *The Bell Curve* are not neutral or objective scientific discoveries. Rather, they reflect the beliefs and values of the cultures—like our own—in which they develop. In turn, the theories that gain acceptance most readily and hold enduring sway over the norms and practices of schooling nearly always serve the interests of those in power. In contemporary schools, such theories are still used to explain a wide range of conditions including, for example, the overrepresentation of students of color and bilingual learners among those designated as having "special needs," and their underrepresentation among those identified as "gifted."[64]

Today's Deficit Thinking About Language

Such ideologies about race, merit, intelligence, and cultural deficits are also embedded in the "English-only" movement of the last few decades, which has helped pass "official English" measures in thirty-one states. James Crawford, a longtime analyst of language policy issues, has traced contemporary English-only activism back to early-1980s efforts to resist racial and cultural diversity—for example, the 1983 creation of the citizens' action group U.S. English. Group founder S. I. Hayakawa, a former California senator, argued that language offers the most respectable tool for curtailing potential cultural degradation at the hands of Latinx immigrants, whose "deficits," beyond language, included failure to use birth control, disregard for the environment, and low "educability."[65] In this sense, Crawford maintains that public debates over language policy often reflect an aversion to non-English-speaking immigrants that is based on underlying fears and prejudices, as well as fundamental struggles for employment and power. Not surprisingly, then, these debates tend to intensify during times of economic downturn.

Alongside proliferating English-only sentiments, anti-immigrant actions at the federal level (e.g., increased numbers of deportations) and legislative efforts at the state level (e.g., as in Arizona, Georgia, Utah, Indiana, and Alabama) continue and intensify anti-immigrant sentiment. Upticks in such sentiments are not necessarily as tied to unemployment as they were in the past; they have become key to appeals made by populist politicians who tie, often troublingly, immigration to matters of national prosperity, personal safety, terrorism, and whatever other fears or resentments seem to connect with disaffected voters. Of all efforts, Alabama's have been among the most strident; House Bill (HB) 57 bars undocumented immigrants from receiving any state or local public benefits, attending public colleges, or applying for or soliciting work. The law also renders it illegal to employ or rent property to undocumented immigrants, and requires—as in Arizona—that police check the immigration status of those they stop and suspect may be in the country illegally. Concerning K–12 education, HB 57 requires that school officials verify and report to the state education board the number of students who are "illegal immigrants."[66]

Although anti-immigrant movements will likely endure, so too will activism aimed at resisting the policies and practices they advocate. In fact, efforts to use schools as mechanisms for identifying or discouraging undocumented immigrants have faced legal challenges in the past. The 1982 *Plyler v. Doe* ruling, for example, forbade public schools in Texas from charging undocumented students attendance fees on the grounds that those fees denied students their fundamental right to an education.[67] Likewise, the 2011 California Dream Act granted qualifying undocumented students access to state-funded financial aid for college and thus protected their rights to an education.[68] Although similar legislation has yet to pass in other states or at the national level, concerted efforts to support such legislation are ongoing among undocumented students and their advocates.

Racial Superiority and White Privilege

Most scientists today agree that race is not a useful scientific category because the genetic differences between races are insignificant compared to those within them. In essence, most consider race "a social construct without biological meaning" and find racial categories to be "weak proxies for genetic diversity,"[69] and yet Whites in U.S. society continue to experience numerous privileges. These are rooted not in biology but in long-standing beliefs that associate more or less moral and intellectual capacity with different racial groups. Onto these beliefs are layered powerful social preferences (not held exclusively by Whites)—for example, consistent messages about the relative aesthetic value of lighter versus darker skin.

White privilege is a difficult concept for many White people to understand because its benefits are indirect, and without a strong critical perspective it may feel unpleasant to acknowledge how one benefits from race-based advantages. In addition, "privilege" doesn't necessarily produce an immediate tangible benefit that registers on a conscious or subconscious level; privilege is often so ingrained that it goes unrecognized—a freedom from deficit biases that other groups experience on a daily basis.

A Direct Challenge to the Myth of Merit

Since the 1980s, critical race scholars like Derrick Bell and Kimberlé Crenshaw have pressed members of academic and legal communities to analyze the complex intersections of race, law, and power. Others, like Gloria Ladson-Billings, have explored how these intersections relate to education in particular. These scholars have argued that by focusing on individual and intentional acts of racism, people have tended to overlook the broader conditions of inequality and racism that permeate social structures, institutions (like schools), and face-to-face relationships in all facets of life in the United States. Thus, their arguments work to unsettle mainstream assumptions about why our society—and its distribution of wealth and opportunity—looks as it does. As mentioned at the start of Chapter 1, Ladson-Billings, for example, has argued that the term *education debt* offers far more accuracy than the term *achievement gap* because it locates the source of contemporary achievement disparities in this country's long history of having disproportionately denied people of color equal educational opportunity.[70]

Analyses like these pose profound cultural questions. Scholars Richard Delgado and Jean Stefancic summarize some of these: Who counts as White? How has the category of Whiteness changed over time? At what point does pride in being White cross the line into White supremacy? What can Whites concerned over racial inequity or White privilege do about it? One answer they provide is that race is largely relational—that "Whiteness" often serves as the norm against which other races are evaluated. As a result, understanding what it means to be White depends on also understanding what it means to *not* be White.[71]

"The Invisible Knapsack"

Notably, it is not only academics and scholars who address Whiteness. Many White people—including some of the new teachers profiled in this text—have worked to process, understand, and redress how Whiteness works to their advantage. Two scholars in particular have written at length and in accessible terms about the structural dimensions of their own White privilege. Likening White privilege to the male privilege she studied as a professor of women's studies, Peggy McIntosh offered in the late 1980s a still-timely framework for grappling with these issues in one's own life. In her most famous essay, she recounts her realization that being White brings considerable advantages that she had previously taken for granted as simply normal features of her life. McIntosh wrote:

> As a white person, I realized I had been taught about racism as something that puts others at a disadvantage, but had been taught not to see one of its corollary aspects, white privilege, which puts me at an advantage.
>
> I think whites are carefully taught not to recognize white privilege. . . . So I have begun in an untutored way to ask what it is like to have white privilege. I have come to see white privilege as an invisible package of unearned assets that I can count on cashing in each day, but about which I was "meant" to remain oblivious. White privilege is like an invisible weightless knapsack of special provisions, maps, passports, codebooks, visas, clothes, tools, and blank checks.[72]

McIntosh made a list of fifty everyday privileges she believes came with the color of her skin. She noted that some of the items on the list were "what one would want for everyone in a just society," and that others allowed Whites to be "ignorant, oblivious, arrogant, and destructive." See Focal Point 2.1 for a selection of those fifty privileges.

Focal Point 2.1
The "Invisible Knapsack" of White Privilege (Excerpt)

1. I can if I wish arrange to be in the company of people of my race most of the time.
2. If I should need to move, I can be pretty sure of renting or purchasing housing in an area, which I can afford and in which I would want to live.
3. I can be pretty sure that my neighbors in such a location will be neutral or pleasant to me.
4. I can go shopping alone most of the time, pretty well assured that I will not be followed or harassed.
5. I can turn on the television or open to the front page of the paper and see people of my race widely represented.
6. When I am told about our national heritage or about "civilization," I am shown that people of my color made it what it is.
7. I can be sure that my children will be given curricular materials that testify to the existence of their race.
8. If I want to, I can be pretty sure of finding a publisher for this piece on white privilege.
9. I can go into a music shop and count on finding the music of my race represented, into a supermarket and find the staple foods which fit with my cultural traditions, into a hair-dresser's shop and find someone who can cut my hair.
10. Whether I use checks, credit cards or cash, I can count on my skin color not to work against the appearance of my financial reliability.
11. I can arrange to protect my children most of the time from people who might not like them.
12. I can swear, or dress in second hand clothes, or not answer letters, without having people attribute these choices to the bad morals, the poverty, or the illiteracy of my race.
13. I can speak in public to a powerful male group without putting my race on trial.
14. I can do well in a challenging situation without being called a credit to my race.
15. I am never asked to speak for all the people of my racial group.
16. I can remain oblivious of the language and customs of persons of color who constitute the world's majority without feeling in my culture any penalty for such oblivion.
17. I can criticize our government and talk about how much I fear its policies and behavior without being seen as a cultural outsider.
18. I can be pretty sure that if I ask to talk to "the person in charge," I will be facing a person of my race.
19. If a traffic cop pulls me over or if the IRS audits my tax return, I can be sure I haven't been singled out because of my race.
20. I can easily buy posters, post-cards, picture books, greeting cards, dolls, toys, and children's magazines featuring people of my race.
21. I can go home from most meetings of organizations I belong to feeling somewhat tied in, rather than isolated, out-of-place, outnumbered, unheard, held at a distance, or feared.
22. I can take a job with an affirmative action employer without having coworkers on the job suspect that I got it because of race.
23. I can choose public accommodation without fearing that people of my race cannot get in or will be mistreated in the place I have chosen.
24. I can be sure that if I need legal or medical help my race will not work against me.

25. If my day, week or year is going badly, I need not ask of each negative episode or situation whether it has racial overtones.
26. I can choose blemish cover or bandages in "flesh" color and have them more or less match my skin.

McIntosh explained that her recognition of these racial privileges challenged her understanding of the United States as a meritocratic society.

> For me white privilege has turned out to be an elusive and fugitive subject. The pressure to avoid it is great, for in facing it I must give up the myth of meritocracy. If these things are true, this is not such a free country; one's life is not what one makes it; many doors open for certain people through no virtues of their own.[73]

Notably, McIntosh realized that these privileges are structural, not simply a matter of individual prejudice. She also understood how hard such structures of privilege are to change.

> In my class and place, I did not see myself as a racist because I was taught to recognize racism only in individual acts of meanness by members of my group, never in invisible systems conferring unsought racial dominance on my group from birth.
>
> Disapproving of the systems won't be enough to change them. I was taught to think that racism could end if white individuals changed their attitude. But a "white" skin in the United States opens many doors for whites whether or not we approve of the way dominance has been conferred on us. Individual acts can palliate but cannot end these problems.[74]

McIntosh's provocative observations have since caught the attention of many educators seeking to explain to themselves, colleagues, and students why and how, decades after the end of legalized segregation and racial discrimination, race still plays such a powerful role in enhancing or limiting access to education and life opportunities. And of course, because race manifests in different ways at different historical moments, it's always worth asking what McIntosh's list, or your own, might include at present—for example, as revealed in mass and social media, wars around the world, activism in opposition to police brutality, and so on.

Race, Privilege, and Teaching

Christine Sleeter offers another, and more historical, example. A scholar of multicultural education, Sleeter has written about reconstructing her family history with the following questions, among others, in mind:

> Can family history help members of the dominant society, especially Whites, gain a deeper insight into the history as well as contemporary workings of power and privilege? Can an understanding of how one's inherited privileges were constructed over time generate a willingness to work against those privileges as they exist today?[75]

Through her examination, Sleeter learned that her current circumstances could, in fact, be traced back to wealth her ancestors had accrued on an uneven playing field. She learned that, like other English immigrants, her ancestors had "appropriated Indian land and Black labor" and that such actions were sanctioned and even encouraged by U.S. lawmakers. However, she also learned about positive, antiracist actions taken by some of her ancestors. Sleeter argues that by reconstructing one's own history, Whites can mine and cultivate the more positive aspects of their identities, while also owning up to and moving beyond patterns of privilege that limit their capacity to participate justly in society. She explains:

> As a white middle class woman of mixed (mostly) European ancestry, my history is more different from the standard history I learned in school than I had anticipated. My history includes narratives of perpetrating from and benefitting from various forms of oppression, to be sure, but it also includes narratives of challenging discrimination and navigating around discriminatory laws and customs, preserving cultural heritage, burying aspects of ourselves that are not middle class, and trying to pass on to the next generation the tools for a better life. And in the process of doing all of this, a good deal of historical memory has been erased—at times intentionally and at other times not. But it is, in part, through our historical memory and the legacies of our families that we, as white Americans, might be able to refashion ourselves, not by breaking with the families on whose shoulders we stand, but rather by claiming tools that some of our ancestors can give us, while letting go of legacies that trap us in insulated cocoons.[76]

Judy Smith, whom we met in Chapter 1, is another such educator. The community where she teaches high school struggles with racial and ethnic tensions compounded by poverty. Conscious of her own privilege and the deficit thinking about students of color that pervades our culture, Judy works to position the diversity in her classroom as an asset for learning, rather than a source of tension.

> As a White teacher of students of color, I am aware of White privilege, or what Peggy McIntosh calls an "invisible package of unearned assets." In my classroom, there are two power structures. Not only am I a member of the dominant culture, but I also represent authority as the teacher of the class. . . .
>
> The students provide me with the opportunity to learn more about the content, the issues that affect their lives, the truths and the impact of various societal problems, and, most important, the reason teachers teach. Together we make meaning of content, day-to-day issues, and grow as human beings.
>
> Learning does not happen without risk taking. I have to take risks and encourage my students to take risks. It is challenging to discuss racism, sexism, and homophobia. However, for a truly effective learning community, we must address the very topics that maintain the status quo. My students and I work together to understand the gross economic and social inequities that exist and what we can do about them.
>
> —Judy Smith
> High school social studies

These are not simply academic issues with which some teachers must wrestle; they affect the lives of all teachers and students. Another of the teachers we introduced in Chapter 1, Mark Hill, has also experienced firsthand our culture's troubling thinking about race. Mark, like many of his students, has struggled to make sense of racial categories that place Whites in a privileged position, attribute deficits to people of color, and generally oversimplify the complex identity that he embraces. His words from Chapter 1 resonate here, as well:

> I remember as a child wanting others to "see" me the same way I saw myself. Because of this, I make a tremendous effort to "see" students as individuals and accept them on their own terms, regardless of preconceived notions of race, gender or age. This is very important for adolescents who are struggling with their identity and are looking for acceptance.
>
> —Mark Hill
> High school mathematics

These educators' stories remind us that race in the United States affects everyone, teachers and students alike, on both structural and personal levels.[77]

Teaching for Democracy

> The forces of inequity and democracy are perpetually in tension within our schools. . . . Ignoring the power that lies in our position as teachers, not examining our theories about children and learning, and ignoring the political dimensions of our work perpetuate in our own classrooms the social inequality that plagues our society.
>
> —Laura Silvina Torres
> First-year teacher, grade 2

In the midst of well-justified concern, and outrage about the nation's contradictory history and traditions, the twenty-first century also shows signs of an energizing hopefulness that gives reason for optimism. We are fortunate to have among these contradictory traditions one that speaks—if not always loudly and clearly—to the role of democracy's core values in education. Teachers like Laura Silvina Torres and others in this book help to bring those democratic values to life, even in the midst of antidemocratic—and yes, sometimes disappointingly racist and xenophobic—political and social outbursts. They speak out against the deficit ideologies that constrain the diverse young people they teach. They touch the lives of countless students who contribute to and carry this important work forward.

We conclude with the words of Matthew Eide, who, like every other teacher, has to solve the seemingly mundane question, "What do I teach on Monday morning?" But drawing on his understanding of history and culture, he poses other questions, too. These are essential questions not just for beginning teachers but for every educator committed to educational justice.

> As a teacher, I must question everything I do. All my classroom practices must be open to a critical examination. How do issues of race, class, language, and gender influence what I do? How does my classroom resist and perpetuate the institutional racism, classism, linguicism, and sexism of education and society? I must ask myself who benefits from the structure of my class. Yet with this awareness must also come action. I must commit myself to multiculturalism and a culturally relevant pedagogy that affirms and legitimizes the language and culture of my students. I must try to create a democratic classroom, where students actively construct their own knowledge. Finally, I must be a teacher who helps students discover their possibilities and urges them to claim their role as transformative members of society.
>
> —Matthew Eide
> First-year teacher, high school history

Digging Deeper and Tools for Critique

www.routledge.com/cw/teachingtochangetheworld

Notes

1 Most of Jefferson's specific recommendations came in the form of proposals for education in his home state of Virginia. See, for example, Thomas Jefferson, *Notes on the State of Virginia* (1781, reprint Richmond, VA: J. W. Randolph, 1853). For a good collection of Jefferson's writings, see James Gilreath, ed., *Thomas Jefferson and the Education of a Citizen* (Washington, DC: Library of Congress, 1999, distributed by University Press of New England).

2 Carter Godwin Woodson, *The Education of the Negro Prior to 1861: A History of the Education of the Colored People of the United States From the Beginning of Slavery to the Civil War* (1919, reprint Project Gutenberg, 2004), 24, www.gutenberg.org/etext/11089/.

3 David Tyack and Elisabeth Hansot, *Managers of Virtue: Public School Leadership in America, 1820–1980* (New York: Basic Books, 1982).

4 *Plessy v. Ferguson*, 163 U.S. 537, 1896.

5 *Brown v. Board of Education of Topeka*, 347 U.S. 483, 1954.

6 Brenda J. Child, *Boarding School Seasons: American Indian Families, 1900–1940* (Lincoln: University of Nebraska Press, 2000); David Wallace Adams, *Education for Extinction: American Indians and the Boarding School Experience 1875–1928* (Lawrence: University Press of Kansas, 1997).

7 David Tyack, *The One Best System: A History of American Urban Education* (Cambridge, MA: Harvard University Press, 1974).

8 Recorded uses of the term *melting pot* date back to the late eighteenth century, and the term was used in intervening years by the likes of writer and philosopher Ralph Waldo Emerson and historian Frederick Jackson Turner. However, the phrase became popular after its use in the play *The Melting Pot: The Great American Drama*, written by Israel Zangwill and performed in Washington, DC, in 1908.

9 Paula Fass, *Outside In: Minorities and the Transformation of American Education* (Oxford and New York: Oxford University Press, 1989).

10 Quoted in James Crawford, *Language Loyalties: A Sourcebook on the Official English Controversy* (Chicago: University of Chicago Press, 1992).

11 *Plessy v. Ferguson*, 163 U.S. 537, 1896.

12 Olivia N. Saracho and Bernard Spodek, *Contemporary Perspectives on Language Policy and Literacy Instruction in Early Childhood Education* (Charlotte, NC: Information Age, 2004), 3.

13 *Brown v. Board of Education of Topeka*, 347 U.S. 483, 1954.

14 *Mills v. Board of Education of District of Columbia*, 348 F.Supp. 866 (D.D.C.), 1972.

15 Quoted in James Crawford, *Language Loyalties: A Sourcebook on the Official English Controversy* (Chicago: University of Chicago Press, 1992), 131.

16 *Board of Education of Oklahoma City v. Dowell*, 498 U.S. 237, 1991.

17 *Who Built America?* CD-ROM produced by the American Social History Project, City University of New York, as cited in *Rethinking Schools*, Summer 1996. The project is also online at www. ashp.cuny.edu.

18 James Crawford, "Anatomy of the English-Only Movement," in *Language Legislation and Linguistic Rights*, ed. Douglas A. Kibbee (Amsterdam and Philadelphia: John Benjamins, 1998).

19 WNYC News, *Allegations of Islam Indoctrination in Public Schools Spread to New Jersey*, April 2017, www.wnyc.org/story/allegations-islam-indoctrination-public-schools-spread-nj/.

20 See, for example, NPR Staff, National Public Radio, *Politics and Religion Mix in Presidential Primaries*, www.npr.org/2011/09/16/140533708/politics-and-religion-mix-in-presidential-primaries/; Bill Keller, "Asking Candidates Tougher Questions About Faith," *New York Times*, August 25, 2011, www.nytimes.com/2011/08/28/magazine/asking-candidates-tougher-questions-about-faith.html?_r=2; Michael B. Berkman and Eric Plutzer, "Defeating Creationism in the Courtroom, But Not in the Classroom," *Science* 331, no. 6016 (2011): 404–405.

21 In 2002, for example, the Bush administration delegated all decisions and funding related to bilingual education to individual states when it replaced the Bilingual Education Act (BEA) with the English Language Acquisition Act (ELAA), a move representing increased hostility toward bilingual education in the national discourse. Indeed, the shift in rhetoric alone—from "bilingual" to "English language acquisition"—implies that using one's native language in the classroom necessarily impedes English language learning. See Patricia Gándara and Megan Hopkins, eds., *Forbidden Language: English Learners and Restrictive Language Policies* (New York: Teachers College Press, 2010).

22 See, for example, Shankar Vedantam, "Bilingualism's Brain Benefits," *Washington Post*, June 14, 2004, A07; Claudia Dreifus, "The Bilingual Advantage," *New York Times*, May 30, 2011, www. nytimes.com/2011/05/31/science/31conversation.html.

23 "Arizona Ethnic Studies Classes Banned, Teachers With Accents Can No Longer Teach English," *Huffington Post*, June 30, 2010, www.huffingtonpost.com/2010/04/30/arizona-ethnic-studies-cl_n1_558731.html; Miriam Jordan, "Arizona Grades Teachers on Fluency," *Wall Street Journal*, April 30, 2010, http://online.wsj.com/article/SB10001424052748703572504575213883276427528.html.

24 Christine E. Sleeter, *The Academic and Social Value of Ethnic Studies: A Research Review* (Washington, DC: National Education Association Research Department, 2011); Thomas S. Dee and Emily K. Penner, "The Causal Effects of Cultural Relevance Evidence From an Ethnic Studies Curriculum," *American Educational Research Journal* 54, no. 1 (2017): 1–40, https://doi.org/10.3102/0002831216677002.

25 Kris Gutiérrez, Jolynn Asato, Maria Santos, and Neil Gotanda, "Backlash Pedagogy: Language and Culture and the Politics of Reform," *Review of Education, Pedagogy and Cultural Studies* 24, no. 4 (2002): 335–351.

26 "Full Text of Obama's Education Speech," *Denver Post*, May 28, 2008, www.denverpost.com/ci_9405199/.

27 Ibid.

28 Bill and Melinda Gates Foundation, *Education and the Workplace*, www.gatesfoundation.org/postsecondaryeducation/Pages/education-and-the-workplace.aspx.

29 Bureau of Labor Statistics, *Occupational Outlook Handbook, 2010–11 Edition, Overview of the 2008–18 Projections*, www.bls.gov/oco/oco2003.htm.

30 Joel Spring, *American Education* (Boston: McGraw-Hill, 1996).

31 National Commission on Excellence in Education, *A Nation at Risk: The Imperatives for Educational Reform* (Washington, DC: U.S. Department of Education, 1983), 1.

32 The Goals 2000: Educate America Act (PL 103-227), paragraph 3A, https://www2.ed.gov/legislation/GOALS2000/TheAct/sec102.html.

33 Deviation from the official text of the speech given October 2001, as cited in E. H. DeBray, *Politics, Ideology, and Education: Federal Policy During the Clinton and Bush Administrations* (New York: Teachers College Press, 2006).

34 "Full Text of Obama's Education Speech," *Denver Post*, May 28, 2008, Document 2.

35 Nadia Pflaum, "Trump: U.S. Spends More Than 'Almost Any Other Major Country' on Education," *Politico Fact Ohio*, September 21, 2016, www.politifact.com/ohio/statements/2016/sep/21/donald-trump/trump-us-spends-more-almost-any-other-major-country/.

36 Richard Kluger, *Simple Justice* (New York: Vintage, 1977).

37 Title I of the Elementary and Secondary Education Act of 1965.

38 Title IX of the Education Amendments of 1972 (discrimination based on sex), 20 U.S.C.A. §§ 1681–1688.

39 *The Individuals With Disabilities Education Act of 1975*, http://idea.ed.gov/explore/view/p/%2Croot%2Cdynamic%2CTopicalBrief%2C23%2C/.

40 It is worth noting that the term *ideological* is often used in debate to describe—and dismiss—opponents' arguments or approaches as being rooted in efforts to legitimate their own claims to, or critiques of, authority and power.

41 Alexander Stille, "The Paradox of the New Elite," *New York Times*, October 22, 2011, SR1.

42 Gunnar Myrdal, *An American Dilemma: The Negro Problem and American Democracy* (New York: Harper and Brothers, 1944).

43 Jay MacLeod, *Ain't No Makin' It* (Boulder, CO: Westview Press, 1995), 3.

44 Richard Fry, D'Vera Cohn, Gretchen Livingston, and Paul Taylor, *The Rising Age Gap in Economic Well-Being: The Old Prosper Relative to the Young* (New York: Pew Foundation, 2011), www.pewsocialtrends.org/2011/11/07/the-rising-age-gap-in-economic-well-being/1/.

45 Carter Godwin Woodson, *The Mis-Education of the Negro* (Washington, DC: Associated Publishers, 1933).

46 See, for example, ibid.; Pierre Bourdieu and Jean Claude Passeron, *Reproduction in Education, Society and Culture* (Thousand Oaks, CA: Sage, 1990); Samuel Bowles and Herbert Gintis, *Schooling in Capitalist America: Educational Reform and the Contradictions of Economic Life* (New York: Basic Books, 1977); and Raymond Allan Morrow and Carlos Alberto Torres, *Social*

Theory and Education: A Critique of Theories of Social and Cultural Reproduction (Buffalo, NY: SUNY Press, 1995).

47 Gunnar Myrdal, *An American Dilemma*. Myrdal's massive report (more than 1,500 pages) concluded that a deeply troubling dilemma in America was the fundamental contradiction between the nation's democratic ideology and its pervasive racism. However, Myrdal also saw racism as a cultural anomaly that Americans could and should excise.

48 Michael Harrington, *The Other America: Poverty in the United States* (1962, reprint New York: Collier Books, 1997).

49 Gary Orfield and Susan Eaton, *Dismantling Desegregation: The Quiet Reversal of "Brown v. Board of Education"* (Boston: New Press, 1996); Gary Orfield, Mark Bachmeier, David James, and Tamela Eitle, *Deepening Segregation in American Public Schools* (Cambridge, MA: Civil Rights Project, Harvard Graduate School of Education, 1997).

50 *Brown v. Board of Education of Topeka*, 347 U.S. 483, 1954.

51 Jonathan Kozol, *The Shame of the Nation: The Restoration of Apartheid Schooling in America* (New York: Crown Publishing, 2005); Gary Orfield and Chungmei Lee, *Historic Reversals, Accelerating Resegregation, and the Need for New Integration Strategies* (Los Angeles, CA: UCLA Civil Rights Project/Proyecto Derechos Civiles, 2007).

52 See, for example, Michael Katz, *The Undeserving Poor: From War on Poverty to War on the Poor* (New York: Pantheon, 1989).

53 Stephan Thernstrom and Abigail Thernstrom, *No Excuses: Closing the Racial Gap in Learning* (New York: Simon and Schuster, 2003).

54 MacLeod, *Ain't No Makin' It*, 126.

55 Charles Darwin, *On the Origin of Species by Means of Natural Selection, Or, the Preservation of Favoured Races in the Struggle for Life* (London: J. Murray, 1859).

56 Quoted in Stephen J. Gould, *The Mismeasure of Man*, 2nd ed. (New York: Norton, 1996), 24.

57 Ellwood P. Cubberley, *Changing Conceptions of Education* (Boston: Houghton Mifflin, 1909), 15.

58 Ibid.

59 Quoted in Gould, *The Mismeasure of Man*, 190.

60 Richard Valencia, ed., *The Origins of Deficit Thinking: Educational Thought and Practice* (London, UK: Falmer Press, 1997).

61 Excerpted from "Mental Ability Test, Stanford University, Test 1, Information (World Book Co, 1920)," as reprinted in Bill Bigelow, "Testing, Tracking, and Toeing the Line," in *Rethinking Our Classrooms: Teaching for Equity and Social Justice*, ed. Wayne Au, Bill Bigelow, and Stan Karp (Milwaukee, WI: Rethinking Schools, 1994), 121.

62 Quoted in Gould, *The Mismeasure of Man*, 221.

63 Richard Herrnstein and Charles Murray, *The Bell Curve: Intelligence and Class Structure in American Life* (New York: The Free Press, 1996), 436.

64 For a review of the literature, see A. J. Artiles, E. Kozleski, S. Trent, D. Osher, and A. Ortiz, "Justifying and Explaining Disproportionality, 1968–2008: A Critique of Underlying Views of Culture," *Exceptional Children* 76, no. 3 (2010): 279–299. For specific information about English Learners and disproportionality, see A. J. Artiles, J. Klingner, A. Sullivan, and E. Fierros, "Shifting Landscapes of Professional Practices: English Learner Special Education Placement in English-Only States," in *Forbidden Language: English Learners and Restrictive Language Policies*, eds. P. Gándara and M. Hopkins (New York: Teachers College Press, 2010).

65 Crawford, "Anatomy of the English-Only Movement."

66 Alabama State Legislature, *Beason-Hammon Alabama Taxpayer and Citizen Protection Act*, HB56, 2011.

67 Carlos R. Soltero, "Plyler v. Doe (1982) and Educating Children of Illegal Aliens," in *Latinos and American Law: Landmark Supreme Court Cases* (Austin, TX: University of Texas Press, 2006), 118–132; see also *Plyler v. Doe*, http://dictionary.sensagent.com/plyler+v.+doe/en-en/.

68 Patrick McGreevy and Anthony York, "Brown Signs California Dream Act," *Los Angeles Times*, October 9, 2011, http://articles.latimes.com/2011/oct/09/local/la-me-brown-dream-act-20111009/.

69 Megan Gannon, "Race Is a Social Construct, Scientists Argue," *Scientific American*, February 5, 2016, n.p., www.scientificamerican.com/article/race-is-a-social-construct-scientists-argue/.

70 Gloria Ladson-Billings, "From the Achievement Gap to the Education Debt: Understanding Achievement in U.S. Schools," 2006 American Educational Research Association Presidential Address, *Education Researcher* 35, no. 7 (2006): 3–12.

71 Richard Delgado and Jean Stefancic, *Critical White Studies: Looking Behind the Mirror* (Philadelphia, PA: Temple University Press, 1997); *Critical Race Theory: An Introduction* (New York: New York University Press, 2001).
72 Peggy McIntosh, "White Privilege and Male Privilege: A Personal Account of Coming to See Correspondences Through Work in Women's Studies," *Working Paper 189, Center for Research on Women, Wellesley College*, 1988, n.p.
73 Ibid., n.p.
74 Ibid., n.p.
75 Christine Sleeter, *Critical Family History: Placing History in a Sociocultural Historical Context*, n.p., https://sites.google.com/a/christinesleeter.org/critical-family-history/Home/critical-family-history-theory/. See also Christine Sleeter, "Becoming White: Reinterpreting a Family Story by Putting Race Back Into the Picture," *Race, Ethnicity and Education* 14, no. 4 (2011): 421–433.
76 Sleeter, *Critical Family History*, n.p.
77 Tara Yosso, *Critical Race Counterstories Along the Chicana/Chicano Educational Pipeline* (New York: Routledge, 2005).

Chapter 3

Politics and Philosophy

The Struggle over the School Curriculum

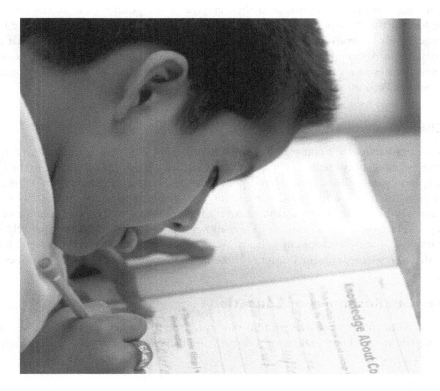

As a social justice educator, I challenge the traditional educational practice of suppressing important "funds of knowledge" [my] students possess, such as languages other than English. It is my responsibility to recognize, respect, and use the home languages to facilitate learning. The respect I place on the home languages will afford my students greater opportunities to develop a strong sense of self-worth.

As a social justice educator, I challenge the traditional practice of excluding people of color, especially women of color, from the curriculum. I include my students' voices in the curriculum. Many literacy activities revolve around students' personal and family histories. Women of color with professional degrees visited our classroom, including a Latina doctor, Latina professional singer, and two Latina teachers. Their presence in our classroom was critical because they are visual and physical proof that my students' high expectations of themselves are realistic and attainable.

—Mauro Bautista
Middle-school bilingual education coordinator

Mauro Bautista is not a traditional teacher. His stance toward curriculum can be characterized as progressive, even critical, as he draws on theories of schooling that challenge ideas that have governed education since the colonial period. Mauro rejects, for example, the idea that the only knowledge worth teaching is that of the dominant culture and that the primary purpose of schooling is to pass that dominant culture on to society's children. He also rejects the idea that cultural knowledge and languages that students bring with them to school are not worthy of incorporation into the curriculum.

What schools teach, *why*, and *how*—conventionally called curriculum and instruction—reflect deep philosophical commitments that touch every aspect of society. In a country as diverse as the United States, the journey from philosophy to practice is highly political. Whether challenging dominant modes of education or struggling to preserve worthy approaches and content, teachers must recognize and then engage in the politics of education. In this chapter, we look at this "politics" broadly, in the sense of the people and ideas that have had relatively more or less *power* in influencing teaching and learning and in determining what becomes the curriculum. Although it may seem that influential educators and policymakers are constantly inventing new ways of thinking about education, some ideas are woven throughout the long history of Western society.

Chapter Overview

Western societies have complex views of schooling and knowledge. In this chapter, we describe different educational philosophies, and then we briefly illustrate how people in the United States have struggled—philosophically and politically—over the curriculum. Most of the time, when we hear teachers use the word *curriculum*, they're referring to the programs or content they teach day-by-day in their classrooms; later chapters explore classroom content in much more depth. Here we focus on how key ideas and events shape beliefs about what schools ought to teach and what students ought to learn. We conclude with an overview of recent debates related to these very issues and the impact of those debates on teachers committed to social justice.

Basic Philosophies of Education

Reduced to their essentials, centuries-old arguments about education reflect philosophers' differing views on (1) the nature of reality, (2) humans' ability to "know" reality, and (3) what's worth knowing.

The Roots of Western Educational Philosophy

Throughout history, people have sought organizing principles to help make sense of the world. People have looked to God, the king, community norms, nature, science, their own intellect, political or economic systems, and more to forge coherent systems of thought and to manage their lives. American traditions and institutions, including schools, were born out of *modern* systems of thought that developed in the eighteenth-century European period known as the Enlightenment. At that time, Western thought turned increasingly to science and reason as central organizing processes.

The European Renaissance, from roughly the fourteenth to the seventeenth century, marked a transition from medieval to modern thought—from people as subjects in God's world to people who could initiate astonishing achievements in architecture and art, mathematics, commerce, cities and government, and more. New questions arose that previously were unimaginable, or at least suited only to a rarefied elite. What, besides divine gifts, allowed those achievements? What or who was the source of knowledge that made the achievements possible?

Even asking questions about the source of knowledge entailed a powerful shift in culture and politics because it implied that orthodoxies and authority were open to challenge. Through the suggestion that reason was an inborn and individual capacity and that humans could discover or construct knowledge, knowledge itself took a democratizing turn. The giants of Enlightenment philosophy—including René Descartes (1596–1650), John Locke (1632–1704), and Immanuel Kant (1724–1804)—articulated key questions that influenced the centuries that followed.

- Are some forms of knowledge inborn or innate?
- What truths can be known through reflection, or by examining our own thoughts?
- Is there a mind or soul that is spiritual or separate from the physical body? If so, do they interact?
- What is the difference between physical sensations and ideas?
- How do smaller bits of experience become organized into broader ideas and concepts?
- How do we study something (like the mind) that we can't see?
- Does science dispute or defend religious teachings based on new kinds of evidence?

Descartes emphasized the mind as a region that is separate from the body and inspects ideas. He argued that some forms of knowledge are inborn (and reside in the mind) and that the mind's reasoning was the most reliable source of that knowledge. Following Descartes, philosophers known as "idealists" took the position that reality is essentially spiritual, and knowledge a product of human reason; the most valuable ideas are those that stand the test of time since they are exposed to reason the longest.

Locke, in contrast, questioned the concept of innate ideas and turned to "empirical" evidence for knowledge. Empirical knowledge is that which can be detected by the senses. Locke argued that the mind is a blank slate that becomes written on through experience. Following Locke, philosophers known as "realists" have argued that reality (facts, truth) exists "out there," and humans come to know it by carefully examining the empirical world. This knowledge is already organized according to universal laws that govern the workings of the universe. The job of scholars is to discover those laws.

Kant, in the idealist tradition, challenged all these ideas. He saw the mind as an organ that was equipped with processes for creating orderly thought and understanding (rather than blankly awaiting experience). The mind mediated, categorized, and represented sensations and ideas, making sense out of chaotic, concrete experience. Unlike Descartes, Kant found the outside world relevant to thinking because it provided the raw material for the mind to organize.[1]

Philosophy in the History of U.S. Schooling

Benjamin Franklin, Thomas Jefferson, and other American intellectuals of the eighteenth and nineteenth centuries were influenced by deism, a religious perspective that conceived of God as the rational architect of an orderly world. After the initial work of creation, God had little to do with the day-by-day (or eon-by-eon) operations of the universe. Something like a "Master Watchmaker," God created a perfect mechanism and left the universe to run on its own. God was similarly absent from the daily affairs of people. Deists believed every human was born with all necessary spiritual knowledge, making the teachings of any church unnecessary. Only human reason was necessary to gain access to spiritual and physical truths. Of course, while the universe was complete and orderly, human reason was incomplete and imperfect. Thus, education in the United States was influenced by the belief that humans—imperfect though they are—can, through science and reason, discover, organize, and control for their own benefit and enlightenment the mysteries of the universe and human existence.

Although most nineteenth-century American educators had little or no training in how to teach, metaphors drawn from the work of Descartes, Locke, Kant, and other Enlightenment thinkers guided classroom practice. For example, following Locke and the realists, many educators thought about their young students' minds as empty vessels to be filled or as blank slates to be written on as they explored the empirical world. Following Descartes, Kant, and the idealists, educators embraced the belief that studying certain subjects would strengthen faculties such as memory, reasoning, will, and imagination. It is to this view that we owe the still popular metaphor of the "mind as a muscle" and the notion that the study of classical languages, geometry, and so on causes learners to "exercise their brains" and produces stronger, more capable minds.[2]

To be sure, not many who were engaged in education were strict (or necessarily knowledgeable) "Lockeans," "Cartesians," or "Kantians." Rather, these philosophical ideas circulated in the intellectual environment, and people drew from them, often picking and choosing to suit their everyday sense making. Further, these positions were challenged in the late nineteenth century by two new sets of ideas—pragmatism and behaviorism. Both perspectives grew out of the emerging science of psychology.

The pragmatist John Dewey and his colleagues, like the realists, believed in the idea of a reality and in the power of humans to know it through interacting with that "real" world. However, unlike realists, who placed the greatest value on knowing the unchanging laws of nature, pragmatists emphasized the importance of understanding how the physical world changes and how to solve problems. Behaviorism received a boost when psychologist Edward Thorndike combined the results of his scientific studies of animal learning with philosopher and psychologist William James's theory that systematic exercise and drill could build proper habits of thought in humans. Unlike the pragmatists, behaviorists viewed humans as mostly passive. Whereas pragmatists saw humans as learning through acting—often by solving problems in their environment—behaviorists saw learning as something that happened *to* people when they were acted upon by external stimulation, and thus saw people's habits as shaped by rewards or punishments.

Both pragmatism and behaviorism regarded science as benefiting society. Despite the horrendous social problems and inequality that accompanied industrialization, mass production, and urbanization at the turn of the twentieth century, Americans were optimistic that, by bringing more of life's variables under control, rational and scientific methods would also bring individual and social benefits.

At the beginning of the twenty-first century, scholars across many different disciplines now view the linear nineteenth- and twentieth-century habits of thought, born of the scientific method, as just *one* of many ways of knowing, not the *only* way. Thus, we can no longer be so certain (or arrogant) about what is progress, what is good, or even what is real to others. Indeed, multiple versions of progress, goodness, and truth might be credible both to different people and to ourselves. Formerly unquestioned modern and Western ideas of universal truths, regularity, and progress are gradually giving way to an emphasis on particularity, difference, and unpredictability. As we will discuss later in this chapter, this shift in thinking has influenced educational philosophy and curriculum as well.

Six Philosophies of Education

In the past century, many specific philosophies of education have developed from these broader philosophical trends. As Concept Tables 3.1 and 3.2 depict, each philosophy holds a somewhat different view of the purpose of schooling, its curriculum, and the roles teachers and students

Concept *Table 3.1* Three Traditional Philosophies of Education

Philosophy	Roots	Education's purpose	Preferred curriculum	Role of the teacher	Role of the student	Examples today
Essentialism	Idealism	Transmitting the culture from one generation to the next; training basic intellectual skills	Knowledge and basic skills necessary to preserve the culture and to enable constructive participation in it	Serve as the authority in the classroom, conveyor of knowledge, and administrator of tests to ensure that knowledge has been acquired	Receive transmitted knowledge—i.e., an "empty vessel" that accumulates knowledge	E. D. Hirsch's Cultural Literacy, standards-based curriculum
Perennialism	Idealism and realism	Cultivating the mind, instilling timeless virtues, and advancing the search for truth	Enduring ideas, universal truths, classic intellectual achievements	Instill virtues; know and teach subject matter to all students; convey received wisdom and knowledge, often through Socratic questioning	Receive knowledge—i.e., a mind waiting to be developed; perhaps think critically but never challenge intellectual authority	The Coalition of Essential Schools— "habits of mind"
Behaviorism	Realism	Building proper habits of thought	Individualized program; carefully paced, linear instruction	Train students, by providing stimuli and reinforcement for learning	Respond to stimuli and develop habits of thought and behavior	Direct instruction

Concept *Table 3.2* Three Progressive Philosophies of Education

Philosophy	Roots	Education's purpose	Preferred curriculum	Role of the teacher	Role of the student	Examples today
Child- and community-centered schooling	Pragmatism	Learning to solve the problems of society and democratic living	Problems faced by society and by children, informed by the academic disciplines	Create an environment rich with opportunities for student-directed learning and group problem solving	Engage actively in deciding what to study; learning by doing, rather than by listening	Constructivist teaching and learning
Social Reconstructionism	Pragmatism	Solving critical social problems that limit equality, justice, and democracy	Community and societal problems that are amenable to social and political action	Raise consciousness about social problems and provide tools for social critique and social action	Engage actively in analyzing social problems and acting to solve them	Critical pedagogy
Multiculturalism/ Sociocultural approach	Pragmatism/ Postmodernism	Promoting a just, multicultural democracy through the recognition of diverse cultures	Broad array of knowledge in the traditional subjects, with an emphasis on respectful understanding of cultures and peoples	Build on the "funds" of knowledge students bring from home; provide experiences that allow for diverse ways of learning	Construct knowledge by participating in ways that connect home culture and language with school experiences	Bilingual education, antiracist pedagogy

play. Each is manifest in one or more contemporary approaches to schooling. The first three philosophies—essentialism, perennialism, and behaviorism—inform what we consider traditional conceptions of schooling (see Concept Table 3.1). These have firm roots in Enlightenment thinking and frame the purpose of education as passing on to the young the knowledge, skills, and virtues prized by the dominant culture. These first three also tend to frame learning as a process of acquiring knowledge and skills.

The second three philosophies—child-centered and community-centered education, social reconstructionism, and multiculturalism—have informed what we consider progressive perspectives (see Concept Table 3.2). Their roots lie in pragmatism and postmodern thought. They frame the purpose of education as developing knowledge and ways of thinking that will move society toward realizing democracy or advancing social justice. These second three philosophies tend to frame learning as a social process of constructing knowledge and an apprenticeship into social and cultural practices.

The comprehensive educational timeline in Chapter 2 includes some of the history of these six philosophical traditions and their roles in the struggle over the school curriculum. The timeline highlights some of the thinkers who profoundly influenced what schools taught, how, and to whom over the first 200 years of American schooling.

Philosophy and Politics in the Struggle for the School Curriculum

Except for social reconstructionism and multiculturalism, these educational philosophies are not typically described as being political. It is characteristic of essentialist and perennialist thinkers to overlook the political elements of their own views. After all, if you see the curriculum as "basic" or enduring across all time, it is hard to imagine that others might view it differently; therefore, asserting your essential or perennial values and perspectives is not an exercise of power but a simple expression of truth. However, as the remainder of this chapter makes clear, proponents of these philosophies have all tried—and still do—to instill their own values and beliefs in the educational system and, by extension, to exclude the values and beliefs of others. In that sense, all educational philosophies are political.

Interwoven with struggles over which philosophical positions should govern U.S. schooling have been debates about whether all students should experience the same kind of schooling. For most of our history, most Americans have believed they should not. As education scholar Lauren B. Resnick observes, we "have inherited two quite distinct educational traditions—one concerned with elite education, the other concerned with mass education. These traditions conceived of schooling differently, had different clienteles, and held different goals for their students."[3]

These "distinct educational traditions"—elite and mass—have carried with them social and political consequences, as well as educational ones. While elite education has tended to lead to university studies and professional jobs, mass education has tended to restrict such access.

Much in our democratic rhetoric—including our promise of public schooling for all—claims to diminish the power of social class in determining who has access to schooling and who does not. However, the reality—a long tradition of separate "mass" and "elite" education—makes it much easier for individuals with wealth, power, leadership, and higher education to succeed in transferring to their children these advantages. The political tensions between equal opportunity and social stratification intertwine with philosophical debates over the purpose and conduct of schooling in the United States.

Essentialist Mass Education in the Eighteenth and Nineteenth Centuries

In the fifty years following the American Revolution, much of the United States' population either dispersed through westward expansion or concentrated in urban centers to work in a rapidly expanding trade and manufacturing economy. Fully tax-supported schools were still a long way off, and communities that had compulsory education rarely enforced it. All students, including the masses, were expected to learn their sums and perhaps a little accounting; to read well enough to understand the Bible, newspaper, and almanac; to understand a smattering of natural history (biology); and to be familiar with at least some national, European, and classical stories or history. This emphasis on the basics (or essentials) included the prevailing moral and religious predilections that teachers were expected to transmit—typically, those of northern European Protestant denominations.

In the 1780s Noah Webster—of dictionary fame—authored an enormously popular series of textbooks, notably the "blue-backed speller." Commonly referred to as the "Schoolmaster of America," Webster was passionately committed to an America free of decadent European influence and to strong, uniquely American citizenship and institutions. Starting as a schoolteacher himself, he fashioned a system of instruction that, in addition to providing lessons in reading and writing, aimed to develop patriotic citizens and create a unified national spirit. Webster argued that children should be educated in distinctive American language and social perspectives to set our culture apart from less acceptable European ones.

The speller attempted to instill respect for hard work and property rights. Its political and moral catechism required students to memorize the following series of questions and answers:

- Q: What is a moral virtue? A: It is an honest upright conduct in all our dealings with men.
- Q: Can we always determine what is honest and just? A: Perhaps not in every instance, but in general it is not difficult.
- Q: What rules have we to direct us? A: God's word contained in the Bible has furnished all necessary rules to direct our conduct.
- Q: In what part of the Bible are these rules to be found? A: In almost every part; but the most important duties between men are summed up in the beginning of Matthew, in Christ's Sermon on the Mount.[4]

By 1875, 75 million copies of Webster's blue-backed speller had been sold. Its popularity both reflected and shaped what people thought children should learn. Once the speller became the standard (there were not many choices), it established the tradition of infusing political and moral content into the teaching of basic skills.

Throughout the 1800s, schooling beyond the rudimentary basics—like those in the blue-backed speller—was available only to those who could pay for private tutors and schools. Most private schools favored a classical European education and prepared students for high schools and universities. Also following an essentialist philosophy, these schools taught the basic knowledge of mathematics, science, Latin, Greek, English grammar, geography, perhaps rhetoric, and so on.

However, some elite private schools took on a character more distinctive of the United States. Benjamin Franklin and other rationalists of the revolutionary period urged a departure from traditional courses in religion and classics and toward more useful and practical studies. Franklin, not surprisingly, envisioned an education consistent with his values for self-improvement. These values depended less on mastering facts through rote learning and more on accumulating

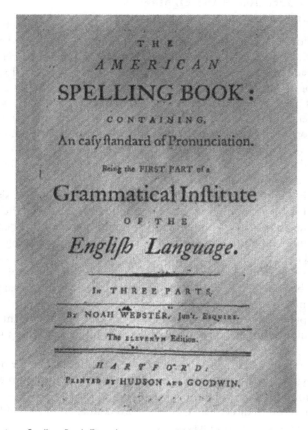

Noah Webster's *American Spelling Book* First Appeared in 1829

learning processes that would serve, as they did in Franklin's own case, a lifetime of learning. Franklin favored a breadth of utilitarian knowledge such as modern languages and the study of commerce and trade. Thus, Franklin advocated an education for elites that would later hold strong appeal for the masses. He also advocated a process-oriented approach and a focus on complex and practical knowledge, thereby providing some of the earliest hints of a problem-solving curriculum that might serve social justice goals.

Many people found Franklin's and others' ideas appealing, but when the first public high school was established in 1821, most Americans had not subscribed to the idea that education for everyone should extend beyond basic literacy and moral training. So, when public high schools began to appear, schoolmasters patterned them after the private academies, and thus relatively few children had access to them.

The Emergence of the Common School

The key idea of the *common* school suggests a public space dedicated to achieving educational goals held in common by all Americans. Precisely what should go on within such a space was and remains disputed. Likewise, such spaces embodied then, and still do, an enduring oxymoron, with students sorted within and segregated across them. As mentioned in Chapter 2, based on principles outlined by Horace Mann, the first so-called common schools emerged in the 1830s and 1840s, and soon became the dominant symbol of American education. The common school curriculum, including the use of textbooks for older youth, paved the way for today's public elementary and secondary schools.

The common school—which required some literacy and math for all—appealed to nearly everyone, but for different reasons. Working-class people, immigrants, and those outside the dominant culture who lacked resources for their own private schools saw the common school as a potential path to the American dream. People of greater wealth and status viewed common schools as enhancing their own well-being as well. Everyone would benefit, they reasoned, if schools could turn out productive workers and good citizens. However, then as now, when determining "how much" education and "how much for whom," the tradition of separate education prevailed, with private schools appealing to and meeting the expectations of the country's educated elites.

An Essentialist Curriculum

Essentialist schooling components reinforced one another in the common schools: Moral truths, cultural certainty, nationalism, capitalism, Protestant Christianity, and the view of children as "empty vessels" formed a tightly compatible whole. Imagine the overlapping influence of Webster's blue-backed speller and 122 million copies of McGuffey's Readers. Between 1836 and 1920, McGuffey's Readers taught rules for reading and proper speech; practical moral precepts; God's active participation in death, nature, and the distribution and withholding of wealth; the rules of capitalism; and—in a time before separate textbooks for different subjects—science, history, biography, geography, and more.

McGuffey's Readers did it all. Elites could be comforted since the readers, though educating large numbers of students from previously uneducated classes, offered academic and social lessons that preserved important social class distinctions. Consider historian Joel Spring's comments on and selections from two excerpts and what both rich and poor children would likely learn from them:

> In "The Rich Boy," students learned that the rich boy knows "that God gives a great deal of money to some persons, in order that they may assist those who are poor." In keeping with the idea that the rich are elected by God, the rich boy is portrayed as being humble, kind to servants, and "careful not to make a noise in the house, or break any thing, or put it out of its place, or tear his clothes." The reader is also told that this model of virtue "likes to go with his parents to visit poor people, in their cottages, and gives them all the money he can spare."[5]

In "The Poor Boy," meanwhile, Spring explains:

> Unlike the rich boy wanting to help the poor, the poor boy dreams of earning his own living. He likes his food of bread and bacon and does not envy the rich little boys and girls "riding on pretty horses, or in coaches." At the end of the story, the poor boy states his acceptance of his social position: "I have often been told, and I have read, that it is God who makes some poor, and others rich—that the rich have many troubles which we know nothing of; and that the poor, if they are but good, may be very happy. Indeed, I think that when I am good, nobody can be happier than I am."[6]

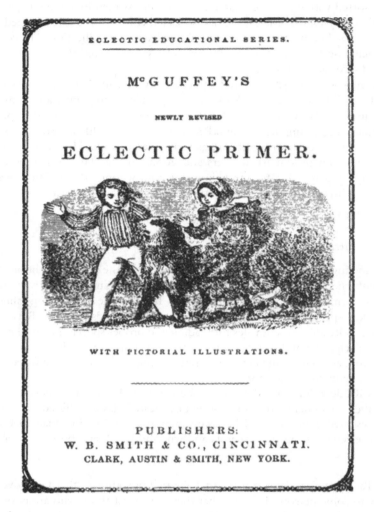

McGuffey's Reader

During the latter half of the 1800s, Webster's spellers and McGuffey's Readers amounted to national textbooks, with the readers remaining popular until World War I. These texts helped unify social, moral, political, and educational values, just as their authors had very pointedly intended. Educational and political leaders, educated as youth according to these same values, retained power and influence well into the twentieth century. Many were active in resisting change or in shaping reforms to keep schools aligned with nineteenth-century educational values. Further, throughout most of the twentieth century, the public continued to see as sensible McGuffey's and Webster's rote learning, as well as their heavy-handed political and moral indoctrination, including their decidedly male, Anglo, and Protestant orientation.

Efficiency in the Essentialist Common School

William Torrey Harris, a respected scholar and philosopher as well as superintendent of St. Louis schools and U.S. commissioner of education from 1889 to 1906, argued persuasively that schools could best pursue democratic principles through strict discipline, orderly behavior, and mastery of the school subjects that we recognize today as the core of the modern essentialist curriculum: mathematics, geography, literature, art, grammar, and history. Harris also believed that if schools were scientifically and rationally organized by age and ability, this curriculum would produce people better equipped for life in a democracy. His ideas were taken up by school systems around the nation.

What did such a curriculum look like? In 1893, pediatrician and school critic Joseph Mayer Rice gave the following description of a geometry lesson in a New York City school:

> Before the lesson began there was passed to each child a little flag, on which had been pasted various forms and colors, such as a square piece of green paper, a triangular piece of red paper, etc. . . . Upon receiving the signal, the first child sprang up, gave the name of the geometrical form upon his flag, loudly and rapidly defined the form, and fell back into his seat to make way for the second child, thus: "A square; a square has four equal sides and four corners; green" (down). Second child (up) "A triangle; a triangle has three sides and three corners; red" (down). . . . The rate of speed was so great that seventy children passed through the process of defining in a very few minutes.[7]

The efficient, orderly process described by Rice reflects the principles of scientific organization and efficiency that many at the turn of the twentieth century believed would ensure students' mastery of academic content, moral development, and general preparation for democratic citizenship.

Perennialism and Essentialism Intertwined in Secondary Schools

As more and more students began attending secondary schools, questions about what students should learn in secondary education and whether all students should learn the same things became more urgent. In 1893, an influential report from the National Education Association's Committee of Ten recommended that secondary schools offer more than one curriculum, but that all offerings be highly academic and lead to university training for those who desired it.[8] The committee argued that all young people—regardless of their future social position—would benefit from a mix of classical and modern studies that would transmit the western European intellectual tradition.

This approach to secondary schooling blended perennialist ideals with the prevailing essentialist curriculum. Perennialists wanted to build on the "basics" curriculum embraced by essentialism and include universal, everlasting principles and habits of thinking such as scientific reasoning. Perennialists saw the need to help students interact with natural, physical, and social worlds, and to prepare them for changing vocations and technology. Intellectual development, rather than the essentialists' basic skills, was the goal of a perennialist curriculum.

The Progressive Education Movement

At about this same time (the late 1800s and early 1900s), still other educators were struggling to fashion an education that would meet the needs of a rapidly urbanizing and industrializing society. Educators rooted in science and pragmatism proposed educational responses that veered in various directions—some toward behavioral psychology, some toward efficient school management, and others toward child- and community-centered schooling. They all considered themselves part of the progressive education movement.

As different as they were from one another, progressives shared some core beliefs. They cared more about applying rational, scientific advancements to the *delivery* of knowledge and to the organization of schools than did the essentialists and perennialists, who tended to focus primarily on *what* was taught. In particular, progressives looked to the emerging science of psychology to guide their practices and considerations as to how educators might contribute to long-term and changing needs of students and society.

Progressives with essentialist views focused on the science and efficiencies of behaviorism to maximize students' accumulation of mostly basic facts and skills. Child- and community-centered progressives built from the perennialist idea that conferring universal truths—scientific or cultural—should be the goal of education. Thus, progressives drifted in diverging directions, with essentialism and behaviorism gaining dominion over mass education, and perennialism influencing education for elites. We say more about this below.

Progressives' Emphasis on Efficiency

A hallmark of scientific practice is to organize, categorize, and rank the subjects or objects under study to build a robust explanatory theory. For example, G. Stanley Hall, founder of the "child study movement" at the end of the nineteenth century, argued that children's development occurred in stages that were fundamentally distinct. His work misinterpreted Charles Darwin's theory of biological and species evolution as applying to different stages of cultures', races', and individuals' aging and development. Thus, childhood, adolescence, and adulthood mirrored the "savages" and the "civilized." He provided the foundation for the idea of adolescence—a stage of life when children have markedly different needs and require distinctive treatments in school (since individuals between postpuberty and marriage have characteristics of both savages and the civilized). The invention of the junior high school as a separate institution with curriculum and instruction designed to match the young adolescent's developmental needs and interests—think peer culture, identity development, rebelliousness, hormones and hygiene, and so on—followed directly from Hall's science.[9]

Another efficiency advocate, Franklin Bobbitt, said that a curriculum designer should be like a "great engineer."[10] In 1918, Bobbitt published *The Curriculum*, outlining a scientific approach to curriculum development. In accordance with "machine theory" and behaviorism, Bobbitt laid out principles of curriculum planning that included specifying the knowledge considered important for students to learn, the specific behavioral objectives that students would meet, and the activities that would enable students to do so. In 1920, Bobbitt elaborated on his theory in *How to Make a Curriculum*, a book that offered 800 curriculum objectives and activities designed to help students meet them.

Bobbitt's colleague W. W. Charters advocated a similar scientific, behaviorist approach in his book *Curriculum Construction*. Mirroring "efficiency experts" in factories, the "job analysis" approach to curriculum planning proposed by Charters began with measurable objectives, analysis of the tasks that would be required to meet those objectives, and activities designed specifically to accomplish those tasks. Together, Bobbitt and Charters laid the groundwork for curriculum that is built around the ideals of science and efficiency.

Perennialism for the Few, Essentialism for the Masses

By 1918, vast numbers of workers' and immigrants' sons and daughters were attending public secondary schools, where they joined a much smaller group of students from more established elite families. While these schools were common, the tradition of separate mass and elite education reestablished itself under one roof. Most progressive educational leaders believed that only the elites had the mental capacity to learn a rigorous perennialist curriculum that looked to science and technology as tools for addressing ever-changing challenges and progress, and thus that only they would occupy the social roles that required such knowledge. Social efficiency advocates, influenced by behaviorism, sought a scientifically designed curriculum that would give most students (nonelite) direct instruction in the academic basics and prepare them with the specific skills they would use as adults.

Thus, children of the elites gained access to an academic curriculum, while children of the masses (including most immigrants) gained access to practical and vocational knowledge and skills, infused with a heavy dose of American patriotism. For that vast majority of students, the 1918 National Education Association's Commission on the Reorganization of Secondary Schools established seven curricular goals: (1) health, (2) command of fundamentals (basic skills), (3) worthy home membership, (4) vocation, (5) citizenship, (6) worthy use of leisure, and (7) ethical character. The commission used the loftiest attributes of democracy—especially freedom and self-determination through effort and merit—to guide schools toward teaching the masses practical competencies and sound moral character.[11]

Child- and Community-Centered Progressivism

The progressive approach of John Dewey, the philosopher and reformer still most closely associated with the term *progressive education*, emerged at this time. Like other progressives, Dewey emphasized the social and pragmatic nature of schooling and learning. However, recognizing that children's development and learning were anything but rational and orderly, he and his followers advocated a child-centered and community-centered curriculum to give students learning experiences that make rigorous intellectual demands in the context of democratic social living.

Child-Centered Schooling

Child-centered reforms emerged as early as 1873 in response to an examination administered by the Quincy, Massachusetts, school board. Historian Lawrence Cremin explains, "The results were disastrous. While the youngsters knew their rules of grammar thoroughly, they could not write an ordinary English letter. While they could read with facility from their textbooks, they were utterly confused by similar material from unfamiliar sources."[12] Shocked, the Quincy board, under the leadership of Superintendent Francis Parker, made a number of changes:

> [The] set curriculum was abandoned, and with it the speller, the reader, the grammar, and the copybook. Children were started on simple words and sentences, rather than the alphabet learned by rote. In place of time-honored texts, magazines, newspapers, and materials devised by the teachers themselves were introduced into the classroom. Arithmetic was approached inductively, through objects rather than rules, while geography began with a series of trips over the local countryside. Drawing was added to encourage manual dexterity and individual expression. The emphasis throughout was on observing, describing, and understanding, and only when these abilities had begun to manifest themselves—among the faculty as well as the students—were more conventional studies introduced.[13]

In short, Parker had introduced a curriculum that "began" with the child's understandings and then sought out appropriate content, materials, and experiences to support academic learning. This differed markedly from conventional approaches that began with inflexible content, materials, and approaches and expected the student to adjust to them. After only a few years, Quincy students achieved excellent scores in reading, writing, and spelling on an exam administered by the Massachusetts State Board of Education.

As head of the Cook County Normal School in Chicago, Parker went on to prepare teachers. A few years later, he stated that his academic goals had a clearly social character. The school, he argued, should be a "model home, a complete community, and an embryonic democracy."[14] In Parker's experimental school, children created stories that became their "texts" for reading, spelling, penmanship, and grammar. Science took the form of nature study, including field trips to Lake Michigan, where the students wrote descriptions and made drawings of what they saw. Back in the classroom, these observations became the basis of laboratory work, where the children also learned mathematics as they constructed the equipment they would use in scientific study. Teachers introduced all subjects by connecting them with activities or experiences that already held meaning for the children.

It was to Parker's experimental school in Chicago that University of Chicago philosopher John Dewey sent his own children, and there that Dewey gathered ideas for the University Laboratory School, which he began in 1896. As at Parker's school, Dewey introduced children to learning through familiar activities of the family. An early account gave this description of Dewey's classroom for 4- and 5-year-olds following a trip to a farm:

> Part of the group played grocery store and sold fruit and sugar for the jelly making of the others. Some were clerks, some delivery boys, others mothers, and some made the grocery wagons. The clerks were given measuring cups with which to measure the sugar and cranberries and paper to wrap the packages to take home. . . . A wholesale house was constructed out of a big box. Elevators would be necessary, a child volunteered, for storehouses have so many floors; and these were made from long narrow corset boxes, a familiar wrapping in every household of the day.[15]

Dewey had extraordinarily high regard for knowledgeable teachers and was certain that they could find a way for each child to get to the heart of the academic disciplines. Although many critics claimed that "child centered" meant neglecting valued knowledge and skills, this was clearly not the case.

As students grew older, teachers applying Dewey's approach guided them through integrated activities filled with increasingly sophisticated opportunities to learn mathematics, science, and

John Dewey

the other disciplines. Six-year-olds constructed a model farm and raised wheat. Seven-, eight-, and nine-year-olds explored the history of Western civilization and the United States through concrete human activities, such as occupations, trade, and the building of cities. Teachers integrated these thematic activities with lessons in the arts, science, music, history and geography, foreign language, and literature. History illuminated human successes and failures, and literature conveyed the hopes of people in various social contexts. The oldest children specialized in a particular discipline, developing in-depth, yearlong projects.

Thus, Dewey's curriculum began with familiar experiences, then moved to more distant and abstract ideas, and finally led children to grapple with broad social themes. Such an approach, Dewey argued, would prepare students to understand society *and* improve it.

Dewey was just as interested in shaping character as those who preceded him—Webster, McGuffey, and Harris, for example. However, Dewey was less interested in preventing or correcting undesirable traits than others had been. Rather, he sought to develop in students a character that would build democratic and interdependent communities. Given Dewey's emphasis on learning through activity, he argued that schools should themselves be miniature democratic societies—places where children *live*, rather than "only a place to learn lessons."[16]

Community-Centered Schooling

Dewey and other early-twentieth-century reformers also argued for cultural pluralism in the curriculum. In 1899, Jane Addams founded Chicago's Hull House, the best known of the big-city settlement houses that helped immigrants adjust to life in the United States. Addams created a community in the Chicago slums that was rich in intellectual and cultural opportunities. Together she and Dewey sought ways to help immigrants adapt to mainstream American culture without losing contact with the cultures they left behind. They argued that while everyone should learn the common culture—English, U.S. history, and the American political system— immigrants should also retain and be proud of their home cultures.

Schooling figured prominently in Jane Addams's reform efforts. She argued that education for immigrants must go beyond the basics of English language instruction and civics, to provide for the social and moral well-being of the poor. That meant attending to their social and aesthetic needs with lectures, discussions, concerts, and art gallery visits; providing vocational training; and giving workers an understanding of the history and significance of the industrial life to which they and their families belonged. In 1908, Addams explained in an address to the National Education Association how schools should address social concerns:

> The schools ought to do more to connect these children with the best things of the past, to make them realize something of the beauty and charm of the language, the history, and the traditions which their parents represent. . . . If the body of teachers in our great cities could take hold of the immigrant colonies, could bring out of them their handicrafts and occupations, their traditions, their folk songs and folk lore, the beautiful stories which every immigrant colony is ready to tell and translate. . . . Give these children a chance to utilize the historic and industrial material they see about them and they will begin to have a sense of ease in America, a first consciousness of being at home. I believe if these people are welcomed upon the basis of the resources which they represent and the contributions which they bring, it may come to pass that these schools which deal with immigrants will find that they have a wealth of cultural and industrial material which will make the schools in other neighborhoods positively envious.[17]

Jane Addams at Hull House

Critical Contributions From Communities of Color

During the first half of the twentieth century, many educators and scholars of color also tried to make the curriculum more community centered and multicultural. These efforts, often contentious, aimed to include the perspectives and achievements of people of color and to reduce bias and misrepresentation in the curriculum. Carter G. Woodson—an African American high school teacher, professor, and historian—had perhaps the greatest influence on this approach to the curriculum. Woodson popularized African American history and promoted its study in African American schools. In 1926, he initiated Negro History Week, which later became Black History Month. Woodson also created the *Negro History Bulletin* to inform teachers about Black history, and he authored textbooks that were used in schools serving Black youth.[18]

Among other public intellectuals, W. E. B. Du Bois challenged the biased accounts of U.S. history featured in most textbooks, as well as African American students' unequal access to quality schools. Around this time, the formation of the National Association for the Advancement of Colored People (NAACP) in 1909 brought together diverse educationalists including its founder, W. E. B. Du Bois, and John Dewey, an involved supporter. Critiques by scholars of color—like Du Bois and Woodson—remained for the time at the margins of mainstream thinking about schools. However, these ideas would emerge openly and with vigor at the mid-century mark, when the rigid constraints of segregation began to weaken.

Social Reconstructionism

In the 1920s, Jane Addams, John Dewey, and other public intellectuals spoke out against social and economic injustices. By the 1930s, progressive reforms had taken an even more political turn. As the Great Depression made injustice highly visible, George Counts, a professor at the

W. E. B. Du Bois and Carter G. Woodson

University of Chicago, and Harold Rugg of Teachers College, Columbia University, with Dewey's support, captured the curriculum reform spotlight with their calls for a "social reconstructionist" curriculum.

In a manifesto called "Dare the Schools Build a New Social Order?" Counts railed against the emphasis on property rights over human rights and against society's emphasis on the individual over the collective. He indicted essentialist and perennialist curricula and the push for scientific efficiency, which he saw as cementing unequal economic and social power. Counts argued for the school curriculum to critique social institutions, including capitalism, that do not further democracy, and that teachers must act as a militant force for change. It is easy to see why social reconstructionists, given their openly transformative aims, met criticism for having a political agenda; of course, they were hardly the only educators for whom schooling was a political matter. Opposition to their goals to change the education status quo was typically powerful, and therefore political, as well.

In sum, the social reconstructionists struck a chord in U.S. social thought, and yet barely penetrated the school curriculum. Their main achievement came with the widespread adoption of Harold Rugg's textbooks. These texts were the first that wove together the disciplines of history, geography, civics, economics, and sociology—all previously taught as separate subjects—as integrated "social studies." Rugg believed that a curriculum centered on real social problems, informed by ideas from across the social sciences, would lead students to more independent thinking and to informed social action. For example, his books described the plight of African slaves and included vivid descriptions of conditions on the slave ships. His unit on economic disparity included photographs of wealthy and poor neighborhoods in the nation's capital.

Rugg's books were very popular during the 1930s, but most educators and the public did not sympathize with the social reconstructionists' anticapitalistic ideology. And with World War II bringing both economic prosperity and a resurgence of American patriotism, Rugg's texts were attacked as un-American by conservative newspapers and organizations such as the American Legion and the Daughters of the Colonial Wars. Blasted in the media, including in an *American Legion Magazine* article titled "Treason in the Textbooks,"[19] the reconstructionist ideas of Rugg and Counts, and even Dewey, stood little chance of mass adoption.

Despite considerable ferment around Dewey's progressivism and social reconstructionism— and despite organizing and activism among scholars and communities of color—the dominant curriculum throughout the first decades of the twentieth century remained a combination of basic academics, organized and taught separately and efficiently according to William Torrey Harris's design, and an unyielding Anglo-American perspective on U.S. history and culture. This dominant curriculum also incorporated the vocational and life skills training that became part of U.S. high schools following the 1918 publication of the "Cardinal Principles of Secondary Education." Appointed by the National Education Association, the authors of those principles argued that separate curriculum "tracks" for elite and mass education should exist side by side in "comprehensive" secondary schools.[20]

Post–World War II Progressivism

The 1940s and 1950s brought little curricular change. Progressives continued to search for ways to connect students' school learning with the rich and relevant learning opportunities that could be found at home and in the community. Ralph Tyler, the nation's leading curriculum scholar, argued that the highest curriculum priority should be to teach about the practical concerns of daily living, for example, the chemistry of detergents, the servicing of an automobile, and the functioning of local utility services. This "life adjustment" curriculum suffered the fate of many progressive reforms. A fundamentally sound idea that was only superficially implemented opened itself to (sometimes justified) ridicule and reaffirmed traditionalists' opposition to reform.

The Intergroup Education Movement

Striving for fairness, dignity, and justice has motivated many organized attempts to improve public education. Though never fully successful, each has left its unique mark. After World War II, the continuing "great migration" of southern Blacks who were escaping severe southern racism, along with returning Black servicemen, met the deep fear and resentment of northern Whites, who perceived threats to their jobs, housing, and segregated lives. The result was racial conflict and even greater segregation than had existed previously. A consortium of religious groups founded the Intercultural, or Intergroup, Education Movement to address these issues.

Sharing many of the ideals espoused by Woodson and Du Bois, the Intergroup Education Movement nonetheless differed in important ways. Education scholar James Banks explains,

> The major aim of the Intergroup Education movement was to reduce prejudice, to develop interracial understandings, and to foster a shared national American culture. . . . Intergroup educators, most of whom were liberal White academics who worked in mainstream American institutions, placed more emphasis on a shared American identity than did Black scholars, who were more concerned about creating accurate images of African Americans, empowering African Americans, and building African American institutions.[21]

Ultimately, the Intergroup Education Movement faded in the 1950s alongside the diminishing heat of postwar racial tension. The movement also lost momentum because its mostly White membership tended to advocate a less radical, more pluralistic, and tolerance-oriented stance toward diversity than seemed relevant to the urgent problems facing communities of color.

Unsuccessful attempts to change the curriculum at this time in U.S. history meshed with the country's resistance toward progressive change, in general. The Cold War of the 1950s, marked by the anticommunist sentiment of the McCarthy period and the oppressions of Stalinist Russia, made the national climate inhospitable to progressive schooling. It was a time when the progressives' vocabulary—including "reform," "social justice," "democratic," and "progressive"—could be (and was) labeled un-American. Finally, complacency brought on by post–World War II prosperity left little room for mainstream thinking about the need for schools to improve. But all that changed in the late 1950s when the Soviet Union shocked the world and U.S. educators by sending a small ball of steel into space.

The Post-Sputnik Curriculum

The launching of the space satellite Sputnik in 1957 foreclosed further debate between the progressive and traditional camps, at least temporarily. That Russia—the source of Cold War anxieties and the ever-present communist threat—beat the United States into space could only mean that our schools had failed. Many citizens believed that the nation had fallen from educational and scientific preeminence. Clearly, education was no longer a need only for individual prosperity and an informed citizenry; as discussed in Chapter 2, education, especially in political rhetoric, had become a matter of national security. High school graduation and college entrance standards were raised, and mathematicians and scientists around the country developed rigorous new courses of study for elementary and secondary schools.

Drawing from the emerging cognitive learning theories of Jerome Bruner and the developmental theories of Jean Piaget, "new" math, science, and social studies programs asked students to engage with knowledge through increasingly sophisticated "spiral" curricula, where ideas were introduced for exposure and then circled back on later for proficiency and eventually

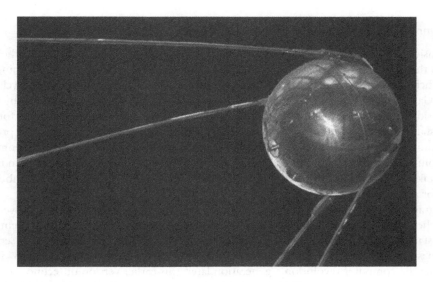

Sputnik: A 184-Pound Satellite Sent Into Orbit by the Russians in 1957

mastery. In short, Bruner contended that children at every stage of cognitive development could learn some form of the most important ideas in the academic disciplines *if* the curriculum mirrored the structure and the inquiry processes of the discipline.[22]

Implementation of these new, more academic curricula was spotty, however, and interest in them was short lived. The Bruner-inspired reforms of the 1960s and 1970s chafed against the prevailing common sense. This turn toward rigorous and demanding intellectual work for U.S. youth was quickly ridiculed with disdain like that previously heaped on the life adjustment curriculum. Curriculum materials that encouraged attention to the social nature of in-depth learning (as embodied in "new math" and discovery-oriented social studies) attracted a firestorm of criticism—chiefly that the programs were flaky and neglected important facts and skills.

Even less inspiring of confidence (among traditionalists especially) were pockets of passionate interest in so-called open classrooms, in which students' interests drove the curriculum. A. S. Neill's 1960 book, *Summerhill*, had captured the imaginations of many who were critical of traditional schools; the book described a "free school" in England where young people constructed their own learning experiences in a democratic community.[23] In some quarters, the briefly and barely implemented curriculum of "new" math, science, and social studies, together with what was seen as the "do your own thing" approach to open schooling, received the blame for many of the country's educational "ills," including the civil rights and anti–Vietnam War student activism that outraged much of the nation.

Back to Basics

Given these sentiments, the 1970s unsurprisingly ushered in a back-to-basics movement—a return to a strong essentialist philosophy and behaviorist approach to curriculum. Once again, a skills-based curriculum, largely accomplished through memorization and enforced through tests, became the order of the day. With this return to tradition, critics hoped to restore stability and predictability to schools (and society), and to increase the achievement of the most disadvantaged children. This back-to-basics emphasis remains powerful still, as we describe later in this chapter and in Chapters 4 and 5.

"Programmed" Learning

This "basic" and skills-oriented approach to instruction quickly found allies among those who believed that scientific methods and technology could make skills instruction and learning vastly more efficient. Based on the work of behaviorist B. F. Skinner and educational psychologist Robert Gagne, reading "labs" sprang up in schools throughout the country. Spurred by reports that President Kennedy endorsed a popular, widely advertised speed-reading method for White House staff, capable readers along with nonreaders were soon exposed to expensive programs that promised to increase reading speed a hundredfold or more. The labs and classrooms filled with "controlled readers"—machines that would flash word groups on a screen to train readers' eyes to take in more words, more quickly. Tachistoscopes would blink words or numbers on a screen for a similar effect.

"Programmed" and individualized reading and math kits emphasized monitoring over teaching; teachers spent much of their class time administering diagnostic tests to place students at the "right" starting point in the kit, handing out and scoring answer sheets in the proper sequence, giving mastery tests, and keeping extensive records of students' progress in relation to kit goals. Much like the computer revolution a generation later, this earlier version of technology reform produced limited benefits for student learning.

Compensatory Curricula

As usual, the benefits of a back-to-basics curriculum were proclaimed most loudly for students of color, students with learning disabilities, students who were poor, and students who otherwise did not fit in with conventional schooling. By the 1970s, the back-to-basics curriculum took on new importance as educators received new federal funding from Lyndon Johnson's War on Poverty and the corresponding Elementary and Secondary Education Act, which sought to remedy low achievement among the nation's poorest children.

Cultural deficit ideology, discussed in Chapter 2, was widely embraced by educators during this time. Thus, the preferred approach for young children was to offer preschool programming that would compensate for the alleged cultural deprivation students suffered at home and would help their parents acquire middle-class parenting skills. For older children, school personnel turned to rote instruction emphasizing drill-and-practice in orderly, teacher-directed classrooms, supplemented by pull-out programs for remedial instruction.

These back-to-basics approaches of the 1970s brought about new problems for schools and those seeking to reform them. Indeed, the chosen "cure" for an undereducated nation was destined to limit the achievement of the nation's fastest-growing demographic sectors: children of color, poor children, and children whose first language was not English. Clearly, new thinking was needed. And, in fact, out of this context a group of educators and education scholars forged a new progressivism, emphasizing multicultural and socially just principles and values.

Multicultural Education

The 1970s were marked by increased ethnic diversity, increased economic and political power for women, efforts to racially integrate public schooling, and reemerging debates about constitutional issues such as the meanings of privacy, separation of church and state, civil rights, and so forth. New thinking on these matters brought new laws expanding educational and economic opportunities for historically underserved groups. Title IX of the 1964 Civil Rights Act made no mention of equal treatment for women; however, Congress corrected that omission in 1972 by amending Title IX to forbid discrimination against students based on sex.[24] The Individuals With Disabilities Education Act of 1975 required a "free and appropriate public education" for students with special needs.[25] Societal changes also encouraged activists to seek curriculum changes, including attempts to make the curriculum more multicultural.

Multiculturalism emerged slowly but steadily in the mainstream education discourse; there was not, as education scholar Carl Grant reminds us, a single moment that marked its beginning.

> The links of the chain . . . are scattered across the United States (and throughout the world), as were those who sought [a] democratic society. . . . For instance, it can be argued that multicultural education was born when enslaved African American people began to educate themselves about their history in Africa and the United States and how their role and participation in these histories, as well as their racial identity dictated their treatment in U.S. society. Multicultural education also began when members of Native American tribes began to educate themselves on how to resist, survive, and get along with White European colonizers and other cultural groups, including other Native American tribes. It also began when Asian Americans, particularly Chinese, communicated with their families in their homelands about life in the United States, and learned to resist, survive, and get along with White Americans, and other people of color. Similarly, multicultural education began for Mexicans in the Southwest . . . when they engaged in various interactions (e.g., work, open border) with Native Americans, African Americans, Asian Americans, and White Americans.[26]

Grant writes about traditions of struggle that were established long before the 1970s. In the 1950s, W. E. B. Du Bois called for groups that were denied full representation in politics, education, and culture to fight, examine their history, and insist upon their rights.

> We should fight to the last ditch to keep open the right to learn, the right to have examined in our schools not only what we believe; not only what our leaders say, but what the leaders of other groups and nations, and the leaders of other centuries have said. We must insist upon this to give our children the fairness of a start which will equip them with such an array of facts and such an attitude toward truth that they can have a real chance to judge what the world is and what its greater minds have thought it might be.[27]

Emerging out of this long history of struggle, multicultural education as we know it today took popular hold in the 1970s, during a time of widespread and growing concern about racism and civil rights. In the 1960s, many mainstream and progressive reformers still were using deficit theories to explain the plight of underserved groups. Trying to equalize opportunity, they developed "compensatory" programs and curricula meant to offset "cultural deprivation" by providing the dispositions, experiences, and family environments that would make it possible to achieve in and beyond school. Well-intentioned social and school programs missed the mark when they ignored or tried to eliminate cultural differences they did not value or understand.

However, some successes of the 1960s and 1970s were not tainted by deficit views. To the contrary, ethnic studies programs in higher education were making a powerful case about how Eurocentric bias overshadowed (or ignored) the knowledges, historical contributions, and contemporary capacities of individuals from Asian American, Black, Latinx, and Native American communities. Progressive educators began to infuse the elementary and secondary school curriculum, and the curriculum of teacher education, accordingly. Primary goals included supporting *all* students to learn more about the nation's diversity and to understand that cultural difference does not equate to cultural deprivation. Reformers also wanted students in desegregated and racially isolated White schools to develop positive attitudes toward people of other races and cultures, as well as the skills to engage in productive intergroup relations. Educators continue to bring multicultural sensibilities to curricula, as when they strive to expose students to the multiple perspectives diverse groups hold on a single topic or issue.[28]

Traditional Approaches to Multicultural Curriculum

It is important to note that in most traditional classrooms, what has typically passed for a pluralistic or multicultural curriculum is little more than a "heroes-and-holidays" approach to teaching about diversity.[29] This typically involves a sprinkling of superficial attention to the contributions of immigrants and other minoritized communities in a sanitized, Anglocentric way, as well as an uncritical recounting of U.S. history and culture. For example, schools may celebrate (or simply announce) "ethnic" holidays like Cinco de Mayo and Ramadan. They may use Black History Month to recognize "events" such as Harriet Tubman's nineteenth-century smuggling of slaves to freedom on the Underground Railroad or Martin Luther King Jr.'s "I Have a Dream" speech.

Teachers may also focus on the accomplishments of individual people of color while ignoring the importance of whole communities of people who have experienced and fought against discrimination. For example, educator Herbert Kohl challenges the usual characterization of Rosa Parks as a lone hero who sat in the front of the bus because she was "tired" and who single-handedly spurred the "elimination" of discrimination and segregation in the United States. A more accurate portrayal would address Parks's role in a broad and well-organized social movement and her decision to stay seated as a planned act of civil disobedience; it would also require a deeper analysis of the realities of racism in the United States, then and now.[30]

The tendency for teachers to engage students in a heroes-and-holidays approach rather than a *critical* approach to multicultural education reflects broader debates among policymakers, curriculum developers, educators, and community members about what multicultural education is and ought to entail. For example, while King, Tubman, and Parks often appear as "appropriate" historical representatives of African Americans in mainstream (and frequently sanitized) accounts of U.S. history, W. E. B. Du Bois and Malcolm X usually do not. Not only is their social criticism less palatable to mainstream tastes, far fewer people (including many teachers) hold deep knowledge of their contributions. Without such knowledge, educators are limited in their capacity to "do right by" the contributions of people of color or to support students of color to learn about and draw on those contributions, as scholar Sonia Nieto notes, on "their own terms."[31] Fortunately, there is no expiration date on learning; educators can and should always be seeking to build those knowledge bases that their own schooling and life experiences left hidden. Even so, as the discussion about standards-based reform later in the chapter illustrates, tensions about what content teachers should cover in U.S. classrooms, particularly concerning diversity, are far from resolved.

Critical Multiculturalism

The voices of Woodson and Du Bois, among others, echo through today's more *critical* approaches to multicultural (and often bilingual) education. Like the traditional multicultural curriculum, a *critical* multicultural curriculum helps students know and value the nation's diversity. Likewise, it engages students in learning about and maintaining their own heritages and languages. However, in contrast, a critical multicultural curriculum explicitly challenges the disproportionate social and economic power that derives from adherence to Eurocentric and Anglo-American perspectives, traditions, and cultural practices.

Critical multicultural educators see the hallmarks of the traditional curriculum—the absolute certainties and universal truths of Western culture—as problematic guidelines for deciding what and how students should learn. Furthermore, they argue that students themselves must actively identify, analyze, and confront the cultural norms that perpetuate racism, classism, sexism, and other -isms, and they must do so by drawing heavily on their own knowledge and experience, as well as the knowledge and experience of minoritized communities.[32]

The following quote from teacher Kimberly Min shows how such priorities can influence curriculum in ways that go beyond the superficiality of heroes and holidays.

> In honor of the anniversary of the landmark *Brown* decision, my students examined oral histories to better understand the schooling experiences of people then and their own experiences now. My students interviewed adults who were bused or who attended schools that were in the midst of desegregation. This examination culminated in a PowerPoint presentation and play they created about a little black girl who was bused to a desegregated school in the 1960s.
>
> The guiding questions for these investigations were: What was schooling like then? How is schooling now? Has anything changed? With literature circles developed around books such as *The Story of Ruby Bridges* and *Freedom School, Yes!*, students connected their knowledge of civil rights activists, what schools were like in the past, and their own experiences now.
>
> —Kimberly Min
> Third-grade teacher

Kimberly's lesson shows that individual teachers can make powerful and critical contributions to multicultural education.

Schools Organized for Critical Multiculturalism

Even more ambitious efforts are possible when schools and districts support reforms that extend beyond individual classrooms. For example, in school-wide two-way bilingual programs, native English-speaking children, those children with another primary language—say, Spanish or Korean—and children who may be simultaneous bilinguals, meaning they have been learning English and another language for all or most of their lives, become fully literate in both languages. These programs don't consider the "other" language a problem or regard bilingual education as a way of remediating the language "deficits" of those learning English as their second language. Rather, such programs treat the cultural and linguistic practices of *all* students as valuable—even essential—for everyone's learning.

This is not a simple matter of pluralism—where student differences are "honored" and children are admonished if they show disrespect. Rather, this requires, in daily practice, exposing biases and their sources and elevating the knowledge, status, and common humanity of all learners. In keeping with these commitments, some schools place the knowledge and experiences of their own communities of color at the center of the curriculum. Several big cities (e.g., Detroit, Chicago, Milwaukee, Washington, DC, and Baltimore), for example, have developed Afrocentric elementary schools; these schools offer a curriculum that builds from students' membership in proud and powerful cultural communities. The principal and teachers at Chicago's Woodlawn Community School, for example, wear African dress; the hallways display African murals, posters, and flags; and the curriculum gives prominence to African and African American history, culture, and current events. Elsewhere, even without an official mandate for an ethnic emphasis, individual schools and teachers have shifted the school curriculum to construct greater relevance and resonance between what students are expected to learn *at* school and what students bring *to* school based on their own cultural backgrounds and everyday practices. Not surprisingly, such shifts often take place under the stewardship of accomplished teachers of color.

While few secondary schools have adopted school-wide ethnic studies programs, many in racially mixed as well as racially isolated communities offer courses to counterbalance the Anglocentric mainstream curriculum. Sometimes the White community mounts a severe reaction against that counterbalance. Thus, in the midst of evidence that ethnic studies approaches improve school success for students of color, hostile voters and state policymakers sometimes seek to eliminate such programs. As discussed in Chapter 2, for example, the Arizona legislature described one district's celebrated Chicano Studies program as "treasonous" and reflecting "ethnic chauvinism" and ultimately banned the program,[33] despite its demonstrated positive outcomes.[34] In August 2017, a federal judge overturned this ban, demonstrating that the ban violated students' constitutional rights and was motivated by racial discrimination.

Explicit Attention to the "Codes of Power"

Common criticisms of traditional multicultural education are that it isn't academically rigorous and that it focuses on raising students' self-esteem at the expense of academic learning. It's correct that a multicultural approach to schooling can be superficial and lack serious content in the hands of educators who themselves are not critical thinkers. A critical approach to schooling asks students to examine race, ethnicity, gender, and so forth, while applying a rigorous critique to literature and the arts, the social sciences, and even science, sports, and more. This approach gives students intellectual tools to learn (and often to *correct*) the standard curriculum. Teachers who practice critical multicultural education do not require students from marginalized groups to "leave who they are at the door." Instead, they help students understand the relationship between their homes, families, languages, neighborhoods, and so forth, and the knowledge and credentials that public schools offer as gateways to jobs, higher education, and civic participation.

Gloria Ladson-Billings's *The Dreamkeepers* offers examples of teachers such as Patricia Hilliard, who attends to the power of Standard English *and* respects the dialect (African American Vernacular English, or AAVE) her students speak outside of school:

> I get so sick and tired of people trying to tell me that my children don't need to use any language other than the one they come to school with. Then those same people turn right around and judge the children negatively because of the way they express themselves. My job is to make sure that they can use both languages, that they understand that their language is valid but the demands placed upon them by others mean that they will constantly have to prove their worth. We spend a lot of time talking about language, what it means, how you use it, and how it can be used against you.[35]

Patricia's teaching reflects sociological theory and research on the relationship between the content of schooling and the dynamics of social class and racial stratification. This research highlights the role of *cultural capital*—or the knowledge, dispositions, and values associated with elevated social class. In the United States, the cultural capital that is most prized for high-status professions, for example, is that of the White middle and upper class. Having the "right" cultural capital—for example, speaking the "King's English" or knowing how to play golf or pick a good red wine—matters quite a bit in terms of the opportunities one receives and what one is able to make of them. Just as in the market, where dollars may be exchanged for goods or services, cultural capital can "buy" acceptance or favored treatment in schools and social interactions generally. Like Patricia, first-year teacher Kay Goodloe is determined not to perpetuate this pattern.

> As an African American female, and a product of the public school system, I am bi-dialectical. But do not jump to conclusions and assume that Black English was my primary home language. It was not. I learned Ebonics on the playground and on the streets of Los Angeles. Our working/middle-class community expected children to use mainstream English. I use the word *community* because all of the mothers shared the duty of policing our language. I have clear recollections of being reprimanded by a neighbor for using "slang" and being questioned as to where I had learned such language. As children, we became adept at code-switching. We used mainstream English at home and in the presence of our parents and other authority figures, but we used Ebonics freely among our peers and at school. To be able to talk "jive" became a sign of group membership and demonstrated an individual's level of "coolness." It was also a form of resistance. We could communicate with our peers, ridiculing Whites and other authority figures with the realization that they were absolutely clueless.
>
> I vowed never to deliberately silence my students' voices. This vow is not easy to keep; it is something I struggle with daily. I am committed to creating a safe environment within my classroom, where my students feel comfortable expressing themselves regardless of the language that they bring with them, be it Ebonics, Spanglish, or other English dialects. But, to facilitate my students' acquisition of mainstream English, all of their assignments must be written in "standard" English. The majority of the time, I communicate with my students using Standard English, but I feel that it is also necessary to model code-switching in the classroom.
>
> To achieve success in mainstream American society, bicultural students need to acquire "mainstream" English. But in exposing bicultural students to Standard English, we also need to expose the relationships of power inherent in these forms of discourse. When

Standard English is discussed as "proper," society fails to acknowledge the cultural hegemony implicit in this definition. An effective teacher cultivates a classroom in which all student voices are valued.

—Kay Goodloe
First-year teacher, history, grade 11

As Patricia and Kay demonstrate, a good deal of cultural capital is wrapped up in language. Standard English and formal diction function as quick indicators of social class, parental influence, aspirations, school behavior, and academic potential. It can also be as simple and yet subtle as knowing and being willing to say "please" and "yes, ma'am" (and knowing when it is not worth the bother).

The pivotal nature of cultural capital in gaining wealth and power has led some reformers to reassert the value of teaching minoritized youth the knowledge and skills of White middle- and upper-class culture. These reformers are not reverting to the traditionalist agenda in the usual sense, however. In fact, most of them support a critical multicultural curriculum. At the same time, they are suspicious of curriculum that cultivates students' own language and culture *to the exclusion* of mainstream language and culture. They also reject the usual approaches to teaching mainstream language and culture as *assimilationist*—designed to obliterate other cultures and languages, and preserve dominant group privileges.

Scholar Lisa Delpit, for example, frames much of (noncritical) multiculturalism as well-intentioned liberalism run amok. In her book *Other People's Children*, she famously asks, "Will Black teachers and parents continue to be silenced by the very forces that claim to 'give voice' to our children?"[36] Delpit and teachers like Kay Goodloe believe that all children should have access to the knowledge and skills that they need to participate fully in society—as long as they understand that they are learning codes of power and not simply the "right" or "best" cultural knowledge and linguistic practice.

Social Critique and Transformative Social Action

Critical multicultural education has been strongly influenced by *critical pedagogy*, an educational approach most often linked to Brazilian educator Paulo Freire. Freire is perhaps best known for his work with disenfranchised farmworkers—specifically, his anchoring of farmworkers' literacy development in the social, political, and economic circumstances of their lives, focusing most concertedly on the oppression that kept them poor and made wealthy landowners even wealthier. In that context, Freire conceptualized literacy broadly, as a way for learners to understand the social order and their place in it—what he referred to as *conscientization*—as well as a tool to challenge social hierarchies. The combination of "reflection and action upon the world in order to transform it" is what Freire called *praxis*.[37]

Praxis, in its simplest expression, involves thinking and doing, theory and practice, understanding problems and working to solve them. Praxis is a powerful concept and tool for teaching and learning because it treats the content of the curriculum and life beyond school as one and the same. Through critical analysis, students grapple with oppression in local and world events, both past and present, which helps them understand the meaning of and threats to democratic life. From this perspective, mainstream multiculturalism can appear superficial if it treats oppressive social structures, such as institutionalized racism, as challenges that can be overcome by greater tolerance and respectful appreciation of cultural differences. Such treatment would represent the very kind of "miseducation" that Carter G. Woodson, among others, so critiqued.

For those who advocate a critical multicultural curriculum that teaches students about systematic discrimination and oppression, the goal is not merely to expose injustice or to generate guilt

Teachers John Paul Arellano, Catherine Bradshaw, and Scott Lyons Under an Image of Paulo Freire

among White and affluent citizens. Rather, it is to help students accomplish traditional public school goals (coursework, cultural and technical knowledge, credentials for work and college), all in the service of the broader goal of transforming oppressive structures.

Many people find the language of critical pedagogy inaccessible and at times off-putting. To some, "oppression" and "domination," for example, seem like more suitable descriptors for enemies abroad than for our own country or schools. Scholar Sonia Nieto comments on the unique obstacles to gaining a clear view of U.S. society and history:

> Textbooks in all subject areas exclude information about unpopular perspectives, or the perspectives of disempowered groups in our society. For instance, there are few U.S. history texts that assume the perspective of working-class people, although it is certainly true that they were and are the backbone of our country. Likewise, the immigrant experience is generally treated as a romantic and successful odyssey rather than the traumatic, wrenching, and often less-than-idyllic situation it was and continues to be for so many. . . . And finally, we can be sure that if the perspectives of women were taken seriously, the school curriculum would be dramatically altered. Unless all students develop the skill to see reality from multiple perspectives, not only the perspective of dominant groups, they will continue to think of it as linear and fixed and to think of themselves as passive in making any changes.[38]

Nieto's analysis has implications for the most fundamental aspects of school and classroom life. For the teachers, it means scrutinizing school procedures, relationships, course content, and materials and asking questions.[39] These might include the following: Who benefits from this content being taught this way? Who benefits from this version of the story? Whose prior knowledge and cultural experiences are best matched to the most important principles of the lesson, and whose are excluded?

Such questions move beyond the realm of abstract ideas and help students associate current social arrangements and distributions of power with the self-interests of people and groups that benefit from those arrangements. Students learn that history and current events don't "just happen"; rather, they follow patterns of interests and power and reflect social constructions that preserve those patterns, or what we call the "status quo." Such questions are also intensely engaging to students from all cultural backgrounds, and make their classroom contributions especially valuable because they often have seen or experienced social arrangements, beliefs, and values that stretch beyond the status quo.

First-year fourth-grade teacher Lucy Patrick used an experiential lesson on the gold rush to draw students into taking the perspectives of others.

> We also dealt with power and justice. After the excitement of panning for gold in the school yard, I asked the students, "How do you think the kindergarten children felt when you took over their sandbox, and what happened when they wanted to play, too?" We discussed our greediness and how we can all get caught up with "gold fever," but we had taken over an area that really did not belong to us. When the kindergartners saw us, they were intimidated, and one fourth grader snatched a gold piece from a kindergartner. I asked my students to connect this oppression to our readings about the people from the east taking over parts of California inhabited by the Spaniards, Mexicans, and Indians. My students made some powerful statements:
>
>> "We took over the kindergarten yard like the forty-niners did from the Indians. In a way, we were greedy, greedy for gold. . . . We were greedy, we didn't care, but we didn't realize whose 'home' we were actually destroying."
>> "Now I know how the Indians and Spaniards felt when pioneers took over their land."
>> "Today we went mining for gold in the kindergartners' sandbox. It was just like what the forty-niners did to the Spaniards and Indians. I don't think it was fair!"
>> Students considered the issue in depth, exchanged views and opinions, and debated the implications. Through role playing and class discussions, students were able to generalize principles, such as fairness and justice, and apply them to present situations.
>
> —Lucy Patrick
> First-year teacher, grade 4

Lessons like Lucy's draw on the theories and thinking of scholars like Paulo Freire and Sonia Nieto, as well as on a postmodern view of knowledge as socially and politically constructed, rather than fixed or objective.

Given critical pedagogy's emphasis on analysis and action, many critical educators incorporate community projects or support students to participate in local political processes so they can develop skills and ideas to contribute to social change by participating, not just learning about what *others* do, but doing *themselves*. For example, first-year teacher Armi Flores describes how she helped her students act on their growing knowledge of racism.

> In the past year, we have had many bouts with racism in our classroom. Light-skinned students have ganged up on darker-skinned students. And those who are more "American" by virtue of the amount of time they have been in the United States have a higher social status within our classroom. . . . When I informed them that the entire class was designated "Latino or Hispanic," the majority of the light-skinned students were outraged. They didn't want to be associated with "Latinos": They believed that they were "White." In an attempt to create some sort

of wall of protection around themselves from the dark-skinned students, one student called out, "Well, what about Douglas? He's not Latino, he's Black." When I informed the class that Douglas, although he was dark skinned, was also Latino, the class fell silent. . . .

This discussion launched us into discussions about definitions of race and ethnicity, and about discrimination. . . . They were making connections from history, from the social studies text, from their personal experiences, from the media, and then wrestling with the issues orally and in writing. Marcos wrote a letter to the president voicing his concern about the current issue of the burning of Black churches. . . . They all wrote letters to influential people who they thought could ameliorate the problems of discrimination. Students wrote to the president, the Marines, the police, a judge, God, or their parents. One student suggested that the answer was within themselves—that they had to take responsibility for discrimination and act against it. They weren't writing hypothetically.

—Armi Flores
First-year teacher, grade 4

James Banks is among those scholars who have been working in multicultural education as it has developed from a focus on tolerance for diversity toward an emphasis on critical ethnic studies and now into a full-blown field of study. Focal Point 3.1 offers one of Banks's more recent multidimensional representations, which makes clear that multicultural education today requires far more than simply adding cultural contributions to the traditional curriculum.

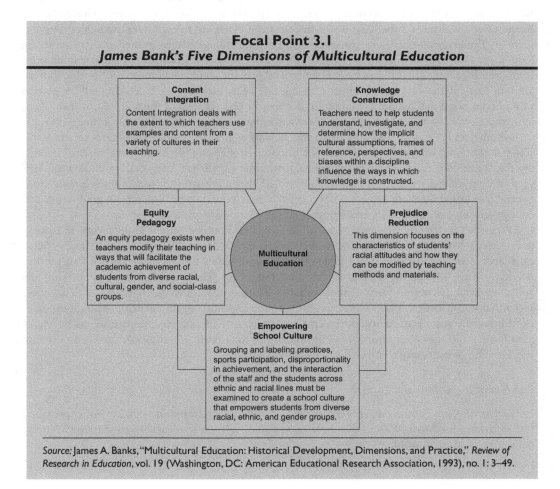

Focal Point 3.1
James Bank's Five Dimensions of Multicultural Education

Content Integration
Content Integration deals with the extent to which teachers use examples and content from a variety of cultures in their teaching.

Knowledge Construction
Teachers need to help students understand, investigate, and determine how the implicit cultural assumptions, frames of reference, perspectives, and biases within a discipline influence the ways in which knowledge is constructed.

Equity Pedagogy
An equity pedagogy exists when teachers modify their teaching in ways that will facilitate the academic achievement of students from diverse racial, cultural, gender, and social-class groups.

Multicultural Education

Prejudice Reduction
This dimension focuses on the characteristics of students' racial attitudes and how they can be modified by teaching methods and materials.

Empowering School Culture
Grouping and labeling practices, sports participation, disproportionality in achievement, and the interaction of the staff and the students across ethnic and racial lines must be examined to create a school culture that empowers students from diverse racial, ethnic, and gender groups.

Source: James A. Banks, "Multicultural Education: Historical Development, Dimensions, and Practice," *Review of Research in Education*, vol. 19 (Washington, DC: American Educational Research Association, 1993), no. 1: 3–49.

Standards and Accountability

As teachers like Lucy Patrick and Armi Flores work to bring the ideas of critical multiculturalism to life in their classrooms, they do so in a public education context shaped by nearly four decades of standards-based reform. Since the early 1980s, political conservatives have championed a return to an essentialist curriculum focused on a set of indisputable, unchanging ideas, values, facts, and works found in past generations of history, literature, and even science and mathematics instruction.

Although many of those arguing for such a curriculum claim to value higher-order thinking and interpretation—a perennialist theme—most conservatives today believe that public schools should stick to the basics and avoid a curriculum that questions dominant cultural values or that questions rules governing correct procedures and right answers. Many are vehemently opposed to any suggestion that knowledge is dynamic, socially constructed, necessarily subjective, and resistant to a set of objective "truths." These arguments can limit the experiences, exploration, and voices of individuals, particularly those from nondominant groups.

Mounted under such themes as "excellence," "cultural literacy," and "standards," resistance to multiculturalism—and associated social and cultural theories of learning—has been quite successful over the past thirty years.

Defining "Excellence"

Ronald Reagan's 1980 election brought a new and hostile assault on schools in the United States. Reagan was eager to end the federal role in education by trying to eliminate the federal Department of Education, which was consistent with a political agenda to minimize or remove the federal government's involvement in people's lives. The administration consistently attempted to discredit federal efforts to promote equality and provide additional funding for poor children, arguing that such efforts had brought a "rising tide of mediocrity" to U.S. schools.[40] A *Nation at Risk* (discussed in Chapter 2) pointed to declines in SAT scores and the nation's poor showing in international test score comparisons as evidence that schools required tough-minded reforms.

The curriculum was the first line of attack. *A Nation at Risk* called on the states to stress traditional academic subjects. All high school students should complete the "new basics," including four years of English; three years each of mathematics, science, and social studies; and a half year of computer science. The report also argued that elementary teachers must spend more instructional time on these subjects. States quickly enacted stringent high school graduation and college entrance requirements and lengthened the school day and year.

In the rush to restore excellence—as well as economic competitiveness and national security—few noticed that the report's authors overlooked data that could have altered their conclusions and recommendations. The shame of the United States' low ranking was not that schools needed to be told what to teach, but that they taught an "elite" curriculum to a few students and a "mass" curriculum to many more students. Thus, it was not so much a matter of education *policy* that was at fault as it was education (and political) *philosophy* that distributed high expectations unevenly among students. In the end, *A Nation at Risk* may have kept students in school a bit longer and raised requirements, but it did little to address U.S. schools' failure to offer all students the opportunity to receive a high-level education.

Preserving the Dominant Culture

A Nation at Risk, combined with the spread of multiculturalism and backlash to it, provided fertile ground for Allan Bloom's perennialist and E. D. Hirsch's essentialist explanations for the nation's educational problems.

In the late 1980s, Bloom, author of the influential book *The Closing of the American Mind*, resurrected the "culture wars," an expression that describes the nineteenth-century idea that maintaining national unity required immigrants to abandon their native language and culture and assume an "American" ethos. The expression also applies to just about any significant value divisions among the population—unity versus diversity, rural versus urban, traditional gender roles versus gender equity, conservative versus progressive, and so on. Writing that "culture means a war against chaos *and* a war against other cultures,"[41] Bloom declared war on mid- and late-twentieth-century reforms that brought multicultural sensibilities to education, particularly higher education.

Bloom argued for an undergraduate college curriculum focused on the "Western canon," a binding and unchanging set of core principles and works most highly valuing Western literary classics, capitalism, American democratic governance, the nuclear family, and so on. Without such a curriculum, Bloom argued, students in the United States would continue their decades-long lapse into cultural relativism, thus further undermining the nation's moral grounding. From a conservative perspective, *cultural relativism*—viewing another culture from the point of view of that culture itself—is deemed a downfall, as if to understand another's perspective necessarily requires abandoning what you or your own country hold dear. If Bloom's prescriptions for what college undergraduates should learn were translated into a curriculum for late-elementary and secondary schools, the result would look quite a lot like E. D. Hirsch's *Cultural Literacy* lists.

In his 1988 and 1996 best-selling books, Hirsch argued that progressive reformers' emphasis during the 1960s and 1970s on projects, "discovery learning," and other "anti-subject matter" methods had brought curricular anarchy and low achievement to U.S. schools. Teachers working from multicultural and social justice perspectives were the primary targets of Hirsch's outrage.[42]

To restore uniformity and predictability to the curriculum, Hirsch outlined the "core knowledge" that he believed all American students should learn. In a series of grade-by-grade books, beginning with *What Your First Grader Needs to Know: Fundamentals of a Good First Grade Education*, he specified the essential names, phrases, dates, and concepts that children should learn in each grade. In behaviorist fashion, topics were carefully sequenced so that students might master supposedly simpler content before being exposed to more complex concepts. And rather than having students critically analyze or discover this knowledge through a problem-based approach, Hirsch argued that teachers should simply present the information they expect children to practice and memorize.

Hirsch's "core knowledge" curriculum included some contributions "from" African Americans and Native Americans (really, they were contributions as determined by Hirsch). However, it did not view multiple perspectives on knowledge as legitimate or permit debate about the dominant perspective. Rather, the curriculum was designed to enable others to adopt the traditional, largely Anglo-American culture as their own, both to enforce cultural unity and to enable the kind of communicative exchanges that fortify it (and in which people can count on their "fellow" Americans having certain kinds of knowledge in common). As designed, it would ideally lead all children to accept—without deliberation or debate—that the land Columbus came to was a new world, that manifest destiny was progressive national expansion, and that civil rights law (though not the civil rights movement that brought about such laws) solved racial problems in the United States.

From Hirsch's perspective, there are two forms of multiculturalism: (1) the ethical, progressive, cosmopolitan, and unifying form that he advocated and (2) a regressive and ethnocentric form that "tends to set group against group" and "hinders the educational excellence and fairness it was conceived to enhance."[43] Hirsch's view of multiculturalism—as embodied in his core knowledge curriculum—considers diversity of ethnicity, religion, language, and so on as an accident of history that should have little to do with how one defines one's identity and culture. Consequently, according to Hirsch, the desirable form of multiculturalism encourages empathy for other cultures and respect for one's own, but stresses "competence in the current system of language and allusion that is dominant in the nation's economic and intellectual discourse."[44]

The regressive, undesirable form of multiculturalism, Hirsch claimed, cultivated ethnic loyalty over national identity. It allowed children to learn a lot about their cultural past, instead of learning to read, write, solve mathematical problems effectively, and understand natural science. He argued that this regressive multiculturalism—of which he considered bilingual education a prime example—might raise children's self-esteem but would ultimately victimize them by impeding their participation in the mainstream culture.

Hirsch's ideas proved enormously popular and were widely promoted by the Reagan and Bush administrations of the 1980s and early 1990s. While Hirsch must be credited for his sincere insistence that all children be given access to "high-status" knowledge, his popularity among political conservatives came mostly from the comfortable familiarity of his lists (both what they included and excluded) and the teacher-centeredness those lists codified in the classroom.

Diane Ravitch, an educational historian and assistant Secretary of Education under the first Bush administration, was also a major player in the culture wars during this time and likewise had a strong influence on public discourse regarding what students ought to learn. Like Hirsch, Ravitch advocated a curriculum that included multicultural contributions and advanced a pluralistic or "melting pot" view of the United States. In her influential contributions to history and social studies standards, Ravitch argued against an approach to multicultural education that threatened national unity, and for an approach that highlighted Americans' "common set of political and moral values."[45]

Developing Standards for Curriculum, Teaching, and Learning

In 1989, President George H. W. Bush and the fifty state governors held an educational summit to set goals for the year 2000 that would spur the nation to improve students' academic performance. Among the goals was to make U.S. students first in the world in mathematics and science achievement. As mentioned in Chapter 2, the Clinton administration's passage of the Goals 2000 Act in 1994 further crystallized these efforts. Although the year 2000 came and went without those goals being met, Goals 2000 had an enormous impact on the debates around what students should know and be able to do. Perhaps most important, the summit and subsequent act spawned the standards movement that has engaged policymakers, businesspeople, and educators in defining what students should learn in each subject area.

The idea of standards, it turns out, appealed to nearly everyone—at least at first. Traditionalists like Hirsch and Ravitch believed that standards would restore clarity and correctness to the school curriculum. Many progressives—especially those who had fought hard for civil rights—believed that setting high standards for all children and holding schools accountable for reaching them might be the best tool for gaining equitable schooling for minoritized students.

Throughout the 1990s, teachers and subject matter experts gathered at national, state, and local meetings to deliberate and formulate the standards in each subject. These groups offered the results of their work as "new standards" to guide curriculum and testing programs. But much to the disappointment of traditionalists, these expert groups framed the standards, by and large, in the form of a "meaningful" curriculum that reflected many of the child-centered and social reconstructionist principles described earlier. As each of these expert reports came forth, conservatives became further outraged. They saw that the new standards for tough, rigorous learning (as they envisioned it) had strayed far from a behaviorist- and essentialist-inspired, fact- and skills-based curriculum. Rather, the standards seemed to encourage schools to move toward more progressive curriculum and teaching.

To stop these standards-based reforms, conservative advocates campaigned aggressively to persuade policymakers and the public that the standards were dangerous. Their tactics included belittling expert involvement in favor of common sense and then calling on their own experts to support their views. They garnered considerable media attention as they caricatured the standards' featured instructional approaches—approaches we describe in Chapters 5 and 6 as reflections of current understandings about sociocultural and constructivist theories of learning—as mindless games, "invented" spelling, and "fuzzy" math without numbers. Illogically, they blamed these new methods for the persistent low standardized test scores of students who had been taught with mostly conventional approaches. By the mid-1990s, the backlash against progressive curricula had captured enormous public sympathy and policy clout. Antireform advocacy groups such as Mathematically Correct in California and Arizona Parents for Traditional Education began using the Internet as a forum to fight the standards.

No Child Left Behind Act and Standards

Despite controversy, the federal No Child Left Behind Act of 2002 reinvigorated the push for academic standards. The law required each state to adopt challenging content and achievement standards for English language arts, mathematics, and, eventually, science. However, it stopped short of pushing particular standards.[46] Rather, in a nod to local control, states were asked to create and adopt standards of their choosing. And, by 2005, every state had adopted standards. In some states, the standards mirrored the national standards constructed by subject matter groups; in others, they conformed to more conservative views of knowledge and learning; in other states, they reflected a mix of perspectives. As a result, states' standards (and the assessments used to measure students' proficiency on those state standards) varied widely in content and in rigor, precision, and transparency. As varied as they were, the No Child Left Behind Act tied federal funding for the education of low-income students to scores on states' assessments. Test results were then used to determine each school's performance status, to judge teachers' effectiveness, and to levy sanctions on schools.

Standards or Standardization?

Over time, teachers' early support for standards eroded. Teachers struggled with the fine line between standards and unproductive *standardization* of teaching and learning, which scholar Christine Sleeter argues can occur when prepackaged curricula, mandated textbooks, and high-stakes standardized tests are linked to standards or used to enforce specific (and generally rigid) approaches to teaching them.[47] Such standardization is also likely when standards documents are developed at a great distance from the students they are meant to serve, the teachers who are meant to implement them, and the communities they are meant to represent.

In fact, many scholars worried about the marginalization of minoritized cultures and ways of knowing that standards-based reforms may threaten. Educators working in schools labeled as low performing, especially, realized that the strict monitoring that accompanied standards and high-stakes testing made it increasingly difficult to teach from a critical multicultural perspective or respond to students' individual strengths and needs.

Nearly all teachers lamented that neither the federal government nor individual states provided the resources necessary or the support they needed to fulfill the promise of standards—that all children would learn at very high levels.

Articulating a "Common Core"

Despite teachers' growing concerns, advocates (many with resources and support from the Bill and Melinda Gates Foundation) pressed their agenda forward. The next step was the creation of K–12 mathematics and English/language arts Common Core State Standards (CCSS)—an effort to resolve the unevenness in quality and rigor across states' standards documents and tests.

In 2009, the National Governors Association and the Council of Chief State School Officers launched an initiative to build support for a common set of standards that states could adopt voluntarily. Much like subject matter groups had done in the 1990s, these state leaders put together "work groups" of university professors, leaders of education advocacy groups, experts from testing companies, and (some) K–12 teachers. To develop a CCSS-aligned assessment system, the federal government funded two groups or consortia of states—the Smarter Balanced Assessment Consortium and the Partnership for Assessment of Readiness for College and Careers (PARCC)—to develop new assessments to measure students proficiency. That the states were doing this work—rather than the federal government—was politically important, since it had become clear that a national curriculum was anathema to those who feared federal government intrusion into state and local authority over schools.

During the Obama administration, however, Secretary of Education Arne Duncan made clear his strong support for a centralized system of standards, arguing that increased uniformity would enable educators to "accelerate learning and close achievement gaps nationwide." Following the trend to link education in the United States to the global economy, Duncan said, "As the nation seeks to maintain our international competitiveness, ensure all students regardless of background have access to a high-quality education, and prepare all students for college, work and citizenship, these standards are an important foundation for our collective work."[48]

Although the federal government could not require states to adopt the CCSS, the Department of Education did everything it could to persuade them. It tied the adoption of the standards to states' eligibility for "Race to the Top" grants (totaling $4 billion) as part of the federal stimulus package following the great recession. It also gave states more flexibility under the No Child Left Behind Act if they adopted "college and career" standards, which was "code" to many for the CCSS. And it worked. By 2011, forty-six states had replaced their home-grown state English/language arts and mathematics standards with the CCSS.[49] Forty-five states signed on to use the newly developed PARCC and Smarter Balanced Assessments.

The Standards Backlash (Again)

By 2015, however an enormous backlash had ensued. Several states rescinded their adoption of the standards, and nearly half backed out of their commitment to use tests designed to measure mastery of them. What happened?

Many educators and experts in the field had substantive concerns: that some of the standards were not developmentally appropriate, that the English/language arts standards privileged nonfiction over literature, that the math standards weren't rigorous enough, that the standards addressed diverse learners only superficially, and more. However, those substantive concerns paled in comparison to worries about the assessments being tied to the standards. As the first states tried out the PARCC and Smarter Balanced Assessments, teachers and parents became aware of how time-consuming and burdensome they were. They also learned that they were far more difficult than the previous state tests, resulting in far fewer students being scored as "proficient" or above.

In an interesting turn of events, Diane Ravitch, the aforementioned conservative advocate of standards-based reform and high-stakes accountability, emerged as a leader of strong public and teacher opposition to this latest wave of standards- and test-based reforms. She explained her change of position as rooted in the tensions and unintended negative consequences such reforms generated.[50]

Ravitch and others argued that if the CCSS and tests focused exclusively on mathematics and English/language arts, schools would feel pressure and focus only on these subject areas and neglect untested subject areas such as science, social studies, music, art, and physical education. As Ravitch explained,

> Our schools will not improve if we continue to focus only on reading and mathematics while ignoring the other studies that are essential elements of a good education. . . . Our schools will not improve if we value only what tests measure. . . . What is tested may ultimately be less important than what is untested, such as a student's ability to seek alternative explanations, to raise questions, to pursue knowledge on his own, and to think differently.[51]

This became a very difficult problem to address. As the standards development efforts turned to science, the standards pertaining to climate change and evolution were perceived in many states as threats to the economy or conservative religion.

Other political opposition mounted. Progressives objected that large textbook and testing corporations that stood to profit from the standards and assessments had been too deeply involved in their development. Conservative, states'-rights advocates were angry about the Department of Education's involvement—what many considered overreach of the appropriate federal role. This conservative opposition has received substantial support from the Koch brothers, who directed funding to several of the ultra-conservative Tea Party groups that railed against what they called "Obamacore," as part of their overall efforts to discredit the former president. A recent Brookings Institution report characterized this response as follows:

> Outlandish, paranoid claims about the Common Core are rampant on the far right (e.g., that the Common Core calls for iris scans of children and facial recognition technology to read students' minds, that it promotes communism, homosexuality, gay marriage, teaches children Islamic vocabulary, advances global warming propaganda, equates George Washington with Palestinian terrorists, indoctrinates children into the New World Order, data-tracks students from kindergarten on, etc.).[52]

The result was that, by 2015, tens of thousands of students boycotted PARCC and Smarter Balanced tests, and many states withdrew their pledge to participate in CCSS altogether.[53]

Unsurprisingly, the CCSS became a major political issue in the 2016 presidential campaign, too. Republican Jeb Bush, a longtime supporter, touted them as part of his education agenda. In response, then-candidate and now-President Trump appealed to the party's most conservative wing by making the abolition of the CCSS a key campaign promise and posting statements like "I will end common core. It's a disaster" on his Facebook site.[54] The political strategy may have worked, in part, because by the November 2016 election few Americans understood that the president could not abolish the standards, since the federal government had no formal role in their creation or adoption by the states.

So, after a broadly positive (or neutral) bipartisan reception, enthusiasm for the CCSS has cooled, with conservatives becoming especially hostile. The complex reasons include the following: the standards are associated with Obama-era reforms; the standards represent undue federal influence; the standards are a "Trojan horse"—a way to sneak into the curriculum a liberal agenda such as study of climate change and evolution; the standards support soft pedagogies such as inquiry and discovery learning in contrast to direct teacher transmission of facts.

Without doubt, almost no one understood the standards' deep roots in conservative, essentialist philosophies of education.

A Call to Critique and Action for Those Who Are Teaching to Change the World

Teachers today stand at the center of curriculum battles. The traditional curriculum often does not match the way students learn; shaped by traditional understandings of merit, efficiency, competition, and progress, as well as political interests and ideologies, it tends to favor those of wealth and power. But it could be otherwise. Each day, teachers in the United States critically analyze standards and engage in critical multicultural curriculum development that, in effect, "un-standardizes" the curriculum.[55] Each day, teachers confront and win curriculum battles, as they engage students around rich and powerful ideas that touch their lives. That is one reason that teachers and students return to schools each day. In the coming chapters, we feature examples of teachers engaged in and winning this worthy battle and explore the knowledge, skills, and dispositions they draw on in that crucial work.

Digging Deeper and Tools for Critique

www.routledge.com/cw/teachingtochangetheworld

Notes

1 See, for a general review, Denis C. Phillips and Harvey Siegel, "Philosophy of Education," *The Stanford Encyclopedia of Philosophy* (Winter 2015 Edition), ed. Edward N. Zalta, https://plato.stanford.edu/archives/win2015/entries/education-philosophy/.
2 Herbert Kliebard, *The Struggle for the American Curriculum: 1898–1958* (New York: Routledge, 1983).
3 Lauren Resnick, *Education and Learning to Think* (Washington, DC: National Academy Press, 1983), 3.
4 Quoted in Joel Spring, *The American School: 1642–1990* (New York: Longman, 1996), 41.
5 Ibid., 149.
6 Ibid.
7 Joseph Mayer Rice, *The Public School System of the United States* (New York: Century, 1893), 34.
8 Kliebard, *The Struggle for the American Curriculum.*
9 For a detailed analysis of these movements, see Kliebard, *The Struggle for the American Curriculum.*
10 Quoted in David Levinson, Peter W. Cookson, and Alan R. Sadovnik, *Education and Sociology: An Encyclopedia* (New York: Routledge, 2004), 467.
11 Bureau of Education, *Cardinal Principles of Secondary Education: A Report of the Commission on the Reorganization of Secondary Education, Appointed by the National Education Association*, Bulletin, 1918, No 35.
12 Lawrence Cremin, *The Transformation of the School: Progressivism in American Education 1876–1957* (New York: Knopf, 1961), 130.
13 Ibid.
14 Francis Parker, *Talks on Pedagogies* (New York: E. L. Kellogg, 1894), 450, as quoted in Cremin, *Transformation*, 132.
15 Katherine Camp Mayhew and Anna Camp Edwards, *The Dewey School* (New York: Appleton-Century, 1936), 64–65, as quoted in Cremin, *Transformation*, 137.
16 John Dewey, *School and Society* (Chicago: University of Chicago Press, 1900), 28.
17 Jane Addams, "The Public School and the Immigrant Child," in *The Educating of Americans: A Documentary History*, ed. Daniel Calhoun (Boston: Houghton Mifflin, 1969), 421–423.
18 James A. Banks, "African American Scholarship and the Evolution of Multicultural Education," *The Journal of Negro Education* 61, no. 3 (1992): 273–286.

19 O. K. Armstrong, "Treason in the Textbooks," *The American Legion Magazine*, September 1940, 8–9, 51, 70–72, as cited in Kliebard, *The Struggle for the American Curriculum.*

20 Bureau of Education, *Cardinal Principles of Secondary Education: A Report of the Commission on the Reorganization of Secondary Education, Appointed by the National Education Association*, Bulletin, 1918, No 35.

21 Banks, "African American Scholarship."

22 Jerome Bruner, *The Process of Education* (Cambridge, MA: Harvard University Press, 1960).

23 A. S. Neill, *Summerhill* (Oxford, UK: Hart Publishing, 1960).

24 Title IX, or the Patsy T. Mink Equal Opportunity in Education Act, www.dol.gov/oasam/regs/statutes/titleix.htm.

25 *The Individuals With Disabilities Education Act (IDEA)*, http://idea.ed.gov.

26 Carl Grant, *The Evolution of Multicultural Education in the United States: A Journey for Civil Rights and Social Justice*, www.iaie.org/download/turin_paper_grant.pdf.

27 W. E. B. Du Bois, "The Freedom to Learn," in *W. E. B. Du Bois Speaks*, ed. P. S. Foner (New York: Pathfinder, 1970), 230–231. This 1949 speech came to our attention because Linda Darling-Hammond uses it to set the tone of her book *The Right to Learn.*

28 See James A. Banks, "Multicultural Education: Historical Development, Dimension, and Practice," in *Handbook of Research on Multicultural Education*, 2nd ed., eds. James A. Banks and Cherry McGee Banks (San Francisco: Jossey Bass, 2004).

29 Enid Lee, Deborah Menkart, and Margo Okazawa-Rey, eds., *Beyond Heroes and Holidays: A Practical Guide to K–12 Anti-Racist, Multicultural Education and Staff Development* (Washington, DC: Network of Educators on the Americas, 1998).

30 Herbert Kohl, "The Politics of Children's Literature: What's Wrong With the Rosa Parks Myth," in *Rethinking Our Classrooms: Teaching for Equity and Justice*, Vol. 1, eds. Bill Bigelow, Linda Christensen, Stan Karp, Barbara Milner, and Bob Peterson (Milwaukee, WI: Rethinking Schools, 1994), 137–140.

31 Sonia Nieto, *Affirming Diversity: The Sociopolitical Context of Multicultural Education*, 2nd ed. (White Plains, NY: Longman, 1996), 312.

32 Barry Kanpol and Peter McLaren, *Critical Multiculturalism: Uncommon Voices in a Common Struggle* (London: Bergen and Garvey, 1995).

33 "Arizona Ethnic Studies Classes Banned, Teachers With Accents Can No Longer Teach English," June 30, 2010, www.huffingtonpost.com/2010/04/30/arizona-ethnic-studies-cl_n_558731.html.

34 For links to various research reports documenting the success of ethnic studies, see *Mexican American Studies Stats Show Program Works*, http://saveethnicstudies.org/proven_results.shtml.

35 Quoted in Gloria Ladson-Billings, *The Dreamkeepers* (San Francisco: Jossey-Bass, 1994), 82.

36 Lisa Delpit, *Other People's Children: Cultural Conflict in the Classroom* (New York: The New Press, 1995), 46.

37 Paulo Freire, *Pedagogy of the Oppressed* (New York: The Continuum International Publishing Group, 1970), 36.

38 Nieto, *Affirming Diversity*, 319.

39 Peter McLaren, *Life in Schools: An Introduction to Critical Pedagogy in the Foundations of Education* (New York: Longman, 1998).

40 National Commission on Excellence in Education, *A Nation at Risk: The Imperatives for Educational Reform* (Washington, DC: U.S. Department of Education, 1983).

41 Quoted in Lawrence W. Levine, *Opening of the American Mind: Canons, Culture, and History* (Boston: Beacon Press, 1996), 19.

42 See E. D. Hirsch, *Cultural Literacy: What Every American Needs to Know* (Boston: Houghton Mifflin, 1988); and E. D. Hirsch, *The Schools We Need and Why We Don't Have Them* (New York: Doubleday, 1996).

43 E. D. Hirsch, *Toward a Centrist Curriculum: Two Kinds of Multiculturalism in Elementary School* (Charlottesville, VA: Core Knowledge Foundation, 1992), n.p., www.coreknowledge.org.

44 Ibid., n.p.

45 Diane Ravitch, "Diversity and Democracy: Multicultural Education in America," *American Educator* 14, no. 1 (Spring 1990), 18.

46 *NCLB Elementary & Secondary Education, Part A—Improving Basic Programs Operated by Local Educational Agencies, State Plans*, www2.ed.gov/policy/elsec/leg/esea02/pg2.html#sec1111.

47 Christine Sleeter, "Reform and Control: An Analysis of SB 2042," *Teacher Education Quarterly* 30, no. 1 (2003): 19–30.

48 Arne Duncan, *Statement on National Governors Association and State Education Chiefs Common Core Standards*, June 2, 2010, www.ed.gov/news/press-releases/statement-national-governors-associationand-state-education-chiefs-common-core-/.

49 Common Core State Standards Initiative, www.corestandards.org.

50 Diane Ravitch, "In Need of a Renaissance: Real Reform Will Renew, Not Abandon, Our Neighborhood Schools," *American Educator*, Spring 2010, 10–22, www.aft.org/pdfs/americaneducator/summer2010/Ravitch.pdf.

51 Ravitch, "In Need of a Renaissance," 14.

52 David Whitman, *The Surprising Roots of the Common Core: How Conservatives Gave Rise to "Obamacore"* (Washington, DC: The Brookings Institution, Brown Center on Education Policy, 2015), 4.

53 Editorial Projects in Education Research Center, "Issues A-Z: The Common Core Explained," *Education Week*, September 28, 2015, www.edweek.org/ew/issues/common-core-state-standards/, retrieved on October 1, 2017.

54 Donald Trump, 2017, www.facebook.com/DonaldTrump/videos/10156570856100725/, retrieved on June 15, 2017.

55 Christine E. Sleeter, *Un-standardizing the Curriculum: Multicultural Teaching in the Standards-Based Classroom* (New York: Teachers College Press, 2005).

Chapter 4

Policy and Law
Rules That Schools Live By

No Child Left Behind has had a pronounced impact on the mathematics department at my school—both good and bad. With No Child Left Behind, each high school gains or loses points based on what percentage of students are at grade level and scoring at high levels on the tests given at the end of those courses. Our school was losing points for the ninth graders taking the Introduction to Algebra class. Therefore, the district decided to eliminate that class and place all ninth graders in algebra or higher. This policy has worked to the benefit of the students, as many of them are able to handle the curriculum and benefit from the higher expectations.

To help struggling students the district created a support class. This is a class the students take in addition to their regular algebra class that provides additional time to fill the gaps in their knowledge or allows them additional time to process the material. Sounds good, in theory. However, the class was not designed for the students most at need. Rather, the "middle third"—the students deemed to have the greatest chance of reaching "Proficient" status on the algebra state test—were placed in the support class. This decision was made to maximize state scores to avoid being placed on the dreaded "schools in need of improvement" list.

The net effect is that No Child Left Behind has led to one policy that provided students access to algebra, but it also led to another that denied them additional support to succeed.

—Mark Hill
First-year teacher, high school mathematics

The No Child Let Behind (NCLB) law is now history. The federal law that labeled half the schools in the United States as failing was replaced in 2015 by a new law—the Every Student Succeeds Act (ESSA). ESSA softened some of the most draconian test-and-punish provisions of NCLB, but its new rules will challenge the education system in other ways. We discuss these laws in more detail later in this chapter. For now, we point to them as recent examples of how government uses laws and policies to encourage, support, and require that schools meet the public's expectations. These laws and policies range from overarching federal laws such ESSA to state, school district, and school-site rules such as whether students wear uniforms, which textbooks are used, what role teachers' union plays, and so on.

As Mark Hill's comments suggest, laws and policies can lead to both positive and negative, intended and unintended consequences. In Mark's school, as in many others, NCLB pushed educators to provide more students access to rigorous academic curricula; it also had the perverse effect of prompting educators to target resources and support toward particular students whose test scores would help the school meet its NCLB numerical targets, rather than to distribute resources and support according to all students' learning needs.

Today, we want our schools to teach more than minimal literacy and citizenship skills. We expect our schools to meet the needs of the workforce, solve social problems, ensure the brainpower necessary for national security, and keep the nation competitive in a global economy. These expectations are constantly shifting. In response, education laws and policies are shifting, too. ESSA, for example, raises expectations considerably. NCLB expected that all students would become proficient in language arts and mathematics by 2014; ESSA now expects all students to graduate from high school ready for college and a career.

Teachers who stay informed about policy—keeping track of where policies come from, who shapes their creation, and how they stand to impact teaching and learning—can place the day-to-day activities at their school in their larger political context. Such teachers also can use their voices and activism to contribute to the development of policies that will serve students better in the future.

Chapter Overview

In this chapter, we describe the roles and responsibilities of local, state, and federal government, as well as the role of the courts. We also identify ideologies that compete and exert influence in the education policymaking process. The chapter concludes with a focus on high-stakes accountability policies, how accountability is not just an educational matter but a heated political one as well, and the impacts accountability has on students, schools, and teachers. We pay most attention to public policies and public schools because public schools serve nearly 90 percent of students nationwide. We also discuss the changing landscape around private schools. Even though private schools are exempt from most government policies, the growing political interest of President Trump's administration in sending public money to private schools has pushed them into the education policy spotlight.

The Complex Education Policy System

In Chapters 2 and 3, we noted the growth of public schooling in the United States during the nineteenth century. For much of that century, the country had what education historian David Tyack called "village schools."[1] That is, schools were governed by their local communities. In accordance with the Tenth Amendment to the U.S. Constitution, the authority for education officially belonged to the states.[2] For the most part, however, states delegated the running of schools to local communities. Typically, community members joined local school boards or committees and decided where schools should be built, selected teachers and told them how to behave, and determined the curriculum. Local taxes covered the costs.

By the middle of the nineteenth century, this began to change. As the nation shifted from a rural to a more urban society, city school districts formed, and many states pressed rural schools to consolidate into larger districts. In these larger districts, many local community school boards gave way to centralized district boards and professional superintendents. At the same time, states and the federal government became more involved in schooling.

Increasingly, state leaders looked for uniformity in their rapidly expanding school systems. Massachusetts led the way by establishing a state board of education in 1837 (with Horace Mann appointed as state commissioner) and by passing the nation's first compulsory-attendance law in 1852. In the South in the 1830s, Louisiana, Georgia, Virginia, Alabama, South Carolina, and North Carolina all passed laws that prohibited teaching slaves to read.

Federal involvement in education began during the Civil War. Using the rationale that the Constitution's Preamble required the federal government to "promote the general welfare," Congress established the Bureau of Education in 1867. The bureau's mission was to collect data and report the "condition and progress of education."[3] For some, however, one important purpose was to give the federal government knowledge of whether the southern states would comply with the "equal protection" provisions of the Fourteenth Amendment. However, the bureau did not push aggressively for equal education, and in 1886, the Supreme Court's *Plessy v. Ferguson* decision made it legal to maintain segregated school systems. For decades, the U.S. Bureau of Education remained a small agency that did little more than survey and write annual reports about the nation's schools.

Three Levels of Educational Governance

Today, the U.S. educational system has grown into a large and complex enterprise, in which federal, state, and local government all play powerful roles. Although the decision-making process differs somewhat in every state—since each state system is independent—there are common patterns of policymaking among the three levels of government.

What Do Local School Districts Do?

There are approximately 15,000 local school districts in the United States. Most are governed by elected school boards that hire a superintendent or a commissioner to lead the day-to-day administration of the system. In the last decade, mayors in some large cities like Boston, New York, Chicago, and Washington, DC, have taken over responsibility for the schools and appointed either the board members or the superintendent.

Now as in the past, local school districts raise a significant portion of the funds needed to support their schools, and they develop and manage district budgets that include state and federal funds. The districts build their own schools, hire teachers and other staff, and negotiate with teachers' and other employees' unions to set salaries and working conditions. They—for the most part—decide what curriculum to offer, how to group students for instruction, and what textbooks to use. They set policies about homework, discipline, and extracurricular activities.

The largest portion of schools' funds comes through state governments, and the states are responsible for maintaining schools. Local school districts can only do what the state government delegates to them, and districts are accountable to state laws and regulations. In practice, though, for most of our history, local school districts have had considerable autonomy over their schools, and most observers still characterize schooling in the United States as locally controlled.

However, since the 1970s, the states and the federal government have become increasingly involved in determining policies and practices in local schools.

What Do States Do?

States have the primary authority for providing education, and as long as they do not violate the U.S. Constitution, they are free to run their schools as they like. Nevertheless, the school systems across the states are far more similar than different.

Every state has a state school board and a chief state school officer (a superintendent of public instruction or a commissioner of education). In every state, these officials administer state laws and regulations that determine how districts should be organized and governed, and they oversee standards for educational programs, instructional materials, graduation requirements, and achievement testing; attendance rules; the length of the school day and school year; teacher credentialing, certification, tenure, and pensions; the construction and maintenance of school buildings; school district finances and budgets; school safety; and parents' and students' rights and responsibilities.

Every state also delegates most of the day-to-day operation of schools to local school districts (except Hawaii, which has only one statewide school system). At the same time, every state has steadily increased its control over local school policies and programs. In California, the State Education Code, which contains all of the state laws and regulations governing education, is fourteen volumes long.

The states' current high level of involvement in local school policies and practices began in the late 1960s when the federal government gave states the responsibility for administering a collection of federal programs related to the War on Poverty and civil rights; several of these programs are discussed in depth in Chapter 10. These federally funded programs changed the relationships between state education officials and local school systems. The unobtrusive technical assistance that the state had provided previously—mostly to rural school systems—morphed into a far more assertive role as overseer of programmatic and funding mandates.

Since the 1980s, states have become more involved in teaching and learning, as well as setting regulations. The dire warnings of *A Nation at Risk*—described in Chapters 2 and 3—led many states to raise graduation requirements, mount school reform initiatives, lengthen the school year, and place greater emphasis on student achievement, effectively taking these policy decisions away from local school boards. By the 1990s, many governors began placing education high on their policy agendas. It cannot be said that education policy became *more* political with this trend; indeed, education policy has *always* been political, even when it has had a lower (and more local) profile. Nevertheless, education policy has come to play an increasingly prominent role in state and national politics.

State involvement in teaching and learning has also increased because of changes in the way many states fund their schools. Until quite recently, local property taxes were the major source of school funding, with states contributing a much smaller share. However, because lower-wealth communities cannot raise as much local money as higher-wealth districts, states have made some efforts to equalize funding between rich and poor districts. Often, it took a court decision to determine that schools' grossly unequal resources violated a state's obligation to treat students equally and fairly. In most cases, equalization has meant that states pay a larger share of educational costs. Or, more precisely, tax money now funnels through the state for redistribution to local areas. The state's increased role in collecting and distributing education money has meant that state lawmakers are more likely to determine how the money is spent.

In the past twenty-five years, states have also experimented with delegating the authority for running schools to groups wanting to start up new public schools that operate outside the rules and regulations imposed by local school districts. In 2010, forty states and Washington, DC, had laws establishing charter schools that agree to be held accountable for student achievement in exchange for greater autonomy. By 2015, charter schools numbered 6,750 and enrolled about 2.7 million of the nation's approximately 50 million public school students.[4]

What Does the Federal Government Do?

Today, as in the past, the federal government collects and reports information on the nation's schools. It also maintains its role of ensuring that states and local school districts do nothing that violates the U.S. Constitution. However, growing national concern about the quality of U.S. education generally and the inequalities we described in earlier chapters has led to an expansion of the federal role. Today, much of what states and local school districts do is shaped, even controlled, by federal policy. Although only about 11 percent of the funding for education comes from federal sources, most states and local districts cannot afford to pass up those funds.[5] Because the funds now come with tight restrictions, the federal government can leverage a comparatively small investment into a lot of influence.

Federal programs providing additional funds for low-income children began during the War on Poverty in the 1970s with the Elementary and Secondary Education Act (ESEA). ESEA evolved into the NCLB Act in 2001 under Republican President George W. Bush, and into ESSA in 2015 under Democratic President Barack Obama. Both laws were supported by a bipartisan coalition of legislators. In a major change from earlier versions of the federal legislation, both laws require that states hold schools accountable for increasing student test scores and closing the achievement gap among racial and economic groups.

NCLB required that every state develop academic standards and standardized tests aligned to the standards, and test every student in grades 3 through 8 in reading and mathematics. The act required states to set a numerical target for each school specifying how many points its scores must increase each year, and it required schools to increase the scores of every subgroup of students (racial, ethnic, income, disability, and grade level). NCLB also required states to choose among four methods of intervening in schools that failed to meet their targets. NCLB expected that all U.S. schools, by 2014, would have 100 percent of their children score "proficient" on reading and math tests.

Many applauded NCLB's basic premise (i.e., its insistence that schools focus on achievement and equity), but others blamed it for undermining high-quality curriculum and teaching, particularly for low-income students and students of color. Critics quickly observed that standardized tests were powerful tools that states and local districts used to encourage the adoption of teaching methods and materials thought to yield higher test scores. Also, the tests were oftentimes used for purposes they were never designed to meet—for example, as we discuss later in the chapter, using a single test to determine whether students pass, fail, or graduate; whether schools remain open or close; and whether teachers get to keep their jobs. As a result, the *consequences* of the tests often overshadowed students' learning and future schooling prospects. Thus, tests used for these flawed purposes became known as "high-stakes" tests, distinguishing them from tests used to inform policies and teaching practices that would result in more and better learning for students. Finally, nearly everyone agreed that too few resources came with NCLB's demands and that most schools could not possibly meet the test-based benchmarks set out for them.

And, in fact, schools did not reach those goals. Each year the proportion of schools identified as failing grew, and by 2011 had reached 50 percent. Rather than continue this demoralizing and clearly ineffective process, the U.S. Department of Education gave most states waivers from these harsh accountability provisions. Congress struggled until the end of 2015 to come up with a replacement.

The 2015 ESSA law pulled back the strictest federal requirements of NCLB. While it maintained the goals of promoting accountability, closing gaps, and intervening in struggling schools, it gave states the responsibility for developing accountability plans with multiple indicators including achievement test performance, English-language proficiency, graduation rates, and another academic indicator of their choosing. In addition, the law requires states to hold schools accountable on at least one nonacademic indicator of school quality, such as student engagement, educator engagement, access to and completion of advanced coursework, postsecondary readiness, and school climate/safety. ESSA also lets the states decide how much these various indicators will "count" in determining whether schools are failing (in need of improvement, in the language of the law), as long as academic achievement counts the most. States must also identify the bottom 5 percent of low-performing schools and develop strategies for helping them improve. Whether these new rules give states and local schools the flexibility they want will, of course, depend, in part, on how the current administration chooses to enforce them.

The federal government also influences state and local school systems by funding particular types of research and innovation aimed at improving educational quality and by requiring that federal money be spent only on those "evidence-based" interventions. Federal policymakers set research priorities, use funding opportunities to send strong signals about what they deem "best" practice, and create incentives for states, districts, and local schools to adopt the innovations they favor. For example, as part of the American Recovery and Reinvestment Act of 2009, which provided money to help the nation recover from the "great recession," the Obama administration earmarked over $4 billion for what they called a Race to the Top fund to improve schools. States were not required to apply for funds, but the Department of Education determined that "winning" would require that states commit to developing standards, assessments, and data systems; ensure teacher and principal effectiveness; and adopt plans for "turning around" low-performing schools. The Race to the Top competition convinced many states to make these significant policy changes, expanding the federal government's reach into state and local education policy and practice.

Concept Table 4.1 summarizes the key roles and responsibilities at each of the three levels of educational governance.

How Do Policies Work?

At each of the federal, state, and local levels, different types of officials are responsible for governing public school systems—elected policymakers, appointed and career administrators, and the courts. As policymakers, Congress, state legislators, and local school boards pass laws and policies establishing the goals of schooling and allocating resources to achieve the goals. The president, governors, and mayors help shape this agenda, usually by using the power and public visibility of their office to press forward ideas for policies that they believe will make schools better.

Federal, state, and local policymakers use a handful of strategies to translate their ideas about what schools should do into policy. The most straightforward strategy is to issue *mandates* that simply tell districts and schools what they must do—such as requiring schools to be in session for a minimum number of days and for a minimum number of minutes each day. A second much-used strategy is to offer *incentives* or *inducements* in the form of funding or other advantages in exchange for schools and districts adopting preferred policies or, conversely, to threaten schools and districts with *sanctions* if they do not adopt such policies. A common incentive is to offer grant funding to states, districts, and schools if they institute a particular program (as Race to the Top did). A third strategy is to *build the capacity* of districts to enact particular policies or programs by providing resources, offering training, or helping them to do things differently.

Concept Table 4.1 Three Levels of Education Policymaking

Level	Policy actors	Responsibilities
Local	School board	Raise funds
	Superintendent and staff	Build and maintain facilities
		Hire, assign, and provide professional development; evaluate administrators, teachers, and staff
		Negotiate with teachers' and other employees' unions to set salaries and working conditions
		Establish basic operational rules for schools—hours, holidays, school organization, curriculum, textbooks, homework, discipline, extracurricular activities, dress codes, etc.
		Administer federal and state programs and achievement testing
		Report to the state and federal governments on spending of funds, student achievement, and other required information
		Publish and distribute public "report cards" about each school
State	Legislature	Enact constitutional obligation to maintain schools
	Governor	Certify educators
	School board	Provide funding for schools
	Chief state school officer	Delegate the operation of schools to local school boards
	State Department of Education	Administer local implementation of federal and state categorical programs
		Collect data from schools
		Report civil rights data to U.S. Department of Education
		Intervene when local school systems experience fiscal, management, or other crises
		Establish curriculum standards, testing programs, and accountability mechanisms
		Report achievement test scores, graduation rates, and teacher quality to U.S. Department of Education
		Take over, reconstitute, or "charterize" failing schools
Federal	Congress	Serve as a "bully pulpit" to spur states and schools to meet expectations
	President	
	Secretary of Education	Fund and oversee support programs for English Learners, low-income students, and students with disabilities
	U.S. Department of Education	
		Collect basic data about school enrollment, staffing, funding, etc.
		Conduct the National Assessment of Educational Progress
		Monitor states' and schools' compliance with federal civil rights laws
		Withhold federal funds to states (and, thereby, local schools) that do not comply with provisions in the federal laws (including ESSA and others)
		Collect accountability data on state indicators
		Require that federal funds be spent only on programs that have been proven effective—i.e., that are evidence based

A common example is to provide professional development to increase teachers' knowledge and skills in a subject area. A fourth policy strategy is to make federal- or state-level *system changes* that alter key elements of local practice. An example is the introduction of standards and standards-based tests that have a strong impact on how and what teachers teach.[6]

In addition to those who make policy, each level of government has education officials who work out the details of how policies should be implemented and then help to make sure that they are. At the federal level, Congress funds the U.S. Department of Education under the leadership of the Secretary of Education to implement and oversee federal educational policy. The departments of education in each state play much the same role, under the direction of the state superintendent or commissioner of education. These state departments of education translate the policies into a set of regulations for local districts, allocate the funding for programs and initiatives, provide support and guidance for schools and districts to implement regulations, and follow up to make sure they do. At the local level, the superintendent of schools and his or her staff in the district office take the federal and state policies and regulations and create the day-to-day procedures that school principals, teachers, and students follow. They also support local schools with professional development for teachers, curriculum development, administration of state tests, and coordination of special programs, such as those for students identified as needing special education.

The Courts Also Make Education Policy

Most education policy and law is established by elected federal, state, and local officials and the professionals they appoint to administer school systems. However, as noted in prior chapters, for more than 100 years, the courts have allowed and disallowed policies and required policymakers to formulate new laws that affect education equity. Their primary role has been to establish and protect the rights of those whose educational rights may be ignored or even violated by elected and appointed school officials. Examples of this include the court's mediating role in cases such as *Brown v. Board of Education* (1954), *Lau v. Nichols* (1974), *Plyler v. Doe* (1982), and *Williams v. California* (2001).

The comprehensive educational timeline (see Chapter 2) highlights some of the court decisions that have played a role in the struggle for equitable schools. Most of these decisions relate to three fundamental questions: Are separate and unequal educational opportunities provided to students on the basis of race, disability, and language permissible under U.S. or state laws? What constitutional rights of children and young people must be protected while they are at school? Do federal or state laws require that all students have an adequately funded education? The courts have not always provided a clear or consistent set of answers to any of these important questions. But their decisions have shaped education policy profoundly.

Most of the equity-related court cases in the second half of the twentieth century were federal cases focused on the rights of minoritized groups to equal education and on the legality of racially segregated schools. Until about 1980, court decisions consistently advanced racial desegregation as a strong and appropriate remedy. After 1980, however, the court retreated, and today education rights activists are well aware that the U.S. Supreme Court can limit progressive schooling policies, as well as advance them. One recent example is the 2007 U.S. Supreme Court decision in *Parents Involved in Community Schools v. Seattle School District No. 1.* That decision invalidated voluntary school desegregation plans in Seattle, Washington, and Louisville, Kentucky—setting a precedent that threatens to undermine decades of work in the service of racial integration and equality.

Another set of cases during this period focused on clarifying the rights of individual students. Here, too, many decisions have advanced students' rights, but not all of the rulings have been decided in the students' favor. The courts have upheld students' rights to freedom of expression in the area of dress and to a hearing before being suspended, but they have also ruled that paddling students is not "cruel and unusual" punishment and that school officials can search students' possessions, restrain students' speech, censor student journalists' articles in school newspapers, and subject student athletes to random urinalysis testing for drug use.

By the beginning of the twenty-first century, the most prominent educational equity cases challenged the fairness and adequacy of school funding. Because the states, not the federal government, have the constitutional obligation to operate school systems, these cases have been filed in state courts. By now, school finance lawsuits had been filed in forty-five states. In about two-thirds of the cases settled since 1989, the courts have found that the state failed to ensure that all schools, and particularly those enrolling the most disadvantaged students, had enough resources to provide the basic education their state constitutions require.[7]

Over the past sixty years, the courts have established that education is a critically important right in U.S. society. The goal of most education finance litigation is similar to segregation and inequality cases, and therefore harkens back to the principles articulated by Chief Justice Earl Warren in the unanimous *Brown v. Board of Education* Supreme Court decision: "In these days, it is doubtful that any child may reasonably be expected to succeed in life if he is denied the opportunity of an education. Such an opportunity, where the state has undertaken to provide it, is a right which must be made available to all on equal terms."[8] The courts are called on to make sure that school policies do not abridge the fundamental constitutional rights of individuals or politically powerless minoritized groups, even if they reflect the will of the majority.

Partly because education is so central to our notions of egalitarian democracy, a whole community of education lawyers and advocates has emerged to ensure that education reflects democratic values as well as economic ones. Like Thurgood Marshall, the lead attorney for Linda Brown in the *Brown v. Board of Education* case, these advocates are among the many allies of teachers who are committed to advancing social justice. At the same time, these advocates work to ensure that the rules set by policymakers and judges make it possible for teachers to engage all children in the educational experiences that are key to personal success and civic participation.

Cultural, Political, and Economic Forces Shape Education Policy

Education policymaking is a constant process of designing and redesigning rules and strategies to make the educational system effective, efficient, and equitable. But the meanings of educational effectiveness, efficiency, and equity are not a given. Neither are they determined by neutral or scientific processes (although they may be influenced by them). Instead these meanings are constructed and reconstructed in an ever-changing stew of ideas, values, and politics.

We noted in Chapter 2 the rising, changing, and often conflicting expectations Americans have for public schools. We also discussed the broad and corrosive ideologies of meritocracy, deficit thinking, and racial superiority that have been considered natural and common sense throughout the country's history. These expectations and ideologies have profound effects on the meanings of educational effectiveness, efficiency, and equity. Likewise, today's efforts to craft sound and just education policy must contend with powerful remnants of an unjust past.

Consider, for example, the influence of Ron Unz, the California software developer who, using the rationale that schools are expected to preserve American culture, founded, funded, and led the anti-bilingual organization English for the Children. Unz's organization mounted successful campaigns to replace bilingual education with policies specifying that instruction could be conducted only in English in California (1998's Proposition 227) and in Arizona (2000's Proposition 203); he attempted unsuccessfully to do the same in Colorado in 2002 and elsewhere.

Policymakers have long sought to make schooling policies that respond to a false choice that schools can either be instruments of justice and democracy *or* optimally serve a competitive economy. The result has been the creation of policies that seek to serve all children equally alongside individualistic, competitive structures and practices that produce "winners" and "losers." Such structures and practices are often rationalized as *meritocratic* and necessary to address certain students' alleged *deficits*. They are nearly always premised on an assumption that White students' privileges are deserved, merited, and indicative of indisputable superiority.

Moreover, no elected or appointed federal, state, or local policymaker makes policy in a vacuum free of these normative and political forces. In addition to their personal histories and upbringing, elected officials answer to supporters and constituents, on whose financial contributions and votes they rely. Appointed officials' views usually reflect those of the elected, who appoint them, or the bosses who hire them. Accordingly, education policies are shaped by what the public (especially its most politically powerful and monied segment) thinks about and expects from schools at any moment in time. And as much as we like the courts to stand apart from such pressures, they too are subject to changing tides of public opinion and political pressures.

Schools Mirror Economic Enterprise

Since the industrial revolution in the mid-to-late nineteenth century, Americans have been captivated by rising economic productivity and the strategies used by industry and business to fuel it. In Chapter 2, we noted that, with the rise of industrialization, the public and policymakers expected schools to prepare young people with the knowledge, skills, and dispositions they would need fit in and contribute to the industrial economy. But that's not all. Increasingly, the public (and especially those with the most political clout) believed that the structures and practices used in the economic sector were what made industry and business effective producers and efficient profit generators. Schools, in contrast, were viewed as lacking the structures and practices that would make them effective and efficient. So, it's not surprising that, over the twentieth century, policymakers crafted education policies that aim to make schools function more like industry and business.

For more than a century, education policymakers have looked to industry and business for models of how to make the best possible schools. This legacy continues to dominate the thinking of today's advocates for choice, competition, and privatization. Although few policymakers would argue *against* "social justice," most have been oblivious to how ideologies of meritocracy, deficit thinking, and racial superiority have distorted their conceptions of effective, efficient, and equitable schooling.

Schools as Factories

As the nation industrialized in the late nineteenth century, factories began producing cheap, labor-saving products that liberated most people from what was considered the drudgery of making basic goods with their own hands. Industrial efficiency caught the public's imagination through the writings of Frederick Winslow Taylor and the example of Henry Ford. Tough-minded factory management practices were touted as hastening the end of deprivation and poverty, as productivity, efficiency, profits, and worker well-being would go hand in hand.

Basing their practices on careful record keeping, "scientific" managers established the "best methods," which replaced the rule-of-thumb approaches that workers had developed over time. Managers trained and supervised workers and were themselves trained in techniques of scientific control and efficiency. People called the techniques "scientific" because they were systematic and precise and allowed few individual judgments and little variability. Factory owners and managers centralized decision making and authority at the top, divided labor by specializing tasks, and governed every aspect of the enterprise with rules, regulations, and an impersonal (more "efficient") attitude toward the individual. Ford's assembly-line autoworkers were easily trained and supervised by managers who used standardized methods to perform small tasks. In this way, "Fordism" became the apex of scientific production and management.[9]

FACTORY-MODEL SCHOOLS

The nation found compelling the metaphor that children were raw materials that could be processed into useful products in schools that operated like factories. University professors and school administrators set about conducting scientific studies of schools, copying what Taylor had done in industry. They used their findings to develop schemes for running schools more like efficient factories. They divided schools' large auditorium-like spaces into today's familiar "egg crate" classrooms and separated students by ages, subjects, and abilities. Texts such as readers and spellers proliferated, making it possible to standardize curriculum. Colleges began to specify sequences of courses that would prepare students for admission. Normal schools—the first teacher education institutions—started training teachers in correct and efficient teaching methods.[10]

Education administrators of the early 1900s, especially those in urban areas, relished scientific management partly because it cast them in the role of experts and enhanced their personal status and political clout. They, as experts, were the factory bosses who supervised low-skilled, low-paid workers (teachers). Increasingly, as women entered the workforce, they filled the ranks of the teaching profession. Given the times, women could be counted on to work for less money and to rarely leave for better jobs (since so few were available to them); they also were thought to be naturally more nurturing. Men, on the other hand, served as principals, superintendents, and members of school boards; they were also considered better suited than women to teaching older students in elite schools and subjects that required intellectual acuity and academic training.

FACTORY-MODEL SCHOOLS TODAY

In assembly-line fashion, schools still separate students into classes by age, grade, and ability. Most teachers teach all students in the room the same material, at the same pace, and in the same way. Curriculum specialists, school district administrators, and even state legislators, acting like industrial production designers, design curriculum sequences and instructional processes for teachers and students to follow, subject by subject, grade by grade. Everyone specializes. One is a reading specialist, one is a third-grade teacher, one teaches social studies, and another is a giftedness expert. Careful supervision by administrators keeps all the parts running smoothly.

Report cards provide an efficient, if not terribly informative, shorthand of letter grades and checklists that sum up and communicate students' learning to parents. State standardized achievement tests report productivity to school boards and state legislatures, as well as to parents, real estate marketers, and so forth. All are reminiscent of scientific management practices.

EQUITY AND THE FACTORY MODEL

As we described in Chapter 3, equity at the turn of the nineteenth century was conceptualized as making sure that factory-like schools provided different and suitable types of curriculum and instruction for students with different family backgrounds, IQs, and future roles in society.

To use the factory metaphor, these would be different but equitable assembly lines. As we described in Chapter 2, deficit thinking related to race and language, and the science of IQ influenced these policies. The tracking practices and approaches to categorical programs we discuss in Chapter 10 are contemporary remnants of this factory-like effectiveness and equity. Indeed, these practices and programs established different parts of a linear schooling process that would prepare different students in different ways for different roles in the postschooling workforce.

Schools as Well-Managed Corporations

In the 1970s, Henry Ford's factory model of production lost its luster. The traumatic mid-1970s upheaval in the Middle East created severe oil shortages. Images of U.S. cars waiting in long, slow lines for rationed gas served as a wake-up call for U.S. business and industry. Confidence in the United States' industrial prowess diminished as Japanese and German car manufacturers moved quickly to supply the U.S. market with smaller, more fuel-efficient alternatives. Foreign competitors easily outpaced Ford, General Motors, and Chrysler. These U.S. companies' rigid, hierarchical ways of organizing and managing work made them extraordinarily slow to notice, let alone respond to, the crisis. Businesses in the United States finally did adapt to these new conditions, but slowly and in their uniquely "American" way.

SYSTEMS THINKING

As business leaders tried to figure out what had gone wrong and how to fix it, they looked to new theories of corporate management and the emerging academic field of management science. In 1945, management professor Peter Drucker wrote a book that popularized the concept of the "corporation," and by the 1960s, Drucker's books and articles were challenging the fundamentals of U.S. business.[11] Known as the "father of modern management," Drucker, along with his colleagues in university business schools, developed a "systems" approach to managing large enterprises.

Moving away from the beliefs of Taylor and Ford, systems theorists saw business enterprises as interrelated and interdependent elements. More important than an assembly line of well-functioning parts was whether the parts added up to a coherent whole. Importantly, systems theorists went beyond the mechanical and technical parts of production and focused on the social and human dimensions of the workplace. Smart, highly motivated workers, whose innovative ideas affect the work, matter most.

Systems thinking caught on in the 1970s because it seemed to explain why the Japanese, and to some degree the Scandinavians, had become so successful. Japanese companies had been using many elements of systems thinking to organize and manage their work, and they credited it for their innovative and nimble performance. Rushing to compete with the Japanese, U.S. companies began to reorganize into cooperative work teams, adopt such policies as employee flextime, and pay closer attention to the ideas of workers. Some of the innovations were successful; some were not. Many business leaders failed to recognize the difficulty of maintaining non-hierarchical, cooperative, and interdependent workplaces in this country's highly individualistic, competitive social and business culture.

SYSTEMIC EDUCATION REFORM

After the 1983 release of *A Nation at Risk*, which depicted American education's low international standing, many business and political leaders blamed schools for the nation's perceived fall from world economic dominance. After all, Japan's economic ascendancy and its besting of the

U.S. consumer electronics and automobile industries mirrored Japanese students' higher scores on international achievement tests. What was needed to restore the economy, many argued, was a radical improvement in the educational system.

Scholars like David Berliner and Bruce Biddle, authors of the award-winning book *The Manufactured Crisis*, would later challenge the validity of the arguments made in *A Nation at Risk*.[12] But, at the time, the public and many policymakers were persuaded by them. In response, most states lengthened school years and school days, increased graduation requirements, and upgraded teacher preparation. Taken individually, these policies may have had some value, but by the late 1980s, they had proved disappointing. They had not significantly improved the *quality* of education, particularly for millions of underserved students in undersupported schools.

Given decades of copying apparently effective and efficient factories, it's not surprising that education policymakers looked to corporate reforms for school improvement strategies. At the same time, education researchers and policymakers began exploring the emerging systems thinking being used in corporations. Many concluded that systemic reform would revolutionize schools in ways that piecemeal reforms (longer days, increased requirements, etc.) could not. Policy analysts argued that states must develop a set of coherent policies that would work together so that each part of the educational system would support all the other parts: (1) set high academic standards; (2) provide schools with the tools, skills, and resources needed to help students meet the standards; and (3) hold schools accountable for the results. Following the example of well-managed organizations, these policies would also provide districts and schools with maximum flexibility in how they achieved results.[13]

School administrators eagerly borrowed two concepts, "learning organizations" and "continuous improvement," from organizational scholar Peter Senge. Senge wrote that these concepts characterized the highest-functioning and most innovation-rich organizations: "organizations where people continually expand their capacity to create the results they truly desire, where new and expansive patterns of thinking are nurtured, where collective aspiration is set free, and where people are continually learning to see the whole together."[14]

Such ideas challenged the command-and-control management strategies of the factory-model school. They suggested, instead, that education officials should build school cultures that would encourage learning and innovation among the adults as well as the students. The 1990s witnessed a proliferation of books and professional development programs claiming to teach school administrators how to put these ideas into practice.

Ultimately, recommendations for systemic reform appeared in major documents of the National Governors Association, the Business Roundtable, and the Council of Chief State School Officers. Systemic reform was also the central rationale behind major initiatives of the National Science Foundation, several major philanthropic foundations, and congressional legislation.

SYSTEMS THEORIES, NCLB, AND ESSA

Reflecting the popularity of systemic approaches to reform, the Clinton administration's 1994 version of the ESEA required states to adopt standards that made clear what students should know and be able to do and that would press schools to upgrade content and instruction. We describe these standards in some detail in Chapter 5.

What's worth mentioning here is that many progressive policymakers and educators assumed that new standards for what students should learn would be accompanied by standards for the *resources* that schools, teachers, and students would need in order to meet the new standards. These came to be called "opportunity-to-learn" standards.

Opportunity-to-learn standards and accountability for meeting them were resisted strongly. In 1994, conservatives (mostly Republicans) in Congress threatened to stall federal education legislation if liberals (mostly Democrats) insisted that states establish standards for resources and learning conditions. Some conservatives argued that such requirements would curtail states' rights to conduct education as they saw fit. Others argued more pragmatically—that "opportunity standards" would open the door to increased education spending. These opponents prevailed. Standards-based policies specified what students should learn, and standardized achievement tests were designed to hold schools accountable for teaching that content, but policies would not speak to the resources and conditions that such learning requires.

NCLB in 2001 and ESSA in 2015 both retained elements of systemic reform. Federal law has continued to require states to set standards, administer standards-based tests, and hold schools accountable for students' test scores. The only "opportunity" required by NCLB was ensuring a "highly qualified" teacher in every classroom. And even that provision was eroded in many states by very weak definitions of "highly qualified" and has since virtually disappeared in ESSA.

Unfortunately, education policymakers and many practitioners embraced the broad concept of "learning organizations" while falling back on tightly controlled, top-down practices. One particularly contradictory example involved policies mandating "scientifically based" scripted literacy curricula that harkened back to factory-model schooling. Such policies constrained teachers' opportunities to use their experience and expertise to fashion rigorous lessons best suited to their students.

EQUITY AND SYSTEMS CHANGE

By the 1960s, the federal government had responded to the *Brown v. Board of Education* decision and the civil rights movement by seeking ways to better serve students of color. It wanted information about the harms of racial segregation that it could use to guide educational policy toward equity.

The U.S. Department of Education commissioned sociologist James Coleman to study the issue. Coleman and his team investigated whether *countable* school resources such as buildings, library resources, teachers' qualifications, class size, and so on were related to students' achievement test scores. Coleman hoped this approach would reveal connections between systemic inequalities in opportunity and achievement gaps. Coleman also studied whether attending school with students of other races influenced students' achievement.

Many of the study's findings surprised everyone, especially Coleman. His now famous "Coleman Report" concluded that differences in tangible school resources were not systematically related to students' test scores. For example, neither the number of books in the school library nor the level of teacher training seemed to explain test score gaps. But if not resources, what? Coleman and his colleagues found that when it came to gaps in academic achievement, school resources mattered far less than students' race and their parents' income or the racial and economic backgrounds of their classmates. This argument was consistent with systems thinking, in that the people in the system are more important than the system's technical features.

Coleman was partly right but mostly wrong. Like Coleman, many researchers since have found that students of all socioeconomic classes do better on tests if they attend schools where most of their classmates are not poor. However, the available social science methods of the time limited the power of Coleman's analysis.[15] Coleman failed to understand that while resources like books and teachers are critical to education, increasing any *one* resource may not be sufficient to raise test scores. For example, simply reducing class size may not improve outcomes if teachers continue to teach as they did before. On the other hand, smaller classes are helpful when teachers take advantage of them to improve instruction and spend more time with individual students.

Because Coleman found that academic outcomes were higher for Blacks who attended desegregated schools, his findings were used as part of the scientific rationale for school desegregation—a system-changing reform of the late 1960s and 1970s. Policymakers developed integration plans, many of which included programs to develop positive relationships within integrated schools. But Coleman's study was also used to provide political and scientific cover for those who resisted increasing resources for desegregating schools—either because they sought to keep education spending low or because they wished for desegregation to fail. That misuse of the report undermined the civil rights victory that Coleman hoped for because it reinforced existing beliefs that schools had no control over the factors that mattered most for achievement, namely, a family's race and wealth.[16]

By the 1980s, systemic reform policies aimed at promoting equity largely abandoned desegregation to focus on promoting "effective schools" within low-income communities of color. In contrast to Coleman's finding about the positive impact of desegregated schools, "effective schools" policies emphasized changing the culture of segregated schools by establishing high expectations ("all children can learn"), a focus on academics, strong leadership, and so on— rather than ensuring racial integration and equitable distribution of high-quality resources and opportunities to learn.

Schools as Markets

By the late 1990s, the United States' overall prosperity was soaring again, with at least some credit due to the deft responses among U.S. businesses using systems theories to improve. Many bureaucratic organizational structures had been replaced by more flexible staffing, patterns of production, and labor markets. Specialization, or "niche" marketing, had replaced some large-scale mass production. At the same time, the accelerated speed at which information, goods, and people could travel was allowing small-scale enterprises and foreign producers to compete alongside large centralized U.S.-based businesses.

These new conditions put new pressures on companies. To lower costs and increase profits, companies began relying on more fluid job descriptions and replacing salaried employees with temporary and/or nonunion workers. Seeking to beat the global competition with quicker turn-around times and decreased labor costs, many industries adopted new employment practices, such as downsizing to smaller workforces and outsourcing or contracting portions of their production to foreign manufacturers or businesses that paid lower wages. They began relocating to "friendlier" business climates—states and countries with fewer regulations, lower taxes, weaker workers' unions, and minimal environmental restrictions.

These trends continue today and reflect the increasingly mainstream view, especially prevalent among conservatives and members of the business community, that secure jobs, wage controls, and other regulations constrain U.S. businesses' ability to be innovative or compete successfully in a global marketplace. Increasingly "free-market" forces are considered the engines of excellence and economic prosperity through increased competitiveness, cost savings, and an explosion of choices among goods and services. This neoliberal view has become increasingly dominant, even as critics call attention to the downsides of market forces—particularly for workers whose jobs are less secure, whose employers are less likely to provide health insurance and pension benefits, and whose interests are less likely to be represented by labor unions.

PRESS FOR AN EDUCATIONAL MARKETPLACE

As sketched earlier, the interests of the business community and other elites—those with economic means and connections to people of significant government power—have always influenced decisions about who U.S. schools should educate and how. They've pressed over the past 100 years for schools to mimic successful industry and business practices. So, it's not surprising that many such influencers now argue that free-market strategies would generate much-needed school improvement. In the last few decades, many philanthropic and advocacy groups have joined in shaping public discourse and public policy favoring education marketplaces.

Overwhelmingly, private interests have galvanized in support of market-based education policies. Wealthy business leaders such as real estate mogul Eli Broad, Walmart's Sam Walton, and media giant and three-term New York City mayor Michael Bloomberg have acquired enormous influence in shaping education policy. Also greatly influential have been the advocacy and money of a whole generation of new billionaires led by Microsoft founder Bill Gates and a host of others. The reforms they advance emphasize parent choice, competition among schools for student enrollment, opening up public school management to the private sector, and limiting teacher tenure and the role of teachers' unions. Generally, these reforms have favored top-down or corporate control rather than public regulation, which they argue inhibits innovation, as well as effectiveness, efficiency, and equity.

Nonprofit advocacy organizations (and some political action committees) such as Stand for Children, the 50-State Campaign for Achievement Now (50CAN), Democrats for Education Reform (DFER), and the Foundation for Excellence in Education (FEE) routinely solicit financial contributions—many from financial and corporate entities—to promote the proliferation of market-based reforms. With branches in states around the country, these well-funded groups and others like them exercise increasing sway over education policymaking, dwarfing the influence of less well-endowed small local groups and even large national ones like the Parent Teacher Association. Historian Diane Ravitch argues that this trend "threatens to destroy public education" by exposing it unduly to "the whim of entrepreneurs and financiers."[17]

MARKET-BASED REFORMS

As today's policymakers seek cures for low-achieving schools, they increasingly look to market-based strategies that business and industry have used to maximize profitability and efficiency. Businesses, thought to thrive under fewest regulations, balance their obligations to broad social principles (equal opportunity, social justice, etc.) with their drive to maximize growth and profit. Likewise, deregulation and local control are thought to free schools from the constraints of centralized bureaucracy and open up possibilities for innovative practice. Other business strategies include accountability for productivity (with standardized test scores as the "bottom line"), niche marketing and choice, competition, and the adding of new markets through increased privatization. These strategies and the policies that support them advance the idea that the lowest-performing public schools should "go out of business" if they don't do well on externally set standards and traditional measures of achievement in comparison with other schools. Their test score results, it follows, should be made public so that "customers"—parents and students—can choose another school if the one assigned doesn't measure up.

Private and public charter schools have become increasingly salient in market-based education policy debates. Charter school advocates want to replace much of the government-run public school system, which they see as an overly regulated monopoly, with a market system that would allow private and charter schools to compete with traditional schools. Some advocates, including Secretary of Education Betsy DeVos and other appointees in the Trump administration, want voucher or tax-credit plans where the government's financial support for schooling goes directly to students, who can then enroll in the school of their choice—public or private. They also see hope in the growing number of charter schools that operate outside the regulations imposed by many school district and state policies. Their advocates believe that freedom from central authority will foster healthy competition and increase the quality of all schools. Many are also unabashed advocates for sectarian agendas that include fundamentalist religious ideologies, biblically based science, "traditional" marriage and gender assignments, and so forth. The logic is that school entrepreneurs can appeal to niche interests unconstrained by public schools' civic mission of forging inclusiveness among diverse populations.

The marketplace theory behind these programs (to be sure, there are also other ways that people defend them) is that the most successful will thrive, and those that do a poor job will disappear. Skeptics point out, however, that in the traditional marketplace of goods and services, harmful or wasteful products do not necessarily disappear or improve but are often the most popular.

Proponents have great confidence that this "rational-choice" process will bring equity to students in low-income communities currently underserved by public schools. However, other social theorists point out that the basis for school choice is a local and individual matter—and not always what market advocates would consider to be rational. For example, some parents might choose to send their children to a neighborhood school even though its test score averages are low and its resources limited. For these parents, having their children close to home instead of attending school in an unfamiliar neighborhood may be rational. Other parents might choose to send their children across town, in part because that is where the mayor's daughter attends—an informal indicator, perhaps, of the school's quality. Still others might be wooed to a particular school on the basis of "advertising"—what the school promises to provide children vis-à-vis other available options. Depending on the depth, accuracy, and accessibility of the information made available to them, parents' decisions about where to send their children to school might seem on the surface more or less rational.[18]

As Ravitch and others argue, the most significant change that market ideas bring to education is to distance schools from their connection to the tradition of common public schools. There have always been ideological opponents to the very concept and institution of a "public" school system, but the new confidence in competition and market forces is a relatively recent phenomenon—one that mirrors changes in the economic sector.

MARKET IDEAS, NCLB, AND ESSA

Free-market ideas are at work in current federal and state policies. NCLB, for example, required schools to document their productivity with large-scale testing, publish the results, compete with private providers of supplemental services when schools didn't score well, and face the consequences that come with providing families the choice to find better schools for their children. ESSA maintains most of these policies.

Neither law insists that schools provide adequate and necessary resources, conditions, and opportunities for learning. Instead, both rely on high-stakes tests and school-rating systems to create competitiveness among schools and to motivate individual teachers and students to teach better and study harder in order to gain rewards and avoid sanctions, such as being closed or subjected to an externally developed "turnaround" plan. Under NCLB, parents in schools that failed to meet their test score targets could use the federal funding to purchase tutoring services, either from the school or from private companies. If that didn't raise test scores sufficiently, parents could send their children to a more successful school. Eventually, failing schools could be taken over by the state, turned into charter schools, and/or "reconstituted" by removing the current administrators and teachers and replacing them with new staff. Market ideas were also evident in the Race to the Top initiative that was part of the recession stimulus package. Race to the Top not only was conceived as a competition among states but also encouraged states to use market-based reforms, such as increasing the number of charter schools.

EQUITY AND MARKET-BASED EDUCATION REFORM

Viewing schools through the lens of a market economy, choice and competition are the mechanisms for ensuring equity. The rationale is as follows: When public school systems assign students to attend specific public schools, those schools are guaranteed their "customers." With no other schools competing for their students, these schools feel little pressure to be excellent. Thus, families whose children are assigned to bad schools have only one choice: "buy" their way out in one of two expensive ways. They can pay the tuition and send their children to private schools, or they can buy a house in a neighborhood with a better school. This situation creates inequities because the families of low-income students (many of whom are also students of color) can't afford to buy their way out of bad schools.

When the Trump administration took office in 2017, Secretary of Education Betsy DeVos and others advanced voucher and choice policies as the best way to equalize students' chances to attend good schools. Advocates of publicly funded vouchers or tax credits that enable parents to pay the tuition at private schools touted them as allowing low-income parents to have the same choices as high-income parents, including choices beyond the public school system.

The choice and voucher approach to ensuring equitable access to good schools fails on several counts. Research on voucher programs consistently finds that students using vouchers to attend private schools do no better (and sometimes worse) than their peers who remain in the public system.[19] Moreover, theories of choice as an avenue to quality and equity make clear that choosers must be fully informed in order to make good choices. Unfortunately, in the absence of accountability and transparency in public reporting about schools' resources and learning conditions, test scores provide parents with very limited information with which to determine the "better" schools. Additionally, social justice advocates argue that the burden of finding a good school should not be placed on families, and insist instead that policymakers must ensure that *every* school provides students with high-quality education.

PUSHBACK AGAINST CHARTERS, CHOICE, AND PRIVATIZATION

Over the past several years, pushback against market reforms has accelerated, even as advocacy for them has increased. Criticism has been fueled by evidence that charters overall have failed to create higher-quality schools, raise student achievement, and serve as models of innovative practice for the rest of the public system, as was originally promised. In fact, some—including a number of for-profit virtual charters and homeschooling charters—have been exposed for extremely low academic quality, inadequate accountability for such basic things as student attendance, and profiteering.[20] Moreover, numerous charters have failed to play by rules of fairness—for example, limiting access for students learning English as a second language, and encouraging (or insisting) that challenging students transfer to other schools.[21] Charters have also been found to increase racial segregation in many locales.[22] And, as the number of charters has grown, they are increasingly seen as threatening the viability of the regular school system by reducing funding to neighborhood schools and increasing taxpayers' burdens as private charter managers push administrative costs out of control.[23]

In response to such concerns, civil rights groups and teachers' unions have adopted firm stances against charter school abuses and have called for a charter school moratorium. In the summer of 2017, the National Education Association adopted a forceful statement in support of state and local efforts to limit charter growth, increase charter accountability, and slow the diversion of resources from neighborhood public schools to charters. The statement lays out three criteria that charters must meet; it states that charter schools must

- be authorized and held accountable by the local school board as only a local, democratically accountable authorizing entity can ensure that a charter is actually needed to meet student needs in a way that other alternatives available to the district could not, and only a local authorizer can monitor charter performance on an ongoing basis to ensure accountability and spread charter innovations to other public schools;

- demonstrate that it is necessary to meet the needs of the students in the district, and meet those needs in a manner that improves the local public school system; and
- comply with the same basic safeguards as other public schools, including open meetings and public records laws, prohibitions against for-profit operations or profiteering, and the same civil rights, employment, labor, health and safety laws, and staff qualification and certification requirements as other public schools.[24]

This statement by the National Education Association echoed concerns expressed in the NAACP's 2016 resolution protesting charter school harms. The resolution called for a nationwide moratorium on charter schools until they are subject to the same accountability requirements as traditional public schools and develop a funding system that does not hurt other schools. It also calls for charter schools to end harsh discipline practices that push students out and selection practices that segregate high-performing children from others.[25]

Diane Ravitch, a former supporter of charter schools, in 2016 summed up as follows the strong and principled opposition that many other critics share:

Despite the absence of any advantages and the presence of scandals, frauds, and discrimination, more and more states are falling victim to the false promise of "school choice." As one Florida superintendent explained it to me, charters enable parents to keep their children away from "those children." Both charters and vouchers increase racial segregation, religious segregation, and economic segregation. These trends are ominous for our democracy.[26]

Concept Table 4.2 provides a summary of how efforts to make schools function like economic enterprises have shaped U.S. educational policy.

Concept Table 4.2 Making Schools Work Like Economic Enterprises

Policy assumption	Schools as factories	Schools as well-managed corporations	Schools as markets
Underlying theory	Scientific management	Systems theory	Free-market economics
How to maximize effectiveness	• Structure school as linear sequence of standardized and scientifically determined procedures that transform students' "raw material" into responsible citizens and good workers.	• Organize schools into well-aligned and coordinated systems, where the whole is more than the sum of the parts. • Promote organizational learning.	• Set goals. • Deregulate schooling processes. • Provide good information about schools' results. • Allow families to choose their schools to infuse competition into the system.
How to maximize efficiency	• Divide the system into small, manageable parts; grade levels; subject areas; ability groups. • Train specialists in the best practices for each part.	• Set standards, provide adequate resources and ample local flexibility, and hold educators accountable for results.	• Provide results-based incentives and sanctions to motivate schools and students.
How to achieve equity	• Match students to classes/ programs according to their abilities and needs, thereby providing for all an equal opportunity for the education that best suits them.	• Provide the supports and resources for all students to meet the same high standards, including additional supports for those with greater needs.	• Hold schools accountable for reducing gaps in achievement test scores. • Allow low-income families to leave low-performing schools.

Effects of Current Policies and Laws on Students, Schools, and Teachers

The whole point of education policy is to ensure that schools meet society's goals effectively, efficiently, and equitably. Of course, policies do not accomplish these goals directly, but only through their effects on educators and students. The most dominant current policies are high-stakes test-based accountability policies. They have been the key driver of NCLB, and will remain powerful under ESSA, albeit softened somewhat by the inclusion of other indicators. We turn now to looking at how these policies impact teachers and students in today's schools. We pay particular attention to how these policies affect teachers who believe schools should bring social justice to those most disadvantaged by U.S. society.

Accountability for Results: Large-Scale Tests and High Stakes

In the past two decades, the business concept of "accountability for results" has become enormously popular as an education policy strategy. Today, results-based accountability has taken the form of policies requiring schools to administer large-scale achievement tests and attaching high stakes to students' performance on those tests. In the case of students, such tests can determine their chances for promotion, graduation, or preparation for college. In the case of schools, student scores can determine reputation, funding, or even whether the school stays open. Both the federal government and many states have adopted high-stakes test-based accountability policies.

The underlying idea of accountability for results comes out of systems-theory management. In the case of education, information from large-scale achievement tests provides feedback that educators and policymakers can use in their efforts to continually improve their performance and meet standards. However, high-stakes accountability policies also fit with the market-based assumption (mostly wrongheaded, in our view) that the problem of low and unequal achievement is attributable primarily to the lack of motivation exhibited by students, teachers, school districts, and parents in a system with no competition or consequences. The theory is that if test scores have high-stakes consequences, educators and students will be motivated to perform well in order to reap rewards or avoid punishing sanctions. Such policies also fit well with efforts to create an educational marketplace with parental choice, as market reformers assume that test scores provide essential information about school quality that parents can use to guide their choices.

Advocates also claim that accountability for results makes the system more equitable since schools must hold all students to the same high standards and demonstrate results for vulnerable groups (low-income students, students designated English Learners, etc.), ending what former president George W. Bush's administration called the "soft bigotry of low expectations."[27] Unfortunately, this motivational perspective has led or allowed officials to ignore serious inadequacies and inequalities in resources, conditions, and capacity. Indeed, some of the strongest supporters of a market view of schooling claim that there are now (or will be very shortly) enough resources and investment in the system to deliver an education to all students, once high-stakes testing has leveraged sufficient motivation.

High Stakes for Students

As we describe in Chapter 7, educators have long relied on test results as a source of information to help them make important decisions about students—determining whether they should be placed in an advanced class or program, promoted to the next grade, designated for special education, classified as an English Learner, admitted to college, and, in some cases, gifted with scholarship money. However, some of today's high-stakes testing policies make students' performance on a test the *only* factor in very important decisions, such as grade promotion, course placement, and high school graduation.

GRADE PROMOTION AND COURSE PLACEMENT

Today, states and school districts increasingly use standardized tests as the basis on which students are promoted into higher grades. For example, under Texas's Student Success Initiative, students in grades 5 and 8 are required to pass the State of Texas Assessments of Academic Readiness (STAAR) in reading and mathematics in order to meet grade promotion requirements. In Florida, students in third grade must pass the Florida Comprehensive Assessment Test (FCAT) to be promoted to fourth grade. Some local school districts in Florida use the tests to determine promotion at other grade levels, as well. Texas and Florida policymakers, like those in fourteen other states (as of 2017) with mandatory retention policies, hope such policies will stop the practice of social promotion and motivate schools, teachers, and students to make greater efforts to reach grade-level proficiency.

Social promotion means that students move from one grade to another with others of their age, regardless of their achievement. Policymakers often point to social promotion as an irresponsible education practice, and in 1999, the Clinton administration announced that it was time to end it. Actually, few school systems have social promotion as an explicit policy, and few educators think it's a good idea. Yet, in most bureaucratic and inflexible schools, the only alternative—grade retention—may be even worse. Neither social promotion nor grade retention identifies or addresses the underlying problems that prevent students from learning. And considerable research shows that grade retention *increases* the likelihood that students will drop out of school, perhaps because of the stigma associated with being older than their classmates.

Such tests oftentimes determine not only promotion but placement into different courses or tracks, particularly at the secondary level. Importantly, once such decisions are made, students tend to be locked in, with little if any power to move into different classes or tracks. Thus, as with promotion, such decisions have long-term implications for students—a topic we discuss in more detail in Chapter 10.

The most educationally sound policies do not base decisions about social promotion, grade retention, or course placements on single high-stakes tests. Rather, they provide students with the supports and conditions they need to learn and be successful. FairTest, an advocacy organization that monitors the use of tests across the nation, recommends the alternatives to high-stakes testing listed in Focal Point 4.1. Coming chapters—especially those in Part II: The Practice of Teaching to Change the World—delve more deeply into the supports and conditions that teachers and schools can put in place to ensure that all students receive educationally sound learning experiences.

Focal Point 4.1
Policy Alternatives to High-Stakes Testing
for Grade Promotion

Both social promotion and grade retention do a grave disservice to students. Both fail to ensure that all students acquire the educational skills and knowledge they need to succeed in school and beyond. However, there are alternative methods that provide help to students who need it before they are passed and prevent students from being harmed by retention. Some of these include:

- Targeted supports and services that are available to students when they need them, which may include tutoring, after-school programs, Saturday classes, or other support services. These services need to be studied to ensure that they are effective in enabling students at risk to catch up and that they are not merely test coaching programs.
- Professional development for teachers to enable them to address a broader range of diverse student needs. Research shows that teachers are the single most important factor to student success.
- Mixed-age classrooms where students at different levels work together on common problems.
- Continuous relationships with teachers. Research has shown that students do better in school when their teachers know them well and when they work with the same teacher for two or more years.
- Developing a variety of assessment skills and tools for classroom use (such as performances and portfolios) to help teachers and parents assess what students are learning, to find gaps, and to address problems immediately. High-quality classroom assessment used to help each child has been shown to be a powerful tool for improving student learning.

Source: FairTest, http://fairtest.org/arn/retenfct.htm.

HIGH STAKES FOR ENGLISH LEARNERS

It is also common for schools and districts to rely on high-stakes assessments to make important decisions about the educational pathways of students they identify as English Learners. As that population grows nationwide, such practices potentially imperil educational opportunity for increasing numbers of U.S. schoolchildren.[28]

A variety of high-stakes tests influence whether students deemed English Learners gain access to grade-level curriculum or remain in remedial classes. Families of newly enrolled students, for example, are expected to complete a home language survey, indicating which languages are spoken in the home. Results from the survey typically determine which students require further testing. For example, federal law requires states to administer screening (or placement) exams to incoming students who speak languages other than English at home. Some states use state-specific assessments; for example, California uses the California English Language Development Test (CELDT), while Arizona administers the Arizona English Language Learner Assessment

(AZELLA). Other states administer tests developed for use across contexts and used by more than thirty states.

Such tests *can* provide useful information about students' home language practices—information that districts and schools can use to ensure students' strengths are recognized and their needs are met. However, as with other high-stakes tests, districts and schools frequently use the resulting information to limit students' access to academic content. In some states, particularly places like Arizona where bilingual education has been outlawed, students whose scores designate them as English Learners are placed automatically in structured English-immersion classes, where they are expected to learn English through intensive English instruction, absent a focus on academic content.

These approaches are problematic for various reasons. Expecting students to learn English without simultaneously learning content puts them at a double disadvantage: It delays their exposure to the language they need to understand disciplinary content, and it delays their exposure to that content, making it unlikely that they will catch up to their native English-speaking peers, who gain access to such content much earlier in their schooling. Indeed, research indicates that authentic and effective language teaching and learning must occur in *conjunction* with—not separate from, or as a precondition for—teaching and learning academic content.

Once students are labeled "English Learners," schools also administer language proficiency tests, typically on an annual basis. Results indicate what "level" of English proficiency students have attained and inform high-stakes decisions such as class placement, program placement (e.g., bilingual, Structured English Immersion, English Only), and reclassification from English Learner to Fluent English Proficient.

In addition, such students are required to take the same standards-based standardized tests as their peers. As mentioned earlier, because such tests are typically administered only in English, they often measure English language proficiency as much or more than they measure anything else, and thus fail to assess students' progress vis-à-vis the standards. Although these validity problems are increasingly recognized by the public and by mainstream testing entities, such as ETS, scores continue to factor (inaccurately) into schools' performance rankings.[29]

While test results may appear official and therefore accurate, schools and teachers have an important role to play when it comes to acting on them. This is crucial given how racial and language ideologies intersect in test design and in the interpretation of results. For example, it's fairly common for schools to assume that students from homes where Spanish is spoken are English Learners, when many are actually *simultaneous bilinguals*, meaning they come to school speaking two languages, such as Spanish *and* English. These deficit-laden determinations can lead schools to push students into courses or programs erroneously, shunting them away from learning experiences better tailored to their actual needs. These determinations additionally perpetuate the embrace of language separation models within dual language programs, despite growing evidence that such models fail to recognize or build on the authentic languaging practices of bilinguals. Teachers can act as advocates for students just by looking beyond test scores and making efforts to get to know students and their language backgrounds and practices on a deeper level.

GRADUATION OR "EXIT" EXAMS

The most visible, and perhaps most consequential, high-stakes testing policies are those that make high school graduation contingent on passing tests. These tests are used to determine whether high school seniors who have met all their high school's graduation requirements will be awarded diplomas. As in the case of other high-stakes testing policies, graduation tests reflect a lack of trust in schools, teachers, and students to meet high standards without significant outside pressure. Advocates for the high-stakes tests often argue that diplomas must "mean something" and that tests prove to the public and to employers that graduates have mastered state-prescribed knowledge and skills.

During the 1990s and 2000s, so-called exit exams were very popular in state policies. But the number of states requiring them has shrunk by half over the past few years. Fourteen states have (or plan to have) such tests in place for the graduating class of 2017; this number is down from a high of twenty-seven states in 2010, when 74 percent of U.S. public school students, including 84 percent of students designated English Learners, 83 percent of students of color, and 78 percent of low-income students, had to pass an exit exam in order to receive their high school diplomas.[30]

Notably, the pass rates of those designated as English Learners and students with educational disabilities were far below those of other students. This is not surprising, because the tests are in English only and thus conflate students' language abilities with their content knowledge. Likewise, few states make testing accommodations for students with special needs. African American and Latinx students, who generally receive fewer educational resources and opportunities than other students, also failed the tests at higher rates.

In California, for example, the highest rates of exit exam failure occurred for students at schools with shortages of qualified teachers and other resource problems.[31] Thus, the exam's underlying premises—that it motivates students and teachers to try harder, and preserves the meaning and value of the diploma—have been highly questionable, and its very administration has proven patently unfair to students whose schools do not provide meaningful opportunity to learn the tested material. Certainly, even if trust in schools is not present or warranted, there are many more just and productive ways to address that problem than unjustly and unproductively punishing students whom the school system has failed.

Today, there is increasing interest in having high school students also pass social studies or civics tests. As of 2017, fifteen states required students to pass a social studies or civics test to graduate.[32] And since ESSA permits academic indicators beyond tests in reading and mathematics, several other states may opt to include such test scores in their accountability systems.

Overall, a number of prominent researchers believe that there is no research evidence to justify high-stakes graduation tests as a means for increasing achievement.[33] Some research on mandated civics exams does show that they can increase students' knowledge of basic facts, but they show little effect on students' later civic participation.[34] It's hard to say that the slim benefits of these tests outweigh the costs of denying diplomas to students who don't earn a passing score. And as we explain next, there are multiple other reasons for not using tests to make high-stakes decisions about students.

Educators in America's public schools obviously are under tremendous pressure to improve their students' scores on whatever tests their states use for accountability purposes. With few exceptions, however, the assessments many states have chosen to implement are national standardized achievement tests or state-developed standards-based tests. As we noted in Chapter 3, many states that had agreed to participate in the federally funded, CCSS-aligned tests that were developed by two state consortia—PARCC and Smarter Balanced—have since retracted their agreement to participate.

Over the past few years, adverse classroom consequences have emerged in states where such tests are used with high stakes attached. In Focal Point 4.2, assessment expert W. James Popham sums up the high instructional price that schools are paying as a consequence of policymakers' pursuit of school improvement via attaching high-stakes consequences to large-scale tests. Popham's sobering observations have been documented in other research.[35]

Focal Point 4.2
The Negative Effects of High-Stakes Testing
on Curriculum and Teaching

- *Curricular Reductionism:* In an effort to boost their students' test scores, many teachers jettison curricular content that—albeit important—is not apt to be covered on an upcoming test. As a result, students end up educationally shortchanged.
- *Excessive Drilling:* Because it is essentially impossible to raise students' scores on instructionally insensitive tests, many teachers—in desperation—require seemingly endless practice with items similar to those on an approaching test. This drilling often stamps out any genuine joy students might (and should) experience while they learn.
- *Modeled Dishonesty:* Some teachers, frustrated by pressure to raise scores on tests deliberately designed to preclude such score raising, may be tempted to adopt unethical practices during test administration or scoring. This teaches students that when the stakes are high enough, it's OK to cheat—a lesson that should never be taught.

These three negative consequences of using instructionally insensitive standardized tests to measure learning, taken together, make it clear that today's widespread method of judging schools by test scores does more than lead to invalid evaluations. Beyond that, such tests can dramatically lower the quality of education.

Source: W. James Popham, "F Is for Assessment," 2005, www.edutopia.org/assessment/.

The civil rights community has also raised serious legal questions about whether high-stakes testing denies educational opportunity to students based on their race, national origin, sex, or disability. The NAACP Legal Defense Fund, MALDEF (Mexican American Legal Defense and Education Fund), and dozens of other civil rights organizations have made easing the impact of high-stakes tests on minoritized students a priority. In 1999, the Office of Civil Rights drafted a resource guide that laid out some of the professional and legal standards for educators and policymakers.

The guide raises legal principles articulated in the Fourteenth Amendment to the Constitution and in federal statutes and regulations—namely, that intentional discrimination is prohibited, as are programs with a discriminatory, disparate impact. Additionally, the guide discusses the legal obligation to provide for the special needs of those designated as English Learners and students with disabilities, and the need to ensure Fifth Amendment due process rights for all students subjected to high-stakes testing decisions. The guide makes clear that testing can advance learning and help safeguard educational opportunity. However, it insists that good educational results are compatible with the enforcement of principles of nondiscrimination.

Unfortunately, this useful document has never been distributed. When the George W. Bush administration took office in 2001, the Office of Civil Rights placed the guide into a new category on its website—"archival file retained for historical purposes"; it remains there today. Although this does not mean that the document will never see the light of day, it adds additional evidence about just how political the testing of students has become. As with opportunity-to-learn standards, the government resists placing into policy any measure that might support advocates who decide to sue the government.

High Stakes for Schools

High-stakes testing policies for schools are those that use students' test scores to label schools "good" or "bad" relative to other schools or to levy sanctions against schools if they don't show improvement. Under NCLB, every school has an achievement test score target and, in the case of high schools, a graduation rate target that it must meet each year in order to satisfy the law's requirement for adequate yearly progress. As we explained earlier in this chapter, ESSA maintains this approach, but allows states some latitude in determining what indicators to use to target schools that need improvement. As with NCLB, ESSA requires states to intervene in the bottom 5 percent of schools, but, here too, states have more discretion than under NCLB. Although the federal government has systematically avoided using the word *failing* to describe these schools, that is how most of the public and most educators interpret the label of "in need of improvement."[36]

Advocates of high-stakes tests apply naive behavioral theory to motivate hard work, attentive learning, and better teaching. As explained elsewhere, rewards and punishments might work in the very short term for very discrete tasks. But they are not viable approaches for changing complex systems and ensuring worthwhile learning. If they were, teaching and parenting would be wonderfully easy so long as there were plenty of spankings and ice cream on hand. The next section details some of the considerable evidence that high-stakes tests have negative effects on the teaching and learning climate—factors that really do matter—at those schools where students have a history of unequal opportunities and low achievement.

THE PRESUMPTION OF ADEQUATE RESOURCES

If a lack of resources, appropriate supplementary help, or qualified teachers diminishes student performance, it makes no sense to believe that a test will motivate students to overcome these educational constraints. Accounts shared by Kimberly Min and Mauro Bautista, both

of whom teach in schools designated as "low performing," illustrate the situation well. Kimberly reports:

> When people ask me why I think my school is low performing, I can rattle off a list of reasons: lack of resources (I have worked without textbooks and with broken chairs and broken desks. Last year a desk collapsed on two students who were writing, and it was reported to the office. It took the office three days to respond); lack of supplies (there is a shortage of supplies, and many teachers have to purchase their own materials. Teachers cannot rely on the school to have the items that they need to teach); lack of teacher training and professional development (teachers sign in at meetings and sign out, and you are considered "professionally developed"); lack of this and that. All these things are true, but I think that people do not want to acknowledge an underlying cause for these deficiencies: We still operate in a racist school system where students of color are not only neglected but set up to fail. The test is designed to distinguish high-performing from low-performing schools—not to give students the best possible education.
>
> The educational system must change so that schools receive needed resources before second language learners, bilingual students, and others perceive themselves to be low-performing individuals.
>
> —Kimberly Min
> Third-grade teacher

Mauro's report is similar, even though his school has made considerable test score gains:

> Yes, my school is a low-performing school, but students have shown dramatic improvement over the last three years. The current administration has emphasized rigor in the curriculum, has invested funds in extracurricular programs (such as drama, sports, music, art), and sometimes has deviated from district mandates if we feel the mandates do not help students. We still face important challenges. One, we continue to have a high teacher turnover rate. Thus, each year we have inexperienced teachers. At times we lose teachers in the middle of the year, and thus our students have long-term subs. Two, we continue to struggle with low expectations. We say we have high expectations, but as soon as there is a challenge, we are quick to place blame on the students instead of reflecting on our own practices. Three, we continue to struggle with low parent involvement. Four, classroom instruction continues to rely too heavily on lecturing, textbooks, and individual and silent work.
>
> —Mauro Bautista
> Middle-school bilingual education coordinator

CURRICULAR DISTORTION AND DRILLING

Teachers have little control over test-based accountability policies, but they certainly feel their effects—both in their classrooms and in their public image. For example, pressure to raise test scores can influence teachers, principals, and school districts to favor subjects that are tested (e.g., mathematics and English/language arts or civics), while pulling resources and attention away from subjects that are not tested (e.g., science, foreign language, and art). (See Focal Point 4.2.) In this way, a *testing* policy decision intended for accountability purposes can become a *curriculum* policy that determines what students learn, not just how their learning gets assessed.

Some groups of students are much more likely to have their curriculum distorted in this way: students attending schools labeled "low performing," students who are learning English as a second language, students from poor families, students with various disabilities, and students of color. A curriculum driven by eventual test performance oftentimes leads to the adoption of prepackaged, test-aligned lessons that emphasize discrete facts and skills. It can also lead educators to favor drills and memorization over critical thinking and conceptual understanding. Such "teaching to the test" violates good teaching, generally, and contradicts what we know about teaching minoritized youth. For example, elementary school teacher Magda Gonzales describes how high-stakes accountability tests influence her work with students.

> My students are very smart; they are problem solvers and critical thinkers. They use their Spanish when they speak and write, and they express their thoughts with meaning and value. It infuriates and frustrates me that standardized assessments step in the path of the exciting, high-level critical thinking skills my students have acquired. I will continue to teach my students strategies for taking these tests, but I will also continue to struggle to find ways to incorporate a safe, multicultural learning experience for them.
>
> —Magda Gonzales
> First-year teacher, grades 3 and 4

DISHONESTY

Well-publicized reports from Texas, New York, and Atlanta suggest that James Popham's third consequence—dishonesty—is occurring on a fairly large scale. In Texas, for example, state investigators revealed that educators at twelve Houston high schools and four middle schools had altered students' records to hide the fact that they had dropped out of school. At the time (the early 2000s), Houston was using "performance contracting" to provide school administrators with incentives that would spur higher productivity in Houston schools. Under performance contracting, principals forfeited job security for higher pay; in other words, principals could lose their jobs—no questions asked—if they didn't reach measurable objectives, including raising test scores and lowering dropout rates. The pressure on Houston educators to fudge the numbers was great, and they did.

Similarly, in July 2003, investigators for the *New York Times* found that thousands of the city's lowest-achieving students were being pushed out by officials desperate to make their schools look good on the state's graduation tests. After "encouraging" students who were likely to fail to leave school, the educators covered their tracks by falsely reporting that the students had "transferred to another educational setting." The *Times* concluded that, faced with low graduation rates followed by loss of some federal funding, schools succumbed to the temptation and tried to make their results look good by getting rid of low performers.[37]

Although these early scandals sent school officials a strong message on the risks of cheating, nothing has changed to lessen the illogic or pressure of trying to motivate excellence with threats of job loss or embarrassment. In one of the saddest cases, a 2011 state investigation into scoring irregularities in Atlanta found "unethical behavior across every level" of the school system. Investigators implicated a total of 178 educators (including 38 principals), 80 of whom reportedly "confessed" to having cheated in some manner, and some of whom had reaped performance-based financial bonuses, while attempting to silence potential whistle-blowers.[38] Several were indicted. One, former Atlanta superintendent Beverly Hall, who always denied any wrongdoing, was too ill with cancer to participate with twelve colleagues in her 2013 trial. She died in 2015. Notably, in 2009, Hall had been named National Superintendent of the Year by the American Association of School Administrators.

BURDEN ON LOW-INCOME COMMUNITIES

Under NCLB, parents in schools that failed to meet their targets two years in a row had the right to transfer their children to more successful schools. ESSA also permits this where the state laws allow it. Thousands of parents requested such transfers, but in many cities there were simply no other schools that could or would take their children. In Chicago, for example, only 500 spaces were available for the 200,000 students eligible for transfers in 2004.[39]

This policy falls short because it gives parents a sequence of responsibilities that are all but impossible to fulfill. First, parents must monitor whether or not their child's school has been labeled as "in need of improvement." Next, they must decide if good alternatives exist and are realistic for their family. Then, should they decide to switch, they must negotiate school bureaucracies to effect a transfer to a school that is likely to be farther away from home, ensure reliable transportation, and subject their children to the perhaps wrenching experience of leaving a familiar environment and friends.

School closures also place a disproportionate burden on low-income communities. To some, closing low-performing schools that have failed to make adequate test score improvements multiple years in a row may seem like common sense. However, social justice advocates argue that even struggling schools often represent key hubs of community interaction, and that failure to meet test score targets signals the need for more and different supports and services rather than eliminating one of the community's key resources.

School closures have generated vigorous debate in urban centers where educators, parents, and community members often disagree with districts' decisions about which schools to close and why. Even those who recognize the urgent need for improvement acknowledge that closing schools can put students at greater risk of educational, social, emotional, and physical harm by fracturing community ties and critical relationships between educators and students.

According to Jitu Brown, a community organizer from Chicago's Southside, school closures in his community led to increased levels of school violence and student dropouts, as surviving schools struggled to absorb new students and students struggled to renegotiate everything from new routes to school to new relationships with peers and teachers.[40] Organizers like Brown also argue that closures often seem to benefit private interests—by giving charter organizations access to "closed" public schools and displacing long-term low-income residents from their homes in newly gentrified communities.

Vouchers or school closures might work well for parents and students who have the financial means, knowledge, skills, and power to take advantage of available options, as well as to participate effectively in school board elections, local decision-making councils, and other avenues for civic involvement. But students who have the greatest need for better school opportunities are usually those least likely to benefit. Even when low-income families are given the "choice" to leave a failing school, better choices are available for only a few.[41]

THE END RESULT OF HIGH-STAKES TESTS FOR SCHOOLS

As we noted earlier in the chapter, the Obama administration issued waivers from NCLB's draconian policies in order to avoid a tsunami of failing schools in every state, and ESSA has modified those policies significantly.[42] Analysts had predicted that by 2014, 99 percent of California schools and 80 percent of Minnesota schools would be labeled as failing under NCLB.[43] Equally grim predictions were made for Massachusetts, Connecticut, Kentucky, Illinois, Indiana, Michigan, Ohio, and Wisconsin.[44] No state was expected to escape.

The impending disaster wouldn't result from the fact that students are incapable of learning or that schools can't help them learn. What we report throughout this book provides evidence that they *can* learn and, under the right circumstances, *will* learn well. Rather, the disaster was an inevitable result of problems embedded in the high stakes that NCLB imposed. Of course, if high standards and high-stakes accountability tests were accompanied by an infusion of new resources into schools and into the social and physical supports that children need outside of school (health care, decent housing, jobs for their parents, etc.), such projections would not be so grim.

The use of test-driven high-stakes policies has brought an outcry of criticism that almost equals the enthusiasm of supporters. The concerns range from the technical (e.g., concerns about tests being inaccurate or biased) to the political (e.g., disagreement that tests will "motivate" improvement) to the philosophical (e.g., objections to an overemphasis on a narrow set of measurable outcomes as opposed to the larger democratic purposes of schooling). This widespread protest in part prompted the changes ushered in by ESSA. However, protests have done little to stem the use of high-stakes testing as the cornerstone of school reform. Educators are left to grapple with the painful consequences for students, schools, and the nation's confidence in public education.

High Stakes for Teachers

As mentioned previously, teachers like those profiled in this book grapple daily with the consequences of high-stakes accountability as they strive for instructional quality and resist pressures to "teach to the test." However, teachers are not just agents of high-stakes accountability; they are also targets of it. Mainstream critiques of teacher tenure—policies that grant teachers permanent contract status after a period of probationary employment and then protect them from being fired without "just cause"—have become more common, alongside efforts to tie teachers' promotion and pay to their performance in the classroom, as discussed below.

By 2015, forty-three states required "objective" measures of student achievement to be included in teacher evaluations, in part because the U.S. Department of Education required this as one condition for receiving a waiver from NCLB. Sixteen states included such measures as the "preponderant criterion" in teacher evaluations, and nineteen states made them a "significant criterion." These states used complex statistical estimates of the impact that teachers have on students' standardized test scores.

Not only is it problematic to use standardized test scores as the metric of teacher quality, because of all that tests *can't* and *don't* convey about teaching and learning, but these tests were not created to evaluate teachers. Using a test for a purpose other than the one for which it was designed automatically compromises its validity, a topic we return to in Chapter 7. In addition, the statistics being computed to estimate teacher impact are notably unreliable.

Nevertheless, some proponents also seek to make teachers' "value-added" scores public. In August 2010, the *Los Angeles Times* published over 6,000 teachers' names and scores, rating teachers on a five-level scale, from "least effective" to "most effective."[45] This prompted a flurry of responses, positive and negative. Many claimed that parents of public school students have a right to these data. Others felt the information should remain private and be used to help teachers improve. Those who knew about the flaws in such measures raised concerns about the whole process.

Certainly, teachers should be held accountable for ensuring that their students learn; neither we nor any of the teachers profiled in this book would argue otherwise. Yet measuring teaching and learning in one narrow way—with annual standardized exams—is problematic for various reasons. (We discuss these reasons, as well as alternative and equitable approaches to assessment, in Chapter 7.)

Yet, despite many scholars' and educators' concerns, current policy trends indicate that this practice may be here to stay. Fortunately, ESSA eliminates the *requirement* for teacher evaluation systems that include such measures of student achievement. However, it does *permit* states and districts to develop and implement such systems.

PAY FOR PERFORMANCE

A related policy development involves merit pay for teachers—paying teachers based on their students' achievement, usually students' standardized test results. Advocates of merit pay claim that the traditional salary scale that rewards teachers for education and years of experience is outdated; teachers should be paid based on performance, they argue. Additionally, they claim that rewarding teachers for high student test scores will motivate them to improve their performance. In the words of Jason Kamras, former Teacher of the Year and currently chief of instructional practice for the District of Columbia public school district, "[w]e want to make great teachers rich."[46]

In alignment with its broad embrace of market-based education reform, the Obama administration supported merit pay for teachers, maintaining that rewarding the best teachers will encourage more talented individuals to begin and remain teaching after graduating from college.[47] We expect that the Trump administration will continue in this vein. Yet, despite the popularity of merit pay among politicians and policymakers, the research on merit pay is mixed on its effectiveness for increasing student test scores.[48] In addition, most teachers do not support merit pay. In keeping with their knowledge of learning theory, many feel that rewarding individuals undermines teamwork and collaboration—key elements of a productive school culture. Such concerns find strength in studies showing the relative effectiveness of merit-pay programs in which teachers work together to earn incentive pay versus those in which individual teachers compete against one another.[49]

As of 2016, although several states have adopted merit-pay policies, only about 5 percent of school districts have implemented them. Florida, however, requires that districts place all new teachers on a performance-pay system that will give teachers deemed highly effective salary increases that outsize those conferred through the traditional contract-bound salary scale.

It is too soon to tell if merit pay will become a foundational element of schooling in the United States. It is, however, probable that the idea, along with evaluating teachers using students' test scores, will remain on the policy agenda in the near future, especially given its overwhelming bipartisan support.

Such policies can seem intimidating at first, but knowledge really *is* power. For new teachers especially, it is critical to stay abreast of policy discussions because the decisions made at the federal and state levels have direct effects on your students, on your school, and on you. The more you know about these policies, the better equipped you will be to navigate and shape them.

Digging Deeper and Tools for Critique

www.routledge.com/cw/teachingtochangetheworld

Notes

1 David Tyack, *The One Best System: A History of American Urban Education* (Cambridge, MA: Harvard University Press, 1974).
2 The Tenth Amendment says that any power not delegated to the federal government in the Constitution belongs to the states.
3 *The Bureau of Education: Its History, Activities, and Organization*, https://archive.org/stream/bureauofeducatio008925mbp/bureauofeducatio008925mbp_djvu.txt.

4 U.S. Department of Education, *The Condition of Education, 2017*, http://nces.ed.gov/programs/coe/.

5 U.S. Department of Education, *Overview: The Federal Role in Education*, www2.ed.gov/about/overview/fed/role.html.

6 Lorraine McDonnell and Richard Elmore, "Getting the Job Done: Alternative Policy Instruments," *Educational Evaluation and Policy Analysis* 9 (Summer 1987): 133–152.

7 Education Law Center, *Is School Funding Fair? A National Report Card, 2010*, www.educationjustice.org; SchoolFunding.Info, *A Project of the Campaign for Educational Equity*, Teachers College, Columbia University, 2017, http://schoolfunding.info/.

8 *Brown v. Board of Education of Topeka*, 493.

9 Lawrence Cremin, *The Transformation of the School: Progressivism in Education 1876–1957* (New York: Knopf, 1961).

10 Cremin, *Transformation*; Tyack, *One Best System*.

11 Peter Drucker, *The Concept of the Corporation* (New York: John Day, 1946); Jack Beatty, *The World According to Peter Drucker* (New York: The Free Press, 1998).

12 Bruce Biddle and David Berliner, *The Manufactured Crisis: Myths, Fraud, and the Attack on America's Public Schools* (New York: Addison-Wesley, 1995).

13 Marshall Smith and Jennifer O'Day, "Systemic School Reform," in *The Politics of Curriculum and Testing, Politics of Education Association Yearbook*, eds. S. H. Fuhrman and B. Malen (London: Taylor & Francis, 1990), 233–267.

14 Peter M. Senge, *The Fifth Discipline: The Art and Practice of the Learning Organization* (London: Random House, 1990), 3.

15 James S. Coleman, *Equality of Educational Opportunity (COLEMAN) Study (EEOS)*, 1966, ICPSR06389-v3 (Ann Arbor, MI: Inter-university Consortium for Political and Social Research [distributor], 2007), https://doi.org/10.3886/ICPSR06389.v3.

16 Ibid.

17 Diane Ravitch, *The Death and Life of the Great American School System* (New York: Basic Books, 2011), 222.

18 Amy Stuart Wells, *Time to Choose: America at the Crossroads of School Choice Policy* (New York: Hill & Wang, 1993).

19 Center on Education Policy, *Keeping Informed About School Vouchers: A Review of Major Developments and Research*, July 2011, www.cep-dc.org/index.cfm?DocumentSubTopicID=16.

20 B. Baker and G. Miron, *The Business of Charter Schooling: Understanding the Policies That Charter Operators Use for Financial Benefit.* (Boulder, CO: National Education Policy Center, 2015), http://nepc.colorado.edu/publication/charter-revenue, retrieved on July 7, 2017.

21 Kevin G. Welner, "The Dirty Dozen: How Charter Schools Influence Student Enrollment," *Teachers College Record*, April 2013. [online], http://www.tcrecord.org ID Number: 17104.

22 Gary Orfield, Jongyeon Ee, Erica Frankenberg, and Genevieve Siegel-Hawley, *"Brown" at 62: School Segregation by Race, Poverty and State* (Los Angeles: UCLA Civil Rights Project/Proyecto Derechos Civiles, May 16, 2016).

23 Valerie Strauss, "Three Big Problems With School 'Choice' That Supporters Don't Like to Talk About," *Washington Post*, May 3, 2017, www.washingtonpost.com/news/answer-sheet/wp/2017/05/03/three-big-problems-with-school-choice-that-supporters-dont-like-to-talk-about/?utm_term=.06f47fefd308.

24 NEA Policy Statement on Charter Schools, Adopted by the 2017 Representative Assembly July 4, 2017. Online at https://ra.nea.org/nea-policy-statement-charter-schools/.

25 Statement Regarding the NAACP's Resolution on a Moratorium on Charter Schools, October 15, 2016, www.NAACP.org/latest/statement-regarding NAACPs-Resolution-Moratorium-charter-schools/.

26 Diane Ravitch, "The South's New Re-segregation Plan: The Koch Brothers, ALEC and the Sneaky Scheme to Undo Brown v Board of Education," *Salon*, April 14, 2016, www.salon.com/2016/04/14/the_souths_new_re_segregation_plan_the_koch_brothers_alec_and_the_sneaky_scheme_to_undo_brown_v_board_of_education/.

27 George W. Bush first used the phrase "soft bigotry of low expectations" during a 2000 campaign speech given to the NAACP. He repeatedly used the phrase over subsequent years as he advocated for particular education policies, including NCLB.

28 Patricia Gándara and Megan Hopkins, eds., *Forbidden Language: English Learners and Restrictive Language Policies* (New York: Teachers College Press, 2011).

29 ETS, "Guidelines for the Assessment of English Language Learners," 2009, www.ets.org/s/about/pdf/ell_guidelines.pdf.

30 Center on Education Policy, *State High School Tests: Exit Exams and Other Assessments*, December 2010, www.cep-dc.org/displayDocument.cfm?DocumentID=34.

31 John Rogers, Jennifer Jellison Holme, and David Silver, "More Questions Than Answers: CAHSEE Results, Opportunity to Learn, and the Class of 2006", *UCLA's IDEA*, 2005.

32 Education Commission of the States, "ESSA: Mapping Opportunities for Civics Education," 2017, www.ecs.org/essa-mapping-opportunities-for-civic-education/.

33 See, for example, Sharon Nichols, Gene Glass, and David Berliner, "High-Stakes Testing and Student Achievement: Problems for the No Child Left Behind Act," *Arizona State University Education Policy Studies Laboratory*, 2005; Angela Valenzuela, *Leaving Children Behind: How "Texas-Style" Accountability Fails Latino Youth* (Albany: State University of New York Press, 2005).

34 David Campbell, "Putting Civics to the Test: The Impact of State-Level Civics Assessments on Civic Knowledge," *American Enterprise Institute*, 2014.

35 Gary Orfield and Mindy L. Kornhaber, eds., *Raising Standards or Raising Barriers? Inequality and High-Stakes Testing in Public Education* (New York: Century Foundation Press, 2001).

36 Public Education Network, *Open to the Public: Speaking Out on "No Child Left Behind,"* 2004, www.publiceducation.org/portals/nclb/hearings/national/Open_to_the_Public.pdf.

37 Tamar Lewin and Jennifer Medina, "To Cut Failure Rate, Schools Shed Students," *New York Times*, July 31, 2003.

38 Kim Severson, "Systematic Cheating Is Found in Atlanta School System," *New York Times*, July 5, 2011, www.nytimes.com/2011/07/06/education/06atlanta.html.

39 Ibid.

40 Since 2001, roughly fifty public schools have been closed city-wide in Chicago; Benjamin Herold, "At Ford Foundation, a Harsh Critique of Urban School Closures," *The Notebook*, March 31, 2011, www. thenotebook.org/blog/113500/ford-foundation-harsh-critique-urban-school-closures/; Rebecca Vevea, "Emanuel's Point Man on School Closings," *Chicago News Cooperative*, November 22, 2011, www. chicagonewscoop.org/emanuels-point-man-on-school-closings-prepares-to-release-list/.

41 Related to this, school lotteries are increasingly impacting middle-class parents as well, particularly in areas where schools are overenrolled and cannot admit all youth in their catchment zones and/or where school admissions policies require the use of test scores to admit a proportion of students at each performance level.

42 "Press Briefing by Press Secretary Jay Carney, Domestic Policy Council Director Melody Barnes, and Secretary of Education Arne Duncan," August 8, 2011, www.whitehouse.gov/the-press-office/2011/08/08/press-briefing-press-secretary-jay-carney-domestic-policy-council-direct/.

43 Gerald Bracey, *Setting the Record Straight* (Portsmouth, NH: Heinemann, 2004).

44 See, for example, MassPartners for Public Schools, *Facing Reality: What Happens When Good Schools Are Labeled "Failures"? Projecting Adequate Yearly Progress in Massachusetts Schools* (Boston: Author, 2005); Edward W. Wiley, William J. Mathis, and David R. Garcia, *The Impact of the Adequate Yearly Progress Requirement of the Federal "No Child Left Behind" Act on Schools in the Great Lakes Region* (Tempe, AZ: Education Policy Studies Laboratory, 2005).

45 "Los Angeles Teacher Ratings," *Los Angeles Times*, http://projects.latimes.com/value-added/.

46 Sam Dillon, "In Washington, Large Rewards in Teacher Pay," *New York Times*, December 31, 2011, www.nytimes.com/2012/01/01/education/big-pay-days-in-washington-dc-schools-merit-system.html?pagewanted=all.

47 "Obama's Remarks on Education," *Wall Street Journal*, March 10, 2009, http://blogs.wsj.com/washwire/2009/03/10/obamas-remarks-on-education-2/.

48 National Center on Performance Incentives, "Teacher Pay for Performance: Experimental Evidence From the Project on Incentives in Teaching," September 2010, www.performanceincentives.org/data/files/gallery/ContentGallery/POINT_REPORT_9.21.10.pdf; Julie Marsh et al., *A Big Apple for Educators: New York City's Experiment With Schoolwide Performance Bonuses*, Rand Corporation, 2011, www.rand.org/content/dam/rand/pubs/monographs/2011/RAND_MG1114.pdf.

49 Matthew Springer, L. Pham, and T. Nguyen, *Teacher Merit Pay and Student Test Scores: A Meta-Analysis*, Unpublished paper, 2017, https://my.vanderbilt.edu/matthewspringer/working-papers/.

Part II

The Practice of Teaching to Change the World

In the words of longtime educator and activist Deborah Meier,

> Teaching, more than virtually any activity (aside from parenting, perhaps), depends on quick instinctive habits and behavior, and on deeply held ways of seeing and valuing. Correcting a child's writing, calling on children who don't have their hands raised, complimenting a child on his or her clothing, deciding whether to intervene in a quarrel, pretending not to overhear a cruel tease—all carry messages of import and all involve decisions that must be made instantaneously.[1]

These moment-by-moment decisions may happen too fast for teachers to analyze each one as it occurs. But the teachers you meet in these chapters do stop and reflect on how consistent their actions are with their core knowledge, values, beliefs, and purposes for teaching. Through reflection, these teachers deepen their understanding about the relationships between their own practices and educational history, culture, politics, and policy. This understanding, in turn, informs the decisions they make moving forward as teachers.

Building on the foundation established in Part I, the next four chapters explore subject matter, instruction, assessment, and classroom management. These chapters highlight some of the ways that teachers can make curriculum and instruction meaningful to students and make classrooms humane and caring places.

Chapter 5, "The Subject Matters: Constructing Knowledge Across the Content Areas," introduces readers to the content areas of mathematics, language arts, social studies, and science and reviews current professional and political debates concerning these subjects. The chapter also describes how the standards movement and current emphasis on test-based, high-stakes accountability have shaped teaching and learning in each of these four major academic subjects.

Chapter 6, "Instruction: Teaching and Learning Across the Content Areas," begins with a bit of history detailing how teaching has changed—and hasn't changed—over the past 200 years. The chapter then discusses recent advances in our understandings about learning. The remainder of the chapter focuses on instructional principles that help teachers to structure multidimensional, active, and interactive experiences that facilitate learning among culturally and linguistically diverse students.

Chapter 7, "Assessment: Measuring What Matters," describes the way educators measure student learning and explores the basic ideas underlying these practices. The chapter begins by explaining a few basic assessment concepts and reviewing the history of testing, including the nineteenth- and early-twentieth-century efforts to define and measure intelligence. It then discusses today's standardized achievement tests—their construction, meaning, and use in twenty-first-century education. Finally, we look inside classrooms and offer a set of principles and practices that can help teachers use assessment to foster learning and social justice.

Chapter 8, "Classrooms as Communities: Developing Caring and Democratic Relationships," surveys the legacy of management, discipline, and control that many teachers still rely on to organize classroom life. It also examines a second tradition—creating child-centered, caring, and democratic classrooms—that, while less common, also has deep roots in this country. The chapter concludes with attention to the contributions of critical theorists, whose insights can help teachers respond with agency to issues of power and domination as they strive to make their classrooms socially just.

Finally, in Part III, we place these aspects of practice in the context of the school culture and organization, the local community, and the profession. There we continue profiling teachers who are putting their philosophies into practice in their daily work. Their efforts illuminate what's possible when teachers draw on foundational knowledge (addressed in Part I) and knowledge of teaching and learning (addressed in Part II) as they strive to make schools, communities, and the teaching profession what socially just, democratic principles suggest they can and should be.

Note

1 Deborah Meier, *The Power of Their Ideas: Lessons for America From a Small School in Harlem* (1995, reprint Boston: Beacon Press, 2002), 139.

The Subject Matters

Constructing Knowledge Across the Content Areas

As teachers, we decide what to teach our students. Yet there are times when we do not have a choice. . . . Curricular back-to-basics, achieved by implementing oppressive language arts and math programs, are used throughout urban schools. This narrow emphasis is a site of contention for many teachers and students. . . . What are teachers to do? How are students to cope? It is in these moments that we must be critical and creative.

We must present the histories of our students, of our country, and of our realities in a context that is critical and truthful. Including marginalized ethnic groups into our curriculum, students of color can identify with powerful histories that mirror their realities. This avenue of identification with the subject matter not only legitimizes students, but also enhances the curriculum by demonstrating the myriad ways that different people have influenced our world.

—Kimberly Min
Third-grade teacher

Teachers like Kimberly Min see themselves as both curriculum implementers and curriculum creators. They think critically about academic subjects, standards, and mandated teaching materials. They strive to make school knowledge meaningful for their diverse students and to remain true to their own commitment to socially just schooling.

Chapter Overview

This chapter focuses on teaching the academic subjects. It describes the debates that swirl around progressive teachers like Kimberly Min. Today as in the past, debates about what and how to teach are very political. They arouse the public's interests, passions, and fears about how schooling portrays society and how society might be changed by what schools teach. Clearly, teachers are not merely technicians parceling out a preestablished, neutral commodity called subject matter.

As noted in Chapter 3, on opposing sides of curriculum debates are "traditionalists" (people who hold conservative views of culture and essentialist and behavioral views of curriculum and teaching) and "progressives" (people who hold postmodern views of culture and critical multicultural perspectives on curriculum and teaching). Although connections between beliefs about schooling and political party affiliations are complicated, traditionalists still tend to be on the conservative end of the political spectrum, and progressives tend to be liberal.

Traditionalists and progressives can find common ground on broad curriculum questions, but consensus often breaks down about the specifics. For example, people across the political spectrum may favor curriculum standards but part over the details: What should the standards be? Who should develop them (teachers, experts, policymakers), and at what level (school, community, state, or federal)? When should students meet various standards? What resources should be required to ensure the opportunity to meet them? How should mastery of the standards be assessed? What should the consequences be for failing to meet them?

Take, for example, nearly every state's adoption by 2012 of the Common Core State Standards (CCSS) in language arts and mathematics—a trend suggesting agreement across states and political parties. Yet most states—some of which have since abandoned the CCSS—did not reconcile progressive and traditional differences about how standards should be used. Inevitably, well-intentioned people differed when it came to translating the CCSS into learning goals, curriculum plans, and assessments. As we describe in this chapter, standards-based reforms have been riddled with disagreements about what and how students should learn in mathematics, English language arts, social studies, and science.[1]

Mathematics

During a 2007 debate, presidential candidate Barack Obama responded to a question about how he would "change the system to make American students more competitive on the world scene:"

> [One thing is] emphasizing math and science instruction, finding innovative ways to make it interesting for students. This is an area where the president has the power to use the bully pulpit and to make math and science interesting and vibrant again.[2]

Obama's words reverberate today as politicians, policymakers, and members of the business community press schools to raise student achievement in mathematics and science and to increase access to science, technology, engineering, and mathematics (STEM) fields, particularly for girls and students of color. The 2011 America COMPETES Act, reauthorized in 2015, responded to what President Obama characterized as a contemporary "Sputnik moment." It presumed that improvements in STEM education would help to "raise American students from the middle to the top of the pack and to make sure we are training the next generation of innovative thinkers and doers."[3]

Although consensus about the importance of STEM education holds firm, decades-old debates about what and how math and science should be taught in U.S. schools drag on today.

The Math Crisis

In the early 1980s, the Second International Study of Science and Mathematics Education rocked the math education community and the public.[4] Its findings showed U.S. eighth graders lagging far behind their counterparts in most developed nations.

The math and science communities responded to the apparent deficiencies in American mathematics instruction. In 1989, the National Research Council (NRC), the research and policy arm of the National Academy of Sciences, published *Everybody Counts*, advising the nation to overhaul mathematics education. That same year, the National Council of Teachers of Mathematics (NCTM) concluded a consensus-building process with thousands of math teachers and mathematicians and published standards laying out what U.S. students should know and be able to do. The NCTM thought these standards would improve mathematics teaching and learning dramatically.

Soon, however, traditionalists were engaged in (and, by many accounts, winning) a full-scale war against the NCTM standards. In August 1997, Lynne Cheney, who became second lady in the second Bush administration, was a fellow at a conservative Washington think tank, the American Enterprise Institute. In an essay about mathematics reform, Cheney used the following story to make a caustic judgment about the progressive mathematics curriculum:

> "They lied to me," says Madalyn McDaniel of Atascadero, California. "They completely betrayed me." At parents' night at the local high school, McDaniel was told about a great opportunity for her son: *The Interactive Mathematics Program*, in which he would be learning everything taught in traditional math courses only in a more effective way. But after signing him up, McDaniel realized the program was not at all what it was advertised. Instead of learning rules and formulas, her son and his classmates were presented with problems and expected to invent their own ways of solving them. "He was very frustrated," McDaniel says. "I'd say, 'Look in the book, it will explain.' He'd say, 'Mom, there is not a book.'"
>
> McDaniel had encountered "whole math." Also known as "fuzzy math" or "new-new math," whole math is based on the idea that knowledge is only meaningful when we construct it for ourselves. . . .
>
> The whole-math disaster began in 1989 when the National Council of Teachers of Mathematics issued a set of standards declaring a new approach to be in order. No more "drill and kill," as whole-math people like to call traditional teaching. Instead, from kindergarten on, there would be a calculator in every hand so that young minds would be free of irksome chores like addition and multiplication and thus able to take on higher-order tasks such as inventing their own personal methods of long division.[5]

Cheney's story provides a glimpse into the substance and rancor of the debate. Since then, two more international studies have shown that although U.S. students have improved since the 1990s, they still lag.[6] The NCTM standards have been revised to clarify that basic arithmetic knowledge and skills matter, and many states and textbook publishers have used these revised standards to develop curriculum. Nevertheless, critics still object and call for a return to traditional math.

For much of the public, the problem and solution seem straightforward. U.S. teachers aren't making students learn as much math as they should; teachers need to have higher expectations, upgrade their own knowledge, spend more time teaching math, and suffer negative consequences if their students do not perform.

The mathematics education community counters that intensifying a fundamentally flawed traditional approach won't solve the problem. They believe that the traditional focus on memorizing rules and procedures and solving abstract problems keeps students from understanding principles and purposes, and that explains why so few students remember and use the mathematics they are taught.[7] They argue that even students who are proficient at remembering facts and performing algorithms—and who score well on tests—often understand little. They note that the U.S. mathematics curriculum is fragmented and incoherent compared to that in Japan, Finland, and Singapore, where math achievement is consistently high.[8] Progressives also fault U.S. ability-grouping practices that keep many students from being taught higher-level math, noting that most high-scoring countries shun that practice.[9] In sum, progressives argue that the traditionalists' "cure" is just more of what schools already do and won't make things better. Traditionalists counter that progressive threats to age-old "truths" of mathematics are part of a general trend toward a disintegrating educational and social order.

Traditional Mathematics: Skills Based and Sequential

Mathematics conventionally consists of orderly, enduring facts and logics that describe patterns and relationships in the physical world—arithmetic operations, algebraic manipulations, geometry terms and theorems, and so forth. Traditional math curriculum lays out a hierarchical sequence of topics and skills that allows students, step-by-step, to master this body of knowledge.[10] For example, a conservative member of California's standards commission once argued, "Mathematics is a cumulative, hierarchical subject; learning new skills and concepts often depends on mastery of previous ones. . . . [Students] must enter each grade in possession of all the prerequisite skills."[11] The prerequisite skills—often referred to as the basics—include math facts and the rules (algorithms). For example, long division is an algorithm of orderly steps that require basic mathematical skills, including multiplication and subtraction.

Traditionalists argue for "balanced instruction in mathematics: basic facts and skills, conceptual understanding; and problem-solving ability."[12] But "problem-solving ability," like many catchphrases in curriculum controversies, means different things to different people. Traditionalists accept correct answers as the only legitimate confirmation of a student's mathematical knowledge and believe there is only one way to solve any problem. Progressives don't deny that mathematics offers useful, precise solutions. But most also see, for example, *estimation* as an integral guide to mathematical reasoning, and believe that there are many correct ways to solve a problem. Progressives value students' explanations of their own reasoning and understanding as key indicators of students' mathematical competency.

Traditional elementary schools stress number facts and algorithms for addition, subtraction, multiplication, and division and for computing fractions, decimals, and percentages. Most middle schools review or reteach these basic operations. Beginning in middle school, however, the curriculum diverges for different students. The "best" math students are placed on a path that leads to high school trigonometry and calculus. Those who haven't mastered the basics take general math classes, where they review the basic math skills of elementary school. Both progressives and traditionalists have severely criticized these dead-end remedial courses, and many schools now channel low-achieving students through separate and slower pathways that may include first-year algebra.

Progressive Mathematics: Meaningful Knowledge in Context

At the end of her first year of teaching, Zeba Palomino wrote a letter to her high school students explaining how she views mathematics and why she strives to teach it as she does.

> Mathematics has a history, and it is deeply rooted in cultures all over the world. Mathematics is logical and controversial at the same time. Mathematics is a beautiful cycle of connections; it is not a linear study of fragmented pieces. Mathematics is connected to, a foundation for, and dependent upon philosophy, communication, art, science, language, and more. Mathematics is not just numbers and letters, and it is not a set of rules to be memorized; it is a world of ideas and patterns to be discovered and played with. Mathematics is not a right or wrong answer; it is an infinite collection of strategies from which to choose to use as we develop our own ideas and make our own sense of the world. It is because these beauties exist within and around the field of mathematics that I choose to use mathematics as a means for critical education.
>
> My intention is to use a constructivist approach to mathematics and the power of collaborative learning to help you develop the intellectual and moral capacities and the commitment to shape your places in the world. Through your own construction of mathematics knowledge, you can become experts in understanding, reasoning, communicating, analyzing, imagining, examining, connecting, and proving. And by learning collaboratively, you learn and achieve more, you respect and care more about each other and your communities, and you take more pride in your responsibilities and capabilities. As you build these academic and moral capacities, my hope is that you are opening doors for yourselves to countless possibilities.
>
> My biggest struggle is staying true to these goals. I know that I often fall into just teaching mathematics skills and concepts because it is much easier to do. I know that many of you would prefer that I continue to do it that way—just let you sit in rows, give you the algorithms, and give you individual work to practice those new math rules. But, please understand, it is unfair and unjust of me to do that to you. When I "teach" that way, you are not truly learning or empowering yourselves. You are only "learning" a meaningless concept with no deeper significance to you and which you will soon forget. You are not building or exchanging ideas, and you are not participating in a critical transformative education.
>
> —Zeba Palomino
> First-year teacher, high school mathematics

Zeba echoes the progressive reform advice. Mathematicians have achieved (with the aid of computer technology) breakthroughs in number theory, logic, statistics, operations research, probability, computation, geometry, and combinatorics that reach far beyond the traditional areas of mathematics (algebra, analysis, and topology).[13] Such dramatic changes, the NRC reasoned, mean that mathematics education must also change:

> The transformation of mathematics from a core of abstract studies to a powerful family of mathematical sciences is reflected poorly, often not at all, by the traditional mathematics curriculum. One can hardly blame students if they rarely see evidence of its full power and richness.
>
> As mathematics is more than calculation, so education in mathematics must be more than mastery of arithmetic. Geometry, chance, and change are as important as numbers in achieving mathematical power. Even more important is a comprehensive, flexible view that embodies the intrinsic unity of mathematics; estimation supplements calculation; heuristics aid algorithms; experience balances innovation. To prepare students to use mathematics

in the twenty-first century, today's curriculum must invoke the full spectrum of the mathematical sciences.[14]

The NRC also rejected the view that "the best way to learn how to solve complex problems is to decompose them into a sequence of basic skills which can then be mastered one at a time."[15] *Everybody Counts* argued, "There is abundant evidence that mastery of necessary skills is rarely sufficient for solving complex problems."[16] Recent scholarship frames mathematics as a dynamic knowledge domain and a way of thinking that emphasizes reasoning and problem solving, rather than computations and static, procedure-driven rules and formulas.[17]

Mathematics as Purposeful Activity

The 1989 NCTM standards defined mathematics as using mathematical algorithms and ideas during *purposeful activity*—that is, across disciplines and in real-life situations.[18] They emphasized that *knowing* math is inseparable from *doing* math.

Computation remains critical in both mathematics and daily life. However, the NRC and the NCTM argued that complex computation can be done by calculators and computers. Having quick mental calculating ability is not a prerequisite for success in many daily situations or even in some complex problem solving.[19] That means students should not be denied opportunities to learn advanced mathematics because they are slower to develop traditional "basic" skills.

The NCTM's 258-page document spelled out what mathematics teaching and learning should be. Throughout the grades, mathematical ideas should be embedded in familiar and meaningful problems. Teachers should link foundational math ideas to math procedures repeatedly, instead of teaching a topic or concept and then dropping it, never to be seen again. From kindergarten on, students should learn (in age- and skill-appropriate ways) about whole numbers, fractions and decimals, geometry, measurement, statistics and probability, and patterns and functions. Number systems, number theory, algebra, trigonometry, discrete mathematics, and calculus should be added as students' mathematical understanding grows. In the hands of well-taught students, computers and calculators should be at the core of learning. Those fearing that these tools are used to avoid rigorous work are out of step with current mathematics and technologies.

The NCTM standards made clear that learning mathematics is no more linear or sequential than learning how to dance. Certainly, there are concepts. There are big ideas. There are facts and processes to be memorized over time and become automatic (i.e., performed without conscious thought). And it is best to approach certain ideas after one is competent with previous ones. That said, traditional mathematics instruction might be compared to teaching someone to dance with a lecture and a book; it is not quite the real thing.

Mathematics for Everyone

On the question of *mathematics for whom?* the NCTM was unequivocal. Core mathematical ideas are necessary and appropriate for *all*. Schools cannot use differences in students' talents, test scores, prior opportunities, or interests as excuses for some students not learning math.

In 1999, an NCTM task force found that inequalities in curriculum, instruction, and expectations for student performance constrain mathematics achievement. Recent studies corroborate these findings.[20] Believing low-achieving students to have low math ability, educators consider it sensible to teach such students low-level math. This rationalizes an uneven distribution of qualified math teachers—assigning highly qualified math teachers to students who are already successful. The result is depressed math achievement.

Progressive teachers, in contrast, search for teaching materials and approaches that make mathematics accessible to and engaging for all students, not just those who have excelled in math. Such teachers understand that learning must be relevant to students, and they know that connecting mathematical knowledge to students' everyday knowledge, interests, experiences, and understandings (or cultural knowledge) can aid mathematics learning.[21] Approaches that bridge everyday knowledge with mathematics knowledge, and that tie mathematics to social justice goals, are crucial for students representing groups (e.g., African Americans, Latinx, girls, etc.) that are underrepresented in STEM fields or assumed to have low math ability. Mathematics educator Eric (Rico) Gutstein and progressive educator Bob Peterson's coedited book, *Rethinking Mathematics: Teaching Social Justice by the Numbers,* includes teaching ideas, lesson plans, and reflections that teachers can use to weave social justice principles into the math curriculum, as well as integrate math and social justice into other curricular areas.[22] The book's approach provides high-level math opportunities to all students and, at the same time, prepares students to be critical, active members of a democratic society (see Focal Point 5.1).

The Math Standards: The Politics of Mathematics Continues

California's traditional/progressive mathematics battles of the late 1990s hold lessons for the rest of the country, even today. As the state developed its own mathematics standards, traditionalist organizations lobbied against any influence of the NCTM standards.

Accusations flew across the Internet and in letters to newspaper editors. Teachers were attacked for teaching math without numbers, denying children access to conventional ways of multiplying and dividing, and paying more attention to how students feel than to whether they can do math. The battle concluded with a policy fight over verbs. The California standards writers used verbs like "model, estimate, interpret, classify, explain, and create," arguing that each is a strategy for thinking about, learning, and solving problems using mathematics. However, the conservative state board of education rejected these verbs in nearly every case. One board member declared that the way to "get children to do more and better and higher math" is with such phrases as "do it, solve it, know it."[23]

The revised standards embodied the traditional view of mathematics learning. An outraged official at the National Science Foundation wrote a letter to the California board stating that the board's action was "short sighted, and detrimental to the long-term mathematical literacy of children in California."[24] Nevertheless, the board adopted standards that emphasized basic skills, memorization, and practice and discouraged invention, estimation, and solving nonroutine problems. They denied the early use of calculators and cautioned against their later use.

In the effort to eliminate what they called "fuzzy math," the traditionalists also sought to remove the College Preparatory Mathematics (CPM) texts from the state's classrooms. Some argued that because these texts are more effective with low-income students and students of color, they sacrifice the math learning of more advantaged students.

Similar campaigns occurred elsewhere. Responding to the pressure, the NCTM revised its standards in 2000. Called *Principles and Standards for School Mathematics,* the revised standards place more emphasis on memorization and rote computation, although the council insists that these revisions remain consistent with the theories of mathematics and mathematics learning that underlie the first set of standards. Most states used the revised standards as the basis for their own standards; few followed California's more traditional path. In 2005, the politically conservative Fordham Foundation graded every state's mathematics standards. California's standards were given an A, largely because the state rejected the NCTM's standards. Eighteen states received Ds, and eleven received Fs, largely because they patterned theirs after the NCTM's.[25]

Focal Point 5.1
Teaching Social Justice by the Numbers

Mathematics: An Essential Tool for Understanding and Changing the World

To have more than a surface understanding of important social and political issues, mathematics is essential. Without mathematics, it is impossible to fully understand a government budget, the impact of a war, the meaning of a national debt, or the long-term effects of a proposal such as the privatization of Social Security. The same is true with other social, ecological, and cultural issues: You need mathematics to have a deep grasp of the influence of advertising on children; the level of pollutants in the water, air, and soil; and the dangers of the chemicals in the food we eat. Math helps students understand these issues, to see them in ways that would otherwise be impossible; for example, visually displaying data in graphs that otherwise might be incomprehensible or seemingly meaningless.

As an example, consider racial profiling. This issue becomes meaningful only when viewed through a mathematical lens, whether or not the viewer appreciates that she or he is using mathematics. That is, it is difficult to declare that racial profiling occurs unless there is a sufficiently large data set and a way to examine that data. If, for example, 30 percent of drivers in an area are African American, and the police stop six African American drivers and four white drivers, there is weak evidence that racial profiling exists. But if police stop 612 African American drivers and 423 white drivers, then there is a much stronger case.

The explanation lies in mathematics: In an area where only 30 percent of the drivers are black, it is virtually impossible for almost 60 percent of more than 1,000 people randomly stopped by the police to be black.

The underlying mathematical ideas—(dis)proportionality, probability, randomness, sample size, and the law of large numbers (that over a sufficiently large data set, the results of a probability simulation or of real-world experiences should approximate the theoretical probabilities)—all become part of the context that students must understand to really see, and in turn demonstrate, that something is amiss. Thus, with a large data set, one can assert that a real problem exists and further investigate racial profiling. For youth, racial profiling may mean being "picked on," but the subtleties and implications are comprehensible only when the mathematical ideas are there.

When teachers weave social justice into the math curriculum and promote social justice math across the curriculum, students' understanding of important social matters deepens. When teachers use data on sweatshop wages to teach accounting to high school students or multidigit multiplication to upper-elementary students, students not only learn math but also learn something about the lives of people in various parts of the world and the relationship between the things we consume and their living conditions.

Source: Eric (Rico) Gutstein and Bob Peterson, eds., introduction to *Rethinking Mathematics: Teaching Social Justice by the Numbers* (Milwaukee, WI: Rethinking Schools, 2005). More information about *Rethinking Mathematics* is available at the Rethinking Schools website at www.rethinkingschools.org.

The battle continued in 2011, when forty-five states adopted the mathematics CCSS. In many ways, reactions to the CCSS mirror prior traditionalist and progressive disagreements. The CCSS sought to correct the shortcomings of prior standards, and make them less incoherent and fragmented—"a mile wide" (covering a lot, and perhaps too much, material) and "an inch deep" (failing to address concepts with sufficient depth or complexity). With fewer standards and increased "clarity and specificity," the CCSS authors argue that the standards will cultivate students' mathematical understanding: their "ability to justify, in a way appropriate to the student's mathematical maturity, why a particular mathematical statement is true or where a mathematical rule comes from."[26]

The NCTM's official response has been mostly positive. The NCTM has, on multiple occasions, praised the CCSS for their consistency and coherence and the "unprecedented opportunities" they present for systemic improvement in mathematics instruction.[27] Yet the NCTM has also criticized the CCSS's failure to "adequately weave the mathematical practices throughout the document," address "mathematical connections both across and within content areas," or acknowledge "the power and place of technology in a 21st-century school mathematics experience."[28] Ultimately, the NCTM supported the CCSS when it released *Making It Happen: A Guide to Interpreting and Implementing Common Core State Standards for Mathematics*, drawing connections between the NCTM's standards and the CCSS, and offering guidelines to districts, schools, and teachers for CCSS implementation.[29]

Some progressives, however, condemned the CCSS math standards for promoting abstract instruction and sequencing, which they believe underlies U.S. students' poor international ranking. They prefer laying the groundwork with an applied curriculum to support students' mathematical thinking and skills in the context of real-world problems.[30] As described in Chapter 3, others worry about the potential of national standards to standardize curriculum and increase the time and resources dedicated to high-stakes standardized testing, as well as about the CCSS's corporate ties and allegedly undemocratic development process.

Meanwhile, traditionalists have mostly supported the mathematics CCSS, touting their national reach and the extensive material they expect schools to cover. The Fordham Institute, for example, described them as "exemplary" for their deep and rigorous "coverage" of mathematical content.[31] This positive assessment is not surprising given the Fordham Institute's deep ties to the individuals and organizations that, as described in Chapter 3, helped to fund CCSS development and implementation.

What Teachers Do With Math Standards

Clearly, teachers are expected to teach standards that, to different degrees, support and/or challenge their students' learning and their own visions of effective, equity-minded mathematics instruction. Because standards are guides for *what* to teach and cannot specify *how* to teach or the *conditions* and *resources* for teaching, teachers must interpret and adapt the standards as they put them into practice with their own students. Education policy scholars David Cohen and Heather Hill concluded from their large-scale study in California that teachers shape the implementation of mathematics standards in consequential ways.[32] The NCTM's multiple efforts to support teachers' use of the CCSS reflect this finding, as do other efforts to help use the standards to facilitate the learning of students representing nondominant groups, such as Emergent Bilinguals.[33] However, most standards documents make recommendations for an imagined "average" or general student population that leaves out or marginalizes the range of learners who populate U.S. public school classrooms. In response, mathematics education scholar Rochelle Gutiérrez calls on teachers, in urban schools especially, to engage in *creative insubordination*, a practice of finding "loopholes" in mandated policies and practices where teachers can make sound, locally responsive instructional decisions and assert their advocacy for historically underserved students.[34]

So, how have mathematics teachers responded to the politicizing of their subject? Math teacher Mark Hill offers one account.

> My school has been making strides toward improving the scores on the [standards-based] tests that California uses to rank school achievement, but we are still classified as a "low-performing" school. Because of this, there has been a lot of pressure to "teach to the test" and focus the curriculum on the material that the state has decided will be on the tests. The result is a pacing guide that stresses breadth over depth.
>
> Many content teachers shy away from teaching critical thinking skills during class due to these intense curriculum deadlines. I experienced this myself. I was often unable to explore a concept in depth, even when my students were struggling, in favor of starting the next section in the allotted time frame. I was afraid that if I took time away from my content area to teach problem-solving strategies, I would fall behind the pacing guide. The result was a shallow conceptual understanding among most of my students.
>
> —Mark Hill
> First-year teacher, high school mathematics

Even under the worst political deluge, teachers like Mark weather the storm and strive to teach math well. Mark tried various approaches and found that students had an easier time learning the mathematics procedures that are on the state test when he spent time helping them develop as critical thinkers. He concluded, "Problem-solving strategies enable students to remember and use the procedural knowledge they are exposed to." Perhaps the best defense against politically driven mandates is an articulate, knowledgeable, and highly competent generation of mathematics teachers—elementary and secondary. With care, courage, and competence, such teachers negotiate traditional mandates strategically—using standards as guides rather than rules, and adapting them to their students' interests and needs.

English Language Arts

Webster's Encyclopedic Unabridged Dictionary of the English Language gives twenty-eight definitions of the word *read*. The first two sum up traditional conceptions:

> 1. To peruse and apprehend the meaning of (something written, printed, etc.): *to read a book*; 2. To utter aloud or render in speech: *reading a story to his children*.[35]

Progressive English language arts teachers and theorists pay attention to the other twenty-six definitions, as well. A few examples show how varied and deep their broader conception of reading is:

> 5. To make out the significance of by scrutiny or observation: *to read the dark and cloudy sky as the threat of a storm*. 6. To foresee, foretell, or predict: *to read a person's fortune in tea leaves*. 7. To make out the character, motivations, desires, etc. . . . as by interpretation of outward signs. 8. To infer (something not expressed or directly indicated) from what is read or considered . . .: *He read an underlying sarcasm into her letter*. 25. To admit of being interpreted: *a rule that reads two different ways*. 26. (Of an electronic computer) to read data. 27. Read in, to introduce information into a computer.[36]

Webster's gives a similarly long list of definitions for "write." And as with reading, traditional educators prefer a narrow conception of writing—rejecting many writing-related events and competencies that progressives favor.

The traditional curriculum frames reading as acquiring information from the printed page, and writing as mastering spelling, grammar, and form. Progressive curriculum sees young readers and writers as bringing to school with them resources, personal histories, and individual and collective voices that already qualify them as literate, even though they may lack some competencies that have a high "exchange rate" or value in mainstream society.

Traditional Language Arts: Mastering Skills, Rules, and Forms

Traditionally, schools expect young children to learn phonics. They should hear and manipulate sounds in spoken words, and master the rules (and many exceptions) that govern how such sounds translate into letters and letter combinations. Teachers emphasize skills for decoding letters, combinations of letters, and whole words. They teach a hierarchy of discrete skills—from recognizing beginning consonants, to consonant blends, to inexplicable words like *cough* and *height*. They expect students to master Standard English conventions by memorizing correct spellings; dividing words into syllables; alphabetizing; capitalizing; punctuating; recognizing synonyms, homonyms, and antonyms; and identifying parts of speech and sentences. They ask students to practice writing sentences, paragraphs, stories, and reports.

Building From Parts to Whole

These basics cycle and recycle throughout the grades and into middle and high school, with teachers focusing on rules, mostly out of context. The result is a progression of more and more difficult spelling, capitalization, punctuation, usage, and grammar lessons, often absent the relationship between such conventions and a text's authentic purpose or meaning. Teachers teach formulas for writing—paragraphs with topic sentences, three- and five-paragraph essays, and,

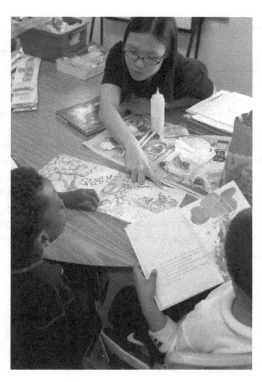

finally, structured research papers. They teach common writing styles—descriptive, persuasive, analytic, critical, personal, "practical" (business letters), and narrative. They assess students' writing for its correct use of formulas and conventions, rather than its success in conveying meaning. Vocabulary lessons ask students to memorize words for recall on tests and to copy dictionary definitions, often without opportunities to understand the meaning or use of words in authentic communication.

As in mathematics, traditional reading and writing instruction focuses on parts that combine into wholes. The alphabet is more specific, and therefore more basic, than recognizing the sounds of parts of words, which are more basic than whole words. Letters are analogous to numbers. Phonics, or the sounds of letters and groups of letters, is elemental, perhaps like counting or even addition and subtraction. Grammar and sentences are akin to more complex algorithms, such as algebraic formulas.

Traditionalists assume that meaning-rich literacy experiences and adult-like tasks come *after* one has mastered the basics. Thus, a student struggling with decoding, for example, could go through twelve years of schooling without ever becoming "ready" for reading and enjoying whole stories or books, writing about what matters, or critiquing media. Emergent Bilingual students and students from other historically underserved groups are among those most likely to experience rote, decontextualized instruction.

The conventional curriculum also treats reading, writing, speaking, and listening as universally applicable skills that do not change much in different contexts. However, people need and use speaking, reading, and writing competencies differently across settings and with different audiences. Comprehending a novel, an advertisement, an e-mail, and a science textbook require markedly different kinds of reading skills. An academic research paper requires a different structure, authorial voice, and vocabulary than a letter to a friend. Likewise, effective speaking differs when one is being interviewed by a potential employer, talking with a family member, or arguing in a debate team competition.

Extracting Meaning From Traditional Texts

The traditional curriculum also includes literature. Elementary students learn basic literary genres—stories, poems, newspaper articles, and novels (known to many younger students as "chapter books"). Older students learn Western literary conventions, like plot, setting, characters, theme, and so on, and they read classics and established twentieth-century writers who are part of the cultural canon: William Shakespeare, Charles Dickens, Ralph Waldo Emerson, Emily Dickinson, John Steinbeck, and Ernest Hemingway. Often what passes for contemporary literature turns out to be twenty to fifty years old. Teachers ask students to discover or simply tell them the author's intended meaning, and students learn to identify conventional literary devices (irony, foreshadowing, metaphor, etc.). Even when canonical texts include topics that could stimulate critical discussions and elicit multiple interpretations (as in *To Kill a Mockingbird*, for example), teachers with traditional views of literacy are still likely to focus on literary conventions and to privilege mainstream interpretations. This has become more common as teachers feel pressure to prepare students for high-stakes standardized tests that emphasize conventions and value low-level comprehension more than analytical thinking.[37]

Reading Traditional Textbooks

Textbooks form the traditional curriculum's bedrock. Basal readers and language arts texts provide simple stories and practice exercises to cultivate young students' sequential development of decoding, vocabulary, comprehension, and related skills. In later grades, the basal reader merges into the familiar literature anthology that contains longer and shorter works—many of which are excerpts rather than whole texts—and includes a range of genres, encompassing fiction and nonfiction, poetry and drama, essays, and so on. Some anthologies feature themes, such as exploring life in cities; others focus on traditions, such as American, British, or world literature. Like basal readers, anthologies target particular grades and usually include pieces based on their level of difficulty.

Some textbooks come with detailed manuals that give teachers step-by-step "direct instruction" strategies, including questions to ask, ways to motivate, assignments, tests, worksheets, posters, videos, software, websites, and more. Some include "scripts" for teachers to follow, a trend we describe in more detail below. State legislatures and local school boards often select traditional texts to ensure that teachers teach reading and writing comprehensively, competently, and uniformly. Many decision makers see scripted approaches to reading instruction as "damage control" for teachers who know little about how to teach reading. It's not surprising that, with the concentration of underqualified teachers in overcrowded high-poverty schools, many high-poverty school districts have adopted such materials.

Progressive Approaches to Language Arts: Developing Literacies

Progressives worry that a narrow focus on skills causes students to miss the essence of literacy—the pleasure and power of expressing and understanding ideas. They argue that learning language arts is as much about *practices* as it is about *skills*—and that practices and skills cannot be separated. They also lament that the traditional literature curriculum favors the elite, White cultural canon and is too narrow to allow the fullest range of learning opportunities that students are capable of exploiting.

Progressive educators consider language, in its multiple expressions, as something people *do* and *use* to accomplish meaningful purposes or needs, rather than something people learn about and store for future use. Thus, the rules, words, and conventions that make up much of the language arts curriculum must be situated in contexts that include ideas, problem solving, engagement with others, and reflection.

Leveraging Students' Own Literacy Practices

Decades of research on learning provides language arts teachers with overwhelming evidence that all students come to school with experiences that prepare them for full adult literacy.

Professor David Pearson of the University of California, Berkeley, notes, "Even the three-year-old who recognizes that if an arch is in sight, a hamburger is not far away has learned the basic principle of signs—that our world is filled with things that 'stand for' other things."[38] Similarly, 3-year-olds who sees their parent pick up a book might know that sitting on a lap and being told a story are soon to follow. Children can read the environment long before they can read the book. Also, children have likely learned that they are active agents in determining the full meaning of their "reading." How they sit (still or squirmy) and how they "reward" their parents (by pointing to the illustration that matches the text being read) show that relationships are inseparable from most literacy events.

Middle and high school students, too, come to school with extensive literacy practices. A challenge for schools is to recognize these practices as fully formed, rich, and valuable, and to treat them as academically generative—as resources that teachers can leverage to facilitate students' development of new knowledge and literacy practices. Pearson argues that when teachers act on their belief that youth are already literate, they "engage them in tasks in which they can demonstrate their literacy and use those successes as bridges to even more challenging literacy activities."[39] This is particularly important for Emergent Bilinguals and for students who schools consider non–Standard English speakers, as these students are among the most likely to be incorrectly labeled as illiterate, even learning disabled, because of teachers' and others' failures to recognize and build on their existing capacities.

Emergent Bilinguals and bicultural youth often come to school accustomed to engaging in especially sophisticated language practices. UCLA professor Marjorie Faulstich Orellana, for example, has found that schools and teachers often fail to recognize and maximize the language and literacy practices bicultural children develop as they translate and paraphrase for others—whether during parent-teacher conferences, doctors' appointments, peer interactions, or routine consumer exchanges.[40] These and other local language and literacy practices are among those that progressive teachers seek to recognize, understand, and use in supporting students' continued language and literacy development.

Translanguaging, or "accessing different linguistic features . . . in order to maximize communicative potential"[41] represents another rich language practice for many multilingual students. This practice typically involves multilinguals' use of "hybrid" language practices—or the strategic meshing of what are viewed by many as autonomous or distinct languages. It reflects the wide range of linguistic resources multilinguals have at their disposal.

In the past, many considered this practice "code-switching," and claimed it represented multilinguals' (problematic) use of less "pure" forms of English and/or their failure to develop any language fully. However, recent research underscores the legitimacy of hybrid language practices and the tremendous intelligence and flexibility—cognitive and otherwise—that multilinguals must exercise to translanguage. It shows how critiques of "code-switching" were seriously misguided.[42] Today we understand that, for multilinguals, languages do not exist as autonomous entities, but rather as one holistic system. The multiple languages one knows are always at play during meaning making and communicative exchanges.

Teachers can use these understandings to encourage multilingual students to draw on their full linguistic repertoires as they engage in learning; these understandings can also help teachers view bilingual students from an asset orientation, rather than assuming they are deficient or limited in some way.

Language practices are not only tied to heritage languages; youth culture also plays a significant role. Media literacies such as texting, blogging, and tweeting are good examples of experiences and skills that are as unfamiliar to some adults as they are essential and life affirming to adolescents. Schools often regard these experiences and skills as irrelevant, or even disruptive, to students' academic learning. Yet blogging and forum formats, for example, could house students' analyses of literary texts. Internet usage and communication that transpire over social media could be understood as second (or third or fourth) languages with linguistic, structural, cultural, social, and other similarities and differences. For the savvy teacher, having students analyze personal media can serve as a powerful bridge between conventional curriculum goals and students' own "literate lives." Imagine a teacher asking her students to consider: *How does the medium influence the content of your message? How do you balance pragmatic informational messages with your expression of style or humor? What rules do you follow to be clear, avoid offending, and so forth? How would William Shakespeare's, Marie Curie's, James Baldwin's, or a family member's life have been different if they communicated via text-message phone at age 17?*

Building From the "Texts" of Students' Lives

Using the Internet and other media as an entrée to literacy development can help teachers reach students from a range of backgrounds—perhaps better than printed text. However, the content of the media also matters a lot. One way to increase the relevancy of the English language arts curriculum via any medium is to incorporate critical, multicultural literature and draw from texts that connect with students' personal, lived experiences. Although highly productive for all students, it is especially crucial for students whose languages and cultural practices are not reflected in the traditional curriculum. Such texts can be taught as valuable examples of human expression and as bridges to more traditional works.

Northwestern University professor Carol Lee encourages teachers to engage students first with texts that are close to home (written by authors representing students' own group(s) and/or life experiences), and move gradually to less familiar ones (canonical texts, such as those written by William Shakespeare).[43] In one example, Lee explains how students moved from an analysis of symbolism in a rap song by the Fugees to an analysis of symbolism in works such as Toni Morrison's *Beloved*, Shakespeare's *Macbeth*, and Ralph Ellison's *Invisible Man*; short stories by William Faulkner, Amy Tan, and Sandra Cisneros; and poems by Dylan Thomas, Emily Dickinson, and Dante.

First-year English teacher Kelly Ganzel used contemporary, culturally relevant novels with her mostly Latinx ninth graders because of the richness and literary power such books offer. Kelly also leveraged students' interest in and engagement with such texts as part of her efforts to cultivate students' interest in and access to canonical literature:

> Pairing classic texts like Shakespeare's *Romeo and Juliet* with contemporary, ethnically diverse young adult literature like Laura Esquivel's *Like Water for Chocolate* is a valuable approach. Such pairing affords the opportunity for teachers to collaborate with their students in choosing a contemporary novel to study. Through multicultural literature, I invite my students to share their knowledge about their history, traditions, and community.

Similarly, Kelly selectively incorporated other texts, like films, to help engage students and activate their prior knowledge, thereby increasing their interest and investment in more traditional (canonical) written texts, as well as their familiarity with salient literary themes.

> As I prepared to teach Harper Lee's *To Kill a Mockingbird*, I decided to capture my students' attention through a portrayal of African American women's experiences in the South during the Depression. After showing *I Know Why the Caged Bird Sings*, the film version of Maya Angelou's youth, Nancy [an African American student with a history of school failure] was bursting with questions and comments. Nancy approached me after class with a smile on her face. "I really like that stuff." The next day, she had written a reflection about how she would have felt had she been in Maya Angelou's shoes.
>
> —Kelly Ganzel
> First-year teacher, high school English

Similarly, first-year English teacher Jessica Wingell engaged her predominantly Latinx ninth graders with texts by Latinx authors Sandra Cisneros (*The House on Mango Street*) and Luis Rodriguez (*Always Running*).

> I wanted my Latino students to see themselves in the literature. Additionally, there is some Spanish included in many of the works I've taught this year, and I don't speak Spanish. My students (including students who are not Latino but are taking Spanish classes) love to show what they know. . . . I often ask my Spanish speakers for help, and I think they appreciate having their bilingualism acknowledged and used.
>
> In the unit on magical realism, specifically, I wanted the students to experience the pure enjoyment of the stories. I also wanted them to understand what magical realism is (the imaginary becomes real), and why it originated in Latin America (according to Gabriel

Garcia Marquez, events in Latin America have been so extraordinary that realism was not adequate to describe people and events). The culminating project for the unit was a research project on an author, an event, or a historical figure. They needed to find the connection between their topic and the events or circumstances in Latin America that led to the development of magical realism.

The strength of this unit was the material—the students really liked the stories because they were unusual, lyrical, and challenging. In addition, my Latino students in particular enjoyed the opportunity to explore aspects of their heritage that they wanted to know more about. . . . This approach is powerful because it combines students' home culture and high-status knowledge in an English curriculum.

—Jessica Wingell
First-year teacher, English, grade 9

Many traditionalists would object to the texts that scholars like Carol Lee advocate using and that teachers like Kelly and Jessica and their students find compelling. Traditionalists and progressives disagree over whose perspective, whose voice, and whose knowledge most belong in the curriculum.

A case in point was the 1998 decision by the San Francisco Board of Education to require teachers to assign books by non-White authors to high school students. At the time, the only required books were Chaucer's *Canterbury Tales*, Shakespeare's *Romeo and Juliet*, and Mark Twain's *Huckleberry Finn*. Although no one disparaged these works, board members thought it reasonable to broaden the list of readings, particularly since 87 percent of the district's students were students of color. Their proposal exploded onto headlines nationwide and became the target of derision by talk-show hosts. The president of a conservative San Francisco think tank told the *New York Times*, "They [students] have to go on to college and the work world, and this [reading books written by racially and ethnically diverse authors] would destroy their opportunities."[44]

Despite the vibrant tradition of Black American literature and a growing group of Latinx American writers (as well as an extensive body of Latin American literature), U.S. students rarely hear these voices in school. In January 1998, two Maryland school systems removed books by African American authors—Nobel Prize–winning Toni Morrison and poet Maya Angelou—from the curriculum after parents complained that the works were "trash" and "anti-white."[45] Parent protests in response to required reading lists, as recent as 2016 in some states (including Florida, New Jersey, and Virginia), reveal continuing tensions about what students should read in school. As part of recent conservative campaigns to eliminate ethnic studies programs statewide, officials in Arizona's Tucson Unified School District went so far in early 2012 as to ban a list of books including Sandra Cisneros's *The House on Mango Street* and Laura Esquivel's *Like Water for Chocolate* (both of which were used by the teachers quoted earlier), as well as Pulitzer Prize winner Junot Diaz's *Drown*, Shakespeare's *The Tempest*, and numerous other texts within which "race, ethnicity and oppression" were deemed central themes.

Integrated and Authentic Reading and Writing

Providing realistic and useful reading and writing experiences, and embedding skill instruction within them, starting in the earliest grades, is at the heart of a progressive approach. Previously referred to as "whole language," this approach is now more likely to be called "literature based" by progressives, in part to offset the misconception that it ignores students' literacy skill development. Teachers who teach from progressive perspectives focus on writing as a multistep, cyclical process of reflecting, drafting, editing, getting feedback, engaging in more reflection and drafting, and so on. These processes are not linear, have no clearly defined beginning and end, and at their best are intensely interactive.[46]

Central to these approaches are principles of integration and authenticity.[47] *Integration* means that literacy events and acts are not broken down into decontextualized subskills (thus the "whole" in "whole language"); that reading, writing, speaking, and listening are treated as different aspects of the same fundamental linguistic and cognitive processes; and that literacy is part and parcel of every school subject. For example, mastering science requires mastery of discipline-specific academic language, as well as the ability to read and create key "text types," such as lab reports, that are at the heart of "doing" science. *Authenticity* means that students should engage in literacy activities that allow them to communicate about real things of interest that have relevance beyond school. Students in all grades should read and produce real stories, expository texts, and other forms of genuine communication—even if they don't yet have all the conventional skills.

National Standards in the Language Arts

In 1992, the International Reading Association (IRA) (now called the International Literacy Association) and the National Council of Teachers of English (NCTE)—professional organizations for elementary and secondary teachers—led the development of national English language arts standards.[48] In 1994, they circulated drafts of the *Standards for the English Language Arts* to hundreds of reviewers, including literacy organizations, state departments of education, and scholars and practitioners. Despite overwhelmingly, but not exclusively, favorable reviews, the federal government refused to continue its sponsorship. The government cited "non-performance," but some leaders believed that the problem was political resistance, akin to what the mathematics community had experienced.[49]

With private funds and their own resources, the IRA and the NCTE continued developing their standards, seeking widespread reviews, and building consensus. They published their standards in 1996, and the NCTE reaffirmed them in 2012.[50]

The IRA/NCTE standards reflect progressive perspectives (which we link to sociocultural theories of learning in Chapter 6) and current research on how students develop literacy. They press schools to respect, and help students leverage, the literacy they have developed in their own lives. Many standards are expressed in terms of developing *practices* ("apply," "adjust," "conduct," "develop," etc.), rather than mastering *skills*. They ask teachers to engage students actively rather than just telling them what they should know, and to situate skill instruction within authentic literacy activities.

The standards pay attention to different historical periods, various literary genres, and a range of classic and contemporary, fiction and nonfiction works. In addition to the basic skills of spoken, written, and visual language, they expect students to conduct research by generating ideas and questions, posing problems, gathering information through a variety of technological and informational resources (e.g., libraries, databases, computer networks, video), and synthesizing and communicating what they've learned. They emphasize literature from the many rich cultural traditions that comprise U.S. society.

A Conservative Backlash

Shortly after the NCTE and the IRA published the standards in 1996, a professor from Missouri wrote an angry commentary for *Education Week* (a weekly newspaper with wide circulation in education circles):

> One would have hoped that the leading language arts standards-setting group in the country would have stated in plain English that our schools expect all students to use proper spelling, grammar, and punctuation in written communication. Indeed, any normal person

would have assumed that such fundamental matters would have been at the top of the list of concerns treated by language-arts teachers. However, if one reads the roughly 100-page document, one finds virtually no mention of such things.[51]

This critic closed by noting,

I am a product of the "drill and kill" school of literacy training complete with weekly spelling and vocabulary tests throughout K–12, along with 20- to 30-page research papers done on weekends at the public library (as opposed to the one- to two-page journal-writing exercises that now dominate English instruction). I, like so many others, somehow managed to overcome this seemingly "stifling" and "boring" education to develop a love for the written word and to author several books and numerous other publications.[52]

Another professor commented, "I can't imagine any other profession promulgating a practice that ends up harming literally hundreds of thousands of children."[53] As had happened in mathematics, these professors joined a rising chorus that attributed all manner of social and educational ills to a supposed departure from traditional, skills-based instruction.

The debate about how to teach language arts gathered advocates and resources far afield from the public schools and their mission to educate everyone well. Commercial companies like Sylvan Learning Centers filled the airways trying to "educate" the public to believe that schools had neglected an easy method for improving reading. Right-wing entities like the *Blumenfeld Education Letter* and the Eagle Forum Education and Defense Fund became strong back-to-basics advocates.[54]

The opposition to "whole language" made its way into policy as progressive and conservative groups jockeyed to have their views represented in state content standards. In California, Nebraska, North Carolina, Massachusetts, Texas, and Ohio, traditionalists mounted concerted efforts to mandate explicit phonics instruction and to eliminate the use of whole-language instruction; some, as in California, succeeded.[55]

Reading First

No Child Left Behind (NCLB) had a profound impact on early literacy instruction by establishing requirements that states and schools must abide by to receive federal funding for low-income students' K–3 reading instruction. The U.S. Department of Education (DOE) required that certain funds be spent on materials, professional development, and testing associated with "scientifically based" reading programs.

Under the NCLB-mandated Reading First program, only a limited set of reading programs qualified according to the DOE's definition of "scientifically based," and these were listed in its online database, called the What Works Clearinghouse.[56] Those that qualified fell squarely into a traditional, behavioral, skills-based approach to teaching and learning and rejected the constructivist approach to language arts recommended in the NCTE/IRA standards.

All approved programs were required to demonstrate with scientific studies that they could improve students' test performance in five discrete reading skills: phonemic awareness, phonics, vocabulary development, reading fluency (including oral reading), and reading comprehension strategies. All had to have a coherent design that included "explicit instructional strategies that address students' specific strengths and weaknesses, coordinated instructional sequences, ample practice opportunities and aligned student materials."[57] The DOE also required that the programs be taught in a protected, uninterrupted block of more than ninety minutes per day.

Perhaps the biggest concern about this mandate is that curricula considered to be scientifically based often "scripted" the teacher's role to guarantee consistent implementation across settings. "Scripting" specifies the precise words, content, presentation, and materials that teachers are meant to use. Such centralized control over lessons has great appeal for some but is a dreadful prospect for others. A scripted program can increase students' chances of having consistent educational experiences from teacher to teacher and potentially across schools, districts, and even states. Their prescriptiveness can help in schools lacking well-prepared teachers. However, a "script" is no substitute for highly competent teachers who use responsive, relevant, creative, and situationally appropriate teaching to help students meet standards.

A Progressive Perspective: Seeking Balance

What do progressives see as wrong with decoding phonetics, having both a subject and a verb in one's sentences, using conventional spelling, and learning the traditional protocols for writing research papers? Nothing! Contrary to the fears and accusations of traditionalists, most progressive teachers and researchers seek a "balanced" approach to literacy that neither neglects skills nor discounts the knowledge of the past thirty-plus years about literacy and learning.

David Pearson places the search for a balanced approach to language arts instruction in a historical perspective:

> I am convinced that we are capable, as a profession, of developing an approach to phonics that is respectful of the journeys we have taken since the early 1980s [when] phonics was a major component of literacy instruction. We are not the same profession now as we were then. Our views of reading have changed. In the 1960s, we regarded reading as fundamentally a perceptual process—taking in visual stimuli and recording them into verbal representations. In the 1970s, we discovered that reading was a cognitive process. In the 1980s, we added a distinctly socio-cultural perspective. And in the 1990s, we discovered a literacy perspective. Today we are learning more and more about reading as a political phenomenon. We need a phonics that respects these roads we have traveled.[58]

The National Academy of Sciences and other experts agree that the explicit teaching of phonics is only one among many strategies needed to assist young children to become literate. Effective teachers use multiple approaches to teach content and skills, integrate test preparation into meaningful lessons, make connections between what students learn at school and their lives outside of classrooms, help students think about their work as they are doing it, and press them to probe deeper into what they have learned. At best, teachers and students engage in "cognitive collaboration" to "push one another's thinking, challenge one another, or bounce ideas off one another."[59]

We see this balance in first-year teacher Benji Chang's struggle to infuse his understanding of how students construct literacy into the scripted Open Court Reading program, a program approved under Reading First that Benji was required to use with his first graders.

> Initially, I was overwhelmed and sometimes fell into the trap of just following along with what the Open Court teachers' guide told me to do. Because the program required my students to sit still for extended periods of time, I found myself thinly disguising its rote phonics drills and dry grammar lessons as games or with the use of a puppet. Although these strategies did not put lessons in the context of my students' lives or tap into their background knowledge, they were somewhat successful at engaging my class.

By late November, I was more familiar with my students and the Open Court structure, and I had learned to work my way around the program's subtractive nature. I developed integrated lessons using multicultural literature. For example, I used *The Legend of Hua Mu Lan* to engage students in practicing synonyms by trying to retell the story. Because the students were exposed to different types of literature, by mid-January they could take a critical look at some of the literature provided by Open Court. In the basal reader, there is a story about an African boy named Jafta. It is one of the first encounters that students have with a character of African descent in the reader and one of the rare stories that identifies the ethnic or racial background of a character.

During a shared reading of the story, I asked the students if they thought the story was fantasy or reality and why. Students said the story was fake because a little boy would not run around with hippos and elephants in his underwear. They said that he would probably have to help his family at home and do homework because that is what they would do. My students were not simply reciting the words on the pages of a story that reinforces stereotypes of Black Africans. They were developing a critical lens through which to view the world. My students were not just developing literacy, but critical literacy as well.

—Benji Chang
First-year teacher, grade 1

Scholars Gloria Ladson-Billings and Lisa Delpit, widely known advocates of progressive and critical multicultural curriculum, provide another important reason for a balanced language arts curriculum. They use the term *codes of power* to describe the traditional skills and conventions of reading, writing, and speaking in Standard English. Ladson-Billings, Delpit, and others worry that if teachers don't teach these codes of power to students of color at the same time as they are building on students' home languages and cultures, they will limit the opportunities of students whose families and communities speak something other than formal Standard English.[60] They argue that nothing can ever justify an education that denies students the power to communicate skillfully to all people.

CCSS in English Language Arts

The introduction of the CCSS in English Language Arts and Literacy in 2011 represents the latest national policy development in literacy education. The CCSS in English/Language Arts address reading, writing, speaking, listening, and language and purport to ensure students' college and career readiness. Some key goals are to increase K–12 students' exposure to and engagement with informational texts; increase the complexity of the texts they read (beginning in the second grade); enable them to craft arguments that are supported by textual evidence; and develop and use "academic language." The CCSS also call for higher-order thinking, as well as increased collaboration and communication among peers.[61]

Some literacy scholars, including David Pearson, have praised the CCSS for their rigorous and research-based approach to reading comprehension, their strong focus on oral language, and their assertion that teachers from all disciplines ought to be considered and supported to develop as literacy teachers.[62] Some language acquisition scholars have pointed to the CCSS's potential to raise expectations for historically underserved students, like Emergent Bilinguals, whom schools have long treated as less capable than their peers.[63]

Yet criticisms appear to be as widespread as endorsements. Numerous educators and scholars have argued that the standards' intense focus on text complexity and informational texts limits students' exposure to literary texts—arguably detrimental for all, but especially for young learners. Relatedly, many argue that the CCSS's definition of text complexity fails to draw on research and relies on overly narrow measures of complexity.[64] Some have suggested that the CCSS's "text complexity staircase" fails to capture key characteristics of texts for young readers, and therefore may direct early childhood educators to select inappropriate texts.[65] Meanwhile, literacy scholars have faulted the exemplar texts associated with the text complexity staircase for overemphasizing "classics" written predominantly by European and male authors and overwhelmingly presenting "dominant, heterosexual and able-bodied" perspectives.[66]

Literacy experts have also questioned the CCSS's recommendation that teachers privilege an instructional strategy called *close reading*, which requires that teachers forgo prereading activities and that students withhold prior understandings and experiences as they make meaning of new texts, relying instead on what appears "within the four corners of the page." In 2012, the NCTE cautioned against relying exclusively on close reading, pointing to the strategy's limited capacity to "ensure that students will develop deep understandings of what they read."[67]

Teachers of historically marginalized students need to be especially vigilant about how they use the CCSS. The standards' monolingual focus (which fails to recognize the linguistic resources of Emergent Bilinguals), recommendations that students ignore connections between their prior knowledge and new texts, and the high stakes attached to student performance on CCSS-aligned standardized tests all put minoritized students at more risk than their peers.[68]

With the CCSS having been adopted by so many states, the NCTE is currently focused on supporting teachers to teach in adaptive and student-centered ways, "helping teachers and schools interpret the Common Core State Standards, contextualize and connect to the CCSS, and plan units of instruction keeping students at the center and teachers as decision-makers."[69] Similarly, IRA past president Kathryn Au reminds educators and policymakers that rigorous standards are only the first step in a three-part process that includes quality assessments that reflect the standards, as well as professional development for teachers. Without these other components in place, it is unlikely that the CCSS or any standards-based reform will improve student learning.[70]

Social Studies

Hannah Cha had just begun teaching first graders in a Latinx immigrant neighborhood in Los Angeles. In the fall, Hannah, like many first-grade teachers in the United States, wanted to teach her students about Thanksgiving and tie her reading and writing lessons to this historical event. But Hannah's understanding of children's learning led her in a less traditional direction.

> Thanksgiving is more than just the picturesque scene of European pilgrims sitting at a table eating turkey with Native Americans standing, almost hiding or blending, into the background. . . . My class considered the Pilgrims as immigrants seeking a life of more opportunities. They concluded that we are all pilgrims. Most of our families journeyed here from another country in search for a better existence. . . .
>
> We had just read *How Many Days to America?* by Eve Bunting, and Marissa strongly identified with the story. It is a book about a Latino family that underwent many tribulations to immigrate to America. Although Marissa did not remember [her immigration], the experience was very alive to her through her mother's stories. She shared some of these stories with the whole class and concluded that she is American and Mexican—she is American even though people tell her that she is not. When a writing activity followed the story, Marissa went straight to work. Usually she is easily distracted . . . but she connected with this activity and took some risks. She achieved the critical awareness that she is just as much an American. . . .
>
> —Hannah Cha
> First-year teacher, grade 1

In Hannah's social studies lesson, first grader Marissa is both learning the traditional story of Thanksgiving and developing a sense of pride and an academic identity grounded in her own and her family's experiences and ways of knowing. But this lesson would be judged differently by those who hold traditional, progressive, or critical multiculturalist perspectives. At one end of the spectrum, traditionalists want social studies lessons to preserve traditional versions of the past, to teach Marissa and other students basic historical "facts," as they were established in generations past, and to instill patriotism. At the other end of the spectrum, most progressive and multicultural social studies educators want Marissa and other students to understand and think critically about traditional Anglo-American history and to have access to historical knowledge *about* Americans from a range of backgrounds, and on their *own* terms.

At the secondary level, Judy Smith teaches her high school seniors a required course in economics. Judy pursues the traditional goals of U.S. schooling; in her words,

> [to] educate and guide our students to recognize their potential, provide them the skills and strategies to be successful after high school and college, and understand their role in our democratic society; . . . educate students that our democracy should not be taken for granted, and that it requires constant vigilance and responsibility.

Yet her lessons are anything but traditional. Judy also believes that social studies teachers "need to direct students towards critical consciousness—of their potential, of their freedom, of ongoing injustices, and of the obligation to ensure our democracy and improve on it for future generations."

Like Hannah, Judy teaches both basic concepts and critical consciousness. In one three-week unit, students considered the economic and social effects of colonialism and neocolonialism, including how consumer habits and beliefs in wealthy countries impact the environment, other cultures, and people. In addition to basic economic concepts, her students grappled with the connections among their own buying habits, business ethics, and social injustices.

> Students analyzed economic development indicators and questioned why persons living in the North are the "haves" and people in the South are the "have nots." We discussed racist reasons for colonialism and how it continues in different forms today. Students read about sweatshops and indigenous cultures and how corporations take advantage of people of color. Finally, we talked about what our roles are in the global marketplace, what changes in our own behaviors we could make, and what additional steps could be taken to address some of the social injustices.
>
> Many of my female students love shopping. They want to go into business for themselves or become clothes designers. Some also work at retail stores. Two lessons, a reading that focuses on a popular Los Angeles clothes store and a video called *Zoned for Slavery*, showcased brand name stores (Gap Inc., OshKosh, and Eddie Bauer) exploiting female workers in their sweatshops. The brand name recognition makes the content accessible to students. They could feel the pain of the sweatshop workers. They could also look at themselves as consumers and decide if they want to change any of their purchasing habits.
>
> —Judy Smith
> High school social studies

As with mathematics and English language arts, intense political controversy has swirled around the social studies curriculum. Here, too, traditionalists and progressives have debated what and whose history and culture should be taught to young Americans.

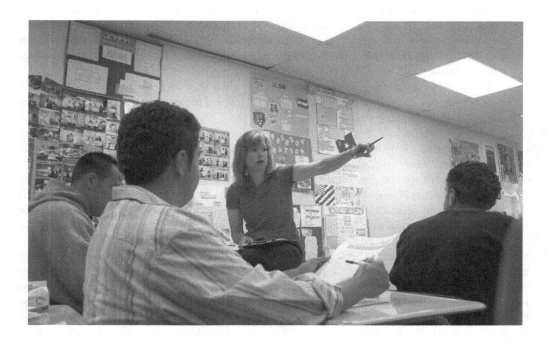

Traditional Social Studies: Facts and Figures Framed by the Dominant Culture

At the core of the traditional curriculum are facts about U.S. history and government to be memorized, appreciation for citizens' rights and responsibilities, and acceptance of the basic values and ideas in the nation's core documents—the Declaration of Independence, the Constitution, and the Bill of Rights. Elementary school teachers teach units focused on the Founding Fathers and the Westward Movement. Middle schoolers take classes in U.S. history and government, including a hefty unit or whole course on state history. High school students take required courses in U.S. history and government, supplemented by electives in psychology, world history, economics, sociology, and law.

Traditionalists want a focus on the traditional disciplines of history, geography, and civics (government). History lessons, for example, should emphasize how government and the values embedded in its founding documents have endured over time, as well as accounts of how the values and courage of leaders and heroes have shaped this country.[71] This attention to solutions and victories reflects the traditional view of history as a story of progress.[72]

Traditionalist history focuses on the perspective of leaders and the dominant culture. And though some presidents, generals, tycoons, and inventors had humble origins and improved the lot of "common folks," school history provides few insights into what it was like to live a working person's life during Reconstruction, the Great Depression, the 1950s, and so on.

Immigrant and minoritized groups may be included, but the focus is often on assimilation into White culture. For example, a 1965 fourth-grade California history textbook about indigenous peoples' experience in the California missions reveals how traditional history results in an inaccurate account that would differ substantially if told from another's perspective:

Indians helped the settlers, and the settlers helped the Indians. The Indians had better food and clothing than they had ever had. They were more comfortable than they had ever been.

Once in a while a mission Indian had to be punished for something he had done. Sometimes such Indians ran away. Some of them took guns with them. Sometimes they took horses with them, too. The runaway Indians taught the wild Indians how to steal animals and other things from the missions. Once in a while soldiers had to protect the missions from an Indian raid.

The Indians at the missions ate more regularly than they had when they were wild. The padres took care of them in many ways. . . . They learned to do many things as the Spaniards did. They learned many new skills.[73]

This text was used for many years. Children who learned these "facts" and attitudes are now at the height of their economic, social, and political influence. They are the parents and grandparents of today's students, and they are veteran teachers and curriculum designers. We must wonder if, when, and how they changed their views of history, conquest, and Indigenous people. We hope that their reflections on the California missions do not bring forth images of simple, benevolent settlers and happy, grateful native people who sometimes were very bad and had to be punished.

The traditional curriculum includes leaders representing minoritized groups, but the predominant focus is on the progress they've made toward solving social problems. Students may learn that Cesar Chavez led protests to improve the conditions of migrant farmworkers. However, they often learn little about the exploitive conditions that farmworkers faced and continue to face or the poverty that remains. Similarly, students may learn overly simple lessons: that the mistake of the Japanese internment camps won't be repeated or that Rosa Parks and Martin Luther King, Jr. acted as lone heroes to end segregation, without understanding how their actions were connected to broader political, strategic efforts.

One review of multicultural curriculum in social studies classrooms concluded:

> Students have little knowledge of the history of race relations in the United States. What they do know is the character of the relations between enslaved African Americans and their White masters. Focusing on the "evils" of slavery—cruel masters, the brutal treatment of slaves, belief in the inferiority of slaves—is important to be sure. But it provides a history that is too narrow and limited to be of much use in discussing contemporary American society. It provides very weak links to issues of racism, discrimination, and the denial of political and civil rights.[74]

In one example, college students revealed their limited understanding of African Americans' experiences with racism.

> Jean wrote about southern slavery as the "era of racism, prejudice, and slavery"; Eric wrote, "less than ninety years later [after the Civil War], black people were the target of racism once again"; Diana wrote, "that was the past"; and Sue, summing up African Americans' experiences, wrote "in the end, as you know, there is no more slavery anymore."[75]

These students don't see racial segregation and prejudice as enduring social problems, but rather as historical moments that came and went.

Finally, traditionalists prefer that teachers teach controversial topics from the perspective of dominant values, rather than as complicated issues to explore, discover, or clarify. AIDS, for example, is rarely presented as emerging in a historical and political context of homophobia. Drug and alcohol abuse are usually portrayed as resulting from character flaws. These are not invitations to explore or to solve problems from a social science perspective as much as they are conclusions the curriculum asserts.

Many traditionalists lament that today's schools focus on current moral and political trends, values, and issues and neglect historic events. They worry that the process of *doing* social science and constructive teaching methods (simulations, projects, etc.) opens the door to multiple interpretations of history, rather than a unitary and unifying story that preserves the country's foundational norms. In fact, many object to the term *social studies* as relativistic and interpretive instead of sticking to the "facts" of history, geography, or economics. They might criticize the progressive teachers quoted in this chapter for emphasizing dilemmas and shortcomings instead of building positive and pride-worthy impressions of American culture and society.

Progressive Social Studies: Critical and Multicultural Approaches

In contrast, progressives want students to learn to think like historians, political scientists, geographers, anthropologists, sociologists, and economists. They hope students will learn how social scientists construct and understand knowledge. They may ask students to do original research and reenact society's decision making and problem solving around critical social issues. They may ask students to support historical arguments with evidence. They may ask students to place their personal and family histories in the context of current and historical events.

Progressives prefer a curriculum that helps students "place the human story in larger context."[76] Many, like Hannah Cha and Judy Smith, have students use history and social commentaries to observe and make sense of their own lives. Teacher Erik Korporaal's class included 10- and 11-year-old students, some of whom were Latinx and Catholic and some of whom were Black and Protestant or Muslim. Erik connected the standard sixth-grade social studies unit on Egypt with the rich and complex knowledge that the children could share about their own backgrounds and cultural practices.

> My students were learning about Egyptian burial practices. They researched the burial customs of their own families and cultures, shared information, and compared their own customs with those of other students. The students now had real-life contexts that they could relate to new understandings of Egypt. They were able to critically analyze their burial customs and form deeper understandings about their history and origin.
>
> —Erik Korporaal
> First-year teacher, grade 6

Progressives also challenge students to view history from the perspective of those at the bottom of the social ladder, particularly those who may not have benefited from the technological advances, territorial expansion, and economic progress that traditional histories highlight. First-year teacher Jennifer Garcia asked her eleventh graders to consider how the industrial age affected workers and immigrants. She included their stories alongside more conventional accounts of the rise of industrialists' power and the making of new economic policy.

> Throughout the unit on "Industrialization, Unionism, and Immigration," I attempted to incorporate critical multiculturalism—not in one or two activities but as a central theme. The goal was for students to be exposed to and appreciate the period's social complexities. Activities and discussions based on themes such as factory life, union organizing, political machines and corruption, and urban living conditions challenged students' preconceived notions about workers, immigrants, and politics. By the end of the unit, students had not only been exposed to the social complexities of the late 1800s but developed a measure of

empathy with the people and issues through critically examining social, political, and economic issues.

—Jennifer Garcia
First-year teacher, history, grade 11

Moreover, progressive educators stress that *all* students—not just students of color, not just older students—need a multicultural curriculum that goes beyond a more traditional "let's include everyone" approach. Jeffrey Madrigal found a way to engage fourth graders in such an approach:

The study of music quickly expanded into a study of international and domestic politics and geography. The class explored the African roots of hip-hop and learned about the trials and accomplishments of Nelson Mandela. We used the strong social commentary present in some music to study the politics of South Africa (South African revolutionary music), to learn about the Rastafarian religion of Jamaica (Reggae), and to look at Black nationalism in America (hip-hop). After the lesson, a simple rap song took on historical roots and sociopolitical meaning. We explored social commentary [in] jazz and Middle Eastern music.

—Jeffrey Madrigal
First-year teacher, grade 4

Critical multiculturalists go further. They, like teacher Martha Guerrero in the next vignette, critique traditional historians, geographers, and anthropologists as mostly White men who learned and work in the tradition of the European Enlightenment. They believe that students draw energy and optimism from grappling with history and contemporary issues from multiple perspectives. They think that schools have an important activist role in challenging the status quo and improving society. They argue that the pursuit of social justice does not require one to be dispassionate, passive, or neutral.

My unit on slavery begins with the idea that historical texts give diverse subjective and objective information. My goal is to encourage students to begin questioning information that commonly remains unexamined. Thus, students are asked to consider who writes history, who is excluded from history, and why history is written as it is. We analyze history by looking at slavery as an economic mode of exploitation. Students examine how slavery is depicted by different authors. I explain the difference between primary and secondary sources. In groups students analyze firsthand accounts of African American slaves. By looking at these primary documents, we validate the history and culture of our ancestors. As a class, we outline the textbook section on slavery. We then compare the different ways that slavery was presented.

—Martha Guerrero
First-year teacher, high school history

Progressives like the teachers quoted here have had an impact on the social studies curriculum over the past few decades. For example, the 1991 revision of the California social studies text made quite a few changes to the 1965 account of Indigenous peoples at the California missions:

Although some Indians were content in the missions, many others were unhappy with this new way of life. By living at the missions the Indians gave up their own culture, the way of life they had known in their tribal villages. They could only leave the mission grounds with permission from the padres. They were not free to hunt or to pick berries.
   Mission Indians were not allowed to return to their tribes once they agreed to take part in mission life. Some ran away but soldiers usually brought them back and sometimes whipped

them. Others wanted to revolt. They wanted to rise up against their leaders, the Spanish padres and the soldiers at the mission communities.

Sometimes Indians revolted violently.

Six years after its founding, the San Diego Mission was attacked by Indians. They set the mission on fire and killed one of the padres.

Many Indians died of diseases brought by the Spanish. When crops failed, Indians didn't have enough to eat. Some became sick from the change in their diet on the missions. By the end of the Mission period, the California Indian population was half the size that it had been when Father Serra raised his first cross at San Diego Mission.[77]

However, even this newer version, more than twenty-five years after the prior edition, waffled as it portrayed the stunning violations of decency and human rights that the Indigenous peoples of California endured. The revised text still situated Native Americans as living only in the past and within the White American story of westward expansion that brought progress to the wilderness. Native American deaths seem sanitized, kept at a safe distance from their killers; disease, crop failure, and a change in diet—not theft of land or enslavement—reduced the Native American population by half. Native Americans were framed as uncivilized; they revolted "violently," attacked and burned missions, and killed padres. These accounts are not the only ones that have been challenged for inaccuracy and misrepresentation. Critics opposed California's standards and aligned textbooks for framing the transatlantic slave trade as an "immigrant experience," minimizing and precluding discussions of racism then and now.[78] Still others noted the standards' failure to identify American imperialist ideology.[79]

The National History Standards: Seeking a Middle Ground

The historians and educators at UCLA's National Center for History in the Schools knew they had walked into the middle of a contentious debate when they launched their development of national curriculum standards in history. Hoping to avoid being labeled as part of either camp, the center included both traditional and progressive groups in the standards-setting process. In 1994, after two years of work, the group had framed standards for teaching U.S. and world history from kindergarten to the twelfth grade.

Historical Thinking and Historical Understanding

To be balanced, the group specified two types of standards. One focused on the progressive goal of developing historical thinking skills. Stanford University educational historian Sam Wineburg explains that historical thinking,

> goes against the grain of how we ordinarily think, [which is] one of the reasons why it is much easier to learn names, dates and stories than it is to change the fundamental mental structures we use to grasp the meaning of the past. . . . Mature historical knowing teaches us to go beyond our own image, to go beyond our brief life, and to go beyond the fleeting moment in human history into which we've been born.[80]

The second type of standard focused on the traditionalists' goal of acquiring knowledge of historical events. They defined them as follows:

> *Historical thinking skills* . . . enable students to evaluate evidence, develop comparative and causal analyses, interpret the historical record, and construct sound historical arguments and perspectives on which informed decisions in contemporary life can be based.

Historical understandings . . . define what students should know about the history of their nation and of the world. These understandings are drawn from the record of human aspirations, strivings, accomplishments, and failures in at least five spheres of human activity: the social, political, scientific/technological, economic, and philosophical/religious/ aesthetic. They also provide students the historical perspectives required to analyze contemporary issues and problems confronting citizens today.

Historical thinking and understanding do not, of course, develop independently of one another. Higher levels of historical thinking depend upon and are linked to the attainment of higher levels of historical understanding. For these reasons, the standards . . . provide an integration of historical thinking and understanding.[81]

Despite the effort to forge a middle ground between traditional and progressive camps, the battle over these standards was intense. At the height of the controversy, the U.S. Senate even condemned the standards.

"The End of History"—Traditionalists Attack the Standards

Two weeks before the public release of the standards, Lynne Cheney (the same Lynne Cheney who railed against the NCTM math standards) published a *Wall Street Journal* editorial, "The End of History." In it, she accused the National Center for History in the Schools of writing standards that promoted a left-wing political agenda. Among other things, she complained that Harriet Tubman was mentioned six times, while Ulysses S. Grant was named only once and Robert E. Lee not at all—evidence, she argued, of a politically correct emphasis on women and people of color.[82]

Rush Limbaugh, the popular conservative radio talk-show host, picked up the attack, saying the standards should be flushed "down the sewer of multiculturalism."

> When you bring [students] into a classroom, and you teach them that America is a rotten place . . . and they don't have a chance here . . . you have a bunch of embittered people growing up, robbing and stealing and turning to crime because they've been told all their young lives that there's no future for them. . . . This country does not deserve the reputation it's getting in multicultural classrooms, and the zenith of this bastardization of American history has been reached with the new standards.[83]

Not all criticism came from politically conservative voices, but the traditionalist argument was made most vehemently by those with antigovernment, pro–free market, and fundamentalist religious ideologies. Former Reagan White House policy adviser Gary Bauer, later the head of the conservative organization American Values, declared:

> It is hard to overstate the magnitude of the failure. For the Department of Education, this embarrassing public fiasco is indisputable evidence of bureaucratic ineptitude. If we adopt these amnesiac history standards, we will succumb to a kind of national identity crisis. We will cease to remember who we are and why it matters that there is an America.
>
> . . . There is an anti-free enterprise bias to the history standards. Students are encouraged to put John D. Rockefeller on trial for his sharp business tactics. But where do the standards lead young Americans to an understanding of the most productive and free economic system in history? Nowhere.
>
> It goes without saying that the history standards' emphasis on race, gender, and class forces young Americans to accept a secular world view. The history standards panel clearly failed to comprehend the influence of religion in American life.[84]

What called forth such impassioned concern? Were the writers of the standards that ill informed, that un-American, and that irreligious? Following is a brief sample of the kind of language in the standards that set off the critics. Indeed, it encourages not only questioning but questioning of values:

> Value-laden issues worthy of classroom analysis include not only those irredeemable events in human history from which students can most easily draw clear ethical judgment—the Holocaust, for example, or the Cambodian genocide under the Pol Pot regime. These analyses should also address situations of lasting consequence in which what is morally right and wrong may not be self-evident. Was it right, for example, for Lincoln, in his Emancipation Proclamation, to free only those slaves behind the Confederate lines? Because of the complicated way values act upon people confronted with the need to decide, the full moral situation in a past event is not always immediately clear. Students should understand, therefore, that their opinions should be held tentative and open to revision as they acquire new insight into these historical problems. Particularly challenging are the many social issues throughout United States history on which multiple interests and different values have come to bear. Issues of civil rights, equal education opportunity, reproductive rights, and criminal justice have all brought such conflicts to the fore.[85]

Clobbered by political backlash, the National Center for History in the Schools agreed to revise the standards and in 1996 issued a document that fared better with conservatives. American history was cast in a more positive light, and many previously absent names were included.[86] The center dropped the "teaching examples" and some of the wording that others had found offensive.

Unlike the national English language arts standards, the history standards (revised in 2010) have retained their U.S. Department of Education sponsorship. Even after being vindicated, however, many textbook publishers shied away from using the standards as a blueprint for standards and curriculum.[87]

Individual states have drawn on the national standards to different degrees as they formulated their own social studies standards. As a result, the standards vary considerably across states. California's current standards, for example, frame social studies as a lengthy list of dates and facts—implicitly favoring instruction that has students memorize events, dates, and people.[88] Meanwhile, New York's state standards lead students to question, analyze, organize, and explore big ideas in relation to one another.[89]

In 2016, California's State Board of Education adopted a new History and Social Science Framework, authored by members of the California History-Social Science Project.[90] Although the state's traditional standards remain, the new framework reflects progressive attempts to incorporate new content (such as the election of Barack Obama), as well as revised content about minoritized groups (such as the history of the LGBTQ community). To increase support for California's Emergent Bilingual students, who comprise more than 20 percent of the state's students, the framework makes explicit connections to the state's English Language Development standards.[91] Also significant, the framework incorporates the CCSS disciplinary literacy standards that are specific to history and social science. Because these standards encourage teachers to have students conduct research, read primary (historical) documents, and engage in analytical thinking, their incorporation into the framework stands to support more progressive approaches to teaching history/social science than the state standards endorse.[92]

Not surprisingly, the framework was not accepted without debate. Traditionalists, and especially those affiliated with conservative religious groups, have been vocal. Some consider the framework "biased" for minimizing references to Judeo-Christian traditions and acknowledging the multiple religions that have influenced U.S. society; framing religion as socially constructed rather than "revealed"; and attributing U.S. culture and progress to more than European traditions.[93]

Similar battles have occurred in New York, Texas, and elsewhere.[94] Conservative Texas school board members criticized the state's social studies curriculum for leaning "too far to the left" and recently made more than 100 amendments to the social studies standards "that stress the superiority of American capitalism, question the Founding Fathers' commitment to a purely secular government and present Republican political philosophies in a more positive light."[95] In contrast, University of Texas education professors Anthony Brown and Kefferlyn Brown analyzed nineteen Texas fifth-, eighth-, and eleventh-grade social studies textbooks, and found that these allegedly "left-leaning" texts attended only minimally to acts of racial violence against African Americans. Even in cases when acts of racial violence were included, explanations tended to be distorted, portraying perpetrators as different from the average citizen, thereby limiting students' understanding of the institutionalized aspects of such actions.[96]

The debate about *what* social studies and *whose* history should be taught will not likely be settled soon. As of 2011, fewer than half the states explicitly identified the 9/11 attacks in their high school social studies standards. Some schools and teachers shy away from this and other potentially controversial content; others work hard to tackle such events, even when standards and textbooks do not (or haven't yet).

The best hope, as always, lies with teachers who acquire the confidence and commitment that come with preparation, experience, and scholarship. Indeed, teachers may have more influence over how social studies is delivered to students than for other subjects because social studies is rarely included in high-stakes standardized tests. Teachers who want to support students to think deeply and ask hard questions about social life have good options for help. Progressive historians, such as the late Howard Zinn, write history from the perspectives of the traditionally disenfranchised.[97] Used with care and thoughtfulness, the Internet is also a rich resource for escaping the chilling effects of curriculum and standards battles. Multicultural educator and scholar Christine Sleeter suggests "un-standardizing" the curriculum. Focal Point 5.2 offers sample questions that teachers interested in this approach might pose and provides a structure for standards-based critical multicultural curriculum planning.[98]

Science

My integrated, coordinated science class is centered on a "survivor" theme. The students and I are stranded together on Santa Rosa Island—one of the larger Channel Islands off the coast of California. The first day of class I introduced the situation, showed them a map, and asked them what they wanted to learn. My students brainstormed topics that they wanted to study that would better equip us for survival on the island. They decided on three topics: water, food, and shelter. We decided that we needed to farm to sustain ourselves, and that to be efficient farmers we needed to be experts on plants. The students also wanted to study medicinal plants so that we could make medicine. Every lesson we did was tied to surviving on the island.

I wanted my students to be able to describe why humans and plants are dependent on each other, and what a plant needs to photosynthesize. If we understood how plants work, then we would be good farmers on the island. My objectives matched the district standards.

My goal for scientific literacy guided many of my activities. I wanted my students to acquire the academic language needed to talk about plant structures and their role in photosynthesis—terms including *absorption, xylem, phloem,* and *glucose.* The students learned by doing, and the content was learned as students used materials to test out hypotheses. The experiments forced students away from passive listening to active participation.

. . . Having an overarching theme of "survival" helped my students to understand scientific principles. Facts they learned were not discrete bodies of knowledge, but rather related principles that supported each other. There was always a purpose to learning. Having a theme also helped me to select science concept depth over breadth.

—Jennie Lee
First-year teacher, high school science

Jennie Lee's science unit would not please everyone. As in the other disciplines, long-standing debates permeate the science curriculum. Some of the most hotly debated questions are:

- Should science curriculum focus on depth or breadth of coverage?
- Should schools teach the traditional science disciplines—earth science, biology, chemistry, and physics—separately or integrated around themes or concepts?
- Should lessons connect science with related social issues?
- Should all students learn the same science, and can they learn it?

Focal Point 5.2
Un-standardizing the Curriculum

Questions to Guide Analysis of Curriculum Documents for Ideology

1. Who produced this document, resource, or website (if it is possible to tell)? Can you tell where the authors or producers are coming from?
2. How is this document, resource, or website intended to be used? By whom?
3. What is it trying to accomplish? What is its purpose?
4. What key concepts does it use? What problems, issues, and points of view does it direct attention toward? What does it direct attention away from? Whose view of the world does it tend to support? Whose view does it undermine or ignore?
5. How would you describe the ideology of this document, resource, or website?
6. Whose knowledge isn't here that could be here? What is left out?

Curriculum Planning Guide

1. Write down a potential concept you could teach.
2. Brainstorm what you could teach, or want students to know, related to that concept.
3. Classify the ideas above according to whether they are
    - worth being familiar with (W);
    - important to know and/or do (I); or
    - essential to enduring understanding (E).
4. Rewrite the central idea, based on the work you did above. Write this as a central question, where possible.
5. What sociocultural groups' knowledge do you have a good grasp on, related to the "enduring understandings" above? Which do you *not* have much of a grasp on?
6. List three to six things you would like students to be able to do with these understandings by the end of the unit.
7. What do you anticipate students already know or can do, related to this central idea? What would you like to know about their existing knowledge, conceptions, or experiences?

8. List key ideas, understandings, and skills students probably don't have that they will need to learn in order to fully comprehend what you've identified as "enduring." (Many of these might be what you classified as "worth being familiar with" or "important to know.") Your unit will need to teach these things.

9. For each of the items above, list at least one potential form of evidence of student learning. This forms the basis of your unit assessment plan.

10. What teaching/learning experiences will help students successfully master the learning outcomes above, given what students already bring?

Source: Adapted from Christine Sleeter and Judith Flores Carmona, *Un-standardizing Curriculum: Multicultural Teaching in the Standards-Based Classroom* (New York: Teachers College Press, 2016).

The answers to the preceding questions, and reactions to Jennie's "survivor" unit, relate directly to theories about knowledge and learning, and they speak precisely to whether social justice values are a legitimate part of the school curriculum.

Traditional Science: Topics, Subtopics, and Facts in Sequence

Traditionalists see science as objective, empirically based, value-neutral explanations of "the way things are." They want teaching to transmit this knowledge through explanation, demonstration, and practice. They prefer the science disciplines to be taught separately.

Traditional science curriculum is organized into sequences of topics, subtopics, and facts, often matched to the table of contents of science textbooks. Students learn scientific terms (e.g., *photosynthesis, osmosis, deciduous*), memorize brief versions of important principles (e.g., plants are green because they contain chlorophyll; plants produce oxygen), and conduct experiments that demonstrate the concepts they are learning. This cycle repeats until the teacher has covered all the topics. In 2000, the National Commission on Mathematics and Science Teaching for the 21st Century, chaired by the late senator and former astronaut John Glenn, found that teachers rarely ask students to learn the powerful and fascinating ideas of science. Instead, they "spend much of their time learning definitions, or the labels that apply to natural phenomena and scientific processes."[99] Almost two decades later, this remains the norm in many classrooms.

Traditional high school science consists of introductory and low-level general science courses; college-preparatory survey courses in specific disciplines—most often biology, anatomy, chemistry, and physics; and advanced placement versions of these survey courses for the science students considered the most capable. Traditionalists judge efforts to integrate the sciences and place them in a social context as disturbing signs of curricular weakness. They fear that such moves erode the rigor of students' academic studies and undermine the structure of the knowledge that has developed through scientific discovery.

The traditional science curriculum has been widely criticized for skimming the surface of science without promoting in-depth scientific understanding. For example, a 1996 international study found that the average American ninth-grade science student covered nearly fifty-five topics in one year. Most of the other fifty nations in the study produced much higher achievement in science and offered far fewer topics. Other reports published by the National Academies reiterate similar claims. For example, a 2007 report, *Taking Science to School: Learning and Teaching Science in Grades K–8*, offered the following conclusion:

> Many existing national, state, and local standards and assessments, as well as the typical curricula in use in the United States, contain too many disconnected topics given equal priority.

Too little attention is given to how students' understanding of a topic can be supported and enhanced from grade to grade. As a result, topics receive repeated, shallow coverage with little consistency, which provides a fragile foundation for further knowledge growth.[100]

Likewise, a 2005 report focused on high school laboratory science concluded that the vast number of topics teachers were expected to cover limited the time available for engaging students in hands-on laboratory experiences that build skills of investigation and experimentation. Both reports suggested that fewer topics studied in depth would result in greater science knowledge.[101]

Teachers face enormous pressure to provide students a taste of many science topics. One source of pressure derives from the familiarity of traditional science classes—the kind we experienced ourselves. Even some distinguished scientists are extraordinarily suspicious of progressive approaches that depart from the traditional, expansive coverage. Textbooks press teachers toward a traditional approach. Publishers try to include all the topics that different schools might want to teach; as a result, no one topic receives in-depth treatment. Thus, texts encourage superficial coverage—breadth over depth—especially if teachers' own science knowledge limits their ability to extend lessons beyond what the text provides.

Progressive Science: Inquiry and Investigation

Some of the nation's most prestigious science organizations, including the National Science Foundation and the American Association for the Advancement of Science (AAAS), have endorsed more progressive approaches.[102]

Progressives argue that science is a product of human understanding and subject to constant revision. Most contend that scientific "truth" lies on a continuum from pretty good hunches to long-enduring, seemingly unassailable (but always open to reinvestigation) facts.

A progressive curriculum is likely to be organized into sustained investigations that cut across specific science disciplines. Students observe, experiment, and interpret what they find. Students work cooperatively, make sense of new concepts through the lens of their prior experiences, and offer predictions based on articulated reasons. Different experiments occur simultaneously, and students follow the progress of those that relate to their own hypotheses. For example, imagine a life science unit in which students cultivate plants so that they can observe and make sense of the processes by which plants grow. Hands-on work (e.g., altering light, water, nutrients, and other growing conditions) while observing, recording, and forming and testing hypotheses anchors students' engagement with traditional knowledge sources (e.g., lectures, films, and textbooks). Students also investigate the real-life consequences of plant growth for farmers, the public, the environment, businesses, and the government. Students consider the careers and lifestyles of those whose work centers on plants: farmworkers, growers, wholesalers, retailers, experimental botanists, chemists, conservationists, rangers, teachers, florists, and so on. Students present formal oral reports of their observations and conclusions. The teacher holds students accountable for core concepts that they all should master (photosynthesis, osmosis, the nature of cells, plant reproduction, etc.) and for the concepts and foundations of their independent research.

Progressive science educators argue that old distinctions among the science disciplines should not drive the curriculum. The late Paul DeHart Hurd, a leader of progressive science education, argued that integrating the science curriculum reflects changes in science:

Disciplines have been replaced by research fields, and most research is done by teams of investigators. A team represents a cognitive system that is phasing out the traditional notion of scientific inquiry. Much of scientific research is strategy or problem oriented rather than theory stimulated. For example, the Hubble telescope has made a wealth of observations, and it may take scientists a century or more to find theoretical explanations for them. A blending of science disciplines is taking place, such as biophysics, biochemistry, and biogeochemistry. The most active areas of research today are cross-disciplinary. . . .

Changes in the practice and culture of today's science go unnoticed. Professional science educators, as well as most scientists, pay little attention to what these revolutionary transformations in science ought to mean for a citizen's education in the sciences.[103]

In the past two decades, many secondary schools have converted the traditional "layer cake" of separate physical science, biology, chemistry, and physics courses into a sequence of integrated classes organized around themes. Others have integrated science and math since the real-world application of one often requires facility with the other.

National Standards: Integrated, Socially Relevant Science for All

In the 1990s, the federal government charged the National Academy of Sciences with developing national science standards. The first edition, published in 1996, specified eight content categories necessary for a high-quality science program. Physical science, life science, earth and space science, and science and technology are four categories that sound familiar, and their adoption into school programs would not have upset traditional views of teaching science. However, the other four categories, described below, turned traditional science education on its head.

Joining Content and Process

The *National Science Education Standards* introduced four "new" provocative and exciting conceptions of science content:

- The content of science cannot be placed outside of science's unifying concepts and processes.
- Participation in inquiry is scientific content, not just process.
- Scientific knowledge is not distinct from societal challenges.
- The history of science is science content that underscores science as a human and social enterprise.

Each of the four standards specified associated core skills and concepts. For example, upon entering high school, students would develop and enact the following abilities for scientific inquiry:

- Identify questions and concepts that guide scientific investigations.
- Design and conduct scientific investigations.
- Use technology and mathematics to improve investigations and communications.
- Formulate and revise scientific explanations and models using logic and evidence.
- Recognize and analyze alternative explanations and models. Communicate and defend a scientific argument.

In addition to these "abilities to do scientific inquiry," the standards specified the *understandings* that students should develop. For example, students in grades 9–12 should understand how substances exist in or are represented by "three domains of thought—the macroscopic world of observable phenomena, the microscopic world of molecules, atoms, and subatomic particles, and the symbolic and mathematical world of chemical formulas, equations and symbols."[104]

The *National Science Education Standards* also pressed for integration across disciplines. Although they didn't completely blur the distinctions among physical science, life science, and earth and space sciences, the standards did emphasize the crosscutting themes—what the document called unifying concepts and processes:

- Systems, order, and organization
- Evidence, models, and explanation
- Constancy, change, and measurement
- Evolution and equilibrium
- Form and function

These crosscutting ideas were meant to "provide students with productive ways of thinking about and integrating a range of basic ideas that explain the natural and designed world."[105]

Science for All

The authors of the *National Science Education Standards* made clear their position about who can do science:

> The intent of the *Standards* can be expressed in a single phrase: Science standards for all students. The phrase embodies both excellence and equity. The *Standards* apply to all students, regardless of age, gender, cultural or ethnic background, disabilities, aspirations, or interest and motivation in science. Different students will achieve understanding in different ways, and different students will achieve different degrees of depth and breadth of understanding depending on interest, ability, and context. But all students can develop the knowledge and skills described in the *Standards*, even as some students go well beyond these levels.[106]

Similar statements appear in the documents of the National Science Foundation, the National Academy of Sciences, and the AAAS.

As described in Focal Point 5.3, Michigan State professor Angela Calabrese Barton takes standards-based science instruction to students who might not otherwise have access to it.

Focal Point 5.3
Science and Social Justice

Bringing Science Education to the City

Professor Angela Calabrese Barton, author of *Teaching Science for Social Justice*, works to bring innovative science education to students in urban settings. "Science can be fun, but it has an integral role in our society," Calabrese Barton explains. "I want to help children use science to make their lives better."

As one example, for years she ran an after-school program for youth and families living in a local shelter. Through this work, she learned a great deal about students, their concerns, their scientific practices, and the potential for science to play an enriching, empowering, and transformative role in their lives.

One of the program's long-term projects focused on pollution in the local community. The project began with the children listing some of the things they disliked about where they lived and how those things made them feel. They then gathered additional data on these issues from people in the community.

"They took a video camera and interviewed people in the area and asked what they thought about the neighborhood," Calabrese Barton explained. "They studied the quality of water in their building and the ground pollution in a one-block area and devised a plan to clean up that block and add plants. They took experiences they felt bad about and used science to transform them and to help them act on them."

Calabrese Barton's current work reflects the same commitment to making rigorous, relevant, and empowering science experiences a reality for students attending urban schools. Among other things, she now runs Green Energy Technology in the City, or GET City, a year-round program focused on the science and engineering of energy sustainability using advanced information technologies. The program provides youth with the following:

- **Experiences** with advanced information technology (IT) skills (i.e., geographic information systems [GIS], data management and acquisition systems, data analysis tools, and communication tools)
- **Opportunities** to develop scientific research skills and conceptual understandings related to energy technologies, production, and sustainability
- **Job skills** development for the growing IT market and an awareness of STEM careers
- A curriculum for **informal science and IT** education that can be adapted for other urban communities

Through GET City, students present their scientific data and analyses to city officials, interact with Green Roof Technology experts, and tour a local coal plant and power station. The project's website documents these experiences, alongside youth-designed resources, including public service videos in which kids conduct an "energy audit" of a local school, perform their own rap lyrics about the process and environmental impact of coal harvesting, and explain how electric cars work. The website offers downloadable unit plans on topics such as electrical production and consumption, transportation and power, building design that is LEED (Leadership in Energy and Environmental Design) certified, and alternative energy. Each unit plan includes the following:

- A twelve-week authentic investigation around a driving question that covers core ideas and practices in science, engineering, and IT
- Individual lessons plans and student activity sheets
- Examples of cybertools that youth can create to educate others

Source: Quotes excerpted from *TC Today* 23, no. 1 (1997). GET City information compiled from http://getcity.org.

The Conservative Backlash

As in the other academic subjects, the national science standards generated controversy. Once again, the debate was particularly heated in California.

Despite widespread agreement among scientists and science educators about science content, skepticism about "who can do science" prevented a unified effort to reform science education.

The nuclear physicist who was leading the writing of the state's standards argued that a major problem that too many students—particularly low-income and minoritized students—give up and never become scientifically literate. He said that California's standards must change an existing curriculum that leaves behind "all these kids who don't get it."[107]

However, three Nobel laureates, led by the late Glen Seaborg, protested California's plan to model its science standards on the national standards.[108] They charged that the progressives were bent on "dumbing down" science to make it appealing to students. They claimed the standards would compromise rigor and undercut learning about great, though difficult-to-understand, scientific discoveries. One charged, "Educational content is continually diluted in a failed effort to produce palatable bits of information for progressively less skilled students. It is essential that we take a stand and insist on educational standards with greater content."[109]

These traditional critics appeared to be judging the quality of the curriculum based on who they expected to master it. At the end of a rancorous process, Seaborg and his group were successful in securing a set of standards far closer to the traditional science curriculum than what the national standards had sought to inspire.

Next Generation Science Standards

In 2012, sixteen years after the *National Science Education Standards* were adopted, the NRC released the *Framework for K–12 Science Education*. Spurred by a need for the curriculum to reflect scientific progress, as well as by the widespread adoption of the CCSS in Mathematics and English/Language Arts, the framework was the first step toward new national standards for K–12 science education.[110] As intended, the framework served as the foundation for the Next Generation Science Standards (NGSS), which were released in 2013, and by 2017 had been adopted by eighteen states. As with the CCSS, a consortium of governors and business leaders known as Achieve launched the development process. However, unlike the CCSS, which were developed by working groups composed largely of members of the testing industry, the framework and the NGSS were developed through a process that involved the states and various stakeholders in science, science education, and industry.[111]

The framework and the NGSS build on the foundation established by previous AAAS reports, *Science for All Americans* and *Benchmarks for Science Literacy*, as well as the *National Science Education Standards*. But several features distinguish the NGSS from previous standards. To encourage a more "integrated approach" than previous standards, the NGSS are organized around three dimensions of science learning: (1) crosscutting concepts, (2) science and engineering practices, and (3) disciplinary core ideas. Crosscutting concepts refer to such ideas as cause and effect, energy and matter, stability and change, and structure and function that have application across all domains of science. The aim of this feature, like the "unifying concepts and processes" in the *National Science Education Standards*, is for students to organize interrelated knowledge from different science fields into a "coherent and scientifically-based view of the world." Science and engineering practices aim to capture the behaviors of real scientists and engineers, and to "better explain and extend what is meant by 'inquiry' in science." These practices, which intentionally intertwine, include asking questions and defining problems, developing and using models, and planning and carrying out investigations, among others. Disciplinary core ideas focus teachers and students on the "most important" aspects of science, grouped in four domains: physical science; life sciences; earth and space sciences; and engineering, technology, and applications of science. These three dimensions combine to form each standard, or what the NGSS call "performance expectations."[112]

Through these dimensions, the NGSS reflect the progressive ideals of science education described earlier, specifically by promoting science as an ongoing process that is always subject to revision, and by encouraging science instruction that is organized around complex ideas that cut across science disciplines.

The framework takes a clear position on equity, claiming that everyone can do science and that the NGSS make science accessible to all. Progressives have touted the framework's and the NGSS's efforts to advance equity; some recommended how teachers might use the NGSS to facilitate rich science learning among students from minoritized communities. For example, several language scholars suggest that the NGSS emphasis on science and engineering practices creates opportunities for Emergent Bilingual students by requiring them to communicate about science, thereby cultivating a rich language-learning environment.[113] However, concerns have also been raised. Professors Thomas Philip and Flávio S. Azevedo argue that the type of equity advanced by the framework and standards risks perpetuating the belief that increasing science achievement among minoritized youth serves to legitimize scientific and economic dominance; color-blind racial ideologies; and misconceptions about social injustice as a problem of the past, rather than of the present.[114]

Another distinguishing feature of the NGSS is that they address long-standing and heated debates about climate science. Five standards at the middle and high school levels address climate change explicitly by drawing connections between the earth and human activity. As explained below, the inclusion of climate change in the NGSS has contributed in no small part to challenges with NGSS implementation.

NGSS adoption and implementation have been far from smooth. The NGSS require significant science and science-teaching knowledge from teachers—more than many multiple-subject teachers and out-of-field teachers currently have. The organization of the NGSS into three intersecting dimensions makes the standards difficult for some teachers to navigate. NGSS advocates have responded with concerted calls for NGSS-specific professional development to bolster teachers' knowledge of the NGSS as well as their confidence in teaching the sort of science the NGSS advance.

An additional implementation challenge concerns assessment. As of 2017, researchers and educators were working hard to figure out to best way to assess three-dimensional learning, an endeavor that stumped most psychometricians. How will students be assessed on the NGSS? Will NGSS tests have high stakes attached to them? Critics have raised questions about how tying a high-stakes assessment to the NGSS might tempt teachers to privilege those standards thought to carry more weight on tests.

An additional implementation barrier is the inclusion of standards that deal with controversial science content such as evolution and climate change. Reactions from religious organizations to the NGSS's inclusion of such topics have been swift and powerful. Legislation aiming to obstruct NGSS adoption on the grounds of such topics being "controversial" rather than "proven" has been introduced in multiple states. Some, such as South Dakota, have written their own state science standards that closely mirror the NGSS, but include revisions of politically charged topics such as evolution and climate change. We discuss the debates at the heart of these curriculum battles below.

Enduring Debates

Perhaps the most enduring science curriculum controversy has been about evolution. Almost seventy-five years after biology teacher John Scopes was arrested for teaching evolution in violation of Tennessee law, the state board of education in Kansas voted in 1999 to remove evolution from the state's science standards.

Although the board did not ban evolution outright, it did eliminate evolution from the topics on which Kansas students would be tested. The conservative board majority argued that evolution is not a proper science topic. Science, they insisted, is the investigation of the natural world, whereas evolution examines humankind's origins—a topic that falls under the purview of the supernatural. One board member said, "I don't want my children's biology teacher talking about religion."[115]

Kansas governor Bill Graves called the board's decision an "embarrassment," and most school districts ignored it. In November 2000, Kansas voted in new board members who promised to restore evolution to the state's standards, and in February 2001, the new board reversed the antievolution decision of 1999.

Following Kansas's lead, however, Nebraska eliminated evolution from its state science guidelines, and Alabama required that science textbooks note that the theory of evolution is "unproven." In other skirmishes, New Mexico banned the teaching of creationism (after voting to allow it four years earlier), and Louisiana upheld teachers' rights to not read a disclaimer that evolution is an "unproven" theory.

In 2004, the Dover, Pennsylvania, school board required its high school biology teachers to read a four-paragraph statement to their students that questions the accuracy of Darwin's theory. This statement pointed to "intelligent design" as a competing theory for the origin and evolution of life. Intelligent design argues that gaps in current scientific knowledge point to an intelligent force (commonly understood to be God) responsible for the life forms we see today. Some parents took the board to court, claiming that the statement tried to "repackage" creationism and interject religion into the science curriculum. And, in fact, the six members of the Dover board who approved the policy were open about their belief that "the origin of life was guided by a heavenly hand."[116]

In 2005, a federal judge ruled "intelligent design" to be religious belief, rather than scientific theory, and that teaching it in public school science classrooms violates the Constitution. However, many expect the U.S. Supreme Court to rule eventually on this case.

Meanwhile, a conservative Kansas state board of education petitioned to change the science standards yet again in 2005.[117] Pushing to include intelligent design and guidelines for using a "teach the controversy" method, board members claimed that the amended standards—strongly informed by the religious policy organization the Discovery Institute[118]—would ensure balance. Although the board voted overwhelmingly to adopt the standards following hearings that were boycotted by the science community,[119] four of the six conservative board members lost their seats in 2006. The new board rejected the amended standards in 2007.

In 2010, the American Academy of Religion established *Guidelines for Teaching About Religion in K–12 Public Schools in the United States*, which recommended that schools refrain from teaching intelligent design. It argued, "Creation science and intelligent design represent worldviews that fall outside the realm of science that is defined as (and limited to) a method of inquiry based on gathering observable and measurable evidence subject to specific principles of reasoning."[120] Nevertheless, the battle surrounding the teaching of evolution has continued. In fact, in 2011, at least seven states considered bills that would limit its teaching in public schools. And in January 2012 alone, two bills that would require teaching evolution as a philosophy more than an established science were introduced in New Hampshire, as well as a new bill promoting the teaching of "creation science" in Indiana.

As is evidenced by the NGSS battles, conservatives increasingly protest the inclusion of climate change, and particularly global warming, in the science curriculum. Tying climate change to evolution, members of the religious right lambast claims that human activity has caused global warming. Some argue that it is "antibiblical" to assume human beings can negatively impact God's creations,[121] while others contend that the focus on climate change is a thinly veiled attempt by progressives to divert the church from its primary focus.[122] Conservative politicians looking to protect corporate polluters from environmental regulation have joined these efforts, as well.[123]

Climate change denial has gained more traction since Donald Trump was voted into office in November 2016. This is (again) largely the result of political and religious convergence among President Trump's "base," largely comprising evangelical Christians and members of economically stressed communities where job losses are often tied directly to sectors like coal mining that have been subjected to environmental regulations. To appeal to this base, President Trump has repeatedly referred to climate change as a "hoax,"[124] while Scott Pruitt, the head of the Environmental Protection Agency, has stated that carbon dioxide does not contribute to global warming.[125]

Against this political backdrop, it's not surprising that climate change currently sits front and center in science curriculum battles. According to the National Center for Science Education, for example, it is becoming common for legislators to file "academic freedom bills" (more than seventy were filed between 2004 and 2017) with the aim of bringing climate change denial and creationism into the classroom.[126] As of April 2017, new legislative measures that allow for the rejection of science, including specific phenomena like global warming, were pending in multiple states, including Texas, Florida, Indiana, Oklahoma, Alabama, South Dakota, and Idaho. Oklahoma's Senate Bill 393 would allow teachers to treat evidence-based science on evolution and climate change as "controversial," even though "97 percent of actively publishing, accredited climate scientists agree that global warming trends over the past century are directly attributable to human activity."[127] Although it had been introduced seven times previously, the Oklahoma bill made progress toward passage only after the "antiscience" rhetoric of the Trump administration took hold. Texas's pending bill similarly treats as controversial "climate change, biological evolution, and the chemical origins of life."[128]

Legislation isn't the only barrier to teaching accurate science. Teachers increasingly report resistance from students during lessons related to evolution and climate change. Like the "academic freedom bills" filed by legislators, students increasingly cite their own "choice" and "freedom" as reasons for rejecting the science taught in schools. A recent *New York Times* article describes the struggles teachers face, including trying to convince students that science is "not about opinions . . . it's about the evidence." These clashes are especially difficult because they represent the culture wars currently at play in the United States, as well as deep-seated ideologies that reflect students' identities and family ties.[129]

Yet teaching climate science, even to resistant students, isn't a lost cause; as with the other subject areas explored in this chapter, teachers are best positioned to effect change. Learning experiences that enable students to see the effects of climate change close to home seem to have some impact on shifting students' understandings.[130] Organizations like the National Center for Science Education, which names as a goal "defending the integrity of science education against ideological interference," offers teachers instructional resources as well as strategies for analyzing political propaganda (e.g., like that distributed by the conservative Heartland Institute) and for becoming politically active.[131] Explicit attention to climate change in the NGSS supports teachers to engage students around these topics.[132]

Access to High-Quality Science Instruction

Another serious problem with science is that schools teach so little of it. For example, a National Center for Educational Statistics survey found that children in elementary school average less than two and a half hours a week learning science.[133] As we noted earlier, many elementary teachers have little more scientific knowledge than the public, and they feel uncomfortable teaching science. Similarly, many who teach older students were not science majors or are not credentialed to teach science. Because reading and math dominate elementary school "accountability," science rarely shows up on high-stakes tests; thus, teachers may be less motivated to teach it, and school policies do not encourage it. Many middle-school students take science for only one semester, and many senior high schools require only one science class for those not planning to attend college. For these reasons, some science educators welcome the prospect of mandated science testing because of its potential to press schools to teach more science.

Often, even skilled science teachers resort to science shortcuts. If resources and time are not adequate, they may opt to *tell* students about science rather than let them *do* science. When this happens, science gets reduced to memorizing names and facts. The authors of the *National Science Education Standards* and the NGSS had these concerns in mind when they proposed standards for the entire science education system. In science, as in all the disciplines, the content of the curriculum must be considered in light of who teaches the subject, how they teach and assess it, and what conditions must prevail for students to learn.

The Struggle for the Subject Matter

Professional responsibility obliges teachers to be articulate participants in public, political, and professional arenas of curriculum inquiry and debate. Sheridan Blau, former president of the NCTE, cautions and advises:

> Our profession as seen from inside teachers' lounges and in the conversations of professionals and in the presentations and workshops at conferences . . . is not a bloody battleground of competing ideas, but it has been made to appear so by a press hungry for dramatic stories and by impatient policy makers and a frustrated public looking for the same kind of simple answers that popular opinion often demands—answers that offer scapegoats and saviors. . . . The true ideological battleground for our profession, then, is not in the field where teacher-educators and teachers debate about the most effective teaching strategies nor in the labs and research sites where scholars offer different theoretical perspectives, different methodological procedures, and competing findings. Disagreements in these arenas can and do lead to dialogue and thereby to the advancement of learning.[134]

Dialogue and advancement of learning in and across the content areas, in the classroom and outside of it: This is the work of teachers.

Digging Deeper and Tools for Critique

www.routledge.com/cw/teachingtochangetheworld

Notes

1 Although we don't discuss them here, the other central disciplines—the arts and foreign languages, for example—also matter. No less critical to a democratic education and to social justice, these disciplines are usually the first to be cut when budgets or reading scores are inadequate. And although sound arguments can be made that school graduates and society benefit equally from multilingual citizens who understand and create music and art and from citizens who can solve quadratic equations, it is success in algebra that is a gatekeeper for students, and it is "verbal analogies" that suppress scores on gatekeeping tests such as the SAT. For this reason, we focus our attention on the subjects that determine which students schools will consider "good students."

2 "Mashup Transcript: Barack Obama," September 13, 2007, https://www.huffingtonpost.com/2007/09/13/mashup-transcript-barack-_n_64321.html.

3 John P. Holdren, "COMPETES Passage Keeps America's Leadership on Target," *The White House Blog*, January 3, 2011, https://obamawhitehouse.archives.gov/blog/2011/01/06/america-competes-act-keeps-americas-leadership-target.

4 Curtis C. McKnight, F. Joe Crosswhite, and John A. Dossey, *The Underachieving Curriculum: Assessing U.S. School Mathematics From an International Perspective* (Indianapolis, IN: Stipes, 1987).

5 Lynne V. Cheney, "The Latest Education Disaster: Whole Math," *Weekly Standard*, August 4, 1997, A22.

6 International Association for the Evaluation of Educational Achievement (IEA), "Trends in International Mathematics and Science Study (TIMSS)," 2015, http://timss2015.org/timss-2015/mathematics/student-achievement/; Organisation for Economic Co-operation and Development (OECD), "International Outcomes of Learning in Mathematics Literacy and Problem Solving: Programme for International Student Assessment PISA 2012 Results," www.oecd.org/pisa/keyfindings/pisa-2012-results.htm.

7 For example, one study found that third graders lacking conceptual knowledge of the multidigit subtraction procedure were more likely to make performance errors such as subtracting the top smaller digit from the bottom larger digit. K. M. Cauley, "Construction of Local Knowledge: Study of Borrowing in Subtraction," *Journal of Educational Psychology* 80 (1988): 202–205.

8 Richard Shavelson, "The Splintered Curriculum," *Education Week*, May 7, 1997, 38. Shavelson places some of the blame on textbook publishers that "produce textbooks that are a mile wide and an inch deep" to promote sales across the diverse U.S. market, and some on standardized tests that cover a wide range of material. Shavelson's essay draws on material in William Schmidt, Curtis C. McKnight, and Senta Raizen, *A Splintered Vision: An Investigation of U.S. Science and Mathematics Education* (Dordrecht, The Netherlands: Kluwer Academic, 1997).

9 McKnight, Crosswhite, and Dossey, *The Underachieving Curriculum*. For a comparable international comparison and analysis, see the report from the Third International Mathematics and Science Study, William Schmidt, *Facing the Consequences: Using TIMSS for a Closer Look at U.S. Mathematics and Science Education* (Dordrecht, The Netherlands: Kluwer Academic, 1999).

10 National Council of Teachers of Mathematics, *Curriculum and Evaluation Standards for School Mathematics* (Reston, VA: Author, 1989), 7.

11 "Mathematics Content Standards for Grades K–12," submitted by Bill Evers, commissioner to California State Academic Standards Commission, September 15, 1997, www.dehnbase.org/hold/platinum-standards/altintro.html.

12 "Mathematics Content Standards for Grades K–12."

13 National Research Council, *Everybody Counts: A Report to the Nation on the Future of Mathematics Education* (Washington, DC: National Academy Press, 1989), 34. The National Research Council was established in 1916 by the prestigious National Academy of Sciences, whose own mission is to further knowledge and advise the federal government.

14 National Research Council, *Everybody Counts*, 43.

15 Ibid., 60.

16 Ibid.

17 See, for example, Dionne I. Cross, "Alignment, Cohesion, and Change: Examining Mathematics Teachers' Beliefs Structures and Their Influence on Instructional Practice," *Journal of Mathematics Teacher Education* 12 (2009): 325–346; Jeffrey A. Frykholm, "The Impact of Reform: Challenges for Mathematics Teacher Preparation," *Journal of Mathematics Teacher Education* 2 (1999): 79–105; Azita Manouchehri and Terry Goodman, "Implementing Mathematics Reform: The Challenge Within," *Educational Studies in Mathematics* 42, no. 1 (2000): 1–34.

18 National Council of Teachers of Mathematics, *Curriculum and Evaluation Standards for School Mathematics*, 7.

19 Ibid., 44–45.

20 See, for example, Ben W. Dalton, Steven J. Ingels, Jane Downing, Robert Bozick, and Jeffrey Owings, "Advanced Mathematics and Science Coursetaking in the Spring High Schools Senior Classes of 1982, 1992 and 2004," *NCES Publication No. 2007–312*, 2007, http://nces.ed.gov/pubs2007/2007312.pdf; and Steven J. Ingels, Ben W. Dalton, and Laura LoGerfo, "Trends Among High School Seniors, 1972–2004," *NCES Publication No. 2008–320*. Washington, DC: National Center for Education Statistics, 2008, http://nces.ed.gov/pubs2008/2008320.pdf.

21 Na'ilah Suad Nasir, Victoria Hand, and Edd Taylor, "Culture and Mathematics in School: Boundaries Between 'Cultural' and 'Domain' Knowledge in the Mathematics Classroom and Beyond," *Review of Research in Education* 32, no. 1 (2008): 187–240.

22 Eric (Rico) Gutstein and Bob Peterson, eds., *Rethinking Mathematics: Teaching Social Justice by the Numbers*, 2nd ed. (Milwaukee, WI: Rethinking Schools, 2013).

23 Richard Lee Colvin, "State Endorses Back-to-Basics Math Standards," *Los Angeles Times*, November 30, 1997, 1, 18, 19, 26.

24 Luther S. Williams, Letter to the California State Board of Education, December 11, 1997.

25 David Klein, Bastiaan J. Braams, Thomas Parker, William Quirk, Wilfried Schmid, W. Stephen Wilson, Chester E. Finn Jr., Justin Torres, Lawrence Braden, and Ralph A. Raimi, *The State of Math Standards 2005* (Washington, DC: Fordham Institute, 2005).

26 Common Core State Standards Initiative, www.corestandards.org/the-standards/mathematics/.

27 National Council of Teachers of Mathematics, "Supporting the Common Core State Standards for Mathematics," http://www.nctm.org/News-and-Calendar/News/NCTM-News-Releases/NCTM-Issues-Position-Statement-Supporting-the-Common-Core/.

28 National Council of Teachers of Mathematics, "NCTM Public Comments on the Common Core Standards for Mathematics," www.nctm.org/about/content.aspx?id=25186.

29 www.nctm.org/store/Products/Making-It-Happen—Common-Core-Standards-%28PDF%29/.

30 See, for example, Grant Wiggins, "Common Core Standards Don't Add Up," *Education Week*, September 27, 2011, www.edweek.org/ew/articles/2011/09/28/05wiggins.h31.html; Sol Garfunkel and David Mumford, "How to Fix Our Math Education," *New York Times*, August 24, 2011, www.nytimes.com/2011/08/25/opinion/how-to-fix-our-math-education.html?_r=1.

31 Thomas B. Fordham Institute, "Our Review of the Common Core State Standards," http://standards.educationgadfly.net/commoncore/math/.

32 David Cohen and Heather Hill, *Learning Policy: When State Education Reform Works* (New Haven, CT: Yale University Press, 2001).

33 See, for example, Judit Moschkovich, "Supporting ELLs in Mathematics: CCSS-Aligned Mathematics Tasks With Annotations and Other Resources for Implementing the Common Core State Standards," Understanding Language, Stanford University, 2013, http://ell.stanford.edu/sites/default/files/math_archives/Full%20set_UL%20Math%20Resources%2010-28-13%20updated.pdf; and Judit Moschkovich, "Mathematics, the Common Core, and Language," Understanding Language, Stanford University, 2013, http://ell.stanford.edu/sites/default/files/pdf/academic-papers/02-JMoschkovich%20Math%20FINAL_bound%20with%20appendix.pdf.

34 Rochelle Gutierrez, "Why (Urban) Mathematics Teachers Need Political Knowledge," *Journal of Urban Mathematics* 6, no. 2 (2013): 7–19.

35 *Webster's Encyclopedic Unabridged Dictionary of the English Language* (New York: Gramercy Books, 1989), 1195.

36 Ibid.

37 Dorothea Anagnostopoulos, "Testing and Student Engagement With Literature in Urban Classrooms: A Multi-Layered Perspective," *Research in the Teaching of English* 38, no. 2 (2003): 177–212.

38 P. David Pearson, "Reclaiming the Center," in *The First R: Every Child's Right to Read*, eds. M. F. Graves, O. van den Broek, and B. M. Taylor (New York: Teachers College Press; Newark, DE: International Reading Association, 1996), 259–274.

39 Ibid.

40 Marjorie Faulstich Orellana, *Translating Childhoods: Immigrant Youth, Language and Culture* (New Brunswick, NJ: Rutgers University Press, 2009).

41 Ofelia García, "Education, Multilingualism and Translanguaging in the 21st Century," in *Multilingual Education for Social Justice: Globalising the Local*, eds. Ajit Mohanty, Minati Panda, Robert Phillipson, and Tove Skutnabb-Kangas (New Delhi: Orient Blackswan, former Orient Longman, 2009), 128–145 (140).

42 Ramón Antonio Martínez, "Spanglish as a Literacy Tool: Toward an Understanding of the Potential Role of Spanish-English Code-Switching in the Development of Academic Literacy," *Research in the Teaching of English* 45, no. 2 (2010): 124–149.

43 See, for example, Carol D. Lee, "Is October Brown Chinese? A Cultural Modeling Activity System for Underachieving Students," *American Educational Research Journal* 38, no. 1 (2001): 97–142; Carol D. Lee, "Literacy in the Academic Disciplines and the Needs of Adolescent Struggling Readers," *Voices in Urban Education* (Special Issue on Adolescent Literacy) no. 3 (Spring 2004).

44 "Multicultural Book List Proposed in San Francisco," *New York Times*, March 11, 1998; see also "S.F. Board OKs Reading of Works by Nonwhites," *Los Angeles Times*, March 21, 1998, 1.

45 Annie Gowen, "Maryland Schools Remove 2 Black-Authored Books," *Los Angeles Times*, January 11, 1998, A6.

46 Melanie Sperling and Sarah W. Freedman, "Research on Writing," in *Handbook of Research on Teaching*, ed. V. Richardson (Washington, DC: American Educational Research Association, 2001), 370–389.

47 Pearson, "Reclaiming the Center."

48 International Reading Association and National Council of Teachers of English, *Standards for the English Language Arts* (Champaign, IL: Author, 1996), 75.

49 Karen Diegmueller, "English Group Loses Funding for Standards," *Education Week*, March 30, 1994; Miles Myers, "Where the Debate About English Standards Goes Wrong," *Education Week*, May 15, 1995.

50 Diegmueller, "English Group Loses Funding for Standards"; Myers, "Where the Debate About English Standards Goes Wrong."

51 J. Martin Rosser, "The Decline of Literacy," *Education Week*, May 15, 1996.

52 Ibid.

53 As quoted in Karen Diegmueller, "The Best of Both Worlds," *Teacher Magazine*, March 1996.

54 Karen Diegmueller, "War of Words," *Education Week*, March 20, 1996.

55 Ibid.

56 What Works Clearinghouse, http://ies.ed.gov/ncee/wwc/.

57 U.S. Department of Education, "Reading First," www2.ed.gov/programs/readingfirst/index.html.

58 P. David Pearson, "The Politics of Reading Research and Practice" (conference presentation, Houston, TX, May 15, 1997), http://ed-web3.educ.msu.edu.cdpds/pdpaper.politics.html.

59 Judith Langer, as quoted in Deborah Viadero, "Researchers Flag Six Elements of Good Secondary English Instruction," *Education Week*, June 14, 2000, www.edweek.org.

60 Ladson-Billings's and Delpit's work is discussed in more detail in Chapter 3.

61 Common Core State Standards, www.corestandards.org.

62 P. David Pearson, "Research Foundations of the Common Core State Standards in English Language Arts," in *Quality Reading Instruction in the Age of Common Core State Standards*, eds. Susan B. Neuman and Linda Gambrell (Newark, DE: International Reading Association, 2013), 237–262.

63 Lily Wong Fillmore and Charles J. Fillmore, "What Does Text Complexity Mean for English Learners and Language Minority Students?" Paper presented at the *Understanding Language Conference*, Stanford University, January 2012, http://ell.stanford.edu/sites/default/files/pdf/academic-papers/06-LWF%20CJF%20Text%20Complexity%20FINAL_0.pdf.

64 See, for example, Heidi Anne E. Mesmer, James W. Cunningham, and Elfrieda H. Hiebert, "Toward a Theoretical Model of Text Complexity for the Early Grades: Learning From the Past, Anticipating the Future," *Reading Research Quarterly* 47, no. 3 (2013): 235–258.

65 See, for example, Elfrieda H. Hiebert, "The Common Core's Staircase of Text Complexity: Getting the Size of the First Step Right," *Reading Today* 29, no. 3 (2012): 26–27.

66 See, for example, Melissa Schieble, "Reframing Equity Under Common Core: A Commentary on the Text Exemplar List for Grades 9–12," *English Teaching* 13 no. 1 (2014): 158.

67 National Council of Teachers of English (NCTE), "Reading Instruction for *All* Students," National Council of Teachers of English, 2012, www.ncte.org/library/NCTEFiles/Resources/Journals/CC/0221-sep2012/Chron0221PolicyBrief.pdf.

68 See, for example, Terrence G. Wiley, "In What Ways Are the Common Core State Standards De Facto Language Education Policy?" in *Common Core Bilingual and English Language Learners: A Resource for Educators*, eds. Guadalupe Valdés, Kate Menken, and Mariana Castro (Philadelphia: Calston Publishing, 2015), 10–11; Kate Menken, "What Have Been the Benefits and Drawbacks of Testing and Accountability for English Language Learners/Emergent Bilinguals Under No Child Left Behind, and What Are the Implications Under the Common Core State Standards?" in *Common Core Bilingual and English Language Learners: A Resource for Educators*, eds. Guadalupe Valdés, Kate Menken, and Mariana Castro (Philadelphia: Calston Publishing, 2015), 246–247; Jamy Stillman and Lauren Anderson, *Teaching for Equity in Complex Times* (New York: Teachers College Press, 2017).

69 National Council of Teachers of English, *Resources for Student-Centered Instruction in a Time of Common Core Standards*, www.ncte.org/standards/common-core.

70 International Reading Association, *IRA Calls for Three-Part Initiative to Raise Literacy Achievement Through Common Core State Standards*, www.corestandards.org/assets/k12_statements/StatementK12IRA.pdf.

71 Gary B. Nash, Charlotte Crabtree, and Ross E. Dunn, *History on Trial: Culture Wars and the Teaching of the Past* (New York: Knopf, 1997).

72 Catharine Cornbleth, "An American Curriculum?" *Teachers College Record* 99, no. 4 (1998): 622–646.

73 California State Department of Education, *California's Own History* (Sacramento: Author, 1965).

74 Hugh Mehan, Dina Okamoto, Angela Lintz, and John S. Wills, "Ethnographic Studies of Multicultural Schools and Classrooms," in *Handbook of Research on Multicultural Education*, eds. James A. Banks and Cherry A. McGee Banks (New York: Macmillan, 1995), 129–144.

75 John S. Wills, "The Situation of African Americans in American History: Using History as a Resource for Understanding the Experiences of Contemporary African Americans," as quoted in Hugh Mehan, Dina Okamoto, Angela Lintz, and John S. Wills, "Ethnographic Studies of Multicultural Schools and Classrooms," in *Handbook of Research on Multicultural Education*, 163–183.

76 As quoted in Ron Brandt, "On the High School Curriculum: A Conversation With Ernest Boyer," *Educational Leadership* 46, no. 1 (September 1988): 6.

77 *Oh, California* (New York: Houghton Mifflin Co., 1991), as cited in "Tragic Side of Mission Era Being Told," *Los Angeles Times*, September 2, 1997.

78 Joyce Elaine King, "Diaspora Literacy and Consciousness in the Struggle Against Miseducation in the Black Community," *Journal of Negro Education* 61, no. 3 (1992): 326.

79 Christine Sleeter, "Standardizing Imperialism," *Rethinking Schools Online* 19, no. 1 (2004): 1–6.

80 Sam Wineburg, *Historical Thinking and Other Unnatural Acts: Charting the Future of Teaching the Past* (Philadelphia: Temple University Press, 2001), 24.

81 National Center for History in the Schools, *National Standards for United States History* (Los Angeles: UCLA National Center for History in the Schools, 1994); italics added.

82 Lynne Cheney, "The End of History," *Wall Street Journal*, October 20, 1994, A26.

83 Rush Limbaugh, as cited in Nash, Crabtree, and Dunn, *History on Trial*, 5.

84 Gary L. Bauer, *National History Standards: Clintonites Miss the Moon* (Washington, DC: Family Research Council, 1995).

85 National Center for History in the Schools, *National Standards for United States History.*

86 The United States is not the only society that struggles to protect a spotless version of its history. Perhaps we can have a higher regard for teaching new insights into our own past when we see the dissembling of another country (happily corrected in this case). The following appeared in "Japan's High Court Rules Against Rewriting History," *Los Angeles Times*, August 30, 1997: "[The Japanese Court] ruled that the Education Ministry acted wrongly in ordering a textbook writer to delete accurate descriptions of Japanese atrocities during World War II, including a mention of the notorious Unit 731 that conducted gruesome medical experiments on human guinea pigs and quoted one of Japan's most famous novelists, Ryotaro Shiba: 'A country whose textbooks lie will inevitably collapse.'"

87 Kathleen Kennedy Manzo, "Glimmer of History Standards Shows Up in Latest Textbooks," *Education Week*, October 8, 1997.

88 California Department of Education, *History—Social Studies Content Standards for California Public Schools: Kindergarten Through Grade Twelve*, 1998, www.cde.ca.gov/be/st/ss/documents/histsocscistnd.pdf.

89 *New York Learning Standards and Core Curriculum in Social Studies*, www.p12.nysed.gov/ciai/socst/ssrg.html.

90 *2016 History-Social Science Framework for California*, www.cde.ca.gov/ci/hs/cf/sbedrafthssfw.asp.

91 Nancy McTygue, "What You Need to Know About California's New History Social Science Framework," *California History-Social Science Project*, Blog post, July 14, 2016, http://chssp.ucdavis.edu/blog/what-you-need-to-know-about-california2019s-new-history-social-science-framework.

92 John Fensterwald, "A Great Awakening for History and Social Studies," *EdSource*, April 2015, https://edsource.org/2015/a-great-awakening-for-history-and-social-studies/77748.

93 "Concerns About the *Proposed History-Social Science Framework*," www.gtbe.org/blog/wp-content/uploads/2016/06/Concerns-about-the-Proposed-History-Social-Science-Framework.pdf.

94 See, for example: Thomas Sobol, "Revising the New York State Social Studies Curriculum," *Teachers College Record* 95, no. 2 (2003): 258–272.

95 James C. McKinley, "Texas Conservatives Win Curriculum Change," *New York Times*, March 12, 2010, www.nytimes.com/2010/03/13/education/13texas.html.

96 Anthony L. Brown and Kefferlyn D. Brown, "Strange Fruit Indeed: Interrogating Contemporary Textbook Representations of Racial Violence Towards African Americans," *Teachers College Record* 112, no. 1 (2010): 31–67.

97 Howard Zinn, *Teaching a People's History*, http://zinnedproject.org.

98 Christine Sleeter, *Un-standardizing Curriculum: Multicultural Teaching in the Standards-Based Classroom* (New York: Teachers College Press, 2005).

99 National Commission on Mathematics and Science, *Before It's Too Late: A Report to the Nation From the National Commission on Mathematics and Science Teaching for the 21st Century* (Washington, DC: U.S. Department of Education, 2000), 20.

100 National Research Council, *Taking Science to School: Learning and Teaching Science in Grades K–8* (Washington, DC: National Academies Press, 2007), 286.

101 Schmidt, McKnight, and Raizen, *A Splintered Vision*; National Research Council, *Taking Science to School: Learning and Teaching Science in Grades K–8* (Washington, DC: The National Academies Press, 2007); National Research Council, *America's Lab Report: Investigations in High School Science* (Washington, DC: The National Academies Press, 2005).

102 The AAAS considers science literacy as (1) being familiar with the natural world and recognizing both its diversity and its unity; (2) understanding key concepts and principles of science; (3) being aware of some of the important ways in which science, mathematics, and technology depend on one another; (4) knowing that science, mathematics, and technology are human enterprises and knowing what that implies about their strengths and limitations; (5) having a capacity for scientific ways of thinking; and (6) using scientific knowledge and ways of thinking for individual and social purposes. See AAAS, *Science for All Americans* (Washington, DC: Author, 1989).

103 Paul DeHart Hurd, "Science Needs a 'Lived' Curriculum," *Education Week*, November 12, 1997, 48.

104 National Research Council, *National Science Education Standards* (Washington, DC: National Academy Press, 1996), 113.

105 Ibid., 115.

106 Ibid., 2.

107 Roland Otto, as quoted in Richard Lee Colvin, "Spurned Nobelists Appeal Science Standards Rejection," *Los Angeles Times*, November 17, 1997, A25.

108 The group, composed of Glen Seaborg, Dudley R. Herschbach, and Henry Taube, filed a formal appeal to the state Commission for the Establishment of Academic Standards in November 1997. See Colvin, "Spurned Nobelists Appeal Science Standards Rejection," A25.

109 Colvin, "Spurned Nobelists Appeal Science Standards Rejection," A25.

110 Committee on a Conceptual Framework for New K-12 Science Standards, Board on Science Education, Division of Behavioral and Social Sciences and Education, and National Research Council of the National Academies, *A Framework for K-12 Science Education: Practices, Crosscutting Concepts and Core Ideas*, www.nap.edu/read/13165/chapter/1.

111 Next Generation Science Standards, www.nextgenscience.org.

112 Ibid.

113 Helen Quinn, Okhee Lee, and Guadalupe Valdés, "Language Demands and Opportunities in Relation to Next Generation Science Standards for English Language Learners: What Teachers Need to Know," *Understanding Language*, Stanford University, 2013, http://ell.stanford.edu/sites/default/files/pdf/academic-papers/03-Quinn%20Lee%20Valdes%20Language%20and%20Opportunities%20in%20Science%20FINAL.pdf.

114 Thomas Philip and Flávio S. Azevedo, "Everyday Science Learning and Equity: Mapping the Contested Terrain," *Science Education* 101 (2017): 526–532.

115 Janet Waugh, as quoted in "Kansas Restores Evolution Standards for Science Classes," *CNN.com/U.S.*, February 14, 2001, http://articles.cnn.com/2001-02-14/us/kansas.evolution.02_1_science-standardskansas-board-sue-gamble?_s=PM:US/.

116 Michael Powell, "Pa. Case Is Newest Round in Evolution Debate: 'Intelligent Design' Teaching Challenged," *Washington Post*, September 27, 2005, A03.

117 Jodi Wilgoren, "Kansas Board Approves Challenges to Evolution," *New York Times*, November 9, 2005, www.nytimes.com/2005/11/09/national/09kansas.html?scp=1&sq=Evolution%20of%20Kansas%20science%20standards%20continues%20as%20Darwin&st=cse.

118 The Discovery Institute, www.discovery.org.

119 *Kansas Evolution Hearings Transcripts*, www.talkorigins.org/faqs/kansas/kangaroo1.html.

120 American Academy of Religion, *Guidelines for Teaching About Religion in K-12 Public Schools in the United States*, 2010, 16, www.aarweb.org/sites/default/files/pdfs/Publications/epublications/AARK-12CurriculumGuidelines.pdf.

121 Leslie Kaufman, "Darwin Foes Add Warming to Targets," *New York Times*, March 3, 2010, www.nytimes.com/2010/03/04/science/earth/04climate.html.

122 Barbara Bradley Hagerty, "Evangelical Voters May Be Up for Grabs in '08," *National Public Radio*, May 16, 2007, www.npr.org/templates/story/story.php?storyId=10215580.

123 Kaufman, "Darwin Foes Add Warming to Targets."

124 Dylan Matthews, "Donald Trump Has Tweeted Climate Change Skepticism 115 Times. Here's All of It," *Vox*, June 1, 2017, www.vox.com/policy-and-politics/2017/6/1/15726472/trump-tweets-global-warming-paris-climate-agreement.

125 Phil McKenna, "EPA Head Pruitt Denies the Basic Science of Climate Change," *Inside Climate News*, March 9, 2017, https://insideclimatenews.org/news/09032017/scott-pruitt-epa-donald-trump-climate-change-denial-co2-global-warming.

126 National Center for Science Education, https://ncse.com.

127 NASA, "Scientific Consensus: Earth's Climate Is Warming," https://climate.nasa.gov/scientific-consensus/.

128 Emmalina Glinskis, "Climate Denial in Schools," *Vice News*, April 25, 2017.

129 Amy Harmon, "Climate Science Meets a Stubborn Obstacle: Students," *New York Times*, June 4, 2017, www.nytimes.com/2017/06/04/us/education-climate-change-science-class-students.html?hp&action=click&pgtype=Homepage&clickSource=story-heading&module=second-column-region&region=top-news&WT.nav=top-news&_r=0.

130 Ibid.

131 National Center for Science Education, https://ncse.com.

132 Next Generation Science Standards, *HS-ESS3 Earth and Human Activity*, www.nextgenscience.org/dci-arrangement/hs-ess3-earth-and-human-activity.

133 Rolf K. Blank, "Science Instructional Time Is Declining in Elementary Schools: What Are the Implications for Student Achievement and Closing the Gap?" *Science Education*, October 2013, n.p.

134 Sheridan Blau, *Toward the Separation of School and State* (inaugural address, 1997 NCTE Convention, Detroit, MI, November 20–25, 1997).

Chapter 6

Instruction
Teaching and Learning Across the Content Areas

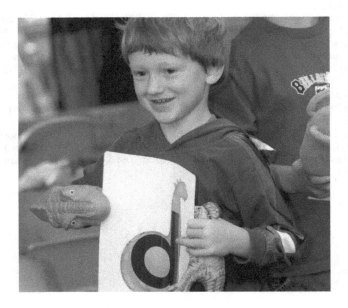

In the Round Robin review activity, I gave each group of four students a math problem. Once the group arrived at a solution, I checked their work. If it was correct, I gave the group the go-ahead to copy their problem onto a big sheet of paper and place it on the wall. When every group had finished, each group chose two members to stay at their problem and be explainers, while the other two rotated. Every three minutes the rotators moved in a circle to a new problem, where they would copy the problem on the wall while a group member talked through their solution. Once the rotators had been through all the problems, they switched places and explained their problem solution while the remaining members circled the room.

I listened to student reflections throughout the activity and looked for improvements in the students' abilities to articulate their ideas about the concepts they encountered. Afterward, we talked about how, in order to explain a problem to someone else, you first need a good understanding yourself. As the students reflected on their learning, they were especially confident about the problem that they presented, and said that the activity helped them identify which concepts they were comfortable with and which they needed more practice [with]: "It helps me by sorting out what I know and what I don't"; "I find that the problem I have to explain, I get right on the test"; "It gives me ideas about how to remember the problem."

—Mark Hill
First-year teacher, high school mathematics

Chapter Overview

This chapter focuses on classroom instruction. It begins with a bit of history of how teaching has changed—and how it hasn't changed—over the past 200 years. It then discusses theories of children's learning, introduces key principles of "authentic" instruction, and reviews some related instructional approaches. Together, these theories, principles, and approaches—coupled with deep, worthwhile content, as described in Chapter 5—encourage effort and persistence, promote intellectual rigor and democratic dispositions, and help students see themselves as competent learners.

How Teachers Taught[1]

Imagine you are a city schoolteacher in the early 1800s; your teaching is nothing like the activity that Mark Hill describes in the opening vignette. Instead of moving around listening to students explain to one another how to solve problems, you likely sit on a raised platform at the front of a cavernous room designed for 450 students of various ages. Below your desk are three rows of monitors' desks and, behind them, rows and rows of students in assigned seats. You direct the monitors, who, in turn, instruct and hear recitations from platoons of students who march forward, slates in hand, to the monitors' desks. In precise sequences, students march, listen, and recite—all under your watchful eye. You "motivate" with rewards and punishment, including administering "the rod" (corporal punishment), to keep your charges orderly and industrious. You teach basic skills such as arithmetic, reading, spelling, and penmanship, but your "real" job is to steer your charges away from evil influences, train them for good moral conduct, and protect the rest of the city from the crime and disease these children would allegedly cause if they continued to cling to their foreign or rural habits.

You were not hired because of your intellectual or pedagogical skills, but because you were "of pure tastes, of good manners, of exemplary morals."[2]

A century later, as a teacher in an early 1900s urban public school, you are following new "scientific" and efficient school reforms. Your pupils are divided by age into grades and by ability into classes, and you have forty to fifty of them sitting in rows of desks bolted to the floor. Since you have been to a special training or *normal* school for your teacher preparation, you know some theory (e.g., the mind needs exercising as if it were a muscle) and pedagogical skills (e.g., drill and recitation) to guide your teaching. But you follow the uniform curriculum and classroom routines dictated by your principal. The rules might be similar to those expected of Bronx teachers in the 1920s: Size the children and assign seats, make a seating plan of the class, drill on standing and sitting and putting the benches up and down noiselessly, and place your daily lesson plan and your time schedule on the desk where you can refer to them frequently.[3]

You help students build strong habits of mind through drill and repetition. You reward correct answers with high grades, praise, and preferred seating. You measure progress with tests. Any fact the curriculum specifies as important, your students memorize and recite in unison. However, there are increasing pressures for you to teach students to analyze and decode texts. You are also expected to pay attention to how well students communicate with and persuade others, as these become important business skills. You follow popular classroom management methods such as lining students up and marching them with good posture to assigned spots at the blackboard. Like your counterparts a century earlier, you are more concerned about developing character than intellect. Your focus is mostly utilitarian, preparing students—many of whom are immigrants—with the habits, language, and dispositions for industrial urban life.

As archaic as these portraits of past classrooms may seem, some aspects are quite familiar. Tables and chairs may have replaced bolted desks, and desks in U shapes or groups of four may have replaced rows. However, individual teachers still instruct large groups of students, and

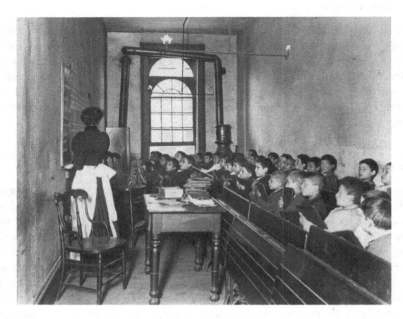

Classroom on the Lower East Side of New York City

students mostly work alone. Teachers transmit knowledge to students in an orderly sequence of steps, often prescribed in school or school district policy.[4] Students memorize and recite answers, and the mind-as-a-muscle metaphor still holds sway. End-of-unit tests assess whether learning took place. Mastery is rewarded, mistakes are corrected, and unlearned material is retaught. Then everyone moves on to the next topic or skill.[5] Although today's time-outs and behavior cards and contracts are improvements over corporal punishment, the underlying theory of control through reward and punishment remains. For low-income and culturally and linguistically "different" students, teachers often stress basic skills and good work habits rather than high intellectual achievement. Children of the wealthy and children of the poor mostly sit in different classrooms, even when they attend the same schools.

If you imagine your own most satisfying learning, in or out of school, you probably picture experiences very different from those just described. Those cherished experiences might have been challenging, but were likely connected to your interests and possibly to authentic adult activities, as well. Most likely, the adults involved believed that you *could* learn, that you *wanted* to learn, and that you *would* learn by observing and participating with others. Most likely, you received help when you needed it. If so, your learning was probably similar to that experienced in societies *without* mass education; in other words, your learning occurred socially, through what anthropologist Jean Lave and Etienne Wegner call "participation in communities of practice."[6] Today's teachers can tap the power of such participation; however, doing so requires teaching based on up-to-date learning theories rather than theories that guided schools in centuries past.

Theories of Learning and Their Implications for Teaching

There are multiple broad ways of thinking about learning and how it occurs; this is what we mean by *theories of learning*. For most of the twentieth century, *behavioral* theories of learning shaped how teachers taught. These theories focus on how stimuli elicit responses and how, if rewarded, those responses become habitual or "learned." Stimulus-response theory, for example, conceives of learners as passive and assumes that if learners' correct response is rewarded with something pleasant—a smile or candy, for example—they are more likely to repeat the response. From this perspective, the teacher's job is to transmit knowledge in small chunks, provide constant rewards or reinforcement, monitor (test) whether chunks of knowledge have been learned, and reteach whatever was missed.

Behavioral theories have some value in explaining a narrow range of learning; however, the last fifty or so years of scientific research on learning have revealed that so much more is both possible and necessary. Fortunately, most teachers have never been so mechanical or limited in their actual practice that they exclusively apply behavioral rules; nevertheless, behavioral and transmission models for instruction remain at the center of conventional teaching.

In the coming paragraphs, we explain what it means to teach from *sociocultural* and *constructivist* perspectives. These theories provide teachers with an alternative to the obvious and documented failures of purely behaviorist practices. Indeed, they inform the work of many teachers who believe it is their job to help *all* students develop the intelligence, understanding, and problem-solving capacities necessary to fill important roles in a diverse and democratic society.

Learning Is Developmental, Social, and Cultural

Since the 1960s, psychologists, linguists, neuroscientists, and anthropologists have learned a great deal about intelligence and about how children learn. All now agree that learning is not simply responding to stimuli. Learning is an active experience; that is, people learn as they interact with others to make sense of, or *construct* meaning out of, the world and their experiences in it. Teachers can do quite a lot to provide appropriate learning opportunities and productive learning environments for children. That is the starting point for good teaching.

The idea that learning takes place through interaction is not new. In the early twentieth century, John Dewey, Jean Piaget, and Lev Vygotsky saw engagement within a social environment as the key to learning.[7] In 1896, philosopher John Dewey wrote an essay for the *School Journal* called "My Pedagogic Creed." In it, Dewey tied children's learning to the social context in which they learn. Dewey wrote:

> I believe that all education proceeds by the participation of the individual in the social consciousness of the race. This process begins almost unconsciously at birth, and is continually shaping the individual's powers, saturating his consciousness, forming his habits, training his ideas, and arousing his feelings and emotions. Through this unconscious education, the individual gradually comes to share in the intellectual and moral resources which humanity has succeeded in getting together. He becomes an inheritor of the funded capital of civilization. . . . I believe that the only true education comes through the stimulation of the child's powers by the demands of the social situation in which he finds himself. . . . Through the responses others make to his own activities, he comes to know what those mean in social terms. . . . I believe that the psychological and social sides are organically related and that education can not be regarded as a compromise between the two, or a superimposition of one upon the other.[8]

Piaget and Vygotsky devoted themselves to understanding how children develop cognitively. Piaget saw the child as very much an independent learner, already equipped to draw in and make sense of the environment, including relationships with others. According to Piaget, children, like "little scientists," investigate and learn pretty much on their own, using the environment as their laboratory. One of Piaget's most important contributions was his theory that children think in fundamentally different ways from adults and that their thinking *develops* as they make sense of experiences. He documented how children represent the world differently as they proceed through different *developmental stages*.

Vygotsky stressed a much more essential and interdependent relationship between child and adult. He blurred the distinction between social experiences and mental processes, emphasizing that learning and problem solving occur *between* a learner and others. From this perspective, social participation does not simply provide external stimulation for one's own thinking; it is part of, and in some respects indistinguishable from, one's thought process. Thus, Vygotsky claimed that all meanings stem from interactions. Another way to make sense of this concept is to think of cognition as *distributed* throughout a person's social world—home and community, the workplace, and school.

Vygotsky also proposed the idea of the *zone of proximal development* (ZPD). Simply put, the ZPD represents the difference between what a learner (or learners) can do and understand independently and what a learner (or learners) can do and understand with targeted assistance. The idea is that learning—the development of higher mental processes—is most likely to occur at this critical juncture.

Like Dewey, Vygotsky placed great importance on the teacher's role in organizing activities and social groupings that would keep students stretching productively within their ZPD. Students must be challenged beyond problems they can already solve, but they should not be *overly* challenged by problems that are beyond their ZPD and therefore too difficult to resolve, even with assistance or what many socioculturalists refer to as *scaffolding*.

Psychologists today continue to explore the interplay between social interactions and mental processes. Among other things, scholars study how cognitive processes differ across cultures that stress different kinds of knowledge, values, social organization, or work. Thus, their research builds on the ideas of Dewey, Vygotsky, and others—for example, the idea that children learn as they interact with their culture and its *use* of knowledge. Contemporary *sociocultural* and *cultural historical* theorists assert that social and cultural contexts determine learning and that mental processes *are*, in and of themselves, both social and cultural.[9] Throughout his life, Jerome Bruner, for example, became increasingly convinced that people create and transform meanings (learn) as members of particular cultural groups.

> Learning, remembering, talking, imagining: all of them are made possible by participating in a culture. So, in the end, while mind creates culture, culture also creates mind.[10]

According to this perspective, it would be impossible to separate *how* thinking takes place from *what* knowledge is available in the context *where* learning happens. Drawing heavily from cross-cultural studies of learning (comparing how people think and solve problems in different societies), sociocultural theories fuse learning, intelligence, and culture into a single, complex entity.

Intelligence Is Acquired and Multidimensional

Scholars today have demonstrated quite convincingly that people develop intelligence as they interact with others and as they use the tools and symbols of their culture to make sense of the world and their experiences in it.

Contemporary psychologists have also developed theoretical models that discount the idea of a *single* intelligence and instead emphasize our use of many mental capacities and *intelligences*. For example, Robert Sternberg proposes three types of intelligence that vary in strength among people. One intelligence promotes analytical and critical thinking, one leads to the development of creative new ideas, and one enables humans to respond quickly and productively to everyday events and experiences. Howard Gardner, meanwhile, identifies multiple intelligences that include but are not limited to one's facility with language, mathematics and logic, visual and spatial perception, physical movement, and sensitivity to others. Gardner argues that everyone inherits the capacity to develop these intelligences and that these intelligences should be understood as the *mastery* of competencies or skills, rather than the underlying abilities or quality of one's mind. Of course, when it comes to mastery, Gardner and others acknowledge that individuals vary, as do the kinds of intelligence emphasized and valued by different cultural communities.

Although innate and universal predispositions may enhance the development of some abilities, people are generally more concerned about whether children develop those particular abilities deemed most important by the dominant culture. Because different cultures provide children with different learning situations, and because different cultures value the mastery of different tasks, differences in IQ among groups of people actually explain little about what those people can and do learn.

While conducting research in West Africa in the 1970s, for example, cultural psychologists Sylvia Scribner and Michael Cole initially assumed that the Vai people were mathematically deficient because of their struggles to successfully complete a U.S. standardized test in mathematics. Upon further examination, Cole and Scribner found that the same individuals who performed poorly on the test demonstrated sophisticated mathematical capacities while buying and selling goods in the local marketplace—capacities that did not map neatly onto the standardized test's questions. This led Cole and Scribner to arrive at what was then a revolutionary conclusion: "When people performed poorly in one of our tasks . . . it was the task and our understanding of its relationship to locally organized activities, not the people's minds that were deficient."[11] In other words, they came to understand that competence and intelligence are context dependent. This point has special relevance for teachers whose students may or may not demonstrate the kinds of ability and intelligence that are typically recognized and valued by schools.

Knowledge Is Constructed and Becomes Meaningful in Context

Another point of departure from traditional, behaviorist, passive notions of learning to progressive, sociocultural, and active approaches is the concept of *construction*. From a constructivist perspective, knowledge is not fixed, is not the same for everyone, and varies in different contexts and over time. This claim, that knowledge and even what might be called "facts" are human constructions, makes many uncomfortable. "What about 2 plus 2 equals 4?" people might ask. Yet there *are* multiple ways to "construct" even this simple equation so that it can have different meanings (e.g., mixing 2 liters each of ethanol and water results in only 3.84 liters of the mixture; similarly, doubling the numerals used to measure intelligence or weather temperature does not make a person twice as smart or twice as hot). Thus, in principle, we want children to explore the reasoning and meaning behind even simple problems rather than settling for the simplest or most common answer and moving on. Reasoning and meaning making are at the heart of what learning theorists call *constructivism*.

Traditional schooling typically poses problems that have right procedures to follow and right answers to find. Constructivist-oriented teachers do not dispute that such answers have their place—in spelling, math facts, and so on—but they object to a curriculum where attention to narrow, single-answer tasks displaces opportunities to generate multiple right answers, identify exceptions to the rule, or select among varied problem-solving approaches. Success in the real world, they argue, requires flexibility, creativity, and learning in context.

Of course, facts—names, events, dates, formulas, algorithms, and so on—are important, but they have meaning (and often are recalled) only when connected to or embedded in ideas, narratives, or experiences that already mean something to students. Educational and social critics frequently tout surveys showing that a shamefully low percentage of teenagers know basic historical facts, such as the century in which the American Civil War was fought. It isn't that these facts were never taught. More likely, they were taught in isolation from any meaningful context.

By situating student learning in the context of meaningful, *authentic* tasks, teachers support students to construct new knowledge. A rough analogy to learning a second language might be helpful: Consider memorizing vocabulary and studying grammar as a less authentic process for learning a second or third language. A more authentic experience might involve classroom practice in speaking the language and perhaps reading literature. The most authentic experience would be to navigate daily life in a city in which the language is primarily spoken—as the language of commerce, education, entertainment, and conversation.

Of course, teachers face limits in providing most-authentic experiences, but pursuing the *principles* of authenticity and meaningful knowledge construction can push student learning in the direction of higher-level thinking and social competence. Solving authentic, real-life problems requires basic information but also tends to extend students' thinking. Real-life solutions require complexity; they have to be compatible with multiple ideas, fit specific contexts, and suit the knowledge and opinions of various people. Not only will different people resolve the same problem in different ways, the same person often will not select the same solution twice if given the chance to change their mind or learn from the experience. In the real world, people need to figure things out by using trial and error, as well as by relying on memorized and automatic routines.

Another key idea in constructivist theory is that students actively construct or make sense of new knowledge in relation to the formal and informal knowledge they already possess. Prior knowledge and experience are valuable curriculum resources, as first-year teacher Ramón Martínez discovered when he began a geography unit with his first graders.

> My students are Latino first graders who have been classified as limited English proficient. All of them come from low-income homes, and most live in the projects. My unit "¿Donde Estamos?" builds on my students' knowledge of their community to help them understand basic concepts in geography. We made a "mural map" as the centerpiece of the unit. Instead of telling my students what to include, I allowed them to decide. Many students supplied me with details about their community that would have otherwise gone unnoticed. One saw that I had forgotten to put a particular store on the map. I encouraged her to make it and put it where it belonged, which she did in amazing detail. Another noticed that the Chinese restaurant near her house did not appear. Not surprisingly, she knew exactly where to put it. My students began noticing maps everywhere. Once my students realized that I welcomed their knowledge, they began to participate more actively. They showed me maps in the hallway and interrupted during journal time to show me maps in books. One brought back a map from Disneyland and insisted on sharing it. After I introduced the cardinal directions, they were constantly notifying me every time that they saw the cardinal directions in print.
>
> —Ramón Martínez
> First-year teacher, bilingual grade 1

Whereas a traditional curriculum might *enrich* lessons by acknowledging diverse and multiple cultures, sociocultural and constructivist theories invite teachers to place inclusive and democratic principles at the *center* of their curricula and from that core develop daily learning opportunities. Such an approach may present a challenge to teachers who are not accustomed to more expansive conceptions of meaningful knowledge or are not used to departing from the subject matter in textbooks and curriculum guides. As Ramón illustrates, however, students learn best when they can relate new experiences to what they already know. Ramón leveraged students' *individualized* and *collective* knowledge of the surrounding community to teach academic facts, skills, and concepts related to maps, mapmaking, and cardinal directions.

Contemporary Theories in the Classroom

Given these new understandings of learning, it's not surprising that most teachers entering the profession today seek community-like relationships within classrooms rather than the factory-like relationships of the past. This does not mean that students are set free from learning the valued traditions, facts, and skills of the mainstream culture. However, sociocultural and constructivist theories do encourage a broader view of culture and suggest that teachers have a powerful role to play in providing opportunities for students to learn about, participate in, and benefit from society's diverse cultures.

Six principles—summarized in Concept Table 6.1—guide teachers in this work. Each principle draws from a distinct body of research. Eliminate any one, and socially just teaching collapses like a house of cards. In the remainder of this chapter, we explore the first three of these principles. In chapters that follow, we examine the remaining three: assessment, caring and interdependent relationships, and socially just talk and action.

Seeing Diversity as an Asset and Every Child as a Capable Learner

Learning is a social endeavor; it is also a matter of individual sense or meaning making. In fact, social and individual learning go hand in hand. Thus, tailoring instruction for *individual* students' differences brings benefits both to individuals and to the entire classroom. To accomplish this requires professional knowledge, strong personal relationships, appreciation for diversity, and a commitment to social justice. In essence, the ways teachers think about and respond to students' differences can either work against or foster students' confidence, hard work, persistence, and learning.

Traditional Treatments of Difference

Even in schools where everyone pretty much "looks" alike, students are still very different. Indeed, there tends to be even more diversity *among* members of a particular group than between groups. Prior experiences, attitudes and expressions, charm and sociability, shyness and

Concept Table 6.1 Six Principles That Guide Socially Just Classroom Learning Communities

| Teachers see diversity as an asset and every student as a capable learner (Chapter 6). | Instruction provides opportunities for active, social, multidimensional, and scaffolded learning (Chapter 6). | Teaching and learning build on students' cultural and linguistic knowledge (Chapter 6). | Authentic assessment plays a central role in teaching and learning (Chapter 7). | Relationships are caring and interdependent (Chapter 8). | Talk and action are socially just (Chapter 8). |

silliness, and mastery of sophisticated knowledge, as well as surprising, even funny misunderstandings, all vary among the students in any classroom. In many classrooms, students also differ in the languages, cultures, and community resources they bring to school. These differences, no less delightful, influence how students approach classroom learning, and yet they bear no relation to whether students are capable learners.

TREATING DIFFERENCES AS PROBLEMATIC

Differences among students are often neutral, but schools almost always place a positive or negative value on those differences. Traditional teaching makes students acutely aware of how their personal characteristics create problems or benefits for themselves and for the teacher. In fact, traditional teaching *requires* these differently valued distinctions to be made. For example, traditional teaching assumes that all students *should* learn the same things in the same way at the same time. Such lessons make students' differences conspicuous and troublesome, and they virtually guarantee that the teacher and class will lose confidence in at least some students' capacity or willingness to learn.[12]

COMPARING STUDENTS

In traditional classrooms, one of the most common ways of addressing differences is to compare students. When such comparisons take place, learning and succeeding (or not) can become very public. Who finishes quickly, who gets the most correct answers, and who never seems to be able to respond when the teacher calls on them are obvious to everyone in the room. Even when teachers appropriately challenge students, students risk making mistakes and suffering public judgments. Focal Point 6.1 discusses some of the problematic ways children's status is constructed and becomes public in schools.

Public comparisons of students also influence how peers view and treat one another; impressions about individuals soon solidify as a classroom consensus about each student's role and value. Each day brings a greater distinction between those students whom the classroom culture expects to meet the class's highest standards and those from whom that culture expects little. These classroom status differences trigger easy social comparisons between students who are perceived as "smart" and those who are not. From there, it is only a short step for students and teachers to conclude that some students simply can't or won't learn well and to blame students' differences (intelligence, race, effort, prior schooling opportunities, etc.), rather than faulty instruction or less-than-ideal classroom relationships and routines.

Focal Point 6.1
How Status Becomes Public in the Classroom

Consider the countless classroom routines that expose students to public scrutiny. A glance at student work stuck on the wall immediately tells who are top students and who are not. In addition, teachers sometimes read scores aloud or permit student helpers to return graded papers to their classmates. Gradebooks are often open for students to peruse classmates' grades. Results of aptitude, achievement, and other standardized tests become public when students or their parents offer their scores voluntarily. A teacher's public display of annoyance is noted by all, and signals sent by peers are always salient. Posted grades and other symbols of students' progress—letters, numbers, stars, smiley faces—likewise make public comparisons of students. Take, for example, this letter written by a veteran teacher to one of her former teachers. The letter illustrates how evaluative acts and symbols can quickly lead students to sum up their own ability in a subject and their school worthiness in general.

> Dear Mrs. DeVries,
>
> You most likely don't remember me. I was one of the many "quiet and sweet" girls who sat in the rows of desks that filled up your second-grade classroom in . . . 1957.
>
> Do you remember the Book Chart you displayed? I do. I can see where it was hung in the room over by two tall bookshelves in front of the classroom. It had all our names in alphabetical order by family name: Jimenez, Alessandra; Lundberg, Anne; Medina, Max. It was hard for us to find our names and record our gold star stickers because we never used our last names and because some of us couldn't read yet. I recall Alessandra lightly drawing a little flower next to her name as a self-help device. But this chart wasn't for us. It was for you, wasn't it? I am writing today because of this chart and to share with you some other thoughts about teaching.
>
> I can still recall walking into the classroom on the first day of school. It was all work; boring workbooks mostly, or whole group lessons. But I entered your room as a reader, so I could escape to my books once my work was done. Maybe you remember me, not because I stood out, but because I didn't. I was compliant. I was a good little girl. I did what you asked, I learned quickly and easily, and I took care of my own boredom. I had an imagination. Yet I doubt you ever knew this about me.
>
> One day I had to speak with you about a problem. My column for gold stars on your Book Chart was full and I had finished another book. *Mrs. DeVries, where should I put this sticker? There's no more room.* You were aghast. How could it be full? How could I have read so many books? There were, after all, 12 slots! You called me a liar. You made me stay in from recess and go through the library shelves and pull out all the books I said I had read and then sit next to your desk while you tested me on the contents of the entire dozen. The other children came back from recess and tried to ignore us. I could not look at them. I was embarrassed.
>
> As you tested me, I could feel the heat of your rage for being defied or duped by this child. You did not apologize. You asked me how it was possible that I had read so many books. I said, *I return one and pick a new one each morning before class starts. I read it when I'm done with my workbook and then finish it up on the 2-hour bus ride home.* You told me to double star the slots and return to my seat.
>
> I am a teacher myself now. I work with young children and their families, and I have been doing this work in cities and rural settings, in classrooms and in natural environments, in and outside the United States, since 1969. And I use charts a lot—to compare and contrast information or to visually record data. But I have never used one to publicly record individual achievement in a competitive way. I wonder why? If I could tell you one thing today, it would be: Take down your Book Chart.

Source: Sonia Nieto, *What Keeps Teachers Going?* (New York: Teachers College Press, 2003), 32–33.

The most far-reaching, as well as ironic, effect of public comparisons in the classroom is that these comparisons communicate that school is a place where imminent failure is possible for *any* student. The very existence of the resulting status hierarchy can also negatively affect the highest-achieving students, who may become chiefly motivated by a desire not to fall to a level where they are treated like others. Such conditions do not help students become fully engaged in their own learning or care about others' success. No wonder so many students, older ones in particular, spend their time applying some of school's "real" lessons: Work hard for others' approval, and if that does not produce results, find another "game"—for example, disruption, resistance, or failure—at which you can succeed.

COMPARING STUDENTS ON THE BASIS OF RACE AND ETHNICITY

For all students, public comparisons are often onerous and rarely beneficial. These comparisons become particularly dangerous when they target students' race or ethnicity, explicitly or in more subtle ways that reflect deep-seated beliefs and biases and may be enacted by well-meaning classmates and teachers. UCLA sociologist Daniel Solórzano refers to such *microaggressions* as racially laden attitudes, comments, and actions of peers and teachers who would likely deny that they were prejudiced or acting hurtfully. Solórzano offers the following examples:

"When I talk about those Blacks, I really wasn't talking about you."
"You're not like the rest of them. You're different."
"If only there were more of them like you."
"I don't think of you as a Mexican."
"You speak such good English."[13]

Makeba Jones, a professor at the University of California, San Diego, describes how her identity as an African American woman increased her vulnerability in a school environment where "differences" were not treated as neutral:

As a teenager, I questioned my abilities in comparison to my peers. Despite the fact that my large public high school was racially mixed, I was the only person of color in my white and affluent Honors level courses. I felt conspicuous and out of place, or rather misplaced. When I did not understand an assignment, I felt sure my peers could see both the confusion on my face, and that I was only pretending to write an essay when I was staring at a blank page.

I accepted the belief that only individual ability and merit would bring high grades and teacher praise. I was naive about race as an adolescent. I am not sure if I felt so inadequate because I was the only black girl in the class, but I felt self-confident outside of my advanced classes. I battled the contradiction between what I knew in my heart was true about me, Makeba, and what I perceived that my peers and teachers thought about me and my "place." This struggle of identity and self-examination pushed me to drop out of Honors English my senior year. I felt relieved the second semester as I passed by the Honors English classroom on my way to a classroom that didn't suddenly fall silent when a student answered a question wrong. But I also felt as though the American Dream only applied to those whose stamina and ability allowed them to flourish under such pressure, and not those, like me, who needed more reassurance and sensitivity.[14]

As Makeba Jones observes, schools do not have to be overtly prejudiced to perpetuate social stereotypes. For example, a school counselor might not tell girls to *avoid* advanced mathematics classes, but staff also might not make the needed effort to overcome the stereotype that girls are less well suited for math. When a student decides to avoid advanced math, the counselor may just say (and believe), "OK, that's your choice." On the one hand, it *is* a free and individual choice; on the other hand, it is a choice that potentially reflects problematic cultural assumptions and most likely translates into limited opportunity. Further, the student who does decide to take advanced math may be aware that her performance in class not only carries the usual risks of exposing flawed math knowledge but also leads others to see her as somehow representative of all girls who take math. Psychologist Claude Steele argues that this combined awareness may impinge on the student's concentration and confidence, despite other evidence suggesting that she is well suited for success.[15]

Steele's studies help explain how stereotypes can negatively impact students' performance and limit their opportunities. In one experiment, high-achieving African American men and women were given intelligence tests and asked to specify their race. They did less well than other similar African American students who were not asked about their race and therefore did not expect to be judged according to racial stereotypes.[16]

Steele also found that most everyone is vulnerable to stereotypes. In another experiment, for example, White males—unaccustomed to being intellectually stigmatized—were told that Asians achieved higher scores than Whites on a mathematics test. That group of White males then achieved lower scores on the test than a control group of White males who were not told anything about previous test results.[17]

Importantly, as with other social science research, Steele's findings are not meant as predictions of what will surely happen in specific instances. That is why the term *vulnerability* proves so apt. Everyone is vulnerable, but *how* vulnerable depends on the prevalence and depth of the stereotype as well as a host of individual characteristics and contextual factors. In sum, the significance of stereotypes extends beyond what *other* people think; stereotypes can affect one's *own* thinking and learning, too.

Sociocultural Treatments of Difference

Sociocultural theory offers another way to think about difference; simply put, it presumes that there is no central "normal" by which others are compared and judged. In this sense, a Muslim and a Christian are equally different from each other; Black and White students are racially different, but one is not more "normal" than the other, regardless of their relative numbers in a particular classroom; and students' varied pathways to learning are (within reason) neither more nor less normal, relatively speaking.

TREATING DIFFERENCES AS ASSETS

In socially just classrooms guided by sociocultural theory, dimensions of difference can exist and should serve as the source of rich learning interactions. Indeed, much of the delight of teaching and learning comes from observing and interacting with these differences. Teachers make each student's particular competencies visible and available to others as resources. Social interactions allow students to support or scaffold one another's learning and to combine their different knowledge and experiences into the collective knowledge and experience of the learning community. Such lessons set in motion a positive cycle that encourages student confidence, effort, risk taking, persistence, and learning.

SETTING HIGH EXPECTATIONS AND SUPPORTING ALL STUDENTS TO MEET THEM

Teachers' beliefs about children's ability to learn have enormous power. This was first documented in Robert Rosenthal and Lenore Jacobson's landmark study, *Pygmalion in the Classroom*.[18] Rosenthal and Jacobson told a group of elementary teachers that a few students in their classes were "late bloomers." They said that although these students were not exceptional now, they would make substantial strides in the future. In fact, the researchers randomly selected students who were neither more nor less ready to "bloom" than the others. By the end of the year, the students who had been labeled late bloomers and expected to shine academically outperformed their classmates.

The study's central assertion—that teachers' expectations influence students' performance—has held up over the years. Adults respond to initial cues from students about what to expect from them and how much to push or encourage them; in other words, adults set high or low expectations, and then students either rise or drop to meet them. A student's well-groomed or unkempt appearance, compliant or disruptive behavior, standard or nonstandard language use, native or nonnative accent when speaking English, and so on can all act as cues that elicit positive or negative reactions and expectations among teachers.

Teachers communicate expectations in many subtle ways. For example, teachers may give some students extra time if they are confident a correct answer will follow, while quickly moving on from students whose hesitation matches the teacher's view of the student as "slow." Sometimes, to avoid embarrassing a student judged to have little to offer, a teacher will skip over the student or quickly supply a correct answer. Receiving a good-natured call back to the task versus a scolding glare can powerfully influence a distracted student's self-concept as a learner.

David and the late Myra Sadker's research documents the extent to which teachers communicate different expectations for boys and girls, specifically. Particularly in math and science, teachers tend to enact the larger society's gender stereotypes in subtle ways that, when pointed out, often astonish the teachers themselves. For example, teachers ask boys more questions and allow them to dominate laboratory experiments. When students encounter difficulties, teachers encourage boys to press on and try harder but are more likely to console and comfort girls.[19] Low-income children and children of color face similarly inequitable expectations.[20] Such responses affect students' willingness to participate, take risks, and work hard.[21]

Sometimes, acting on high expectations requires teachers to challenge "normal" procedures that reflect institutionalized low expectations. This is particularly true in the case of Emergent Bilinguals, where schools often act as if students who speak languages other than English lack intelligence and can't learn math, science, social studies, or other school subjects without mastering English first.

Racial and other stereotypes, along with perceptions of academic ability and acceptance of diversity, are all tightly linked. Most teachers value and want to be sensitive to student differences, but as Laura Silvina Torres and Marilyn Cortez have learned, working productively within the social world of their classrooms requires more than tolerance or acceptance. It often involves publicly advocating for students and explicitly challenging the status quo.

> I focus on what students can do instead of what they are not doing. Then I give them opportunities to recognize their strengths and support for critical thinking. A colleague of mine, whose deficit thinking is both explicit and subtle, approached me. Frustrated with his students' writing, he asked what we were doing, and I explained my students' analytical writing. He immediately said, "Oh, you guys are doing that? That is way too sophisticated. . . . My kids are not going to be able to do it." He glanced over my students' work and asked, "So, what's the trick? If there are any tricks you can tell me, I'd love to hear them." I was upset with his implication that my students could not think at those levels without having some trick taught to them, so I said, "Well, it's not about any tricks, it's starting from a belief that they can do it."
>
> —Laura Silvina Torres
> First-year teacher, grade 2

Discussions that focused on logic and reason helped students to make sense out of math-ematics. The challenges students faced in my classroom gave them a sense that their math class was no longer a place for "dummies." Rather, it was a place that challenged them to reason things out. I would hear them bragging about this to their friends outside of our class. Although several students would complain about the difficulty of the work, they were proud to be doing it.

—Marilyn Cortez
First-year teacher, high school mathematics

Of course, high expectations by themselves do not generate high academic outcomes. Teach-ers must also hold themselves accountable for supporting students to meet those expectations. Sociocultural and constructivist theories help guide teachers as they get to know their students and scaffold students' learning accordingly. Indeed, even when teachers hold the same rigorous learning goals for all students, students' differences require different instructional approaches—what educators often call *differentiated* instruction. Differentiating instruction does not mean always supporting every student in the same way; rather, it involves designing instruction that leads to equitable *outcomes* among all students.

Increasingly, social justice–oriented teachers also draw on *Universal Design*, a framework developed within architecture as part of efforts to design spaces that are accessible to all. Applied to education, the framework is known as *Universal Design for Learning* (UDL). UDL is geared toward helping teachers design instruction that considers students' differences *from the outset*, rather than modifying instruction or making accommodations for students as afterthoughts or interventions. Instead, UDL supports teachers to understand that all students possess some form of difference, and that there is no "normal" student around which instruction ought to be designed. UDL is also based on the assumption that all learners can and will achieve at high levels if they are supported appropriately.[22] In this respect, high expectations can be thought of as a contract between student and teacher that requires of both parties whatever it takes to realize success.

DESIGNING AND DELIVERING COMPLEX INSTRUCTION

One key approach for supporting students to meet high expectations involves helping them develop confidence in their academic abilities. For more than twenty years, Stanford sociologists Elizabeth Cohen and Rachel Lotan studied elementary and middle-school classrooms to deter-mine the instructional principles that sustain confidence. Cohen and Lotan took one of these principles—engaging students with rich and complex knowledge—and made it the foundation for their program Complex Instruction.

Complex Instruction involves attending to students' status as learners and teaching in ways that address a variety of student abilities. Consider the following assignment: "Read the chap-ter and answer the questions at the end. Test on Tuesday. Don't forget the vocab." This work requires skills related to low-level reading comprehension and memorization. Because the test will measure those skills alone, it is easy to predict who will score high and low. In classrooms dominated by such instruction, teachers and students know within just a few months who is "smart" on this kind of test and who is not.

Conversely, multi-ability instructional tasks include elements that require distinctly differ-ent skill levels, as well as elements that all students can engage in and benefit from. Such tasks can be short range and relatively simple, or they can be embedded in richer, long-range, often project-based instruction that involves multiple tasks and subassignments. This kind of instruc-tion incorporates work that students can do individually, as well as work that students must do together. It involves hands-on activity, traditional book-and-paper scholarship, and research. It also makes use of students' informal and prior knowledge. Because of this complexity, all students are able to participate and find areas in which they have particular strengths. The teacher and other knowledgeable helpers are ready to step in when some students struggle or when others are ready to forge ahead. Of course, no one lesson or task ever reaches an ideal. There is always another opportunity for student investigation, another theme to explore, more resources to consult, and a teacher's wish for just a little more time.

That said, Cohen and Lotan have proposed that the Complex Instruction approach allows teachers to engage students in discussions that address the many different intellectual abilities and skills a given task requires. Cohen and Lotan found that when teachers do this, and consistently associate students' participation with competence, students increasingly identify one another and themselves as "smart" on a wide range of attributes, weakening the power of traditional classroom hierarchies. Of course, the goal is not to assign or label individual students as being good at one thing and not another. That would just create new status hierarchies. Rather, the goal is for students to see one another as competent, support one another to contribute, and understand that individual competence results from *participating* in the classroom learning community.[23] The work of Cohen and Lotan, among others, makes clear that students' initial degree of competence does not matter as much as their engagement in activities that scaffold their learning.

In an ideal setting, everyone's status is that of a highly competent learner. However, students themselves have much to say about the classroom's learning environment and the status of other students. The self-concepts students bring with them into the classroom, coupled with their habits of judging one another, are often so powerful that teachers must address issues of self-concept and status head-on. Thus, Cohen and Lotan have encouraged teachers who use Complex Instruction to *assign* competence to low-status students explicitly.

To do this, teachers watch for instances of capable performance on various relevant tasks by students with low status and/or low expectations of themselves. The teacher then gives the student a specific, favorable, and very public evaluation, pointing out to others in the class that the student can serve as a resource to others in that area.[24] First-year bilingual teacher Benji Chang used just this strategy to boost students' confidence in themselves and one another.

One day a student who has a lot of difficulty speaking English spoke. I did not understand him and was reminded of the trouble he had acquiring English in my class, while speaking mostly Spanish at home and studying Cantonese at Chinese school. As I often do, I replied to him in his home language, saying, "What?" in Spanish. He then rattled off a beautiful description of a bird building its nest on a rooftop, and he connected it to an integrated lesson we had a month earlier. To the casual observer, it might not have seemed like any success in developing language. For me, it was poetry—the student's description of a bird building a nest to take care of eggs that would someday hatch. He engaged his classmates in a real-life situation and connected it to what we had done in class. He not only got his Spanish-speaking peers to speak in their home language, the rest of the class became interested. Despite not being able to understand Spanish, other students were excited and tried to figure out what was being said. This led the Spanish speakers to explain in English and Spanish. As I looked at this class at that moment, I saw twenty smiling faces engaged in a spontaneous language arts lesson led by a peer who was speaking just two of the languages he was going to master.

—Benji Chang
First-year teacher, grade 1

Assigning competence disrupts students' cycle of low expectations, low status, and low participation. Of course, the assignment must be genuine and credible. Quick praise for something mediocre or not central to the task (such as decorating a journal cover) will not prove convincing and may well have the opposite effect. Admittedly, these positive public evaluations carry some of the risks associated with traditional rewards and praise. However, if a teacher has worked consistently to build a sense of community and has established their role in class as a "broker" of knowledge—one whose main job is not to evaluate but to ask questions and point out knowledge sources—then they can present a student as a resource rather than as a shining example.

The remainder of this chapter and the next two explore additional strategies that teachers can use to make their classrooms places where students are confident about their ability to learn and where they are supported to meet high expectations.

Providing Opportunities for Active, Multidimensional, and Social Learning

> During our study of civil rights in U.S. History, my students wrestle with essential questions such as "How should we liberate ourselves? How should we gain civil rights?" I number students off, and they become different historical figures of the era (in this case, Marcus Garvey, Ida B. Wells, W. E. B. Du Bois, Booker T. Washington, etc.). The students have a goal—to convince the rest of the class that their historical figure has the best answers to these questions. Together they read the readings and produce speeches and questions for the other characters. They also create some piece of artwork. Because of the variety of the tasks and singularity of the tasks, the students usually remain on task and work well together.
>
> —Judy Smith
> High school social studies

Many teachers, striving for quiet and efficient classrooms, organize their instruction to control or minimize activity and social interaction. These teachers talk to the whole class at once, and they walk around the room giving individual help. They call on students to read aloud to the class, answer questions, or write on the board. Students quickly learn to identify the behaviors that school adults want from them. Some students learn to listen for the answers that please adults, and they become skilled at repeating them. Meanwhile, others sit quietly, hoping to avoid the teacher's eye and the pressure to participate. After only a short time in school, such students often come to believe that "real" learning happens only when they are working on their own and are able to show what they know by offering the teacher the "right" answer.

In contrast, considerable research demonstrates how active, multidimensional, and social instruction, like the instruction Judy Smith described in the preceding vignette, supports all learners to be successful. Roland Tharp and his former colleagues at the Center for Research on Education, Diversity, and Excellence (CREDE)—a federally funded University of California research center—distilled this research into five principles characterizing lessons that promote academic excellence for all students: (1) engaging teachers and students together in the production of knowledge, (2) developing language and literacy across the curriculum, (3) making meaning by connecting school content to students' lives, (4) teaching complex thinking, and (5) teaching through conversation. Putting these principles into practice requires that teachers create settings where diverse learning activities, including small-group experiences, occur simultaneously. Working in small groups, the teachers integrate students' out-of-school experiences with new learning, and all students are appropriately challenged. In such settings, teachers can then draw on students' diverse backgrounds and experiences so that differences become an asset rather than an obstacle; in the process, classrooms become active, social, and multidimensional.[25]

These principles are woven into the various approaches we discuss in the remainder of the chapter.

Students Learning Together

Kimberly Min's third-grade students in the photo at the bottom of the page are counting one another's teeth in an investigation designed to help them meet one of California's then third-grade science standards. In the process, they are working together to *construct* knowledge about human development.

The traditional view, however, is that teaching is all about transmitting knowledge. In this case, that could mean *telling* students facts—for example, that around age 6 humans begin the long process of acquiring thirty-two adult teeth—and then requiring that they memorize and recite those facts. Similarly, traditional classrooms focus on getting students to approach learning as a solitary effort. Schools abound with admonitions that reflect individualistic values, such as "Be sure to do your own work," "You need to become an independent thinker," and "He's just not a self-starter."

In contrast, sociocultural theories lead teachers to structure classroom lessons that are active and social. Following the ideas of Dewey, Vygotsky, and others, many teachers now think of their classrooms as "learning communities." They pay special attention to activities and relationships that give students access to adults and knowledgeable peers. They design instruction that encourages students to interact and engage in authentic problem solving. Rather than retaining authority, they share authority appropriately with students. In sum, they organize classrooms with the goal of preparing students for participation in a just, democratic society.

TWO LESSONS

Consider how two different teachers might approach the teaching of measurement to upper-elementary-school students. The first teacher—one who is grounded in traditional theories and practice—explains to the class how to add feet and inches and demonstrates the process by working through several sample problems step-by-step on an overhead projector she keeps at the front of the room. As she goes through the examples, she elicits students' ideas about what comes next, and as much as half the class gets to respond at least once. A few students are clearly enthusiastic and strive to answer every question.

The teacher then gives the students a few minutes to do a problem by themselves at their desks and asks two volunteers to come to the board to model how they worked the problem. She corrects any errors they make and asks the rest of the class if they understand. Seeing mostly positive head nods, she assigns a page of twenty practice problems for them to work on quietly for the rest of math time, while she circulates and monitors their work.

The second teacher proceeds quite differently. She had a measurement lesson planned, but she modified it two days earlier, after one of her students came late to class, having been delayed in the school office while getting his cut knee bandaged. On the way to school the student was running across a littered empty lot and fell. The class talked about the problems of the lot; they decided that it was ugly, dangerous, a waste of space, and so on. The teacher asked them to imagine what could be done with the lot to solve its problems and improve the community. The students decided that a playground would be nice, with benches for old people to sit on. However, their interest was not just self-serving or charitable; they marshaled their anger and social consciousness. They wondered why they had no nice parks close by, and these authentic questions added energy to their project.

Enlisting the supervision help of two parents, the teacher took her class, organized into teams, to the lot to measure its dimensions and locate and sketch topographical features (a small hill, an abandoned refrigerator, etc.). Back in the classroom, the students designed and located play equipment, paths, perimeter fencing, and other features. They calculated necessary amounts of materials—in some cases enlisting the help of parents with construction experience. They telephoned and visited lumberyards, asking questions and gathering information. They figured costs and prepared a budget.

To some degree, this teacher used the same instructional strategies as the first teacher: lecture and demonstration, question and answer, drill and practice. But these strategies were used more sparingly and in the context of solving real problems. Never did she allow them to become ends in themselves or to dominate large blocks of time. Often she used them with just a portion of the class.

The second lesson also illustrates several of the principles laid out by Vygotsky and Dewey, as well as Roland Tharp and his colleagues. It required that students engage in "joint productive activity" as they worked together to generate ideas for transforming the empty lot into something beneficial for their community. Their participation was authentic because the task had immediate meaning and because of the complex social and academic problems it presented. In doing this work, students became members of a mathematical community. As members of that community, they came to see themselves and each other as math-using specialists in the real, math-using world. This rich mix of relevance, collaboration, assistance, learning of new skills, and encouragement mirrors how work is accomplished in productive workplaces and communities. Two instructional elements stand out as particularly important: authentic, multidimensional tasks and instructional assistance or scaffolding.

Multidimensional Tasks

The elaborate measurement lesson just described provides complex mathematical tasks in abundance. It allows all students to succeed by situating new knowledge in relation to what they already know—in this case, the vacant lot in their community. The lesson involves tasks that are complex enough to offer multiple entry points for students with different levels of experience and expertise. It invites students, with the help of adults, to collaboratively tackle problems that they would likely struggle to solve on their own. In addition, opportunities for the teacher to assess students' learning (a topic we discuss at length in Chapter 7) are embedded within the tasks themselves.

Elizabeth Cohen referred to these carefully constructed tasks as "multidimensional." Drawing from her own and others' research, Cohen has identified the following common characteristics of multidimensional tasks. Not surprisingly, these characteristics overlap with the five principles that CREDE has used to characterize lessons that lead to academic excellence. Such tasks:

- include more than one answer or more than one way to solve the problem;
- are intrinsically interesting and rewarding;
- allow different students to make different contributions;
- use multimedia;
- involve sight, sound, and touch;
- require a variety of skills and behaviors;
- require reading and writing; and
- are challenging.

The following lesson that Kimman Thi Pham describes illustrates some of the advantages of incorporating multidimensional tasks that meet these criteria. It also shows that such tasks require that teachers both plan thoroughly and think on their feet. Her class had just finished investigating the relationship between the United Farm Workers Union and the Chicano Movement, and her students were working in small groups and preparing to present to the class what they'd learned.

> The room is alive with activity. Desks are pushed to the edge of the classroom, accommodating various groups. Some students discuss how to share their recent experience of working with migrant farmworkers in the fields. One student patiently charts a graph showing the economic breakdown of maintaining a large farm. Two students and I plan the presentation order. Other students complete a poster on the United Farm Workers, focusing on the leadership of Cesar Chavez and Philip Vera Cruz. Their photographs, news clippings, and markers are sprawled across the floor. Laughter erupts from the back of the room where four students debate the idea of dressing up as fruit while presenting information on the movement of farmworkers across the state following the peak harvest times of the fruit and vegetable season. Someone asks me if she can give her classmates a test after the presentation. "Certainly," I reply, "but consider—'What do you want them to know?'" The student thinks about the question while slowly returning to the group. Activity continues unabated until the final minutes. I remind students to document progress with a short journal entry highlighting individual concerns and feelings. Students write until the end of class.
>
> —Kimman Thi Pham
> First-year teacher, history, grade 11

Basic skills—like "charting a graph" or decoding a text—remain important in multidimensional classrooms; however, they are learned, applied, and enhanced through students' participation in multidimensional tasks. Cohen offered numerous examples of such tasks, including role playing, building models, drawing "mind maps" of the relationships between ideas, and using equipment or objects to explore or communicate a concept—tasks like those Kimman planned for her students. Hands-on science lessons that ask students to observe, manipulate, collect and record data, hypothesize causes and effects, and write up findings also often qualify as multidimensional, given the range of activities they encompass and the skills they require. According to Cohen, if tasks can be done more quickly and efficiently by one person than by a group, involve simple memorization or routine learning, and/or have a single right answer, teachers can be pretty sure they are unidimensional and will inhibit many students' learning.[26] That said, working alone, practicing skills, reflecting quietly, and even memorizing are not by definition unidimensional if they are incorporated into a larger, multidimensional context.

Scaffolded Participation

In classrooms guided by sociocultural theories of learning, the teacher's principal role is to support, or *scaffold*, students to acquire knowledge and skills that they cannot learn on their own but can learn with targeted assistance. As with an apprentice's relationship to an accomplished member of the community, the novice's contributions—no matter how small—are valued.

For example, as Mauro Bautista works to help one of his Emergent Bilingual students with writing, he employs one of the most effective forms of scaffolding: targeted questioning. Mauro might ask a question such as, "This sentence says 'ran home' but I am having a hard time understanding what you mean. Who or what ran home? Knowing this will help me develop a deeper understanding of your story." As this student's skills develop, Mauro will ask him increasingly sophisticated questions and encourage him to try increasingly complex problem-solving strategies. Some call this scaffolding because it provides a temporary structure around the student's knowledge "construction" (new learning) and helps hold concepts together during the early stages of "sort of" knowing something but not yet having it "all together."

Math teacher Juliana Jones is mindful of these interactions as she guides her students through social learning. Her work underscores how a teacher's active involvement depends upon her specific lesson preparation, on-the-spot reliance on theory, and knowledge of students. There is no way for a teacher's plan alone to prepare her for the spontaneous and idiosyncratic questions and responses her students are likely to offer. Theory without preparation (and subject knowledge) will fall flat. Experience helps, too.

> No matter how student centered the classroom may be, I still have an important job to facilitate discussion and cognitive conflict by asking a tough question or challenging their conjectures. I must know how to support the "stretching of their minds." I need experience to do this effectively, but it also takes preparation. Before a lesson, I brainstorm ways to extend understanding, or compose questions to push students a little farther. I think about questions they may ask and devise ways to help them come to an understanding. One never knows exactly how students will respond—that is the excitement of teaching.
>
> I have gotten the students to volunteer ideas, and some of them ask the most wonderful questions. However, I must ask rich mathematical questions and pose interesting problems. I must field their wonderful questions (and by wonderful I mean they stop me in my tracks and leave me wondering how in the world I can answer them) by using a counterexample and asking questions, or articulating why what they say is correct or incorrect. And I must rely on what I know about the student's personality and prior struggles to figure out where they are getting lost, ask them a question that lets them rethink the situation, use a manipulative or drawing to clear something up, or tell them, "You know, that is a really good question, and I'm not sure how to answer it, so let's explore some possibilities. What does the class think?" I learn so much as I facilitate mathematical discourse. The fodder for years of reflection lies in these class discussions.
>
> —Juliana Jones
> First-year teacher, middle-school mathematics

By setting classroom norms to guide math talk, Juliana has developed a community of math learners whose members scaffold one another's understanding of mathematics strategies, explanations, and algorithms. These norms are consistent with the teachings of Vygotsky, who proposed

Concept Table 6.2 Popular Scaffolding Techniques

Activating prior knowledge	A teacher activates students' prior knowledge about a topic to "prime" them to learn new information. The students discuss what they already know about a topic before the teacher introduces new material, because connecting new learning to previous knowledge facilitates student understanding.
Modeling	Teacher modeling consists of teachers demonstrating ("modeling") the strategy or skill they want students to learn or practice. Modeling frequently involves teachers thinking aloud about the process involved in implementing a particular strategy or skill.
Questioning	Questioning is the deliberate instructional technique of asking students questions at varying levels of difficulty. If a student is unable to answer a more sophisticated, inferential question, the teacher may ask several more straightforward, explicit questions that lead the student to understand the original question.
Mapping concepts	Concept maps organize information visually, making the relationships between pieces of information more explicit. Placing one concept in a box and drawing arrows to connect the various related concepts creates a typically hierarchical diagram. Words that define the relationship between concepts accompany the arrows (e.g., includes, leads to).
Using graphic organizers	Graphic organizers are another way to visually organize information and include a variety of formats. A graphic organizer could be a T-chart (e.g., a pros and cons list), a story map with story elements (e.g., characters, setting), a cyclical flowchart (e.g., depicting a life cycle), or a Venn diagram (e.g., illustrating comparison), to name a few possibilities.
Offering sentence frames	Sentence frames support students in expressing (verbally or in writing) their ideas when they might be struggling with language. Sentence frames provide students with partial sentences so they can fill in the blanks with their thoughts. Examples of sentence frames include: "I agree that _ because _." "First I thought _, but now I believe _." As is the case with all scaffolds, the support that sentence frames provide should be temporary, changing as students learn and develop.

that learning occurs "out there" as much as inside the head. More precisely, Vygotsky viewed thought as the internalization of experiences in the social context. In other words, the "location" of Juliana's students' mathematical learning and knowledge cannot be specified as being exclusively in individual students' heads, in the classroom culture at large, or in the relationship among students. It is, in a word, sociocultural. The internalization of the social interaction *becomes* the cognitive process. Questioning is but one of many ways teachers scaffold. Concept Table 6.2 offers a selection, though by no means an exhaustive list, of popular scaffolding techniques. Of course, none of these approaches should replace opportunities for students to work together and/or on multidimensional tasks. To the contrary, the success of these approaches depends on their application in social, active learning communities that embrace sociocultural theories *and* social justice principles. Their success also depends on avoiding what University of California, Berkeley, education professor Kris Gutiérrez calls "hypermediating"—or providing too much scaffolding such that students feel condescended to or miss the chance to think critically and creatively and to problem-solve. To avoid over- or underscaffolding, teachers try to stay attuned to students' ZPD and to be strategic about when and how to scaffold in relation to learning goals.[27]

Instructional Approaches That Incorporate Multidimensional Tasks and Scaffolded Participation

As we described in Chapters 3 and 4, there is considerable interest in teachers using research-based instructional strategies—those that have been identified as effective according to empirical research. The following four strategies have been the subject of rigorous research demonstrating that students' achievement increases when teachers emphasize active and social learning, incorporate multidimensional tasks, and provide appropriate scaffolding. While they should not be viewed as recipes for "good" teaching, these approaches are worthy of brief explanation.

SUBSTANTIVE CONVERSATION

A team of researchers headed by Fred Newmann at the University of Wisconsin spent five years studying hundreds of classrooms, trying to understand what particular classroom conditions enhance the intellectual quality and the authenticity of students' schoolwork.[28] Newmann and his colleagues found that one of the most powerful strategies was *substantive conversation*. By that, they meant times when "students engage in extended conversational exchanges with the teacher and/or their peers about subject matter in a way that builds an improved or shared understanding of ideas or topics."[29] They stressed that these subject-matter conversations went beyond reporting facts, procedures, or definitions; they focused on making distinctions, applying ideas, forming generalizations, and raising questions. In other words, substantive conversation mirrors the idea of teaching through conversation—one of the six CREDE principles—and supports students to engage in what Tharp and his colleagues deemed complex thinking.

When teaching through conversation, teachers do not script or control the discussion. Rather, conversations flow from a sharing of ideas among the participants as they work to understand a concept or finish a project. The teacher's skill, artistry, and knowledge of both the students and the subject help guide the conversation, connect it to the teaching goals, and extend important themes and principles. These conversations may appear to be self-sustaining—requiring little more than the students' interest and urge to participate. But the teacher's role is no more effortless than that of skilled athletes (say, a diver, a golfer, or a tight end) at the peak of their performances. Teachers are attending to many factors at once—noting, for example, the contributions of individuals and the collective, and what those contributions reveal about students' understandings (and misunderstandings). They are also making myriad decisions—for example, whether and when to interject or redirect or yield to the flow of conversation. Substantive conversations *can* take place at any grade level, and in any subject area, but their success depends mightily on the knowledge, experience, and relationships that teachers bring to the equation.

RECIPROCAL TEACHING

The late Ann Brown and her husband, Joe Campione, both professors at the University of California, Berkeley, and Annemarie Palincsar, a professor at the University of Michigan, developed strategies that use cognitive and sociocultural learning theories as a basis for teaching reading. One of their strategies, *reciprocal teaching*, teaches children to ask for assistance when they encounter unfamiliar words, to stop and summarize the text periodically, to ask questions about the content, and to predict what they expect to find next. Students work together in groups of six or so. Each student takes a turn leading a discussion about an article, a video, an excerpt from a textbook, or other material they are using to gather information. The leader begins by asking a question and perhaps requesting that the group members make predictions. Clarifying and summarizing help ensure comprehension. Reciprocal teaching, if well organized and thoughtfully planned, can be used with adolescents and even with young learners and in any subject area where information gathering represents the heart of the work.

Brown, Campione, and Palincsar argued that this strategy works because it

> provokes zones of proximal development within which readers of varying abilities can find support. Group cooperation, where everyone is trying to arrive at consensus concerning

> meaning, relevance, and importance, helps to ensure that understanding occurs, even if some members of the group are not yet capable of full participation. . . . The task is simplified by the provision of social support through a variety of expertise, *not* via decomposition of the task into basic skills.[30]

That is, students are successful not because the learning goals have been reduced but because expectations remain high and students' participation and learning are scaffolded in strategic ways. Of course, here too the teacher's role is crucial in establishing the norms and routines involved in reciprocal teaching, monitoring students' participation, assessing individual and collective learning, and providing (or organizing for) targeted assistance.

COGNITIVELY GUIDED INSTRUCTION

A third approach comes from Tom Carpenter and Elizabeth Fennema, University of Wisconsin researchers, and from Megan Franke, at UCLA. *Cognitively guided instruction* (CGI) places students' reasoning at the center of teachers' instructional decision making. Teachers who apply CGI in their own classrooms use cognitive theories of learning to help them investigate their own students' thinking about mathematics. In essence, teachers become *students* of their own learners. Teachers learn all they can about how their students make sense of mathematical concepts and tasks, as well as what obstacles students encounter as they use various strategies for problem solving. Rather than simply assessing "*what* they know," teachers gather through questioning, discussion, and observation evidence of students' mathematical reasoning. They then use their understanding of *how* students think about mathematics to inform their instructional planning.

Teachers who apply CGI in their classrooms spend a good deal of time developing skills that help them uncover the often tacit, or unspoken, knowledge and strategies that students use to solve problems. They watch closely as students take steps to solve problems. They encourage students to explain, to show how, and to consider alternatives. They listen carefully to the way students talk to each other about math and how they represent mathematical ideas through talking, writing, drawing, and building (often using "manipulatives" like counters or cubes). From what they see and hear, teachers then ask incisive questions that probe students' explanations and press students to reconsider or extend their thinking.

In CGI classrooms, "figuring out" becomes an interactive or relational experience rather than an individual one. In fact, "figuring out" becomes the heart of mathematics and replaces the old paradigm of "doing problems."[31] In these classrooms, students often work together, both because this supports their learning and because it helps make their reasoning more transparent (visible, audible) to their teachers. As a result, CGI classrooms are usually alive with mathematical talk and activity. It's from this talk and activity that teachers extract information that can help them align their instruction more closely with students' needs. While CGI has its origins in mathematics teaching, its principles are applicable to teaching generally.

COOPERATIVE LEARNING

Considerable classroom research documents the advantages of students working together in small groups.[32] In fact, although vigorous disputes remain over how and when groups ought to work and be formed, researchers and education policy advisers mostly agree that sharing, talking, and working with others should be central to the learning process, rather than peripheral.

First-year teacher Marilyn Cortez explains some of what can emerge when students are pressed to collaborate.

In the first activity of the Pythagorean theorem unit, I gave students a chance to explore the relationships in the theorem. Working in pairs and trying to convince each other of their responses, students helped each other see things from different perspectives. It was interesting to watch and listen to students claim their version had more area. It was more interesting to hear their reasons why. Because they were required to explain why and how they knew, students needed to fully analyze the situation while forming their final responses. They were confronted with situations where problem solving was difficult to do alone. I saw students working together and expanding each other's ideas. There appeared to be both a competitive spirit and a cooperative one at the same time. Although students worked together on finding solutions, they still wanted to be the first ones to discover them and explain them to the class.

—Marilyn Cortez
First-year teacher, high school mathematics

As students work together, they take charge of the assignment. All students have an opportunity to make valuable contributions to classmates' work and have their work appreciated by others. Despite (or perhaps because of) all the interactions among students, any one student's strengths and weaknesses need not become fodder for comparison or embarrassment. When working with others, students can safely watch and learn how others become successful. In addition, well-designed cooperative lessons offer a variety of tasks and paths to success, so they stand a good chance of accommodating students' differences. Not surprisingly, students learn more under these conditions.

Combining the idea of cooperative group work with Vygotsky's and Piaget's theories of cognitive development, Brown and Campione used the "jigsaw" strategy to develop students' individual and shared expertise. A jigsaw strategy involves having students develop areas of expertise and then share that expertise with others through collaborative work. For example, a class of second graders was studying the animals in their habitat. Students had to select independent "research" topics related to that broad area of study. Some students chose to become experts on how animals protected themselves from predators; others focused on animal communication or reproduction. The teacher then organized design teams composed of students with different areas of expertise. Within teams, students shared their knowledge and used it to design a habitat or invent an "animal of the future." The teacher, meanwhile, served as a more knowledgeable other who guided individual and group activities with questions and prompts.[33]

In a similar vein, high school teacher Douglas Pollock assigns heterogeneous groups in his twelfth-grade composition classes to write a documented critical essay on a single author. Students in a group read different combinations of, for example, James Baldwin's works. Each student is responsible for their own independently produced paper, but the group develops a shared online database of resources gathered from library research and the Internet. As students read, they are quick to point out useful information for others' projects. Various editing, critiquing, and interim reporting requirements keep students in tune with others' thinking and progress. Considerable common knowledge develops, and students draw on one another's ideas as they develop new, more sophisticated critical analyses. Students become aware of the power and extent of their group's literary "intelligence," and that intelligence becomes the most important resource for their own work. Pollock's conversations with students help them articulate their problems and frustrations and formulate questions that the database of resources or other students can help answer.

The jigsaw approach—like any instructional strategy—can and should be tailored to suit the needs of different groups of students and different learning goals. In one classroom, for example, a teacher might have students engage in a jigsaw to deconstruct and decipher a difficult

Concept Table 6.3 Principles of Cooperative Learning

Small groups	Students engage together in groups of three, four, or five—large enough for diverse perspectives but small enough so that everyone can engage fully.
Positive interdependence	Students engage in a task that cannot be successfully completed without cooperation, and each individual's success is dependent on the success of the group.
Accountable talk	Asking questions and providing explanations to one another about what is being learned are central to the learning process.
Group social skills	Knowing how to work together is not taken for granted but is an explicit part of what teachers teach and students learn.
Debriefing	Students discuss and evaluate how well they have worked together as a group, as well as judging how well they have learned.

piece of text, whereas another might use the same technique to assign multiple related readings that students then report on and build knowledge across.

The jigsaw method, which was developed by independent researcher Spencer Kagan, is one of many popular cooperative learning strategies. Others include "team learning," developed by Robert Slavin and his colleagues at Johns Hopkins University, and "learning together" strategies, developed by David Johnson and Roger Johnson at the University of Minnesota. Although these approaches differ in their particulars, they all enact a common set of principles, which are summarized in Concept Table 6.3.

Regardless of the particular strategy, good cooperative lessons require and develop knowledge that is complex and rich in meaning. Simple group goals such as memorizing a list of terms do not necessarily serve all students well, since there are bound to be some who can memorize better on their own, some who already know the meanings, and others who need more time to learn than the group can allow.

Productive cooperative groups must seek rewards from achieving a group goal that students cannot reach unless each group member does their own best work. While some assume that this must hold skilled students back or slow them down, such lessons actually offer those students more challenge than competitive lessons do. In productive group work situations, merely doing better than others no longer brings easy rewards. All students, regardless of skill level, are able to contribute in areas of strength, and all can receive help in areas in which they do less well. Even the most advanced students make considerable intellectual gains when they work with students of all skill levels.

However, organizing students for productive group work requires attention to detail, to sociocultural principles, and to particular skills. Most students, even those who have spent lots of time in groups, need an induction into *cooperative* group work. All members, not just the students considered most skilled, must help others, must feel safe with their peers, and must be able to receive help from them. Everyone must find value in what others offer and view their own success as interdependent with that of their collaborators. Conflicts inevitably occur, necessitating new social skills and practices. Successful cooperative work depends on far more than teachers simply telling students to move their chairs and work together. Absent thoughtful induction, group work may not be an improvement over working alone. Eric Korporaal recognizes that developing social skills is essential to support learning.

I began by having my students work on simpler, shorter activities in teams of two. For instance, the small groups worked on math problems that they were already familiar with.

I did this so that they could focus on working together rather than struggling to understand the problem. Gradually, I increased the difficulty of the tasks as well as the size of the groups. I reinforced positive behavior and pointed out the types of interactions that led to successful groups. Over time students began to realize the sorts of interactions (e.g., effective communication, listening, delegation of responsibilities, and attention to each member's contributions) that needed to occur in order for their group to succeed.

—Erik Korporaal
First-year teacher, grades 4 and 5

What does an academic and socially productive cooperative lesson look like? No single lesson can cover the entire range of possibilities, but the literature unit briefly sketched in Focal Point 6.2 illustrates some essentials. In a ninth-grade English class, groups of four students worked together for nearly ten weeks. They practiced the necessary social skills—how to ask for help and give explanations, share ideas and not dominate, withhold judgments and not put down their classmates and others—and although certain groups still had problems to work out, most had achieved easy familiarity. The teacher had created intentionally heterogeneous groupings, mixing students who differed according to race, gender, and skill level. She also had mixed high-energy, gregarious students with shier, quieter ones.

Focal Point 6.2
A Cooperative Learning Lesson

To Kill a Mockingbird

The class read *To Kill a Mockingbird*, an engaging and intellectually demanding classic that is nearly always on high school reading lists. The novel includes themes of racism (including whether the book's treatment of racism is racism itself), justice, early education, one-parent families, small-town life, courage, sexism, maturation, perspective, and more. Soon after the class started the novel, the special education resource teacher (who had several students "mainstreamed" in the class) arranged a lunchtime showing of the movie adapted from the novel. Most students didn't want to give up their lunch periods, but several did—including all the students from special education. Having seen the movie, these students had an easier time reading the book than they might have otherwise. Furthermore, because they had an overview of the novel, they were well positioned to make valuable contributions in their groups.

After reading one-third of the book, each group member adopted a different character to follow. As they finished reading, the students wrote short compositions describing their characters and linking them to the book's themes. They took notes on their reading and exchanged ideas in "expert groups"; that is, they conferred with their classmates from other groups who had chosen the same character. Although the students could get help and ideas from their classmates, the teacher held all students individually accountable for the brief composition.

The next part of this assignment emphasized group interdependence; that is, no student could successfully complete their own work without the participation and cooperation of the other group members. The students wrote a longer composition, entitled "Exploring Themes in *To Kill a Mockingbird* Through Four Characters," using the short pieces that each of the four group members had written as source materials. In the longer assignment, the students who were most skilled in literary analysis found sophisticated differences and commonalities as they explored the characters and themes. Those most skilled in the area of research modeled for others how to attribute ideas to their sources—quoting from both the novel and their classmates. Supported by their group members, less experienced students stretched beyond their inclination simply to summarize their group's four papers and successfully engaged in deeper analysis.

Throughout, the interaction was intense. Students were questioning, explaining, and arguing. Given the nature of the assignment, they had good reason to engage others and expect solid work from their fellow group members. As the individual compositions neared completion, the students grew increasingly interested in what their peers were writing. After all, their own ideas were being represented. It's hard to squelch your curiosity when you see your own name in the text or footnote!

When they had finished their compositions, each group wrote a skit loosely based on their characters. Each picked a common conflict at school that concerned them. The groups selected such problems as social cliques, dating, drug use, grade pressure, intimidation and violence, and parent-student trust. Then each student had to imagine how their character would fit into the school conflict. (They could take liberties with the character's age or gender.) Each student wrote the dialogue for their own character. Finally, the groups performed the skits for the class. Because the skit had a group rather than an individual goal, the group shared a single grade. As with the compositions, each student achieved something by working with others that could not have been achieved by working alone.

Work in small cooperative groups will not solve all the problems that ail typical classes. Nonetheless, successful cooperative groups enable learning to take place while presenting the fewest limits to students, and they help ensure many essential conditions for learning. When cooperative groups are successful, it is likely that there is a teacher who has a deep knowledge of the subject, who has designed rich and complex multi-ability lessons, who scaffolds students' learning, who openly values treating others with respect and dignity, and who frequently engages students in democratic participation and decision making.

The Role of Technology in Twenty-First-Century Teaching and Learning

Technology clearly has become a fundamental part of education. All fifty states now include technology in their state standards, and some states have separate standards for technology. In both cases, state standards for technology mirror national technology standards that were developed (and updated in 2007) by the International Society for Technology in Education (ISTE). Increasingly, state technology standards include the skills that students need to take the Smarter Balanced Assessment Consortium (SBAC) or the Partnership for Assessment of Readiness for College and Careers (PARCC) computer-based assessments, which, in 2016, were used by twenty-one states to measure student mastery of the Common Core State Standards.[34]

As of 2009, thirteen states required that schools test students' technology skills.[35] In addition, teachers increasingly report valuing blogs and student-created websites as tools for facilitating academic learning; over 97 percent of teachers surveyed in 2011 report that they use some form of digital media for instruction.[36] Not only does nearly every school across the nation see computers and the Internet as basic equipment for teaching and learning, students are increasingly using computers—and expected to use computers—to learn at home. In 2009, a study conducted by the Federal Communication Commission Broadband Taskforce, for example, reported that 70 percent of teachers in the United States assigned homework that required students to have access to (high-speed) Internet.[37] Previously, a 2007 National School Boards Association report claimed that 95 percent of school districts reported that at least some teachers use web pages to communicate with students about assignments, curriculum content, and other information.[38]

Research also indicates that technological devices in schools are proliferating at staggering speeds. *Education Week*'s 2017 "Technology Counts Report," for example, reports that the number of laptops, smart pads, and netbooks shipped to K–12 schools increased by 363 percent between 2010 and 2017. While this may seem like good news, the report also noted that most teachers surveyed were underprepared to use such technologies to facilitate deep learning because neither their preservice programs nor their inservice professional learning experiences provided them with the necessary training. Even worse, the percentages of teachers prepared to use technology to facilitate deep learning may be dropping, despite the surge of new devices and technologies present in schools.[39]

Like any educational tool, electronic technologies can serve either traditional or progressive approaches to teaching and learning. Many software packages for classrooms, or "distance learning" offerings, provide nothing more than traditional instruction wrapped up in electronic packages. The same holds true for new media technologies such as blogs, wikis, and online social networks. In the wrong hands, such technologies can be used to uphold traditional approaches to teaching and learning or even as a way to keep students busy and docile. On the other hand, used in the context of authentic and active learning communities, these same technologies can help scaffold learners' explorations beyond the bounds of their current knowledge. They can provide multidimensional routes for investigation and forums for authentic literacy development, concept attainment, individual and/or collaborative sense making, social justice projects, and community building, to name but a few possibilities.

Thoughtfully engaging students with such technologies can develop "new media literacies"—forms of literacy that have emerged alongside new technologies and that expand on rather than replace traditional literacies like reading and writing.[40] Henry Jenkins, a professor of communications at the University of Southern California, has delineated a set of core new media literacy skills (see Concept Table 6.4) that he argues are critical to full participation in today's technology-based culture.

The North Central Regional Educational Laboratory (NCREL) has provided technology guidance to teachers and schools around the country. Its charge has been to translate the best research on the educational uses of technology into practical guidelines for schools. One of its online publications, *Plugging In*, has helped teachers judge whether a technological offering will promote students' active engagement and scaffold their learning.[41] A selection of the criteria used is included in Concept Table 6.5.

NCREL makes note of researchers' reluctance to name the "right" amount or "correct" use of technology in the classroom. Indeed, the ever-changing technology landscape, including the continuous development of new technologies, makes it hard for research to keep pace. Thus, few firm guidelines exist to guide teachers' decisions about appropriate uses of technology. This places great responsibility on teachers' own judgments concerning which technologies to use, and how to use them, to support their students' engagement and learning.

Concept Table 6.4 Core Media Literacy Skills

Core skill	Definition
Play	Ability to experiment with one's surroundings as a form of problem solving
Performance	Ability to adopt alternative identities for the purpose of improvisation and discovery
Simulation	Ability to interpret and construct dynamic models of real-world processes
Appropriation	Ability to meaningfully sample and remix media content
Multitasking	Ability to scan one's environment and shift focus as needed to salient details
Distributed cognition	Ability to interact meaningfully with tools that expand mental capacities
Collective intelligence	Ability to pool knowledge and compare notes with others toward a common goal
Judgment	Ability to evaluate the reliability and credibility of different information sources
Transmedia navigation	Ability to follow the flow of stories and information across multiple modalities
Networking	Ability to search for, synthesize, and disseminate information
Negotiation	Ability to travel across diverse communities, discerning and respecting multiple perspectives, and grasping and following alternative norms

Source: Henry Jenkins, with Katie Clinton, Ravi Purushotma, Alice J. Robison, and Margaret Weigel, "Confronting the Challenges of Participatory Culture: Media Education for the 21st Century" (occasional paper), www.macfound.org/media/article_pdfs/JENKINS_WHITE_PAPER.PDF.

Concept Table 6.5 Educational Technology That Engages Students

Purpose of technology	Examples
Provides challenging tasks, opportunities, and experiences	Complex problems and cases; links to unique resources such as museums and libraries; opportunities to examine contrasting events or databases
	Access to experts, peers, and community members who can guide, mentor, tutor, broker, share, inform, and involve students in meaningful ways
	Access to rich media sources for data manipulation or presentations
	Tools for interactive browsing, searching, and authoring
Allows students to learn by doing	Engages students in planning, reflecting, making decisions, experiencing consequences, and examining alternative solutions and ideas
Provides guided participation and content customized to suit the particular needs or interests of students	Socratic questioning
	Intelligent tutoring
	Diagnosing and guiding an analysis of mistakes
	Adaptations or changes that respond to students' actions

THE DIGITAL DIVIDE

Though new technologies hold promise for learning, they are not evenly distributed across students and schools. In fact, recent reports indicate that high-speed Internet access continues to vary widely across schools and districts.[42] And even when schools serving low-income students and students of color do have Internet access and nearly as many computers as schools serving more advantaged students, the actual use of technology in such schools lags behind technology use in more advantaged schools.[43]

One study in an urban midwestern high school, for example, found that a group of White boys considered "gifted" had claimed the computing lab and was using it as an informal clubhouse.[44] These students were encouraged by teachers who often relied on them to help set up equipment, troubleshoot, and teach. Meanwhile, girls and African American students felt unwelcome in the lab. Other research suggests that teachers tend to infuse technology into lessons much less with low-achieving students than with high achievers and that students of color and Emergent Bilingual students receive particularly limited access to technology in schools. UCLA researcher Jane Margolis and her colleagues, for example, found that relatively few African American and Latinx high school students receive the kind of encouragement, opportunities, and preparation needed to pursue postsecondary studies in technology-saturated fields like computer science. This "virtual segregation," they argue, maintains underlying inequalities and perpetuates the underrepresentation of certain populations in certain fields.[45]

According to a 2016 report, homework is another area within which inequities appear to be expanding. Despite teachers' growing tendencies to assign homework requiring high-speed Internet access, around 5 million homes with school-age children—the majority of whom were students of color and low-income students—were without such access in 2009. Students surveyed more recently reported that lacking home Internet access sometimes prevented them from completing homework assignments, which also led to lower grades. Nevertheless, 75 percent of the districts studied were taking no action to address the problem, and students were mostly expected to manage the "homework gap" on their own.[46]

Technology is deeply ingrained in society in the form of cell phones, the Internet, chip or card-based commerce, and so forth. Yet not all students have the chance to develop the same deep level of useful knowledge, experience, and confidence with technologies. Thus, as new technologies proliferate, new disparities emerge. One study, for example, found that more than half of teenagers had created media content, and many had shared that content.[47] Such experiences confer numerous potentially beneficial opportunities, including opportunities for peer-to-peer learning, cultural expression and exchange, and development of skills that are valued in the modern workplace, just to name a few.[48] Similar opportunities may be limited for students who engage less, or in less dynamic ways, with technology.

Thus, observers have begun to emphasize students' *engagement with* rather than mere *access to* technology. *Engaging* students sets them on a path toward using technologies as empowering and transformative tools, whereas providing *access* might allow a more limited role—perhaps only as a passive consumer. This distinction is an important one, because it helps focus attention on what youth are encouraged and supported to do with technology. The 2017 Technology Counts Report indicates that, despite this understanding, the problem of engagement may be becoming worse. In addition to the lack of consistency in teachers' technology use that exists across classrooms, the report suggests that "students are still largely using technology for drill and practice rather than for more complex tasks, such as creating projects, conducting simulations, or doing extensive research."[49] As mentioned above, the report ties teachers' capacities to *engage* students with technology to their training, while also pointing out that teachers in high-poverty schools are among the least likely to have received training on how to integrate technology into instruction.

When it comes to supporting students to *engage* in complex ways with technology, teachers' expectations can play a particularly consequential role. For example, in earlier work, Margolis and Fisher found that male and female college students, as well as teachers, expected males to be better at computing. These expectations damaged girls' confidence and impacted their engagement with computers and computing.[50] Such expectations can lead to inequities, even when access to computers (say, the ratio of computers to students) might suggest otherwise. If schools don't expect girls, low-income students, or less experienced students to achieve in technology-saturated fields, schools won't provide opportunities that fully engage those students, and students may not build confidence as empowered technology users.

Just a few years ago, computer science, engineering, and a few other fields came to mind as the only ones that required high-tech knowledge and skills. But, increasingly, nearly all fields incorporate, value, and/or require significant technological engagement. In light of this, setting high expectations for technology learning and technology use represents an important first step that teachers and schools can take. Supporting students to meet those expectations must then begin with recognizing students' diverse strengths as foundations on which to build technology-related expertise. Sociocultural theory suggests that students' cultural and linguistic practices are among those strengths.

Building on Students' Cultures and Languages

First-year history teacher Matthew Eide could have had his diverse high school students memorize important facts about turn-of-the-century immigration but instead chose an approach that built on what they and their families already knew.

> I had students interview a recent immigrant, ideally a family member or a close friend. About 80 percent of my students were able to interview a family member. The students asked how the immigrants navigated a new life in a sometimes-hostile environment, and specifically how they used their family and social networks to survive. The students then wrote essays comparing the experiences of the immigrants they interviewed with those of the turn-of-the-century immigrants. This essay had the highest completion rate of any I had assigned. I believe that's because students used their cultural and linguistic knowledge in a way that was legitimate in the classroom.
>
> —Matthew Eide
> First-year teacher, high school history

Matthew's students conducted their interviews in person, but examples abound of teachers using new technologies—like those just discussed—in similarly powerful ways. Some are supporting students to conduct interviews with native-language "penpals" through e-mail and wikis and via simple videoconferencing tools like Skype or FaceTime. Others are supporting students to use digital technologies to conduct and document original research. Indeed, such efforts supported Los Angeles high school students Jenny Aguilar, Marco de la Torre, Whitney Reynolds, Francisco Romo, and Tanyea Thomas in creating an edited video (including excerpts from interview footage), a photo slideshow, and a web-published written report (with data analysis figures and charts) documenting their investigations into the experiences of youth in one South Los Angeles neighborhood. Such efforts are also at the core of work being done school-wide at Chula Vista Learning Community Charter School in San Diego, where teachers and students are using videos of their own classroom interactions to deepen their dialogue and build community.

Chapter 1 described the increasing diversity of U.S. schoolchildren. What the prior examples begin to show are some of the myriad opportunities for learning that can arise from such diversity and be tapped into by teachers using technology and other tools. As sociocultural theory suggests, all students bring powerful prior knowledge, social and cultural practices, and salient experiences to school; and as constructivist theory suggests, these represent the essential foundation for students' future learning. Thus, it's a teacher's job to learn about the knowledge, practices, and experiences that students bring to school, and to support students to make connections between what they bring and what the academic curriculum expects of them.

This part of every teacher's job is particularly important for teachers serving students whose language, culture, abilities, and so forth are different from those of the majority or the mainstream culture. Schools often send such students the message that the resources they bring to school—including their ways of learning and solving problems—are inferior to those of the dominant (or school) culture. Meanwhile, the social and cultural resources that many White, middle-class children bring from home map more readily onto schools' expectations. This often occurs to such a degree that these students' social and cultural resources seem almost invisible and are considered "just normal." If teachers do not recognize the value of the social and cultural resources that all students possess, and do not encourage all students to develop and use those resources, teachers deny students the very assets that are essential to their learning and development.

"Funds of Knowledge" and Cultural Competencies

Professors Luis Moll and Norma Gonzalez's research at the University of Arizona illustrates how students' social and cultural resources serve as a rich and robust foundation for learning. Much of this work has involved studies conducted with Mexican American families in a low-income community in Tucson, Arizona. Moll, Gonzalez, and their colleagues assessed the knowledge and other resources that children from this community had available to them *outside* of school. Because of the generally low expectations schools hold for children of low-income and working-class parents, these children performed "as expected." They were considered low achieving, and they found in school little relevance to their lives.

As Moll studied the children's extended families, however, he found rich "funds of knowledge." Each household had developed expertise in particular domains. In fact, Moll identified nearly fifty areas of expertise, including soil and irrigation systems, minerals, renting and selling, budgets, design and architecture, first aid, moral knowledge and ethics, and so on. Children participated in everyday tasks and chores, all the while observing, asking questions, and receiving assistance as needed. At times, adults scaffolded children's participation in relatively difficult tasks, and because help was available when needed, the risk of failure was low.

Moll and Gonzalez argue (as does Cindy Kauionalani Bell, the teacher in the following quote) that the secret to effective instruction is for schools to tap into students' and families' funds of knowledge and leverage everyday cultural practices to facilitate academic learning.[51] This approach represents a significant departure from traditional practice, which is to see "different" cultural knowledge and practices as not useful or as an obstacle.

> Neither my students nor I enter our classroom empty-handed. We come, as Luis Moll says, "con nuestras mochilas llenas, no están vacías (with our backpacks full, not empty)." I not only carry pedagogical theories about teaching and learning, but I also carry assumptions and ideas about people: what learning looks like, what a teacher looks like, what schooling looks like and why. . . . No classroom practice exists in isolation of a social and cultural history.
>
> —Cindy Kauionalani Bell
> First-year teacher, grade 2

First-year English as a Second Language (ESL) teacher Maria Chiping Hwang used students' local knowledge to help them learn about Mexico in light of what they know about where they live.

> My curriculum on Mexico begins in Los Angeles, a point of reference for the students. They explore and rediscover the familiar in order to establish a foundation for new information

that will be introduced in their [studies about] Mexico. Understanding the influences of Mexico manifested in Los Angeles, students can absorb the authentic source from which the influence derives.

—Maria Chiping Hwang
First-year teacher, high school ESL

As mentioned above, "funds of knowledge" is an idea firmly rooted in sociocultural and constructivist learning theories, and emphasizes the teacher's role in leveraging the knowledge students acquire at home and in the community to enhance school learning. Scholars of culturally relevant and critical pedagogy—like Gloria Ladson-Billings, Geneva Gay, and others described in Chapters 3 and 8—make similar points about the role of the teacher.[52] First-year teacher Benji Chang describes some of his efforts in this area—specifically how he got to know students well enough to provide them with curriculum and instruction that was responsive to what they and their families know and value.

I went to work right away to become familiar with my students' backgrounds. I observed and asked questions. I wanted to communicate a sense of respect for my students' diverse communities and put their backgrounds in the forefront of my lessons. I made it a point to be visible off campus, and before and after school. From day one, I talked with parents and guardians outside of class, and sent home the first of my weekly home letters, explaining and requesting a home visit. I eventually visited, and usually shared a meal, at eighteen of my twenty students' homes. In these visits I forged stronger home-school connections and uncovered invaluable information that would shape my curriculum and instruction. I communicated to parents and guardians that they were the experts on their child. I asked about their child's strengths and areas needing improvement.

—Benji Chang
First-year teacher, grade 1

This quote illustrates how developing relationships with students can also involve building relationships with families. The late Vivian Paley, a renowned kindergarten teacher, in *Kwanzaa and Me*, shows how middle-class White teachers can talk directly and honestly with parents, colleagues, and children of color about their experiences. Paley describes how bringing family- and community-based curriculum into classrooms requires that teachers learn about and confront the racism and discrimination that many students and their families experience in communities and schools.

Paley's racially and culturally sensitive kindergarten classroom practices began with a conversation with a former student. This young African American woman, now an adult, shared her painful recollections of loneliness and worry in Paley's kindergarten class. Paley, on the other hand, remembered her as a happy member of her racially integrated classroom. What had Paley missed? To find out, she began a series of honest conversations about racism with her students' parents. Their stories were so rich and powerful, revealing enormous joy and sadness, that Paley invited parents to bring the stories of family traditions and daily life into her diverse classroom. The *Kwanzaa* stories that emerged became the basis for students bridging their multiple worlds with one another and their schoolwork.[53]

First-year teacher Christina Haug made stories like Paley's an important part of her lessons.

Kenny, a Latino student, has a close relationship with his grandmother, who tells him stories about family members, folk tales, and cultural legends. He is a valuable resource for oral storytelling. He also learns that his culture is not being ignored in the classroom. . . . As he shares family stories, he becomes a teacher for our class, educating us about his home culture and language.

—Christina Haug
First-year teacher, grade 2

High school social studies teacher Judy Smith also integrates family and community knowledge into the curriculum of her economics course:

In my economics class, students used their parents' knowledge and experience to help them. For the project "How to Make a Living," students asked parents about utility bills, late rent payments, and car-buying procedures. Students generated a six-month budget to live financially independently. In their write-ups, many of them referenced their parents as a source of information.

In the international economics unit, students compared consumer habits now with economic life twenty to thirty years ago. Many students realized that they own more and have freedoms their parents did not have.

In still another class assignment, students create their own businesses. I pushed students to think like producers rather than consumers. They create a business plan and discuss business ownership with their parents. Many students used their parents' work experience to write their plans. One student modeled her business after her father's boat repair business. Another student opened a business that competed with his father's spark plug store. A third student, familiar with her mother's work in a beauty salon, documented her plan for opening a nail shop.

Our field trips exposed students to both opportunities and social problems in the larger community. We traveled to downtown Los Angeles to Homeboy Industries [a community-based organization that engages former gang members in running a thriving bakery business] and the Los Angeles Central Library. At the library, they attended "Choosing to Participate," a Facing History exhibition that emphasized the individual's power to make a difference.

—Judy Smith
High school social studies

Vivian Paley and the teachers quoted above demonstrate how their sociocultural orientation draws them into addressing social justice issues that they care deeply about. It is possible to see their actions as pedagogical approaches—that is, they address social justice to fully educate their students. However, their social critique—similar to that discussed in Chapter 3—is just as much a matter of personal commitment and values as it is a matter of pedagogy. The two cannot be separated. Scholars like James Banks have long encouraged teachers to engage students in social action as part of a multicultural instructional approach.[54] More recently, teacher educators like Bree Picower have addressed this same theme. Picower, for example, presents six elements of social justice education at the elementary level. These elements, described in Concept Table 6.6, help illustrate how sociocultural and constructivist learning theories, commitments to multiculturalism, and critical pedagogy come together in social justice teaching.

"Additive" Instruction for Emergent Bilinguals, Among Others

Some of students' most significant cultural resources are the languages they use in their everyday lives and with the people closest to them. Thus, connecting students' home culture to the academic content of the curriculum is especially important for multilingual students, particularly in

Concept Table 6.6 Six Elements of Social Justice Curriculum Design for Elementary Education

1. **Self-love and Knowledge:** Teachers provide opportunities for students to learn about who they are and where they come from. A sense of dignity in their culture, heritage, ethnicity/race, religion, skin tone, gender etc. is cultivated in the classroom. Students learn about different aspects of their identity and history associated with it. Negative stereotypes about students' identities are deconstructed. Potential classroom activities include: where I come from poems, self-portraits that include skin tone identification, name poems, family interviews, grandparent guest speakers, cultural ABC books.

2. **Respect for Others:** Teachers provide opportunities for students to share their knowledge about their own cultural background with their classmates. The goal is to create a climate of respect for diversity through students learning to listen with kindness and empathy to the experiences of their peers. Students deconstruct stereotypes about their peers' identities. Potential classroom activities include: sharing of cultural ABC books, diverse family structures that include LGBT families, field trips to cultural museums, guest speakers from children's families and cultural centers.

3. **Issues of Social Injustice:** Teachers move from "celebrating diversity" to an exploration of how diversity has differently impacted various groups of people. Students learn about the history of racism, sexism, classism, homophobia, religious intolerance etc. and how these forms of oppression have affected different communities. Teachers make links that show how the historical roots of oppression impact the lived experiences and material conditions of people today. Potential topics of study include: Native American genocide, slavery, the Holocaust, anti-immigration policies and sentiment, media (mis) representations, issues that face their own communities such as gentrification, police brutality, etc.

4. **Social Movements and Social Change:** Teachers share examples of movements of iconic and everyday people standing together to address the issues of social injustice they learned about in Element Three. Rather than leaving students feeling overwhelmed and defeated, teachers help students understand that working together, ordinary people have united to create change. Potential topics of study include: abolitionism, civil rights movement, the L.A. janitors' strikes, various labor movements, 1968 and 2006 Chicano student walkouts.

5. **Awareness Raising:** Teachers provide opportunities for students to teach others about the issues they have learned about. This allows students who feel passionately about issues to become advocates by raising awareness of other students, teachers, family and community members. It is important to recognize that while raising awareness is a necessary and important precursor for action, it by itself does not by itself translate into change. Potential activities include: newsletters, public service announcements, letter writing campaigns, creating documentaries, blogging.

6. **Social Action:** Teachers provide opportunities to take action on issues that affect students and their communities. Students identify issues they feel passionate about and learn the skills of creating change firsthand. Potential activities include: letter writing campaigns, petitions, linking with local grassroots organization campaigns, speaking at public meetings, attending and/or organizing protests.

Source: Bree Picower, "6 Elements of SJE," *Using Their Words*, www.usingtheirwords.org/?page_id=180/.

schools with English-only policies. Judy Smith (shown in the photo on the facing page) teaches high school Emergent Bilingual students. She uses her own fluency in Spanish to help make these important connections.

Because language is at the heart of culture, educators must pay attention to students' languaging practices. Vygotsky made clear that learning language and literacy is a never-ending process of communicating with others and internalizing content and meaning. Drawing on Vygotsky's ideas, linguist James Cummins developed the principle of "additive bilingualism," based on the theory that language is learned in contexts where communication is meaningful and purposeful and has social value.

Additive bilingualism is premised on the idea that heritage languages are essential and authentic aspects of culture and a powerful means of communication in communities and families. In an additive approach, great efforts are made to preserve students' heritage languages, which, in

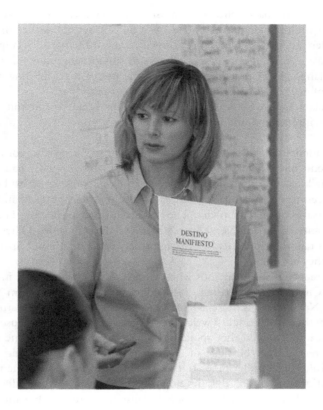

addition to their inherent value, are also understood to be crucial resources for learning additional languages. In other words, children acquire new languages best as they simultaneously strengthen and enrich their primary language(s).

Cummins contrasts an additive approach with a "subtractive" approach, in which one language *replaces* the other and often results in language loss, as well as minimal literacy development in either language. A subtractive approach additionally reflects the hegemony of English in the United States and promotes a *monoglossic* ideology, by sending students the message that their heritage language is worth less than English, and that becoming fluent in English is more valuable than becoming bilingual.[55]

Increasingly, well-prepared teachers are expanding an additive approach to support the development of not just students' bilingualism, but also their biliteracy. Reflecting growing understandings about the value of biliteracy, schools and districts in twenty-six states now give students who have "studied and attained biliteracy by high school graduation" the *Seal of Biliteracy*—an award developed by the advocacy organization Californian's Together.[56] An additive approach to language learning also guides teachers in responding to schools' changing demographics. As mentioned in Chapter 1, schools today are far more likely than schools of the past to serve students who are native-born *simultaneous bilinguals*, meaning that they come to school already somewhat proficient in more than one language, and are thus poised to develop both languages simultaneously.[57] For these students, subtracting one of their languages in order to learn the other makes even less sense than it does for *sequential bilinguals*, or those students who come to school familiar with their heritage language exclusively, who used to comprise the majority of language-minoritized students in U.S. schools.

Finally, an additive approach reflects the most recent research on language learning, specifically the idea that multiple languages operate as a holistic system, rather than as autonomous entities. This understanding challenges previous views about the need for language separation in bilingual programs; instead, it encourages schools to support multilingual students to tap into their authentic "languaging" practices, including the use of their full linguistic knowledge as they make sense of new topics and communicate with others.[58]

Cindy Kauionalani Bell, who teaches in a Latinx immigrant community, used an additive approach to guide interactions and learning in her classroom.

> When my students talk to each other, they engage in purposeful conversation. Whether to help a friend find a word in the dictionary or to discuss what game they will play at recess, they talk to communicate. They know that they must speak to be understood, and they must listen to understand. The students develop their speaking and listening skills by developing conversational strategies. They ask each other questions. They repeat the most important points. They emphasize words and give them meaning. They also identify their audience and tailor their words by switching between English and Spanish depending on with whom they are talking.
>
> This last practice is most obvious when we welcome new students into our classroom's Community Circle. Lali, who recently arrived in the United States from Mexico, joined our classroom in November. As our class introduced ourselves to her, the students immediately changed from their usual English welcomes to Spanish greetings, because, as they discussed, Lali wouldn't understand if they spoke in English. Even Maria, my one monoliterate English student, recognized the value of communicating for meaning and asked someone to translate so Lali would understand. In this group interaction and in many others, language acts as a functional social skill that develops oral literacy skills. My students understand that both English and Spanish are social tools because they are valuable and meaningful forms of communication.
>
> —Cindy Kauionalani Bell
> First-year teacher, grade 2

Theorist Stephen Krashen has studied students' emotions when they are learning a new language, especially if their primary language itself is disparaged. He explains that students' anxiety and self-doubt "filter" or limit the language they can understand and produce. Krashen argues that Emergent Bilinguals must feel secure before they can open themselves to the risks of failure. When students feel that their heritage language is important and that school is relevant to them, their anxiety is likely to decrease, thereby lowering their "affective filter" and supporting learning.[59]

First-grade teacher Benji Chang describes the learning challenges he faced in his first year in the classroom and how his understanding of the affective filter helped him to deepen students' problem solving, understanding, and participation.

> Two days before school started, I finally received my class roster. Four of my students are African American with roots in Texas, Georgia, and Alabama. Seven are Latino, with parents born and raised in Guatemala, El Salvador, and Mexico. Other families come from countries in Asia and the Pacific, such as Vietnam, Cambodia, Thailand, Hong Kong, the Philippines, and China. Six of my students are biracial or triracial, with families from all of these areas, as well as Belize and Puerto Rico. Within each category of race and ethnicity, I also learned about substantial linguistic diversity in my class (ten languages). . . . I was surprised, but it was a challenge I was eager to take on.

One idea that supported my effort to research and access my students' languages and cultures is Krashen's concept of the "affective filter." As I have come to know more about my students and their families, I have been able to connect what I learned outside the classroom with what we are doing in the classroom. For example, to learn about nouns and adjectives, I asked students to pretend they were going to the store with their *lola* (Tagalog for grandmother) or some other family member. With all of the different domestic practices and foods in my students' homes, this context for learning about different word types also became a social studies lesson.

The result was a group of engaged students learning about and appreciating their differences as well as learning the official language arts curriculum. A simple assessment lets me know if I have been successful in lowering affective filters. It is the twinkle in their eyes, and the smiles on their faces. Their faces light up in a way that is unlike anything else. Neither ice cream, nor stickers, nor extra recess minutes can produce the expression on my students' faces when I ask them how to say a high-frequency word in their own language or when they answer questions in the context of their homes and families.

—Benji Chang
First-year teacher, grade 1

When teaching an English-only class, Kimberly Min noted that her African American students spoke a variety of English that schools often interpreted as incorrect. However, Kimberly recognized students' languaging practices as legitimate and understood that her students had to feel seen and secure with their home languages and cultures if they were to risk engaging in new learning at school.

Mainstream Academic English (MAE) is not only considered the standard language, it is also a code of power. African American Language (AAL) is also a legitimate form of language, with a sociocultural history that is culturally significant for African Americans.[60] The majority of my students use AAL, which most teachers deem as slang or as an unacceptable form of English. There is a great deal of neglect in terms of language acquisition because many teachers do not acknowledge that African Americans are standard language learners.

I counter this by allowing my students to express themselves in both AAL and MAE, while I teach the contexts in which to use both languages appropriately. . . . During writing assignments and oral language activities, these students demonstrate that they can successfully use MAE. For instance, Aaron is aware of his language use and the language use of his classmates, as he constantly reminds them of the rules of MAE. Yet, on the basketball court, Aaron successfully code-switches back to AAL to convey his anger or happiness to his peers. This ability to switch languages depending on their contexts is what I hope to teach my students.

—Kimberly Min
Third-grade teacher

Benji and Kimberly have found ways to help students feel secure and positive enough about the language competencies they bring from home to take the risks necessary to develop new language competencies at school. In this sense, they defy traditional "subtractive" approaches to teaching Emergent Bilingual youth—approaches that either ignore or try to *subtract* from students the languages and cultures they bring with them to school. Instead, teachers like Benji and Kimberly embody a commitment to "additive" instruction—instruction that recognizes, enhances, and actively adds to the cultural resources, including language, their students bring to school.

No Easy Recipes

This chapter has focused on important characteristics of classrooms that are consistent with sociocultural and constructivist theories of learning. How teachers enact these theories in their classrooms profoundly influences students' willingness and ability to apply their natural learning processes to formal school learning and makes a critical difference in allowing all students in a diverse society to succeed at school.

Basing classrooms on sociocultural and constructivist learning theories, as well as principles of social justice, is an ideal in much the same way that democracy is an ideal—something to be pursued, but something never quite attained well enough to satisfy us. And so it's not surprising that teachers who act on what they know about learning and what they believe about social justice are often dismayed by the gap between their ideals and what they are able to realize in their classrooms. Even so, such teachers steadily move their classroom worlds closer to their ideals, and those ideals are what fuels their continued struggle for social justice.

Digging Deeper and Tools for Critique

www.routledge.com/cw/teachingtochangetheworld

Notes

1 The heading for this section as well as much of the content here is from Larry Cuban's book by the same name: *How Teachers Taught: Constancy and Change in American Classrooms, 1890–1990* (New York: Teachers College Press, 1993).
2 As quoted in Joel Spring, *The American School, 1642–1990* (New York: Longman, 1990), 120.
3 Larry Cuban, *How Teachers Taught* (New York: Teachers College Press, 1993).
4 Philip Jackson, *The Practice of Teaching* (New York: Teachers College Press, 1987).
5 Cuban, *How Teachers Taught*.
6 Jean Lave and Etienne Wenger, *Situated Learning: Legitimate Peripheral Participation* (New York: Cambridge University Press, 1991).
7 John Dewey, *How We Think* (Boston: D. C. Heath, 1910); Jean Piaget, *The Science of Education and the Psychology of the Child* (New York: Orion Press, 1970); Lev Vygotsky, *Mind in Society* (Cambridge, UK: Cambridge University Press, 1978).
8 John Dewey, "My Pedagogic Creed," in *The School Journal* 65, no. 3 (January 16, 1897), 71, reprinted in John Dewey, *Early Works*, Vol. 5 (Carbondale, IL: Southern Illinois University Press, 1989).
9 See, for example, Jerome Bruner, *Culture and Education* (Cambridge, MA: Harvard University Press, 1996); Michael Cole, *Cultural Psychology: A Once and Future Discipline* (Cambridge, MA: Harvard University Press, 1996); Jean Lave and Etienne Wenger, *Situated Cognition: Legitimate Peripheral Participation* (Cambridge, UK: Cambridge University Press, 1991); Barbara Rogoff, *Apprenticeship in Thinking: Cognitive Development in Social Context* (New York: Oxford University Press, 1990); Etienne Wenger, *Communities of Practice: Learning, Meaning, and Identity* (Cambridge, UK: Cambridge University Press, 1999).
10 Jerome Bruner, *Culture and Education*, xi, 166.
11 Sylvia Scribner and Michael Cole, *The Psychology of Literacy* (Cambridge, MA: Harvard University Press, 1981), 80.
12 See Elizabeth Cohen and Rachel Lotan's book, *Working for Equity in Heterogeneous Classrooms* (New York: Teachers College Press, 1997), for an elaborated discussion of these issues.
13 Daniel G. Solórzano, "Critical Race Theory, Race and Gender Microaggressions, and the Experience of Chicana and Chicano Scholars," *Qualitative Studies in Education* 11, no. 1 (1998): 121.

14 Makeba Jones, *Rethinking African American Students' Agency: Meaningful Choices and Negotiating Meaning* (PhD diss., UCLA Graduate School of Education and Information Studies, 1998), 1–2.

15 Claude Steele, "Race and the Schooling of Black Americans," *Atlantic Monthly*, April 1992, 68–78.

16 Claude Steele, *Whistling Vivaldi: And Other Clues to How Stereotypes Affect Us* (New York: W. W. Norton and Company, 2010).

17 Ibid.

18 Robert Rosenthal and Lenore Jacobson, *Pygmalion in the Classroom* (New York: Holt, Rinehart & Winston, 1968).

19 Myra Sadker and David Sadker, *Failing at Fairness: How America's Schools Cheat Girls* (New York: Macmillan, 1994).

20 One of the first and best-known studies documenting these patterns is Ray Rist, "Student Social Class and Teacher Expectations: The Self-Fulfilling Prophecy of Ghetto Education," in *Challenging the Myths: The Schools, the Blacks, and the Poor*, Reprint Series No. 5 (Cambridge, MA: Harvard Educational Review, 1971).

21 See, for example, Jere Brophy and Thomas Good, *Looking in Classrooms*, 7th ed. (New York: Longman, 1997), especially Chapter 3.

22 Center for Applied Special Technology (CAST), *Universal Design for Learning Guidelines, 2.0*, Wakefield, MA, 2011, www.udlcenter.org/sites/udlcenter.org/files/updateguidelines2_0.pdf.

23 Elizabeth G. Cohen and Rachel A. Lotan, "Equity in Heterogeneous Classrooms," in *Handbook of Research on Multicultural Education*, 2nd ed., eds. J. A. Banks and C. M. Banks (San Francisco: Jossey-Bass, 2004), 736–750; Elizabeth G. Cohen, Rachel A. Lotan, Beth A. Scarloss, and Adele R. Arellano, "Complex Instruction: Equity in Cooperative Learning Classrooms," *Theory Into Practice* 38, no. 2 (1999): 80–86.

24 Elizabeth G. Cohen, Rachel A. Lotan, Beth A. Scarloss, and Adele R. Arellano, "Complex Instruction: Equity in Cooperative Learning Classrooms.

25 Roland Tharp, *Transforming Teaching: Achieving Excellence, Fairness, Inclusion, and Harmony* (Boulder, CO: Westview Press, 2000).

26 Elizabeth Cohen, *Designing Groupwork: Strategies for the Heterogeneous Classroom* (New York: Teachers College Press, 1994).

27 Kris Gutiérrez and Lynda Stone, "Hypermediating Literacy Activity: How Learning Contexts Get Reorganized," in *Contemporary Perspectives in Early Childhood Education*, Vol. 2, eds. O. Saracho and B. Spodek (Greenwich, CT: Information Age Publishing, 2002), 25–51.

28 Fred M. Newmann, Walter G. Secada, and Gary Wehlage, *A Guide to Authentic Instruction and Assessment: Vision, Standards, and Scoring* (Madison, WI: Wisconsin Center for Education Research at the University of Wisconsin, 1995).

29 Ibid., 35; see also Fred M. Newmann, ed., *Student Engagement and Achievement in American Secondary Schools* (New York: Teachers College Press, 1992), 8.

30 Ann L. Brown, Kathleen E. Metz, and Joseph C. Campione, "Social Interaction and Individual Understanding in a Community of Learners: The Influence of Piaget and Vygotsky," in *Piaget-Vygotsky: The Social Genesis of Thought*, eds. Anastasia Tryphon and Jacques Voneche (East Sussex, UK: Psychology Press, 1996), 160.

31 Thomas P. Carpenter, Megan Loef Franke, and Linda Levi, *Thinking Mathematically: Integrating Arithmetic and Algebra in Elementary School* (Portsmouth, NH: Heinemann, 2003).

32 See, for example, Robert Slavin, *Cooperative Learning: Theory, Research, and Practice* (Englewood Cliffs, NJ: Prentice Hall, 1995).

33 Ann Brown and Joseph Campione, "Guided Discovery in a Community of Learners," in *Classroom Lessons: Integrating Cognitive Theory and Classroom Practice*, ed. Kate McGilly (Cambridge, MA: MIT Press, 1994), 229–272.

34 "State Testing: An Interactive Breakdown of 2015–2016 Plans," *Education Week*, April 1, 2016, www.edweek.org/ew/section/multimedia/state-testing-an-interactive-breakdown-of-2015-16.html.

35 "The Technology Counts Report," *Education Week*, 2009, https://myaccount.edweek.org/epe/main.pl?action=ProductDisplay&iProdId=257&searchstring=.

36 Public Broadcasting Systems 2011 Survey on Media and Technology Use, *Deepening Connections: Teachers Increasingly Rely on Media and Technology*, www.grunwald.com/pdfs/PBS-GRUNWALD_2011_ANNUAL_ED_TECH_STUDY.pdf.

37 Federal Communications Commission, www.fcc.gov/general/national-broadband-plan.

38 National School Board Association, *Creating and Connecting: Research and Guidelines on Social—And Educational—Networking*, 2007, https://cdn-files.nsba.org/s3fs-public/reports/CREATING-CONNECTING-Research-and-Guidelines-on-Online-Social-and-Educational-Networking.pdf?uWboUuaGF3I1xHt6.Vlnq4D9HnfutHyF.

39 "Technology Counts 2017: Where Schools Stand," *Education Week*, www.edweek.org/ew/toc/2017/06/14/index.html.

40 Henry Jenkins, *Confronting the Challenges of Participatory Culture: Media Education for the 21st Century*, www.macfound.org/media/article_pdfs/JENKINS_WHITE_PAPER.PDF.

41 Beau Fly Jones, Gilbert Valdez, Jeri Nowakowski, and Claudette Rasmussen, *Plugging In* (Oak Brook, IL: North Central Regional Educational Laboratory, 1995).

42 "Technology Counts 2017: Where Schools Stand."

43 "The Technology Counts Report," 2009.

44 Janet Ward Schofield, *Computers and Classroom Culture* (New York: Cambridge University Press, 1995), 134–190.

45 Jane Margolis, *Stuck in the Shallow End: Education, Race and Computing* (Boston: MIT Press, 2008).

46 Clare McLaughlin, "The Homework Gap: The 'Cruelest Part of the Digital Divide,'" *NEA Today*, April 20, 2016, http://neatoday.org/2016/04/20/the-homework-gap/.

47 Amanda Lenhardt and Mary Madden, *Teen Content Creators and Consumers* (Washington, DC: Pew Internet & American Life Project, 2005), www.pewinternet.org/files/old-media/Files/Reports/2005/PIP_Teens_Content_Creation.pdf.pdf.

48 Jenkins, *Confronting the Challenges of Participatory Culture*, 3.

49 "Technology Counts 2017: Where Schools Stand."

50 Jane Margolis and Allan Fisher, *Unlocking the Clubhouse: Women and Computing* (Cambridge, MA: MIT Press, 2002); Jane Margolis, *Stuck in the Shallow End: Education, Race, and Computing* (Cambridge: Massachusetts Institute of Technology, 2008).

51 Luis Moll, "Funds of Knowledge for Teaching: Using a Qualitative Approach to Connect Homes and Classrooms," *Theory Into Practice* 31, no. 2 (1992): 132–141.

52 See Gloria Ladson-Billings, *The Dreamkeepers* (San Francisco: Jossey-Bass, 1994); and Geneva Gay, *Culturally Responsive Teaching: Theory, Research, and Practice* (New York: Teachers College Press, 2000).

53 Vivian Gussin Paley, *Kwanzaa and Me: A Teacher's Story* (Cambridge, MA: Harvard University Press, 1996).

54 James Banks, "Approaches to Multicultural Curriculum Reform," in *Beyond Heroes and Holidays: A Practical Guide to K–12 Anti Racist, Multicultural Education and Staff Development*, eds. Enid Lee, Deborah Menkart, and Margo Okazawa-Rey (Washington, DC: Teaching for Change, 1998).

55 James Cummins, *Language, Power and Pedagogy: Bilingual Children in the Crossfire* (Clevedon, UK: Multilingual Matters Ltd, 2000).

56 *Seal of Biliteracy*, http://sealofbiliteracy.org.

57 Jie Zong and Jeanne Batalova, *Frequently Requested Statistics on Immigrants and Immigration in the United States*, Migration Policy Institute, 2017, www.migrationpolicy.org/article/frequently-requested-statistics-immigrants-and-immigration-united-states.

58 Ofelia García, "Education, Multilingualism and Translanguaging in the 21st Century," in *Multilingual Education for Social Justice: Globalising the Local*, eds. Ajit Mohanty, Minati Panda, Robert Phillipson, and Tove Skutnabb-Kangas (New Delhi: Orient Blackswan, former Orient Longman, 2009), 128–145 (140).

59 Stephen Krashen, *Second Language Acquisition and Second Language Learning*, 1981, www.sciencedirect.com/science/article/pii/0346251X83900131.

60 The terms *AAL* and *MAE* were coined by Dr. Noma LeMoine; see Noma LeMoine, *English for Your Success: A Language Development Program for African American Children Grades PreK–8* (Saddle Brook, NJ: The Peoples Publishing Group, 1999).

Chapter 7

Assessment

Measuring What Matters

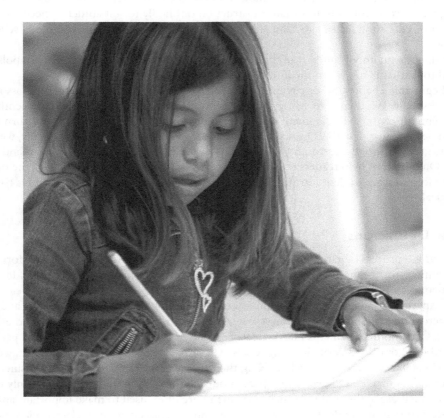

In my classroom, we do presentations, tests, simulations, projects, quizzes, seminars, quick writes, debates, etc. I am always on my feet talking to students, looking at their work as they do it, spontaneously adding more questions/thoughts for them to wrestle with. I am constantly adjusting my teaching plans because, as I read quick writes or other class work or listen in on group and partner dialogues, I know whether I need to go back and review or I can push ahead. Recently, I postponed a test for three days because I knew the students weren't ready (everything from their body language to a practice test were dead giveaways). I worked with them to teach each other the material and explain how they would study for the test.

—Judy Smith
High school social studies

What most people think of as "testing" is just one of many techniques that Judy Smith uses to keep track of student learning, to evaluate the success of her instruction, and to figure out what she and her students should do next. Teachers like Judy, committed to social justice, use assessment of various kinds to inform their daily classroom practice.

Chapter Overview

We assess students to answer key questions: What do students know, and what can they do? How does that knowledge relate to what they are expected to learn? How can teachers use that information to make decisions that support every student's growth and development? In this sense, assessments fuel teaching and learning. Without them, teachers cannot refine tomorrow's lessons, plan next month's unit, or tailor instruction on the fly to suit students' needs; without assessments, education leaders and the public can't know much about the health of a school or the nation.

Assessment is an important part of the science, craft, and art of teaching. It is also a politically charged topic that is subject to the interests and biases of the larger culture.

We begin this chapter by discussing some concepts and vocabulary commonly associated with assessment. We then give a brief history of assessment, focusing on the nineteenth- and early-twentieth-century development of testing to determine intelligence. Next, we turn to the modern descendants of early IQ tests, today's standardized achievement tests. Finally, we focus on what goes on inside classrooms, illustrating how assessment can foster learning and social justice. Our aim is to help readers put contemporary assessment in context, identify the options available for assessing student learning, and recognize the power of classroom teachers to assess authentically.

A Few Definitions

Assessment is a process of gathering, describing, or quantifying information about performance. By "quantify" we mean express numerically the amount or accuracy of a student's learning. Assessments can be divided into two major categories: (1) *large-scale assessments* developed by testing experts, "standardized," and administered to individuals or groups in schools and classrooms across the country and (2) *classroom assessments* that teachers use to support and evaluate learning. Classroom assessments may be teacher made or commercially produced and packaged with textbooks or other instructional materials. They can also be informal, for example, gauging students' readiness to answer or recognizing their furrowed brows. Large-scale assessments are mandated, designed, conducted, and reported outside the classroom. Teachers are only one of many intended users; the results of such assessments are often used to make important administrative decisions about students, such as grade promotion, placement into classes, identification for special education, or high school graduation. As mentioned in Chapter 4, large-scale assessments are also used to make consequential decisions about school performance: Is a school "low performing" or "high performing"? Does a school require instructional intervention (e.g., a different curriculum or a targeted approach to raising test scores)? Should a school be "reconstituted" or closed altogether? Increasingly, students' scores on large-scale assessments are also being used to evaluate teachers' effectiveness.

Traditional assessment typically includes multiple-choice, fill-in-the-blank, true-false, and matching test items—all of which have predetermined correct answers. Students' knowledge is assessed on the basis of their demonstrated recall of information—in other words, their selection or production of the expected "right" answers. Traditional assessments may be standardized or created by teachers, and they may be administered in classrooms or across schools, districts, states, or countries. With a focus on recall and limited choices, the assumptions underlying traditional assessment fit well with *behaviorist perspectives* on learning, which we described briefly in Chapters 3 and 6 and explain further in this chapter.

Tests, the most common form of traditional assessment, are specific, formal procedures by which a teacher or other test administrator obtains a sample of what a student knows, and generalizes from this sample to the student's broader knowledge—as when students' answers to a few multiplication problems are used to indicate whether they understand multiplication or when students' ability to identify grammatical errors in sentences is used as a proxy for their writing skills.

In contrast with traditional assessments, *alternative assessments* often include tasks or questions with a variety of acceptable answers, and they often reflect more concern for how well students explain or justify their responses. Thus, alternative assessments often demand higher-level thinking from students, and they support educators to assess not just whether students identify "right" answers or solutions, but *how* they approach and solve problems.

Psychology professor Jon Mueller summarizes key differences between traditional assessments and alternative assessments that are also *authentic*.[1] (See Concept Table 7.1.) Authentic alternative assessments align with sociocultural perspectives on learning and can better accommodate students' diversity. While many educators, like Mueller, prefer authentic alternative assessments for these reasons, they are not easily *standardized*—making them less useful for many traditional, large-scale testing purposes.

Performance assessment is one of the more popular forms of authentic alternative assessment. Performance assessments allow students to apply skills and knowledge they have learned to complete real-life tasks—for example, demonstrating writing and research skills by producing a newspaper article; demonstrating skills of analysis, synthesis, and argumentation by participating in a debate; demonstrating mathematical thinking and scientific inquiry skills by completing an experiment; and so forth. Student performance is then compared with that of experts—journalists, litigators, scientists, and so on—who are accomplished in those areas. A performance assessment can involve something as straightforward as having students write an essay in response to a question or prompt. Or it can involve more complex tasks. For example, a group of students might design and maintain their own stock market mutual fund; at the end of the semester, they might then present a report to convince new investors to join their fund. Or, more simply, students might craft letters to community members about issues of interest—perhaps expressing

Concept Table 7.1 Contrasting Traditional and Authentic Alternative Assessments

	Traditional	*Alternative and authentic*
How does a student display competence?	Selecting or supplying a "right" response	Performing a task with more than a simple "right" response
Is the task contrived or similar to real life?	Contrived task	Real-life task
What type of knowledge or skill is measured?	Recall/recognition	Construction/application
Who determines what is offered as evidence of competence?	Teacher determines what evidence must be provided	Student determines what evidence to provide, within parameters
What type of evidence is the basis of judging competence?	Indirect evidence (inferred from a selected/supplied response)	Direct evidence (inferred from a performance of knowledge or skill)

views on new school rules or desires for more playground space. Performance assessments—and other alternative assessments—are considered *authentic* only when the instructional objectives (e.g., clear, persuasive, factual writing) and the tasks themselves closely connect to real-life, meaningful activities.

Like many alternative assessments, performance assessments often include a *rubric*, or list of criteria by which performance should be judged. Although rubrics do not lay out predetermined correct responses, they do specify characteristics of performance at various levels of competence, along with guidelines for scoring. For example, "Relates evidence to conclusions" might be one rubric item for an essay asking students to combine scientific evidence for global warming with suggestions for solutions. A student might receive all or partial credit for that rubric item. A team-project rubric might include items for both group *and* individual contributions and might specify values or "points" that correspond with particular learning goals—for example, crafting a clear thesis statement, using statistics appropriately, and accurately citing research. Sharing such rubrics with students helps them gauge their performance against clearly articulated academic expectations that are also tied to meaningful standards of accomplishment in the world beyond school. This poses difficulties for both technical and political reasons. Policymakers have long favored traditional assessments, partly because they are easier than alternative assessments to administer, score, and report over very large groups of students. This tension is a theme that we explore throughout this chapter.

Evaluation, which is usually the end product of assessment, is the interpretation of a student's performance. Evaluation involves applying established criteria to determine the quality, value, or worth of that performance. Grades are one example of evaluations, since they convey whether a student has done well, average, or poorly; but they say nothing about the particulars of what a student has learned.

Test-based accountability is the term used to describe controversial systems like our own in which assessment results are provided to officials and the public as a means for demonstrating whether schools and teachers have fulfilled their responsibility to promote student achievement. Typically, states and the federal government use large-scale assessments for these accountability purposes. To date, most of these assessments have been traditional, although many are hopeful that the next generation of large-scale assessments will usher in needed change, including more performance-based measures.

Two assessment consortia, both of which won competitive federal funding in 2010 under Race to the Top, described in Chapter 4, have been developing, piloting, and implementing performance-based measures for inclusion in the latest standardized assessments, which are aligned to the Common Core State Standards (CCSS). In addition, the recent reauthorization of the federal government's centerpiece education policy, the Every Student Succeeds Act, described in Chapter 4, requires that assessments measure higher-order thinking and understanding; allows for integration of portfolios, projects, or extended-performance tasks; and invites states to apply for a pilot to develop new approaches to large-scale assessment.

These efforts, however, continue to pose technical and political difficulties. Policymakers have long favored traditional assessments, partly because they are easier to administer, score, and report on for large groups of students; they also believe that these tests give them (officials and the publics they represent) independent oversight of public education without having to rely on or entirely trust educators. Educators, meanwhile, have tended to favor assessments they create, administer, and analyze, and to question the resource demands incurred by externally imposed, large-scale assessments. This tension—between substance (i.e., what assessments address and ask of students) and scale (i.e., how readily assessments can be administered en masse, and with what costs)—is a theme that reappears throughout this chapter.

The History of Educational Testing

Because tests have dominated assessment for more than 100 years and continue to do so, a bit of history is useful for seeing tests as human constructions, created and used in particular contexts, rather than as natural or inevitable parts of teaching and learning.

Testing in Early China

Large-scale tests began in China, starting around 1100 BC. A system was devised to select the "best" people to hold high public office and, thereby, become part of the elite class. By about AD 1100, most of the population was eligible to take the exams, although those in a few occupations and their children were excluded, including watchmen, executioners, torturers, laborers, detectives, jailers, coroners, play actors, slaves, beggars, boatpeople, scavengers, and musicians.[2] Throughout the Chinese empire, thousands of candidates took a series of rigorous examinations hoping to qualify for important government posts. Those taking the exams subjected themselves to grueling conditions, as described by anthropology professor F. Allan Hanson in his fascinating history of testing:

> Examinees were crowded into huge, walled compounds that contained thousands of tiny cells. Huddled in his cubicle for three days and two nights, under the scrutiny of guards who prowled the lanes and watched from towers, the candidate would write commentaries on the Confucian classics, compose poetry, and write essays on subjects pertaining to history, politics, and current affairs. No one could enter or leave the compound during an examination.[3]

To "pass," candidates had to score well on a sequence of increasingly difficult examinations, each lasting a few days. Very few did. The examinations began as oral assessments and later— about 200 BC—became written exams. The topics included law, military, agriculture, finance, geography, and Confucian classics, and handwriting was weighed heavily.[4]

Testing developed much later in the West. Medieval European craft guilds required those seeking to attain the status of master craftsman to submit their work to juries who would judge whether their workmanship qualified them. Similar processes were used in universities, where students took oral examinations to prove their mastery of knowledge.

Despite this long history of examinations, educational tests did not appear on the U.S. schooling scene until the mid-nineteenth century, and the technology of large-scale standardized testing was not refined until early in the twentieth century.

Testing in Nineteenth-Century U.S. Schools

In colonial times, teaching and learning were quite individualized, and so was assessment. In small village schools, teachers taught students of all ages, providing different instruction to individuals and small groups. Generally, they knew what their students had learned and what they had not. Students were often called to the schoolmaster's desk individually or in small groups to demonstrate their learning by reciting what they had memorized. Teachers communicated this informally to parents, most of whom they knew well.

In the early 1800s, large urban "monitorial" schools also had students do recitations to demonstrate their mastery of facts and skills. Monitors, under the supervision of the schoolmasters, listened to recitations as students marched by their desks. For much of the nineteenth century, the end of the school day was the time for recitation and oral quizzes. And, at the end of each school term, public "recitation days" provided parents and community members a chance to witness displays of children's learning in spelling, grammar, rapid arithmetic, geography, history, and penmanship.

The quest for efficient and fair ways to assess large numbers of students drove the development of large-scale examinations in nineteenth-century U.S. schools. As schools were divided into grades, many began to expect that students in the same grade should master the same material. Visiting examiners conducted annual oral examinations in many city elementary and secondary schools to ascertain whether students should be promoted to the next grade.[5] Those who failed were held back, regardless of their age.

As urban systems grew in the mid-nineteenth century, oral examinations were no longer practical. So, for example, in 1845, when Boston enrolled over 7,000 children in nineteen schools, the system turned to written examinations.

> It was our wish to have as fair an examination as possible; to give the same advantages to all; to prevent leading questions; to carry away, not loose notes, or vague remembrances of the examination, but positive information, in black and white; to ascertain with certainty what the scholars did not know, as well as what they did know.[6]

Hanson describes some of the challenges that accompanied the early administration of written examinations in Boston schools in 1845.

> There were a few practical wrinkles at the beginning. The same test was given in all schools, and although it was printed, it did not occur to the committee to have it administered in all schools simultaneously. Instead they gave it in the schools one at a time, rushing as quickly as possible from one school to the next in an effort to prevent knowledge of the questions reaching some schools before the test did.[7]

Recitation for Inspectors in a Nineteenth-Century Common School

Nineteenth-century school leaders saw these examinations as a major advance in U.S. education. In 1845, for example, Horace Mann praised the tests as uniform and impartial tools for evaluating students and schools. Written tests reduced the risk of bias and protected against interventions by teachers who might be inclined to offer suggestions during the exam or show favoritism to some students. He also welcomed them as a means for permitting a more thorough understanding of what students had learned and documenting that for evaluation against objective standards.

System-wide written tests soon became common practice in cities across the nation. Schools in San Diego, California, for example, began to base students' promotions and graduation on annual exams developed by the county board of education. Teachers gave the tests and graded the students' responses, but the answers were all predetermined, and students had to respond correctly to 75 percent of the items to be promoted to the next grade. When San Diego ended its countywide annual examinations in 1891, the school board authorized teachers to administer exams for promotion.[8] In New York, the statewide Regents exams—named after the state's governing education board, whose members are called regents—began in 1878 and are still administered today.

Nineteenth-century schools also developed more systematic and efficient ways to report the results of tests and other assessments to parents. By the 1890s, teachers were less likely to know their students well, and increasing numbers of parents didn't speak English. So teachers began to report students' accomplishments graphically, with letter grades. Report cards sent home several times a year became standard, and they evolved only slightly over the twentieth century. Most often, teachers assigned letter or number grades in the various subjects, although as the twentieth century proceeded, many schools replaced grades with phrases such as "exceeds expectations," "satisfactory," or "needs improvement," and added comments to describe behaviors such as effort, conduct, and personal habits.[9]

All these forms of assessment relied heavily on behavioral theories of human learning. Recitations and written tests were viewed as the "end" of a transmission process in which knowledge began with the sender (teacher) and finished with the receiver (student). Resembling a straightforward one-directional conduit or pipeline, this process asks that teachers break down and

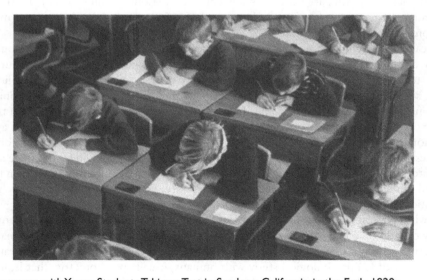

Huge Classroom with Young Students Taking a Test in San Jose, California, in the Early 1920s

organize the facts (through curriculum creation and lesson planning), send facts to students (teach), and monitor whether facts have been received (test). Although faulty transmission could occur anywhere along the pipeline, the fact that *some* students learned made it seem logical that those who didn't learn as well were responsible for their own failures.

The Development of Scientific Testing

Today's professionally developed standardized aptitude and achievement tests are direct descendants of nineteenth- and early-twentieth-century attempts to understand and measure intelligence. As we discussed in Chapter 3, the nineteenth-century fascination with empirical investigation included developing a scientific understanding of humans. Even though the mind could not be observed directly, understanding mental functioning held great appeal. In its quest to measure the mind—and, in particular, intelligence—psychology shifted away from its previously philosophical roots and toward the methods of the natural sciences. As history makes clear, the prevailing racism of the time powerfully influenced this new science of psychology, the evolution of which we trace in more detail below.

Early Behavioral Psychology: Measuring the Observable

The first scientific studies of the human mind were a curious mix of crackpot invention and increasingly sophisticated study of learning and intelligence. Phrenology, for example, represented an attempt to make practical use of an early version of psychological theory. Yes, some believed that they could feel the bumps on one's skull and know something about that person's mental faculties and character traits. Franz Gall, a noted nineteenth-century phrenologist, combined his pseudoscience with a systematic study of anatomy. Other investigators studied the brain and brain functions—sometimes correctly identifying parts of the brain that had specific functions such as speech or sight.

Throughout the 1800s, enthusiasm mounted about the prospect of knowing with precision a person's mental and behavioral characteristics. Might scientists predict who was compassionate, uncaring, or intelligent? Could they establish with certainty how people come to know (learning), and could they compare people's knowledge and reasoning (intelligence)? By the end of the century, the new science of psychology was born, focused on investigating the mind and mental processes, including learning.

Whereas early psychology had been a blend of folk wisdom, philosophy, anthropology, introspection, and biological science, psychologists in the early years of the twentieth century strove mightily to bring order and "scientific" respectability to their discipline. No longer limited to thought scenarios, general scholarship, and study of the classics, scholars were becoming systematic in their observations, recording their findings, and building on (or refuting) the work of other observers. In 1913, American psychologist John Watson argued against an approach being pioneered by European psychologists, in which human participants might "cooperate" with investigators by reporting about their mental processes. He maintained that since impartial investigators could not *observe* the working of the mind, asking people about their own thinking produced unreliable, unscientific information. Therefore, Watson contended that psychologists should stick to examining observable behaviors.[10]

Following Watson's caution, much of psychology in the first half of the twentieth century followed two traditional lines of scientific inquiry: (1) laboratory experiments with animals, often investigating response times and other physiological responses (blood pressure, respiration, eye blinks, etc.); and (2) psychological study with humans, usually psychometric, that is, involving tests that could be scored and converted to statistics.

Assessment and testing in nineteenth-century schools had been focused on measuring what and how much knowledge students acquired. Psychologists had somewhat different goals. They wanted to understand the learning process itself and to measure intelligence—the mental power that psychologists believed to govern human capacity to learn. As we describe next, intelligence was of particular interest to psychologists because they wanted to assess the "differences" among people. They were not as interested in any one person's intelligence as they were in measuring how much *more* or *less* intelligent people were in relation to one another—in scientific terms, the "variation" in intelligence across individuals and groups.

The Science of Intelligence

Charles Darwin (1809–1882) argued that the human species transmitted intelligence along with other traits, and that natural selection favored its most intelligent members. Darwin's nephew, Sir Francis Galton (1822–1911), later applied Darwin's ideas to his own study of intelligence. He gathered data about the British royal family and concluded that intellectual capacity runs in families. To measure intelligence, he also developed tests of sight, hearing, reaction time, and sensitivity to touch. Galton's studies were empirical; they relied less on subjective judgment and more on recorded observation. Galton's quest to measure inherited abilities dominated psychology in the early twentieth century.

Around that time, the U.S. school population was on the rise. In 1890 only 10 percent of young people pursued schooling beyond the basic primary years. But by 1920 that percentage had nearly quadrupled. Similarly, France had instituted mass education and expanded its educational goals to reach many more students. In both the United States and France, schools continued to educate children from prosperous families, who were assumed to learn easily; at the same time, both countries were now teaching children from families who had never attended school and who were deemed unable to learn or behave.

Partly in response to this diversity among students, the French government asked psychologist Alfred Binet (1857–1911) to devise a test to help schools identify those students who might benefit from greater assistance and attention in school—thus increasing their chances of achieving success. Binet's test included a range of questions designed for different-aged children. An 8-year-old who could pass most of the questions designed for a 12-year-old was said to have a *mental age* of 12. The reverse could be said as well—a 12-year-old could have a mental age of 8, thus indicating a need for special help. Binet cautioned that the test was strictly a screening device for students with severe cognitive deficiencies; it was not intended for use with "normal" children or for broad application in schools.

Although they imported Binet's intelligence test, educators in the United States—in alignment with the prevailing thinking of the time—were looking primarily for educational efficiency and were less motivated by sentiments of helpfulness or fairness. Within a few years, the field of psychology made intelligence the cornerstone of its new scientific orientation. Many refinements of Binet's original tests followed—each one giving test makers more confidence in their tests' accuracy and descriptive power. One refinement, for example, led to greater understanding and confidence among intelligence researchers and the public. That refinement involved reporting the test result as a ratio of mental age to chronological (actual) age. Thus, a 6-year-old who scored a mental age of 4—in other words, who knew as many correct answers as the average 4-year-old—received a score of 4 over 6, which, expressed as a ratio, would produce an intelligence quotient, or IQ, of 67. Likewise, a 4-year-old with a mental age of 6 would have an IQ of 150. Of course, the test results did not say anything more about children than how many questions they could answer relative to other children of the same age. However, the convenient "IQ" shorthand created the impression that IQ captured the essence of a child's prospects for school achievement, occupational fitness, and adult success.

Once imported to the United States, Binet's test was utilized for purposes beyond its original intent. The test quickly became linked to scientific authority and existing social power and prejudices. At the center of this were men of high regard in the world of science. Their views and work employed statistical analyses along with novel, often twisted, interpretations of Darwin's evolution theories and those of another profoundly influential scientist, Gregor Mendel (1822–1884), who established principles of biological inheritance. In particular, H. H. Goddard (1866–1957), Lewis Terman (1877–1956), and Charles Spearman (1863–1945), among others, drew on theories of evolution and inheritance to fashion a scientific theory of eugenics. *Eugenics*, or the shaping of a population through selective breeding, included stipulations regarding who should not be allowed to have children—all purportedly to improve the mental and moral qualities of the human race.

Prior to World War I, psychologist H. H. Goddard used a version of Binet's tests on youngsters in a large New Jersey mental institution, as well as on their relatives, to explore whether "feeblemindedness" ran in families. His work was responsible for popularizing Binet's ideas in the United States. But Goddard went much further than Binet, applying Mendel's ideas of biological inheritance to intelligence. Binet's scale provided Goddard a single number to represent how much intelligence a person inherited. Goddard concluded that the poor and criminals had low intelligence, which they passed on to their children:

> Our thesis is that the chief determiner of human conduct is a unitary mental process which we call intelligence: that this process is conditioned by a nervous mechanism which is inborn: that the degree of efficiency to be attained by that nervous mechanism and the consequent grade of intellectual or mental level for each individual is determined by the kind of chromosomes that come together with the union of the germ cells: that it is but little affected by any later influences except such serious accidents as may destroy part of the mechanism.
> How can there be such a thing as social equality with this wide range of mental capacity?[11]

As the final line suggests, Goddard and others theorized that the variation in what they considered "heritable" intelligence made social inequality somewhat inevitable—an idea that could be used, at least by some, to rationalize injustices.

Despite Binet's admonitions, educators worked intelligence testing into our school system's structure and ideology. In particular, Lewis Terman, a professor at Stanford University, developed and promoted intelligence tests for U.S. schoolchildren.

As mentioned in Chapter 2, Terman purported that his Stanford-Binet IQ tests measured innate abilities. Yet test items were written in such a way that children from educated, culturally mainstream families were more likely to earn high scores. Answering an item correctly, for example, might hinge on familiarity with highly specific content and vocabulary drawn from business and literature. Thus, children of color and children from poor families often scored lower than their more socially advantaged peers. Terman then used the test results to bolster his claims that heredity determined intelligence and his arguments in favor of low-level schooling for those who tested poorly and population control for those he deemed feebleminded.

As also noted in Chapter 2, the conclusions that Terman drew after testing a group of boys who lived in an orphanage reveal his unwavering belief in the validity of IQ testing and the threads of racism and classism woven through his interpretations.

> The tests have told the truth. These boys are ineducable beyond the merest rudiments of training. No amount of school instruction will ever make them intelligent voters or capable

citizens. . . . Their dullness seems to be racial, or at least inherent in the family stocks from which they came. . . . [O]ne meets this type with such extraordinary frequency among Indians, Mexicans and Negroes. . . . Children of this group should be segregated in special classes and be given instruction which is concrete and practical. . . . There is no possibility at present of convincing society that they should not be allowed to reproduce, although from a eugenic point of view they constitute a grave problem because of their unusually prolific breeding.[12]

Despite being subject to critique and periodic modification, IQ tests would continue to support views similar to Terman's well beyond the 1920s.

Charles Spearman, an English military engineer before he was a psychologist, tested schoolchildren with a wide variety of measures to determine whether people who were good at one thing tended also to be good at others. Through statistical analysis of test results, Spearman inferred an entity that he called g, for general intelligence. He conceived of g as a kind of inherited energy or power within the brain that activated other entities he called s, which referred to more specific abilities for which one could be trained. Spearman then used his theory to draw conclusions about different groups of people.

According to Spearman, in 1927,

the general conclusion emphasized by nearly every investigator is that as regards "intelligence" the Germanic stock has on the average a marked advantage over the South European. And this result would seem to have had vitally important practical consequences in shaping the recent stringent U.S. laws as to admission of immigrants.[13]

Spearman's statistical methods were inventive at best. Biologist and historian of science Stephen J. Gould, who systematically deconstructs these and other methods in his aptly titled text *The Mismeasure of Man*, calls Spearman's "a bankrupt theory" that treats intelligence "as a unitary, rankable, genetically based and minimally alterable thing in the head."[14]

Treating a Prejudicial Construct as Truth

Many late-nineteenth-century scientists were attracted to the study of intelligence because they sought rational and scientific explanations for the social class differences among racial and other groups. They had previously argued that the poor and "other" races were less capable and meritorious due to small brain size, moral depravity and wickedness, recent descent from apes, eastern European or southern European lineage, or religious background. In many ways, they were seeking to explain in new ways the existing social order.

Soon, *psychometric measurement* of mental traits, abilities, and processes took hold as a specialized field of study. IQ was elevated to a valid scientific measure of a real human attribute—the substance or quality of mind that defines the upper limits of one's learning ability. This attribute had a home: the brain. It had an origin: heredity. It could be measured with precision: IQ scores indicating how much intelligence different people as individuals, or groups on average, possessed. Because psychologists considered intelligence to be a natural endowment—like hair color or height—it was seen as fixed; people were more or less stuck with their intelligence from birth. These ideas about intelligence—measured by scientifically developed standardized tests—fit well with the prevailing logic that people's wealth and privilege was due to their greater intelligence, as opposed to wealth and privilege being largely responsible for high scores on intelligence measures. This reasoning recalls Calvinist religious views, in which wealth and privilege were seen as blessings from God, and not much was to be done about the poor because they clearly lacked those immutable blessings.

However, there was always some nagging indication that parenting and experiences in early childhood might also play a role in development. Thus, *nurture* as well as *nature* (inherited abilities) together or in competition came to be seen as for responsible for whether and how children acquire intelligence and make use of it over time. Consequently, a child born to a supposedly culturally impoverished family might not blossom intellectually because the parents would not provide adequate intellectual stimulation.

Recent genetic research has added a new scientific layer to the nature versus nurture debate. The science of epigenetics examines how environment affects genes and, in turn, human functioning. Some of this work suggests that biology and life experiences cannot be seen as independent determinants of the outcomes measured by intelligence tests. In particular, scientists are investigating how negative factors—stress, toxins, poor living conditions—and positive factors—healthy diet, social interactions, physical exercise—influence or activate genes that contribute to brain development and learning.

Given this old and emerging "science," we need to sound a loud note of caution: the idea of "intelligence" has been around for so long, and has served social and political interests so powerfully, that in spite of debates and complex new understandings, the culture has a hard time keeping up. "Intelligence" is an abstract idea cemented in popular understanding, and it can't easily shake off the myths and baggage of past centuries. In short, this popular concept has not kept up with science or social justice.

As teachers, it's important to avoid defining our students according to abstractions that are convenient for education institutions to organize their work. Intelligence, for example, has become seen as a tangible thing, reified as IQ and defined as a score on an IQ test. However, reified ideas are not real in any material sense. Rather, they are abstractions—what social scientists call *constructs*. According to the late researcher and measurement expert Kenneth Sirotnik, many educational constructs begin as narrowly defined, specialized measures—like IQ, for example—that researchers and theorists use for limited purposes. Then, as these constructs make their way from research to professional journals and popular media and then to the everyday talk of policymakers and the public, they lose their narrow definitions and specialized uses. "Pretty soon," Sirotnik notes, "people talk and make decisions about other people's *intelligence, achievement,* and *self-concept* as if these attributes really existed in the same sense as, for example, people's height and weight."[15]

Sirotnik argues that this reification—treating abstract constructs as if they have concrete, material reality—distorts people's thinking about education. Once reified, categories such as "gifted," "high ability," and "average," whether they began with specific and technical definitions or as loose and informal ideas, become deeply embedded features of students' identities—in both their own and others' minds. Often, educators and others fail to examine the origins and limits of the specialized meanings of these designations, and they exaggerate and overinterpret them. These dangers have plagued makers and users of intelligence tests and other, similar tests from the outset.

In 1927, Harper and Brothers published the book *Tisn't What You Know, But Are You Intelligent?*, whose back cover proclaims, "Rate yourself on the actual tests used in the Department of Applied Physiology at Yale University." The preface, written by a Yale psychologist, explains that intelligence is the "capability to do productive thinking" and that intelligence is not knowledge but "an inborn capacity of the mind." In the section on feeblemindedness, the author declares, "By the principle of heredity, two feebleminded parents have nothing but feebleminded children and usually in large numbers."[16] Although no explicit claims are made about the racial basis of intelligence, there are some overt and troubling assertions about gender:

> The introduction of a strain of low mentality into an intelligent family sometimes shows up in later generations. This strain of feeblemindedness is usually introduced into the family on

the female side. This statement is not one of misogyny. Its reason lies in the fact that many of the qualities in the male which make him a desirable mate, his abilities and his earning capacity for example, are related to intelligence. These qualities are not always expected in the female. A girl of moron intelligence may have the physical beauty and grace that lead quickly to matrimony even though her conversation is limited to, "I've had a perfectly glorious time"; "Isn't it too wonderful"; "You dear"; and, "Oh, anything you say!"[17]

The remainder of the book consists of intelligence tests, plus a table that provides test scores, corresponding intelligence ratings, and a list of the average number of correct answers given by members of different occupations—from laborers at the bottom, with "low average intelligence," to accountants and doctors at the top, with "superior intelligence."

What were the questions on the Yale tests like? They were much like those included in Terman's early tests, and, perhaps not surprising, some are quite a lot like the questions that turn up on today's aptitude tests like the SAT. Here are some examples:

1. It is wiser to save some money and not spend it all, so that you may (a) gamble when you wish? (b) prepare for old age and sickness? (c) collect all the different kinds of money?
2. How long will it take a man to walk 42 miles if he walks at the rate of 3 miles per hour?
3. The Percheron is a kind of (a) goat, (b) horse, (c) cow, (d) sheep.[18]

The reification of IQ and other constructs is destructive because they reinforce our cultural habit of deficit thinking. IQ is meaningless unless there exists "high" and "low" IQ. And that distinction is useless unless IQ has explanatory or predictive power. More broadly, deficit thinking has us look at students in terms of what they do not have, or who they are "less than," and we use those deficits to explain and predict their futures. Compare deficits of abstract constructs (intelligence, motivation, cooperation, etc.) with deficits of things that are real and tangible (food, medical care, shelter, etc.). Addressing these latter deficits, when they exist, has real and reliable power to explain, predict, and correct.

IQ and Scientific Schooling

As we described in Chapters 3 and 6, beginning in the early twentieth century, educators found great use for behavioral psychology and intelligence tests. They helped make education seem more scientific at a time when "being scientific" brought increased respectability and higher status. Psychologists and educators alike agreed that scientific tests enabled teachers to address students' particular mental capacities and prepare them for particular social roles based on those capacities.

The public bought into the idea that IQ tests gave educators expert authority to measure students' capacity for thinking and learning. For several decades, group IQ tests were administered routinely to U.S. schoolchildren as the basis for determining their intellectual potential and assigning them to "appropriate" classes and programs.

As this brief account makes clear, the twentieth-century Western world invented a peculiar way of thinking about a person's capacity for learning: intelligence represented an upper limit, a ceiling, on how successful a student might become. Especially important for most Americans, who struggle to balance concerns for democratic equality with the preservation of privilege, the tests appeared to be scientific and fair: the same tests were administered under similar conditions, and scores were calculated with impartial mathematical formulas. But, of course, the tests were hardly fair, and the science behind them was suspect. Nevertheless, in mainstream science, social discourse, and public policy, IQ scores were seen for a time as accurately representing individuals' intelligence, and averages of individuals' IQs were used to compare groups of children. Such averaging gave the broader society an explanation and justification for inequalities across many social domains beyond education, including income, employment, housing, health, and so forth.

As discussed in Chapter 2, IQ remains a powerful construct. The serious reception given to the 1994 book *The Bell Curve: Intelligence and Class Structure in American Life*, claiming that African Americans' disadvantaged circumstances stem, in part, from lower inherited IQ, is one example of how persistent such ideas can be, despite ample evidence to the contrary and considerable advances in our understanding, which we discuss later in this chapter. The 2005 reference by Lawrence Summers, then Harvard University's president, to IQ differences as a potential contributing factor in long-standing gender gaps in science and engineering,[19] and Harvard's 2009 approval of a doctoral dissertation reportedly "dedicated to the proposition that Hispanics have lower IQs than White people,"[20] are but two examples of IQ's enduring salience in scholarly and public discourse.

Contemporary Large-Scale Assessment

In recent years, the widespread use of IQ tests in school has fallen into disfavor. When they are used—for example, for identifying students with special needs—they are used far more carefully than in the past. However, IQ tests have also spawned large-scale aptitude and achievement tests—the SAT, the ACT, and an array of basic skills tests that are variations of IQ tests themselves. Like IQ tests, these tests shape judgments about students' abilities, and they play an important role in rank-ordering students and deciding what their future schooling opportunities will be. So, although most students today are unlikely to be tested for IQ, per se, their schools have similar measures by which to judge them.

Although it is difficult to obtain exact data on the extent of standardized testing in schools nationwide, an estimate in 1990 of 200 million per year vastly underestimates the number of standardized tests given today.[21] Indeed, more recent analyses have found that students in major cities take about 112 required standardized tests, or roughly eight per year.[22] Researchers found 1,110 minutes an *under*estimate of the time New Yorkers in grades 3–6 spent per year completing standardized tests.[23] This prevalence is one result of test scores having become the single most important indicator of whether students and schools are doing well.

In addition to state and local tests, the National Assessment of Educational Progress (NAEP), a national test given every few years, gathers new data to document the educational achievement of U.S. students. Recently, NAEP has been nicknamed "the Nation's Report Card," and when NAEP scores are released, they make the front page of newspapers across the country, with the ranking of states by their students' scores capturing widespread attention. International tests like the PISA, given periodically, provide rankings of nations according to how well their students perform in reading, writing, math, and science.[24] Scores from these tests, too, increasingly make headlines, drawing more and more visitors to higher-scoring countries, such as Finland and Singapore, where policymakers and educators travel to learn which policies and practices lead to impressive test performance.

Federal officials decry the nation's standing on international math and science tests; state policymakers proclaim a crisis when their state's achievement scores are lower than those of other states; federal and state governments threaten sanctions such as school closures when a school's scores lead to a "low-performing" designation; real estate agents compare and share local schools' scores when enticing home buyers; and parents trumpet high scores as irrefutable proof of their children's merit or lament low scores as evidence that their children are being underserved by schools. In short, tests continue to play a huge role in how we think about teaching and learning, intelligence and achievement, and schools and schooling.

Standardized Tests

In their design, today's standardized tests follow much of the same logic and statistical procedures that were pioneered by IQ test developers. They obtain a sample of students' responses and behaviors that are used to generate more global judgments about students' abilities. Most of these tests, like IQ tests, are *norm referenced*, meaning that they compare a student's performance with that of other students of the same age or grade. Some, however, are now *criterion referenced*; this newer breed of achievement tests, developed in conjunction with curriculum standards, compares student performance against a fixed standard.

Whether norm or criterion referenced, standardized tests rely on a particular "technology"—a set of practices, rules, and standards for test construction, administration, and scoring. In their development, they must meet technical requirements of validity and reliability. *Validity* refers to whether the information being collected is trustworthy for the assessment purpose. For example, does a high score mean that a student is actually really good at what is being measured? Does the format allow students to show what they can do? Are the instructions clear? Has the test been administered under uniform conditions?

Reliability refers to whether the results of the assessment can be trusted to be consistent. For example, will the results be similar if the assessment is repeated at another time? Will the outcome be the same if another person administers or scores the test? Do students answer consistently questions seeking to measure the same knowledge or skills?

Standardized tests also make claims to *objectivity*, meaning that a test's answers are not open to interpretation, discrimination, or dispute. The assumption is that item development and scoring procedures guard against the influence of irrelevant factors (e.g., background, language) or bias. Objective tests, in theory, provide all students a fair opportunity to show what they have learned.

Norm-Referenced Standardized Tests

For *norm-referenced* standardized tests, the test development process includes a national sample of students—called the "norm" group. The scores of this group make up the standard against which the performance of subsequent test takers is compared. The scores on norm-referenced tests don't reveal what or how much a student actually knows but, instead, reveal how that student compares with the norm group.

There is no good, everyday synonym for *norm*, probably because most people are not accustomed to thinking in strictly statistical terms. That's what *norm* is—a statistical term that combines elements of *normal, usual*, and perhaps *most common*. And yet it is really quite different from the everyday understanding of those ideas. For example, a student's (norm-referenced) percentile score on the SAT tells what percentage of the norm group the student outscored; someone who scores in the 80th percentile provided more correct answers than 79 percent of the students in the norm group. Grade-level scores work the same way. Students who score "at grade level" did about as well as the average person in their grade; those who are "above grade level" did better than most of their peers.

Because norm-referenced tests aim to place students precisely within peer groups, the tests are designed to spread scores out over a wide range, so there will be enough difference among test takers to rank them. The tests are constructed so that most people score in the average range, with fewer getting scores above and below average, and even fewer at the two extremes. This is why the distribution of scores on these tests can be described as a *bell curve*. The large number of average scores forms the highest point of the curve, and the smaller number of extremely high and low scores flatten out on either side. The two most well-known types of norm-referenced tests are aptitude tests and achievement tests.

APTITUDE TESTS

Aptitude tests are designed to predict an individual's ability in relation to a particular skill or area of knowledge. The SAT (formerly known as the Scholastic Aptitude Test) and the ACT, the American College Testing Program's college admissions test, are aptitude tests. Their goal and claim is to predict how a student is likely to perform in the future—specifically, to predict the grades that high school students will earn when they get to college. While the College Board maintains the validity of the SAT—both the prior and the revised edition—for admissions decisions, some scholars question the test's fairness, given its underwhelming correlation to first-year college grades and its over- and underprediction of how many students fare well in college.[25]

The SAT and the ACT include some questions that are aligned to the school curriculum, but, like IQ tests, they purport to measure general knowledge and skills. SAT developers, for example, have long argued that studying for the SAT is not really worthwhile because the test measures general competencies—verbal and mathematics aptitudes—not specific subject knowledge. Recent efforts by the College Board, in collaboration with Khan Academy, to "level the playing field" by making free SAT prep materials available online, indicates some shifts in thinking about the relationship between practicing for the SAT and faring well on it. Still, as *aptitude* tests, the SAT and the ACT claim to predict future school success; they do not claim to accurately measure what students have learned or how intelligent students are.

In reality, such tests measure a complex, and often misunderstood, mix of factors. The following SAT "mathematical reasoning" question, for example, blends together—and requires of students—school knowledge (math), reading ability (general comprehension and specific vocabulary), cultural background (familiarity with playing cards, and perhaps prior experience solving problems for no practical purpose), and reasoning:

> Seven cards in a pile are numbered 1 through 7. One card is drawn. The units digit of the sum of the numbers on the remaining cards is 7. What is the number of the drawn card? (The choices are numbers 1, 3, 5, 6, or 7.)[26]

Whether a student can answer such a question correctly depends on many things.

ACHIEVEMENT TESTS

Achievement tests are designed to measure individuals' knowledge of or proficiency with skills and/or concepts they have learned. Most standardized achievement tests assess how well students have acquired knowledge and mastered skills that are taught in school, compared with others at the same grade. However, because many of these tests have important reading comprehension components, such as the California Test of Basic Skills (CTBS) and the Iowa Test of Basic Skills (ITBS), they measure similar skills to the SAT. In fact, since scores on reading comprehension tests typically correlate strongly with scores on IQ tests, they are often interpreted similarly. In other words, high reading scores—even ones on, say, kindergarten reading readiness tests—are taken to mean high ability in general, just as high scores on an IQ test are taken to mean high intelligence.

Standards-Based Standardized Tests

As mentioned previously, many of the more recent achievement tests, particularly those administered by states in the last few decades, are intended to determine whether students have become proficient on state-determined standards. In other words, they are both *standardized* and *standards based*. Although they are not constructed to compare students with one another, aggregated scores nevertheless are used to compare and even rank schools. Unlike general aptitude tests or basic skills tests, these tests purport to measure whether students have acquired the state-specified knowledge in the curriculum for their grade level. Tests that compare student performance against a standard, or an expectation of particular knowledge, are called *criterion-referenced* tests. Students' performances on standards-based tests are reported in categories—for example, "below basic," "basic," "proficient," and "advanced"—that specify students' relative levels of mastery vis-à-vis the standards. Whereas norm-referenced tests require a spread of scores from highest to lowest, it is possible with standards-based tests that all students or none will score at a particular level.

Even though standards-based tests avoid some of the problems of norm-referenced standardized tests, they, too, are flawed. They focus narrowly on limited academic goals and often do a poor job of measuring them. They require instruction that prepares students to understand subjects in ways that will produce strong results within a traditional testing format. This, in turn, creates pressure for schools and teachers to rely on traditional teaching methods, as discussed in Chapters 4 and 6. Pressure to produce high scores also makes it difficult for teachers and students to look critically at the content of the standards or the test questions that are meant to represent them. Teachers have limited opportunity (except, perhaps, by offering input to distant committees) to shape the knowledge they are tasked with teaching or the standardized assessments they must administer. Students' lives and experiences often get sidelined in the process, despite the fact that connecting students' lives and experiences to academic content, instruction, and assessment is a key component of critical multicultural and sociocultural teaching.

Indeed, most standards-based assessments to date have been paper-and-pencil tests consisting of traditional items that require students to select or supply a predetermined correct response. For example, the following is a sample question from a standards-based test—in this case, New York State's Regents test in biology:

1. The excretory organelles of some unicellular organisms are contractile vacuoles and
    Cell membranes
    Cell walls
    Ribosomes
    Centrioles

    (Study guide for the 1995 New York Regents test in high school biology)[27]

The question is technical and specific, seems intellectually challenging, and appears to measure knowledge contained in the state's biology standards. Although such items may seem intellectually challenging, they display what researcher Linda Darling-Hammond calls the "trappings of intellectual rigor." Like the school examinations of the nineteenth century, they measure little more than whether a student has memorized words unique to the discipline (i.e., *organelles, ribosomes*). They do not measure whether students actually understand and can do science at all. As a result, Darling-Hammond argues, standardized tests such as these often undermine students' motivation and crowd out opportunities for making academic knowledge meaningful and useful.[28]

In addition, standards documents themselves—like those developed by most states in response to the No Child Left Behind Act of 2001 and in place until the adoption of the national CCSS in 2010—have posed challenges for the development of reliable standards-based assessments. Many contained far too many standards for any test to measure, and thus test results didn't provide an overall sense of which standards students met and which they did not. High scores, for example, mean only that students answered questions correctly about those standards that were represented on the test. These dynamics create conditions for people to make broad inferences about standards being met (or not) based on insufficient information.

Critiques of Standardized Tests

Standardized tests have become increasingly controversial, even as they continue to be the most influential assessments in U.S. schools. Many of the reasons, summarized below, stretch across norm-referenced and standards-based assessments. All are important to consider as the United States works to develop and implement its "next generation" of large-scale assessments, discussed in the subsequent section.

FLAWED THEORIES OF LEARNING

A major critique of standardized tests is that they embody nineteenth-century behavioral psychological theories and ignore new scholarship on learning as a complex sense-making process that involves connecting new information to prior knowledge and experience. The prevailing assumption behind standardized tests is that students' learning (or knowledge) can be represented by their facility in selecting or providing predetermined right answers. Such tests must ignore complex understandings (or knowledge) or break learning up into shorter, simpler chunks for the purposes of testing and statistical analysis. As testing expert Robert Mislevy once put it, "The essential problem is that the view of human abilities implicit in standard test theory . . . is incompatible with the view rapidly emerging from cognitive and educational psychology."[29]

Contemporary scholars generally believe that intellectual competence encompasses a richer and deeper collection of abilities than standardized tests can measure. Psychologist Robert Sternberg, for example, argues that the most important kinds of intelligence needed for success at school and on the job are poorly revealed by standardized tests. Developmental psychologist Howard Gardner likewise offers evidence that the kind of intelligence often measured by standardized tests pales in importance when compared with more reflective mental processes. Gardner suggests that while some of the most successful CEOs, schoolteachers, and surgeons may have received high test scores, scores typically don't predict an individual's ability to seize a business opportunity, ask the right question at the right moment, or wield a scalpel assuredly.[30]

In fact, as noted earlier, norm-referenced aptitude and achievement tests, like IQ tests, are *designed* to ensure a wide range of scores, which allows for the ranking and grouping of test takers into percentiles. By definition, such tests include finite items ranging from easy to difficult. Scores reveal only the ability of test takers to answer the included questions, which may or may not address what test takers know about the content at hand. Given these design issues, the questions that best *distinguish* test takers—especially those with high scores—end up being those to which the fewest people know the answers. As a result, consequential decisions may be unduly influenced by rarefied facts with little real-life import or connection to meaningful student learning.

CULTURAL BIAS

Because different cultural contexts provide children with different learning situations, and different cultures value the mastery of different skills and knowledge, it is unimaginable that a standardized test, useful for schooling purposes, could be designed to work across all cultures.

In light of this, much attention has been given to so-called culturally sensitive standardized tests; however, these often represent reductive notions of culture and overinflated ambitions for tests.

Stephen J. Gould—who published *The Mismeasure of Man* nearly four decades ago—details the scientific and statistical flaws of intelligence testing and traces the links between IQ, bigotry, and oppression.[31] These same linkages still plague many tests used today to indicate aptitude and ability gaps between racial and cultural groups. Even tests that purport to measure what's been taught at school typically tell us more about students' socioeconomic status and cultural background than about what students have learned in the classroom.

Poverty and oppressive social conditions—factors that *do* vary according to race, as explained in Chapter 1—*are* significantly related to people's performance on standardized tests; scholars agree that this is more reflective of those *conditions* than of test takers' intelligence. Psychologist Jerome Bruner offers an example in support of this very idea. He reports on the interplay between social and economic conditions and IQ among Korean immigrants, who score 15 points lower on average on IQ tests in Japan than in the United States. Bruner attributes this gap to the two cultures' treatment of Korean immigrants; while they are often denigrated as ignorant in Japan, they are often stereotyped as smart in the United States.[32]

As Bruner's example suggests, different cultures hold varied views on what "being smart" means and entails. Middle-class Americans often associate problem-solving speed with intelligence, and speed is a prized attribute when taking most standardized tests; Ugandan villagers, however, describe intelligence with words such as *slow* and *careful*. The Chinese place a high value on the ability to memorize facts; Australians consider this trivial. Middle-class Americans consider intelligence to encompass technical and abstract skills; Kenyans see intelligence as comprising social and personal responsibility, too. Ugandans and the Ifaluk people of the western Pacific consider intelligence to include both knowing socially responsible actions *and* acting accordingly. Such variation raises questions about the limitations of narrow, fact-based, timed standardized tests when it comes to judging something as complex as intelligence.

QUESTIONABLE IMPLEMENTATION AND USE

A final problem with standardized tests is their questionable implementation and use. Although well-constructed tests can provide nuanced information, in the real world of schools and politics, tests are often blunt tools. Indeed, it is difficult to find a school district that complies with testing experts' and test makers' recommendations for how tests should be used. Likewise, policymakers tend to be rather uninformed about the problems inherent in standardized testing and to make excuses for why flawed instruments are better than alternatives.

In addition, standardized test scores increasingly confer serious consequences on students and schools. As explained in Chapter 4, some standards-based test scores can be used to justify retaining students in a given grade and denying them high school diplomas; they can also be used to justify decisions to reconstitute schools or have them taken over by the state. Despite critique, the high stakes attached to standardized tests have become the single most popular policy instrument for pushing schools to raise academic rigor.

Much of the questionable implementation and use of standardized tests contradicts professional standards put forward by experts to inform ethical use of large-scale assessments and thereby minimize potential harm caused by the flaws described above. (See Focal Point 7.1.) Although testing experts have universally endorsed these standards, they have not been effective in halting outright some of the harmful practices. In many states, Emergent Bilingual

Focal Point 7.1
Standards for Educational and Psychological Testing

The American Psychological Association, the American Educational Research Association, and the National Council on Measurement in Education have created a set of professional standards for educational and psychological testing. They revised these substantially in 1999 and again in 2014. The standards set out important principles meant to promote fairness in testing and to ward off unintended consequences. They include:

- Any decision about a student's continued education, such as retention, tracking, or graduation, should not be based on the results of a single test but should include other relevant and valid information.
- When test results substantially contribute to decisions made about student promotion or graduation, there should be evidence that the test addresses only the specific or generalized content and skills that students have had an opportunity to learn.
- For tests that will determine a student's eligibility for promotion to the next grade, or for high school graduation, students should be granted, if needed, multiple opportunities to demonstrate mastery of materials through equivalent testing procedures.
- When a school district, state, or some other authority mandates a test, the ways in which the test results are intended to be used should be clearly described. It is also the responsibility of those who mandate the test to monitor its impact, particularly on racial and ethnic minority students or students of lower socio-economic status, and to identify and minimize potential negative consequences of such testing.
- In some cases, special accommodations for students with limited English proficiency may be necessary to obtain valid test scores. If students with limited English skills are to be tested in English, their scores should be interpreted in light of their limited English skills.
- Likewise, special accommodations may be needed to ensure that test scores are valid for students with disabilities. Not enough is currently known about how particular test modification may affect the test scores of students with disabilities: more research is needed. As a first step, test developers should include students with disabilities in field testing of pilot tests and document the impact of particular modifications (if any) for test users.

Source: American Educational Research Association, American Psychological Association, and National Council on Measurement in Education, Standards for Educational and Psychological Testing (Washington, DC: American Educational Research Association, 2014).

students—even newcomers to the United States—must take tests in English, and test accommodations for students with special needs are often lacking. In other areas, however, some progress has been made; as mentioned in Chapter 4, for example, the number of states using a single high-stakes graduation test as the basis for granting diplomas dropped in recent years from twenty-seven to twelve.[33]

But progress has not been enough to allay the concerns of many people, including those who have spearheaded nationwide efforts to inform parents about their right to "opt out" of standardized testing for their children. (See Focal Point 7.2.)

Focal Point 7.2
United Opt Out

United Opt Out (UOO) is a Florida-based national nonprofit led by current and former public school educators. UOO educates families about their right to opt their children out of standardized testing. Following are some excerpts from UOO's website describing its work and a template "opt out" letter that UOO makes available for public use.

UOO's mission is to strengthen public education, fight corporate based reforms that are threatening the concept and existence of an educational system that is publicly funded, quality in nature and available to all; and, in particular, to end the practice of punitive, high-stakes testing, indoctrinating digital instruction, and related activities that are fraudulently being used as "proof" of the incompetence of public education/teachers.

As part of UOO's mission "to create an environment that leads to the demise of high-stakes testing, indoctrinating digital instruction, and related activities," the group:

- *Promotes students opting out of high-stakes testing and indoctrinating digital instruction;*
- *Provides guidance and support for parents;*
- *Informs educational institutions of the rights of parents/students to "opt out;"*
- *Informs the media about "opting out;" and*
- *Informs media, community leaders, civil rights leaders, and politicians of the reason for students "opting out."*

Sample Opt Out Letter

September 7, 2016
To Whom It May Concern:

Please be advised that our child, _____, will not be participating in all state and district standardized testing nor computer based learning such as _____ during the current school year, 2016–2017. Our child will participate in paper-based lessons and assessments generated by her classroom teacher only.

We believe the following of forced, high stakes testing:

- Is not scientifically-based and fails to follow the U.S. Government's own data on learning
- Is developmentally inappropriate and abusive for early childhood learners
- Fosters test driven education that is not meeting the individual/intellectual needs of students
- Presents a racial and economic bias detrimental to second language students, impoverished students, and students of color
- Violates fiscal fairness in funding schools
- Supports complicity of corporate interests rather than democracy based on public concerns
- Fosters coercion over cooperation with regards to federal funding for public education
- Promotes a culture of lying, cheating, and exploitation within the school community
- Has used the achievement gap to foster a "de facto" segregation that has resulted in separate and unequal education for non-white students

Additionally, we believe that screen time and computer based instruction is damaging cognitively, physically, and socially to early learners and promotes screen addiction in all learners. We understand that federal law provides the parent or guardian the right of choice regarding standardized testing and instruction when such violates beliefs. In contrast to our beliefs, which are firmly rooted in a moral code that embraces equity and fairness, we believe such testing and computer based instruction is not in the best interests of our child since it fosters competition instead of cooperation, contributes to separate and unequal education for minorities, and belies our child's intellectual, creative, and problem-solving abilities, and is damaging while presenting a fictitious picture as to the impact of the pedagogy provided by our child's individual educators.

Ultimately, our state is required to provide our child with an education in a least restrictive environment that does not force us to go against our core beliefs. My child should proceed to learn and develop at an individual pace following education standards that are imparted under the guidance of education professionals, not market-based reformers, who are able to provide quality pedagogy without fear of reprisal if students—who mature at vastly different levels and come from diverse backgrounds that may or may not be supportive of intellectual pursuit—do not hit the bulls' eye of a constantly moving achievement targets.

Therefore, we request that the school provide appropriate learning activities during the testing window, provide only paper-based activities for formative assessment and learning activities, and utilize an alternative assessment portfolio to fulfill promotion requirements.

Sincerely,

The above excerpts are taken from United Opt Out National's website (www.unitedoptoutnational.org), where readers can find additional information about the organization and access the resources it offers.

Alternatives to Traditional Large-Scale Assessments

Over the past few decades, assessment experts have sought to develop large-scale assessments that match current conceptions of learning and intelligence and avoid the problems associated with traditional tests. Although some have the goal of eliminating traditional standardized tests altogether, most seek to augment conventional tests with multiple, alternative ways to assess learning. Some of these efforts have shown great promise, but they have also been plagued, unsurprisingly, with technical and political problems—problems serious enough to severely limit their use.

More recently, with the nearly nationwide adoption of the CCSS, there is renewed energy and hope about transforming large-scale assessment for the better. Before turning to the most recent iterations of CCSS-aligned large-scale assessments, we offer a glimpse into lesser-known efforts forged a few decades back.

In the 1990s, California, Kentucky, Maryland, and Vermont all developed alternative assessment strategies as part of their state testing programs. In California and Maryland, students wrote essays and laboratory reports, and explained their mathematical reasoning instead of taking multiple-choice tests. Vermont and Kentucky had students do group activities, conduct hands-on science tasks, and use tools and manipulatives. Students developed portfolios of their work and identified what they thought were the best work samples to evidence their learning. In some states, teachers helped score these assessments; in others, professional contractors did the scoring.

Teachers generally liked these new assessments because they fit better with a complex curriculum and multidimensional teaching; however, they consumed more instructional time than traditional standardized tests and cost more to develop, administer, and score. The fact that these assessments had fewer actual items than multiple-choice tests also raised technical questions about whether they could validly measure a broad enough scope of the academic subjects they were assessing. Some critics raised concerns that the administration of these assessments (the wording of instructions, the set time limits, etc.) couldn't be standardized as well as the administration of multiple-choice tests, so they might not be fair. Performance assessments also proved challenging to score. In Vermont, for example, different scorers didn't always rate students' performances in the same way, compromising reliability. In Maryland and California, political objections were raised to the practice of giving only a few performance tasks to each child and then assigning the scores to schools rather than to each child.

In all of these states, concerns were raised about the lack of national norms for alternative assessments at the time, which meant that states couldn't compare the performance of their children with that of children in other states. In some cases, like California, charges were also lodged that the nontraditional performance items pried too deeply into students' personal beliefs and paid too little attention to their mastery of core knowledge.

Due in part to the No Child Left Behind provisions of the early 2000s, all of these states reverted in the intervening years to more conventional standardized tests, including norm-referenced tests, in their state assessment systems.

"Next Generation" Standards-Based Assessments

In 2010, then Secretary of Education Arne Duncan announced that two consortia—the Partnership for Assessment of Readiness for College and Careers (PARCC)[34] and the Smarter Balanced Assessment Consortium (SBAC)[35]—had won the $350 million Race to the Top competition to design large-scale assessment systems. As winners, both were charged with developing innovative ways to assess third- through eighth-grade students' achievement in relation to the newly adopted CCSS. Not surprisingly, among numerous others, the four aforementioned states were quick members—Maryland of PARCC, California and Vermont of SBAC, and Kentucky of both (until the last withdrew in favor of administering its own state test).

The consortia worked to develop and pilot assessments for different purposes, with different types of questions, and to gauge students' progress on both the "full range" of standards and the "critical areas." As expected, both focused on using technology and creating systems to provide timely feedback to teachers and students. In addition, after considerable work to resolve earlier technical problems, both consortia incorporated performance tasks, which require that students, for example, *apply* mathematical knowledge and skills to solve actual problems and *use* evidence drawn from provided texts to substantiate claims in English language arts. The resulting pilot- and field-tested, computer-based assessments are a few years into usage and almost fully online— with computer adaptive components, which assign subsequent test items to students based on their answers to prior items, in place or under development.

Both consortia have seen states go the way of Kentucky, peeling off from the group. PARCC's membership dropped from twenty-four to eight states, and SBAC's from thirty to seventeen states, plus three affiliates. In addition, significant numbers of students have opted out of consortia tests in particular. For example, 27 percent of juniors in Washington did not show up for the SBAC in 2015,[36] and more than 97,000 students across Long Island, New York—51.2 percent of those in grades 3 through 8—opted out of the SBAC for English language arts in 2017.[37] Among the core concerns are questions about student data and privacy, demands on time and technology, and tests' validity and reliability in assessing students' actual learning. These are among the very concerns spurring on the "opt-out" movement, as well.

The twenty-seven states currently not affiliated with either consortium are using other assessments—including the SAT or ACT—to gauge students' English language arts and math achievement vis-à-vis the CCSS if they adopted them, or their own state standards if they did not. Likewise, states are in various stages of decision making around the adoption of other new standards, like the Next Generation Science Standards, discussed in Chapter 5, and the aligned assessments now available for use.

As mentioned earlier, when it comes to assessments, federal policy (i.e., the Every Student Succeeds Act) now requires that they measure higher-order thinking and understanding; enables the incorporation of multiple assessments including portfolios, projects, or extended-performance tasks; and offers states an opportunity to apply for inclusion in pilot programs aimed at developing new and innovative large-scale assessments. What this will mean in the coming years, and in the post-Trump election political climate, is up for debate.

Irrespective of what transpires at the state and federal level, it's teachers who do much of day-to-day assessment in classrooms; with this work, they can play an incredibly powerful role in advancing social justice.

Classroom-Based Assessment

> I have come to believe that assessment is one of the most overlooked challenges, especially if one departs from the multiple-choice/pencil-and-paper/procedural tests that are nicely provided in the Teacher's Edition. Do I just walk around the room and give grades based on content of discussion? How do I respond to the author of a journal entry who already understood the concept versus the hardworking author who finally achieved some degree of understanding? Do I respond differently? Will it take me a solid week to grade the test with open-ended questions? What if a good student does a poor job when editing another student's paper? How do I use the results of assessments to guide my teaching or grade student achievement?
>
> As a new teacher, I tried a variety of methods to begin learning how to assess my students' mathematical understanding and use the information to inform my instructional practices. I used writing as an assessment tool as much as I could. Students had to write about their process of solving the problem. Strategies, false starts, steps they took, diagrams that helped—all these items and more were part of the process about which I wanted students to write. Not only did I want to know what they were doing and why, I wanted them to have to reason and justify their thought process. I did learn an incredible amount about how students think about mathematics. By giving students an opportunity to articulate their internal thought processes, I was able to assess understanding of the problem. I could identify strengths or weaknesses in their logic and help them, or comment accordingly.
>
> —Juliana Jones
> First-year teacher, middle-school mathematics

In the midst of all the current attention to large-scale assessments, it is important to remember that teachers still select or make many of the assessments that students experience in school. In their classrooms, teachers can assess student learning in humanizing, authentic ways; their decisions can support students to demonstrate the fullness of what they know and can do. In the remainder of this chapter, we turn to some of the day-in and day-out assessment practices that teachers use. In doing so, we return to the social and cultural dimensions of learning described in Chapter 6. We also revisit the concepts of alternative and authentic assessment, including performance assessment, raised earlier in this chapter. We offer examples of how assessment can support the work of teachers who reject traditional conceptions of intelligence, who are transforming traditional teaching practices, and who are working to advance social justice in their classrooms.

Moving Beyond Traditional Assessments

Since the dawn of behavioral psychology and scientific testing more than a century ago, classroom teachers have used assessment to gather samples of students' knowledge in order to make inferences about the extent to which students have learned the curriculum. Like behavioral psychologists, teachers have often focused their assessments on what they can observe *after* learning has taken place—whether students can recall what they have learned. Assessments like these, which take place *after* learning and serve as *final* evaluations of student performance, are considered *summative* assessments: they summarize what students have learned. In most cases, summative assessments—including those that are teacher made or taken from textbooks (typically including multiple-choice, true-false, and fill-in-the blank items)—end up mimicking large-scale tests.

Like commercial test makers, teachers often call such tests "objective." However, teachers' decisions about which questions to include, how to grade, how much time to allot for instruction and test taking, and how to weigh the importance of a given test are all subjective. In the classroom, teachers typically do not have formal norm groups against which to judge students' performances, but they may have an informal protocol (or "curve") for giving the top few performances As, and the lowest Ds and Fs—based as much on how the class as a whole performs as on a single student's actual number of correct answers.

Of course, most teachers—especially those who view learning as social and cultural—also use *alternative* assessment strategies. They scrutinize essays, performances, and projects in order to assess how well students understand and can apply what they've learned. But, in the tradition of scientific efficiency and behaviorism, even assessments that are more performance based, like these, often have been treated as samples of students' knowledge that can be extrapolated "objectively." Thus, a teacher's reading of an essay might be translated into points (87), the points into a grade (B plus), the grade into a class grade (B), which then is converted back into points in order to calculate grade point average.

Principles to Guide Authentic Assessment

Despite the long history of traditional assessment and today's pressures around standardized testing, many teachers are turning to alternative assessment strategies. To assist with this, the National Forum on Assessment, a coalition of education and civil rights organizations, came together more than twenty years ago to develop a set of foundational guiding principles. Although it hoped to influence large-scale testing, its primary commitment was to help educators put learning at the center of classroom assessment, to integrate assessment with curriculum and instruction, and to ensure that assessments were fair to all of the nation's diverse students. Concept Table 7.2 includes the seven principles of assessment that the forum believed would help achieve these goals.

Educators Carol Ann Tomlinson and Jay McTighe build on these seven principles with an additional three principles of effective assessment. Defining assessment as a process by which teachers make inferences about student learning, Tomlinson and McTighe first encourage teachers to collect a "photo album" (rather than a "snapshot") of evidence for each student, as a means of increasing the reliability of teachers' inferences about student progress. To illustrate this point,

Concept Table 7.2 Principles of High-Quality Assessment Systems

Principle	Characteristics and actions of a high-quality assessment system
1. Assessments' primary purpose is to improve student learning.	Is organized around improving student learning. Provides information about students' progress toward learning goals. Employs practices and methods consistent with curriculum, instruction, and learning. Integrates with curriculum and instruction. Uses methods such as structured and informal observations and interviews, projects and tasks, tests, performances and exhibitions, audio- and videotapes, experiments, portfolios, and journals. Limits use of multiple-choice methods. Limits use of assessments intended to rank-order or compare students.
2. Assessment used for other purposes also supports student learning.	Bases important decisions, such as graduation, on information gathered over time, not a single assessment. Uses information for accountability and improvement that comes from both regular, continuing classroom work and large-scale assessments. Uses sampling procedures in accountability assessments to minimize burden on students. Applies rigorous technical standards to ensure high-quality assessments. Monitors the educational consequences of the particular assessment tools.
3. Assessment systems are fair to all students.	Doesn't limit students' present and future opportunities. Allows multiple methods for students to express knowledge and understanding. Reflects a student's actual knowledge. Is adapted to meet the specific needs of particular populations, such as English Learners and students with disabilities. Uses methods that students have been taught. Has been studied and approved by bias review committees.
4. Professional collaboration and development support assessment.	Helps educators understand the full range of assessment purposes. Helps educators use a variety of methods appropriately. Ensures that educators collaborate. Has the support of states, districts, and schools. Improves educators' capability as assessors. Prepares teachers to assess diverse student populations. Allows educators to score student work at the district or state level.
5. The broader community participates in assessment development.	Draws on the community's knowledge. Discusses assessment purposes and methods with a wide range of people—including parents, community members, and students—who help shape the assessment system.
6. Communication about assessment is regular and clear.	Ensures educators discuss assessment system practices and student and program progress with students, families, and the community. Ensures educators (and experts) communicate, in ordinary language, assessment purposes, methods, and results. Reports information about what students know and are able to do, what they need to do, and what will be done to facilitate improvement. Reports achievement in terms of agreed-upon learning goals. Offers information in translation as needed. Provides examples of assessments and high-quality student work. Provides contextual information such as education programs, social data, resource availability, and other student outcomes.
7. Assessment systems are regularly reviewed and improved.	Seeks to make assessments more educationally beneficial to all students. Adapts to changing conditions and increased knowledge. Focuses cost-benefit analyses of the system on the effects of assessment on learning.

Source: National Forum on Assessment, *Principles and Indicators for Student Assessment Systems,* FairTest: The National Center for Fair and Open Testing, 1991, www.fairtest.org/princind.htm.

Concept Table 7.3 The Six Facets of Understanding

When we truly understand, we:

- can **explain** via generalizations or principles; provide justified and systematic accounts of phenomena, facts, and data; make insightful connections and provide illuminating examples or illustrations.

- can **interpret:** tell meaningful stories; offer apt translations; provide a revealing historical or personal dimension to ideas and events; make it personal or accessible through images, anecdotes, analogies, and models.

- can **apply:** effectively use and adapt what we know in diverse and real contexts—we can "do" the subject.

- have **perspective:** see and hear points of view through critical eyes and ears; see the big picture.

- display **empathy:** find value in what others find odd, alien, or implausible; perceive sensitively on the basis of prior direct experience.

- demonstrate and deepen **self-knowledge:** show metacognitive awareness; perceive the personal style, prejudices, projections, and habits of mind that both shape and impede our own understanding; be aware of what we do not understand; reflect on the meaning of learning and experience.

Source: Excerpted from Carol Ann Tomlinson and Jay McTighe, *Integrating Differentiated Instruction and Understanding by Design* (Alexandria, VA: Association for Supervision and Instruction, 2006), 67.

they explain that teachers interested in gauging students' number sense and ability to complete numerical operations could have students engage in a role-play as store cashiers, complete paper-and-pencil worksheets and quizzes on addition and subtraction, and also provide oral and written explanations for correct and incorrect solutions to addition and subtraction problems.

Second, Tomlinson and McTighe emphasize that assessments must measure what students are expected to know, understand, and be able to do in relation to specific learning goals. This principle presses teachers to consider the question, "How will we know that students *truly* understand what we have aimed to teach?" Concept Table 7.3 provides guidance for answering this crucial but thorny question.

The third principle—that "form" should follow "function"—encourages teachers to consider whether assessments align with their purposes for assessing as well as their goals regarding how results will be used. For example, whereas a summative assessment would need an evaluative component, a diagnostic assessment would need components that effectively gauge students' prior knowledge and understandings about a given topic. Similarly, assessment results meant to be shared with students' families during parent-teacher conferences might need to look different from those intended for district administrators.[38]

The two sets of assessment principles described above—those of the National Forum on Assessment and those of Tomlinson and McTighe—lay the groundwork for a balanced and authentic approach to assessment. Undergirded by these principles, classroom assessments can promote learning and social justice because they support students' beliefs that their hard work will result in learning. Assessments that embody these principles can reinforce instruction that is increasingly rich, complex, and full of meaning; they can encourage and enhance lessons that offer authentic tasks with a variety of routes to success. Further, such assessments can help teachers avoid the easy comparisons made possible by grades, numbers, and rankings, which everyone in the classroom and throughout the school can transform into destructive judgments about who is smart and who isn't. The remainder of the chapter shows how teachers are using assessments in promising ways.

Assessments That Inform Instruction and Promote Learning

Teachers who rely on assessment to inform their instruction oftentimes use *diagnostic* and *formative* assessments in addition to summative assessments. Diagnostic assessments—generally administered before instruction begins—aim to gather information about students' prior knowledge and understandings; teachers then use assessment outcomes to guide future instruction. Formative assessments are administered on an ongoing basis, take place alongside instruction, and attend to the *processes* that occur *during* learning. Similar to diagnostic assessments, formative assessments provide information that teachers can use when designing whole-class instruction and determining how to differentiate instruction for individual learners. Formative assessments can incorporate approaches that are traditional or performance based and formal (e.g., paper-and-pencil tests) or informal (e.g., observations, ungraded quizzes or reflections).

High school social studies teacher Judy Smith uses assessment formatively throughout her lessons to enhance learning, not just at the end to see what students have learned. For example, she began her global economics unit on sweatshops with a diagnostic assessment designed to gauge what her students already knew about the topic.

> I introduced students to the concept of sweatshops by having their teams analyze pictures and cartoons of sweatshops. During this "write around" activity, the students analyzed the pictures, wrote comments, questions, thoughts, and feelings. . . . When they finished, each group explained the images to the class. Then, on the back of the "write around" sheet, I asked, "Now that you have an image of a sweatshop, how would you describe one? What goes on in a sweatshop?" We played with the word *sweatshop* and with the interpretations of the pictures. Students wrote for a while as a way to learn and understand more from the images, their group's knowledge, and classroom discussion.
>
> This informal assessment of their prior knowledge was useful to me. I learned that the students had very little knowledge about actual sweatshop conditions although they did gain some initial impressions.
>
> —Judy Smith
> High school social studies

During the unit, Judy constantly assessed her students' learning. On one occasion, she asked them to write a letter to a CEO of a company that supports sweatshops so that she could assess how the students' knowledge about global economics was developing.

For both formative and summative assessment, first-year history teacher Jennifer Garcia often uses concept maps—an approach where students graphically represent how their prior ideas relate to each other and to new ideas that the teacher introduces. This visual representation of information and relationships was developed by Paul Novak in the 1970s and is solidly based in cognitive (learning) science. Since then, mapping has been widely used in education, the sciences, computer programming (including gaming), and more. Much of mapping's value lies in multiple participants—students and teacher—sharing (contributing, discussing, questioning) different representations of how complex ideas are "put together." In this process, the teacher can gain insight into how a student *thinks about* complex problems and support core understandings in addition to knowing relevant facts.

> I used concept maps in a variety of circumstances—from a quick comprehension check to an alternative way of assessing at the end of my unit on World War I and Progressive Politics. Concept maps allow teachers (and students) to determine whether critical historical connections are being made. They test comprehension, not facts, and focus on what students know and the connections they can make, instead of what they don't know. They ask students to demonstrate historical understandings at a deeper level than a more traditional objective form of assessment (i.e., multiple choice, matching) because students must relate concepts to each other.
>
> One student, for example, connected the events of World War I pre–U.S. involvement to events in World War I post–U.S. involvement. However, his concept map told me that while he was able to recall many specifics from this historical period, he did not address the larger concepts.
>
> This format leaves plenty of room for individual differences; students realize that there is no one "correct" answer and that there is room for individual interpretation and analysis. Allowing for this type of maximum freedom (as much as is possible in a formal assessment situation) allows students of all abilities and types of intelligence to succeed academically.
>
> —Jennifer Garcia
> First-year teacher, history, grade 11

Assessment that promotes learning is often not limited to traditional academic content. Mauro Bautista used assessment throughout a "college and careers" unit he taught his middle-school students who were still learning English. Mauro wanted to be sure that his students had the knowledge they needed to navigate successfully toward their career goals. He also designed the unit to meet language arts standards and his school district's particular expectations. As he introduced the unit, he engaged students in a writing assignment that allowed him to assess what his students already knew about careers. Embracing the principle that assessment's primary purpose is to improve student learning, Mauro scaffolded his students' efforts to develop their knowledge, even as he was assessing it.

> Taking into account that students are generally more engaged when their interests guide instruction, the "big idea" in this lesson was to identify my students' career goals, so that their interests could guide the rest of the unit. I asked students to answer the following question in a free write: Where will your life be in fifteen years? Students had the option of using their home language to document their ideas in detail.

I provided the following support questions: What occupation do you want to have in fifteen years? Why do you want to have that occupation? Do you know anyone who has that occupation? If yes, who? What do you need to do in order to have that occupation? These questions helped me further assess what students knew about their future career goals.

—Mauro Bautista
Middle-school bilingual education coordinator

Mauro noted that very few of his students understood that they would need to pursue higher education if they wanted to achieve their dreams of being teachers, doctors, and architects. He used this information—gathered through diagnostic assessment—to design learning activities that would allow students to understand and to feel competent about what they needed to do to set themselves up for success in their future careers. He later employed formative assessments that measured students' developing knowledge at every step of the process.

In each of these examples, teachers seamlessly integrate assessment into their instruction; that is, their assessment becomes indistinguishable from their efforts to facilitate student learning. In addition, these examples reflect teachers' efforts to align assessments with established learning goals and to gather "photo albums" of evidence that can be used to make accurate inferences about learning and to inform future instruction.

Assessments That Provide Multiple Routes to Success

In Chapter 6, we described multidimensional instruction that allows students to learn and demonstrate learning in multiple ways; we also provided the list of features that Elizabeth Cohen uses to characterize multidimensional tasks. Since these features are as important to assessment as they are to instruction, we repeat Cohen's list here. Indeed, these features characterize assessments that allow for student differences and avoid narrow definitions of competence or mastery.

Assessments that provide multiple routes to success:

- include more than one answer or more than one way to solve the problem;
- are intrinsically interesting and rewarding;
- allow different students to make different contributions;
- use multimedia;
- involve sight, sound, and touch;
- require a variety of skills and behaviors;
- require reading and writing; and
- are challenging.

Role playing, building models, drawing "mind maps" of the relationship among ideas, and describing relationships by manipulating objects all represent potentially powerful methods for facilitating and assessing learning.

Tomlinson and McTighe also emphasize that when teachers respond to student differences, they must also differentiate assessment by providing students with individually relevant feedback "early and often" and by asking students to reflect on their own learning. Students become more deeply engaged when *they* are encouraged to make decisions about their learning and assessment—for example, by choosing from a menu of options for demonstrating their knowledge, skills, and understandings. (Focal Point 7.3 presents a "tic-tac-toe" structure devised by Tomlinson and McTighe for offering product and performance options that keep end learning goals in sight; we have updated it slightly.) Importantly, offering students options is only a first step. Teachers who differentiate assessments must also create *differentiated assessment tools* (i.e.,

	Focal Point 7.3	
	Product and Performance Tic-Tac-Toe	
Written	*Visual*	*Oral*
Research report	Poster	Lesson presentation
News article	Graphic organizer	Oral presentation
Information brochure	PowerPoint	Radio interview
Blog post	Curated Tumblr	Song or spoken-word poem

Source: Excerpted and adapted slightly from Carol Ann Tomlinson and Jay McTighe, *Integrating Differentiated Instruction and Understanding by Design* (Alexandria, VA: Association for Supervision and Instruction, 2006), 74.

rubrics) that allow for the evaluation of features specific to different products and performances (e.g., composition and use of color for a poster, delivery rate and eye contact for oral presentations). At the same time, Tomlinson and McTighe explain that differentiated rubrics must also collect evidence based on *shared* content-related objectives. In other words, differentiated rubrics must contain criteria that vary by product, as well as criteria that are content related and, therefore, universal.[39]

Many of the teachers profiled in this book use the assessment strategies advanced by Cohen and Tomlinson and McTighe. For example, Jennifer Garcia describes how she incorporated student choice in the open-ended concept mapping task she used to assess her students' understandings of important historical concepts and events.

> I created a demonstration project assessment to assess students' historical understandings of the connections between the concepts of industrialization, unionism, and immigration (i.e., how they could tie together themes such as immigration trends, political machines, early union efforts, factory conditions, production changes, changes in gender roles, etc.). I did not set limits on the format, but I suggested some possible ideas.
>
> Students created immigrant journals, posters and advertisements, and original songs that showed they were able to incorporate both the historical evidence and creativity and originality at a deeper intellectual level. In the immigrant journals, students assumed the persona of an immigrant who came to the United States during the 1880s. Common themes included descriptions of what countries they immigrated from, why they immigrated, their immigration journey, living conditions in urban areas, factory working conditions (union vs. nonunion), and so on.
>
> These journals were not re-creations or copies of texts/outside resources—they were original stories that students developed from lectures and their impressions of what experiences real people went through. This was a new form of assessment for many students, and I was unsure about how seriously students would take it. I was impressed with the success, particularly for those who do not test well. I learned that it is a strategy to give students a variety of ways to be assessed so that each student can succeed, allowing their individual strengths to shine through.
>
> —Jennifer Garcia
> First-year teacher, history, grade 11

Likewise, Mauro Bautista recounted asking his students to demonstrate their understanding of their future careers by constructing collages using a wide range of materials. Mauro observed,

"The collages offered an opportunity for students who are artistically inclined to excel. They also provided visual scaffolding for the writing and oral presentations."

Assessments That Emphasize Content First, Language Second

Bryan Brown, an education professor at Stanford University, recently proposed a promising new approach for differentiating assessment so that it supports students to demonstrate what they know and can do. Specifically, Brown's research shows that discipline-specific, "academic" language often gets in the way of students demonstrating understanding. Brown therefore developed a "content-first" approach to assessment that permits students to use everyday language to talk or write about content. For example, if photosynthesis is the focus of instruction, initial assessments (and instruction) might include questions and answers that use commonly understood words such as *light*, *sugar*, *water*, *air humans breathe out*, and *good air*. Delaying the introduction of technical terms allows students to build understanding of new concepts to which they can then attach specialized and often abstract vocabulary. Such assessments avoid confusing students' struggles with vocabulary (or language generally) with determinations of whether they understand the content and concepts.

Of course, learning the academic vocabulary associated with the disciplines is important for understanding and for school success. A content-first approach introduces academic language to deepen students' knowledge—building first from students' understandings expressed in everyday terms. Thus, as in the example above, when students become familiar with the role of "sugar" and "breathing" in plant biology, they will learn about glucose and carbon dioxide. Similarly, subsequent assessments require students to engage with academic content and academic language simultaneously.

This approach to assessment enables teachers to understand whether students need support with language, with content, or with both. With this approach and others, the best clues for assessing students' needs often come from informal assessments, on-the-spot observations, and interpretations of classroom interactions.[40]

Assessments That Are Interactive

As students construct logical answers that include descriptions, facts, experiences, and problems, they *use* their knowledge to sort, form, and conclude. This process complicates and enriches their knowledge, more than if they simply repeated facts or tried to recognize and choose the correct answer on a paper-and-pencil test.

When teachers and students go back and forth during assessments, teachers can adjust on the spot to help students express what they know. Only in an interactive situation can a teacher sense when it is appropriate to say, "Take a few more seconds to think about it" or "Let's skip that for now; we can come back to it later." Such interactions can be open ended. When teachers ask students questions like, "What do you think of that?," "What will you do next?," "Why did you do it that way?," and "How did you figure that out?," teachers get as close as they can to the heart of students' learning. Students, in turn, offer responses that reveal their sense making—not just their conclusions.

Interactive assessments generate responses that guide teachers as they help, explain, and provide feedback. Both teachers and students can make "course corrections" when students get stuck. These exchanges can help students become more comfortable with assessment and increase their efforts to do better. Students can come to see assessment as a process by which a caring and knowledgeable person helps them identify and overcome roadblocks to learning. Jennifer Garcia used journals as a forum for such "informal and comfortable" dialogues.

> I used journal entries as a continuous form of informal assessment, and as a means of communicating more personally with students about what they were learning and how they felt

about it. The goal was not to elicit any particular "correct" response, but to allow students to find their own voices and write about what interested them. . . . Keeping the journal provided an opportunity for students to take time to reflect and opened up an informal and comfortable dialogue between the students and me (particularly for those learning English as a second language, who are often reluctant to participate in other ways). Many commented that they appreciated time to reflect and ask questions in a private way, and . . . that they appreciated the response comments by me. This form of informal assessment can help develop self-confidence and student voice.

—Jennifer Garcia
First-year teacher, history, grade 11

If students receive feedback in the form of new questions and subtle encouragement, it can prompt them to explore beyond their first hunches. Unlike conventional testing, or classroom question-and-answer sessions—where students' first inclination might be to say "I don't know," or to select any answer just to get over the discomfort—interactive assessments can encourage students to raise their own questions as they explain what they have learned.

Teachers can keep interactive assessments nonthreatening and nonjudgmental, in part because they can be negotiable. That is, teachers don't need to ask all students the same questions. Furthermore, teachers can accept many answers at many different levels of sophistication, depending on the questions and on students' prior knowledge.

Assessments That Are Personalized

Teachers can assess individual students' progress without encouraging public comparisons. However, most teachers still work in schools with policies that require traditional evaluations and record keeping. A goal, then, is to use authentic assessments to promote a classroom culture that encourages progress, while also protecting privacy and discouraging unhealthy competition and comparison. One high school teacher discussed such concerns with his class, and the class agreed to this policy: "*Do* inquire about classmates' grades if you are genuinely interested in their progress, if you have worked with or helped them on the assignment, and if you care about them. If you do inquire, do so outside of class. *Do not* sneak a look at someone's grade or shout out 'Wadja get?'"

Increasingly, teachers are balancing traditional evaluations with opportunities for students to demonstrate to others their growing competence. When others can witness and respond to students' work, assessment *and* learning continue together. For example, when Mauro Bautista's students presented their career-focused collages, he supported the rest of the class in answering a set of collectively developed questions about the substance of their peers' work. As language learners, Mauro's students were learning unfamiliar content, how to present academic knowledge, and what was expected of them during different kinds of classroom interaction.

The presenters consistently spoke confidently, referring to their collages as necessary. The "audience" also did an excellent job. We created a personalized chart for each presenter that incorporated the students' personal goals. The audience filled out the chart as their classmates were presenting. The charts kept the audience actively engaged in the presentations.

For instance, when Julia presented, the three questions on her chart were: What is one thing on Julia's collage? What are two things Julia needs to do to become a doctor? What did you like best about her presentation? José answered the questions accordingly, "One thing on Julia's collage is doctor allundando [*sic*] a un paciente [doctor helping a patient]." "Good grades and graduate school." "Me gusto como ella leyó [I liked how she read]."

—Mauro Bautista
Middle-school bilingual education coordinator

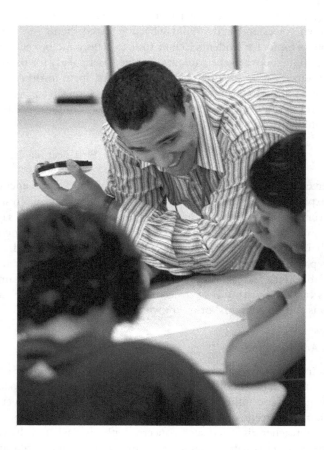

As previously mentioned, many teachers personalize assessment by asking their students to collect samples of their work over time in a portfolio—similar to the practice of artists, who keep samples of their work, and similar to the idea of the "photo album" of evidence put forth by McTighe and Tomlinson. Students might include writing samples, experiments, lists of books they've read, math problems they've solved, and more. Portfolios work well when they go beyond simply collecting all work and instead press students to select work that represents their best achievements and growth, as well as their greatest investments of effort. Here, too, Judy Smith's assessments of her global economics unit provide a useful example.

On the last day of class, students turned in their portfolios. In the folder, they wrote me a letter reflecting on their learning during the unit. I could see whether the students achieved the unit learning goals: learn about international trade and the economic and social results of colonialism and neocolonialism and learn how their individual consumer habits and beliefs impacted the environment, other cultures and peoples, and themselves.

The reflection included three parts. First, the students picked one assignment that they felt best demonstrated what they learned and explained why they picked that assignment over other assignments, what it made them think about, and how it demonstrated their learning. Second, they wrote an essay in which they reflected on their performance during the role-play and on the responsibility we have for what is happening to indigenous groups and rain forests in places like Ecuador. Finally, they reviewed their entire portfolio and wrote about their personal habits of consumption and what they might change. I asked what they thought they would remember in ten years and why. I requested that they document a question that the unit raised for them.

—Judy Smith
High school social studies

Assessment strategies like these allow teachers, parents, classmates, and students themselves to reflect on and discuss what's been learned.

Assessments That Include "Authentic" Tasks

Linda Darling-Hammond, among others, proposes that assessments should be based on "meaningful performances in real-world contexts" and that these performances should be so "closely entwined as to be often inseparable" from the curriculum itself.[41] She points to schools that engage students in demonstrating their learning in exhibitions and portfolios with "products like mathematical models, literary critiques, scientific experiments, dance performances, debates, and oral presentations and defense of ideas."[42] In such performances, students are required to *apply* what they've learned, allowing teachers to assess students' conceptual knowledge and problem-solving skills, neither of which can be easily measured with conventional testing.

Researchers at the University of Wisconsin have established criteria for use in developing high-quality authentic assessments. In their view, students should be engaged in a task that requires they construct knowledge through the use of discipline-specific inquiry that has some value or meaning beyond success in school.[43] Thus, biology students would present their findings as biologists might, by writing a report, presenting at a conference, or demonstrating and discussing an experiment (this, of course, during and after authentic learning experiences in which they have learned as biologists learn—by reading, working collaboratively, reporting and checking findings, etc.).

Judy Smith describes a debate that simultaneously engaged students in deepening and applying their learning and allowed her the opportunity to assess it. It is a performance task that illustrates what Darling-Hammond and the Wisconsin researchers mean by authentic.

> With one week left to go in the unit, I introduced the final project—the role play. I hoped that students would debate progress versus tradition. I also wanted them to experience the ethical dilemmas that corporations face when pursuing profit. Students represented one of six roles—Indigenous Indians, Oil Company, Workers, Missionaries, Environmentalists, and the System of Profit. Fulfilling these roles by writing interior monologues, building alliances, and then debating, students made meaning of the issues and demonstrated their learning in an intellectual space. Students had already learned about profit, capitalism, power, gross domestic product, and neocolonialism. The two-day debate . . . allowed the students to enact a real dilemma that continues to plague our global community today.
>
> —Judy Smith
> High school social studies

As the students participate in these performance tasks, Judy and teachers like her take note of the knowledge and skills students display. They observe how students interact and how they solve problems. They closely follow the nature and appropriateness of students' reasoning as well as the correctness of their answers. They analyze students' responses to uncover gaps and errors in students' thinking, to recognize and address problems in their own instruction, and to help frame new strategies for pressing students forward.

Authentic performance tasks also include performing the real-world tasks that their learning makes possible. As the culminating project in his career and college unit, for example, Mauro Bautista assessed his students' understanding of successful pathways toward college and careers by having his middle-school students fill out college applications that included calculating their grade point average, writing their personal statement, and submitting letters of recommendation. These constituted real drafts of the very applications they now expected to finalize years later.

A Culture of Authenticity

Ongoing authentic assessment challenges students to go beyond the usual classroom study habits of skimming the chapters, doing the problems, studying for the test, and never again bothering with the material. Moreover, reasoning and figuring out take place *as part of* the learning and assessment process, not at the end of the unit and just before the test. Engaging students in authentic assessment also has a way of positively permeating classroom culture. Students' interactions take on the values, habits, and skills that contribute to a vibrant and caring learning community. Not to mention, these methods of evaluating and reporting also help teachers to communicate substantive and meaningful information to parents about what their children have learned, and how well.

Authentic assessment challenges teachers to look beyond single measures or high-stakes tests that rank students and can lead to fixed labels—competent or incompetent, able or unable, intelligent or unintelligent, and so forth. Fundamental to authentic assessment is the teacher's ability and willingness to see all students as capable learners. With that understanding in place, teachers can hold *themselves* accountable for using a variety of assessments to determine what students know and guiding them to reach rigorous learning goals.

Digging Deeper and Tools for Critique

www.routledge.com/cw/teachingtochangetheworld

Notes

1 "What Is Authentic Assessment?" *Authentic Assessment Toolbox*, http://jfmueller.faculty.noctrl. edu/toolbox/whatisit.htm.
2 C. T. Hu, "The Historical Background: Examinations and Control in Pre-Modern China," *Comparative Education* 20 (1984): 17, as cited in F. Allan Hanson, *Testing Testing: Social Consequences of the Examined Life* (Berkeley: University of California Press, 1993), 191, http://ark.cdlib.org/ark:/13030/ft4m3nb2h2/.
3 Hanson, *Testing Testing*, 191.
4 Ibid.
5 Ibid.
6 Quoted in Isaac L. Kandel, *Examinations and Their Substitutes in the United States* (New York: Carnegie Foundation for the Advancement of Teaching, 1936), as quoted in Hanson, *Testing Testing*, 194.
7 Hanson, *Testing Testing*, 194.
8 Rudolph T. Shappee, "Serving the City's Children: San Diego City Schools, the First Fifty Years," *Journal of San Diego History* 37, no. 2 (Spring 1991), www.sandiegohistory.org/journal/91spring/schools.htm.
9 Larry Cuban, *How Teachers Taught: Constancy and Change in American Classrooms 1880–1990* (New York: Teachers College Press, 1994).
10 German psychologist Wilhelm Wundt introduced what might have become in America a third line of inquiry—the systematic analysis of the perceptions, interpretations, and judgments that people report. Wundt was influential in Europe, but American investigators found Wundt's procedures—talking to people and recording what they report—less than scientific.

11 Quoted in Stephen J. Gould, *The Mismeasure of Man*, 2nd ed. (New York: Norton, 1996), 190.

12 Quoted in ibid., 121.

13 Quoted in ibid., 301.

14 Moreover, Gould calls *The Bell Curve*, published in 1994, "little more than a hard-line version of Spearman's *g*." Gould, *The Mismeasure of Man*, 35.

15 Kenneth Sirotnik, "Equal Access to Quality in Public Schooling: Issues in the Assessment of Equity and Excellence," in *Access to Knowledge: The Continuing Agenda for Our Nation's Schools*, rev. ed., eds. John I. Goodlad and Pamela Keating (New York: The College Board, 1994), 162.

16 Howard W. Haggard, preface to *Tisn't What You Know, But Are You Intelligent?* (New York: Harper and Brothers, 1927), 6, 8.

17 Ibid., 8.

18 College Board Online, *Test Question of the Day*, March 16, 1998, http://sat.collegeboard.org/practice/sat-question-of-the-day.

19 Lawrence H. Summers, *Remarks at NBER Conference on Diversifying the Science and Engineering Workforce* (Cambridge, MA: Harvard Office of the President, June 14, 2005).

20 Jon Wiener, "Why Did Harvard Give a PhD for a Discredited Approach to Race and IQ?" *The Nation*, May 11, 2013.

21 Noe Medina and Monty Neill, *Fallout From the Testing Explosion: How 100 Million Standardized Exams Undermine Equity and Excellence in America's Public Schools*, 3rd ed. (Cambridge, MA: FairTest, 1990).

22 Council of Great City Schools, *Student Testing in American's Great City Schools: An Inventory and Preliminary Analysis*, October 2015, www.cgcs.org/cms/lib/DC00001581/Centricity/Domain/87/Testing%20Report.pdf.

23 Robin Jacobowitz and K. T. Tobin, *Time on Test: The Fixed Costs of 3–8 Standardized Testing in New York State* (New Paltz, NY: The Benjamin Center for Public Policy Initiatives, 2015).

24 PISA stands for the Programme for International Student Assessment, a worldwide study of math, science, and reading achievement conducted by the Organization for Economic Cooperation and Development.

25 For example, see Herman Aguinis, Steven A. Culpepper, and Charles A. Pierce, "Differential Prediction Generalization in College Admissions Testing," *Journal of Education Psychology* 108, no. 7 (October 2016), 1045–1059.

26 College Board Online, *Test Question of the Day*.

27 *Regents Exam Study Guides: The Complete Series*, www.studyworld.com/books/study_guides/regents_exam_study_guides_.htm.

28 Linda Darling-Hammond, *The Right to Learn* (San Francisco: Jossey-Bass, 1997), 59–60.

29 Robert J. Mislevy, "Foundations of a New Test Theory," in *Test Theory for a New Generation of Tests*, eds. Norman Frederiksen, Robert J. Mislevy, and Isaac I. Bejar (Hillsdale, NJ: Lawrence Erlbaum, 1993), 1.

30 Howard Gardner, *Frames of Mind* (New York: Basic Books, 1993).

31 Gould, *The Mismeasure of Man*, 24.

32 Jerome Bruner, *Culture and Education* (Cambridge, MA: Harvard University Press, 1996), 77.

33 FairTest, "Graduation Test Update: States That Recently Eliminated or Scaled Back High School Exit Exams," January 24, 2017, www.fairtest.org/graduation-test-update-states-recently-eliminated.

34 Partnership for Assessment of Readiness for College and Careers, www.parcconline.org.

35 Smarter Balanced Assessment Consortium, www.SmarterBalanced.org.

36 John Higgins, "Backlash Against New Math, Reading Tests Ripples Across State," *Seattle Times*, July 9, 2015.

37 "Opt-outs From Common Core Test on English 2017," *Newsday*, March 31, 2017.

38 Carol Ann Tomlinson and Jay McTighe, *Integrating Differentiated Instruction and Understanding by Design* (Alexandria, VA: Association for Supervision and Instruction, 2006), 59–72.

39 Ibid., 72–82.

40 Bryan Brown and Kihyun Ryoo, "Teaching Science as a Language: A 'Content-First' Approach to Science Teaching," *Journal of Research in Science Teaching* 45 (2008): 525–664.

41 Darling-Hammond, *The Right to Learn*, 115.

42 Ibid.

43 Fred M. Newmann, Walter G. Secada, and Gary Wehlage, *A Guide to Authentic Instruction and Assessment: Vision, Standards, and Scoring* (Madison, WI: Wisconsin Center for Education Research at the University of Wisconsin, 1995), 8.

Chapter 8

Classrooms as Communities
Developing Caring and Democratic Relationships

I've observed that some first-year teachers talk about social justice but don't know how to do it when it comes to classroom management. What does social justice look like in the everyday classroom? I think it starts with respect and clear guidelines—when we are together, we learn. We have fun, and we respect each other. This is what we do.

—Judy Smith
High school social studies

Classroom management is relevant, not to empower the teacher, but to empower students—to make them feel that they belong and are safe in the class. I start off the year by asking the students what they think the rules should be. Every year, they give me a laundry list of NO: "No running, no gum chewing, no lighters (that was Jameon's comment my first year teaching), no name calling, etc." After I write down every comment, I ask the students what we are allowed to do. The students then change their language to: "Be nice, take turns, love, etc."

The words take on new meaning, and the students see the rules of the class as rules that we should abide by as humans. The students are not told "no no no"; rather, "love, be kind, etc." I think it shifts the perspective. I have never had a list of rules posted on the door before students walked in. I listen to their ideas and incorporate what I want to see and what they want to see in the class. The students also begin to see the classroom working in a democratic manner and see that I respect their voices.

—Kimberly Min
Third-grade teacher

When we asked Judy Smith and Kimberly Min about classroom management, they did not tell us about special programs or tricks to keep students under control. They told us about their approaches to teaching, their caring and respectful relationships with students, and their deep commitments to learning. For Judy and Kimberly, these are the hallmarks of teaching for social justice.

Chapter Overview

This chapter surveys the behaviorist legacies of classroom management, discipline, and control as well as an alternative perspective that promotes caring relationships and democratic communities. This second perspective makes sense to today's school officials and teachers; it is supported by research findings and personal experience. Yet, in practice, it is easy to fall into familiar behaviorist approaches. A critical perspective helps to identify the authoritarian tendencies that pervade public schools and diminish constructive action; without a critical perspective, behaviorist strategies—like using rewards, punishments, threats of failure, and so forth—may remain persuasive.

Caring and Democratic Classrooms

Like Judy Smith and Kimberly Min, first-year teacher Amy Lee sees the connection between classroom management and teaching for social justice. Her sixth-grade class included several children with serious out-of-school challenges as well as in-class misbehavior. One student, Hector, had been placed in his aunt's care when a local protective services agency decided that his mother was not fit to care for him. Amy's school expected her to follow a discipline system that included a series of increasingly severe consequences for misconduct in the classroom. The first consequence involved having students post cards with their names on them in the front of the class. Hector posted his card nearly every day.

In the beginning, my students didn't trust me. They were sixth graders on the verge of junior high school; many of them were already hardened and embittered toward school and their teachers. Many had been ridiculed, silenced, demeaned, and misunderstood, and to them, I was just another teacher who would continue to do the same. They waved their attitude like a red flag, challenging me to play their game. They expected me to live up to their low expectations of what a teacher should be. I was determined to prove them wrong.

I wanted to build relationships with my students—authentic relationships. Much of what I had read stuck with me: Be fair; allow your students a voice; teach with care, respect, and kindness. I struggled to be tolerant, giving each student the opportunity to voice his or her side. I touted fairness and mutual respect, always telling my students how much I valued their ideas and insights. However, I had to prove to them through my actions that I was sincere. I gave second chances, and, when proven wrong, admitted that I was at fault. At first, none of my efforts made any impact. I think the students believed it was a facade and that soon I would show my true, mean colors. . . .

Hector was my biggest challenge. From the first day, he was in my face, resisting any attempts at kindness. Other teachers, some of whom had never even had him in their classrooms, came and warned me about how awful he was.

Every day Hector stayed with me after school for misbehaving. He seemed surprised that I talked with him. His answers were usually short and inexpressive, or he sat like a stone and said nothing. So, at first, I did all of the talking. I told him that no matter how hard he pushed me away, I would not give up on him. I think that this was the key—not giving up. So many of his teachers in the past hit such a point of frustration with Hector that they threw up their hands and walked away. I was very close many times to doing exactly the same. He yelled at me, threw his binder through the air, and sat in class refusing to do the intelligent work that he was capable of. I quietly but firmly reprimanded him in class, and then in our conversations after school shared with him all of the good things that I saw from him during the day. I called his aunt frequently to praise him, and I visited his home.

Slowly Hector came to realize that I was real, and that I really did care. He gradually let me into his world. He started to change. He no longer sat like a stone after school and said nothing. In class, instead of reacting quickly and irrationally, I found him expressing himself and calmly telling others "how frustrated I got when . . . " instead of yelling and screaming like before. It was a miracle. Over the next few months, Hector blossomed. He became a real class leader and role model, and the other students noticed. "Wow, Ms. Lee, Hector hasn't posted his card in a whole month. He is really different from last year." He made friends and strengthened his "PR" at school. I was really proud of him; he was proud of himself.

Hector is one of the many students who touched me deeply this past year. I believe that it was the time and effort in building caring relationships that made all the difference. I had many moments filled with frustration, anger, disappointment, and apathy, but fortunately, when I was ready to walk away, the pure joys of teaching revealed themselves. I fell in love with my job this year, because I fell in love with the students I teach.

—Amy Lee
First-year teacher, grade 6

Like Judy and Kimberly, Amy has no formula or system that guarantees picture-perfect comportment—that no "Hector" will act out. Like Judy and Kimberly, she relies on trusting relationships and a community-like atmosphere to create a suitable environment for learning. Indeed, it wasn't traditional consequences—like posting a card or staying after school—that supported Hector's growth; it was Amy's relationship building that made the difference.

Management, Socialization, Discipline, and Control: Lasting Legacies

As Judy, Kimberly, Amy, and many others would attest, school administrators and experienced teachers often place enormous importance on first-year teachers' ability to control their classrooms. As a consequence, many new teachers think that without traditional discipline, their reputations will suffer as their classrooms disintegrate into chaos.

Traditional methods may bring some short-term relief from noise or disruption, but the fact that discipline "problems" persist as a constant source of school aggravation indicates that, over time, rewards, punishments, and controls simply do not produce good results.

Traditional discipline has a long history. St. Thomas Aquinas argued in the thirteenth century that schools should shape character and foster moral development—training the wills of the young as well as their minds. That is pretty much what America's earliest White settlers thought, too. Schooling in the United States was always as much or more about teaching children— especially "other" people's children—to act "right" as it was about academic learning.

Classrooms as Well-Managed Factories

Recall the descriptions in Chapters 2 and 6 of early-nineteenth-century classrooms, with students moving in orderly groups to recite their lessons with monitors. Beginning at this early time, schools tried to match the organizational efficiencies of the factories that were producing such abundant manufactured goods.[1] These efficiencies required smooth-running classrooms where many students would all do the same academic work at the same time. In such settings, little movement could be tolerated, and materials other than the most rudimentary texts, slates, tablets, pens, and pencils were either not available, too costly, or deemed unnecessary. Neither children nor adults could be left to follow their own propensities to learn and teach.

Training Dutiful Workers

Teachers in the late 1800s and early 1900s were expected to transmit to students the values and behaviors of industrialized society: respect for authority, punctuality, following directions, performing tasks with precision, tolerating the boredom of repetitive activity, and so on. The assembly-line production used in factories made equal sense for schools. In both settings, benefits were not directed to individual workers or students but to the larger enterprise of training workers for the predominant modes of production.

Between 1907 and 1927, William Bagley's teacher education textbook, *Classroom Management*, was enormously popular. Bagley made explicit connections between classroom order and assembly lines, and he advised teachers to develop rigid classroom routines to build good habits. (See Focal Point 8.1.) For example, Bagley suggested that teachers have students practice packing and unpacking their desks, marching to the blackboard, and filing through the cloakroom to collect their coats as they left the classroom. He urged teachers to march children to the lavatories before recess to develop good habits related to "bodily functions," and to teach them to assume on command a formal pose of attention.

Focal Point 8.1
Classroom Management 100 Years Ago

"One who studies educational theory aright can see in the mechanical routine of the classroom the educative forces that are slowly transforming the child from a little savage into a creature of law and order, fit for the life of civilized society."

Source: William Bagley, *Classroom Management* (New York: Macmillan, 1907), 35; we are indebted to historian Howard Zinn for bringing this quote to our attention.

Bagley and other educators turned to the expanding field of psychology for help in designing strategies that would produce student compliance. For example, Edward Thorndike's behaviorist theories led many teachers to reinforce good behavior with rewards that included conveying approval with talk, facial expressions, and gestures. For the most part, Americans believed that behavior could be "scientifically" controlled or "conditioned," as Ivan Pavlov had demonstrated with his animal research.

Throughout the twentieth century, systems for producing student learning and for producing goods and services followed mostly parallel paths.

Managing for High-Quality Work

In the 1970s and 1980s, the United States' unquestioned dominance of world markets was eroding—particularly in those areas that hit closest to American pride, such as electronics and automobiles. Much of America's faith in the infallibility of traditional business practices diminished. Some business analysts looked to other countries, particularly Japan and Scandinavia, for their "secrets" and discovered that more cooperative and humanistic production models could produce greater job satisfaction and commitment along with efficiently manufactured, high-quality products. This emphasis on respect for the dignity and worth of workers struck a chord with many Americans. They also seemed like good business—a combination too appealing to resist.

Concerning behavior management in the classroom, psychiatrist William Glasser was especially influential. Borrowing from and adding to these enlightened management perspectives, he argued that students take action to meet basic human needs—in his view, survival, love, fun, power, and freedom—and prefer productive choices if those choices are available. The key, for Glasser, was to give students responsibility in choosing those actions that would fulfill their own needs. Glasser's choice theory (originally called control theory) thus emphasizes that a successful teacher-manager's role is to provide students with a "satisfying picture" of the desired activity; to "empower" students by allowing them to choose and experience the consequences of their actions; and to stress cooperation, rather than punishing, overpowering, and enforcing rules.[2] Like managers in successful businesses, Glasser's ideal teachers help students understand high-quality work and its rewards.

Glasser's approach is a great improvement over many overtly behaviorist classroom management programs, some of which we discuss later in this chapter. However, the emphasis on student choice neglects many of the mediating factors that help explain, for example, Amy's effectiveness with Hector and the likelihood that Hector's struggles are far from over. Certainly, it *was* important for Amy to persevere in allowing Hector to make better choices over time, rather than trying to control him through punishment. However, she also realized that Hector's decision making was more complex than basic need fulfillment. His decisions connected powerfully to social *structures* and school *culture*, two dimensions of his life that neither he nor Amy had complete control over. To some degree, Hector and Amy negotiated parameters for acceptable behavior; to some degree, Hector gradually accepted additional scaffolding from his teacher and classmates; and, to some degree, Hector nevertheless continued to be in for a rough time at school.

Given her critical perspective, Amy understood that other teachers' classes would continue to be places that would influence Hector and that Hector would influence—not always positively. She expected, for example, that Hector might try to prove to his next teacher that Amy was an exception. In short, Amy's influence was constrained; and yet she *could* continue to work on Hector's behalf. She *could* share with other teachers how she gained Hector's trust, and she *could* try to maintain a relationship with him. Depending on a school's culture, of course, other teachers might be more or less receptive to hearing about a colleague's success with a trouble-some student, especially when the colleague has spent extraordinary time and energy in that effort.

Classrooms as Places to Socialize Youth

From the beginning, schools punished students to manage their behavior. In the early-nineteenth-century public schools that used the "monitorial" method, teachers might place a wooden log around the necks of children who talked too much or didn't do their schoolwork, or punish more serious offenders by hanging them in a sack or basket from the school roof in a place where their classmates could see them. Other schools would spank, paddle, "switch," or apply any of the typical corporal punishments of the day. Many viewed rigidly enforced behavioral controls as the best way to achieve the common school's goal of suppressing crime and unrest among the lower socioeconomic classes.

Americanizing Immigrants

Strict classroom discipline took on a particularly patriotic tone at the end of the nineteenth century. As noted in Chapter 2, by that time society wanted schools to Americanize a flood of newcomers. By 1909, 58 percent of the students in the nation's thirty-seven largest cities were foreign born, and many longer-standing residents feared a wholesale corruption of the culture. Schools responded by adding a considerable dose of patriotism to the curriculum, but Americanization was far more about behavior and discipline than about learning the substance of American culture. Through character training and strictly enforced discipline, schools aimed to extinguish the threatening foreign ways that immigrant children brought to school and to replace them with the habits, manners, and loyalties considered necessary for proper American life.

Taming the "Unruly"

The widespread adoption of compulsory education laws in the first half of the twentieth century brought into classrooms more and more unwilling students—immigrants and nonimmigrants alike—making strictness and control seem all the more necessary. After all, schools couldn't simply fire recalcitrant students the way industry could dismiss unwanted workers.

The economic trauma of the Depression in the 1930s and World War II in the 1940s damp-ened somewhat the country's worries about wayward, troublesome youth. But by the 1950s, popular films like *Blackboard Jungle* heightened fears of an increasingly belligerent younger generation—particularly in city schools. The concept of the "juvenile delinquent" gained cur-rency and provided new justification for harsh discipline. Predominantly minoritized youth, "delinquents" were a cross-cultural class of antisocial, antischool, antiauthority disruptive young people, vaguely disaffected with modern society. Their lot was to stay in school and be bother-some, drop out to no one's chagrin, or be sent away to reform schools, widely understood as one step before prison.

Correcting for "Cultural Deprivation"

By the 1960s, teachers were learning in their teacher education programs that poor children were "culturally deprived," in part because they came from "disorganized" families that failed to teach punctuality, obedience, cleanliness, respect for personal property, or the value of education.

In short, the stereotypical judgments that had previously been associated with race or nationality were stripped, in part, of their most blatant and odious prejudice (i.e., assumptions of genetic inferiority).

Instead, society adopted a new social science assertion—a nongenetic theory that attributed huge gaps in education achievement to minorities' "faulty" cultures, which "deprived" them of the "requisite" knowledge and experiences valued by White, middle-class Americans. In fact, "poor" in the 1960s served as a powerful code word also denoting race; when policymakers referred to "the poor" or "the culturally deprived," they often meant—and were taken to mean—Blacks and other minoritized groups.

The phrase *culturally deprived*, too, took on a life of its own; social scientists, educators, and the mainstream public came to see children who were not White and middle class as requiring a special set of educational treatments in order to bring them up to par with what White, middle-class children learned in their predominantly suburban communities and at home. To combat their so-called deprivation, such children, many reasoned, needed classrooms characterized by fixed routines, unambiguous rules, and firm disciplinary policies.[3]

Though most evident during the 1960s and 1970s, the rhetoric of cultural deprivation endures. For example, Ruby Payne's *Framework for Understanding Poverty* remains fairly popular, despite being publicly critiqued for its lack of scientific rigor and its stereotypical and classist depictions of lower-income students, families, and communities. According to scholars Jennifer Ng and John Rury:

> [In Payne's] descriptive scenarios, the poor are generally depicted as having a weak work ethic, little sense of internal discipline or future orientation, and leading lives characterized to one extent or another by disorder and violence. In making these characterizations, Payne seems to be unaware of the many studies dating from the late 1960s that challenged the culture of poverty thesis, in many instances directly testing the extent to which traits such as these were more prevalent among the poor than other groups. By and large, these studies found that such characteristics were not more likely to be evident in poor individuals or households. Indeed, people in poverty valued work, saving money, behaving properly, maintaining stable families, and a number of other "middle-class" attributes as much as their counterparts in higher social and economic strata. These results, moreover, held across groups with experiences of differing duration in poverty and across racial and ethnic lines.[4]

Still, Payne's consulting company—staffed by roughly forty consultants—generates significant interest and revenue from districts and schools nationwide.

Classrooms Characterized by Discipline and Control

Since the 1970s and 1980s, college courses, school district workshops, and training from profit-making corporations have offered teachers a range of detailed plans and programs for controlling classroom behavior. Most of these harken back to the theories of nineteenth- and twentieth-century psychologists like Ivan Pavlov, Edward Thorndike, and B. F. Skinner, all of whom believed in controlling behavior through positive and negative reinforcements.

Some programs use fear to intimidate disruptive students and are based on the crude behavioral theory that punishment (or fear of it) will extinguish unwanted behavior. Teachers might use the "stony stare," verbal reprimands, nonverbal signals (e.g., pointing a finger or moving close to an offender), and threats of a failing grade. In the early 1980s, many schools bought the services of Scared Straight, a program that brought teenagers in contact with jailed criminals who intimidated the students with horror stories of prison life. Like nearly every other plan to threaten, scare, and punish, Scared Straight didn't work and didn't last.

Still, many of today's commercially developed classroom management and discipline programs are built on behavioral psychology. These behavior modification programs promise prescribed, foolproof, and scientific techniques that guarantee correct behavior through rewarding, punishing, and otherwise conditioning students' thoughts and actions.

Assertive Discipline

Assertive Discipline, developed by Lee and Marlene Canter, is perhaps the most well known of the commercially available, behaviorist discipline programs.[5] The Canters' approach starts with the premise that teachers have the right and responsibility to define and enforce rules that allow them to teach. Following from this, teachers must communicate clear expectations for students' behavior and establish classroom rules. They must let students know the set of escalating and public consequences (punishments) for undesirable behavior.

Whole-class rewards (parties, candy, etc.) for collective good behavior are intended as reinforcement, as well as a means to bring social control to bear on individual students who might prevent the class from receiving a reward. Proponents claim that the preestablished punishment scheme, along with proper arrangement of classroom time and space, enables teachers to manage misbehavior without diverting their or the class's attention from learning.

Research on traditional, behaviorist programs like Assertive Discipline remains limited and unclear. Such programs may suppress misbehavior in the short term, but even if punishment works in this way, it doesn't teach acceptable behavior or quell all students' desire to misbehave. One often unrecognized effect of behaviorist strategies and their emphasis on teacher control is that when things don't go well (insufficient learning, misbehavior), it's easy to assume that the teacher didn't make the rewards and punishments clear or correct.

What we know about behaviorally oriented disciplinary approaches is that the lessons learned from punishments and rewards tend to be specific, short lived, and shallow. In other words, students learn to make judgments based on what they can "get" and "get away with," rather than learning to read the environment and make complex choices that are appropriate for themselves and the community.

In more recent years, the Canters—and Glasser, too, before his death in 2013—have embraced more community-like and cooperative classrooms. Yet their approaches remain individualistic and teacher centered, where individual students make behavioral choices (with consequences for themselves and sometimes for others, too), and the teacher retains moral and behavioral authority. Other similar systems—including token reinforcement, contingency contracts, and Positive Behavior Interventions and Supports (PBIS) programs—rely more on preventative rewards than reactive punishments. These systems may be less mechanical and rule bound and may offer more opportunity for proactive learning and meaningful sense making. However, they, too, have been criticized for emphasizing teachers' power over students rather than students' capacities for problem solving. In addition, substantial evidence indicates that giving external rewards for good behavior can diminish students' intrinsic motivation to learn and abide by classroom social norms; lacking authentic engagement and "going through the motions" of reward-worthy behavior produces few long-term benefits and possibly cynicism toward school and learning.[6]

First-year kindergarten teacher Javier Espindola initially thought that the reward-and-punish strategies used by many teachers in his school would help him motivate his students. Before long, however, he changed his mind.

When my students were sitting quietly and listening to me or when they were on task writing in their journals, I would give them a sticker or happy face to motivate them to continue that behavior. When I saw them talking with peers and not working, I would put their names on the board or give them a sad face.

At first, these strategies worked. Over time, however, I noticed negative effects. Students . . . began to refuse to follow classroom directions, work productively, and respect and listen to their peers and me if they did not receive any rewards. Labeling was another problem. For example . . . every time Steve broke the classroom rules and directions, I placed his name on the board with a check mark or under the sad face. Soon Steve received a reputation. . . . One day during a lesson, one of my students was shouting out the answer without raising his hand. I asked my students, "Who is shouting out the answer without raising their hand?" A few students shouted out Steve's name, even though he was absent that day! It was evident that Steve's peers had labeled him as the classroom troublemaker, and whenever someone was to blame, they chose Steve. . . .

The first step in removing Assertive Discipline from my classroom was discussing it with my students. I told them that they were no longer going to receive happy faces, stars, stickers, and candies when they were behaving and performing well or consequences such as check marks, sad faces, or names on the board when they were behaving inappropriately. I removed from the chalkboard the chart where I posted check marks when students misbehave and stars when they behave well. The students were extremely happy that the chart was gone. Steve said, "No more check marks," with a big smile. The next step was to let students know how we were going to solve problems when the classroom rules were not followed. I let them know that we would have discussions to decide what needed improvement.

I no longer feel the need to have complete control. . . . I have implemented group activities that encourage my students to interact, share experiences, and work with their peers. . . . Steve is no longer seen as the classroom troublemaker but is now a valuable resource. I have proven to his peers and myself that everyone is capable of improving their academic and social skills in a comfortable environment.

—Javier Espindola
First-year teacher, kindergarten

As Javier's account suggests, Assertive Discipline and similar approaches often create or exacerbate, rather than disrupt, the status hierarchies discussed in Chapter 6. As in the case of Amy and Hector, Javier's experience with Steve suggests that while such approaches may contribute to the appearance of a well-managed classroom—with orderly check marks, stars, and pull cards signaling individual disciplinary infractions—they often do little to build classroom community or improve individual students' behavior.

Zero Tolerance

The most extreme forms of nonphysical behavioral controls on student behavior are zero-tolerance policies. Originally intended to address blatant safety threats such as weapons, such policies trigger automatic severe consequences. The policies are sometimes interpreted to include all manner of forbidden objects and behaviors, some of which are clearly not threatening. For example, some schools use suspensions, expulsions, citations, and arrests to handle minor infractions like bringing cell phones and iPods to school, cutting class, and smoking cigarettes.

Research on these policies makes clear that they are not only ineffective but also unjust and often discriminatory. They lead to increased rates of school dropout/pushout and fuel the "school-to-prison pipeline," by criminalizing youth and bringing them into contact with law enforcement, often for the first time. Such policies have had a disproportionately negative impact on Black students, especially boys, who are suspended and expelled 3.8 times more often than White students, starting as early as preschool.[7]

Zero tolerance may create the illusion that schools are addressing disruptive behavior. In fact, such policies are harmful to the students they directly impact and also to all others, since the policies undermine trust and distract from productively addressing safety concerns. And as Focal Point 8.2 demonstrates, they can limit students' opportunities to learn in the short and long term. Not to mention, children's respect for the rule of law may suffer when adults' actions—as in Focal Point 8.2's profiled stories—seem so arbitrary and patently foolish.

Focal Point 8.2
Zero Tolerance

Here are just a few articles that demonstrate some of the problematic ways zero-tolerance policies have been used and the adverse impact they have had on students. Stories like these have helped fuel recent efforts to replace such policies altogether.

On October 11, 2009, the *New York Times* published the following article about a Newark, Delaware, first grader:

It's a Fork, It's a Spoon, It's a . . . Weapon?

Finding character witnesses when you are 6 years old is not easy. But there was Zachary Christie last week at a school disciplinary committee hearing with his karate instructor and his mother's fiancé by his side to vouch for him.

Zachary's offense? Taking a camping utensil that can serve as a knife, fork and spoon to school. He was so excited about recently joining the Cub Scouts that he wanted to use it at lunch. School officials concluded that he had violated their zero-tolerance policy on weapons, and Zachary was suspended and now faces 45 days in the district's reform school. . . .

Based on the code of conduct for the Christina School District, where Zachary is a first grader, school officials had no choice. They had to suspend him because, "regardless of possessor's intent," knives are banned. . . .

On October 6, 2010, CNN published this story about a 7-year-old Florida student:

Toy Gun Leads to Florida Boy's Expulsion

When Samuel Burgos brought a gun to school last November in Broward County, Florida, the zero tolerance policy kicked in, and Samuel was suspended and then expelled. A just punishment? Did he deserve it?

Well, here's more. The gun wasn't real. It was a toy gun that never left his book bag. And Samuel—he was 7 years old at the time. . . .

Samuel, now 8, has been out of school for almost a year. His parents have home-schooled him since he was expelled for bringing a clear plastic, spring-action toy gun to school. . . .

Samuel told one of his friends the toy gun was there but said he never took it out. . . .

The school board classified the toy gun as a weapon because it fired a projectile device, small plastic beads. The punishment: mandatory expulsion. . . .

The Burgoses worry that this blemish on Samuel's permanent record will follow him. . . . "If he applies to certain colleges and universities . . ." said Burgos family attorney, Alfreda Coward. "They'll know that he was expelled from school for having a class 'A' weapon, and the No. 1 item on that is a firearm."

On December 28, 2010, a local news outlet published the following article about a Sanford, North Carolina, high school senior:

Lunchbox Mix-Up Leads to Charges for Sanford Student

An athletic and academic standout in Lee County said a lunchbox mix-up has cut short her senior year of high school and might hurt her college opportunities.

Ashley Smithwick, 17, of Sanford, was suspended from Southern Lee High School in October after school personnel found a small paring knife in her lunchbox. . . .

The lunchbox really belonged to Joe Smithwick, who packs a paring knife to slice his apple. He and his daughter have matching lunchboxes. "It's just an honest mistake. That was supposed to be my lunch because it was a whole apple," he said. . . .

Smithwick was initially given a 10-day suspension, then received notice that she was suspended the rest of the school year. . . . This month, Ashley Smithwick, a soccer player who takes college-level courses, was charged with misdemeanor possession of a weapon on school grounds. She is no longer allowed to set foot on campus. . . .

Ashley Smithwick is completing her coursework online through Central Carolina Community College. She said she worries the case will affect her college prospects. . . .

Sources: Ina Urbina, "It's a Fork, It's a Spoon, It's a . . . Weapon?" *New York Times,* October 11, 2009, www.nytimes. com/2009/10/12/education/12discipline.html?ref=education; Rich Phillips, "Toy Gun Leads to Florida Boy's Expulsion," *CNN.com,* October 6, 2010, www.cnn.com/2010/US/10/06/toy.gun.expelled/index.html; "Lunchbox Mix-Up Leads to Charges for Sanford Student," *WRAL.com,* December 28, 2010, www.wral.com/news/local/story/8845676/.

The National Association of School Psychologists has concluded that improved learning and safe school communities depend not on draconian, zero-tolerance-style policies but on "school-wide violence prevention programs, social skills curricula and positive behavioral supports."[8] Other education experts agree—so much so that the Department of Education under the Obama administration urged schools to drop zero tolerance and offered guidelines and resources to support transitions to less punitive approaches. Recent political shifts, including the Department of Education's announcement that it will scale back civil rights investigations under the Trump administration, stand to imperil tenuous progress made on these matters.

Corporal Punishment

The most extreme method to control students' behavior is corporal punishment. As of 2017, fifteen states still explicitly permit the use of paddling as a means of punishing misbehavior, and seven more states do not prohibit it explicitly. Figure 8.1, constructed by the national Center for Effective Discipline, shows the declining numbers of students who were struck in school for disciplinary reasons since the 1980s. Between 2000 and 2006 alone, the number of students who were subjected to corporal punishment dropped from about 300,000 to about 220,000. More recent analyses indicate further reductions—to over 110,000 students in 2013–2014.[9]

Figure 8.1 Corporal Punishment in U.S. Public Schools

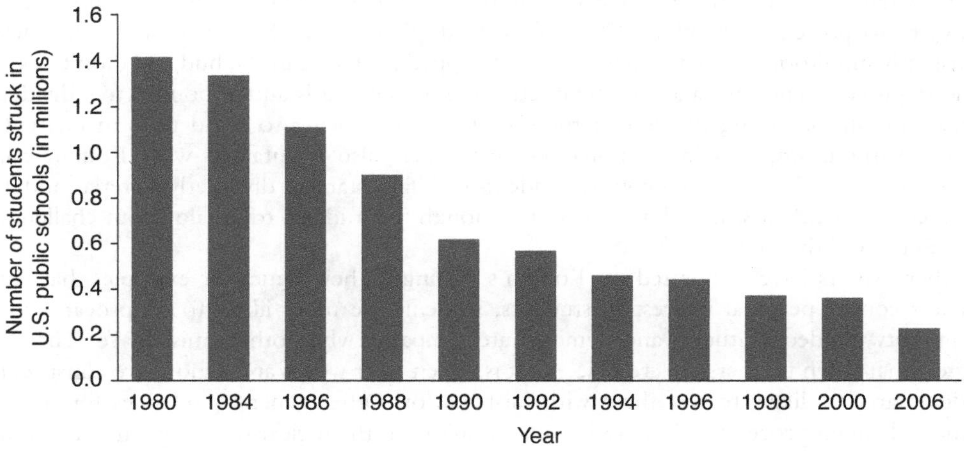

Source: Center for Effective Discipline, www.stophitting.com.

Data for that same school year, however, also reflect long-standing, shameful patterns of disproportionality—namely, that poor children, minorities, and students with disabilities are among those struck most frequently. More than a third of those who experienced corporal punishment in school in 2013–2014 were Black, despite Black students representing only 16 percent of students overall. Black boys and girls were 1.8 and 2.6 times as likely, respectively, than their White counterparts to be subjected to corporal punishment in states where such practices endure.

And, in many ways, formal data such as these likely undercount the punitive physical contact that students—some more than others—are at risk of experiencing in school. In recent years, as cellphone videos documenting police brutality against people of color have circulated with horrifying frequency, so too has footage of school resource officers (SROs) assaulting students. One video from 2015 shows an SRO in Florida slamming a middle schooler to the ground. Another shows an SRO in South Carolina throwing a student from her desk to the ground later that same year. A third from 2016 shows an SRO in Texas body-slamming a 12-year-old. A fourth from 2017 shows an SRO in North Carolina hoisting a female student almost overhead before tossing her down. A fifth from later that year shows a high school student in a chokehold, forced to the ground, and tased by an SRO in Pennsylvania. Each of these incidents, among others, involved students of color—a fact that resonates with racialized realities beyond school and bolsters claims that the presence of SROs may exacerbate rather than reduce danger for students of color, especially.

Classrooms Characterized by Consistency and Attentiveness

In the 1970s, many educators and others began to see that certain classroom management and discipline problems could be avoided when teachers modified their instruction to connect with and engage students. It was becoming increasingly clear that elaborate management and discipline strategies could not overcome irrelevant curricula, boring pedagogy, or general insensitivity to students' personal and learning needs. It also became clear that at some point in time children and adolescents would misbehave, and that the quest for "perfect" classroom comportment was necessarily a work in progress. These instructional modifications and community-building approaches still have much to offer, especially as educators and activists work to realize schools' unfulfilled potential as humane spaces for all children to learn.

Teachers Who Are "With It"

In one well-known and now foundational study, Jacob Kounin analyzed thousands of hours of video footage and found that teachers in smoothly running classrooms consistently used certain strategies to prevent disruption. These teachers displayed what Kounin called "withitness." Constantly monitoring students' behavior, they nipped problems in the bud and didn't hesitate to do so publicly. They managed multiple activities simultaneously and responded to individuals' needs without disrupting the rest of the class (e.g., by moving to stand near an inattentive student without stopping instruction). These teachers also maintained what Kounin called "signal continuity." They didn't confuse students with false starts or disorderly material, and they provided independent seatwork that was easy enough for students to do alone but challenging enough to hold their interest.[10]

Other experts have elaborated on Kounin's findings. They argue, for example, that when teachers convey personal interest in students, students are more likely to reciprocate, adopt community-minded attitudes, and demonstrate sympathy when others misbehave. They also suggest that when teachers are credible—that is, when their words and actions are consistent—students are less likely to test them with misbehavior. Other general guidelines for teachers include planning procedures in advance, communicating them clearly, letting students assume some responsibility for determining rules, returning to those rules occasionally to discuss revisions, developing cooperative relationships among students, minimizing disruptions and delays, and incorporating independent and whole-class activities.[11] Most also emphasize the importance of starting the year off with a friendly but serious, "warm-and-firm" way.

Few people would dispute the value of these practices. Yet they often prove elusive, even in the classrooms of well-intentioned and hardworking teachers.

Problems often arise, in part, because of teachers' tendencies to see these practices as *disciplinary* rather than *instructional* strategies. When the purpose of cooperation, for example, becomes control instead of learning, lesson quality is likely to suffer. Likewise, when students can tell that their participation in co-constructing rules is more about managing behavior than ensuring learning, a genuine sense of community may not develop. And surely students can discern between teachers who stand beside them to redirect attention or ward off disruption and teachers who stand nearby to answer questions or encourage. In short, the success of any strategy depends on the goals and sincerity of the teacher using it.

Teachers Who Make Lessons Interesting

Offering the simplistic solution of "make lessons interesting" hardly addresses the full complexity of classroom management. However, *un*interesting lessons make any challenge, including misbehavior, worse.

Researcher Jeff Gregg investigated how teachers' approaches to behavior management differed across settings and with what consequence.[12] He conducted a yearlong study of discipline approaches in one first-year teacher's general (lower-track) mathematics class. He found that the teacher, not viewing students as college bound, lowered her expectations for their academic performance. She still set high (strict and traditional) standards for their behavior. But, worried about students' potential to be troublesome, she decided not to joke, "be too nice," or offer opportunities for them to participate in fun activities, lest she risk losing control of the classroom. In return, students—many of whom struggled to see the value of math in their lives—became even less eager to please or inclined to engage. Together, she and the class entered a vicious cycle—she would clamp down, students would misbehave more, and she would clamp down even further. Eventually, she gave up trying to enforce her rules, blamed students' negative attitudes and home lives, and decided that she didn't care whether they learned.

This teacher Gregg studied did not consider that the problems she and her students faced might originate from what Gregg calls "the school mathematics tradition"—the prevailing notion that general mathematics is little more than (usually boring) algorithms and procedures. They did not consider that math could be learned outside the usual routine of (1) the teacher leading the class as they check their homework, (2) the teacher providing instruction on the next topic, and (3) the teacher assigning problems for students to work on individually for the remainder of class and as homework. For Gregg, the very nature of school knowledge was one root of the problem.

Another was that the teacher needed more knowledge in order to break from the subject matter and schooling traditions that she followed by default. Mathematics or other subjects stripped down to remedial routine and without any inducements—talk, kindness, and fun, for example—are almost certain to create discipline problems. In Chapters 5, 6, and 7, we described curriculum considerations, instructional approaches, and methods of assessment that can keep knowledge-loving teachers engaged and enthused in helping students direct their energy into learning.

Child-Centeredness, Caring, and Democracy: A Second Set of Legacies

Traditional schooling has had its critics since the early nineteenth century. A big part of that criticism has focused on schools' encouraging desirable behavior and preventing undesirable behavior. For example, Horace Mann argued against physical punishments, generally accepted at the time, because he believed they undermined character development. Many nineteenth-century progressives advocated hiring women teachers because they believed they cultivated more nurturing classroom dynamics. Turn-of-the-twentieth-century progressive reformers, including John Dewey, argued for child-centered schools that would foster a well-educated and civic-minded populace and ward off disaffection. Advocacy for child-centered, caring, and democratic schools and classrooms remains strong today.

Child-Centered Schooling

As noted in Chapter 3, some eighteenth-, nineteenth-, and twentieth-century school reformers argued that students' essentially good nature would cause them to behave well in school if their needs were met. French philosopher Jean-Jacques Rousseau (1712–1778), for example, theorized that humans are naturally good and that it is society that corrupts. Since discipline represents a society's efforts to impose goodness, Rousseau's followers argued that it has no place in education. Instead, those and other progressive reformers believed that schooling practices should align to children's developmental needs rather than focus on preserving social order.

Prioritizing Children's Development

Johann Pestalozzi (1746–1827), a Swiss educator with a strong following in the United States throughout the nineteenth century, translated Rousseau's ideas into pedagogy. Pestalozzi believed that students learn best when schools help them develop self-respect and emotional security. According to Pestalozzi, rather than focusing on abstractions while sitting obediently at a desk, students' learning should emerge from exploration and engagement in activities that connect ideas to real-life objects and events—all under the maternal guidance of a teacher. "Maternal love," in Pestalozzi's view, promised to ensure trust, elevate moral character, and improve the lot of poor children especially.

Friedrich Froebel (1782–1852) built on Pestalozzi's ideas and developed the first kindergarten curriculum aimed at promoting children's development through self-expression and cooperative play. He envisioned *kindergarten*, or "children's garden," as a protected space where children could explore, mature, and grow under the watchful eyes of nurturing adults. Froebel saw the classroom as a miniature society, wherein the cooperation that children learned at school would make them cooperative members of adult society. Thus, Pestalozzi, Froebel, and their followers built schools and classrooms that were grounded in a respect for children—their interests, curiosities, potential, and overall development.

What a contrast these ideas were to those of earlier schooling! Educational historian Herbert Kliebard recounts that in 1913, a factory inspector surveyed 500 child laborers about whether they would prefer to return to school or "remain in the squalor of the factories." Among them, "412 told her, sometimes in graphic terms, that they preferred factory labor to the monotony, humiliation, and even sheer cruelty that they experienced in school."[13]

Meeting Academic and Social Needs

At the turn of the century, the settlement house movement developed an ethic of democratic social service that merged educational, political, and social purposes. Jane Addams's Hull House and other settlement houses functioned more like extended families and communities than traditional schools. Over time, the settlement house reformers persuaded many schools to follow suit by appointing school physicians, offering classes for children with disabilities, initiating school lunch programs, and creating school libraries. John Dewey's friendship with Addams, and his support of the settlement house movement, influenced his thinking that schools might themselves become social centers.

Dewey also wanted schools to provide for the multiple needs of immigrants and especially to respond to the devastating effects of their disconnection from their "Old World" cultures. But Dewey wanted schools to go beyond just ministering to immigrants' needs. The key to social progress, he believed, was for schools to develop children's dispositions and skills to serve a just, democratic society. Dewey wanted schools to support immigrants to become "good Americans, public-spirited citizens, and members of the 'great community.'"[14]

Throughout the twentieth century, progressives continued to emphasize themes of caring and community as counterpoints to the dominant themes of management and control.

Establishing Humanistic and "Open" Classrooms

In the 1970s, the themes of caring and community reemerged in a new movement called *humanistic education*. Spearheaded by humanistic psychologists—most prominently Carl Rogers, Abraham Maslow, and Lawrence Kohlberg—reformers proposed that if schools treated students humanely and respectfully, these qualities would prevail in classrooms. Values, moral development, self-discipline, and personal responsibility thus assumed a major role. One popular method, called "values clarification," engaged students in discussions and simulations to help them discover and examine the principles by which they choose to live.

Closely related to the humanistic movement were the more radical ideas of A. S. Neill, whose school (and 1960 book by the same name), Summerhill, featured "open" classrooms. At Summerhill, students were free to discover and choose for themselves meaningful ways to behave and interact with others, and teachers facilitated and mediated students' freedom.[15] These ideas inspired numerous attempts to replicate Summerhill's features in what were, and still are, often called *alternative* schools. For complex reasons, the experimentation catalyzed by humanism and open schooling, although never widely popular, has taken place more in middle-class, suburban schools than in poorer urban communities.

Attending to Social and Emotional Learning

Over the past decade, educators (and policymakers, too) have increasingly embraced the concept of social emotional learning (SEL). SEL emerged in the 1990s, when Daniel Goleman's book *Emotional Intelligence: Why It Can Matter More Than IQ* popularized the idea of a set of "soft" competencies that enable people to develop healthy, respectful, and caring behaviors and relationships.[16] In 1994, Goleman founded the Collaborative for Academic, Social, and Emotional Learning (CASEL), a nonprofit organization that seeks to advance the science and practice of SEL.

According to the SEL perspective, people with social and emotional intelligence exhibit five competencies. *Self-awareness* enables them to be cognizant of their emotions, recognize their values, and assess their strengths. Their *ability to regulate emotions* means that they can manage a wide range of situations, including stressful ones, without acting impulsively or losing control. *Social awareness* supports them to appreciate the perspectives, diversity, and resources of those around them. *Relationship* skills bolster their cooperation and help giving and, at the same time, increase their resilience to peer pressure and conflict. Finally, *social intelligence* fosters responsible decision making based on ethical standards and respect for others. In schools, these competencies are enormously important; they enable children to calm themselves when agitated, establish friendships, solve conflicts, and make safe choices.

Focal Point 8.3 depicts these core competencies and offers examples of how educators can support students to develop them.

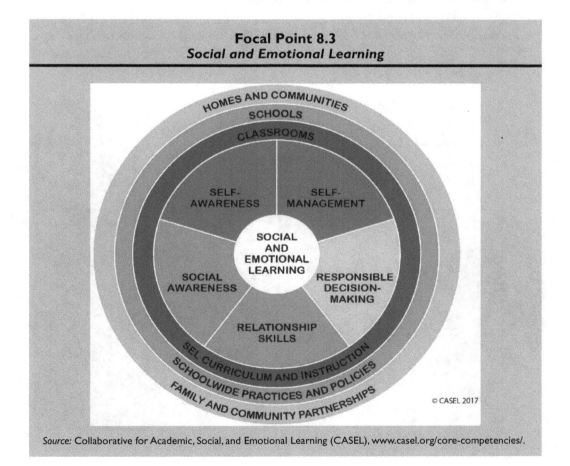

Focal Point 8.3
Social and Emotional Learning

Source: Collaborative for Academic, Social, and Emotional Learning (CASEL), www.casel.org/core-competencies/.

The graphic depicts the five core competencies associated with social and emotional learning (SEL). Teachers can play a huge role in supporting students to develop such competencies. The following are a few examples of active, engaging, and effective instructional methods for teaching SEL skills. Teachers can

- use **modeling and coaching** to teach young children to recognize how they feel or how someone else might be feeling;
- prompt students to use **conflict-resolution** skills in new situations and then guide them through the necessary steps;
- organize **class meetings** that give students authentic opportunities to practice engaging in dialogue, setting classroom rules, and making group decisions;
- help students develop **cooperation and teamwork** skills by supporting them to participate in team sports and games, and other activities involving cooperative groups;
- establish **cross-age mentoring**, in which a younger student is paired with an older one, in order to build self-confidence, deepen students' sense of belonging, and enhance students' academic skills;
- design activities that develop students' **reflective listening skills** by, for example, having students listen to and then repeat or restate others' comments.

Source: Adapted from "SEL FAQs," Collaborative for Academic, Social and Emotional Learning, http://casel.org/why-it-matters/sel-faqs/.

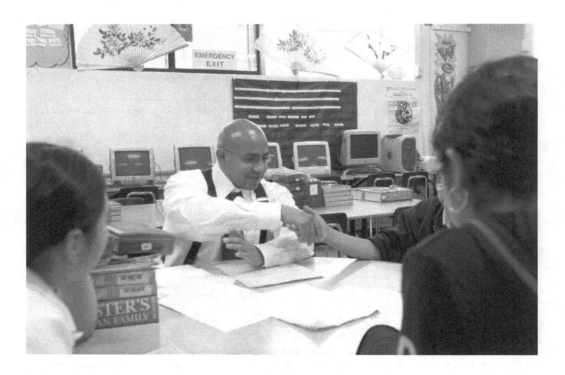

Educators have adopted various programs to support students in developing relationship skills and handling school responsibilities productively. Many of these programs have been rigorously evaluated. CASEL is one organization that assists educators in identifying programs that have met the highest standards of quality and effectiveness, as well as evidence-based strategies that align with the principles underlying SEL.

An Ethic of Care

Among others, Nel Noddings, a professor emeritus of educational philosophy, has long argued that an "ethic of care" should pervade classrooms and schools. She believes that educators must commit themselves to "a great moral purpose: to care for children so that they, too, will be prepared to care."[17] Caring encompasses moral and cultural considerations about how people relate to others, and thus offers a counterpoint to traditional school discipline and classroom management. Noddings proposes that behavioral control strategies like Assertive Discipline destroy care. In her view, such strategies are manipulative and, in their effort to routinize teacher-student interaction, foreclose opportunities to help students learn to be "healthy, competent, moral people."[18] Noddings believes that whether engaged in a math lesson or playing on a field, children must be engaged humanely and holistically—exactly what does not occur in systems with automatic, predetermined consequences for undesirable behavior.

Noddings explains that care includes far more than "a warm fuzzy feeling that makes people kind and likeable."[19] Rather, a caring teacher engages in a "continuous search for competence" that includes fostering in students the knowledge and skills "necessary to make a positive contribution" in whatever field of study or work they might choose. This "search for competence"[20] is a mutual endeavor involving both the student and the teacher. This mutual endeavor requires far more than mere teacher approval, error correction, or supplying of new facts. Instead, it requires that students and teachers *co-construct* student competence. Co-constructing contrasts with the dynamics of one-way "transmission" favored by traditional approaches. As exemplified in Mauro Bautista's comments below, this kind of co-construction demands of teachers a commitment to critical reflection and a willingness to assume responsibility for how relationships develop, or don't, in the classroom.

> When dealing with students, I often ask myself, "How would I want an adult at a school setting to treat my own son in this situation?" Thus, if it is a celebratory occasion, I make sure to praise. If it is a situation where a student needs to be reprimanded, I make sure to do it in a respectful manner. If I need something from a student, I make sure to say "please." If a student does a favor for me, I make sure to say "thank you." Students, like adults, appreciate being treated with respect. In turn, they will treat you with respect.
>
> In the classroom, I had the greatest expectations of my students academically and behaviorally. I made my expectations clear at the beginning of the year, and I often reminded them of those expectations throughout the year. If something occurred that was not in line with the expectations, I made an effort to look at my practices first. Many times classroom management issues occur when a lesson is not properly thought out. Thus, instead of blaming the students, teachers need to look at themselves and ask, "How can I change the lesson to engage all students?"
>
> —Mauro Bautista
> Middle-school bilingual education coordinator

Seeing Relationships as Contexts for Making Meaning

In the book *Developing Through Relationships*, psychologist Alan Fogel explores the crucial role of relationships in human development.[21] In particular, Fogel shows how new bits of information can be understood differently across social settings and relationships.

For example, even a simple demand, "Take out your pencil," can mean different things to different students—based on their relationships with the teacher. For some, it might mean, "Uh, oh, no pencil; I'm in trouble." For others, it might mean, "Great, we are having the quiz I prepared for" or "How rude he is that he never says please." For some, it might bring feelings of defiance: "I don't care if I fail." For others, resignation: "Another forty-five minutes to go." For still others, anxiety: "Should I just get up to sharpen this or raise my hand and ask for permission? Either way some teachers get mad." And so on. None of the preceding meanings exist independent of the classroom culture or the teacher-student relationship. In this sense, even when the given information (the same four words) seems universal, the received information (its *meaning*) can differ among those in the class.

Students do not construct meaning on their own. The sociocultural perspectives of Vygotsky, Fogel, and others emphasize that meaning is *co*-constructed (or, in Fogel's term, co-regulated) *in* relationships. In other words, relationships are an important part of the context where meaning making occurs. In our example, it was *this* teacher, not another, who spoke *these* words in *this* class where she expected students to have *this* kind of writing implement. For the teacher and students, these words have histories, which might include the teacher's annoyance if students do not have pencils, if students have to fish pencils out of their backpacks, and so on. These are different from the histories the same students might share with other teachers in other classes.

In essence, the meanings that students make in the classroom depend on the relationships they have or have had in the past, particularly with teachers. In order for intended learning to occur, both teachers and students must be willing to search for shared understanding, to accept guidance and expertise from others, and to change.

Moving Beyond Rules and Routines to Reciprocal Care

In classrooms that are rigidly structured and rule bound, teachers dispense consequences almost automatically. Teachers might even try to assure students that punishment is "not personal" and is "strictly a consequence of behavior." This is an extreme message to send. It forecloses the possibility of establishing classroom communities in which students develop and apply their own approaches to interaction, interdependence, and problem solving. It also denies a fundamental truth: all classroom interactions are in some way personal. Relationships are not incidental to learning. And their importance extends beyond our conventional sense that if teachers seem friendly and are liked by students, students will try harder and learn more. Desirable characteristics—like friendliness and even kindness—are unlikely to generate learning if teachers neglect the interactive and cooperative teaching approaches that facilitate cognitive and social development.

Complementing the work of scholars like Noddings and Fogel are psychological studies that show the importance of relationships between teachers and students, particularly those who have been traditionally underserved. For example, researchers Carollee Howes and Sharon Ritchie examined how teachers built positive classroom relationships with children who came to school with behaviors and assumptions borne of difficult life circumstances (e.g., poverty, homelessness). Even with children who were initially "hostile, aggressive, and distrustful," teachers were able to establish trust, much as Amy Lee did with Hector.[22]

While novice teachers sometimes feel that they must be consistent in their responses to different students to show that they are not playing favorites, Howes and Ritchie's work indicates otherwise. Establishing trust—especially with students who may have few safe or reliable relationships with adults—requires teachers who are "sufficiently flexible to individualize" their interactions.[23] This flexibility should not be mistaken for confusing, inconsistent, or unpredictable classroom practices. To the contrary, consistency and structure are important parts of demonstrating care. Even things as simple as repeating supportive phrases—for example, "I'm glad you're here" and "I'll help you"—and following through on those phrases can engender trust. Such repetition can communicate affection and signal positive attention.

Sociologist George Noblit and his colleagues studied how two experienced teachers, Martha and Pam, constructed caring relationships with their students. Both worked in the same racially mixed, inner-city school but had quite different classroom manners. Pam, an African American teacher, kept her classroom interactions formal and polite, while Martha, a White teacher, encouraged lots of informal exchange. Yet both exercised what Noblit calls a "dogged determination" to develop caring relationships with troubled students.

Like the teachers that Howes and Ritchie observed and the teachers profiled in this book, Pam and Martha used "no magic tricks, no technical fixes—just consistent day-in and day-out, hour-to-hour, even minute-to-minute" attention to creating opportunities for students to succeed.[24] For example, Martha established daily rituals to communicate her care for Robert, who had recently transferred from a school for students with severe behavioral problems. She waited at the door to greet him; she made sure to chat with him about nonschool matters, like his favorite television programs; and she said good-bye when he left each afternoon. Martha also insisted that Robert participate in classroom learning experiences. In time, her obvious commitment and regular attention helped create a classroom context that supported Robert to behave appropriately, make friends, and achieve more than he ever had before.

Pam used a somewhat different approach to develop a caring relationship with John, a painfully shy special education student who had been mainstreamed into her class (see Chapter 10 for a discussion of the terms *special education* and *mainstream*). In response to John's efforts to avoid interacting with her by hiding behind other students or his desk, Pam insisted in a firm but reassuring way that he participate. She moved his desk closer to her, and she made a practice of standing nearby when he worked with other students. She also sometimes touched his shoulder reassuringly to show her support. Pam's constancy and care over the school year helped John thrive.

Martha's and Pam's students recognized the actions their teachers took to demonstrate care. Students told Noblit that they knew Martha and Pam cared because they helped students "without demeaning them for needing help," talked with them, showed respect by listening, expressed confidence in their abilities, and supported them to persevere to success.[25]

Making Classrooms Communities

In *Beyond Discipline: From Compliance to Community*, former teacher Alfie Kohn describes class meetings during which students agree on how they will work together to solve the inevitable problems that arise in class.[26] By pondering such questions as "What makes school awful sometimes?," "What can we do this year to make sure things go better?," "Suppose you hurt someone's feelings, or did something even worse. How would you want us, the rest of the community, to help you then?," and "What if someone else acted that way? How could we help that person?," students can construct a safe and caring learning community. Kohn argues that such conversations, combined with lots of collaborative work on academic and social issues, can turn classrooms into places where discipline problems are rare.

Kohn draws extensively from the Child Development Project, which developed, studied, and disseminated information about community-like classroom practices. The project emphasized that core values must be experienced, not just taught; thus, participating teachers learned to reflect on their own practice and ask questions that elicit students' thinking. They learned to maintain order without extrinsic rewards and to deemphasize competition by having students set learning goals and establish classroom rules. Students were given substantial responsibility for their own learning. Teachers and students collaborated on an inquiry-based curriculum in which they investigated—through literature, science, and history—what it means to be a principled, caring person. Class meetings were routine, rather than a response to crisis.

Researcher Eric Schaps and his colleagues studied sixth graders who had participated in the program since kindergarten. Compared with peers of the same social class and achievement, these students behaved more considerately toward classmates and worked better together. They also better understood others' perspectives and could better solve interpersonal conflicts. Two years later, when the students were in junior high, the positive effects of the program were still evident. Schools that implemented the project's suggested practices noted substantial decreases in discipline problems, as well. These strategies worked well in both city schools and more affluent suburban ones.[27] And while the Child Development Project no longer exists in its original form, its good works live on through the California-based Center for the Collaborative Classroom, which partners to provide professional development for schools and districts nationwide.[28]

In keeping with these ideas about the centrality of community in learning and in life, first-year teacher Cicely Bingener provided her kindergartners with a series of experiences meant to establish a culture of care in and beyond her classroom.

> The Peace Builders antiviolence curriculum helps teachers teach social, emotional, and thinking skills to help students avoid violence and give them a strategy for handling conflicts peacefully.[29] Using a combination of stories, role plays, discussions, writing activities, projects, positive reinforcements, and exhibitions, the curriculum addresses the causes, effects, and alternatives to violence at both a global and local level. Peace Builders is organized around four principles that serve as guides for how to develop into an effective peace builder: (1) praise people; (2) give up put-downs; (3) notice hurts and right wrongs; and (4) seek wise people. Lessons and activities focus on these ideas.
>
> —Cicely Bingener
> First-year teacher, kindergarten

To enact these classroom norms, Cicely's students discussed peace and violence in their own lives, brainstormed ways to support peace, invented a pantomime to accompany the class-adopted theme song ("I've Got Peace Like a River"), and read big-book stories like *Tillie and the Wall*, "an allegorical tale of a young mouse who bravely crosses a long-accepted wall that separates her community from another."[30] Cicely created a bulletin board to recognize students' peace-building activities and had students construct a giant peace chain to help them visualize their peaceful acts.

While peace represents her central focus, Cicely does not silence herself, or her students, when it comes to addressing issues of violence. To the contrary, she considers it imperative that teachers tackle such issues as they arise.

> Some may argue that bringing the unpleasantness of surrounding violence to the fore of a curriculum for 5-year-olds is ill timed and casts a dark shadow on what ought to be the most carefree time of a child's life.
>
> This assertion might hold up if these young children did not already suffer from exposure to violence. . . . A teacher's silence on these issues is irresponsible. Expecting young children

to interpret the violence they witness and extricate themselves from violence in their own responses to conflict [without the help of adults] is a disservice.

—Cicely Bingener
First-year teacher, kindergarten

Cicely's unflinching approach echoes that of former Chicago kindergarten teacher Vivian Gussin Paley. In her books *You Can't Say You Can't Play* and *White Teacher*, Paley probes the moral mandate to address exclusion in the classroom.[31] Paley's writing reminds us that schools often reinforce children's rejections of one another, including racialized rejections. Adults often accept and, in doing so, condone "small" rejections as natural behavior, and thus often intervene only in cases of blatant physical or psychological harm. Like other "microaggressions" mentioned in Chapter 6, familiar, frequent, and so-called micro incidents of exclusion exact a painful and cumulative toll; teachers are wrong to ignore them.

Tolerating rejection and exclusion is not a minor matter. It teaches students to accept and even perpetrate attitudes and actions that endanger their own and others' well-being. To prevent this, Paley implemented a simple rule that her students proposed when they discussed this problem. That rule—"You can't say you can't play"—forbade them from turning away any student who wanted to participate. A simple mantra like this one is as important now as ever. Indeed, as the country continues to wrestle with discriminatory political rhetoric, entrenched institutional racism, and a rash of hate crimes, teachers have a responsibility to address these issues head-on with students and to teach them what caring, inclusive, justice-oriented attitudes and actions entail.

Restoring Justice—Creating Conditions for Kids to "Do Right"

In any community, people will err, and wrongs will need to be righted. A caring community finds ways to support its members to demonstrate care for one another—even when they've done something wrong. Restorative justice offers concepts and practices for this very purpose. These hold promise as an alternative to demonstrably ineffective traditional school discipline.

Unlike traditional discipline, whereby school personnel administer punishments to perpetrators, restorative justice involves both offenders and victims. With support from trained mediators, both help decide how offenders can make amends. The goal is for victims to feel empowered by their active involvement in the justice process and for offenders to take responsibility by helping to make sense of misdeeds and determine how to remedy the harm.

In many schools, restorative justice approaches have been adopted as alternatives to the excessive suspensions and expulsions that often accompany zero-tolerance policies. They have been used productively to address smaller infractions as well as serious offenses such as bullying and violence. Because they involve both victims and offenders, restorative justice processes can help right the power imbalances that bolster such offenses.

Concept Table 8.1 juxtaposes traditional, punitive approaches with restorative ones. Focal Point 8.4, meanwhile, offers an example of the kind of productive educational outcomes that restorative justice can yield.

Restorative justice represents a rather new approach in education. It has been embraced by educators and activists who seek to bring a human rights framework to schooling, and it has gained more urgent attention amid growing concerns about mass incarceration and its connection to racial disproportionality in school discipline. The Education Subcommittee of the Children's Rights Litigation Committee of the American Bar Association, for example, is leading one effort, the Dignity in Schools Campaign. Invoking international treaties such as the Convention on the Rights of the Child,[32] its members advocate explicitly for child-centered reforms that keep children in school and preserve their dignity.

Positive evidence about restorative justice's impact has emerged from a growing number of school districts. For example, Denver public schools reported a 68 percent reduction in police tickets in schools and a 40 percent reduction in out-of-school suspensions in the few years after they adopted new discipline policies that use restorative justice.[33] Similarly, West Philadelphia High School—a school that had been on Pennsylvania's list of "Persistently Dangerous Schools" for six years—saw dramatic changes after a year and a half of restorative practices. Suspensions dropped by 50 percent, and violent acts and serious incidents dropped even more.[34] In both cases, gains from these early efforts have fortified and fueled forward continued improvement.

Concept Table 8.1 A Comparison of Punitive and Restorative Justice Responses in Schools

Punitive	Restorative
Misbehavior defined as breaking school rules or letting the school down.	Misbehavior defined as harm (emotional/mental/physical) done to one person/group by another.
Focus is on what happened and establishing blame or guilt.	Focus on problem solving by expressing feelings and needs and exploring how to address problems in the future.
Adversarial relationship and process. Includes an authority figure with the power to decide on a penalty, in conflict with wrongdoer.	Dialogue and negotiation, with everyone involved in the communication and cooperation with each other.
Imposition of pain or unpleasantness to punish and deter/prevent.	Restitution as a means of restoring both parties, the goal being reconciliation and acknowledging responsibility for choices.
Attention to rules and adherence to due process.	Attention to relationships and achievement of a mutually desired outcome.
Conflict/wrongdoing represented as impersonal and abstract; individual versus school.	Conflict/wrongdoing recognized as interpersonal conflicts with opportunity for learning.
One social injury compounded by another.	Focus on repair of social injury/damage.
School community as spectators, represented by member of staff dealing with the situation; those directly affected uninvolved and powerless.	School community involved in facilitating restoration; those affected taken into consideration; empowerment.
Accountability defined in terms of receiving punishment.	Accountability defined as understanding impact of actions, taking responsibility for choices, and suggesting ways to repair harm.

Source: Kimberly Burke and Jessica Ashley, Implementing Restorative Justice: A Guide for Schools (Springfield, IL: Illinois Criminal Justice Information Authority, 2009).

Focal Point 8.4
Restorative Justice Program in Action

This is an example of a school peer jury in action, submitted by Art Lobl, teacher and peer jury coordinator at Kelvyn Park High School in Chicago.

A young man named Jose threw his shoe across the auditorium at another student in front of both his music teacher and the school principal. Embarrassed and exasperated, the teacher referred Jose to the discipline office. Jose was then referred to the school peer jury program. As the jurors talked to Jose, they learned that he wanted to go to art school after graduation and was having problems with his music teacher. The jurors decided that Jose would assist the teacher in setting up for a concert the following week so that he and the teacher could meet outside the classroom and get to know each other better. In addition, Jose agreed to use his artistic talents to make a poster to publicize and recruit students for the school jazz band club. The poster was enlarged, copied, and posted around the school. The student and the teacher made peace, Jose saw the error of his ways, and his talents were put to use in repairing harm done to the school and the music program. The poster was later included in Jose's art portfolio and he was accepted by an art school upon graduation.

Source: Kimberly Burke and Jessica Ashley, *Implementing Restorative Justice: A Guide for Schools* (Springfield, IL: Illinois Criminal Justice Information Authority, 2009), 15.

Socially Just Classrooms: Doing Democracy

Throughout the nineteenth century, small and often marginalized groups strove to make schools seedbeds for social justice. Particularly powerful is the long history of activism among African American women educators, often assisted by Black churches and sometimes by liberal Whites like the Quakers, to improve the social, economic, and political circumstances of the African American community. These women used their leadership and their classrooms to teach reading and writing not only to their students but to adults in the community as well—a daring act in the nineteenth century.

For example, teacher Fannie Jackson Coppin organized tuition-free classes for freedmen coming north and founded a school for children of emancipated slaves. Believing that knowledge is power, Coppin intended her teaching to uplift the race. Other Black women educators, such as Anna Julia Cooper and Mary McLeod Bethune, also went far beyond teaching their students technical skills and attempted to teach in ways that would bring about social and political change. At the root of their efforts was the conviction that education was not about individual gain, but about strengthening the community, a view captured eloquently in the motto of the National Association of Colored Women—"Lifting as We Climb."

In the educational mainstream, John Dewey and others also envisioned schools as equalizers and engines of democratization. Dewey stressed that classrooms should be part of life, not merely preparation for it, and that to make society more democratic, students must participate in classrooms that are themselves democratic societies. In other words, teachers must give students a chance to learn how their actions affect the success or failure of the group. And students must develop their sense of civic-mindedness by sharing both the pleasant and trying tasks that complex group projects require. Doing one's part as a member of a classroom project, the argument went, would prepare children to be both leaders and collaborators.

With the civil rights movements of the 1960s came structural changes to schools: racial desegregation programs; bilingual education offerings; inclusion of handicapped children in regular classrooms; and heterogeneous (or mixed-ability) grouping. Each of these changes was met with intense (and enduring) opposition. In response, researchers and teachers began developing cooperative learning approaches that could be used to improve social relationships and ease tensions in diverse classrooms. Today these approaches are at the heart of crucial efforts not to overcome the "problem" of classroom diversity but rather to unleash diversity's power as a *resource* and, in so doing, build rich and more resilient communities.

Reframing Student Resistance

At the end of the twentieth century, critical pedagogy emerged. As a theory of education, it called for the co-construction of classrooms as socially just communities. Introduced in Chapter 3, critical pedagogy begins with the assumption that schooling is not in actuality a "great equalizer." Rather, schooling tends to help privileged families pass on their advantages to their children and to ensure that lower-status and lower-income children follow in their parents' footsteps, too.

When teachers practice critical pedagogy, they support students to analyze historical and contemporary events, institutions, and relationships in order to expose underlying mechanisms of advantage and disadvantage. Critical pedagogy requires that teachers and students seek out voices, versions, and interpretations typically marginalized, or silenced, by the "official" curriculum.

Even though her students are young, Kimberly Min understands that their engagement in school depends on whether they see the connections between what they learn in classrooms and what they live outside school. These understandings inform Kimberly's instructional decisions, including her decision to teach a unit about the landmark *Brown v. Board of Education* case.

> As a critical pedagogue, I strive for my students to be interested and invested in what they are learning and provide a space for my students to have opportunities to create knowledge. The lessons I have developed encompass California state standards and fulfill my goal to actively engage my students in rigorous knowledge making around the implications and the outcomes of the *Brown* case.
>
> Students discussed how history has affected their current educational reality, and although only 8 years in age, they can recognize and express their discontent with their educational experiences. The students also shared their discontent with the type of curriculum, lack of school supplies, and diversity on campus.
>
> —Kimberly Min
> Third-grade teacher

As Kimberly's statements suggest, students are capable of unpacking sophisticated ideas about learning, knowledge, curriculum, diversity, discipline, and control. Developing critical perspectives about their own schooling helps them develop identities as transformative actors—identities that may depart from the labels others might foist upon them. Analysis of this kind—a powerful form of literacy in its own right—can serve as a powerful bridge between students' lived experiences and conventional forms of literacy (e.g., reading, writing, speaking, and listening about topics specified in the formal curriculum) that are demanded for mainstream school success.

Critical educators aim to help students interrogate the beliefs, structures, and routines that influence human behavior, including their own behavior. Such questioning helps students as well as teachers reevaluate what they perceive as problematic or resistant and why.

Developed by Paul Willis, Henry Giroux, and others, (critical) theories of resistance draw heavily on anthropological and sociological studies of schools and classrooms. Both Giroux and Willis, for example, found that working-class students often behaved "badly" in school as an expression of resistance against a system not intended to serve their needs or stoke their capacities.[35] These students knew, on some level, that their schools expected little from them, and would respond to them accordingly. In light of this, theorists like Willis and Giroux argue that students' antischool attitudes and behaviors should be seen as a logical (even creative and resourceful) form of rebellion against an oppressive institution, rather than as a sign of individual psychological problems (e.g., lack of self-discipline, laziness, low ability, etc.), poor parenting, or disorganized neighborhoods. This view presses teachers to consider the potential for even commonly named problems—for example, disengagement and truancy—to be as much about

schools' and teachers' attitudes and behaviors *toward youth* as they are about youths' attitudes and behaviors *toward schools and teachers*. Although critical educators do not believe that all oppositional behavior necessarily has this particular political quality, they do believe that many students act rebelliously to assert the power they feel they have over their destinies.

Creating Critical Classrooms

Critical pedagogy is both theoretical and practical. At the theoretical level, critical pedagogy helps us understand how relationships are shaped by privilege and power, culture and history, and more. Those who practice critical pedagogy in their classrooms, however, also offer down-to-earth examples of how teachers can support children to preserve, enrich, and value their native cultures while contributing to and challenging "common" culture. Years ago, Professor Gloria Ladson-Billings introduced the phrase *culturally relevant* to describe such classrooms.

It is easy to have a commitment to cultural relevance *as a value* but more challenging to act on it—especially when students' cultural backgrounds differ from your own. And yet, if culture is central to learning, then coming to a deeper understanding about culture must be central to teaching, too. This is a lifelong project; while it may seem daunting at first, it is necessary, worthwhile, and exhilarating. And even though we may learn sometimes painful things about ourselves, we grow and earn respect through that part of the process, too.

Some of the more general elements of culturally relevant teaching are woven throughout this book—approaches to schooling, learning, curriculum, and so forth that embrace diversity, equity, and critical social analysis. More specific dimensions of culturally relevant teaching, however, require knowledge that can be gained only by knowing your particular students and their community.

In her now famous book *The Dreamkeepers: Successful Teachers of African American Children*, Ladson-Billings describes the practices of eight teachers (five African American and three White) who created caring and democratic classroom communities with their students. These teachers viewed themselves as artists who "mined" knowledge from capable and knowing learners, rather than technicians who deposited knowledge into empty vessels. They saw and valued students' racial and cultural heritages, supporting them to see how their identities as African Americans connected with national and global ideas, events, and movements. All eight teachers saw themselves as part of and "giving back" to the communities where they taught.

These teachers structured classroom social interactions so that students worked together in ways that we described in Chapter 6. For example, teacher Margaret Rossi used her knowledge about students and the community to encourage connections between current events and their own lives. At the outset of the Gulf War, for example, Rossi pressed her students to figure out how events in Kuwait and Iraq affected them. This might seem like distant history, but notice in Focal Point 8.5 the *timeless* features of this teaching. Notice, for example, how

---

Focal Point 8.5
Successful Teachers of African American Students:
An Excerpt From The Dreamkeepers

Denisha, a small African American girl who was a diligent student but rarely spoke up in class, raised her hand.

"Yes, Denisha."

In a soft and measured voice, Denisha said, "Well, I think it affects us because you have to have people to fight a war, and since they don't have no draft, the people who will volunteer will be the people who don't have any jobs, and a lot of people in our community need work, so they might be the first ones to go."

Before Rossi could comment, an African American boy, Sean, chimed in, "Yeah, my dad said that's what happened in Vietnam—blacks and Mexicans were the first ones to go."

"I'm not sure if they were the first to go," remarked Rossi, "but I can say they were overrepresented." She writes the words on the board. "Do you know what I mean by this?"

None of the students volunteers a response, so Rossi proceeds with an example.

"If African Americans are 12% of the total U.S. population, and Latinos are 8% of the total U.S. population, what percent of the armed services do you think they should be?"

"Twenty percent total," calls out James, beaming at his ability to do the arithmetic quickly. "Twelve percent should be black, and 8 percent should be Mexican."

"Okay," says Rossi. "However, I would call that 8 percent Latino rather than Mexican, because we are also including Puerto Ricans, Cuban Americans, and other U.S. citizens who are from Latin America. But in Vietnam, their numbers in the armed services far exceeded their numbers in the general population. Often they were the first to volunteer to go. Does it seem as if Denisha's comments help us link up with this news item?"

Source: Gloria Ladson-Billings, *The Dreamkeepers: Successful Teachers of African American Children* (San Francisco: Jossey-Bass, 1994), 50–51.

Rossi weaves complex concepts throughout the lesson, including "disproportionality"—basic to mathematics and statistics—plus specific academic language appropriate for describing cultural groups with accuracy and respectful affirmations of students' contributions. Ladson-Billings describes how, under Rossi's skillful guidance, students worked busily together to create by the end of the lesson charts revealing how events in the news might impact their community.

These and similar practices can be found under way in the classrooms of critical teachers nationwide. Consider, for example, some of the curriculum units and resource guides developed by the New York Collective of Radical Educators, which provides teacher-developed tools that critical educators can use to support students in critically analyzing and connecting current events to their lives. (See Focal Point 8.6.)

Teaching tips, published strategies, workshops, study of learning and social theory, guidance from more experienced teachers, and so forth can all help teachers understand and respond to the cultural repertoires of their students. Likewise, interacting meaningfully with people, most especially parents and caregivers who live in students' communities, stands to enhance essential knowledge for teaching. Chapter 11 provides more detail on how schools, teachers, and families build respectful relationships that can yield key insights for responsive teaching. Chapters 9, 10, and 12 elaborate on the importance of new teachers brokering relationships with other educators, too. (Of course, the online "Tools for Critique" also offers questions and suggestions for understanding and leveraging cultural diversity.)

Focal Point 8.6
Examples of Critical Curricular Resources

The New York Collective of Radical Educators (NYCoRE) is "a group of public school educators committed to fighting for social justice in our school system and society at large, by organizing and mobilizing teachers, developing curriculum, and working with community, parent, and student organizations." Over the years, NYCoRE members have developed numerous curricular materials; the names and descriptions of some are included below.

Camouflaged: Investigating How the U.S. Military Affects You and Your Community

We believe that drastic cuts in state and city education budgets are indicative of the war being waged against low-income youth, especially youth of color. Military recruiters see the lack of sound educational institutions in low-income communities as an opportunity to encourage young people to join the military after high school. We as teachers must proactively help students address the camouflaged ways they are affected by the military and ensure that they have information from a variety of sources before considering enlisting in the armed forces. This curriculum provides a critical lens to help students navigate recruiters' messages and to examine the role of the military throughout this country's history to the present.

Revealing Racist Roots: The 3 R's for Teaching About the Jena 6

If all students are expected to learn about our country's justice system, our history, our laws, and our rights, what kinds of lessons can we learn from the Jena 6? (The "Jena 6" were six African American high school students detained and arrested in Jena, Louisiana.) This guide places the case of the Jena 6 within a historical framework. The guide includes and draws connections between the following sections: The Historical Context of American Racism; Literature; Media Literacy; Arts Education; Social Action; Mathematics; and justice-themed organizations and organizing.

No Human Is Illegal!—¡Ningún Ser Humano Es Ilegal!

We must not let our sense of civic duty to engage critical issues begin once the school day is over—we must weave them into our teaching and learning. This resource is best utilized online, as an immigration-themed web resource. It is organized into the following three sections: Engage in Teacher Activism; Encourage and Protect Students' Activism; and Connect your Activism to your Academics.

An Unnatural Disaster: A Critical Guide for Addressing the Aftermath of Hurricane Katrina in the Classroom

This resource encourages teachers as they boldly raise the bar of intellectual questioning in their classrooms. It serves to make available information that will responsibly provide broad and informed perspectives for students to ponder. Teachers must tackle tough issues with students to uncover truths about the nature of power in our society. This is an opportunity for the education community to honor those who are suffering by refusing to ignore them.

Beyond Tolerance: A Resource Guide for Addressing LGBTQ Issues in School

NYQueer and NYCoRE ... [developed this] curricular resource guide to support educators in addressing Lesbian, Gay, Transgender, Bisexual, Questioning and Intersex (LGBTQI) issues and themes in their classrooms. Often, teaching about LGBTQI issues in the classroom is complex and unique—fraught with a variety of fears and uncertainty including fear of retribution and backlash from students, families or administration. But as educators, we must teach these issues because we know it is what is right ... and because we know too clearly what the outcomes are when we don't.

Source: New York Collective of Radical Educators, "Resources," www.nycore.org/resources/.

Ensuring Fair Classrooms

Socially just, democratic classrooms reflect consideration for social differences of all kinds. In their book *Failing at Fairness: How America's Schools Cheat Girls*, researchers David and the late Myra Sadker examine the role that gender, as one example, plays in how teachers treat children, and children treat one another. Specifically, the Sadkers sent "raters" to observe fourth, sixth, and eighth graders and their teachers in more than 100 classrooms. They attended to questions like the following: Whom did teachers call on? How did students get teachers' attention? What did teachers say after they called on students? What level of help or feedback did students receive? If teachers praised students, what was the praise for?

The Sadkers detail "subtle and insidious gender lessons, micro-inequities that appear seemingly insignificant when looked at individually but that have a powerful cumulative impact." These take many forms and begin early. In elementary school classrooms, for example, girls were shortchanged in class discussion, on the playground, and in the curriculum. Boys received from teachers more praise, correction, help, and criticism—all of which foster achievement. Girls received less time, help, and academic challenge. "Reinforced for passivity," the Sadkers argue, "girls' independence and self-esteem suffer."[36]

While these inequities are harmful especially to girls and young women, they are damaging more broadly because they miseducate students about one another's capacities, deservingness, and inherent worth. The same holds true in any situation where explicit (overt) or implicit (hidden) bias advantages some and disadvantages others. Fortunately, teachers can do much to ward against this. Most importantly, they can be vigilant and reflective about their own practices and open to constructive feedback from others who observe their teaching. They can also incorporate strategies—such as longer wait time after asking questions, better monitoring of cooperative groups, and more tailored differentiation, as discussed in Chapter 6—in order to protect against certain students becoming more dominant in the classroom than others.

First-year high school science teacher Lisa Trebasky takes these suggestions to heart as she makes curricular and instructional decisions.

> It is not only what I do but also what I do not do that has a tremendous impact. I have high expectations for all of my students, not just the boys. If I challenge a boy to figure out the answer to a scientifically engaging problem for himself, and then go and give the answer to a girl, I send an unconscious message that I do not think [she] can figure it out by herself. I encourage the girls' active participation when it is easy for them to be drowned out by the louder and more aggressive boys. I encourage girls to ask questions and help them use scientific methodology to find answers. I challenge them to think about why there are more men who do science than women.
>
> —Lisa Trebasky
> First-year teacher, high school science

Of course, ensuring gender-fair classrooms requires more than just ensuring equitable opportunities for girls to participate, communicate, build confidence, and excel. It requires ensuring that such opportunities are available to *all* students. Anything less compromises learning for everyone involved and falls short of emulating the kind of democratic society we aspire to be—one that invites and values multiple voices, rather than elevating only some.

Providing "Apprenticeships in Democracy"

In the introduction to this book, we pointed out that cultural pluralism is not a philosophy or a strategy or, for that matter, a choice. In a society where there are many cultures, it is a reality. Likewise, as critical theories of resistance make clear, students *have* power—power to act, opt out, care, contribute, and so on—whether adults bestow it upon them or not. The question worth asking, then, is, "What will support students and teachers to make the most of this cultural pluralism and power?"

Part of the answer involves affirming and accessing the power of diversity. Critical theorists such as Ira Shor and Antonia Darder emphasize the important but difficult work involved in supporting "resistant" students to channel their energies in directions that benefit them without requiring them to give up what makes them who they are. Darder, for example, calls for teachers to construct classrooms as "apprenticeships in democracy"—places where students can be themselves, so to speak, *and* be contributing members of a learning community. She stresses the need for teachers to take seriously student participation, solidarity, interest, and voice.[37]

Darder also alerts teachers to the right and the need that students have to develop and maintain bicultural (and multicultural) identities—for example, American *and* Lithuanian, working class *and* college going. Darder calls for classroom environments that help students make informed, empowered decisions about how they want to fit in (or not) with the dominant culture. Given students' varied cultures and experiences, there can be no one formula, no "best" approach, except that the classroom culture must begin within the students themselves.

When he was a first-year teacher, Ramón Martínez decided that his first graders were not too young to confront in the classroom the conditions they experienced in their daily lives. Using Darder's approach, he sought to redirect the resistance that his students, as young as they were, had already begun to exhibit.

I witnessed firsthand the way that my students' cultural contexts influence their attitudes and actions in our classroom. Since academic and economic success are uncommon in their community, my students are likely to dismiss academic and economic aspirations as unrealistic. In fact, some of my students seem to have already done just that.

The challenge for me is to use my theoretical understanding of students' behavior to provide a more effective learning environment. In particular, I have been influenced by the notion that student participation and the development of student voice are essential components of a culturally democratic learning environment.

My students' familiarity with alcoholism, drug abuse, and gang violence; their mastery of "Spanglish" and code-switching; and their skillful ability to communicate the subtle nuances of everyday life might not be perceived as knowledge or intelligence by many teachers. However, my students have much to contribute to the construction of knowledge in our classroom. Group discussions, weekly "sharing time," and interactive journals are three ways that I have attempted to validate my students' lived experiences. I have tried to communicate to them that their thoughts, ideas, and experiences are important and worthy of discussion in the classroom. My goal has been for them to feel that they are experts when it comes to their neighborhood and themselves.

For example, although most of my students live in public housing, [when we made our "mural map" of the neighborhood] many of them chose to create large, colorful homes with sloped roofs. Interestingly, one student depicted her building extremely realistically. When I smiled at her house, she insisted that that was how it really looked. I agreed with her and recruited her to make more buildings to fill some of the empty spaces on the map. After she had completed her task, I noticed that one of the buildings had "PR" written on it in large letters. When I questioned her about what the letters were for, she was silent and even seemed a little embarrassed. After an extended pause, she told me that that was what they spray-painted on the walls of her building. I quickly realized that she had attempted to imitate the graffiti of "PF" ("Primera Flats"), one of the eight gangs that reside in the housing projects. I realized that her embarrassment was due to her uncertainty as to how I would react to the graffiti. I reassured her that it was perfectly all right to depict things as she saw them.

To a very large degree, these strategies have been successful. My students share their thoughts, ideas, and experiences with me and with their classmates. They seem to perceive that our classroom is a forum for them to share freely and openly. I feel that I have contributed to their empowerment by encouraging them to express and define themselves.

—Ramón Martínez
First-year teacher, grade 1

Building on Students' Powerful Resources

Obviously, to help students gain access and build on the powerful resources they bring, teachers have to be able to recognize and leverage those resources as Ramón did. In his now classic book, *Empowering Education: Critical Teaching for Social Change*, Ira Shor identifies resources that are worth every teacher's efforts to seek out and support. In the following list, we summarize and elaborate on Shor's ten "student resources for empowering education and critical thought"—resources that stand to flourish and fuel deep learning in caring, democratic classrooms.[38]

1. *Cognitive and affective resources*: Students read, write, listen, and debate with more care, and even *feel* with more depth, in caring, democratic classrooms. Their cognitive and affective resources, in turn, become assets on which the community can draw for learning.
2. *Insight, passion, and authenticity*: In caring, democratic classrooms, students' "talkative habits" become "academic tools." Students speak passionately and insightfully about what matters to them. And they do so in rich and vibrant language that reflects their authentic voices, imaginations, interests, thoughts, and feelings.
3. *Life and work experience*: In caring, democratic classrooms, students share their school, family, community, and social experiences. Their concerns—about sexuality, social media, suicide, and so on—are treated as worthy of inquiry, as are their minor satisfactions and major triumphs. In turn, students learn to see their everyday knowledge as *expertise* and as a powerful *foundation* for their own and others' academic learning.
4. *Self-esteem*: In caring, democratic classrooms, students find in themselves the inherent value they bring. In turn, they become powerful actors on behalf of themselves and their classmates. Their confidence enables them to ask for help and to help others. They learn to leverage that confidence to build the confidence of their peers. Teachers facilitate this by listening and attending to them carefully and evidently—taking notes on their comments, asking them to repeat statements for clarification, having them reread work aloud for peers to hear, referring back in class discussion to things expressed previously, and so on.
5. *Curiosity*: Children come to school curious. Over time, however, many come to feel that curiosity brings risks and reaps few rewards in school. Caring, democratic classrooms reignite curiosity and nurture it in ways that fuel learning—by encouraging students to ask questions that cannot be easily answered, by inviting them to confront taboos and voice silenced perspectives, by asking them to consider unimagined alternatives, and so on.

6. *Democratic dispositions:* To school, students often bring powerful democratic dispositions: distaste for bosses, politicians, and other big shots; sensitivity to indignity, arbitrary authority, and haughtiness; resentfulness toward following rules not of their making; beliefs in justice, equality, fairness, and free speech. Many of these dispositions clash with antidemocratic values permeating our culture, like male superiority, White supremacy, homophobia and transphobia, and more. In caring, democratic classrooms, students come together to make sense of these competing values and to figure out what kind of adults they want to be, what kind of society they want to be part of, and what they can do to help make that a reality.

7. *Varied views on race and racism (and the courage to converse):* In caring, democratic classrooms, students do what many adults avoid; they talk about race and racism. Though they may be reluctant at first, students have things to say, which is why teachers in such classrooms refrain from moralizing lecture, and instead support students to share and question one another. Of course, just "airing" different perspectives is inadequate at best, damaging at worst, and students show us they are capable of so much more. With teachers' support, they can and do answer crucial questions—What is race? What is racism? What causes racism? What can reduce it?—and they work together to raise consciousness and take action. (Focal Point 8.7 offers an example of what even very young students are capable of in this regard; it features courageous race-conscious conversation, facilitated by literacy scholar and early childhood education expert Mariana Souto-Manning, in a caring, democratic first-grade classroom.)

8. *Willingness to act against -isms:* And in caring, democratic classrooms, students actually *do* take action against racism and other *-isms*. Such classrooms capture and deepen young people's willingness, often their *desire*, to be a part of social progress. And while we can conjure ample examples of -isms—racism, sexism, classism, homophobia, xenophobia, religious intolerance, and so on—playing out in schools, we can also conjure ample examples—in caring, democratic classrooms across the country—of young people working against the grain to create socially just learning communities. And we can see in so many other students the untapped potential for classroom-catalyzed social action.

9. *Reservations about the American dream:* In caring, democratic classrooms, students voice their wonderings and frustrations with common-sense ideas and cultural myths, of which "the American dream" is perhaps the most obvious. After all, it's a statistical fact that most students in the United States are not part of the 1 percent and that the majority come from families and communities that struggle to make ends meet. So many students bring to school a sense, often unarticulated, that the American dream (or, simply, school) works in others' favor but not their own. Caring, democratic classrooms support students to explore how culture and identity in this country interact with capitalism and its conceptions of worth and merit. They help students—in the words of Paolo Freire—"read the world," reimagine it, and realize their power and potential as authors of their own lives.

10. *Humor and emotion:* Caring, democratic classrooms invite students to engage their full selves, not just their analytic minds, in the learning process. This is not the norm. As Shor writes, students are often surprised, delighted, shy, or caught off guard when classroom conversation or content invokes emotional, not just analytic, intensity. Classroom life shouldn't, and needn't, be this way. When it is, we are asking students to holster half of who they are, and to leave that half somewhere beyond the classroom door. This undermines learning. Joy and good humor have a rightful and essential place in caring, democratic classrooms.

Focal Point 8.7
Critical Pedagogy in a First-Grade Classroom

Literacy scholar and early childhood education expert Mariana Souto-Manning, a former teacher herself, works closely and collaboratively with practicing teachers to show what young children are capable of when supported by adults with the dispositions, skills, and will to engage children's creativity and cultural and linguistic wealth. The following excerpt is from an article in which Souto-Manning illustrates what critical pedagogy can look like in a first-grade classroom. In the excerpt, we see students drawing connections between the texts they are reading and the way their school functions. We see them analyze—quite explicitly—the racialized dynamics of "pull-out" programs that remove students from their classroom. Ultimately, based on these analyses, the students—with support from the adults around them—successfully petitioned their school's principal to have special education and gifted services "pushed in" to classrooms, so that students could access them together, instead of "pulling out" individuals in an inequitable, segregating, and stigmatizing fashion.

As we continued reading, the children continued to draw parallels and become involved with the structure that curtailed their agency within the sphere of schooling. The Story of Ruby Bridges (Coles, 1995), the first African American girl to attend a New Orleans elementary school after court-ordered desegregation in 1960, describes how a six-year-old walks past angry crowds of white protestors to enter the school only white children traditionally attended. Yet, when she gets in, she is all alone. Parents of the white students kept them home. Ruby "began learning how to read and write in an empty classroom, an empty building." In a somewhat romanticized ending, the story progresses until two boys and then the rest of the students return to school; the mobs disperse by the time Ruby enters second grade. My students engaged in dialogue such as the following one:

William:	I get it. It's just like us.
Teacher:	Like you?
William:	Yeah. It's like when you don't know you goin' special ed, to resource, and you thin' you special. Then you know later that you really dumb. You all alone, ya' know. We all here in yo' class, but when we go to tha' other class, it's not everybody.
Derrick:	And how everyone who goes to Star [pseudonym for the county's gifted education program] is white.
Kary:	Wow . . .
Shaniece:	I don't know . . .
Luz:	But we go to the same school.
Derrick:	Just think . . .
Johnnie:	Yeah, Derrick. I'm not really sure.
Erin:	Well, there's a way. Let's find out.

(Erin goes to the easel and grabs the marker. She writes the names of the teachers who teach in pull-out programs.)

Teacher:	What are you going to do?
Erin:	I am going to find out how many go with each teacher.
Teacher:	How will this help you get to what you want to know?
William:	Yeah. How?
Derrick:	We can choose different color markers for boys and girls, and then

Kary: No, no, I know. If we are talking about black and white, we need to get black and white markers.

Ci'Erikka: White marker?

Madison: Well, like we read, we are not really white. So, let's choose pink.

(Erin grabs a pink and a black marker.)

Jorge: Here is the brown.

Erin: Oh yes, I forgot.

Kary: We can't forget anyone.

Even though the children ignored many of the complexities of the matrix of domination described by Hill Collins (1990) and the way gender, class, and race served as sorting devices in schools and in society (Parsons, 1959; Turner, 1960) they charted themselves and discovered that all children who received gifted services were from white or Asian backgrounds. All the children who received ESOL (English to Speakers of Other Languages) services were Asian or Latinos. All those going to resource (receiving Special Education services) were African American, actually African American boys. They had uncovered racial and gender segregation, covert racism, and sexism in our own school.

Excerpted from: Mariana Souto-Manning, Negotiating Culturally Responsive Pedagogy Through Multicultural Children's Literature: Towards critical democratic literacy practices in a first grade classroom, *Journal of Early Childhood Literacy* 9, no. 1 (2009): 50–74.

Creating School and Classroom Communities Is an Ongoing, Emancipatory Struggle

People often associate critical pedagogy, and accurately so, with an unflinching critique of oppressive structures and practices. What we hear less about, however, is the central role that love for self and others must play. Antonia Darder described this love as "rooted in a committed willingness to struggle persistently with an emancipatory purpose and to intimately connect that purpose with what [critical theorist Paolo Freire] called our 'true vocation'—to be human."[39] This is the kind of "radical love" that teachers can bring to the classroom in order to move beyond the traditions of discipline and control.

Creating caring, democratic communities that work together to advance social justice is no small task. It requires working against the accumulated weight of history—nearly two centuries of schools having been dominated by behaviorist approaches to classroom management. What may seem like small, everyday achievements are important victories in a long and worthy collective project. First-year teacher Janene Ashford, for one, is learning to see the value even in her failed attempts. She's learning to see classroom community as a process, or a living entity—something to which she and her students must consistently tend—rather than a job to finish or a goal to reach.

> Community and community building were important aspects of my educational philosophy, so I knew they had to be part of my practice from day one. I spent the first week of school doing community-building activities. We did people hunts, made and wore nametags, wrote first-day-of-school creative essays, and did other getting-to-know-you activities. By the second week, I felt my students were getting to know each other and me and were developing a sense of trust and security.

As the days passed, I began to wonder when and if my kids were ever going to "learn." I felt such pressure to make sure my students were academically prepared that, by the third week of school, I had placed the idea of community building on the back burner. I did not see any behavior problems in those first weeks, so I felt comfortable that the time we spent building our community was probably enough. I was ready to get down to "business." I watched them work in partners or in groups, and the work was getting done. That was all that I cared about. What I failed to realize, however, was that they were simply completing the work independently, while sitting next to their partners. There was no negotiation, communication, or interaction taking place. It was every student for him- or herself.

By the fifth week, my students were out of control. They were tattling, bullying, name calling, poking, and excluding one another from activities . . . and their antics were affecting the lessons and activities. I spent more time mediating fights than mediating knowledge. I was miserable and angry.

I decided to incorporate a community circle into our schedule. I called the circle to share what I had observed in the classroom and the yard. I used a story, "A Sense of Goose," as a discussion starter. The story describes how geese function as a community, uplifting one another as they fly in a V formation. Interwoven through the story are italicized messages that make the connection between how geese live and how humans should live. But my students spent more time trying to figure out the vocabulary than to comprehend the meaning. Many did not even know what geese looked like or anything about geese. (I marked this as failure number one.) I found myself losing patience with them because they weren't "getting it." I could not believe that my students were not able to take the meaning from the story and apply it to life and our classroom. I could not imagine taking thirty-two students outside and making them flap their arms in a V formation for them to construct understanding. So I tried to draw it on the chalkboard. (I marked this as failure number two.)

Eventually, after a couple of readings a few students understood the meaning, but I didn't want to push it. The idea of community and our classroom as a community of learners was as foreign as another language. I placed the story back into my lesson plan book, feeling defeated. I had my students put the story in their binders, in hopes that one day we would come back to it and really understand its meaning and relevance. . . .

Over winter break, I finally had time to read Alfie Kohn's book *Beyond Discipline: From Compliance to Community*. It could not have come at a better time. I began to find answers to why the "A Sense of Goose" story did not make sense to my students. Whatever form of community we had was enforced by me. I was running a very teacher-centered classroom, where all the power of decision making and conflict resolution rested in my hands.

As the year progressed, my students and I began to realize a democratic classroom community. It was an incredible and sometimes difficult evolution. . . . "Guess what the teacher wants" (under the guise of democracy) evolved into "What should we do?" under guidelines I determined, and then into "I can't/don't need to do it myself, what do you guys think we should do?" Over the next couple of months, my students and I developed and maintained a wonderfully strong community.

Then, once again, I put our community building on autopilot, just as the "change" in sixth-grade students that my colleagues had warned me about occurred. Slowly things crumbled. Best friends were no longer best friends. Rumors and gossip were "destroying" reputations and tearing down trust. Four of my students were put into in-school suspension! I was barely sleeping at night. The "Goose" story began to nag me from the recesses of my mind.

I raced to my classroom and created a space big enough in the center for the thirty-three chairs to be formed into a circle. I stopped the students before they entered and told them to take a seat in the circle. The looks on their faces were priceless. The expression was not the same "What is this crazy lady talking about" look; it was a "something big is about to happen" looks. They did as they were told. I sat down, took a deep breath, and let them know we needed a community circle. I then passed around "A Sense of Goose." Expressions of familiarity washed over their faces. Their responses to the story were incredibly insightful. They understood how the geese worked together in communities, took care of and looked after one another. They shared wonderful examples of how humans should work together. They shared relevant and meaningful stories that revealed how profound their connections were with one another and how deeply those connections had been damaged. We sorted through issues in our classroom community by engaging in dialogue, and began the long and difficult process of making change.

—Janene Ashford
First-year teacher, grade 6

Creating a caring, democratic classroom community takes time, experience, and patience. Even when teachers gain skill and confidence, and their classrooms are more safe and caring than they might have hoped for previously, new challenges will arise. Every year, Janene and other teachers like her call upon themselves for even greater measures of care and skill than they thought possible the prior year. Educational researcher Andy Hargreaves, in his book *Changing Teachers, Changing Times*, offers a valuable perspective on creating better classrooms and a better society. He suggests to us that teachers' work is not just about working with others to *solve problems* in and beyond the classroom, but allowing ourselves to identify and then struggle with a "better class of problems."[40] Struggling to care, we believe, is a far better class of problem than struggling to discipline.

Digging Deeper and Tools for Critique

www.routledge.com/cw/teachingtochangetheworld

Notes

1 Joel Spring, *The American School* (New York: Longman, 1990), 56–57.
2 William Glasser, *The Quality School* (New York: HarperCollins, 1992).
3 See, for example, Frank Riessman, *The Culturally Deprived Child* (New York: Harper & Row, 1962); and Harry Passow, Miriam Goldberg, and Abraham J. Tannenbaum, eds., *Education of the Disadvantaged* (New York: Holt, Rinehart & Winston, 1967).
4 Jennifer Ng and John Rury, *Poverty and Education: A Critical Analysis of the Ruby Payne Phenomenon*, Teachers College Record, 2006, n.p., www.tcrecord.org ID#12596.
5 See, for example, Lee Canter and Marlene Canter, *Assertive Discipline: Positive Behavior* (Santa Monica: Lee Canter & Associates, 1997).
6 See, for example, Alfie Kohn, *Punished by Rewards* (Boston: Houghton Mifflin, 1993).
7 U.S. Department of Education and Office for Civil Rights, *A First Look: Key Data Highlights on Equity and Opportunity Gaps in Our Nation's Public Schools*, October 2016.
8 The National Association of School Psychologists, *Zero Tolerance and Alternative Strategies: A Fact Sheet for Educators and Policymakers*, 2001, www.naspcenter.org/factsheets/zt_fs.html.
9 U.S. Department of Education, Office for Civil Rights, Civil Rights Data Collection (CRDC), 2013–14, 2016, https://ocrdata.ed.gov.
10 Jacob Kounin, *Discipline and Group Management in Classrooms* (New York: Holt, Rinehart & Winston, 1970).
11 Thomas Good and Jere Brophy, *Looking in Classrooms* (New York: Longman, 1997).
12 Jeff Gregg, "Discipline, Control, and the School Mathematics Tradition," *Teaching and Teacher Education* 11, no. 6 (1995): 579–593.

13 Herbert M. Kliebard, *The Struggle for the American Curriculum: 1893–1958*, 2nd ed. (New York: Routledge, 1995), 6.

14 Alan Ryan, *John Dewey and the High Tide of American Liberalism* (New York: W. W. Norton, 1995), 153. Ryan notes that Dewey was far more nationalistic than Addams; he, far more than she, wanted such settings to bring immigrants into the American community, not simply to create community-like settings per se.

15 A. S. Neill, *Summerhill* (New York: St. Martin's Press, 1995, originally published in 1960).

16 Daniel Goleman, *Emotional Intelligence: Why It Can Matter More Than IQ* (New York: Bantam Books, 1995).

17 Nel Noddings, *The Challenge to Care in Schools: An Alternative Approach to Education* (New York: Teachers College Press, 1992), 65.

18 Nel Noddings, "Teaching Themes of Care," *Phi Delta Kappan* 77 (May 1995): 676.

19 Noddings, *The Challenge to Care in Schools*, 20.

20 Ibid.

21 Alan Fogel, *Developing Through Relationships* (Chicago: University of Chicago Press, 1993).

22 Carollee Howes and Sharon Ritchie, *A Matter of Trust: Connecting Teachers and Learners in the Early Childhood Classroom* (New York: Teachers College Press, 2002).

23 Ibid., 77.

24 George Noblit, "In the Meaning: The Possibilities of Caring," *Phi Delta Kappan* 77 (May 1995): 682.

25 Ibid., 684.

26 Alfie Kohn, *Beyond Discipline: From Compliance to Community* (Alexandria, VA: Association for Supervision and Curriculum Development, 1996), 114–115.

27 Child Development Project, *Ways We Want Our Classroom to Be: Class Meetings That Build Commitment to Kindness and Learning* (Oakland, CA: Developmental Studies Center, 1994); Victor Battistich, Eric Schaps, and Nance Wilson, "Effects of an Elementary School Intervention on Students' 'Connectedness' to School and Social Adjustment During Middle School," *Journal of Primary Prevention* 24, no. 3 (2004): 243–262.

28 The Center for the Collaborative Classroom, www.collaboratingclassroom.org.

29 Peace Builders is a commercially available curriculum (Tucson, AZ: Heartsprings, 1995) based on Dennis D. Embry's work in conflict resolution.

30 Leo Lionni, *Tillie and the Wall* (Decorah, IA: Dragonfly Books; New York: Penguin Random House, 1991), n.p.

31 Vivian Paley, *You Can't Say You Can't Play* (Cambridge, MA: Harvard University Press, 1993).

32 United Nations, *Convention on the Rights of the Child*, 2001, www.unicef.org/crc/.

33 The Advancement Project, *Schoolhouse to Jailhouse: On the Ground*, www.advancementproject.org/our-work/schoolhouse-to-jailhouse/on-the-ground/.

34 Sharon Lewis, *Improving School Climate: Findings From Schools Implementing Restorative Practices* (Bethlehem, PA: International Institute for Restorative Practices, 2009).

35 Henry A. Giroux, *Theory and Resistance in Education: A Pedagogy of Opposition* (South Hadley, MA: Bergin and Garvey, 1983); Paul Willis, *Learning to Labour: How Working Class Kids Get Working Class Jobs* (Farnborough, Hants: Saxon House, 1977).

36 Myra Sadker and David Sadker, *Failing at Fairness: How America's Schools Cheat Girls* (New York: Macmillan, 1994), 44.

37 Antonia Darder, *Culture and Power in the Classroom: A Critical Foundation for Bicultural Education* (Westport, CT: Bergin & Garvey, 1991), 67.

38 Ira Shor, *Empowering Education: Critical Teaching for Social Change* (Chicago: University of Chicago Press, 1992), 223–232.

39 Antonia Darder, "Teaching as an Act of Love," in *The Critical Pedagogy Reader*, eds. A. Darder, M. Baltodano, and R. Torres (New York: Routledge Falmer, 2003), 497.

40 Andy Hargreaves, *Changing Teachers, Changing Times: Teachers' Work and Culture in the Postmodern Age* (New York: Continuum, 1994).

Part III

The Context of Teaching to Change the World

As education scholar Sonia Nieto explains,

> Excellent teachers don't develop full-blown at graduation; nor are they just 'born teachers.' Instead, teachers are always in the process of 'becoming.' They continually discover who they are and what they stand for, through their dialogue with peers, through ongoing and consistent study, and through deep reflection about their craft.[1]

This "becoming" requires engaging with others, seeking new learning opportunities, and reflecting deeply; it is a career-long process that provides hope, sustenance, and competence in the day-to-day work of teaching.

In this final section of the book, "The Context of Teaching to Change the World," we explore the possibilities that reside in schools, in communities, and in the profession. We show how teachers can search for the deeper meanings that lie within the education clichés of "teaching one child at a time," "thinking about the children, not the adults," and, yes, even "teaching to change the world." We also, however, acknowledge some of the often-significant challenges teachers face. Rather than sugarcoat these challenges, or explain them away, we show how some teachers are meeting such challenges with agency, ingenuity, and hope.

Chapter 9, "The School Culture: Where Good Teaching Makes Sense," identifies characteristics of schools that support democratic teaching and learning. The chapter describes several current reform efforts aimed at establishing healthy learning environments. The chapter also describes "inquiry"—a kind of dialogue that supports members of the school community to ask questions, reflect, and take action to improve the school's culture and ensure socially just learning.

Chapter 10, "School Structure: Sorting Students and Opportunities to Learn," deals with the often-controversial ways that schools respond to differences in students' abilities, achievements, and behaviors. We explain how the categories and labels schools assign to students reflect social and cultural constructions, rather than natural "facts," and we explain how labeling and sorting students became part of American schooling. We then review some of the evidence showing that these practices often do as much to create differences as they do to meet students' special needs. Finally, we describe the work of educators who attempt to give all students the attention and resources they need without isolating or alienating them.

In Chapter 11, "The Community: Engaging With Families and Neighborhoods," we first consider two dominant (and contradictory) complaints about parents—that they participate too much or not enough. We then examine four traditions that inform relationships between parents and schools. Finally, we argue that school cultures that work well to support all students engage families and communities as partners. Teachers can pursue such relationships individually as they teach and care for their students, and they can act collectively through their own and others' organizing.

Chapter 12, "Teaching to Change the World: A Profession and a Hopeful Struggle," provides an overview of the teaching profession today and describes some of the pressures that teachers face as they begin their careers. We conclude the chapter, and the book, with five strategies that teachers use as they teach to change the world. These include making a commitment to hope and struggle, building a learning community, becoming a social justice activist, expanding your professional influence, and finding satisfaction in the everyday.

It is not by accident that this section, and thus this book, culminates with the idea of a "hopeful struggle." There is likely no better way to describe what teaching to change the world is and involves. Yet, as education professor and experienced high school teacher Jeffrey Andrade-Duncan reminds us, this struggle requires not just any hope but a specific kind: critical hope. This is a hope that confronts rather than denies the injustice and pain that so many students experience—a hope that "stares down the painful path" and propels us forward in the face of adversity. It is this kind of hope that keeps great teachers going and that explains why

> despite the overwhelming odds against us making it down that path to change, we make the journey again and again. There is no other choice. Acceptance of this fact [that there is no other choice] allows us to find the courage and the commitment to cajole our students to join us on that journey. This makes us better people as it makes us better teachers, and it models for our students that the painful path is the hopeful path.[2]

The teachers featured in these final four chapters demonstrate what it might look like to begin moving along that painful, yet hopeful, path—"becoming," as Nieto would suggest, better teachers *and* better people—and inspiring the rest of us to do the same.

Notes

1 Sonia Nieto, *What Keeps Teachers Going?* (New York: Teachers College Press, 2003), 125.
2 Jeffrey M. R. Duncan-Andrade, "Note to Educators: Hope Required When Growing Roses in Concrete," *Harvard Educational Review* 79, no. 2 (2009): 191.

Chapter 9

The School Culture
Where Good Teaching Makes Sense

Our school provides an excellent environment for inquiry, advancement, and staff development. This is due to the largely supportive administration and the strong influence of educated teachers. Just as is the case with students in classrooms, a critical mass of educators will dictate the school's philosophy and culture. Either a "woe is me" or a "can do" attitude will prevail. There is no middle ground. Our site is most definitely a "can do" atmosphere. My colleagues feed off of each other, and defeatism doesn't have a place to gain traction. Whether it is a challenge dictated to us by the district or state, a lack of basic skills by students coming into the school, difficulties at home for the students, or a lack of the appropriate methods and techniques by a teacher, our site focuses on solving the problem. We are highly collaborative within individual departments, and we are working on greater interdepartmental collaboration. We also have a high level of collaboration with other schools during staff development days. The district encourages teachers to participate as workshop leaders, and it provides strong new teacher training and continued support through departmental "coaches."

—Mark Hill
First-year teacher, high school mathematics

Students need committed and capable teachers; a clean and safe environment; up-to-date books, computers, and facilities; and enough time to learn, but they need other things, too. The school's organizational arrangements and routines, attitudes and beliefs, and social dynamics also shape what students accomplish in school. And just as students need a school culture that enables a socially just, excellent education, so do teachers.

Chapter Overview

This chapter focuses on school culture—one of the most important conditions for teaching to change the world. First, we discuss the powerful influence that a school's culture has on the quality of teaching and learning. We then elaborate four key features of "good" school cultures—that is, school cultures that foster high academic quality and social justice. These features include academic press, rich learning opportunities and resources, caring relationships and practices, and conditions that support teachers' inquiry and activism. Chapters 10 and 11 address two additional essential characteristics of supportive, socially just school cultures: (1) flexible, heterogeneous grouping practices and (2) respectful partnerships between schools and the families and communities they serve. Together, these cultural features allow teachers and students to teach and learn in ways that can change the world.

Schools as Cultures

In the following excerpt, a new teacher describes the cultures at two different senior high schools where she has taught. In many ways, the two schools are similar. Both are large urban high schools in medium-sized school systems. Both enroll racially mixed student populations and many students who struggle academically. Nevertheless, this teacher was struck by the contrast between the cultures at the two schools.

Wow. I am still adapting to this new school. The culture is very different from the school where I taught last year. That school had many well-trained teachers and administrators. Teachers formed small communities among themselves, and one hosted a monthly inquiry group meeting. Teachers felt free to speak out at the large monthly staff meetings. We could also give anonymous feedback and ask questions of the principal, and we were given typed-up answers.

There was a tardy policy. There were discipline procedures. Social justice was not only spoken of, it was expected. When I wanted to do a community volunteer project, the principal supported me. When I went outside the norm and departed from the textbook, I felt supported. There was a community liaison and a bilingual newsletter for parents and students. The school's leadership was diverse. I definitely found a community of teachers there.

My new school, in contrast, has had six principals in the last eight years. There is high teacher turnover, and the administration has had a very difficult time finding substitute teachers. Many students sit in the cafeteria waiting for a solution. Because of the lack of consistent leadership, it feels as if the students run the school in some ways. There is little to no school-wide tardy policy. Few discipline procedures seem in place. The school is run by three to eight loudspeaker interruptions a day (management by loudspeaker, I call it). There needs to be stronger leadership about what is expected and what is appropriate. I don't think the school is caring enough.

After only six weeks at this pretty dysfunctional second school, I can see why teachers burn out quickly.

—Name withheld
First-year high school teacher

These two schools are dissimilar in many respects, but the heart of their differences lies in their school cultures. School cultures help shape what people see, how they feel, and what they think is possible. Most people adapt to the culture they are in and see it as pretty much "normal." They often aren't aware of how their familiar culture shapes their thinking and actions until they come face-to-face with cultural changes or differences. Then, life seems out of the ordinary, abnormal, or "not how we usually do things."[1] Teachers who are new to a school may be more attuned to the culture's influence than those who have been teaching at the school for some time and for whom its daily practices and attitudes seem normal. New teachers can make use of their heightened perception, but they must also be aware that the existing culture often does not take happily to those, especially newcomers, who challenge it. After all, to insiders, the culture *is* normal; it's the challengers who are not.

That said, new teachers can be assured that with patience and hard work, school cultures do change. For many teachers, teaching to change the world necessarily involves working to change school culture. The last time we spoke to the teacher quoted above, she told us that she was already doing that work.

As a new hire in a new school, I had planned to be somewhat quiet, but I am finding it increasingly difficult. I have already been a voice of dissent in some meetings (for example, suggesting that we make advisory periods more about the students and their goals), and I am seeking out a new network of like-minded teachers.

School Cultures Shape Sense Making

For decades, psychologist Seymour Sarason studied the power of school culture.[2] He first realized how much school culture matters when his studies of school change in the 1960s showed that schools rarely took reforms seriously. Cultural "regularities"—the opportunities that schools made available to students, the expectations they held, and the relationships already in place—blocked genuine change in most schools. Existing patterns of practice were so ingrained that few people questioned them. Sarason suggested that a visitor from Mars might ask, "Why do you do it this way?" but that few people at the schools he studied would think to ask, or even be able to answer, such a question. To them, cultural regularities—the things they did in school day in, day out—were just considered normal and therefore rarely the subject of reflection.

In fact, when reforms were proposed, administrators and teachers would adjust the reforms to fit their schools instead of changing their schools to fit the reforms. Usually, that meant following along with the outward appearance of change, but changing little else in the hopes that reforms would pass. And usually they did. Over the past forty years, many studies have echoed Sarason's finding that few reforms take hold in ways that produce the intended results.

In today's schools, course offerings, parent conference schedules, teachers' supervision responsibilities, and much else are matters of formal policy—typically decided on and then written by school leadership and committees following a more or less deliberative process. But some of the most powerful cultural regularities are less formalized; that is, rarely does anyone consciously decide, "Let's do it this way." For example, teachers at one school stay late to give students extra help, while the parking lot at another school empties shortly after the last bell. At one school, much to the teachers' delight, the principal pops into classrooms and informally participates in lessons. At another school, similar visits prompt the teachers to feel as if the principal is checking up on them; even the students shape up and appear to concentrate, waiting for the principal to leave before they and the teacher relax. At some schools, teachers follow the required curriculum to the letter; elsewhere, they expand on the curriculum to meet students' needs. At some schools, teachers pitch in to help their colleagues, preferring to work on teams; at others, teachers guard their ideas and materials, preferring to work alone.

A school's culture exerts a powerful effect on teachers, who, like students, learn by observation: how others act, what others see and think, when others agree or resist, and with what consequences. Sometimes, teachers are shocked by the disapproval they elicit as a result of acting or speaking according to their professional norms and values. Always, it is essential that teachers "read" their school culture to determine the best entry points for change.

School Cultures Where It Makes Sense to Teach All Students Well

Good schools have cultures where it makes sense for faculty to teach all students well and for all students to learn well. That doesn't mean that all good schools are alike. A central tenet of the Coalition of Essential Schools, one of the most successful and enduring school reform networks in the United States, is that "good schools do share powerful guiding ideas, principles that are widely accepted even as they take different shapes in practice when people put them to work in their own settings from day to day."[3] So, rather than prescribing lists of ideal practices for schools to follow, educators need to understand the guiding principles, or ideas, that can help schools chart meaningful progress. The various groups that we mention online in Digging Deeper all embrace four key principles, which we discuss in the sections that follow:

- A "press" for learning and social justice
- Access to learning opportunities and resources
- Access to caring relationships and practices
- Conditions that support teacher inquiry and activism

A Press for Learning and Social Justice

Press refers to the influence of a cultural imperative or a social consensus. It suggests an inevitability: that each member of a society, a group, or an institution will be immersed in, and thus *pressed* by, particular cultural values. Some may rebel against this press, some may not "get it," but all will be touched by it. Schools are inevitably pressed by the values, beliefs, and commitments of the larger culture, and, in turn, they create a press of their own on the adults and young people in them.

Some examples are helpful to understand the concept of cultural press. During World War II, American schools were shaped by the strong press for victory in the war, which was manifest in nearly every aspect of daily life in schools. War was woven throughout the content of geography and history classes. Students brought money to school to deposit toward their own federal savings (war) bonds. Clothing, energy use, and school meals were all influenced by wartime rationing—not complied with reluctantly, but as a matter of civic responsibility. Conversations often focused on young people who were at or about to go to war. And so on.

In contrast to the civic orientation of the "war years," popular culture in the 1970s was highly individualized, hence the self-awareness and personal expression valued by what came to be called the "me generation." The curriculum and teaching at many schools reflected, more or less, these broader cultural values; students were asked to look inward, to find themselves.

Emerging cultural norms often press schools in other directions. The current attention to global economic competition emerges in the press to have American students outscore those in other nations on standardized tests. Shifting attitudes about gender roles and relationships press for increased openness and fluidity. Worries about student safety and discipline press for more metal detectors, surveillance, and security on school campuses. Belief in the power of postsecondary education presses schools and students to treat college-going as a necessity.

School cultures also press students to behave in characteristic ways, and if a school's culture is strong enough, it can press students in ways that counter some of the broader culture's influence. Private religious schools offer one example; they tend to exert a distinct cultural press that emerges from the religious norms at their core. At most of these schools, not everything is overtly religious, but religious values are ever-present in students' daily lives and shape how everyone acts, and reacts, in school.

Most schools around the turn of the twenty-first century have crafted statements of their purpose or mission. All express a value for high levels of learning, and almost all voice a commitment to ensuring equitable opportunities to learn. However, a mission statement alone isn't enough to create a strong school-wide press toward ambitious learning and the advancement of social justice. That requires a culture where rigorous academics and equity are simply normal, unquestioned, and reinforced in the details of everyday life.

School Cultures Where Learning Is the Top Priority

Every school's mission statement puts learning first, but schools differ enormously in whether they create a press for students' learning and how they create it. Quiet halls, a litter-free cafeteria, high attendance at sports events, and increased test scores are all worthy-enough goals, but they do not constitute a press for achievement or for social justice. Order and security are essential in well-functioning schools, but some schools can't seem to get beyond their success at "keeping the lid on." What's much more important is whether students are actually engaged in their learning. Listen for what principals, teachers, and students expect and what they take pride in. Do they describe in specific detail rich learning experiences? Can they tell you about innovative practices? Or do they make self-effacing comments about how they really don't understand math very well, or how they are "not good" at English?

Consider the following description of what we observed at a fairly well-off suburban high school, where the press for learning appears quite low:

> The bell has rung, and the last few eleventh graders are sauntering into their second-period class. Several students present "absence slips" to the teacher, confessing truancy or documenting their real or invented illness or family emergency. Three others present passes, respectively, from the school nurse, the counseling office, and the student government adviser. Another student has forgotten her pass, and the teacher sends her to the office. There are seven students absent. A couple might arrive late. Others will receive summonses

from various corners of the school. Only two-thirds of the students actually attend the entire class two days in a row.

Over the public address, a student recites the Pledge of Allegiance. . . . Another student reads announcements. The senior class advertises, as it will each day for two weeks, its fund-raising computer-dating dance. Two students perform a hastily written skit. They are too close to the microphone, and their garbled speech is nearly unintelligible. However, a few adolescent sexual innuendoes manage to get through, and the class receives them with exaggerated, uproarious appreciation. A single academic announcement—the scholarship society will offer tutoring at noon—arouses no apparent interest. An announcer praises a winning sports team and commends the losers for a great effort. The vice principal issues a warning about lunch passes. He adds that makeup testing for the state achievement test will take place in the library, and therefore the library will be closed for the next two days.

Announcements over, instruction begins.

The students at this school score well on standardized tests, and many gain admission to top-rated colleges. Yet there is palpable disdain for many of the school's top students—so much so that even some adults at school are cautious about spotlighting their achievements. The youth held in highest esteem by their peers are better-than-average students, but they are noted as much for their good looks, cars, and popularity as they are for their academics. All students, particularly the large group that simply gets by, would likely achieve more if their school *pressed* the importance of its real business: teaching and learning.

Individual school leaders and teachers have different values and methods. A wonderful, loved leader or teacher can contribute much to a school's culture. Likewise, a single deficit-minded staff member can undermine group norms. And yet, to step back from these individual differences, school-wide practices influence the school's culture beyond any particular faculty member. For example, one national study in the 1980s found that elementary schools scheduled anywhere between eighteen and twenty-seven hours per week for instruction.[4] This range suggests important differences in students' learning opportunities across schools. Furthermore, the study found that most classrooms spent only 70 percent of those eighteen to twenty-seven hours on learning activities—the remainder was spent getting ready, cleaning up, disciplining, and socializing. Thus, while an organized, focused teacher will always provide more learning opportunities than a disorganized, lax teacher at the same school, that same organized, focused teacher will provide more or fewer opportunities depending on where she teaches. School culture, it seems, makes quite a difference.

Patterns of practice across secondary schools reveal a powerful interplay between individual teacher volition and overall school culture. Consider the following questions: Do teachers teach until dismissal, or do students wander out of class a few minutes early? Does a school treat homework time as a legitimate classroom activity or engage students fully in discussion, group work, research, and other learning experiences? Are videos and films judiciously selected and discussed, or, at the start of the period, do the lights go out and the movies go on? Are teachers absent rarely or often? When teachers are absent, do carefully selected substitutes follow well-designed lessons, or are randomly selected substitutes expected to "babysit" students? Again, each school may have teachers who display different levels of concern for keeping students engaged in learning, but each school will *also* display a culture that values students' engagement and learning more or less.

Currently, many schools are experimenting with alternatives to traditional schedules in order to maximize instructional minutes by providing more concentrated learning time and, in secondary schools, freeing teachers from the constraints of fifty-minute class periods. For example, many schools now use "block scheduling," in which teams of teachers have larger chunks of class time each day. Teachers can use this time flexibly to engage students in varied learning experiences and groups.[5]

Not only does the schedule matter, but the prevailing norms about what's most worth spending time on are also important. Some junior and senior high schools excuse students from class for all kinds of reasons. Sports teams may need to dress for a game, or the auditorium may need decorating for a dance. Elementary-level students may get to spend instructional time watching cartoons as a reward for having met a candy-sale goal. And there is no end to the ways that schools can spend time on routines, such as taking roll, checking tardies, lining up properly, and so on. Students can lose as much learning time in the teacher's pursuit of quiet and orderliness as they lose because of noise and disorder.

It's a mistake to think that schools can easily limit these time-consuming activities. Each has its roots in societal traditions and expectations. Americans see social activities and athletics as ways to help students prepare for community participation. Schools view athletics as a vehicle for teaching fairness, competition, and cooperation, as well as building students' self-esteem and sense of belonging. Bureaucratic routines and record keeping are often a response to legal requirements schools can do little to change. How these routine activities get enacted has everything to do with a school's culture.

School Cultures Where Everyone Succeeding Is the Norm

All schools *say* they are committed to *all* of their students learning, and some schools do translate this spoken value into a school-defining theme. When schools offer all students an intellectually rich curriculum and expect them to perform well, students get the message, "We believe you can do it." When a school's staff believes that all its students can learn challenging content, then the collective works very hard to provide conditions that enable that. These efforts pay off.

Unfortunately, many school cultures press in the opposite direction. They assume and behave as if high achievement just wouldn't be normal for all students at their school. Sometimes, well-intentioned teachers maintain low expectations, thinking they are being kind and understanding; for example, they might think and say things like, "Well, given the challenges she's facing, it wouldn't be right to ask this of her." Unfortunately, this kind of thinking endures, even though there is considerable evidence that students learn more—even those in the most distressed schools—when they are offered a challenging curriculum.[6]

Most school cultures foster the belief that although some students can and will learn very well, many will not, and that anything else would be abnormal. Fourth-grade teacher Jeffrey Madrigal had such an experience. His universally high expectations were dismissed by some others as the naïveté of a beginner.

> During the first days of teaching, I was incredibly self-conscious about ignoring convention, constantly experimenting, and changing every week. After the first month, however, it was awesome. I seemed to be making progress. We did group work, hands-on math, and visual social studies; made models; wrote stories and letters; and did a fascinating unit on the workings of the brain.
>
> Then it all began to slip away. Much to my dismay I discovered that my students had not learned much. My test results were fairly standard for the school: 30 percent of the class did very well, 30 percent did passing work, and 30 percent failed. The big question was why. Were my lessons confusing? Was the test too hard? Perhaps I should have given more frequent evaluations.
>
> The school's answer lay in a conversation I had with one of the veteran teachers soon after the test. I told her about my result and how discouraged I was over the lack of mastery.

She chuckled one of those annoying know-it-all chuckles and said, "We all get those same results. That is just how it is." This immediately reminded me of a similar conversation I had with a teacher during my student teaching. This woman had warned me not to expect to "reach them all." "Take off those rose-colored glasses," she said. I sat at a crossroads. What kind of an educator would I be?

—Jeffrey Madrigal
First-year teacher, grade 4

As Jeffrey knows well, low expectations are not simply inert beliefs. They exert their own kind of press; they press educators to take actions that align with those expectations—to translate low expectations into practices that impede student learning.

In sharp contrast, some school cultures, even in the most disadvantaged communities, have an incredibly strong press for learning that translates into powerful actions that enable learning to occur. In these schools, teachers are convinced that if a student does not succeed, the *least* likely explanation is that the student can't. Teachers concentrate less on what students are lacking and more on how instruction can press all students to achieve. They emphasize and model for students the hard work and persistence it takes to succeed.

Sometimes such teachers with high expectations become emblematic of their school and community, and over time they define the culture as much as they work within it. First-year middle-school teachers Lily Kim and Suzanne Markoe found an inspiring mentor in veteran teacher Yvonne Divans-Hutchinson, who helped them translate their beliefs about students' abilities into practices that in turn created rich classroom learning experiences. Here is what they wrote about their mentor:

Yvonne Divans-Hutchinson teaches eighth- and ninth-grade English at Edwin Markham Middle School in Watts, California. Yvonne was born in Little Rock, Arkansas during the height of racial segregation. When she moved to California, she lived in the Imperial Courts Housing Project in Watts and became a member of the first graduating class of the school where she now teaches. She chose to return to her alma mater and has been teaching there for the past thirty years. As one of her respected colleagues stated, "Yvonne is the gate-keeper to Watts. If you want to get out of Watts, if you want to go to college, you need to pass through Ms. Hutchinson; you need to be touched by her."

Yvonne prepares her students for real life by setting high standards and expecting her students to rise to them. Her nickname, "Killer Hutch," came about because of a fight that she broke up, but it has since evolved to describe the type of curriculum that she teaches. One of her students aptly noted that "Ms. Hutchinson helps you to see the deeper side to everything. She makes you think on a higher level." Yvonne challenges her students with engaging literature and demands that they go beyond the literal in analyzing what they read. The students know that they dare not write about what is obvious in what they read. A former student, now at the University of California-Berkeley, remarked: "Even now I check all my papers and ask myself if they are good enough for Ms. Hutchinson."

Providing an emotionally safe classroom is also vitally important to Yvonne. To promote respect of different cultures and ethnicities, her students follow a specific routine in calling on each other. When one student wishes to call on another student, they must choose someone who differs from them in race, ethnicity, gender, or in some other way. Yvonne regularly reminds her students of this policy, and it promotes a respect of diverse cultures in her classroom. Whenever a student dares to utter a racial slur or other form of disrespect to another student, Yvonne will stop the entire class at whatever they are doing because she believes a more important lesson needs to be taught. By the time the class is over, the student and class know not to disrespect another student or culture again.

Instead of seeing her students as so many people see them ("at risk, poverty-stricken, poor, disadvantaged"), Yvonne sees the "thousands of possibilities" that the students possess.[7]

A school anchored by a belief that students embody "thousands of possibilities" is a school likely to show strong press for learning. In such a school—as in a classroom like Yvonne's—the use of students' experiences and backgrounds as resources for learning sends a powerful cultural message: we value what you bring, and we consider it a foundation for future learning. That message alone *presses* not only toward learning but also toward social justice. It's a message embodied by the UCLA Community School, which opened in 2009 as a partnership between UCLA, the Los Angeles Unified School District, and the local community (a point-of-entry neighborhood for many immigrant populations in the region). It now serves more than 1,000 students—a population that is 80 percent Latinx, 14 percent Asian, 81 percent low income, and 55 percent "Limited English Proficient."

The school is based on the premise that to separate individual learning from culture is to diminish both. At the core of its design and daily practice is an asset-based, rather than deficit-laced, view of the children and community it serves; this commitment is reflected and refined by the school's explicit emphasis on self-directed, passionate learning; academic content and skill mastery; biliterate, bilingual, and multicultural competency; and active and critical participation in society.[8] The school's teachers, more than half of whom are teachers of color and many of whom have strong ties to the local community, work hard together to develop curricula that build from students' backgrounds, experiences, and cultural and linguistic repertoires. For example, the school embraces its immigrant families and their home languages, as evidenced in the pro-immigrant imagery displayed throughout the school and the thoughtful discussions of immigration embedded in many teachers' curricula.[9] The school's celebrated outcomes, including a 24 percent increase in college-going among its students, speak to what can happen when a stance like Yvonne Divans-Hutchinson's gets taken up school-wide.

Researcher Linda Darling-Hammond maintains that schools like this one press students every day to "find and act on who they are, what their passions, gifts, and talents may be, what they care about, and how they want to make a contribution to each other in the world."[10]

School Cultures That Foster College-Going Identities

Schools today are expected to prepare all students for both college and careers, since most jobs require some form of postsecondary education. Increasingly, teachers tell all their students, "You can, and should, go to college." Still, many teachers often leave unspoken a cultural assumption that high-status four-year college is really only meant for certain students—those who conform to familiar stereotypes of "the successful college-goer." This stereotype may include receiving high scores on standardized tests; speaking mainstream, grammatically "correct," and unaccented English; having parents who attended college themselves; and so on. Others may be considered as better suited for two-year colleges or the growing number of career and technical (often for-profit) colleges. While these lower-status colleges can provide additional academic preparation and job training for students who want or need it, schools should not steer students in that direction simply because they don't fit the "college-going" stereotype.

Making college-going accessible requires that students see their cultural identities as integral to college preparation, matriculation, and success. Their families, languages, life experiences, and connections to their home communities need to be framed as resources—not something to discard or "overcome." Dozens of studies contradict the commonly held view that low-income students don't value higher education; most want to go to college. But many come to believe that college doesn't want them.[11] For example, a study of low-income high school graduates who were eligible for admission to the University of California, but chose not to attend, found that what deterred students most was their beliefs that the university was "not for people like me," and that they weren't prepared for the university's rigorous demands.[12]

In Chapter 6, we referenced what Claude Steele terms "stereotype threat," whereby students internalize negative attitudes directed toward their own racial and cultural groups; these attitudes can have deep consequences for how students perform, often becoming a kind of self-fulfilling prophecy.[13] Students from underrepresented groups are further affected by their awareness that, unfair as it is, their personal performance will reflect on other members of their race or culture. Students in the majority rarely have to wrestle with such concerns.

To develop college-going identities among students who are underrepresented in higher education, teachers, students, and communities must confront the unspoken beliefs and assumptions about who is fit to attend. Of course, "confronting" means more than talking. For teachers, it means entering the worlds students inhabit and helping them identify supports for college-going. It means finding or creating programs where students can develop and practice the skills needed to succeed in college. And it means collaborating with students, teachers, families, community members, and colleges to create conditions and relationships that will support students' successful preparation, admission, and matriculation. In this day and age of soaring college tuition and crippling student loan debt, it unavoidably means navigating with students the complexities of financial aid—figuring out with students how they can structure their lives so they can maximize their higher education experience at a manageable short- and long-term cost.

The following questions can reveal a school's press for inclusive and equitable access to college-going; fortunately, these are questions that the broader culture is asking more frequently of schools: Are students being intellectually challenged, or can students get by without trying very hard? Is the knowledge that students bring with them to school treated as a powerful resource for high-level learning? Are *all* students—of all genders, races, and socioeconomic backgrounds—expected to acquire gatekeeping knowledge and to study rigorous content like algebra, foreign languages, and advanced science? What percentage of students does a given school—whether elementary or secondary—expect to go on to college? What is students' progress like through high school and into college and careers?

Access to Learning Opportunities and Resources

> The school district is in such dire straits that the teachers can't make photocopies, we don't have overhead projectors, nor do we have enough space for the children. The lack of resources has actually made me a very creative teacher. I learned this year that I didn't need an overhead nor did I need a chalkboard! I've learned that my students don't need paper or pencil. And I've learned to creatively manage and teach a class without these staples of American education.
>
> —Steven Branch
> First-year teacher, grade 5

It has become fashionable, especially in politically conservative quarters, to argue that the problems of American schools cannot be solved with money. Tell that to first-year teacher Steven Branch. Despite his ironic bravado in the preceding quote about teaching creatively with scarce resources, Steven knows better than most the dual truths: that creative teachers can accomplish much with very little and that money matters a great deal.

Access to Adequate Resources

Certainly, upper- and middle-class parents throughout history have understood that if their own children are to become readers, they need classrooms and libraries full of books. Their science learning requires equipment and laboratory space. Their physical development requires things to climb on, toys and sports equipment, and open space in which to play. Their classrooms require the workspaces and technologies teachers need to facilitate learning—for example, safe, clean, well-lit, well-heated or air-conditioned classrooms with room for productive activity.

In spite of the well-known and well-documented knowledge that high-quality resources are essential for all students, Americans have a high level of acceptance for obviously unequal school resources. Those who resist an equal distribution of resources seize on some very narrow and traditional research perspectives that allow them to conclude that resources (and the money spent on them) do not matter. Yet studies of the impact of expenditures on student achievement clearly show that not only does greater school spending yield higher student achievement, but spending on teachers matters most.[14] Of course, school spending is more or less effective depending on many other factors within the school culture.

Access to High-Quality Teaching

In addition to basic facilities and materials, students need enough teachers—and teachers with *knowledge of the subjects* they teach, *and* knowledge and skill in *how to teach* that subject. Too few teachers means classes will be large and difficult to manage. Hiring less knowledgeable and less experienced teachers for less money leaves students less likely to encounter teachers who can teach well. In November 2005, 500 students from Los Angeles's South Gate High School boycotted their classes to protest receiving their quarter grades after many students had experienced a string of unqualified substitutes for math and other subjects, and many did not have textbooks for their courses. The school district quickly arranged to supply the requisite teachers and books, but many observers were left shaking their heads and wondering why it took a two-day student walkout and media exposure to get those results—results that are elusive still, more than ten years later, in many urban and rural schools nationwide.

Most everyone would agree that a string of unqualified substitutes hardly constitutes access to high-quality teachers. Yet teacher quality itself remains a tricky construct. There is nothing to say that a school's newest teacher is the least competent or that "credentials" alone ensure quality. However, well-prepared and experienced teachers *are* valuable resources. Similarly, teachers with good reputations across the school and in the community are not guaranteed to be the best teachers, but they are a better bet than those with the worst reputations.

All students at a school—not just the highest-achieving ones—need excellent educators. And yet it's a not-so-well-kept secret that in many schools teachers are tracked much like students. That is, the most experienced and knowledgeable teachers are often "rewarded" with the "plum" teaching assignments—usually considered to be those in the higher "tracks," which we elaborate on in Chapter 10. New teachers often end up with the classes that others don't want—usually those classes considered lower ability or those with lots of behavioral challenges. However, schools are increasingly making an effort to distribute teacher talent more evenly, recognizing that low-achieving students are further disadvantaged when they are consistently placed in classes with less qualified teachers.

Good teaching depends *on* teachers, but also on the conditions *for* teaching. Considerable research shows that a class size of fifteen students, or fewer, is optimal at the elementary level.[15] Unfortunately, classes that small are rare in any but the wealthiest private schools. Secondary school classes should probably not exceed twenty-five students, although most do. Smaller classes in and of themselves do not cause more learning, but they strongly affect the kinds of instruction teachers can design, the kinds of assessment practices they can use, and the kinds of relationships they can build. The number of students in a class affects not only the time that teachers have available to spend with individuals, but also the teachers' pedagogical flexibility.

In addition to class size, other essential conditions for high-quality teaching include adequate space, supplies, and materials with which to work. Books for students; materials for hands-on learning; functional audiovisual equipment and other learning technologies; Internet access, a telephone and a decent copy machine; and whatever might be found in the office of any well-functioning business can make the difference between a teacher feeling able to do their job well or feeling quite overwhelmed.

Access to a Rich, Balanced Curriculum

If a school has no French class, no one will learn French at school. No music? No computers? Then no one learns to play music or use computers at school. When some students have access to certain subjects and others do not, inequities in opportunities are just as apparent.

We should add that "access" to opportunities doesn't mean a theoretical possibility that, under the best of circumstances, some students could have those experiences if they prove lucky enough or, according to someone's measure, smart enough. Access in this case means the environment is filled with opportunities for arts and music, languages, technology, and so forth, and there is little risk of students getting caught in a clutter of intellectually undemanding—sometimes frivolous—classes.

Sometimes inequities are subtle. For example, all third graders receive reading instruction, but the quantity and quality of that instruction vary. Good sense tells us what will happen when one group reads stories and another does only worksheets, or when students in an advanced history course produce research papers, while students in a "regular" history course fill in the blanks and answer fact-based multiple-choice questions.

It matters how rich the curriculum is and which students have full access to it. As we discuss in Chapter 10, many secondary schools have taken a crude but often effective first step toward giving all students access to rich curriculum by simply eliminating low-level classes. Some now require that all students take courses previously considered advanced—for example, algebra in middle school. Other schools open up their honors programs to everyone or provide rigorous honors-style instruction within heterogeneous classes. These actions are supported by considerable evidence that all students of all races, class backgrounds, and achievement levels learn better when they are provided rich and challenging content and classroom experiences.[16]

While individual teachers may be sensitive to cultural differences and try to bring in academically challenging content that builds from students' backgrounds and interests, the broader school can also do much to make this possible. Department, grade-level, and whole-school commitments help individual teachers diversify literature, present multiple perspectives in history and economics, teach high-level conceptual math, and so on.

A new teacher will not change a school's curriculum single-handedly, but new teachers often bring valuable energy and insights and can find more experienced teachers in their schools who will support their novice efforts (and vice versa). Like Yvonne Divans-Hutchinson (described earlier) and Pat Cady (described next), these veteran educators are not just single teachers with educational influence confined to their classrooms. They are themselves cultural assets. Their presence creates spaces and reveals new possibilities for curricular richness. First-year social studies teacher Kate Castleberry found a mentor in Pat Cady, whose example helped scaffold Kate's own efforts to create culturally relevant curricula.

Pat Cady has been a social studies teacher for more than twenty years. He agrees with Noel Ignatiev's ideas in *Race Traitor* that although people look White, acting and participating in the "White club" only furthers racial segregation, degradation, and depression. He therefore is a White Irishman on the outside, yet his actions and beliefs indicate his affiliation with the entire human race. In his teaching, Pat Cady addresses historical perspectives from many points of view and includes innovative scholars who are also concerned with social justice. His unit on the Vietnam era begins with a study of the African American soldier. He has explored Richard Takaki's *A Different Mirror* and James Loewen's *Lies My Teacher Told Me* with his eleventh-grade class. . . . By sharing his standpoint and his approach to teaching, Pat continually sends the message that White is not "best" and that all students should share and represent themselves in our history.[17]

Access to Extra Help When It's Needed

In many schools, both teachers and students expect that some children just won't keep up with their classmates. But supportive school cultures refuse to let students fall behind. Rather than framing students as "behind," these school cultures frame students as "still learning" and provide the necessary resources for them to catch up with their peers. Ideally, in the elementary grades, most extra help comes during regular class time. Daily classroom instruction offers opportunities to scaffold students' learning in ways that blur the distinction between help and extra help. Still, it is normal for situations to occur when students need more time with and support from a "knowledgeable other." A special resource teacher, a paid aide, or a parent volunteer may provide the needed boost. Or a peer tutor, in the same class or from a higher grade, may provide one-on-one assistance. As with these examples, extra help should supplement classroom lessons and should not substitute a remedial program for the regular one.

Many secondary schools provide extra help for students to master more challenging curriculum. Some offer "backup classes" for low-achieving students; students might enroll in them as an elective alongside an advanced academic course. Such classes provide additional instruction and time for students to make sense of the material in their advanced course. Some schools call this a "double dose" of teaching. Other schools operate homework centers or Saturday schools, staffed with teachers, community volunteers, and peer tutors. Some schools also run summer programs so students can skip to higher-level courses in the fall.[18]

Despite its undisputed benefits, the provision of extra help conflicts with some common ideas about standardization and efficiency. Extra help may require scheduling changes; it might cost more; and, by definition, it may mean some students receive more instruction than others. But *not* helping students keep up is also costly and inefficient. When students repeat a grade, for example, it adds an additional year's cost for that child's education. And since grade retention does not boost students' school success (in fact, retention likely contributes to dropping out of school), the extra expense is money wasted. If students who don't keep up are simply passed along, schools end up providing low-level classes to accommodate them—another ineffective use of school resources. Providing extra help so that students can keep up with the "regular" and more rigorous curriculum is money well spent.

Access to Equitable Learning Time

Time is increasingly recognized as a critical resource for learning. A broad range of educators and policymakers agree that students in neighborhoods characterized by concentrated poverty may need more learning time than is provided in a traditional schedule of six-and-a-half-hour days, 180 days per year. Many see "more time" as an equity reform that can provide every child with academic and enrichment opportunities like those that are commonplace in middle- and upper-class communities (weekend sports, music lessons, math tutors). Lower-income families, which are now more likely than ever to be headed by single parents, are increasingly stretched for time and resources and increasingly unable to provide such learning opportunities beyond the school day.[19]

Adding more and better learning time extends to students more academic instruction and individualized support; more personalized attention to their health, physical fitness, and social emotional needs; and a more well-rounded education. More time spent on academics, engaging learning experiences, and individualized tutoring can accommodate the differences in how quickly students learn; that is, it can make *time* the variable, and *learning* the norm. With more time, schools can incorporate more service learning, self-directed learning, project-based research, and independent reading. Schools also can expand access to subjects—such as social studies, history, world languages, and science—that have been cut back or even eliminated because of standardized testing pressures.

A longer school day, specifically, can also provide time to infuse community resources and caring adults from local art organizations, universities, and businesses into the instructional program, thereby enriching students' sense of connection to the world beyond school. (See Focal Point 9.1, describing Expanded Learning Time in Boston's Edwards Middle School.)

Focal Point 9.1
The Edwards Middle School: Expanded Learning Time

In the early 2000s, Boston's Clarence Edwards Middle School was on the verge of being shut down. The long-struggling school had among the lowest math scores of any middle school in the city. The school's enrollment was dwindling as even neighboring families chose to send their children elsewhere. Faculty and student morale was low, and family engagement was almost nonexistent. As at other middle schools in Boston, students left the building at 1:30 P.M. every day. But by 2009, Edwards had become one of the city's highest-performing middle schools, dramatically narrowing and even eliminating achievement gaps. Test scores showed growth across the board in English language arts, math, and science and across all subgroups of students. The school's enrichment offerings included a band, football team, and student apprenticeships with Google and MIT, and its annual theater production attracted hundreds of community members, including families on the new waiting list for enrollment and fifth graders from nearby schools, who were hoping to enter Edwards the next year.

What accounted for the transformation? After all, the school was in the same building with many of the same teachers, and student demographics had not much changed: 89 percent low income, 88 percent minoritized, 32 percent special education, and 24 percent Limited English Proficient.

As it turns out, in 2006 Edwards had become one of a group of Massachusetts public schools taking part in the Expanded Learning Time (ELT) Initiative. Though Edwards had undertaken some essential reforms already at the time, much of its improvement can be tied directly to its launching in 2006 of a redesigned school day that included 300 more hours of instruction per year. The additional time enabled the following:

- *A data-driven approach that helped increase instructional time for all core subjects.* For students, this meant a social studies and science block every day, in addition to four extra hours per week of academic support. For teachers, it meant opportunities to monitor closely students' progress through more frequent assessments and more individualized attention in areas where they need the most help.

- *Enhanced collaboration that helped teachers make good use of instructional time.* Teachers met in grade-level teams two to three times per week to discuss students' progress (while students took music and art). Students were dismissed early every Friday, enabling robust, all-staff professional development—planned by the school's Instructional Leadership Team, supported by representatives from partnering organizations, and incorporating monthly model lessons taught by teachers for their colleagues.
- *Enrichment programs and community partnerships that helped improve student and family engagement.* Sixth graders participated in a national program focused on developing skills like leadership and oral communication through apprenticeships with professionals. Seventh and eighth graders chose four electives per year from a menu of options including swimming, Latin dance, environmental science, and fashion design. Electives were taught by Edwards teachers and specialists from partnering community-based organizations. At the culmination of each semester, Edwards students exhibited for the entire school what they had learned in their enrichment classes.

Leo, a former eighth-grade student at Edwards, explained the change as follows: "When the Edwards Middle School switched to a longer day, I thought, 'Great, I can barely stand six and a half hours. Who wants to go for nine?' But during the first year I realized that ELT makes school more fun. . . . If I went home at two o'clock, I'd probably be doing nothing. I'd probably sit on the couch with a Mountain Dew watching TV or I'd be out skateboarding. But I'd give up skateboarding and Mountain Dew any day of the week to be here at Edwards. Nothing that you would do out on the streets at two o'clock can compare to what people are doing here at 4:30."

Although continued improvement at Edwards has been uneven—as is often the case when reforms are put into place, school leaders change, and resources are hard to sustain—the school's dramatic gains speak to the potential potency that not just more time, but reimagined time can have.

Source: Adapted from "Clarence Edwards Middle School: Success Through Transformation, National Center on Time and Learning," www.mass2020.org/fles/fle/Edwards%20Case%20Study%20FINAL.pdf.

Access to Caring Relationships and Practices

A group of future teachers visited the high school where first-year teacher Jessica Wingell was teaching. They were struck by the caring relationships they found among many teachers and students—the kind of relationships described in depth in the prior chapter. In particular, they recounted with admiration their interaction with one of the school's counselors, Mr. Joyce, whose approach they considered deeply personal and also emblematic in terms of how it seemed to press students toward success, academic and otherwise.

The group described how during their conversation in Mr. Joyce's office, he stopped five or six times to conduct brief exchanges with students passing by. They noted how at one point, when a student stuck his head in the door and said, "Mr. Joyce, can I talk to you for one second?" Mr. Joyce immediately stepped outside without hesitation or question. They were particularly impressed to learn, in passing conversation, that he had been at one student's home until 11:00 P.M. the previous night, talking at length with her and her parents. They summarized Mr. Joyce's approach as follows: "For him, students come first." And its outcome like this: "The rapport he has developed with his students is amazing."

At one point in the conversation, when one of the future teachers asked Mr. Joyce how White educators especially "can bridge the gap between themselves and students of color," Mr. Joyce invited a student of color, Michael, in from the hallway to join the conversation. He asked Michael if he'd be willing to share with the future teachers what makes for a trustworthy educator. Michael offered Ms. Wingell, the teacher they were visiting, as one example: "Ms. Wingell is good because you know she really wants you to do good," he said, "and she spends time helping you."[20]

Many schools are attempting to establish cultures of caring—places where it's the norm for educators like Mr. Joyce and Jessica Wingell to act on their commitments to know, respect, and support students. School cultures that surround students with caring relationships drive socially just changes in school programs and policies, as well as in classrooms.

Schools as Places Where Every Student Is Known

The school structure—how a school is organized—powerfully influences its culture. For example, academic departments (social studies, math, English, etc.) have long been an organizational structure for middle schools and high schools. Academic departments group teachers and courses by subject, but they are not really designed with as much concern for students' personal and social needs. Because teachers in "departmentalized" schools usually manage large numbers of students, often only the most visible or highly skilled students compete successfully for teachers' attention. Many students drift through classes without developing stable relationships with teachers or other students.

In response, student advocates have sought to replace large and impersonal structures with ones that encourage caring relationships and personalization. Many middle schools now divide students into teams—smaller groups that stay together during the day and are taught by an interdisciplinary group of teachers. Large high schools are increasingly experimenting to give students more sustained contact with teachers and peers, too. For example, many schools have added an "advisory" class—imagine a ramped-up and far more relationship-focused "homeroom"— where a group of students and a teacher connect every day for support as students negotiate complexities in and beyond school.[21]

In some elementary and secondary schools, students and teachers even stay together for two or three years. This is sometimes called "looping." In middle schools, it might mean that a group of teachers begins with a group of fifth- or sixth-grade students and remains with that same group until they move on to senior high.

Access to caring relationships can also be expanded through school-wide curricular and extracurricular activities. Many schools have service-learning programs that engage students in community work—for example, tutoring younger students or working in local organizations (nonprofits, nursing homes, shelters, etc.). Other programs also encourage sustained interaction beyond the classroom. Consider first-year teacher Matt Flanders's experience coaching his school's water polo team. After Matt took over the team, it became one of the more racially diverse settings on campus. Matt created space within this extracurricular activity for students to grapple with issues of success, social difference, and common cause. He also established an ethic of care that drew team members toward helping others.

> Most of my unsuccessful students felt no connection to the campus community. They did not feel that school was important because they were not involved in it. They did not feel as if their presence mattered, so they sank into the shadows of nonengagement.

Water polo had kept me in high school and college, so I knew the value of team involvement in education. My team had been a source of support and friendship for me. Coming full circle, I became head water polo coach. I wanted to do for my student-athletes what my coach had done for me years before. I hired a group of young, energetic assistant coaches to help me out, and we proceeded to coach our team not only in the art of water polo, but in the game of life as well.

We provided a place where students could be comfortable as well as mentally and physically challenged. We connected them to the campus, to the school community. Our involvement with our students did not stop in the pool. We dealt with issues like drug abuse and pregnancy. We helped team members secure admission to college. We became a big part of our students' lives.

Our program is one of inclusion; we do not cut. Our goal is to make the best team and the best group of young people we can. I think that is what draws students to our program. In addition, we have started a middle-school water polo team for our district. Thirty-five children participate twice a week, and they are coached by my senior high school student-athletes. Not only are we strengthening our athletics for years to come, we are reaching into the broader community and connecting with students to help them be successful in high school.

—Matt Flanders
First-year teacher, high school history

In caring communities like the one Matt nurtured, students are known well, by both caring adults and peers. The question that remains, however, is, how might we create whole schools where the culture is that of a caring community?

Creating "small schools" is one reform idea that has gained popularity among many educators and policymakers. In the 1990s, award-winning teacher and principal Deborah Meier began writing and speaking about the incredible experience that she and a group of teachers had over twenty years, creating a handful of small schools in Harlem, New York. (See Focal Point 9.2.) Meier worked with teachers, parents, and students to create schools characterized by rich, rigorous opportunities to learn and strong relationships. Inspiring stories about schools like Meier's Central Park East, along with impressive rates of achievement and college-going, have since captured the imaginations of educators, policymakers, and (for a time) philanthropists like Bill Gates. Through the creation of new schools and the "breaking up" of large schools into smaller ones, these reforms have touched nearly every large city in the United States, and other places as well. Many schools, even ones that are not officially "small schools," have taken on one of the small schools movement's central goals—to ensure that every student is known, and known well.

Schools as Safe Zones

As long as one person does not feel safe—experiences or fears abuse by others—no one is safe. When schools fail to respond to hurtful acts, they offer a kind of tacit approval that further imperils student safety. Likewise, when they fail to *proactively* advocate and plan for the provision of safety to all students—regardless of race, class, gender, gender expression, religion, and so on—they fall short of providing the ongoing attentiveness needed to challenge a multitude of oppressions.

We focus here on two pressing school safety imperatives related to matters of social difference. They are confronting racism and xenophobia, and confronting homophobia and transphobia. We chose these not to exclude other important concerns, but because of their salience at present (and always) and because of the opportunities they present to address themes of exclusion and inclusion, voice and representation, and identity and self-actualization. They also provide space to address bullying as a structurally supported, rather than purely individually perpetrated, phenomenon. Schools must never excuse these oppressions as just an annoying but "natural" part of growing up.

Focal Point 9.2
Deborah Meier on Creating Democratic Small Schools

If we're talking about the creation of a thoughtful school culture, size becomes decisive—especially if we're trying to create a changed culture. Thoughtfulness is time-consuming. Collaboration is time-consuming. The time they both consume can't be private time, late-at-night at-home time. To find time for thoughtful discussion we need to create schools in which consensus is easy to arrive at while argument is encouraged (even fostered) and focused on those issues of teaching and learning close to teacher and student experiences, rather than on procedural rules and processes, elections and nominating committees, building-wide disciplinary codes, detention policies, filling out forms and checklists, scheduling, etc.

Only in a small school can deep ongoing discussion take place in ways that produce change and involve the entire faculty—and even there, it's tough to sustain. For teachers to start thinking through the task before them, collectively and collaboratively, schools must be so small that governance does not become the topic of discussion but issues of education do, so small that the faculty as a whole becomes the decision-making body on questions of teaching and learning.

We bragged for years that the Central Park East (CPE) schools didn't have a single permanent committee. We were a committee of the whole; the time we spent talking had immediate repercussions affecting the way we thought and felt about children, classroom life, our teaching practices. If an issue arose we could meet with almost no notice, and gather together in one room, around one table or one circle, and hear each other out. We didn't need complex governing structures, committees of committees, representatives of representatives, differentiations of staff, classes and subclasses.

And even though on the high school level we now do have one permanent committee (our Cabinet), anyone can join any of its meetings—even kids if they wish. (It would be nice if they did more often.) A third of the faculty is in the Cabinet, which only occasionally takes a vote. Mostly we argue it out and find a solution that all can live with for the time being. We avoid deciding issues better decided elsewhere. And anyone can insist that decisions made by the Cabinet can be reviewed at a schoolwide meeting.

This continuing dialogue, face to face, over and over, is a powerful educative force. It is our primary form of staff development. When people ask me how we "train" new teachers, I say that the school itself is an educator for the kids and staff; it's its own staff development project. And it is by this same token always accessible to the outside world as well as to our students; the school itself is a public deliberative body whose existence is a reminder of the power of reasoning, reflecting, assessing, revising, and planning. The habits of mind, our five essential questions, and the habits of work we encourage in our students are thus exemplified in the daily life of the staff. We too weigh evidence, explore alternative viewpoints, conjecture about other possibilities, make connections, and ask, So what? We too must meet deadlines and keep our word and communicate clearly. We're "demonstrating" the value of what we preach—daily.

The staff spends all year reviewing its 14 graduation requirements, and each fall comes up with new versions of one or another of them. The experience of our alumni/ae, of external visitors, the work of our colleagues across the nation, as well as our own daily practice, all lead to such revisions. At various steps along the way the latest drafts are circulated and debated by students and teachers. We added a new section on computer literacy after considerable debate on whether it should be a part of our requirements or a separate one. Recently we added an emphasis on experimental science and redrafted the math requirements to reflect the latest National Council of Teachers of Math (NCTM) standards.

Similarly, issues of behavior, school management, and student-teacher relations occupy our attention. We spend a good deal of time—even an embarrassing amount of time—debating student "dress codes," mostly shall they or shan't they be allowed to wear hats. But even this issue was argued on terms that allowed students to join us. People brought in articles about the impact of clothes and raised issues about the importance (or not) of worrying about how others see us and whether our informality would make it harder for kids to shift to more formal ways of dressing in more formal workplaces. The opponents of dress codes eventually won, but supporters occasionally still submit interesting pieces of evidence for their side.

In a small school we can dare to experiment without feeling we are treating kids like guinea pigs. After all, what doesn't work isn't irreversible. We can reschedule one afternoon and put a new agenda into practice the next morning. We can undo them just as fast. Changes don't require Herculean coordination or time-consuming bureaucratic arranging. In short, smallness makes democracy feasible, and without democracy we won't be able to create the kind of profound rethinking the times demand.

Source: Deborah Meier, *The Power of Their Ideas: Lessons for America from a Small School in Harlem* (Boston: Beacon Press, 1995), 110–115.

Confronting Racism and Xenophobia

Teachers often shy away from explicit conversations about race. Yet schools are key spaces for students to learn about race as a social construct and to talk about social differences they see in their school and community. Students hear racial slurs and witness (or feel) the impact of racial stereotypes; they notice when resources are distributed unfairly across groups, or when peers exclude them, or others. Kate Castleberry, a first-year high school history teacher, did what many teachers fear: she tackled race head-on and let students take the lead in promoting better race relations among the school's student body.

Kate's students wanted a day of serious inquiry when members of the school community could come together to examine the role of race in all aspects of school life. The school's principal and most of Kate's colleagues lent their support. The events that students organized became a source of pride and catalyzed school-wide efforts to improve the racial climate.

This day of events was not a day to join hands and sing "Kumbaya." It was a time to explore how we thought of others, and our fear and knowledge of different races. It reflected a commitment to stand up for our people and for our brothers and sisters when they are not present.

The day began as a dream of two juniors. One hundred and sixty students were separated into racial groups—African American, Asian/Pacific Islander, Caucasian, Latino, and

Middle Eastern. Pairs of groups met to share and discuss feelings and questions about stereotypes. Students tearfully faced peers and friends and questioned why their "people" held certain thoughts and beliefs. After each group met with the others, the students broke into small, racially heterogeneous dialogue groups with a facilitator and discussed any unresolved feelings. The day ended with an outpouring of willingness to continue the struggle and journey toward racial understanding. A core group of students formed a steering committee to help develop more activities. A week after the event, a lunch meeting reacquainted students who suggested further dialogue at a retreat or sleep-over.

Change will not happen overnight, but students have taken the first steps toward a society that is fair and accepting of all.

—Kate Castleberry
First-year teacher, high school history

Third-grade teacher Kimberly Min saw firsthand how racism undermines the learning culture at school, even at the elementary level. Kimberly's school was rife with racial tension and with deficit thinking about low-income students of color. Unlike Kate, Kimberly didn't have a school-wide program or community that shared her commitment to promoting racial understanding. Like many teachers, Kimberly showed courage and skill as she pressed her students and colleagues to combat stereotypes, think critically, and encourage socially just action.

Misperceptions of race and ethnicity permeate the speech and actions of the staff and students, to the detriment of the whole community. The staff generalizes about African Americans and Latinos—the African American kids are "louder and more physical," whereas the Latinos are more "obedient and reticent." Because I teach African Americans, I receive sympathy from teachers who teach mostly Latino classes. This thinking puts the students in a precarious position, since, when there are tensions or yard fights the African Americans are perceived as the aggressors while the Latinos are seen as the victims. My students at age 7 begin to define what it means to be African American or Mexican in this context.

I use culturally responsive literature to help my students identify with the struggles, successes, riches, and hardships of their collective history. As we read biographies of African American leaders, pictures of segregated drinking fountains brought about genuine interest. I began to ask questions about how segregation began, and Latisha responded, "They [White people] drink out of different water fountains because the Black people were sick and the White people didn't want to get sick." Terrell suggested, "The Black people must have put something in the White people's water, so they didn't want to drink out of the same place." I found it fascinating that students rationalized segregation with negative views of African Americans, and I began to question their responses. . . . They eventually began to see that they didn't always have to associate negative things with the African American community. Unfortunately, many of the teachers at the school, including those of color, do not think that students have anything to say about these issues. If one is aware of how racism is shaped and perpetuated in society, these topics must be discussed. Without continual reflection and dialogue, the racial divide and deficit practices will persist at our school.

—Kimberly Min
Third-grade teacher

It's possible both to admire the approaches of Kate and Kimberly and to feel daunted by them. That's understandable. Most of us haven't come up as children in classrooms where frank conversation about race and racism was encouraged, or perhaps even permissible. Many of us have never seen a teacher broker such open exchange. Conversely, most of us have heard, maybe many times and from many places, that talking candidly about race and racism is too serious or sophisticated for students to handle, especially the young ones. Many of us also have been told that drawing "attention" to racial differences creates problems, because it works against "tolerance" and "colorblindness."

In fact, tolerance and colorblindness are problems themselves—unworthy, and ultimately unjust, aims. Tolerance, for example, usually describes the reserves of patience or acceptance one needs to put up with something at worst toxic or distasteful and at best unpleasant or annoying. Teaching for social justice requires more than teaching students to put up with racial diversity. Colorblindness, meanwhile, is a myth. Not only do we see the color of one another's skin, but, if we're socially conscious, we also see quite clearly the ways that judgments based on skin color have and still do place some at far greater risk than others for disadvantage, discrimination, and physical harm.

Standing back and ignoring aggressions in young children's midst—home, playground, classroom—erodes all positive aspects of the classroom culture. It's safe to assume that micro-aggressions, bullying, expressions of racism and privilege, and so forth will arise regularly. It's what young children do; it's what we all do. Correcting these cultural tendencies is not so much a matter of a singular lesson or unit on "respect" but careful listening each day, and often responding on the fly. Young children might not have the language to define race and racism (yet), but they have much to say and ask about what they see and hear in the world around them, including on the nightly news and social media. To not address race and racism represents a kind of complicity with the racially stratified status quo, and it also takes a toll on justice-minded teachers for whom "standing back and ignoring" is never an easy option. Borrowing from Jerome Bruner's spiral curriculum approaches, it is worth considering that whatever children can see and experience, the teacher can find a developmentally appropriate entry point to engage students with difficult topics. The exchanges in Kimberly Min's classroom and Focal Point 8.7, featuring justice dialogue among Mariana Souto-Manning's first graders, demonstrate this beautifully.

All of the points above also apply to the enduring and increasing xenophobic strands of our culture (as mentioned in Chapter 2). Immigrant and refugee populations have been thrust to the center of political and ideological discourse and discriminatory practices and policies. Educators at all levels have an especially important role to play, by teaching about the inherent dignity and worth of all people and by forging classroom and school cultures that enable and enhance safety for children and their families.

In addition to one's own school colleagues, teachers can look to organizations that have created a range of tools and resources that support teachers who want to connect students with the knowledge and empathy that promote socially just classrooms and schools. The New York Collective of Radical Educators, profiled in Focal Point 8.6, is one example; its members discuss, develop, and disseminate critical curricula, including curricula about immigrant rights and challenging racial injustice.

Many more resources are highlighted online in Digging Deeper. And in Focal Point 9.3, we include a smaller-scale example that provides wise guidance for teachers. We love this example for its content—simple sample language for talking with young children about race and racism— and for its authorship by a group of educators and parents working together in Vermont and yet also in connection with a much larger racial justice project. The example reminds us that, wherever we are, we can find ways to move beyond navigating culture as it is, and contribute to culture as it could be.

Focal Point 9.3
Tools for Talking About Race

"*Equity work*," explains anthropologist and education researcher Mica Pollock, "starts with our words."

Below are some helpful words and images from a zine created by Emma Redden and a group of parents and educators working and living in northern Vermont. "Because children experience and participate in racism as young as 3," the zine creators write, "it is vital to help them understand this system in order to fight it." In their zine, which you can read in full online, they offer advice and examples of the kind of language that adults can use to talk with children about race and racism.

Figure 9.1 Tools for Talking About Race

1. Start with one simple concrete honest sentence. Kids will ask questions as they are ready to hear the answers.

2. Talk to kids about their 5 senses—things they have seen, felt, heard, smelled, or tasted. [Hearing something on the radio or a child only having white teachers at a school with a majority non-white janitorial staff is a child experiencing racism with their 5 senses.]

3. Use vocabulary words children can understand.

"The police made a choice to make the his body stop working. He had brown skin and I wish he was still live because his life is very important."

"Lies were told about people with brown skin to explain why they were made to work without getting paid any money. That is called slavery. Even though people with brown skin now usually get paid money to work, a lot of people with light tan skin, called white people, still tell those lies. This can make it hard for people with brown skin to get important things, like the jobs, homes, doctors, or teachers they need and want."

Figure 9.1 (Continued)

Working definition of WHITE SUPREMACY

White supremacy is a lie that says people with light tan skin are more important, and deserve to have more money, safety, space and power to make decisions for others, than people with brown skin. This is an untrue idea people have, but also an idea that the government, banks, stores and hospitals have, and they use this idea to give more money and power to people with light tan skin, even when they don't need it.

"Race means the color of your skin plus how much the government helps you be healthy and safe".

Confronting Homophobia and Transphobia

In recent years, we have seen substantial shifts in attitudes about gender expression, sexual orientation, marriage equality, and discriminatory speech. Talking honestly and openly about these issues is often just as challenging as talking about racism, xenophobia, and other deeply embedded cultural harms; it's also just as necessary.

According to GLSEN, which conducts a national school climate survey every two years, significant progress has been made since 2001, and yet LGBTQ youth still report that harassment and discrimination remain commonplace. Since continued progress depends on an up-to-date understanding, we offer a quick overview of key definitions and terms in Focal Point 9.4.

Focal Point 9.4
LGBTQ Terms and Tools

Acronyms, and terms in general, shift and change. This happened with "LGBTQ," which gained additional letters over the years, including some that are included less often or left implicit. In light of this, we provide a quick review of terms, including those that apply to LGBTQIA. But before we do, we offer an image, known as *The Genderbread Person*, which has been refined a number of times by activist, educator, and artist Sam Killerman; it depicts the distinctions between gender identity, gender expression, biological sex, and sexual orientation. We close the focal point with helpful words of advice for teachers from A Queer Endeavor, a grassroots, queer-led initiative that provides training and materials aimed at creating safer, more affirming school communities for LGBTQ youth and families.

- **Lesbian:** A female-identified person who is attracted romantically, physically, or emotionally to another female-identified person.
- **Gay:** A male-identified person who is attracted romantically, physically, or emotionally to another male-identified person.
- **Bisexual:** A person who is attracted to both men and women romantically, physically, or emotionally.
- **Transgender:** A person whose biological sex is different from the gender with which they identify.
- **Transsexual:** A person who has physically altered their body in order to better match their gender identity. (This term refers to biology, not identity necessarily; it indicates a change in one's physiology.)
- **Queer:** An all-inclusive term that was once derogatory but has been reclaimed by the LGBTQIA community and now signals rejection of the idea that labels can adequately explain identity.
- **Intersex:** A person whose physical sex characteristics are not categorized as exclusively male or exclusively female.
- **Asexual:** A person who is not attracted to anyone or does not have a sexual orientation.
- **Ally:** A person who does not identify as LGBTQIA but supports those who do.

An important first step toward affirming gender, sexual, and family diversity involves including LGBTQ-themed content and asking questions such as: Am I using texts that include LGBTQ identities and experiences? Do students see themselves and their families represented in the curriculum? Am I using gender-inclusive language? Are there facilities that feel safe and inclusive of everyone? But full inclusion is never possible, and including marginalized identities often leaves the status quo in place. In other words, inclusion does not necessarily disrupt what counts as "normal" and "different" with respect to gender and sexuality and also leaves intersections of identity unrecognized.

In their workshops, the cofounders and directors of A Queer Endeavor, Dr. Sara Staley and Dr. Bethy Leonardi, support educators to *queer* their practice. Thinking *queerly* involves examining the ways in which certain identities, behaviors, beliefs, practices, and expectations are perceived as

The Genderbread Person v3.3

by it's pronounced METROsexual *.com*

Gender is one of those things everyone thinks they understand, but most people don't. Like *Inception*. Gender isn't binary. It's not either/or. In many cases it's both/and. A bit of this, a dash of that. This tasty little guide is meant to be an appetizer for gender understanding. It's okay if you're hungry for more. In fact, that's the idea.

Plot a point on both continua in each category to represent your identity, combine all ingredients to form your Genderbread

4 (of infinite) possible plot and label combos

↙ Indicates a lack of what's on the right.

Gender Identity

○ ⃠ Woman-ness

○ ⃠ Man-ness

How you, in your head, define your gender, based on how much you align (or don't align) with what you understand to be the options for gender.

Gender Expression

○ ⃠ Feminine

○ ⃠ Masculine

The ways you present gender, through your actions, dress and demeanor, and how those presentations are interpreted based on gender norms.

Biological Sex

○ ⃠ Female-ness

○ ⃠ Male-ness

The physical sex characteristics you're born with and develop, including genitalia, body shape, voice pitch, body hair, hormones, chromosomes, etc.

Identity

Attraction

Sex

Expression

Sexually Attracted to

Nobody ← → (Women/Females/Femininity)

Nobody ← → (Men/Males/Masculinity)

Romantically Attracted to

Nobody ← → (Women/Females/Femininity)

Nobody ← → (Men/Males/Masculinity)

In each grouping, circle all that apply to you and plot a point, depicting the aspects of gender toward which you experience attraction.

"normal," and others as "different"; how those norms are produced and upheld; who they benefit or privilege; and who they marginalize. Below are some questions they press teachers to consider:

- What counts as "normal" in this text or lesson? How can I disrupt those norms?
- What assumptions related to gender, sexuality, families, race, ethnicity, class, language, ability, and other identity markers are embedded in this text or lesson? What about their intersections?
- Whose voices are privileged? Whose voices are left out, and how might those voices complicate, trouble, contribute to what counts as normal?
- What ideas will students walk away with that might perpetuate stereotypes? How can I encourage student thinking that disrupts those stereotypes?
- How will students be positioned and how might they position themselves in relation to those norms, stereotypes, and assumptions?
- How can I support students to consider the ways they perpetuate what counts as normal and what consequences that might have on personal, social, and institutional levels?
- What about resistance? How might students resist *un*learning what counts as normal? How can I support students to "lean in" to that discomfort?

For more information and resources for educators, visit the websites of "social justice comedian" Sam Killerman (http://itspronouncedmetrosexual.com) and A Queer Endeavor (http://aqueerendeavor.org/).

As mentioned in Chapter 1, the 2015 National School Climate Survey of over 10,000 middle and high school students nationwide found that nine in ten LGBTQ respondents reported experiencing verbal harassment at school, nearly three-quarters felt unsafe because of their sexual orientation, and nearly a third reported skipping at least one day of school in the past month because of safety concerns. The majority of respondents—56 percent and 66 percent, respectively—reported hearing homophobic comments or negative comments about gender expression from *teachers* and other school adults; and their reports indicate some troubling indication of *diminishing* rates of intervention by other school staff in these instances.[22]

Statistics like these give numerical context for why one parent of a gender nonconforming son described school-going for LGBTQ youth as "like walking through a hailstorm."[23] There's no doubt that these realities adversely impact students' learning, as well as their health and well-being more broadly.[24]

Historically, schools have offered few supportive programs for LGBTQ youth specifically. Even when such support is present, it can be difficult to access because LGBTQ student groups—like Gay-Straight Alliances (GSAs)—are sometimes marginalized or prohibited. Nevertheless, they play a crucial role, and are increasingly present and active, especially in secondary schools nationwide.

Much of the silencing around issues of gender, sexuality, and sexual orientation occurs for all students, but with disproportionately negative impacts on LGBTQ youth. For example, comprehensive health education remains lacking and desperately needed. In many ways, the federal government has played a complicit role here; for example, under President George W. Bush, funding significantly increased for sex education focused on abstinence only until marriage. In many schools, these programs still prevail, as does normative opposition to gay marriage. The implications are profound: while such norms and programs deny *all* youth critical information about contraception, sexually transmitted disease (STD) prevention, and reproductive health, they are particularly troublesome for LGBTQ youth.[25] In some places, heteronormativity and homophobia and transphobia remain so entrenched that teachers are restricted from addressing LGBTQ-related issues. In fact, in 2017 eight states—Alabama, Arizona, Louisiana, Mississippi, Oklahoma, South Carolina, Texas, and Utah—had laws in place to restrict staff from talking about such issues in school.[26] And with the Department of Education under the Trump administration reporting its intent to roll back civil rights investigations and promote voucher and choice programs (including ones that direct federal funds to schools that defend anti-LGBTQ bias on religious grounds), there is concern about the role of schooling in limiting, rather than expanding, LGBTQ rights.

Clearly, social justice educators have their work cut out for them, and clearly, their work will have to take different forms in different contexts. There are, however, some universal components. The first is intervention. Overt and subtle injustices cannot go unaddressed; each time teachers act to interrupt injustice, to make themselves visible allies to students, they impact all the ways that injustice manifests at their schools.

Teachers can also act proactively to help establish or advise ally groups. The Gay-Straight Alliance Network is one organization that "supports young people in starting, strengthening, and sustaining" local chapters; it helps build their capacity to

- create environments in schools where students can support and educate one another about LGBTQ racial and gender justice;
- advocate for just policies that protect LGBTQ youth from harassment and violence; and
- build coalitions with youth groups across identity lines and state and national borders.

Organizations like the Gay-Straight Alliance Network, GLSEN, and Human Rights Watch have long histories of activism and organizing, and offer strong support for intersectional analyses and action.

By appropriating existing structures—like school clubs, for example—teachers can also help create "normalized" and central (rather than marginalized) spaces that counter an oppressive school culture and build a base for broader school change. For example, one veteran teacher, the adviser to his school's Gay-Straight Alliance, reports that the group's *uncommon* efforts to challenge homophobia on campus draw significant strength from the group's *common* conduct and form; like any other campus club, it elects its officers, meets regularly, petitions the administration for support, organizes social activities such as bowling night, and so on. When groups like this one emerge on campus as recognized, visible, and appreciated contributors, it's a strong indicator that a school's culture is moving in the right direction.

Finally, of course, there is the classroom itself, where there is so much great work to be done. For support, teachers and those who work with them can look to organizations like A Queer Endeavor, a grassroots, queer-led initiative housed in the University of Colorado Boulder's School of Education. With its training, materials, and tools, such as the questions featured in the second half of Focal Point 9.4, A Queer Endeavor supports educators in their work to make the silence that has surrounded LGBTQ topics in education unworkable.

Schools in a Violent Culture

Schools are generally safe places—safer than homes and neighborhoods. What, then, are we to make of the headlines and on-the-spot television reporting of school violence, of students and teachers suffering injury or loss of life? Well-publicized acts of violence at schools, whether mass or single shootings; "security" officers enacting violence against students; gangs and other fights; and so forth each have unique causes, but they have many cultural commonalities:

- School violence reflects a violent society, in which violence is a tool available to those who are angry and hurt, who are unskilled in addressing conflict in other ways, or who are inclined to use their power destructively. Any abuse of others *is* violence; downplaying it—treating it as minor, dismissing it as "locker-room talk," or rationalizing that "kids will be kids"—does not diminish the violence done, and often serves instead to condone and perpetuate it. When students are helped to name and talk about these aspects of society and to understand them, then teachers are *doing* something productive about violence both in and out of school.

- Although watchfulness and security are important, prevention is best accomplished in caring school cultures—cultures where it is intolerable to diminish the dignity or security of anyone for any reason, and where any violation of that norm is handled quickly and constructively. Trusted teachers—ones students can approach with reports of actual or potential violence—are the best safeguards.

- Much of the response to fears about school safety—zero-tolerance policies, metal detectors, school-based police officers—is expensive and doesn't address the mental health and social-emotional issues that are often at the root of violence. These are instruments and structures for control of behavior, often harsh and out of line with the actual offense, and they tend to disproportionately impact students of color in low-income communities. Advocating for investments in counseling services, restorative justice programs, and community-based partnerships are ways that educators can help fortify safety in schools.

By working each day to advance caring school cultures, teachers make schools safer as they help students learn more.

Schools in a Fearful Culture

The shattering enormity of some events, like the 2001 destruction of the World Trade Center, cannot be left for students to resolve on their own, with their limited resources and experiences—perhaps some thirdhand news accounts, television commentary, provocative social media posts, youthful maturity, and so on. Young and old alike must find ways to explain and express anger and fears about events like these and their aftermaths (including, for example, our country's decade-plus engagement in seemingly unending war).

The effects of these events are not "local," as they resonate across the entire country. Neither are the effects strictly "national." Crises, wars, genocides, and natural disasters across the globe can (and should) deeply penetrate our consciousness. At best, we hope that our schools help channel emotions and anxieties into productive understandings and action. Good teachers will never be immune to anger, fear, and bafflement when horrifying things occur; we are, after all, human. We should have no illusions that teachers will automatically know the "best" or "right" ways to respond to such events, nor should we assume that teachers can easily turn their personal responses into coherent and healing pedagogy. And yet that must be one of our goals, our struggles, as teachers. In those struggles, our surest guide is to listen persistently, question students, bring them information, and demonstrate care.

After September 11, third-year high school teacher Mary Hendra wrote down some of the personal questions the attacks raised for her—suggesting that these reflections helped her engage students in the most difficult issue of the day. Focal Point 9.5 includes some of her writing, which was published in the *Christian Science Monitor* on September 25, 2001.

If teachers confined their teaching in the aftermath of September 11, or in the aftermath of any other traumatic event, to questions that they knew the answers to, these would be very short lessons indeed. Certainly, students need access to information about the geography, politics, and science involved, but they also need to make sense of humanitarian crises, emotional shocks, and moral quandaries that the prepared curriculum could never have anticipated.

Yet the common response is often to keep things as normal as possible—to maintain schedules, complete assignments, not intrude on students' highly personal responses. In fact, after the September 11 attacks, many teachers were encouraged to proceed with extreme caution—to briefly acknowledge this "current event" and, for the sake of the children, to continue with business as usual.

Focal Point 9.5
A Third-Year Teacher on September 11, 2001

I was on my way to school when I heard the news that would rivet the nation, and the world, for days. Like many throughout the United States, my reaction went from shock to sorrow. But, there was another thought that went through my head that morning: "What will I teach my students today?"

. . . How could I teach about the Industrial Revolution in world history, and the Gilded Age in U.S. history, and ignore the events of this day? I wondered how I would respond to my students' questions, how we could talk about the event without exacerbating fear?

. . . I have urged my students to question—to think critically, to read critically, and to ask questions about the world around them. So they continue to ask me, "Why would people in other countries be celebrating? Why would people want to cause this destruction? How has the United States created these enemies?"

I also have questions. How do we as a nation critically look at why this might have happened, without being seen as "unpatriotic"? Shouldn't it be a sign of patriotism that we seek to improve our nation? The U.S. has certainly not led a pure and perfect existence, but our democracy has been strong enough to change with the challenges brought by women, African-Americans, social activists, and many others. How can the events of September 11 be molded into an opportunity for humanity's progress?

I wonder, if this tragic event was possible in part because of the freedom and openness of our society, whether restricting that freedom could be the best response. My students, many of whom are first- or second-generation Americans themselves, would probably be among the first to complain of heightened immigration controls. They already ask me, "Why should the U.S. restrict immigration? Immigrants are only looking for a better life."

And if my students look to history for understanding, as I frequently tell them to do, what can they—and we—learn? . . .

Can we root out terrorism by government-sanctioned violence, regardless of the magnitude of that violence? The more the U.S. is seen as an aggressor, the more resentment it will engender from around the world—and hence the greater commitment it will foster among thousands of individuals who will become willing to put their own lives on the line.

And that implies a question for my classroom: How can I explain to critical teenagers that violence by a government is OK, but violence by an individual is not? What about the violence that was used by imperialist nations to subdue and exploit the African continent?

. . . I believe that asking these questions helps my students understand. I hope they will see adults around them asking questions, too, as we all work through these events and their repercussions. On September 11, my class talked about questions no one yet knows the answers to, but are worth asking anyway. I gave students space to reflect, to put the events outside on "pause" for a few moments.

One student articulated what was probably one of the underlying reasons for much of the questioning that day. "I'm not ready to go to war," she said.

Source: Adapted from an article by Mary Hendra in the *Christian Science Monitor*, September 25, 2001.

A wiser and more humane alternative is to do as Alfie Kohn urges: "Help children locate themselves in widening circles of care that extend beyond self, beyond country, to all humanity."[27] This is a tall order in a social and political environment rife with fear and calls for revenge. Teachers wonder about the appropriate developmental level for such lessons and discussions. They worry about acquiring the range of knowledge and perspectives necessary to be responsive to students' questions and concerns. They wince at their potential vulnerability and the consequences of supporting students to extend their thinking "beyond self."

For example, immediately after September 11, older students quickly became engaged in discussions and arguments surrounding racial profiling, and even the youngest students struggled to form impressions about who the "bad" people were and what they looked like. Politicians, media sources, and others scrambled to learn about Islam and about the historical and cultural context in which to place and not place the tragic events. Critical thinkers around the world searched for ways to penetrate the meaning and causes of the events without seeming to excuse them. Teachers were no different.

Many teachers are interested in educating their students about the dangers of racial profiling and stereotyping, and helping students place events like 9/11 and its aftermath in a historical, cultural, and global context. Unfortunately, official school curricula are notoriously slow to catch up, and when they do, they tend to proliferate sanitized accounts of historical events—oftentimes accounts that traffic in predictable, but problematic American exceptionalism (the idea that somehow our country is above certain kinds of reproach and criticism).[28] Fortunately, however, many teachers have turned to one another for support in grappling with these issues and have amassed a wide range of resources from education and social justice organizations. Thematic "syllabi" and other tools circulate on social media, offering context and curricular inspiration for teachers seeking to address everything from the Syrian refugee crisis to state-sanctioned violence against indigenous activists and allies protesting pipeline construction in Standing Rock, South Dakota. Like Mary Hendra, these teachers are working against the grain to ensure that students experience curriculum, instruction, and school culture in the service of social justice education.

Schooling in the Face of a Broken Social Contract

In August 2005, soon after Hurricane Katrina hit New Orleans and water broke through the levees in the city's Lower Ninth Ward, the first images and accounts of the floods began appearing on the news. Houses underwater, some with people stranded on top or waving out of second- and third-story windows. Families wading in waist-high water, paddling makeshift rowboats, and sleeping amid squalor in the Superdome, where they were meant to take shelter.

Alongside these images were stories of suffering and rage at the government's failure to rescue so many of the city's mostly African American and low-income residents. Among these stories were, for example, the vivid accounts of nurses and patients who spent five days—without power, and with only meager supplies—waiting for evacuation in one of the city's public hospitals.

Young people across the country brought with them to school hard questions about the events unfolding along the Gulf Coast. In a country so well resourced as our own, why did it take such a long time for the government to rescue its own people? Would the response have been so slow if the hurricane had struck a more affluent community, or a predominantly White one? How come news coverage framed some storm victims as doing what they needed to do to survive, while framing others as looters with questionable moral fiber? Could the more than 1,800 deaths, plus countless injuries, separations, and relocations, have been averted if those outside the area cared more about those living within it? What explains the lagging restoration of the city's public infrastructure, including its public schooling options, like the Dr. Martin Luther King, Jr. Charter School for Science and Technology (featured in Focal Point 9.6)? These questions are profound ones, worthy of serious classroom discussion. They also speak to significant strands of distrust and abandonment that many Americans increasingly feel toward their own government.

In this age of the Tea Party, the Trump presidency, and Black Lives Matter, people are speaking out against corporate greed, racial injustice, and the government's inaction (or worse) on climate change, wars, population shifts, resource distribution, voting rights, and more. Many protest policing practices, including incidents of police brutality that have left far too many Black people, including children, dead or injured, and far too few officers indicted.

For teachers, these complicated issues can feel both vital and daunting, particularly in a mainstream political climate that often characterizes critical questioning and dissent as unpatriotic. Starting in their own classrooms, teachers must gain the skills to exercise, cultivate, and protect these rights. It's up to teachers to create spaces where students can ask hard questions, even—perhaps especially—of their own government. Teachers can be protective and open and honest and bring developmentally appropriate content into conversations with students. They can bring knowledge and build bridges to organizations with knowledge; they can themselves join and organize.

But individual teachers can only do so much. The teacher cannot be the only voice in the school or the classroom to take a social justice position; teachers have to make it possible for students to make just decisions but, unlike for bullying or racist talk, can't step in to squelch students who land on the side of unjust public policies, and such imposition of a teacher's authority can work against a justice agenda. Transforming to politically just positions (even changing racist and homophobic attitudes, for example) requires a large measure of cognitive shift—changes in sense making, and that may take a longer-term, patient process. Schools with truly democratic cultures make it possible for youth and adults to make sense of and learn from their disappointments, fears, and distrust and to channel them into productive, socially just action.

Focal Point 9.6
Community Commitment to Education in New Orleans's Lower Ninth Ward

In 2010, Secretary of Education Arne Duncan stated, "The best thing that happened to the education system in New Orleans was Hurricane Katrina. That education system was a disaster. And it took Hurricane Katrina to wake up the community to say that we have to do better."[31] Yet residents of New Orleans's Lower Ninth Ward—those hardest hit by flooding—have a much longer history and commitment to education than this quote suggests. The news story below details the Herculean efforts of one community to reopen a well-established local school damaged by the storm and its aftermath.

At the time of the article, six years after Hurricane Katrina made landfall, only one-third of New Orleans's public schools had reopened (and only one in the Lower Ninth Ward), and roughly two-thirds of public and private medical health facilities were still not in operation. Since the article's publication, the school has been described as a "symbol of rebirth in the Lower 9th Ward." Its graduated its first senior class since reopening, and in 2015 it became the first school to return to the New Orleans Public Schools district's authority since the state took over jurisdiction of all the city's schools post-Katrina. Its story stands as a reminder of how much some communities have had to endure and why trust—in institutions—might reasonably be fractured; it also reminds us of the role that schools *can* play in anchoring and revitalizing a community in hard times.

First School in Lower 9th Ward Reopened

New Orleans, August 30, 2007

Following numerous months of arduous struggle, Dr. Martin Luther King, Jr. Charter School for Science and Technology finally had something to celebrate. King school is the first to reopen in the Lower 9th Ward since Hurricane Katrina.

. . . Principal Doris Hicks, who was raised in the Lower 9th Ward, was thrilled to finally be home. But Hicks reiterated that the homecoming was bittersweet because over 30 students and family members lost their lives during Katrina. "So, we take this rededication and dedicate it to their memories," she said.

. . . But the journey to reopen the school was filled with struggle. When Hicks and King staff approached school board members and city officials soon after the storm, they responded saying it would take three to five years to repair the damages.

. . . Tired of waiting around for the government, New Orleans relief organization Common Ground decided to organize school repairs alongside the community. In mid-March 2006, hundreds of students arrived to volunteer over their spring break. More than 200 of the volunteers participated in a training, informing them that they may be risking arrest if they stepped foot on the King site, because it was deemed dangerous. On March 16, residents and volunteers took matters into their own hands. Volunteers wore Tyvek suits, all-day cleanup efforts began and community members spoke about the importance of Martin Luther King, Jr. and the history of the school. . . .

The following day New Orleans Police shut down the clean-up operation and threatened to arrest volunteers and community members. A series of meetings took place over the weekend, which connected Common Ground with school district and city officials.

The City Council eventually passed a resolution, affirming that volunteers and Lower 9th Ward residents would have the right to clean up the school for immediate use and with the hope of reopening it sooner than the three to five years originally promised.

Cleaning resumed the following week, but the obstacles continued. The district said it could not rebuild, claiming the school wasn't structurally sound and didn't have enough water pressure. Hicks, however, had a report from engineers who assessed the property in January 2006, declaring it structurally sound. New Orleans Sewage and Water Board confirmed that there was sufficient water pressure, so the police backed down.

. . . While the original school site was being cleaned, the search for a temporary site was also besieged with obstacles. The first few offered sites were in deplorable condition. After visiting numerous buildings, the principal, teachers and residents negotiated to open the school at another old facility that was in appalling disrepair. But then Principal Hicks visited the facility and said, "No, not my babies. My children deserve to be in a school facility that gives them dignity and respects them as human beings."

Promises were made to clean the building but there were numerous delays for opening dates, moving the original deadline of August 11 to September 7, 2006. Despite the building being unfinished, teachers, parents and leaders from the Southern Christian Leadership Conference (SCLC) went to the dilapidated site and held classes for the first day on the school's lawn and front steps, with about 250 to 300 students.

The determination of the school community led to a march and demonstration, during which SCLC members taught students about the history of the civil rights movement.

District officials met with community members and, after a negotiation session, agreed to grant King staff and students access to another temporary school, available immediately. Previously, King staff were told that this temporary school suffered considerable flood damage, when in fact it was minimal compared to the King site which had up to 17 feet of water.

All the while Lower 9th residents watched public schools in other neighborhoods, primarily white neighborhoods, reopen.

While in the temporary site, members of the King school community continued to appeal to the State School Board, lobbying to return to their original home and insisting that the school was worth fixing. "We understood that our school would be the anchor of the rebuilding in the Lower 9th Ward," said King's Dean of Students.

Principal Hicks adds that the battle still isn't over. King staff must now sign a lease written by the district for usage of their building, and Hicks finds the lease completely unacceptable. In the lease, the district requests control of the building or to have another school share the site with King. As a result, Hicks and staff continue in negotiations.

"Why do we have to sign a lease first of all for a school that belongs to us?" asks Hicks. Though Hicks says it is a big step to have the building, "it is more like scratching the surface."

Source: Abridged, amended text of freelance writer and Common Ground Collective volunteer Daniela Rible's *New America Media* article, "First School in Lower 9th Ward Reopened," published August 30, 2007.

Professionalism, Collaboration, Inquiry, and Activism

Despite its rigors and complexities, professional teaching carries with it the burdens of its history, and it suffers from the low status that society gives to its charges—children. Historically, society has not valued children highly. Neither has it valued those who spend their lives with them. In the eighteenth and nineteenth centuries, servants, not professionals, cared for the children of the middle and upper classes. And for most of the twentieth century, teaching was considered women's work and done almost exclusively by women. Community leaders saw women as being dependent on their husbands or other male authorities for leadership—not suited for making important decisions. The feminization of teaching also fit well with scientific management theories. Women teachers provided schools with a class of low-status employees—those who occupied the bottom positions on the organizational chart. They carried out the decisions made by those at the top—male administrators.

In 1908, Felix Arnold published the *Text-Book of School and Class Management*, which explicated theories and practices that should guide school administrators and teachers. Among teachers' duties and responsibilities, Arnold listed these obligations to the principal:

> All instructions, when given by the principal, should be rigidly followed. They may be wrong. They may harm the children. They may be against high ethical standards. But they should be followed. The moment a principal delivers his instructions he becomes responsible for whatever happens when they are carried out. Remonstrance and protest are allowable. But as long as the instructions hold, they should be followed.[29]

Arnold's advice leaves little room for teachers who want to change the world. It also presents the principal as a distinctly male authority figure.

Teachers as Participants and Professionals

Developing school cultures that enhance learning and social justice requires teachers' long-range involvement, rather than their participation in a primarily technical and rational process. Teachers must engage with one another in an ongoing process of inquiry where they examine the assumptions and values that underlie their own practice as well as the school's.[30] In other words, teacher involvement in school culture must entail more than, for example, sitting on a committee that will disband as soon as a specific policy has been written or a specific problem has been temporarily resolved.

Teachers' primary visible task is teaching students in the classroom. This typically occupies five to seven hours a day, five days a week, but teachers must also spend time grading, completing administrative paperwork, supervising, tutoring, preparing for classes and parent conferences, cleaning, and telephoning parents. These activities must take place when teachers are not teaching.

If attending to students and simply keeping up with lessons and logistics consume all of a teacher's time, little time or energy remains for other professional activities. A *professionalizing* school culture is one that requires and ensures that teachers have time for creative, energizing inquiry and learning. Time to read, work with colleagues, and participate in reflection and reform may be structured into some teachers' workday; more likely, teachers themselves have to make tough decisions about where and how to squeeze in such time.

> When I began my first year, I knew that teaching involved more than just planning and delivering a lesson, managing a classroom, grading, and reporting the progress of the students. Teaching included administrative tasks; developing relationships; communicating with fellow teachers, administrators, and parents; and continually striving toward better lessons and instruction. However, I did not understand the constraints, pressures, and demands that these activities would place on my teaching. With so many constraints, pressures, and demands on teachers, no wonder the profession seems so resistant to change. Even though I consider myself one who would like

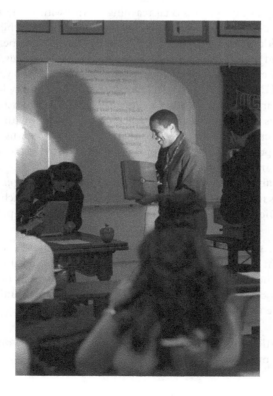

to see changes, I feel pushed toward conservatism because I have so much work. What I want to do on the inside becomes compromised as I deal with the day-to-day reality of the job.

Although I have not completely resolved them, I know that these are important issues that I need to address if I am to achieve my goals for education. They suggest that in order to achieve my goals for education, I must continue to reflect on my teaching practices through a method of inquiry.

—Jasper Hiep Dang Bui
First-year teacher, English, grade 8

Regular meetings with a group of new teachers gave Mark Hill the opportunity to reflect on his practices. Frustrated by his students' level of critical thinking, Mark conducted a study of whether his students might be more effective mathematics problem solvers if he taught them to monitor their own thinking—a process that psychologists call "metacognition." Mark gave students a pretest to determine the extent to which they were aware of their thinking and learning processes, taught them some metacognitive strategies, gave them a posttest, collected students' reflections about the lessons, and conducted a focus group to discuss the study and its results with his students.

The photo on the preceding page shows Mark sharing his study with colleagues for their review. He found that students organized their knowledge more effectively when they used meta-cognitive techniques, but that all sorts of other social and cultural factors also came into play. These intervening factors, he explained to his colleagues, might be the subject of further inquiry.

Conducting a formal study, as Mark did, is one way of engaging in inquiry and reflection on one's practice, but it's not the only way. Teachers who teach and even just plan together often inquire and reflect collectively as a matter of course. And, in many schools, teachers have joined together in inquiry groups or study groups where they examine a wide range of issues at the heart of their teaching and the school culture. We describe some of these inquiry practices in what follows.

Teachers as Partners in Learning

In schools, as in any professional workplace, the most potent force for learning is collaboration with peers. This can take many forms for teachers; a common arrangement is team teaching, as described in the following quotes.

At first, I thought that sharing a room with someone was a horrible thing. I wanted my own class, and I wanted to practice all of the wonderful theories I had learned over the past year. I felt as if all of my plans were ruined because of a lack of space and because I had to com-promise timing, scheduling, and work with this other woman. But, before long, I began to see that we had similar beliefs about how children learn and how we should teach.

The most wonderful thing about team teaching was that we learned an incredible amount from each other about every aspect of teaching, including relationships with students, parents, and other teachers. We have not only shared ideas and resources, but we are there to construc-tively criticize and encourage one another as we deal with the many aspects of being a bilingual teacher. It has been so valuable to my students to see that we two teachers are able to work cooperatively and learn from each other. This is consistent with my belief that teachers are not a source of all knowledge, but, like our students, we are learning and changing daily. We have also been able to build a great sense of community among all of our students. They know that there are two adults who care about them, and a whole class of students who care as well.

—Susie Shin
First-year teacher, grade 1

Team teaching is an unbelievable experience. It is not easy; it requires more time to plan (or maybe my partner teacher and I just have not figured it out yet). It requires patience and good listening skills. There are some days that we wake up on the wrong side of the bed, but that is normal. We have learned to deal with it.

Being able to work so closely with my team teacher makes me realize how important it is to interact, collaborate, and share with other teachers. We were able to work so well together because we believe in the same things about schooling, learning, and community. We have done great, engaging activities with the kids. Each of us can spend more time doing individual assessments (i.e., running records) while the other is doing something else. We have a lot of fun together, and I think that the students do, too. It is just really nice to have another adult in the classroom. Our parent meetings are much more successful because there are two of us.

My partner teacher and I have developed a truly special relationship. She has been my shoulder to cry on, my journal to reflect in, my partner in crime, and one of my most influential mentors.

—Wendy Herrera
First-year teacher, grades 1 and 2

Both Susie Shin and Wendy Herrera convey the personal satisfaction and professional enrichment that come when teachers work closely together.

Teachers as Members of Learning Communities

A productive school culture requires teachers who have the willingness, skills, and structures to examine every aspect of their teaching. This kind of inquiry goes beyond the familiar search for "what works" to make conventional and technical school practice "better." Grounded in socio-cultural views of learning, inquiry approaches reflect broad and collaborative goals.

Inquiry-based professional development differs from typical in-services, trainings, or workshops, most of which replicate transmission models of teaching. Indeed, in typical offerings, teachers are often expected to receive information from experts, rather than actively engage in learning experiences and construct their own knowledge. Scaffolding is minimal, or sessions are stand-alone rather than sequenced to enable follow-through. Scant attention is paid to relationships among colleagues, who inevitably bring different kinds of experience and expertise, and who may know, feel, or learn things that they won't readily share with others.

Conversely, inquiry approaches attend to teachers' capacities as constructors of knowledge and to the complex structures and social systems in which they're embedded. Just as students learn best when their learning connects to issues that are important to them, teachers learn best when professional development supports them to focus on aspects of their practice that are interesting, puzzling, or concerning to them in some way. Inquiry processes support them to ask and answer important questions, such as how their underlying beliefs and understandings impact what they teach and what students learn. They also support them to work with peers to make their practices and problem solving more public and, thus, more potent for collective learning and school improvement.

Positive shifts in school culture are much more possible when teachers (and students) are accountable to each other and have space and support to express themselves authentically, critically analyze taken-for-granted aspects of schooling, and negotiate common understandings that support collective action. This is what a school-wide commitment to inquiry can enable.

One first-year teacher was lucky enough to experience a culture of inquiry at the school where she student-taught. We don't use her name, because the school where she now teaches has a culture that sees such inquiry as a waste of time.

Northern's district used its professional development and reform funds to conduct student and teacher inquiry sessions to address the school's concerns. . . . The guiding focus of these discussions was the "two schools" issue—why do different segments of the student population perform and succeed at different levels?

One English teacher condemned the AP test as the "ultimate canon." He argued that, for teachers, "there are conflicting priorities. Is our goal to build a sense of self—for students—or is our goal to push as many kids into Harvard as possible?" A math teacher responded with his frustration with the current emphasis on testing and how his priorities have been altered. "I refuse to believe that passing a test is a measure of one's intelligence. Let's face it, some of our kids are being prepared to succeed, and others are overlooked."

Several staff members recognized that without reform in how teachers used assessments, the cycle of educational inequality would be perpetuated. A counselor for "at-risk" students explained that not changing would be "most damaging for lower-achieving students—those who don't see themselves as smart because they don't relate to the school environment and don't 'buy into the system.'"

The most striking aspect of Northern's inquiry was the level of comfort in discussing issues of school culture and the ways teachers' practices can negatively impact students. These are not easy topics to discuss, because individuals tend to become defensive about their teaching practices. But in this school, participants explained their frustrations and distress about the impact of some of their classroom practices (particularly concerning assessment). And they did so in a way that demonstrated that they were struggling with these issues and open to change.

At Northern, people honestly want to exchange ideas and hear what others have to say. The environment is safe and supportive enough to deal with difficult issues. Teachers are not blaming administrators, and administrators are not blaming teachers. All are working as a group toward addressing how curriculum, school culture, and assessment impact students. Reform is everyone's priority, and everyone seems to believe that these issues can and will be addressed in a meaningful way to improve the learning environment for students.

—Name withheld
First-year high school teacher

While the excerpt above focuses most on inquiry around structures and policies, other forms of teacher inquiry home in on curriculum and instruction. For example, teachers who participate in cognitively guided instruction (CGI)—described in Chapter 6—might meet regularly in inquiry groups to examine samples of the mathematics work done by students in one another's classes. As they reflect together on their teaching practices and their students' work, such teachers replicate the same processes (describing, explaining, questioning) that they aim to facilitate for their students during classroom instruction.

Creating a Culture of Critical Inquiry

At its broadest, *inquiry* is a way to learn what other people believe and to struggle for common understandings. *Critical* inquiry adds a political dimension—namely, explicit attention to power. Power is always present in relationships, even in the noncoercive, cordial, and cooperative relationships among friends. Typically, when there is a strong commitment to co-constructing understanding (as there often is among friends), power imbalances do not greatly disrupt the democratic, reciprocal nature of the relationship. But schools exist in a world of immense status differences associated with gender, race, age, employment, wealth, background, physical power, and so on. Since educators work in this world—where people do not and cannot simply check their status and power "at the schoolroom door"—it is necessary to create school conditions and cultures that support people to solve problems and learn as equals.

Schools that reflect a commitment to critical inquiry invite and require explicit consideration of how power "works" in any classroom, school, and community. Typical "practical" approaches to school change often involve addressing the problems that seem easiest to solve or that will arouse the least discomfort and debate. As a result, such approaches often yield quick agreements—for example, to follow a certain program or implement a certain solution. Critical inquiry approaches require instead that people look first to the knowledge, routines, and values that exist in a school community and then ask hard questions about what new knowledge might be needed, what routines might warrant change, and what alternative values might be explored. This does not mean that a critical perspective is "impractical." To the contrary, critical inquiry is arguably *more* practical, because it holds potential for meaningful and lasting change in addition to being personally fulfilling for participants.

There is no doubt that critical inquiry embodies different ways of prioritizing problems, directed efforts to empower and give voice to members who are less assertive, different views on useful sources of new knowledge, different time frames for accomplishing goals, and different and greater demands on members' patience along with an elevated need to develop and protect relationships. There are schools that embrace this kind of inquiry and create conditions for teachers to collaborate in pursuit of social justice. In the following excerpt, Chrysta Bakstad describes her participation in an inquiry group at one such school, while Focal Point 9.7 profiles another.

Participating in an "inquiry group" has provided an opportunity for me to reflect with other staff members. I am part of the "Wednesday Inquiry Group" that meets every other Wednesday, from 12:15 P.M. until 3:00 P.M. During this time an "Inquiry Sub," trained in the arts, teaches my class. My group consists of seven teachers, the school nurse, and a site coordinator. The teachers involved represent all grade levels, kindergarten through fifth, and special education and bilingual teachers. The teaching experience of group members ranges from first-year teacher to those who have taught over ten years. The site coordinator is an "external critical friend" to the school who participates in all three inquiry group sessions and serves as the facilitator for the group.

Inquiry has allowed me to reflect on my teaching practices with a group of teachers with whom I typically would not have the opportunity to sit and talk. Topics of discussion center around our school's two "essential questions": (1) "What can I do to ensure that the inequitable pattern of student achievement no longer exists?" and (2) "What can I do to ensure that there is student and parent voice in my classroom?" Still, the topics of discussion are extremely diverse: racial and ethnic issues, creating and sustaining a learning community, critical pedagogy, teaching tolerance, discipline, the school structure, parent involvement, and teaching "growth and development." The group also reads and discusses professional articles and books and agrees to take action as a result of these discussions. For example, at one meeting we agreed to pay attention to how we used "choice" in the classroom. At another meeting, we agreed to pay attention to how we call on students in class. After every such agreement, we report back on our related efforts and findings at the following meeting. This creates a springboard for discussion.

As the youngest member of the group, I am in no way made to feel like I am the least experienced. My opinions and viewpoints are listened to and validated. I feel safe expressing my views, even if I think that they will not be embraced by all of the members of the group. Because this is my first year in the school community as a credentialed teacher, the inquiry group is a good place for me to express my opinions. This experience has given me an opportunity in a small, safe, intimate setting to reflect and find my "voice."

When I contribute to my inquiry group, I bring with me the knowledge from my recent courses. I have had the opportunity to share books, articles, and my research papers with the group. The positive reaction and interest expressed in my contributions have enhanced my comfort and feeling of inclusion.

—Chrysta Bakstad
First-year teacher, grades K, 1, and 2

Focal Point 9.7
A Caring School Culture: The Chula Vista
Learning Community Charter School

Chula Vista School's Turnaround Turns Heads: Elementary Charter Has
Gone From Federal Improvement List to Distinguished Status
by Karen Kucher, Monday, November 21, 2011, San Diego Union Tribune

A charter school in Chula Vista was performing so poorly on state assessments that it made the federal watch list for three years. Now it has staged a dramatic turnaround that is attracting international attention.

Today, the 822-student school has test scores among the highest in the Chula Vista Elementary School District and has been recognized as a California Distinguished School. The dual-language immersion campus has become a type of laboratory where professors from San Diego State University as well as educators from Mexico, England and Switzerland visit, hoping to discover the secret to its success....

At this school, everyone has a role in the education of children. Teachers are encouraged to be "teacher scholars" and are expected to keep up with research being done in the field of education.

Students at the school take half their courses in English and half in Spanish each day, and also get weekly instruction in Mandarin, a third language added two years ago. About 95 percent of students at the K–8 school are Latino, with about 53 percent English-language learners and about half come from families poor enough they qualify for free or reduced lunch.

Parents say they like the school for the language immersion and rigorous instruction. Martha Garcia, whose 4-year-old daughter is in kindergarten, said she's pleased so far. "She reads already in both languages," Garcia said.

Administrators focus on making sure that everyone on staff believes all students can succeed and won't excuse failures because of their students' backgrounds.

Teachers at the school look at the students' cultural and linguistic backgrounds and develop curricula that connect to their experiences.

The school this year is focusing on having students engage in critical discussions with classmates about texts they read and having them explain their thought processes. To prepare for the emphasis on dialogue, every teacher read and discussed the book *Pedagogy of the Oppressed*, written by Harvard professor Paulo Freire about his experiences of teaching in literacy programs in Brazil.

When Principal Jorge Ramirez talks about his teachers, he uses words like "intellectual" and "lifelong learners" and says they are continually seeking to improve their methods.

On the team webpage of fourth grade teachers—John Paul Arellano, Scott Lyons, and Catherine Bradshaw, who plan their interdisciplinary units together—is the following mission statement:

> The fourth-grade team, along with all the staff from CVLCC, have spent the summer analyzing the words of a great educator, Paulo Freire. Due to our reading and re-reading of his work we have decided to highlight 3 central themes in our classrooms. These 3 themes are: the knowledge begins with the student and not the teacher; true learning

takes place through authentic dialogue; and by better understanding our reality we will be able to transform it. Our mission is to have a year in which the traditional view of education is challenged. Inspired by Freire's words we intend to transform the student-teacher relationship!

The class webpage also features photos and videos of students at work, including content students themselves have generated, alongside interactive features that reflect the school and classroom culture. Rather than more typical approaches, which tend to highlight individualistic accomplishments, for example, CVLCC "Students of Week" honors recognize "the valued acts of students who are committed to the strengthening of our classroom and school community" and "who take action" toward "building a *Community Conscious of Others*."

Source: Adapted from Karen Kucher, "Chula Vista School's Turnaround Turns Heads," *San Diego Union Tribune*, November 21, 2011, www.utsandiego.com/news/2011/nov/21/chula-vista-schools-turnaround-turns-heads/?print&page=all/.

Formal inquiry groups and common planning periods for inquiry-oriented educators offer regularly scheduled time away from the classroom, where teachers can forge deeper collective understandings. They can ask hard questions like those Chrysta asked concerning patterns of achievement, parent voice, and so forth. They can identify areas of concentrated and sustained focus, as evident in Focal Point 9.7. And they can encourage the integrated communities evident in both schools, where veteran and novice teachers work together in nonhierarchical ways that acknowledge the wisdom and expertise that different people bring.

While both of these schools have well-established structures that encourage and enable critical inquiry, this isn't always the case. Elsewhere, teachers introduce critical inquiry by becoming members on committees and, generally, participating in school affairs with a critical frame of mind. This is not always easy, even in the aforementioned schools; because *critical* inquiry aims to change and improve the school culture, its purpose is *counter*cultural. Resistance is to be expected, even from well-intentioned educators whose everyday common sense may lead them to accept and passively perpetuate the cultural status quo. And yet, even in the face of resistance, critical inquiry *can* thrive. Becoming informed about one's own and others' practices, connecting practices with theory, and developing trusting relationships with allies are all examples of powerful actions. And these are not just first steps—they are themselves practical achievements that represent progress and promote social justice.

Creating Cultures Where Good Teaching Makes Sense

Some reforms—like creating intentional small schools—have shown particular promise for fostering equitable, caring, and academically rigorous school cultures. Still, not all small schools have been successes. Stanford professor Linda Darling-Hammond warns that it is not the size but the culture that matters:

"Small" is not synonymous with successful. There are ineffective small schools, some of which replicate the very problems they were seeking to solve. Small size is a necessary condition for effective schooling, but it is not enough.[32]

Concept Table 9.1 Principles for Effective Design

Principle	Description/Example
Personalization	Smaller classes and reduced teacher-pupil loads help to personalize learning.
Continuous relationships	Advisory classes and looping—as well as diminished teacher attrition—allow relationships to develop over time.
Standards and performance assessment	High expectations and performance-based assessments help students learn and demonstrate learning.
Authentic curriculum	In-depth learning with real-world connections leads to higher achievement.
Adaptive pedagogy	Teachers adjust their teaching modes to meet students where they are.
Antiracist teaching	Schools embrace diversity and openly challenge racism (and other oppressions).
Qualified teachers	Qualified teachers support students' learning and make a difference.
Collaboration and development	Time provided for teachers to work together develops their expertise.
Family/community connections	Relationships built with families and communities strengthen students' learning.
Democratic decision making	Shared governance allows for the creation of a common vision.

Source: Stanford School ReDesign Network, "Ten Features of Effective Design," www.srnleads.org/data/pdfs/10_features.pdf.

And, indeed, no one condition alone—not smallness or anything else—can ensure a healthy school culture. In this regard, the *principles* developed by Darling-Hammond and colleagues to guide the creation of *successful* small schools are a helpful tool (see Concept Table 9.1). Not surprisingly, they bear a strong resemblance to the elements of school culture discussed throughout this chapter, and thus provide guidelines that any school, not just official "small schools," might use when "taking stock."

Guided by these principles, educators ask important questions such as the following: How well do we really know our students? What are we doing to support all of them to meet high expectations? How do we ensure that our students don't fall behind? Where in our curriculum do we give students opportunities to make "real-world" connections and take socially just action? Are we making the very most of the resources we have for learning? Are we doing enough to collaborate with one another—as well as with students, families, community members, and so on—to provide the most rigorous, responsive education possible?

When school cultures press teachers and others to wrestle with questions like these, positive outcomes follow for students and teachers alike.[33] Likewise, when teachers bring such questions to their colleagues and schools, they open up possibilities and exert their own press for positive cultural change.

Digging Deeper and Tools for Critique

www.routledge.com/cw/teachingtochangetheworld

Notes

1 Cultures permit a broad range of acceptable behavior in some matters, and in other matters only a very limited range of behaviors. A school, for example, may tolerate a wide range of dress for students but sharply limit where they can use mobile phones on campus. Both of these

determinations derive from the school's culture—or general system of beliefs—regarding what it must do to preserve its most important values and ways of life.

2 Seymour Sarason, *The Culture of the School and the Problem of Change*, 3rd ed. (Boston: Allyn & Bacon, 1996).

3 Coalition of Essential Schools, www.essentialschools.org.

4 John I. Goodlad, *A Place Called School* (New York: McGraw-Hill, 1984).

5 Jeannie Oakes, Karen Hunter Quartz, Steve Ryan, and Martin Lipton, *Becoming Good American Schools: The Struggle for Virtue in School Reform* (San Francisco: Jossey-Bass, 2001); Theodore Sizer, *Horace's Hope: What Works for the American High School* (Boston: Houghton Mifflin, 1996).

6 Council of the Great City Schools, *Charting the Right Course: A Report on Urban Student Achievement and Course-Taking* (Washington, DC: Author, 1998).

7 This is the first of several excerpts in this chapter from a booklet compiled by UCLA teacher education students to honor educators and citizens struggling to promote social justice in and through Los Angeles area schools. John Rogers and Carolyn Castelli, eds., *Building Social Justice for a New Generation: Profiles of Social Justice Fellows From UCLA's Teacher Education Program, 1997* (Los Angeles: UCLA, 1997).

8 UCLA Community School, http://cs.gseis.ucla.edu.

9 UCLA Community School, *Research, Practice and Policy Brief* (Spring 2017), http://cs.gseis.ucla.edu/assets/CS17-PolicyBrief-Web.pdf.

10 Linda Darling-Hammond, "The Right to Learn and the Advancement of Teaching: Research, Policy, and Practice for Democratic Education," *Educational Researcher* 26 (August/September 1996): 5.

11 See Laurence Steinberg, *Beyond the Classroom* (New York: Simon & Schuster, 1996).

12 Cathy Krop, Dominic Brewer, Susan Gates, Brian Gill, Robert Reichardt, Melora Sundt, and Dan Throgmorton, *Potentially Eligible Students: A Growing Opportunity for the University of California* (Santa Monica, CA: RAND, 1998).

13 See Claude Steele, "A Threat in the Air: How Stereotypes Shape the Intellectual Identities and Performance of Women and African-Americans," *American Psychologist* 52 (1997): 613–629.

14 Ronald F. Ferguson, "Paying for Public Education: New Evidence on How and Why Money Matters," *Harvard Journal on Legislation* 28, no. 2 (Summer 1991): 465–498. Ferguson's studies are supported by other analyses showing that money does indeed make a difference, including a 1994 study by Larry Hedges, Richard D. Laine, and Rob Greenwald, "Does Money Matter? A Meta-Analysis of the Effects of Differential School Inputs on Student Outcomes," *Educational Researcher* 23, no. 3 (1994): 5–14; see also Bruce J. Biddle and David C. Berliner, *What Research Says About Unequal Funding for Schools in America* (Tempe, AZ: Arizona State University, Education Policy Studies Laboratory, Education Policy Reports Project, 2002).

15 See Gene Glass, Leonard Cahan, Mary Lee Smith, and Nikola Filby, *School Class Size: Research and Policy* (Beverly Hills, CA: Sage, 1982); Jeremy Finn and Charles M. Achilles, "Answers and Questions About Class Size," *American Educational Research Journal* 27 (Fall 1990): 557–577; and Alan B. Krueger, "Understanding the Magnitude and Effect of Class Size on Student Achievement," in *The Class Size Debate*, eds. Lawrence Mishel and Richard Rothstein (Washington, DC: Economic Policy Institute, 2002), 7–36.

16 See, for example, Michael Knapp, Patrick Shields, and Brenda Turnbull, *Teaching for Meaning in High-Poverty Classrooms* (New York: Teachers College Press, 1995); Jeannie Oakes, "Two Cities: Tracking and Within-School Segregation," *Teachers College Record* 96, no. 4 (1995): 681–690; and new analyses of the impact of academic coursework on college entrance test scores reported in "Study: Hard Courses Help Urban ACT's," *New York Times*, January 15, 1998.

17 Rogers and Castelli, *Building Social Justice for a New Generation*, n.p.

18 Jeannie Oakes, Amy Stuart Wells, Susan Yonezawa, and Karen Ray, "The Politics of Equity and Change: Lessons From Detracking Schools," in *1997 ASCD Yearbook: Rethinking Educational Change With Heart and Mind*, ed. Andy Hargreaves (Alexandria, VA: Association for Supervision and Curriculum Development, 1997), 43–72.

19 Sabino Kornrich and Frank F. Furstenberg, "Investing in Children: Changes in Spending on Children, 1972 to 2007," *Demography* 49 (Forthcoming).

20 Rogers and Castelli, *Building Social Justice for a New Generation*. n.p.

21 One of many books exploring these concepts for high school reform is Theodore Sizer's *Horace's Hope: What Works for the American High School* (Boston: Houghton Mifflin, 1996); see also Oakes, Hunter Quartz, Ryan, and Lipton, *Becoming Good American Schools*.

22 Joseph G. Kosciw, Emily A. Greytak, Noreen M. Giga, Christian Villenas, and David J. Danischewski, M.A., *The 2015 National School Climate Survey: The Experiences of Lesbian, Gay, Bisexual, Transgender, and Queer Youth in Our Nation's Schools.* New York: GLSEN, 2016, www.glsen.org/sites/default/files/2015%20National%20GLSEN%202015%20National%20School%20Climate%20Survey%20%28NSCS%29%20-%20Full%20Report_0.pdf.

23 Human Rights Watch, *Walking Through a Hailstorm: Discrimination Against LGBT Youth in Schools*, www.hrw.org/report/2016/12/07/walking-through-hailstorm/discrimination-against-lgbt-youth-us-schools.

24 GLSEN, "Students Still Face Hostility: Considerable School Improvements Show Progress," www.glsen.org/article/lgbtq-secondary-students-still-face-hostility-school-considerable-improvements-show-progress.

25 Michelle Fine and Sara McClelland, "Sexuality Education and Desire: Still Missing After All These Years," *Harvard Educational Review* 76, no. 3 (2006): 297–338, 437.

26 Human Rights Watch, *Like Walking Through a Hailstorm*, 2016, www.hrw.org/report/2016/12/07/walking-through-hailstorm/discrimination-against-lgbt-youth-us-schools.

27 Alfie Kohn, "Teaching About September 11," in "War, Terrorism and Our Classrooms: Teaching in the Aftermath of the September 11th Tragedy," special issue, *Rethinking Schools* 16, no. 2 (Winter 2001/2002): 5, www.rethinkingschools.org/static/special_reports/sept11/pdf/911insrt.pdf.

28 Eric W. Robelen, "Majority of States' Standards Don't Mention 9/11," *Education Week*, 2011, www.edweek.org/ew/articles/2011/08/31/02sept11_ep.h31.html.

29 Felix Arnold, *Text-Book of School and Class Management: Theory and Practice* (New York: The Macmillan Company, 1908), 22.

30 Considerable research has documented the power of collaborative work among teachers in the process of school change and improvement. See, for example, Michael Fullan, *Successful School Improvement* (Philadelphia: Open University Press, 1992); Judith Warren Little, "Norms of Collegiality and Experimentation: Workplace Conditions of School Success," *American Educational Research Journal* 19 (1982): 325–340; Judith Warren Little and Milbery McLaughlin, eds., *Teachers Work: Individuals, Colleagues, and Contexts* (New York: Teachers College Press, 1993); and Karen Seashore Louis and Sharon D. Kruse, *Professionalism and Community: Perspectives on Reforming Urban Schools* (Newberry Park, CA: Corwin Press, 1995).

31 Mary Bruce, *Duncan: Katrina Was the "Best Thing" for New Orleans School System*, 2010, http://abcnews.go.com/blogs/politics/2010/01/duncan-katrina-was-the-best-thing-for-new-orleans-schools/.

32 Linda Darling-Hammond, overview to *Ten Features of Effective Design*, www.schoolredesign.net.

33 See, in particular, Anthony Bryk, *Trust in Schools: A Core Resource for Improvement* (New York: Russell Sage Foundation, 2004); and Anthony Bryk, Penny Bender Sebring, Elaine Allensworth, Stuart Luppescu, and John Q. Easton, *Organizing Schools for Improvement: Lessons From Chicago* (Chicago: University of Chicago Press, 2009).

Chapter 10

School Structure
Sorting Students and Opportunities to Learn

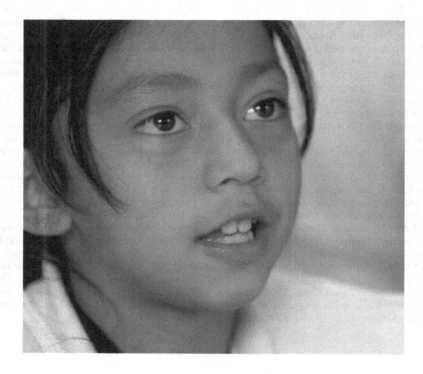

I consider myself a huge advocate for English Learners (ELs). Language classification guides tracking in the twenty-first century. If a student is classified Limited English Proficient (LEP), it is very difficult for her to be reclassified as a fluent English speaker and be placed in a class where grade-level curriculum is taught. As the EL coordinator, I helped my school do two significant things to help EL students have access to rigorous curriculum. One, we've changed the way that graduates from the fifth grade who are classified as LEP are placed into our sixth-grade classes. If an LEP student can perform in grade-level classes (which most can because they rise to the expectations), she is placed into regular sixth-grade English and put on track to take college-preparatory English in high school. Two, we have been reclassifying kids as fluent English speakers by the handful. Last year, we reclassified over 250 students, which allows them to be placed in grade-level English. This year we are looking to surpass that number and become the first large Eastside Middle School to go under 1,000 LEPs. Moreover, we want to continue to lower our LEP population each year.

—Mauro Bautista
Middle-school bilingual education coordinator

Mauro Bautista struggles with one of the most entrenched practices in American education—labeling students according to their perceived competencies and deficits and placing them in classes and programs tailored to meet their needs. Although most people rarely question them, such practices can do as much harm as good. The exclusion from rigorous curriculum that Mauro worries about has long-term consequences for students' future educational opportunities.

Chapter Overview

This chapter describes how and why schools categorize and group students into separate classrooms and programs for instruction. In doing so, it addresses one of the core ways that the school's structure influences students' opportunities to learn. Specifically, the chapter focuses on ability grouping and curriculum tracking,[1] as well as on the multitude of special classes and programs created to respond to differences among students. We explain the socially constructed nature of the categories and labels schools assign to students—labels like special education, gifted, compensatory, and Limited English Proficient (LEP)—and we provide some of the history behind labeling and sorting in American schools. We then review some of the evidence showing that these practices often do as much to *create* differences as they do to meet students' different needs. Finally, we describe the work of educators who seek to avoid these damaging practices and instead use more multidimensional, developmental, and socially just approaches for meeting students' needs.

Labeling, Sorting, and Grouping in Today's Schools

School systems throughout the United States routinely use assessment and evaluation strategies to compare, rank, and assign relative value to students' abilities and achievements both within and across schools, states, and countries, as we described in Chapter 7. Within schools, students are regularly identified as gifted, high achieving, below average, learning disabled, LEP, and more. These labels shape how educators sort students into instructional groups, classes, and programs. Today, ability, previous achievement, postsecondary aspirations, English language competence, and disability status have become almost taken-for-granted, or common-sense, criteria used for grouping students. "Individual choice," "talent," "motivation," various course prerequisites, and other criteria are also used. However, nearly all grouping assignments are ultimately made and justified by the school's prediction of a student's *capacity* to succeed in a particular group. Generally, the intention is to place students in, or encourage students to take, the most demanding courses in which the school thinks they can succeed. These predictions are fraught with inconsistencies and are often just plain wrong.

Although the labels differ from school to school, most schools have ways of publicly identifying students and differentiating their opportunities. First-year teacher Kimberly Aragon's experience, described next, is not unusual.

> Grouping pervades almost every area of my K–8 school. Some students enter a "VISTA" (gifted according to various intelligences) program as early as second grade, and, as those students progress, there will be at least one VISTA class in every grade. Every grade, 2 to 8, also has what is called a "SHARP" class. SHARP is an acronym for "Students with High Achievement in Reading Program." Students are placed in a SHARP class based on their previous years' test scores and their grades in English. Although the rest of the

students at my school are not labeled as "DULL," the implication of the "SHARP" name is obvious.

Moreover, some grades are divided further by placing the Limited English Proficient (LEP) students in one class and all of the rest of the students in another class. In addition, approximately twenty students in grade 1 are pulled out of class for one-on-one Reading Recovery instruction [Title I program]. One-third of the way through this year, the school instituted a middle-school reading elective, which requires ten students who scored in the bottom quartile on the previous year's standardized test to receive extra reading instruction from a credentialed teacher. Those students are then not able to participate in the other electives offered, such as drama, Spanish, communications, art, and computers.

Furthermore, the school's reading philosophy requires that each teacher create ability groups in his or her classroom, based on reading and math levels. As an English teacher, I am required to give each of my seventy students a "Running Record" three times a year and, based only on the records, place students in groups. . . . For instance, if a student's Running Record showed that his instructional level, according to the program, is fifth grade, he should be placed in a reading group that is reading a fifth-grade book.

—Kimberly Aragon
First-year teacher, humanities, grade 8

Of course, there's nothing wrong with Running Records or most other assessments, per se, or with giving students reading material at their reading level. It is appropriate and desirable for middle-school humanities teachers to assess students' literacy competencies one-on-one and then use the information they gain to select appropriately challenging texts and/or to scaffold students such that they can access the content they are expected to learn. The problem comes, as Kimberly describes, when (1) a single assessment is used to determine a student's ability, and (2) the action based on that determination restricts access to the curriculum.

Sorting by Academic Ability and Achievement

Ability grouping (also commonly known as tracking) is the routine sorting of all students into homogeneous groups and classes of "high," "average," and "low" students (or any of the creative euphemisms in vogue, such as "advanced," "accelerated," "opportunity," "basic," "SHARP," "VISTA," etc.). Such sorting typically begins early in elementary school—sometimes even in kindergarten—and continues throughout the grades.[2] Many elementary schools provide separate classes so that students spend the entire day with others judged to be at the same ability level. Other schools group students by ability for part of the day for specific subjects such as reading and math; this kind of grouping might include students from more than one class or grade, or, more likely, it may consist of small ability groups (such as reading or math groups) within a classroom. Sometimes ability groups follow a staggered schedule. A kindergarten class may be divided into early and late birds (separating the more and less precocious readers) so that each group has time alone with the teacher each day.

Nearly all middle schools and senior high schools ability-group some or all academic subjects (typically English, mathematics, science, and, slightly less commonly, social studies) based on students' past grades, test scores, and teacher recommendations. Schools sometimes assign students to blocks of classes all at the same ability level. This typically happens when schools assign a label to the student; a high-ability or low-ability student would then go into all classes that match his or her designation.

Policies affecting ability grouping and tracking have ebbed and flowed over the years, especially since the mid-1980s, when research began in earnest to document the ill effects and inequalities of tracking. Since then, many schools and some scholars have distinguished between tracking and ability grouping—narrowly defining tracking as a permanent, block assignment of students into courses that prepare them for different futures, such as entering two- or four-year colleges, going directly into the workforce, and so on. Because of the clear problems caused by placing students in different tracks that lead to such different opportunities and life outcomes, schools typically try to avoid tracking while favoring ability grouping. On the one hand, grouping students for instruction can be useful, even essential, but only if the groups are flexible, temporary, done within classes for particular assignments or lessons, and do not attach status labels to students such as "fast," "remedial," and so forth. Unfortunately, what some schools call ability grouping is really tracking under a more acceptable name.

National survey data have long indicated what most high school students could tell you—that those taking honors math tend to also take honors English, and that the same overlap prevails in remedial math and remedial or low-level English.[3] Because some subjects like math follow a sequence, students' assignments in earlier grades often still determine how far they can progress by the time they graduate.[4] Students who end up in the top math classes throughout high school are those who have been identified as strong math students by the sixth grade or before. Conversely, those students not placed in the uppermost ability classes by the sixth grade often stand only the slimmest chance of completing upper-level math in high school.

This type of sorting persists even as reforms attempt to interrupt it. For example, the push to have all students take algebra in the eighth grade is often implemented by sorting students into different levels of algebra, sometimes with names such as "basic algebra" or "honors algebra." The many problems associated with these grouping practices are discussed later in this chapter.

Sorting by Postsecondary Prospects

In addition to grouping students by their academic ability or prior achievement in various subjects, high schools have traditionally prescribed different sequences of classes, or tracks, for students with different futures. Thus, students heading for college and those expecting to take jobs right after high school historically ended in different tracks. In some schools, students still enroll in formal or informal programs of study—such as college-preparatory, general, or vocational—that dictate their entire array of courses. The vocational or general (noncollege) track usually coincides with the lower academic levels. College-bound students enroll in the high-ability tracks, since the lower-level courses typically don't satisfy college entrance requirements.

Increasingly, however, schools are recognizing the importance of preparing all students for college—an emphasis reinforced throughout contemporary education policy rhetoric and accountability. Aware that classes in the vocational track often have low status and limited value for gaining college admission, many vocational educators are now working to upgrade classes as needed. Finally, even *within* the college-prep designation, different course sequences often emerge—some designed to prepare students for the most competitive universities, some for less competitive ones, and some for two-year community colleges.

Most senior high schools offer some advanced placement (AP) classes for exceptionally high-achieving eleventh and twelfth graders bound for the most competitive universities. These courses allow students to pursue college-level study in nearly all the academic subjects. The content of AP courses is similar nationwide, since a major objective is to prepare students for the AP examinations, national tests administered by the College Board (the same organization that gives the Scholastic Aptitude Test [SAT], which many colleges require for admission). Most colleges give automatic credits to students who receive high scores on AP tests and excuse them from beginning courses in those subjects. AP classes often overlap with gifted and talented programs at the senior high level and with honors-level courses. Increasingly, schools further distinguish these highest-level courses by giving extra weight to grades earned in them when calculating grade point averages.

In the past decade, taking AP classes has become critical for students wishing to attend the nation's most competitive universities. In many states, the days have passed when getting all As or being class valedictorian could ensure admission to the university of one's choice. Many universities are looking not just for college-prep courses but for honors or AP credits, and students who have not been programmed for these courses thus stand less chance than others of earning admission.

Access to such courses varies widely across schools. Recent studies in California reveal that most of the state's low-income Latinx and African American students still attend schools that offer only a fraction of the courses that wealthier schools do.[5] It took the settlement of a lawsuit for the state to agree to add a minimum number of advanced courses to poor schools; meanwhile, wealthy schools are always gearing up to do more. Developments like these mean that even when standards are applied across the board in an effort to level the playing field, the traditional unfair distribution of opportunity persists. A few elite colleges and some high schools are bucking these trends by asserting that they can make their own good judgments, maintain their reputation for high quality, and attract excellent students without relying so heavily on the College Board.

Sorting by "Giftedness"

In the past, exceptionally precocious students often skipped grades if they outdistanced their peers academically. If they remained with their peers just by age, the logic went, they might make less progress that would otherwise be possible, or they might become unduly discouraged and bored. In the intervening years, federal funding has supported state and local efforts to improve services for students identified as gifted and talented; however, at present, gifted education is neither funded nor regulated at the federal level, leaving states and local districts responsible. In 2015, the National Association for Gifted Children reported that at least twenty-seven states provided special funding for gifted and talented students, and many schools maintain prominent gifted programs where the highest-achieving students are grouped together for enrichment or accelerated instruction, either in separate classes, in pull-out programs, or in gifted clusters within regular classrooms.

Although IQ is the most commonly used criterion for identifying gifted students, *giftedness* is defined in many different ways in different states and by different organizations. Joseph Renzulli, director of the National Research Center on Gifted and Talented, defines giftedness as high ability (including high intelligence), high creativity (ability to formulate and apply new ideas), and high task commitment (motivation and willingness to stick with a project until it is finished).[6] In many states, districts, and schools, to ensure that "talented" students without strong academic skills can qualify for gifted programs, IQ scores or achievement tests may be augmented by teachers' observations of leadership, creativity, or other special abilities and, sometimes, by parents' recommendation. In fact, nineteen states currently require the use of a multiple-criteria model that includes at least two sources of information, the most common of which are IQ scores and achievement data, nominations, scores on state-approved assessments, and portfolios.[7]

Sorting by Disabilities

New disability categories surface and old ones disappear as educators, psychologists, and physicians refine their definitions of conditions that fall outside the normal range in physical, sensory, behavioral, or cognitive characteristics. The 2004 federal Individuals With Disabilities Education

Act (IDEA) specifies thirteen categories of disabilities, and it provides funding to states and local school districts for special programs and services. In 2015, 6.6 million U.S. students, or 13 percent of the total school-going population, qualified for special education services under IDEA. These students' disabilities fall into various categories: specific learning disabilities (35 percent); speech or language impairments (20 percent); health-related impairment (13 percent); and intellectual disabilities (termed *mental retardation* prior to 2010), developmental delays, autism, and emotional disturbance (ED) (5–9 percent each).[8]

Once school personnel determine that a student qualifies for special help, the school is required by law to develop a written individual educational plan (IEP). The IEP states the child's needs, outlines specific learning goals, specifies the help the school will provide, and oftentimes details a role for the student and his or her family. Students with speech and language problems may need one-on-one instruction provided outside the classroom. Students with long-range illnesses might receive teaching at home or in a hospital. Large school districts might staff schools for students with severe intellectual disabilities and for those with vision and hearing impairment. Others might contract with private centers and provide transportation so that students have access to support and equipment that typical classrooms can't offer.

Students with less debilitating cognitive and emotional disorders usually spend all or part of their school day in more typical schools' regular and *resource classrooms.* The latter are places where smaller groups of students with disabilities receive assistance from specially trained teachers and teachers' aides. That said, the law requires that schools provide all students with disabilities the opportunity to receive individualized support in the *least restrictive environment.* This provision presses schools to *mainstream* students with disabilities into classrooms with peers at their grade level for as much of the day as possible.

Cognitive

Students often lag behind their peers in some school skills. In most cases, these lags are within the normal range of individual developmental differences. However, a growing number of students of normal intelligence who have difficulties, particularly in reading, are identified as having a learning disability, and a large proportion of those receiving special education services now fall into this category.[9] These students have unusual and specific struggles thought to result from organic causes, such as the brain's inability to process information with the same efficiency as other children.

The key to identifying a learning disability is not so much how a student performs in any one area as the discrepancy among different areas of performance. Such students, try as they may, have great difficulty accomplishing certain tasks, such as copying correctly, spelling accurately, reading fast, or memorizing details. However, these same students may be skilled at expressing ideas orally and solving problems. Others may have more serious difficulty with language, short-term memory, or visual perception. Students with identified disabilities such as these spend varying amounts of their school time receiving special services, either within a mainstream classroom or in the resource room.

Students identified as having "intellectual disabilities" (officially replacing the term *mental retardation* as of 2010) are those who score substantially below the normal range on intelligence tests. Specific designations range from "mild" to "severe and profound." These students' disabilities so restrict their intellectual functioning that they are projected to never reach typical adult levels. Like students with designated learning disabilities, however, these students differ widely; students with the same IQ scores can possess markedly different capabilities. Some develop strong social skills that enable them to get along and learn far better than those with higher IQ scores. Students with severe intellectual impairments might join other students for parts or all the school day.

Behavioral and Emotional

All students experience occasional mild behavior problems. Some, though, are at odds with their peers and/or with adults on a more profound level, and they are diagnosed formally only after their conduct has become bothersome or potentially harmful to themselves or others. Such diagnoses can result from a range of emotional and psychological conditions that affect students. They also, at times and unjustly, can result from a mismatch between in-class behavior standards and those of a student's home or play group. Students who seem unable to pay attention—who fidget and squirm, run around the room, or doze off during a video—are often the first to capture attention. Chronic inability to pay attention, sit still, and act cooperatively can signal disabilities with serious consequences, including falling behind academically, being socially ostracized by peers, and developing troubled relationships with teachers.

In earlier generations, schools may have labeled older students who consistently acted badly at school "incorrigible" or "delinquent" and sent them to reform schools; most of these students simply dropped out of school altogether. Today schools designate many habitually misbehaving otherwise. For example, attention-deficit/hyperactivity disorder (ADHD) now qualifies students for assistance under federal law. Roughly 12 percent of school-age children and teens had been diagnosed with ADHD in 2011, a 43 percent increase since 2003.[10] Many advocates view ADHD as a discrete genetic disorder, while others see it as a catchall label for the behaviors just described.

Educators categorize students who exhibit more dangerous, unruly, and violent behavior as having other disabilities—for example, as being severely emotionally disturbed (SED). Others are identified as having oppositional defiant disorder (ODD) if they consistently respond to authority by disobeying, talking back, arguing, or being hostile in a way that is excessive compared to other children. Though such behavior disorders are not themselves cognitive deficits, they often go hand in hand with learning difficulties.

Most students with behavior disorders remain in regular schools, where educators assign them to resource or "opportunity" rooms for a portion of the day. Federal law provides guidelines stipulating that schools should apply different, and usually less severe, forms of discipline for students with behavioral disabilities than nondisabled students. For example, schools might be disallowed from expelling students for behavior related to their disabilities, even if the offense warrants expulsion under the school's discipline policy.

Sorting by English Language Proficiency

From colonial times, American schools have struggled to educate students who speak languages other than English. The increasing numbers of immigrant students in the early 1970s fueled support for federal and state assistance for English language teaching and learning. Although the law doesn't require that schools separate students who speak little or no English from their English-speaking peers, English as a Second Language (ESL), also called English Language Development (ELD), programs nearly always do so.

ESL programs typically take the form of special classes in which non-English-speaking students learn English as a foreign language—without the use of the students' primary language for instruction. Supporters of ESL programs believe that students will do better, both academically and socially, if they use English exclusively for their schoolwork. ESL classes usually occupy one or two hours a day. For the remainder of the time, students attend mainstream classes and learn their other subjects in English. This may mean that these students are in special academic classes where teachers use "sheltered" English and other strategies designed to make content area instruction in English comprehensible for those with limited English competency. Because ESL and sheltered academic classes use English for instruction, students with different native languages often take these classes together. Finally, the regular classes that these students attend are far more likely to be low-ability classes (for English speakers) than high-ability classes.

Bilingual education is different. It is based on research showing that students do better in both academic learning and acquisition of the new language if they develop, maintain, and build on native-language and literacy skills. Advocates of bilingual education argue that students can keep up with their peers in subjects like mathematics and science at the same time that they are learning English. They also argue that this happens best when students learn these subjects using their primary language until they can understand those subjects in English. Thus, bilingual classes group students who speak the same primary language, and bilingual teachers teach in that language while gradually introducing English.

Most bilingual programs include an ESL or ELD component as well as native-language instruction in other academic subjects. Several models of bilingual education rely on separate classes. *Maintenance* programs, for example, have three goals—learning English, learning academics, and developing literacy in students' native language. *Transitional* bilingual programs, in contrast, have only the first two goals: learning English and academic content. Their intent is to shift students away from their primary language to English as quickly as possible. *Dual language* programs, which seek to develop biliteracy, group students intentionally such that a Korean-English dual-language class, for example, would be comprised of students half of whom are dominant in English and half of whom are dominant in Korean; this design is meant to ensure that students can serve as language models for one another when the language of instruction shifts from English to Korean and back again.

Why Do Schools Label and Sort Students?

The conventional explanation for labeling students and placing them into groups, classes, and programs accordingly is that teachers then can tailor instruction to groups of students with meaningful similarities, and students can benefit from that instruction delivered in those groups. However, underneath this superficially sensible explanation are cultural and historical patterns that reveal how sorting students connects to cultural conceptions of racial and social class differences.

The Social Construction of Difference

> The way we cut up the world clearly affects the way we organize our everyday life. The way we divide our surroundings, for example, determines what we notice and what we ignore. . . . [T]he way we classify people determines whom we trust and whom we fear. . . . The way we partition time and space likewise determines when we work and when we rest, where we live and where we never set foot. Indeed, our entire social order is a product of the ways in which we separate kin from nonkin, moral from immoral, serious from merely playful, and what is ours from what is not.[11]

Documenting and explaining variation has been a controlling purpose of Western science. Humans cannot resist noticing differences and attempting to make categories for people and things to "fall into." And as sociologist Eviatar Zerubavel notes in the preceding excerpt, our categories affect how we see the world, how we act, and what we value.

Every culture uses such constructs to make sense of and organize their world, but not all cultures create and use the *same* constructs. And even if they do, they often assign different meanings and importance to them. Despite their socially constructed and culturally contingent nature, it is tempting to accept the categories, explanations, and values of one's own culture as real, true, and "common sense." As anthropologists remind us, however, each culture's meanings and values represent that group's particular way of understanding and preserving their society.

Some student differences are real. Some students experience problems so severe that they interfere with learning or social interactions at school, and some have astonishing memories or musical talents. However, most of the educational categories that guide grouping practices in school—practices that affect *all* students, not just a few—bear little resemblance to the wholly justifiable practices that target individual learning problems or talents.

Researchers Harold Stevenson and James Stigler show how ideas about intellectual capacity vary from culture to culture. Comparing American, Chinese, and Japanese cultures, Stevenson and Stigler found that American culture constructs intelligence as a function of innate ability far more than in Chinese and Japanese cultures, both of which emphasize the roles of effort and persistence in being "smart."[12] Partly because of the powerful role that intelligence has played in our culture historically (as described in Chapter 7), Americans typically consider a good student to be a "bright" or "smart" or "quick" student. In contrast, a good student in Chinese and Japanese cultures is more likely one deemed to be "hardworking." Of course, there is no correct answer to the question of what makes a student "good," even though different cultures may treat such constructs and the meanings they assign to them as common sense. Although intelligence (narrowly defined) rarely is the only construct used to categorize students in U.S. schools today, it remains a powerful signifier of students' merit, and it often overshadows other constructs that schools use to categorize students, including achievement, creativity, motivation, ability, leadership, aspiration, self-concept, and more.

Americans have also believed for more than a century that once schools have identified, and to a large degree created, differences, they should respond to the differences by separating students for instruction. Thus, most schools group students homogeneously (i.e., with others thought to be like them), not only by age but also by (perceived) academic ability, educational disadvantage, language proficiency, and college-going potential. This, too, differs dramatically from how the Japanese, for example, treat differences. Until high school, Japanese schools rarely separate students into groups or classes with others who are somehow similar to them. The idea of teaching all types of students in the same classrooms seems perfectly normal and ordinary to Japanese teachers.

Ability labeling and other kinds of grouping and sorting in U.S. schools have always had strong statistical overlaps with students' race, ethnicity, and social class. For example, White and wealthy students are far more likely to be labeled as high ability or gifted and placed in high-level classes and programs for those assumed to be college bound. At the same time, low-income students, African American students, and Latinx students are disproportionately identified as less able and placed in lower-level groups and classes.

Because of these overlaps, no discussion of grouping can take place without paying careful attention to the racial and social class characteristics of the resulting groups. Defenders of ability-grouping practices sometimes claim that group assignments are "objective" or "color-blind," and they attribute the disproportionate assignment of some students into college-prep, remedial, or resource classes to unfortunate differences in students' backgrounds and abilities. But these claims of scientific and bias-free objectivity are not supported when viewed in the context of historical and current sorting practices.[13]

The History of Biased Sorting

The labeling and grouping of students began in earnest in the late nineteenth century. Once classrooms were organized into grade levels, schools sought to teach students the same things at the same time and in the same way. Soon, normal differences among children became a bothersome obstacle to this efficient plan. Grouping students was seen as a way to overcome this obstacle.

As we described in Chapter 2, by the early 1900s, schools were expected to solve a whole array of social concerns that were quite distinct from students' learning of mathematics, literature, science, and so forth. Immigrants needed to learn the English language and American ways. Factories needed trained workers. Footloose urban youth required supervision. Future professionals, nearly always the children of the most advantaged, needed to be taught the high-status knowledge that would prepare them for universities. Despite the rhetoric about schools being the great equalizer, they were also expected to help maintain the current social and economic order with its uneven power and privilege. Policymakers and educators saw homogeneous grouping as a way to help them meet all of these expectations.

Furthermore, the early-twentieth-century culture was, generally speaking, one in which it made perfectly good sense to dislike people who were different. Established American families often did not think much of immigrants; some immigrant groups often thought of themselves as better than other immigrant groups. Nearly every group at the time thought itself superior to African Americans, and most of the wealthiest (White) Americans thought themselves superior to everyone else. Thus, schools had to teach students to get along but only somewhat—in other words, teach everyone well, but teach some students to be better.

By the early twentieth century, industrializing democracies like the United States sought to combine the efficiencies of assembly lines with the fairness of democratic principles. Differentiating using the old indicators of race and family background was expedient but ran contrary to the American creed. Gradually, schools settled on a new view of democratic schooling. They defined *opportunity* as the chance to fulfill, productively and with dignity, one's position in society—albeit a place predetermined by one's race, gender, and class.

Ellwood Cubberley, a prominent educational scholar of the time, wrote,

> Our city schools will soon be forced to give up the exceedingly democratic idea that all are equal, and our society devoid of classes . . . and to begin a specialization of educational effort along many lines in an attempt to adapt the school to the needs of these many classes.[14]

Two increasingly popular ideas bolstered Cubberley's definition of democratic schooling: that IQ tests could assess students' potential for learning, and that scientific efficiency should guide educational practice. We discussed these ideas in earlier chapters, and in what follows, we show their specific influence on grouping practices in school.

IQ and Grouping

The development of IQ tests allowed schools to label and sort students "scientifically" according to their intellectual merit, without involving parentage, race, or wealth directly. Since intelligence tests were increasingly accepted as scientific, accurate, and impartial, there could be no claim of unfairness. However, IQ merely served as a proxy for preexisting ways of sorting, since the questions selected for the tests were those that privileged test takers would be much more likely to get right. Thus, sorting by IQ scores resulted in ability groups made up of students of similar family backgrounds, wealth, and race.

Testing helped institutionalize prevailing stereotypes. Results generally aligned with the popular view that poor and minoritized students were intellectually, morally, and even biologically inferior. Many people adopted distorted versions of Charles Darwin's evolution theories, to argue that darker-skinned, recently arrived immigrants from southern Europe occupied a lower rung on the evolutionary ladder. Recall from Chapter 2 the words of intelligence-test pioneer Lewis Terman: "Their dullness seems to be racial. . . . Children of this group should be segregated in special classes. . . . They cannot master abstractions, but they can often be made efficient workers."[15] Although these views did not go uncontested, schools enacted the prevailing belief that inherent differences caused variation in students' potential for school learning. Grouping practices followed suit.

Most current grouping practices don't rely on IQ, at least not exclusively, but the early practices and views set a pattern that continues today. Standardized achievement tests help divide students into groups and are central to qualifying for compensatory education programs. Standardized language proficiency tests determine the appropriate class levels for students designated as "English Learners." IQ, in conjunction with other measures, remains basic in identifying the "gifted" students as well as those who have cognitive disabilities. Intelligence persists as a widely respected marker in a society that wants to see itself as just and equitable. However, because intelligence has been constructed in a culture characterized by race and class discrimination, using intelligence as an indicator of merit also produces a distribution of power and opportunity that is strikingly similar to the overt racial and social class sorting of earlier times.

Scientific Management and Grouping

Identifying, separating, and treating students differently fit well with turn-of-the-twentieth-century notions of scientific management, too. As educators embraced the "scientific" methods used by managers in the expanding manufacturing sector of the economy, grouping made wonderful sense to school leaders and to boards of education. Educational managers conducted time-and-motion studies: picture efficiency experts with stopwatches and charts noting every aspect of school activity, including the passing out and collecting of materials. They advocated centralization, concentration of authority at the top, setting of rules, and so on. Following the model of the efficient factory, schools increasingly saw children as raw materials out of which they would fashion their product: productive adults.

Homogeneous grouping meant greater specialization, a clearer division of labor, and more mass-produced learning. As in the factory, managers did not value individual differences along the assembly line—differences meant defects in the product.

Universal Education and Grouping

Over the course of the twentieth century, compulsory education laws and the increased necessity of a high school diploma in the job market drew more and more students to school—even those previously considered uneducable. In less enlightened times, affluent families closeted away children who had serious physical and mental problems or sent them to special schools—often boarding schools. Charitable institutions cared for others. Poor children with disabilities—often the objects of strangers' curiosity, fear, and ridicule—were frequently sent to asylums.

Milder problems simply went unrecognized or were dismissed as unimportant. When students had trouble fitting in at school, they quit—often with the school's active encouragement. Until mid-century, most of them found jobs and led productive lives. Adults chalked up students' unexplained difficulties at school to their backwardness, bad character or upbringing, maladjustment, or just being odd. As the century progressed, however, these attitudes changed, and states and local school systems developed an array of special programs for students who were different.[16]

Categorical programs for low-income children and English Learners grew out of the War on Poverty, as we described in Chapter 2. Advocates for the "gifted" piggybacked on this; they used the rationale that these students, too, had such significant differences that they could not be fully educated alongside "normal" students. Their efforts were bolstered by faulty views of intelligence—for example, that an IQ of 100 was a real representation of "normal" youth. Parents, policymakers, and educators alike became convinced that deviation from the norm *in either direction* gave students disadvantages proportional to the number of points. Relying on the appeal of the bell curve, they reasoned that a student with an IQ of 68 had a similar degree of disability as a student with an IQ of 132 had "extra ability." By borrowing equity-minded arguments that were used to justify additional services for students disadvantaged by physical or cognitive handicaps, advocates succeeded in reifying "giftedness"—changing it from a metaphorical abstraction to a legal and educational category.

Educators responded in predictable ways to the new laws and court decisions providing categorical funding and protections for student differences. They scientifically diagnosed students' differences and assigned them to different categories. They then grouped students by category and tailored curriculum and instruction to the abilities of each group, according to what educators thought each group needed. The increasing importance of legally defined groups led to a corresponding increase in schools' grouping consciousness, and additional groups have proliferated beyond the terms of the law.

Grouping Dilemmas

Grouping students according to their similarities, as school policy, is neither efficient nor effective; it never was and is not now. Students who are assumed to be similar to one another are actually different in important ways and do not benefit from any environment that ignores those differences. This array of differences within groups holds true across all groups.

In addition, the standards movement has made the idea of educating students to very different levels unacceptable. Policies such as No Child Left Behind (NCLB) and the Every Student Succeeds Act (ESSA) now demand that schools educate every student to high academic standards, regardless of presumed intellectual ability, disability, social status, gender, or race, as the current push is for all high school graduates to be prepared for both college and careers. Today's grouping practices must be judged by whether they help teachers meet this goal.

The Arbitrariness of Labels and Sorting

States, school districts, and individual schools differ so widely in their definitions of "high," "average," and "low" ability that a student identified as belonging in any one of these categories in one place might wind up in a different category someplace else. Our own research found wide disparities in the cut-off scores that high schools use to decide which students should be admitted to honors, regular, and low-level classes.[17] For example, a student in a lower-performing school may require a lower score on a standardized test to get into an honors class than a student in a higher-performing school. Similarly, the same schools might apply different criteria in different years. California once raised its qualifying score for a gifted designation by 2 IQ points and instantly disqualified thousands of students who would have been designated as gifted just the year before.

Joseph Renzulli, an advocate for programs that develop students' talents, argues against "gifted" as a label both because it excludes so many students and because it creates a misleading (and sometimes detrimental) identity for those labeled with it. Renzulli told an interviewer that the use of the gifted label is something that he rejects outright, and he relayed his frustration with parents who approach him about their "gifted child":

> When a parent comes to me and says, "I have a gifted child," I say, "Wait a minute. Tell me what your child does. Talk to me about their writing, their science, their music. If you begin our conversation by telling me you have a gifted child, you are creating a gulf between us."[18]

Disparities in special education categories are also widely documented. Some states require an IQ score of 69 or less for a student to be classified as having intellectual disabilities (formerly termed *mental retardation*), while others require a score of 84 or below. For that reason, among others, the proportion of students identified as having disabilities ranges from 8 to 15 percent among states. For example, in 2009–2010, Kentucky and Georgia identified only about 2 and 3 percent, respectively, of their students as having specific learning disabilities, while Delaware and Pennsylvania each identified about 7 percent;[19] Rhode Island's rate of disability identification overall was over twice that of Texas.[20] In that same year, West Virginia's percentage of students classified as having intellectual disabilities was more than eight times that of New Hampshire, while Washington, DC's percentage of students classified as emotionally disturbed was more than nine times that of Alabama.[21]

Categories come and go, and each change is thought to represent progress and the triumph of enlightened views. In the 1930s, educators began using psycho-medical explanations of deviant behavior, such as *minimally brain injured*. These labels lasted well beyond mid-century. When research could not bear out a relevant class of defects to support that label, other diagnoses appeared. Today, the categories of "attention deficit disorder" and "disabled" stand alongside "at risk," "disadvantaged," and others.

The learning disability category exemplifies shifting meaning and questionable usefulness (for teaching and learning). It achieved national status in 1963, with the founding of the Association for Children With Learning Disabilities. The organizing parents did not want their low-achieving children identified as mentally retarded, but they did want their children to have extra help. By 1979, learning disabled had become the largest special education category. Christine Sleeter argues that this surge did not result from a scientific discovery of a previously unknown biological disorder but from advocacy by White, middle-class parents who wanted to differentiate their low-achieving children from lower-class children and children of color.[22] These more privileged families did not want their children's learning problems to be attributed to low IQ, emotional disturbances, or cultural deprivation. And, in fact, most students labeled as learning disabled during the first ten years of the classification's existence were White and middle class. Once established, however, the learning disability category soon included most students whom schools would formerly have identified as having mild mental retardation.

Many people respond to the unfairness and imprecision of labeling and grouping as if these systems were ill-functioning machines that needed a tune-up and more careful operators. Calls are made for more exacting diagnoses of students, more precise categories, and more specialized teaching methods and curricula suited to different groups. However, many researchers, like Louise Spear-Swerling and Robert Sternberg, argue that the very construct—learning disabilities—probably causes more problems than it solves.[23] They believe that students would be better served if teachers and other learning specialists could address students' specific cognitive difficulties, such as reading-specific struggles, without the distraction of labels. Other researchers make parallel arguments about the validity and usefulness of behavioral categories like ADHD, SED, and ODD.[24]

The Illusion of Homogeneity

> In my school, reading groups are based on ability. Students cannot progress to another basal reader or transition to English until they pass test after test. This has become a nightmare. Teachers must accommodate large numbers of students who are "not reading at grade level" because they have not been able to pass the tests. I have been able to successfully "test out" four of my third-grade students who were considered to be reading at the second-grade level. I believed them to be at grade level, but the question remains: Were these students labeled as below grade level based on their ability to pass the test, rather than on their actual reading ability?
>
> —Yvette Nuñez
> First-year teacher, grades 3 and 4

Classes designed for specific ability, disability, and language levels are actually filled with a wide variety of students who display noteworthy differences in the speed, interest, effort, and aptitude they bring to various tasks. Furthermore, substantial evidence demonstrates that schools often disregard their own placement criteria—allowing, for example, parent preferences or student behavior to influence academic placements. Thus, schools may actually encourage teaching very different students all in the same way instead of responding to students' inevitable differences.

> Placing students in the correct math class was something I assumed was done with very little discrepancy. I found out over the course of the year that many students had been misplaced and were not aware of it. They knew the course name and number, but they did not know the type of content that would be covered. They just assumed that counselors placed them correctly. Misplaced students are plentiful in my "sheltered" class. It was not until late in the year that I asked students individually whether they spoke Spanish fluently and, if so, whether they considered it their primary language. Three students! Only three students in my entire sheltered course considered Spanish their primary language, and only four others spoke it fluently.
>
> —Marilyn Cortez
> First-year teacher, mathematics, grade 9

As Marilyn Cortez discovered, many school systems designate classes for students at a particular ability level but then enroll students whose measured ability ranges far above or below the stated criteria.[25] Still other powerful factors—including testing, placement criteria, parents' and students' own activism, the school's master schedule, and more—make group assignments prone to error and unfairness.

The Fallibility of Testing

Schools risk enormous unfairness when they use tests to sort students. The most common guideline for identifying a student's learning disability is if his or her achievement lags two years behind his or her grade level. Schools use achievement tests, school performance, or both to arrive at a student's achievement level. If the student's IQ scores show normal intelligence, a low achievement score would indicate a learning disability. (If the student has a low achievement score and a low IQ, they may not qualify for some special programs. The reasoning is that the student is performing at the anticipated level for someone with a low IQ, and thus special attention would not help.) However, these test results do not prove that a student has or does not have a cognitive or neurological disability. Neither do they provide information about what the disability might be.

Difficulties also arise with the measures schools use to identify "gifted" students. Although there is vigorous debate about what constitutes giftedness, technically, gifted students are those who meet criteria set by a state, district, or school. These can include an IQ score and an array of other criteria, such as artistic talent and leadership qualities. Complicating matters further is that intelligence tests are less accurate at the upper end of the curve, where one might expect gifted candidates to be, and a given student's IQ may vary from day to day, year to year. On a good day, the student might qualify as gifted. If tested on another day, that same student might fall short.

The tests used to gauge students' English language proficiency can be similarly problematic, leading to seemingly arbitrary placements of students into so-called ability-grouped classes, as was the case in the class Marilyn Cortez described above.

Attributes Influence Placement

Educators claim to base placements on merit. That is, children's school achievement alone—not irrelevant characteristics like race, social class, or parents' facility with the English language—determines whether they are in a gifted class, a sheltered English class, or a low-tracked class. Some acknowledge that students' own choices, character, and motivation influence track placements, and that social indicators such as maturity and cooperation can sway decisions.

For example, because the process of identifying gifted students often begins with teacher recommendation, students who are outgoing and mature, and more readily noticed, have an advantage over those who are shy or immature. Racial bias plays a role too, which research suggests systematically advantages White students and disadvantages students of color.[26] In addition, schools frequently fail to follow state criteria when identifying students.[27] Often schools place capable but poorly behaved students in low-ability groups. Although this behavioral criterion is rarely stated explicitly in policy guidelines, high-ability groups end up being shielded from disruptive and disaffected students, and those students—despite their strengths—end up being locked out of higher-ability groups.

Parent Activism and Choice

Parents can also play a role in how schools set and apply criteria. The distortion of homogeneity that results from this activism is not random, but skewed to the advantage of White and wealthier families.

Most states and schools allow for parent nominations of potentially gifted students as early as kindergarten. As students get older, parents participate in selecting classes and programs for their children. Often, savvy and/or status-conscious parents who want their children enrolled in the "best" classes and special programs find ways to make that happen, sometimes even by pressuring educators.[28] In a competitive system that offers a small number of high-track opportunities, it is not rare for knowledgeable parents to pit themselves against others in order to acquire what they see as the best educational services. Middle- and upper-income families are especially active in seeking gifted designations for their children. For example, in 1997, the *Washington Post* reported that a third of the students in an affluent Maryland County school district had been assigned to gifted classes: "In Howard, parents can bypass all other criteria by insisting their children be allowed into the more challenging classes. School officials sometimes try to talk parents out of doing so, if they think it's inappropriate, but parents usually get their way."[29]

Gifted students, and their families, often form a quite visible and elite student subgroup. Many schools encourage gifted students to associate with one another, since much of the advocacy literature argues that they feel most comfortable and thrive in one another's company. Often schools or parent associations distribute rosters with telephone numbers to parents of gifted students, and educational meetings for parents (who are usually among the more active in the schools) further support the socializing of gifted students with one another. Because these students often come from the ranks of social and economic elites, some parents work quite hard to have their children included, even if immediate advantages don't follow. For example, in some of today's cash-strapped elementary schools, students continue to be tested and labeled, even though there is no program for those identified as gifted. However, the status remains powerful, as does the promise of future benefits, such as priority placement in a high-status middle school.

Organizational Constraints

Schools often compromise grouping criteria in the face of other organizational constraints. Particularly in secondary schools, administrators juggle many factors that may override accurate placements. For example, they must make sure that each student has a class every hour. Those who want football, beginning strings class, or second-year computer drafting often get those classes even if it means students wind up in low- rather than high-level content area courses, or vice versa. In addition, since each class must have approximately the same number of students, schools may place borderline students or students who enroll last in higher- or lower-level classes more out of convenience than anything else. As Hugh Mehan, Jane Mercer, and Robert Rueda once observed, schools will always find enough students to fill all their allocated slots.[30]

Race and Social Class Bias

First-year teacher Matt Flanders, who teaches at a diverse high school, reveals how sorting practices mirror societal biases about the intellectual potential of low-income students and students of color.

> My teaching assignment is one of the most diverse that I have ever heard of—two sections of United States history (grade 11), two sections of math (grades 10–12), one section of driver's education (grades 9–12), one section of tutorial (grades 9–12), and the head coach of the men's and women's water polo teams (grades 9–12). The math and tutorial classes are the lowest-level classes in the school. . . .
>
> This high school contains "two schools" even though they are not formally distinguishable. First, there is the advanced placement division. Highly motivated, adequately supported and taught, most of the students are White and are expected to go to college. Then there is the second "school" that is not expected to go on to higher education. These students are not motivated or engaged at all by school, are not given the best resources or teachers, and are overwhelmingly Latino and African American. This school's dropout rate is significantly higher than the first school's.
>
> I teach almost exclusively in the second school. These students have lost faith in themselves, in school, in peers, in families, and, in some instances, in life itself. . . . Hearing how many students had been accepted to university, how many teams had won championships, how our music program was second to none, and not participating in these activities because of a lack of previous opportunity or deficient grades/units would keep anyone's self-confidence extremely low. They frequently tell me "I can't do this" or "This is too hard for us."
>
> The most frustrating part of this situation is that I was no more intelligent than these students; I just had learned more about how to make school work for me.
>
> —Matt Flanders
> First-year teacher, grades 9–12

As Matt discovered at his high school, African American, Latinx, and low-income students are consistently overrepresented in low-ability, remedial, and special education classes and programs. Racially isolated schools serving low-income and minority students typically have smaller academic tracks and larger remedial and vocational programs than do schools serving predominantly White, more affluent students.

In desegregated schools, like the one where Matt teaches, African American and Latinx students are assigned to low-track classes more often than White (and Asian) students, leading to two separate schools in one building. In a 1990 study for the National Science Foundation, we found a pattern of racially identifiable math and science classes in racially mixed schools. That is, one would expect to find in any math or science class a similar proportion of White, Black, or Latinx students as in the whole school. Instead, higher-tracked math and science classes had much larger percentages of White students, and lower-ability classes had far larger percentages of Black and Latinx students.[31]

Our more recent studies of racially mixed school systems revealed that the lower participation of African American and Latinx students in high-level classes could not be explained simply by the students' prior learning opportunities or achievement. These students were much less likely than White or Asian students *with the same test scores* to be placed in high-ability classes. For example, in one West Coast school system, White and Asian students with average scores on standardized tests were more than twice as likely to be in "accelerated" classes than Latinx students with *the same scores*. The discrimination was even more striking among the highest-scoring students. Whereas only 56 percent of very high-scoring Latinx were in accelerated classes, 93 percent of Whites and 97 percent of Asians with *comparable* test scores were. In three other school systems, we found similar discrepancies between African American and White students.[32]

For the past several decades, researchers have warned that schools often classify and treat students with identical IQ scores but different racial and social class characteristics differently.[33] By the late 1970s, the misidentification problem triggered both federal and state court decisions requiring due process for students. And in a far-reaching decision, the California courts ruled in *Larry P. v. Riles* that schools could no longer use intelligence tests to identify "minority" students as mentally retarded. However, substantial problems remain, and new ones continue to emerge, including evidence that African American boys are disproportionately identified as having attention deficits, hyperactivity, or emotional disturbance.[34] Office of Civil Rights data gathered in the 1990s, for example, showed that Black students were two and a half times more likely than White students to be classified as mildly mentally retarded.[35] More recent data reveal similar patterns, as well as racial disparities in the identification of "gifted" students.[36] African American and Latinx students remain underrepresented among gifted students but overrepresented among those in special education, and especially so among the most stigmatizing categories. As the director of the Center for Civil Rights Remedies, Daniel Losen, explains, for example, Black students are oftentimes two or three times more likely to be identified for special education, and are disproportionately represented among those designated emotionally disturbed or intellectually disabled while underrepresented among those designated autistic or speech and language impaired.[37]

Parents and students themselves can tilt selection processes to gain placement advantages that an unbiased system would otherwise prevent.[38] Generally speaking, high-achieving, affluent White parents and students are much more knowledgeable about grouping practices. They are more willing to "push the system" if they are displeased with their course assignments, while parents of low-achieving and midrange students (often lower-income students of color) are frequently less comfortable challenging the system, and given their limited clout, some officials feel safe dismissing or ignoring their concerns.

Meanwhile, more well-off parents make use of the resources at their disposal. Some might pay a private psychologist to retest their child if the child missed a "gifted" cut-off on the school's test. Or they might seek private diagnoses of learning disabilities for their children when they think that such identification will help their children succeed, for example, by requiring extra teacher attention or allowing extra time to take tests. In fact, sometimes a disability designation is sought out so that a struggling student in a high-ability class will be able to remain in that group.

In all cases, however, the process of discovering a child's disability, diagnosing it, and deciding what to do is complex and emotionally wrenching for any parent. Low-income parents, those who are not native English speakers, and those who are cautious when interacting with public institutions face additional obstacles. They are the least likely to be active advocates in ways that prompt schools to act on their children's behalf. Consequently, their children may not receive the same careful screening (or repeated diagnostic services) as the children of White, middle-class parents.

Ties to Behavioral Learning Theory and Transmission Teaching

Grouping students according to estimates of their abilities creates a high-stakes cycle that makes it harder for schools to break away from behaviorist approaches to teaching and learning. Because placing students in particular tracks or classes influences their pathways through school and their life chances, educators rely heavily on standardized testing to make these potent decisions seem legitimate. As we discussed in Chapter 7, the tests themselves call for behaviorist approaches that may help students master small units of information and discrete skills, but they do not promote the deep learning that most educators and parents value.

Because homogeneous grouping assumes that students in a given class are similar in nearly all respects, teaching can appear to be a misleadingly simple task—giving teachers little reason to develop multidimensional lessons or tailor instruction to individual students. All students benefit from this kind of teaching, but it makes little sense if all students are presumed to be the same.

Self-Fulfilling Prophecies and Processes

My students believe they are in classes for stupid people. They say things such as, "We can't do this. We're only '103' [low-ability class] students." Most of them ask if they can move up, and some even say they are in the retarded classes. It is important for me to not treat these students as if they cannot handle difficult work. . . .

One thing that has limited my effectiveness . . . is the culture of the school. Many teachers believe not only that low-track students will not do the work but that they cannot do the work. Any readings I assign for them to do at home I have to photocopy since they are not allowed their own books. There is only a class set because someone has decided that they will not do any homework anyway, and they will probably just lose the books. Because of this, students rarely get any homework. Many of them tell me I am the only teacher that gives homework.

During my first semester, I taught my English classes in the print shop. My next room turned out not to be a classroom at all. My students had nowhere to sit, and one of the kids said, "Mr. Alvarez, they always give you the cheap classrooms." She sure was right. Finally, with ten weeks to go in the year, I moved into a [third] room . . . with one window that does not open, no air conditioner, and only one door to let in air. It has been close to 90 degrees every day.

The students are being cheated out of a quality education, and they are seeing a school system that is willing to just throw them anywhere. I look at all the classes that have to endure this environment, and I see they all have one thing in common: They are lower-track classes. The four teachers who were in the print shop and now in the windowless bungalows for the most part have "103" students. . . . The school decided that the kids who need the most attention, the most help, should get the worst environment in which to learn. There is no way that the school would put honors kids in these rooms.

Many people feel that these kids are already lost so we should not waste any time or resources on them. It is for this reason that I have asked to continue teaching the "103" students. They need someone who has not given up on them.

—Michael Alvarez
First-year teacher, English, grade 9

Experiences like Michael Alvarez's reveal how the differentiation that accompanies homogeneous grouping can limit students who are not in the uppermost track. And if the school and teachers buy into the idea that these students are less able, then the students will also. The result is that not all students are seen as warranting similarly engaging learning experiences and opportunities—including access to teachers with reputations for being the most experienced and highly skilled.[39]

Labeling (even if it is masked in local codes such as "103" students) translates into lowered self-confidence and lowered expectations for all students not graced with the highest status label. Placement in a low-level, middle-level, or almost-but-not-quite-top-level class often becomes a self-fulfilling prophecy—a cycle of lower expectations, fewer opportunities, and academic performance that usually matches (but does not exceed) the expected performance.[40] In every aspect of what makes for a quality education, kids in lower tracks typically get less than those in higher tracks and gifted programs.[41] Some of the well-documented differences between high- and low-level classes are listed in Concept Table 10.1.

As described next, when schools adopt heterogeneous or mixed-ability classes, these classes tend to look more like high-ability classes than low-ability classes. To understand why this might be, it's worth looking at what typically happens when teachers are assigned to work with low-ability students in a setting that includes only those students. Although such teachers may have experience or special training and skills to teach students with learning disabilities, they may not have content area expertise. And yet a strong background in and enthusiasm for math, science,

Concept Table 10.1 Grouping-Related Differences in Learning Opportunities

Higher-group advantages	Lower-group disadvantages
Curriculum emphasizing concepts, inquiry, and problem solving	Curriculum emphasizing low-level facts and skills
Stress on students developing as autonomous thinkers	Stress on teaching students to follow rules and procedures
More time spent on instruction	More time spent on discipline and socializing
More active and interactive learning activities	More worksheets and seatwork
Computers used as learning tools	Computers used as tutors or for worksheet completion and other low-level "busywork"
More qualified and experienced teachers	More uncertified and inexperienced teachers
Extra enrichment activities and resources	Few enrichment opportunities
More engaging and friendly classroom atmosphere	More alienating and hostile classroom atmosphere
"Hard work" a likely classroom norm	"Not working" a likely classroom norm

Source: Jeannie Oakes, *Multiplying Inequalities* (Santa Monica, CA: RAND, 1990).

literature, and so forth assist teachers in finding ways to make a subject accessible and engaging for all students. With a commitment to heterogeneity, students stand a much better chance of exposure to high-level knowledge as well as the support they need from regular and resource teachers in order to master the content. None of this happens at the expense of students' "non-disabled" peers. There is abundant evidence that students without disabilities are not at all disadvantaged by learning alongside their peers with learning disabilities.[42]

Students learning English in separate programs might also have fewer opportunities. Although the evidence is clear that they learn better with support in their native languages, the shortage of qualified bilingual teachers makes it hard to implement this approach.[43] As a result, many students end up learning from teachers who are not fully able to teach either English or academic subject matter using the students' native language. Some work mostly with teachers' assistants, often called paraprofessionals, who may be fluent in students' native language but typically don't have the subject matter knowledge or pedagogical expertise of a fully qualified teacher.

Grouping practices help shape students' identities, status, and expectations for themselves. Both students and adults mistake labels such as "gifted," "honors student," "average," "remedial," "learning disabled," and "emotionally disturbed" for certification of overall ability and sometimes personal worth. Of course, these labeling effects are not just a student phenomenon. They permeate the culture. Thus, we have frequent references to "gifted parents." Teachers talk about "my low kids." Parents and educators alike confer greater status on teachers of high-achieving students. For example, at public and professional meetings, teachers may identify themselves as AP calculus teachers rather than as teachers of basic math or of average algebra students, even though they might teach all three classes. Teachers of low-ability classes may be admired for how "tough" their job is, but it is often assumed that they are not—or don't need to be—as accomplished in their content area. Even highly qualified special education and bilingual teachers are not typically thought of as having the background and training needed to work with highly able students.

First-year teacher Lucy Patrick saw the dynamics of homogeneous grouping at work in an unexpected place—her and a colleague's experiment with creating homogeneous groups within their gifted fourth-grade classes.

> Though my teaching partner and I were both teaching gifted fourth graders, we saw a wide range of abilities in our classes. I especially saw a large discrepancy between students in the area of mathematics. I was frustrated, not knowing what to do for a group of students who learned a mathematical concept, while another group of students needed additional explanation or practice.
>
> I felt like the class was a three-ring circus, with one group doing a handout, another group working independently, and the last group still not ready to do their class work. Feeling ineffective, my teaching partner and I decided to divide our classrooms based on math test scores. It seemed like a great opportunity to have two separate groups and teach toward their needs.
>
> Before long we saw the discrepancy between the two groups widening, and I began to reconsider the advantages and disadvantages of having homogeneous grouping based on ability. By separating students, we isolated many of the student leaders into one group, while the other group contained disruptive students. I was meeting my objective to provide additional help to the group that needed it most, yet time spent on management took away from their review or practice, and they fell more and more behind.
>
> Another concern was the effects on their emotional and social well-being. Though we never made it known how we divided the students, the students themselves understood the differences. In my mind, all the students are capable. Yet I am not certain what message the

students received, especially when the class work and homework were not the same for the two groups. I saw an elitist attitude building within the higher-track group. I would hear students say, "I already know this," "This is easy," or "The other group isn't doing this." This attitude disturbed me because I had tried to create a fair and supportive learning environment in my classroom and I felt that I had failed.

What I had done with my classroom was create a microcosm of the tracking used in our school in my gifted classroom. I had managed to track the students even more!

As an educator, I want all my students to reach their potential with heterogeneous grouping instead of more homogeneous grouping. I do not think that I would attempt homogeneous grouping again.

—Lucy Patrick
First-year teacher, grade 4

Simply by rejecting the "solution" of homogeneous grouping, Lucy did not solve her original concern. She still must grapple with what to do with a roomful of energetic, competitive youngsters with varied skills, styles, and personalities. This failed experiment redirected her attention to planning multidimensional lessons and working to improve students' independent and group work skills. For Lucy, making the most of heterogeneous grouping will no doubt be a trying, but deeply rewarding process.

Disappointing and Enduring Outcomes

Over the years of schooling, students who are initially similar in background and skills become increasingly different in achievement when schools put them into separate, ability-grouped classes. Students placed in lower-level courses consistently achieve less than classmates with the same abilities who were placed by schools into higher-level classes. Students with both high *and* low test scores do better when they are in higher-level courses.[44] Clearly, low-ability classes do not promote learning, even if teachers believe they are tailoring instruction to students' ability levels and academic potential.

Achievement gains from compensatory Title I programs also have proven disappointing, at least partly because most compensatory programs work like low-ability classes. That is, they classify students as low achievers, create a separate pull-out structure, and provide a mostly low-level, remedial curriculum.[45]

In some cases, bilingual and ESL programs have generated similar criticisms. As first-year bilingual teacher Yvette Nuñez observes, referencing Jim Cummins, separate programs can restrict students' opportunities to interact in authentic ways with native speakers of English.[46]

I want to tear down the system of isolating Spanish speakers from their English-proficient counterparts. I believe in developing primary language skills, not only because these skills will transfer to English, but also because becoming biliterate and bicultural helps one understand the world.

We do not have high-enough expectations for all our students to learn a second language. Students are able to learn language when it is applied in meaningful contexts, and an optimal environment includes lots of native English-speaking peers.

—Yvette Nuñez
First-year teacher, grades 3 and 4

Of course, not all bilingual and ESL classes have the effect that Yvette describes. Some schools implement bilingual programs, such as dual immersion programs, so that students have ample access to rigorous native language instruction *and* to authentic interactions with English-speaking peers. Others, however, reflect the more problematic aspects of ability grouping and tracking—for example, questionable assessment practices, erroneous placements, near-complete segregation from peers in different groups, low-level academics, and rigid course-to-course sequences that make it difficult for students to move beyond the confines of the program into which they are originally placed. This latter issue is of particular concern.

Given the prevailing structure of schooling, students' hopes for the future still rise or fall in ways that are far too consistent with their early-grade placements. Most students placed in low-ability or even average groups in elementary school continue in these tracks in middle school. Senior high schools usually place these students in non-college-prep tracks or low-college-prep tracks that offer access to less competitive colleges or majors, two-year colleges, or remedial classes as college freshmen. Being in a low-level class most often fosters lower achievement, poor self-concepts, lowered aspirations, negative attitudes, and even dropping out.[47] Because students' track placements rarely change as they move through the grade span, such differences among students accumulate over time until they become most obvious in high school, by which point they often seem natural, inevitable, and irreparable to students and educators alike.

Certainly, there are exceptions to these patterns. Many teachers know of students who become inspired and transcend their labels and classroom placements. Some, by sheer grit, pull themselves out of low-ability classes and succeed in higher classes. However, exceptions occur in spite of group placement, not because of it, and those who do succeed in spite of the odds often carry bitter memories of their struggle.

Homogeneous grouping is not necessarily good for high achievers, either. In fact, students can become destructively competitive—particularly in classrooms that stress individual achievement and grades. Those who are not at the very top sometimes feel like failures when they compare themselves with the "best" students. For other students, being designated gifted or high achieving can impede their learning that effort and persistence bring their own rewards and matter enormously for success in school and beyond. Moreover, many studies show that highly capable students do as well in mixed classes as in homogeneous groupings, particularly when teachers use the instructional strategies described in Chapter 6.[48]

The large, established research base has yielded a consensus that's described well by researcher John Hattie, who conducted a meta-analysis of more than 300 studies of ability grouping that included all grade levels and areas of curriculum. He concluded that "tracking has minimal effects on learning outcomes and profound negative effects on equity outcomes." Hattie also examined the effects on subgroups of students and concluded that "no one profits" from ability grouping, including high achievers.[49]

Controversy Surrounds Homogeneous Grouping

One highly publicized grouping story came out of Selma, Alabama, in 1990 when Rose and Hank Sanders's high-achieving daughter was put in a low-track class. Rose went to school to straighten out the mistake, as most parents would. It took some negotiating, as it often does, but the principal finally agreed to change the girl's placement. Ordinarily, the matter would have ended here. But the Sanders are not an ordinary family. Graduates of the Harvard Law School, they ran a practice together in Selma, and Hank—now in his ninth term—served in the state legislature. Their daughter's class placement seemed suspiciously like a civil rights violation to them, so they investigated further. When they discovered that nearly all of the school's African American students were in the low track, Rose got on the telephone. She advised every Black parent to ask for a class reassignment.

African American school superintendent Norward Roussell agreed to make the grouping system fairer, and he instituted new graduation standards that require all students to take Algebra 1, Biology 1, Geography, and Computer Sciences—courses from which many students had previously been excluded. But Roussell lost the support of White residents and was fired when he tried to bring about change. A White city councilman told a reporter that members of the White community feared that the new system would harm their children: "The basic position of the white community was that they wanted an honest program for the gifted students—for the best students. When they saw that being eliminated and the curriculum being watered down, theoretically, to a different level, they objected."[50]

Before it was over, African American protesters held daily marches, boycotted White-owned businesses, and occupied city hall. Students boycotted and closed down Selma High School. Rose Sanders was arrested, and ninety-one of the students who staged a "peaceful protest" in the cafeteria were reassigned to an alternative school. Since that time Rose and Hank Sanders have mounted a statewide campaign against tracking and educational inequality in Alabama. More recently, Rose Sanders, who was appointed the first African American woman judge in the state of Alabama in 1973, has remained active in the community around issues of civil rights, including recent protests around policing practices.

Efforts to dismantle homogeneous groups usually trigger controversy. Despite the empirical evidence against tracking, many educators still cannot imagine overturning so many school traditions, and other school practices depend on sorting students into different groups. Often, educators haven't seen heterogeneous grouping done well. Additionally, as in Selma, many parents of high-achieving students—often the most powerful and active parents in the community—oppose any changes to grouping practices because they fear losing the relative advantages the current system provides for their children.

To Change or to Fix

The usual response to evidence that current grouping practices don't work and aren't fair is to fix, adjust, or modify them.[51] Many schools, recognizing that tracking harms rather than helps achieve school goals, constantly change the criteria for sorting, add or eliminate classes, "recruit" students of color for the high-track and gifted programs, add resources to the low track, and so forth.

These responses can have merit, but educators report enormous difficulty in making them stick because sorting students appears inevitably to attract fundamental sociocultural and academic features that disadvantage those on the lowest rung. Meanwhile, advantages to high tracks, when they occur, are not attributable to the structure of sorting per se, but to tangible academic, resource, and status differences. As a result, a fair system could improve educational outcomes for all students. Many educators have spent their careers trying to beef up the rigor of the low-track curriculum, to encourage colleagues to adopt more positive dispositions toward the capacities of low-track students, and to alter the reward systems that work against teaching these students (e.g., the most accomplished teachers get to teach the highest-track classes). But few students or adults can overcome the negative perceptions that schools have low regard for students in low-track classes or of their ability and prospects for school success. This does not suggest that teachers necessarily dislike or disrespect students in the low track; rather, the problem rests with the obvious institutional disregard that can carry more weight than individual relationships. Educators' attempts to tweak their sorting systems in ways that are good and fair are not borne out by evidence and long-lasting models.

Accommodating Diversity Without Sorting

> My students represent a wide range of abilities. A dozen are English language learners. In the beginning, they did not participate in class discussion. They remained quiet until they worked with a partner or group, where they often felt more comfortable to ask questions, voice opinions, and grapple with the material. These same students, along with about half of the other students, were struggling readers and writers. Concurrently, one of my students received a silver medal at the Academic Decathlon, and several will attend UCLA this fall. There is one resource student and thirteen gifted and talented students, some of whom are also English language learners. As I plan lessons for this class, I take into account their diversity.
>
> To address diversity and individual needs, I have to think about what I want my students to know and learn and what I want them to be able to do. How can I ensure that all students have access to the information, and that they learn and feel successful? As I put together a unit, I focus on the students (identity and voice), the languages they speak, literacy, and cultural relevancy.
>
> I want students to work with different people because I know that once they graduate, they will not get to choose whom they work with. . . . I attempt to mix skill levels and ethnicities so that students will experience working with both diverse skill levels and diverse people. I always tell them that they are not marrying the people in their group but they must figure out how to work with each other in class.
>
> —Judy Smith
> High school social studies

Like many other educators today, Judy Smith's efforts to make schools more equitable include grappling with students' differences without classifying and sorting.

Since the late 1980s, policymakers and educators have recommended that schools dismantle structures that privilege so-called homogeneous grouping. Those offering recommendations include the directors of the Third International Mathematics and Science Study, who conclude that tracking "fails to provide satisfactory achievement for either average or advanced students";[52] the Carnegie Corporation's prestigious *Turning Points*, which identified heterogeneous grouping as a much-needed middle-school reform;[53] the National Governors Association, whose members proposed eliminating much ability grouping and tracking; the College Board, which argued that grouping practices erect barriers to minority students' achievement and called for eliminating mathematics tracking in 200 racially diverse high schools; and most publishers of standardized achievement tests, which caution about using their assessments to group students.

In addition, the NAACP Legal Defense Fund, the Children's Defense Fund, the American Civil Liberties Union, and the federal Government Accounting Office have all identified ability grouping, gifted programs, and special education as a second-generation segregation issue. Throughout the 1990s, the U.S. Department of Education's Civil Rights Division paid special attention to tracking when determining racially mixed schools' compliance with Title VI requirements.

Today's standards-based reforms should render these grouping practices quite obsolete. They are in so many ways incompatible with initiatives like the Common Core State Standards, which emphasize "college and career readiness" for *all* students, and with efforts among organizations— like those that formed the Pathways to College Network in 2006—working to promote "college preparation, access, and success for students from populations that have historically been under-represented in college."[54] These initiatives and efforts align with the growing support for heterogeneous grouping as a means for eliminating discriminatory practices and ensuring that all students have access to high-quality curriculum, teachers, and learning experiences.

But the means-end relationship signals difficulty as with nearly all equity-minded reforms: for some, the prospect of greater equity taints the programs designed to achieve it.

Implementing Heterogeneous Grouping

Many schools around the country have altered their grouping practices. The most common reforms include reducing or eliminating ability grouping, adopting school-wide reforms instead of targeting groups of students for compensatory education, including students designated as gifted and learning disabled in regular classes, and developing two-way bilingual programs.

Detracking

First-year teacher Kay Goodloe and her teaching partner have joined a large group of educators attempting to "detrack" their schools.

> I have ideological problems with the entire advanced placement (AP) program. . . . My AP students received a much more comprehensive education than my other students did. I find this very disturbing. Every student should have access to a college-preparatory education. By tracking students, we limit their future choices, and that is the true crime. Every student should be allowed to choose whether they pursue a college education, but by denying them college-preparatory classes, we rob them of that choice. My experience with the AP program has strengthened my resolve to provide such an education to all of my students. My partner and I will be detracking our classes next semester and offering a curriculum based on AP to everyone.
>
> —Kay Goodloe
> First-year teacher, high school history

Most schools' first step toward mixed-ability classes is to do away with low-level groups and classes. Some of these schools start to require that all students take a set of core heterogeneous courses in addition to some that remain tracked. Some adopt specialized programs like AVID (Advancement via Individual Determination) that provide schools with curriculum and instructional strategies for including lower-achieving middle and high school students in classes that prepare students for four-year universities. Many open honors programs to all—or almost all—students who wish to take them.

Other schools explore ways for students to earn honors credit within heterogeneous classes (e.g., by doing supplemental assignments and activities). Many schools rearrange their schedules so that struggling students can get the extra help they need to master the more challenging curriculum and keep up academically. Some offer backup classes, tutorial periods, homework centers, and intensive summer programs intended to provide a double dose of instruction.

Many racially mixed schools also develop more multicultural (or critical multicultural) curricula to make rigorous content more accessible to all students. Some high schools, for example, diversify their elective offerings to include such classes as African American or Mexican American history, African American or Latin American literature, ethnic studies, and women's studies.

Many teachers in detracking schools adopt the classroom strategies described in Chapters 6, 7, and 8. These help teachers align their instruction, assessment, and management practices with sociocultural perspectives on learning. Socratic seminars, experiential curriculum (e.g., project-based science and interactive math), and cooperative learning promote instructional conversation. Multidimensional assignments challenge students of varying abilities and provide necessary scaffolding to ensure all students' success. Authentic assessments offer opportunities for students to show what they know and can do and, in doing so, support students' inclinations to work hard. The inclusion of multiple, and oftentimes marginalized, perspectives helps make content accessible.[55] Practices grounded in critical pedagogy draw on students' backgrounds and experiences, build shared expertise among students in the class, and elevate the status of low-status students, in particular. Under these conditions, students with different technical skills in reading, writing, and mathematics come to view differences in skill levels as normal, temporary, and productive.

Research shows that when detracking is accompanied by such changes, both low- and high-achieving students fare very well. One study examined practices and outcomes at a network of "Talent Development" middle and senior high schools in urban Philadelphia. These schools offered a rich, academic curriculum, provided ample opportunities for students to assist one another, and used authentic assessments in heterogeneous classrooms. Their middle-school students showed significantly higher achievement gains than did tracked students in comparable "control" schools. To many observers' surprise, the students with the strongest academic skills seemed to benefit most.[56] Ninth graders in the Talent Development high schools made substantial gains in attendance, academic course credits earned, and promotion rates, and their improvements were sustained as they moved through high school. Student performance on the eleventh-grade state standards assessment also showed improvement.[57] Partly in recognition of its proven success, the Talent Development model subsequently received a major implementation grant from the U.S. Department of Education's Investing in Innovation (i3) competition.

High-Track Classes for All

The standards movement, the goal of ensuring that every child succeeds, and the call to have all high school graduates prepared for college and careers have pressed many school districts to eliminate their lowest-level courses and, at the secondary level, to put all students in college-preparatory classes. Of course, simply putting all students into high-level classes will not by itself bring about sought-after changes. As illustrated in Focal Point 10.1, Rockville Centre Schools in New York were thoughtful and thorough in providing the necessary *conditions* for enrolling all students in the state's high-level Regents curriculum.

Carol Burris, the celebrated former principal of Rockville Centre's South Side High School, now spends a great deal of her time advising other schools. She has become widely known for her research, advocacy, and expertise in detracking and equity-minded education reform more broadly.[58]

School-Wide Improvement Rather Than Remediation

Federal legislation governing compensatory education presses schools to use Title I funding to improve regular programs rather than create separate, specialized ones for target groups. With these funds, teachers can adopt fundamentally different approaches to the "regular" classroom—approaches that make high-quality curriculum, teaching, and learning more widely available.

LINKED LEARNING

Linked Learning integrates rigorous academics and career and technical education for high school students, providing *both* college *and* career preparation. Thus, it openly defies traditional tracking that separates students into either college-preparatory or vocational courses. At the same time, Linked Learning seeks to make high school more relevant, equitable, and interesting for all students.

Focal Point 10.1
Detracking in Rockville Centre

In 1990, Rockville Centre School District, a diverse, suburban school district located on Long Island, New York, began replacing its tracked classes with mixed-ability classes and teaching everyone the curriculum formerly reserved for the district's high-track students. Previously, the high school had three tracks—school level, Regents, and honors—and the middle school had two or more tracks in each subject. As in many districts, African American and Latino students were enrolled disproportionately in the lowest tracks. Superintendent William H. Johnson's and the Rockville Centre Board of Education's ambitious goal was to have 75 percent of high school graduates earn a New York State Regents diploma and to close the district's racial and social class gaps. Doing so would require that students pass at least eight examinations in mathematics, laboratory sciences, social studies, English language arts, and foreign language—examinations tied to the curriculum in the higher-track courses. Tracking stood in the way of achieving this ambitious goal.

The district decided that all students would study the accelerated middle-school math curriculum since the Regents math test posed the greatest challenge. So the middle school enrolled mixed-ability groups in math classes formerly reserved for the district's highest achievers. It provided support classes and after-school tutoring to help struggling students keep up. The results were astonishing. The following year, over 90 percent of incoming freshmen, excluding special education students, entered the district's South Side High School having passed the first Regents math examination. The achievement gap dramatically narrowed, as the percentage of African American and Latino students passing the algebra-based Regents exam in the eighth grade also increased dramatically—from 54 percent to 98 percent. Inspired by but not satisfied with those results, the district pushed further. The following year, the special education students were included as well; detracking expanded to other subjects, and in 1999 it followed students into the ninth and tenth grades. Enrollment in South Side's AP and International Baccalaureate classes was opened up to everyone who wanted to enter them.

During the first decade of detracking reform, the school became a U.S. Department of Education Blue Ribbon School of Excellence, and one of Newsweek magazine's "100 Best High Schools in the United States." By 2003, the gap among Rockville Centre graduates had nearly disappeared. Eighty-two percent of all African American or Latino and 97 percent of all White or Asian American graduates earned a Regents diploma. In 2004, the overall Regents diploma rate increased to a remarkable 94 percent, with 30 percent of the graduating class also earning the International Baccalaureate diploma.

Research on students' pathways through and beyond South Side High School further debunks the myth that detracking compromises the learning of high-track students. To the contrary, researchers offer South Side's case as evidence that a well-executed detracking reform can help increasing numbers of students reach state and world-class standards without adversely affecting high-achieving students. In Rockville Centre, detracking raised the bar for all students. Every group improved at the same time that the achievement gap narrowed dramatically.

Sources: Jeannie Oakes, "Democracy's Canaries," in *Keeping Track: How Schools Structure Inequality* (New Haven, CT: Yale University Press), 261–300; Carol Corbet Burris, Ed Wiley, Kevin G. Welner, and John Murphy, "Accountability, Rigor, and Detracking: Achievement Effects of Embracing a Challenging Curriculum as a Universal Good for All Students," *Teachers College Record* 110, no. 3 (2008): 571–607.

Linked Learning restructures high schools into a variety of theme-based schools and programs, including career academies, industry/career majors in large high schools, magnet schools, and small learning communities. In some cases, community colleges provide "dual enrollment" opportunities for students, enabling them to begin their postsecondary education while still in high school. Various Linked Learning pathways are based on broad industry themes—arts and media, health professions, and law and public service, for example—and differ in their curricular emphasis, in how courses are organized, in the extent to which students spend time on and off campus, in their relationship with colleges, and in their partnerships with business and industry.

Regardless of the particular pathway, all students experience college-preparatory academics, challenging professional/technical/applied studies, rigorous field-based experiences that contextualize learning, and flexible time and support to accommodate differences in academic readiness. By incorporating these four essential elements, every pathway leads to the same destination: preparation to succeed in *both* college *and* career, not simply one or the other. Students and their families choose among alternatives, based on their interests, but they do not choose whether they will go to college.

The core idea is that a combined academic and technical program will increase both the rigor and the relevance of the high school curriculum for a broad range of high school students, and, as a consequence, boost academic achievement, motivate students to stay in school, and improve their workforce outcomes. This claim is supported by considerable recent research on learning, as was discussed in Chapter 6. It assumes that almost all students will eventually end up in the workplace and that most workers will need to learn advanced knowledge and skills to sustain or advance their careers. Although any given student may decide to bypass college in favor of postsecondary training or beginning to work after high school, a Linked Learning pathway offers all students the preparation to seek the college option. (See Focal Point 10.2 for a description of one Linked Learning high school.)

Inclusive Classrooms

Since the early 1990s, a movement called "inclusion" has advocated placing students with disabilities in regular schools and classrooms, and integrating the supports they need into the regular education program. Such supports (e.g., another teacher or aide) then become available to all students. Similarly, many, including advocates for the gifted, have argued that gifted students can be well served in regular classrooms if the curriculum is differentiated, and that the activities shown to be effective for gifted students can and should be extended to other students, too.[59]

Thoughtfully designed heterogeneous classes can do a good job of responding to individual differences in community-like contexts, such as those we described in Chapter 7. With the help of a collaborating specialist, first-year teacher Janet Kim and her middle-school students developed a safe, supportive classroom community within which students were able to take risks and make strides in their learning. Janet offers one account that exemplifies how this community rallied around its members—in this case a particular reticent student with diagnosed learning disabilities.

> He didn't speak a word at the beginning of the year. With the support of the special education teacher and a comfortable, caring classroom, he was able to stand up in front of the class during Author's Chair time and read a five-sentence paragraph. . . . He read that paragraph with every pair of eyes fixed on his face—everyone wanting and hoping that he would finish reading successfully no matter how long it took. That was one of the most memorable and amazing moments. We were all so proud.
>
> —Janet Kim
> First-year teacher, English, middle school

Focal Point 10.2
Linked Learning at Stanley Foster Construction Tech Academy

In San Diego City Schools, the Stanley Foster Construction Tech Academy (CTA) is a career-themed magnet program that serves a diverse, low-income student population. The school was created when Kearny High School—a large, urban, "underperforming," comprehensive high school—was reconstituted because of its failure to meet its test score target. When Kearny shut down, it reopened the next day as four small autonomous schools. CTA is one of them. Its approximately 500 students are 20 percent white, 18 percent black, 14 percent Asian, 1 percent American Indian, and 47 percent Latinx. Roughly 65 percent qualify for free and reduced-price lunch.

CTA's mission is to provide students an opportunity to explore construction, engineering, and architecture through contextual, hands-on, and rigorous curriculum that prepares students for direct entry into college, apprenticeship programs, or a job. The school offers AP classes in thirteen subjects, and students may enroll concurrently in Mesa College while completing high school requirements. The school also offers on-site Regional Occupation Program (ROP) courses. But the students are not tracked; they all take both rigorous academics and Career and Technical Education (CTE) courses in architecture, engineering, and construction management. Graduates are guaranteed admission to San Diego State University.

Courses are blocked together in a "4 × 4" schedule to facilitate a flexible use of class time for math, science, and language arts classes. For students who need extra academic support, tutoring is available before school on Wednesday and Thursday from 7:45 to 8:30 A.M. and after school Tuesday through Friday from 3:35 to 4:25 P.M. Faculty include academic and CTE teachers, a part-time architect, an engineer, a building contractor, and a host of mentors from the construction industry. Throughout the year, students work in teams, using the latest industry design software and sophisticated computer equipment to complete construction, engineering, and architecture projects for real-world clients.

In one recent project, the juniors completely redesigned a real square block of downtown San Diego, as if it had been destroyed in some sort of disaster. They determined the most effective land use in the neighborhood, and then they worked from the underground up. They figured everything, including ensuring functioning utilities, meeting building code requirements, and creating a building design and construction plans. In addition to being graded by their teachers, their work was assessed by panels that included architects, engineers, city building inspectors, contractors, and members of construction trade unions.

The school's partners in the industry contribute regularly to the school's learning materials and opportunities. For example, the San Diego Chapter of the American Institute of Architects (AIA), led by Kevin deFrietas (project coordinator and 2010 Young Architect of the Year, known for designing energy-saving homes), donated hundreds of books for the "Architect's Bookshelf" at CTA, providing students with access to architectural history from Egypt to Frank Gehry. San Diego architects penned inscriptions inside the covers of the books to encourage young people to pursue their dreams of becoming architects. The architects hope, according to deFrietas, "to inspire kids to think big."[60]

Of the graduating class of 2009, 41 percent of students entered four-year universities; 43 percent community colleges; 7 percent apprenticeship programs; and 9 percent military careers. Nearly half were pursuing careers in construction/construction management (26 percent), engineering (16 percent), and architecture (5 percent). The others were choosing other pathways.

Biliteracy Programs

Bilingual specialists advocate various approaches depending on their philosophies and goals and school resources. The most important resources are usually skilled bilingual teachers, who are fluent in students' native languages, and English-speaking peers. In the following quote, bilingual teacher Mauro Bautista describes how he uses the language diversity in his classroom and school as a resource for learning.

> My classes were made up of students who just recently arrived from another country and were diverse in their knowledge of English. I would try to group students whose English skills differed. This was beneficial for students who were limited in English because they could learn from their peers. This was also great for more advanced students because they could take on the roles of experts. In addition, I would encourage them to join extracurricular activities like Students Run L.A., Mariachi, Art, and Leadership. Several of my beginning ESL students were elected class officers. These extracurricular activities placed students in settings where they had to further practice their English.
>
> —Mauro Bautista
> Middle-school bilingual education coordinator

Two-way bilingual education is one highly effective method of providing students the primary language support they need without segregating them from English speakers. This approach brings native English speakers together with students whose primary language is not English. Mentioned earlier, formalized two-way bilingual programs, often called dual immersion programs, aim to develop bilingual proficiency in *all* students, as well as promote academic achievement and cross-cultural knowledge and regard. Available evidence suggests that these programs are quite successful. For example, a study of 160 schools with two-way bilingual programs (most of them Spanish and English) found these programs to be effective for both native and nonnative English speakers.[61]

Importantly, offering *high-quality* bilingual programs is not the same thing as tracking. Whereas tracking based on language ability tends to treat students' limited English proficiency as a deficit that needs to be compensated for, bilingual education is premised on the notion that students are better understood as Emergent Bilinguals whose native language serves as an asset for learning. Indeed, the very goal of bilingual education—that students become *bilingual* and *biliterate*—challenges compensatory programs' goals that students learn English at all costs, even when it means diminishing students' native-language proficiency.

Technical Skills, Norms and Beliefs, Politics and Power

Few teachers entering the teaching profession today have had personal experience in heterogeneous classrooms, and few teaching mentors have answers for how to make such classrooms work. Yet some teachers study these challenges carefully and refuse to settle for merely replicating the familiar. First-year teacher Frank Divinagracia found these challenges engrossing and exciting.

> The Environmental Careers Academy expects innovative and reform-minded teaching. This pushes me to be more hands-off and more creative in my nontracked class, which is 25 percent African American, 45 percent Latinx, and 30 percent Asian. . . .
> I had a geometry curriculum that centered around investigations and students' conjectures. . . . The geometry lessons allowed students to speak and listen to one another

and create their own knowledge. Acting as a facilitator, I want them to think for themselves, defend their ideas, and be confident enough to stick to their beliefs. The beauty of it is they have to draw their own conclusions and use them for further study. I could see deliberateness in my students' actions, a true yearning to understand. The atmosphere was free and relaxed. They still struggled, but they did so without fear of being wrong.

Because these students are getting a good dose of small-group work in all their classes, they are used to being challenged and engaged in both their individual projects and group work. They have been extremely creative and have designed collaborative projects such as researching and painting murals, starting a garden, producing a recycling project on campus, and more. The students are thinking critically about geometry and their environment, and taking action on its problems.

—Frank Divinagracia
First-year teacher, high school mathematics

Nearly all advocates of ability grouping, in particular those who favor gifted or high-track classes, would prefer classes like the one Frank taught (as well as teachers like Frank). Sandra Berger of the Council for Exceptional Children has summarized the research on curriculum and instruction for gifted students and has concluded that gifted learners are served best by the very same types of educational experiences that make all students successful in heterogeneous classes. Berger advocates "thematic, broad-based, and integrative content"—like the blend of math, environmental science, and community-specific content evident in the projects designed by Frank's students and that are found in Linked Learning high schools. According to Berger, this kind of "concept-based instruction" expands students' opportunities to generalize, integrate, and apply new knowledge. Gifted learners, she argues, need to be challenged by "open-ended questions that stimulate inquiry, active exploration, and discovery" and learn best in a "receptive, non-judgmental, student-centered environment that encourages inquiry and independence, includes a wide variety of material, provides some physical movement, is generally complex, and connects the school experience with the greater world." Berger also emphasizes that teachers must provide multiple ways for gifted students to demonstrate what they have learned: "For example, instead of giving a written or oral book report, students might prefer to design a game around the theme and characters of a book."[62]

Those who advocate for heterogeneous grouping make similar arguments. Supported by research, they argue that the commonly touted benefits of gifted classes are attributable not to the classes' separateness or supposed homogeneity but to the kind of instructional practices and environmental conditions described above—practices and conditions that could (and should) be used to facilitate all students' learning. Similarly, they point out that the most common criticisms of mixed-ability classes—that they hold back or bore high achievers—can be attributed to the *lack* of practices and conditions like those described above, not to the particular mix of students.

Competing Norms and Values

Educators attempting heterogeneous grouping must come to terms with the emphasis that American culture places on competition and individualism. These norms bring a winners-and-losers frame of mind to education, and they imply that "good" education channels the most deserving students toward better educational opportunities and then higher income,

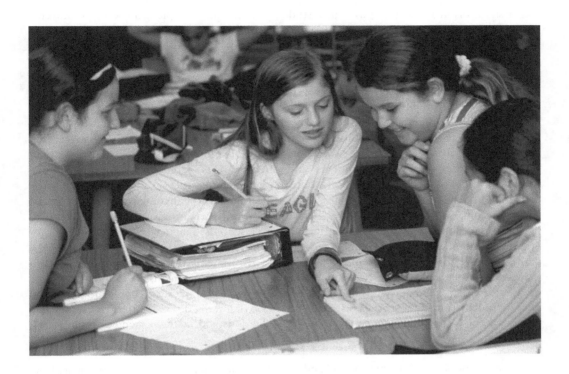

power, and status. If heterogeneous grouping is to work well, schools and classrooms must move toward more democratic norms of cooperation, support, and community. Conversely, if Americans want a society that values cooperation, support, and community, then it must begin in schools.

Why is this so? Conventional views of knowledge, language, and culture harbor deep-seated attitudes about race and social class. Curriculum guides, textbooks, legislative oversight, and typical teacher training more often than not reflect these conventional views. Thus, they help ensure that the curriculum remains consistent with mainstream Eurocentric, male, and White perspectives and can serve as filters that prevent alternative or competing perspectives from reaching students.

Yet, as sociocultural learning theory suggests, students learn best in schools and classrooms that acknowledge and engage students' diverse backgrounds, lived experiences, interests, and concerns. If students worry about being isolated or humiliated because of their differences, they won't take the intellectual and social risks that learning requires. Educators have an important role to play in bringing about necessary shifts so that students gain access to a broader and more inclusive range of perspectives, and do so in the context of heterogeneous groups.

Attention to the Political

Grouping, like all educational policy and practice, is highly political. Homogeneous grouping in particular has had long-term consequences in students' lives. Labels and group designations confer status distinctions and signal which students should, for example, gain access to universities and the enhanced life chances that higher education can bring. Thus, ability grouping and tracking play a powerful role in shaping the distribution of school resources, opportunities, and credentials that have exchange value in the larger society. Because ability grouping and tracking yield predictable comparative advantages for some students and families and not for others, efforts to move away from such practices nearly always engender resistance from those whose children are advantaged by them.

Many educators worry about the political consequences of abandoning homogeneous grouping. That is to say, educators sensibly worry about anger or pushback when they cause different interests to feel that they are losing power to control educational practices. Some worry about losing the support of high-track students' and gifted students' parents, who are often among those with the most social and political clout. In many communities, as the story of the Sanders family in Selma, Alabama, illustrates, this political dimension encompasses highly charged and enduring issues of race and social class stratification. Increasingly, a variety of "choice" policies offer a range of schooling options—charter schools, magnet schools, voucher programs, and homeschooling, to name a few. At least part of their attractiveness stems from the desire—among some educators and families—for environments that are more homogeneous than what public schools, especially ones that practice heterogeneously grouping, stand to offer.[63] First-year elementary teacher Lucy Patrick knows well how such choice models—even ones intended, as magnet schools originally were, to voluntarily diversify otherwise segregated public schools—can ultimately re-create political divisions and material inequities that follow from them.

> At our school, the "magnet-gifted" and "resident" classrooms are physically set apart from each other. I have heard my magnet students argue on the playground with resident students. The resident students had been calling the magnet students "nerds" and "dorks," while the magnet students counter by saying that they are "smarter" and that the resident students are "stupid." There is the attitude in my classroom—that they are smarter and better because they "got in" to the gifted program. Others go so far as to say that there are students in our classroom who do not belong in the magnet. Some staff even "joke" about the magnet teachers, "Oh, the magnets are having a meeting" or "We're not good enough to be magnet teachers."
>
> Some of the tension between the two schools centers around resources. As a magnet school, there are more funds available for extra materials or needed equipment. The magnet has special out-of-town field trips and experts who come in and teach art, music, PE, science, and opera. Teachers within the magnet program make it a point to be different from the resident school, regardless of what is best for students. For example, when we were deciding which publishing company to choose for our new language arts program, teachers suggested that we choose a series that is different from the resident school in order to explain to parents how the program is different.
>
> Only after intense and honest dialogue about what is best for all students will this two-school system change. Next year, I would like to bridge the two schools by having students interact more on a social level. Perhaps I can combine magnet students with resident school students in classes. As long as the school is based on "merit" and "ability," those in power will push for the status quo. It will take the combined efforts of students, teachers, administrators, parents, and community members to come together and engage in thoughtful reflection.
>
> —Lucy Patrick
> First-year teacher, grade 4

In short, the political challenges are daunting. Successful heterogeneous grouping will inevitably require that those who may now see themselves as *competing*—such as advocates for the gifted, for students with disabilities, for students of color, and so on—make *common cause* around serving all students well. Educators like Lucy have an important role to play in building coalitions among these divergent constituencies. They must guarantee that new and different practices will provide all students with opportunities that are at least as rich and rigorous as those previously enjoyed by students (though perhaps rich and rigorous in different ways). No parent would sensibly agree to less. But some parents will also object to changes that take away the *comparative* advantages their privileged children enjoyed because of homogeneous grouping—no matter how good the new approaches might be. Confronting these issues requires astute political leadership by educators. In the subsequent two chapters, we focus on some of the ways that critical, change-oriented educators forge powerful alliances with one another and with parents and community members.

The Struggle for Heterogeneous Grouping

This chapter has explored how sorting students into categories based on students' presumed abilities constrains all students' learning, *regardless* of how extensive and well intentioned the services provided to "special" categories of students are.

Transforming educational grouping practices will require changes similar in magnitude to social shifts like the slow erosion of legal racial segregation, or gender discrimination, or norms regarding cigarette smoking. As with all deeply embedded social practices, knowledge, science, and righteous arguments alone are not enough to bring about rapid change. But coalitions of people who see the harm in these educational practices are forming, and they are finding important success in challenging the status quo. Those with professional knowledge and credible moral standing in the community are joining in the chorus of criticism against tracking and ability grouping. While progress has been made, we still have a long way to go. Ultimately, those who benefit from these practices will not be able to marshal sufficient political power to hold the practices in place. The status quo is changing—by slow, painful degrees, to be sure, but it is changing.

Digging Deeper and Tools for Critique

www.routledge.com/cw/teachingtochangetheworld

Notes

1 "Ability grouping" and "tracking" are often used interchangeably to describe both ability-grouped classes and differentiated programs of study in which schools place students of different abilities. Some make a distinction by suggesting that "tracking" applies only to permanent assignments to a pathway leading to college or work. In practice, assignment to various ability levels is quite permanent and often extends to all of a student's academic subjects, K–12.
2 Although the labels don't always convey it, everyone at a school knows the ability level of various groups.
3 Adam Gamoran, "A Multi-Level Analysis of the Effects of Tracking," paper presented at the *Annual Meetings of the American Sociological Association*, Atlanta, GA, 1988.
4 Michael Garet and Brian DeLany, "Students, Courses, and Stratification," *Sociology of Education* 61 (1988): 61–77; Brian DeLany, "Allocation, Choice, and Stratification Within High Schools: How the Sorting Machine Copes," *American Journal of Education* 99, no. 3 (1991): 191–207. Carol C. Burris, Kevin D. Welner, and Jennifer Bedoza, "Universal Access to a Quality Education:

Research and Recommendations for the Elimination of Curricular Stratification," National Education Policy Center, 2016, www.nepc.colorado.edu/publication/universal-access.

5 Jeannie Oakes, John Rogers, David Silver, Siomara Valladares, Veronica Terriquez, Patricia McDonough, Michelle Renée, and Martin Lipton, *Removing the Roadblocks: Fair College Opportunities for All California Students* (Los Angeles: University of California/All Campus Consortium for Research on Diversity [ACCORD]; University of California Los Angeles, Institute for Democracy, Education, and Access [IDEA], 2006), http://idea.gseis.ucla.edu/publications/eor-06/RemovingRoadblocks.pdf; John Rogers, Jeannie Oakes, Sophie Fanelli, David Medina, Siomara Valladares, and Veronica Terriquez, *California Educational Opportunity Report* (Los Angeles: University of California/All Campus Consortium for Research on Diversity [ACCORD]; University of California Los Angeles, Institute for Democracy, Education, and Access [IDEA], 2007), http://idea.gseis.ucla.edu/publications/eor-07/2007-educational-opportunity-report-the-racial-opportunity-gap/.

6 Joseph Renzulli and Sally Reis, "The Reform Movement and the Quiet Crisis in Gifted Education," *Gifted Child Quarterly* 35 (1991): 26–35.

7 National Association of Gifted Children, *2014–2015 State of the States in Gifted Education* (Washington, DC: National Association for Gifted Children, 2015).

8 U.S. Department of Education, National Center for Education Statistics, *Digest of Education Statistics, 2010*, 2011, http://nces.ed.gov/fastfacts/display.asp?id=64.

9 Candace Cortiella, *The State of Learning Disabilities* (New York: National Center for Learning Disabilities, 2001); Hugh Mehan, Jane Mercer, and Robert Rueda, "Special Education," in *Encyclopedia of Education and Sociology*, eds. D. L. Levinson, P. W. Cookson, and A. R. Sadovnik (New York: Routledge Falmer, 2002), 619–624.

10 Kevin P. Collins and Sean D. Cleary, "Racial and Ethnic Disparities in Parent-Reported Diagnosis of ADHD: National Survey of Children's Health (2003, 2007, and 2011)," *Journal of Clinical Psychiatry* (2016), www.ncbi.nlm.nih.gov/pubmed/26761486.

11 Eviatar Zerubavel, *The Fine Line: Making Distinctions in Everyday Life* (Chicago: University of Chicago Press, 1993), 1–2.

12 Harold Stevenson and James W. Stigler, *The Learning Gap: Why Our Schools Are Failing and What We Can Learn From Japanese and Chinese Education* (New York: Simon and Schuster, 1994).

13 Kevin Welner, *Legal Rights, Local Wrongs: When Community Control Collides With Educational Equity* (Buffalo: State University of New York Press, 2001).

14 Ellwood Cubberley, *Changing Conceptions of Education* (Boston: Houghton Mifflin, 1909), 18–19.

15 Quoted in Gould, *The Mismeasure of Man*, 221.

16 For a fascinating, detailed history of the links between the growth of universal, compulsory education and special education, see John G. Richardson, "Common Delinquent, and Special: On the Formalization of Common Schooling in the American States," *American Educational Research Journal* 31, no. 4 (1994): 695–723.

17 Jeannie Oakes and Gretchen Guiton, "Matchmaking: The Dynamics of High School Tracking Decisions," *American Educational Research Journal* 32, no. 1 (1995): 3–33.

18 Joseph Renzulli, in an interview with Anne Turnbaugh Lockwood, "Beyond the Golden Chromosome," in *Focus in Change*, a publication of the National Center for Effective Schools at the University of Wisconsin, Madison (no. 11 [fall 1993]), 3.

19 Data Accountability Center, *Individuals With Disabilities Education Act (IDEA) Data*, www.ideadata.org.

20 Janie Scull and Amber M. Winkler, *Shifting Trends in Special Education* (Washington, DC: Thomas B. Fordham Institute, 2011).

21 Data Accountability Center, *Individuals With Disabilities Education Act (IDEA) Data*.

22 Christine Sleeter, "Learning Disabilities: The Social Construction of a Special Education Category," *Exceptional Children* 53, no. 1 (1986): 46–54; see also Christine Sleeter, "Why Is There Learning Disabilities? A Critical Analysis of the Birth of the Field in Its Social Context," in *The Formation of the School Subject Matter: The Struggle for Creating an American Institution*, ed. T. S. Popkewitz (New York: Falmer Press, 1987), 210–237.

23 Louise Spear-Swerling and Robert J. Sternberg, *Off Track: When Poor Readers Become Learning Disabled* (Boulder, CO: Westview Press, 1996).

24 See, for example, the special issue of *Phi Delta Kappan* (February 1996) and Thomas Armstrong, *The Myth of the ADD Child* (New York: Dutton, 1985).

25 Mehan, Mercer, and Rueda, "Special Education."

26 Rachel Fish, "The Racialized Construction of Exceptionality," *Social Science Research* 61, no. 1 (2017): 317–334, www.sciencedirect.com/science/article/pii/S0049089X15301642.

27 Donald L. MacMillan and Daniel Reschly, "Overrepresentation of Minority Students: The Case for Greater Specificity or Reconsideration of the Variables Examined," *Journal of Special Education* 32 (1998): 15–24.

28 For example, researcher Elizabeth Useem found that middle-school students' placement in math classes was not necessarily determined on the basis of professionally administered, fair, and accurate assessments of students' actual capacities, but rather on parents' willingness to take steps to ensure that their children were enrolled in upper-level classes even when school personnel recommended against it or their children resisted it. Elizabeth Useem, "Student Selection Into Course Sequences in Mathematics: The Impact of Parental Involvement and School Policies," *Journal of Research on Adolescence* 1, no. 3 (1991): 231–250; see also Susan Yonezawa and Jeannie Oakes, "Making All Parents Partners in the Placement Process," *Education Leadership* 56, no. 7 (April 1999): 33–36.

29 "A New Mix of Gifted Students," *Washington Post*, July 27, 1997.

30 Mehan, Mercer, and Rueda, "Special Education."

31 Jeannie Oakes, *Multiplying Inequalities* (Santa Monica, CA: RAND, 1990).

32 Oakes and Guiton, "Matchmaking."

33 Mehan, Mercer, and Rueda, "Special Education."

34 Luanna H. Meyer, Beth Harry, and Mara Sapon-Shevin, "School Inclusion and Multicultural Education," in *Multicultural Education: Issues and Perspectives*, 3rd ed., eds. James A. Banks and Cherry A. McGee Banks (Boston: Allyn & Bacon, 1996), 369–400.

35 MacMillan and Reschly, "Overrepresentation of Minority Students."

36 U.S. Department of Education Office of Civil Rights, *Civil Rights Data Collection*, http://ocrdata.ed.gov.

37 Jared Greenhouse, *The Complicated Problem of Race and Special Education*, 2015, www.huffingtonpost.com/entry/racism-inherent-in-special-education-leads-to-marginalization_us_55b63c0ae4b0224d8832b8d3.

38 Oakes and Guiton, "Matchmaking"; Susan Yonezawa, *Making Decisions About Students' Lives* (PhD diss., UCLA, 1997); Annette Lareau, *Home Advantage: Social Class and Parental Intervention in Elementary Education* (London: Falmer, 1989).

39 Jeannie Oakes, *Keeping Track: How Schools Structure Inequality* (New Haven, CT: Yale University Press, 1985/2005); Oakes, *Multiplying Inequalities*.

40 Oakes, *Multiplying Inequalities*.

41 This is not to say that *particular* classes for lower-ability students are not given wonderful facilities, a solid curriculum, and well-qualified teachers, but such situations are clear exceptions to the rule.

42 John Hattie, *Visible Learning: A Synthesis of Over 800 Meta-Analyses Relating to Achievement* (New York: Routledge, 2009).

43 Jay P. Greene, *A Meta-Analysis of the Effectiveness of Bilingual Education* (Claremont, CA: The Tomas Rivera Policy Institute, 1998).

44 Jeannie Oakes, "Two Cities: Tracking and Within-School Segregation," *Teachers College Record* 96, no. 4 (1995): 681–690; Kevin G. Welner, *Legal Rights, Local Wrongs: When Community Control Collides With Educational Equity* (Buffalo: State University of New York Press, 2001).

45 David J. Hoff, "Chapter 1 Aid Failed to Close Learning Gap," *Education Week*, April 2, 1997, 1, 29; Robert E. Slavin, "How Title I Can (Still) Save America's Children," *Education Week*, May 21, 1997, 52; Thomas Kelly, "The 4 Percent 'Structural Flaw,'" *Education Week*, June 11, 1997, 44.

46 Jim Cummins, "From Multicultural to Anti-Racist Education: An Analysis of Programmes and Policies in Ontario," in *Minority Education: From Shame to Struggle*, eds. Tove Skutnabb-Kangas and Jim Cummins (Philadelphia: Multilingual Matters Ltd., 1988).

47 Jeannie Oakes, Adam Gamoran, and Reba Page, "Curriculum Differentiation: Opportunities, Outcomes, and Meanings," in *Handbook of Research on Curriculum*, ed. Phillip Jackson (New York: Macmillan, 1992), 570–608.

48 There is disagreement in the academic community about whether high-achieving students benefit academically from high-track placement. Most, however, agree that what benefits might accrue come about because of the enriched opportunities in these classes, not because the students are separated per se. See, for example, the series of articles in the November 1995 issue of *Phi Delta Kappan*.

49 Hattie, *Visible Learning*, 90.

50 William Snider, "Schools Are Reopened in Selma Amid Continuing Racial Tension," *Education Week*, February 21, 1990.

51 For example, researcher Maureen Hallinan argues that "a more tempered response" is for schools to make grouping practices more consistent with the theories behind those practices, and to balance the inherently negative features of grouping with countervailing policies and practices. See Maureen Hallinan, "Tracking: From Theory to Practice," *Sociology of Education* 67, no. 2 (1994): 79–84. See also Adam Gamoran, "Alternative Uses of Ability Grouping in Secondary Schools: Can We Bring High-Quality Instruction to Low-Ability Classrooms?" *American Journal of Education* 102, no. 1 (1993): 1–22.

52 William Schmidt, "Are There Surprises in the TIMSS Twelfth Grade Results?" *TIMSS United States*, Report No. 8 (East Lansing, MI: TIMSS U.S. National Research Center, Michigan State University, April 1998), 4.

53 Carnegie Council on Adolescent Development, *Turning Points: Preparing Youth for the 21st Century* (New York: Carnegie Corporation of New York, 1989).

54 Pathways to College Network, www.pathwaystocollege.net.

55 Jeannie Oakes, Amy Stuart Wells, Susan Yonezawa, and Karen Ray, "Equity Lessons From Detracking Schools," in *Rethinking Educational Change With Heart and Mind*, ed. Andy Hargreaves (Arlington, VA: Association for Supervision and Curriculum Development, 1997), 43–65.

56 Douglas MacIver, Steven B. Plank, and Robert Balfanz, *Working Together to Become Proficient Readers: Early Impact of the Talent Development Middle School's "Student Team Literature Program."* Report of the Center for Research on the Education of Students Placed at Risk (Baltimore: The Johns Hopkins University Press, 1998).

57 James J. Kemple, Corinne M. Herlihy, and Thomas J. Smith, *Making Progress Toward Graduation: Evidence From the Talent Development High School Model* (Washington, DC: MRDC, 2005).

58 Carol C. Burris, Jay P. Heubert, and Henry M. Levin, "Accelerating Mathematics Achievement Using Heterogeneous Grouping," *American Educational Research Journal* 43, no. 1 (2006): 105–136.

59 Joseph S. Renzulli and Sally Reis, *The Schoolwide Enrichment Model: A Comprehensive Plan for Educational Excellence* (Mansfield Center, CT: Creative Learning Press, 1985); Carol Tomlinson, *How to Differentiate Instruction for Mixed-Ability Classrooms* (Alexandria, VA: Association for Supervision and Curriculum Development, 1995); Carol Tomlinson, "Differentiated Instruction in the Regular Classroom: What Does It Mean? How Does It Look?" *Understanding Our Gifted* 14, no. 1 (2001): 3–6.

60 Personal communication.

61 Donna Christian, *Two-Way Bilingual Education: Students Learning Through Two Languages* (Santa Cruz, CA: National Center for Research on Cultural Diversity and Second Language Learning, 1994).

62 Sandra L. Berger, "Differentiating Curriculum for Gifted Students," *ERIC Digest #E510* (Reston, VA: Council for Exceptional Children, ERIC Clearinghouse on Disabilities and Gifted Education, n.d.), 3.

63 For example, see Kate Taylor, "A Manhattan School District Where School Choice Amounts to Segregation," *New York Times*, June 7, 2017, www.nytimes.com/2017/06/07/nyregion/a-manhattan-district-where-school-choice-amounts-to-segregation.html.

Chapter 11

The Community

Engaging with Families and Neighborhoods

Genuine parental involvement is something we struggle with at my school. Recently, we've begun working with the activist community group Inner-City Struggle because we want to move beyond monthly parent meetings and teacher-parent conferences. Inner-City Struggle supports parents in two important ways. One, they provide workshops that give parents the basic information they need to make sure that their children are receiving a rigorous college-preparatory education. For instance, in January they will offer a workshop on the high school graduation requirements. Two, they work to establish a type of student and parent involvement that can lead to social and educational change within the school and the community. For example, Inner-City Struggle sponsors a school service club called United Students Junior. Last year, Inner-City Struggle involved the students and their parents in a successful organizing campaign to ensure that all high school students are enrolled in college preparation courses.

—Mauro Bautista
Middle-school bilingual education coordinator

Administrators and teachers are professionals whom the public entrusts with creating class-room and school cultures that support all students to learn well; educators' actions determine the quality of students' opportunities. However, educators are not the only adults who influence whether schools become academically rigorous and socially just learning communities. Administrators, teachers, parents, community members, and students themselves must all work toward this goal. In the best schools, educators reach out, welcome, guide, and respond to families and community members to make sure that their participation is authentic and meaningful.[1] As Mauro Bautista's account illustrates, this reaching out can include much more than just encouraging parents to help with students' homework or attend meetings at school.

Chapter Overview

In this chapter, we look at several parent and community involvement strategies and examine whether and how these strategies share power in addition to sharing responsibility. We begin by considering two dominant (and contradictory) complaints about parents:

- Parents neglect their responsibility to participate and support their children's schools.
- Parents are disruptive and overly involved in schools.

We then examine four types of constructive parent engagement:

- Parents supporting the work of schools
- Schools serving families' and communities' needs
- Building bridges between the cultures of home and school
- Organizing parents and communities for school improvement and social justice

Each of these four has the potential for helping to build a supportive and respectful synergy between teachers and parents, but each also takes considerable work and patience. Parent involvement means so much more than parents acting as supporters, helpers, or compliant clients for the school's services. Parents must be equal partners in their children's schooling; this is not to say, however, that parents and teachers are supposed to perform one another's jobs. Instead, the entire community needs to get straight how its various members both do their jobs and work together. This isn't easy because, when it comes to schooling, the best distributions of work and power are not familiar or comfortable to most people.

Removing Barriers to Constructive Parent Engagement

Dozens of studies attest to the positive impact of parent involvement on children's school achievements and outcomes. Likewise, parental noninvolvement gets much of the blame when schooling does not go well. When parents participate in their children's education, students' attitudes and achievement improve. Increased parent involvement correlates with higher attendance rates and fewer discipline problems. It can also lead to a stronger curriculum and more positive school and community relations. These positive effects seem to hold regardless of students' socioeconomic status and prior academic achievement.[2]

Given these findings, many states and the U.S. Department of Education have mandated that parent involvement programs be introduced into schools' daily operations as a condition for receiving certain state and federal funds. Yet, despite near consensus on the importance of parent involvement, there is limited understanding or agreement about parents' roles.

Much of this chapter provides an overview of strategies educators have used to involve parents. These strategies are not just about preventing or solving problems; they are positive and generative ways to have *all* parents feel welcomed, empowered, and equally valued. Before addressing those strategies, however, it helps to consider some of the common complaints educators have about parents' involvement in schools, and vice versa.

Common Complaints About Parent Involvement

One complaint—common in schools serving high-poverty neighborhoods—is that parents don't care enough about their children's education. Educators may reference parents' failure to show up at school events, to return paperwork or phone calls, to supervise homework, or to answer phone calls. School personnel and social critics often lament that schools' influence cannot compete with alienated peer groups and dysfunctional families. Sometimes this lack of caring is framed sympathetically, as when educators note the constraints that poverty places on many parents' involvement. Meanwhile, many educators levy a different, but equally powerful, complaint—more common in affluent communities—about parents who are too demanding and care too much, often about the wrong things.

In the following sections, we discuss these two common complaints and then place them in the broader spectrum of contemporary parent involvement practices and perspectives.

Too Little Involvement

When casting about for blame—who's at fault for low achievement in schools—parents share blame with teachers, and they often blame one another. Political and opinion leaders follow suit. In the 1980s, George H. W. Bush's education secretary, Lauro Cavazos, admonished Latino families for their children's high dropout rates.[3] Famous entertainer Bill Cosby, before becoming the subject of several legal suits accusing him of sexual misconduct, spoke at venues nationwide about his belief that the Black-White achievement gap persists in part because "people are not parenting" and, in particular, because "lower economic people are not holding up their end of the deal."[4] President Barack Obama interestingly enough reinforced at least some of these notions. Speaking at a 2008 National Association for the Advancement of Colored People (NAACP) Father's Day event, for example, he called on African American parents to raise academic expectations for their children. He did not follow through by mentioning, even briefly, the corresponding responsibilities for schools, teachers, and society at large to engage parents in meaningful ways.[5]

And yet studies of parents' attitudes toward schooling consistently portray parents differently—education is often their top priority. Low-income parents of all races and ethnicities are clear in their belief that schooling provides the crucial hope for moving their children into meaningful work and out of poverty. Why this gap between common perceptions and families' actual commitments to education? Part of the answer lies with different definitions of parent involvement. Whereas educators stress parents' participation in organized school events and their attention to lessons and homework, parents often see the care, support, encouragement, and cultural values they impart to their children as their involvement *and* the foundation for their children's success in school.[6]

Most parents, regardless of income level, share the exact same assumption about schools: "The school's job is to see that my child succeeds." Where parents differ is in the kind of critique and empowerment they bring to their relationship with the school. Wealthy parents often have highly valued resources—like money and social capital—to leverage, and they believe that they are entitled to use them to their children's benefit. Schools, in turn, respond to these resources and to these parents. Poor parents, for a multitude of reasons, often do not have the same sense of empowerment and entitlement; thus, it makes little sense to interpret the respectful distance they may keep as not caring. Because of these varied cultural views and practices, schools often view parents as not caring about education, and parents often view schools as not caring about their kids.

How can educators and families, who want the same thing for students, stop misreading one another's intentions and connect their efforts? And what can teachers do about it?

When Mauro Bautista began teaching at a middle school in a mostly Latinx community, some of his colleagues cautioned him not to count on parents being involved. But because he had grown up in the neighborhood, he knew that the parents did care, even if they didn't spend much time at school. So he made a point of reaching out to parents in ways they would see as welcoming.

> I invited all my students' parents to the classroom the first Friday of the year. I introduced myself, gave them my home phone number, and invited them to visit the classroom any time. I spoke Spanish because most of the parents spoke limited, if any, English.
>
> When parents visit the classroom, I approach them as soon as possible and we discuss their goals for the visit. Some come to find out how their children are doing. A few ask me how they can help their kids at home. Several invite me to eat at their homes, and one parent invited me for a beer. I have been very humbled by these signs of camaraderie.
>
> I would love to visit all my students' homes. I always try to give positive reports by emphasizing the progress and showing them examples of their child's work. Parents enjoy hearing that their children are doing well in school.
>
> My connections with parents clearly disprove some teachers' belief that parents in this community do not care about their children's success in school.
>
> —Mauro Bautista
> Middle-school bilingual education coordinator

Not all parents may respond as quickly as the parents of Mauro's students did to teachers' goodwill and invitations to become an active part of their children's success in the classroom. And, in fact, Mauro's own success was quite gradual—the product of weeks, months, and years of steadily communicating his desire to connect with parents and his sincerity in inviting them into the classroom community. Mauro had the advantage of knowing the language spoken in his students' homes; others who lack this language facility might need to enlist bilingual allies. Regardless of their language, culture, or prior experiences with the local schools, parents will respond positively when treated with respect and when their participation is valued. Hard work and patience are essential.

Often, low-income parents who grew up in the United States have unhappy recollections of their own schooling, and these can dampen their enthusiasm for getting involved with schools. Given histories of racism in many communities, parents of color may feel reluctant to become a visible presence at school or to trust those who work there. Immigrant parents may understand little about the U.S. school system—they may mistakenly (or correctly) assume that parents are neither wanted nor needed at school, or they may trust that the school will make appropriate educational decisions on their children's behalf. Some families may believe that a "good" parent's role involves leaving school matters to the teacher's discretion. For many, language barriers also may make it difficult or impossible to communicate with teachers.

Schools and teachers often create barriers to parent involvement. The school may be organized in ways that discourage parents from visiting, or that make schools seem inhospitable. Things as simple as a clearly marked entrance and friendly office staff can make a big difference in welcoming parents. School security measures can feel particularly daunting, as they may require signing in with personal information, passing through metal detectors, securing visitor badges and escorts, and more. Teachers may have few resources and little time to connect with parents, especially parents who work more than one job, have limited Internet access or transportation, or speak a language other than English. And, of course, some teachers just don't see cultivating relationships with parents as part of their "teaching" job.

Too Much Involvement

In some neighborhoods, typically middle and upper class, nervousness around grades, test scores, students qualifying for admission to a popular charter school or magnet programs, and other perceived high-stakes achievements can raise parents' anxiety and make them feel that they must be highly involved advocates for their children. Even routine instructional matters such as scores on weekly spelling tests or homework assignments can worry parents even in the earliest grades. The following two anecdotes appeared in a 2005 story about parent involvement in *Time* magazine.

> An Iowa high school counselor gets a call from a parent protesting the C her child received on an assignment. "The parent argued every point in the essay," recalls the counselor, who soon realized why the mother was so upset about the grade. "It became apparent that she'd written it."
>
> A sixth-grade teacher in California tells a girl in her class that she needs to work on her reading at home, not just in school. "Her mom came in the next day," the teacher says, "and started yelling at me that I had emotionally upset her child."[7]

Few educators or researchers openly discuss this side of parent involvement, because it runs counter to the ubiquitous plea for parents to be involved. Because schools need political support for funding and physical resources, they often acquiesce to highly involved parents' demands, even if it means giving special privileges or reining in a reform.[8] In a culture that favors marketplace comparisons—where schools are seen as competing, and parents may be seen as clients or customers—it can be difficult to please parents *and* to preserve fidelity to a school's programs and mission. Of course, just because some parent involvement is too much, or feels like an intrusion on an overburdened teacher or school, does not mean that parents are unjustified in asking for, or perhaps demanding, things. *Every* parent has "correct" insights into their own children's needs, into instruction, into school policy—insight that a teacher or a principal might not have. The school's responsibility is to understand and often negotiate its practices and relationships for the good of all students and the harm of none.

It is rare that parents fail to recognize deeply caring, competent, and hardworking faculty and administrators. Hypercritical parents can soon find themselves isolated in their complaints and see little to gain from continuing their disruptions. Other parents who first approach the school with a complaint can often become allies whose continued engagement turns into powerful, useful support.

In Chapters 3, 4, and 5, we discussed the "wars" over curriculum, which have triggered many parent complaints in recent years. For example, many parents who themselves did well with traditional instruction become apprehensive if their children experience other kinds of teaching.[9] We witnessed this in an affluent community when a highly acclaimed principal became the target of parents because she instituted a progressive mathematics curriculum. The principal took many of the recommended steps for parent involvement that *should have* smoothed the way for reform.[10] She convened a "transformation" study group of twenty-five community members, teachers, and administrators, paying close attention to developing a process for openly discussing difficult issues. This group read and talked about relevant research.

Despite the principal's efforts to include her vocal, upper-middle-class community, some parents still formed an ad hoc group for "educational accountability" and petitioned the board of education to return the school to traditional teaching and curricula. Some parents demanded that specific books be read, and others prescribed specific amounts of time for certain lessons. The innovative math curriculum became a lightning rod for a group of fathers—many with degrees in science and engineering—who blasted the program as failing to prepare their children for the rigors of university. One former student, now attending an Ivy League college, wrote to the local paper blaming the principal for his average math grades in his college class. The principal conceded to parents' demands for a more traditional curriculum, but the controversy still cost her the job.

Parent involvement can reflect the racism and classism in the rest of the culture. Some White and middle-class parents respond to their children's classmates of color or lower socioeconomic background with fear and prejudice. One first-year teacher found herself and her teaching partner in just such a situation.

> Last summer, the district decided to install three portable classrooms to absorb the increasing number of children in the district. A group of White, middle-class parents immediately and adamantly opposed the new bungalows, fearing that they would bring transient children of low socioeconomic status from other, less desirable neighborhoods into their children's classrooms. When the bungalows were installed over their protests, they attempted to rally the neighborhood to turn our school into a charter school. The dissatisfied parents derided teachers in public meetings and sent out inflammatory fliers to convince homeowners without school-age children to vote to change our school to a charter school. The fliers indicated that property values would rise if the measure passed.
>
> Although the charter school proposal died—most teachers and other parents were happy with the school—the problems continued. My teaching partner had one of these parents come to her requesting her child's seat be changed because it was located in the same group as Rosa, a Spanish-speaking child who had recently moved here from Mexico. Rosa always completed her work and had not been a source of problems in this group. The school climate affected our decisions most profoundly during a unit on the migration of groups of people—in this case slaves in the American South. . . . Excitedly, my teaching partner and I prepared everything for the simulation, including a paper rendition of the Ohio River; then, as we were taping it to the floor, she said, "What about the parents? I don't want any more phone calls to our principal. I just know they're not going to go for this." We canceled the simulation.
>
> —Name withheld
> First-year teacher, grade 2

Parents often seek educational advantages for their children where those advantages are built into the school structure. In schools with ability-grouped classes, tracking, or pull-out programs for gifted students, for example, savvy parents invariably want their children enrolled in the "best" classes. Because so many schools permit only a small percentage of slots in high-track classes, many parents feel they have few options but to push for access.

We know of no strategies or programs that directly address the problem of parents who exercise a disproportionate amount of influence over a school's programs and over decisions advantaging their own children. Teachers or principals often struggle to manage these parents unless *enough* other parents are involved to check their power. In such cases, parents themselves may effectively subdue the most bothersome, intrusive, or self-serving individuals and cliques.

Relationships Between Families and Schools: Four Traditions

The relationships between schools and families typically involve an imbalance of power or control. When a school or a set of parents retains power in ways that cannot be rebalanced, those with less power remain disadvantaged. Sometimes the family-school relationship is that of parents being *helpers* who support or give services to the school. Schools try to manage the helpers, but some parents inevitably and inequitably leverage their help (time, material resources, political support, etc.) to generate improvements for the school or advantages for their own children. At other times, the school treats families as *clients*; in this case, the power relationship is clearer— the school is in charge even if some students benefit. There is also a tradition, not a widespread one, for schools to construct *bridges* between the cultures of schools and those of the diverse communities they serve. Finally, in some cases, outside groups or schools themselves engage in *organizing* parents for broad-based social and educational change within and beyond the school itself. All four traditions—engaging parents as helpers, engaging parents as clients, bridging cultures, and community organizing—have a role in promoting both learning and social justice.

Parents Supporting the School's Agenda

Schools are most active when it comes to getting parents to support the school's agenda for students. Through letters sent home, pleas at parent meetings, websites, and so on, the theme is that schools can't do it alone; parents must take an active role in their children's schooling. This traditional parent involvement asks parents to send children to school ready to learn—rested, well fed, with proper materials, and with supervised homework completed. It calls on parents to attend parent conferences, back-to-school night, Parent Teacher Association meetings, and other school events. It solicits parents' support at school (making photocopies, supervising on the playground) and expects them to help raise or donate money through bake sales and candy sales, organized fund-raisers, check writing, and so on. More recently, it has invited parents to participate in *certain* areas of school governance.

Joyce Epstein, a prominent researcher on schools and families, concludes that educators need better strategies for involving parents. Productively rethinking parents' roles, Epstein cautions, requires more time, organization, and effort than schools are used to committing.

To assist schools in understanding and developing partnerships with families and communities, Epstein has developed a typology of involvement. (See Concept Table 11.1.) She argues that each type of involvement presents challenges that must be met and leads to different results for students, families, and teachers. Notably, most of these strategies focus on having parents and communities support and enhance the work of schools.

Joyce Epstein's work became popular in the last decade of the twentieth century and has done much to refine the traditional ways that schools engage parents. Types 1 and 2 in her typology echo a century-long effort to strengthen families' capacity to improve student learning, school behavior, and socialization into mainstream culture. Types 3, 4, and 5 focus on teaching parents about and engaging them in the actual work of the school—whether it be the content of the curriculum or the procedures of school life.

These strategies have grown in popularity since the 1980s when, not coincidentally, political leaders began to emphasize families as children's first and most important teachers. The

Concept Table 11.1 Joyce Epstein's Parent Involvement Typology

Parent involvement type	What do schools do?
Type 1—Parenting	Assist families with parenting and child-rearing skills, understanding child and adolescent development, and setting home conditions that support children as students at each age and grade level; assist schools in understanding families.
Type 2—Communicating	Communicate with families about school programs and student progress through effective school-to-home and home-to-school communications.
Type 3—Volunteering	Improve recruitment, training, work, and schedules to involve families as volunteers and audiences at the school or in other locations to support students and school programs.
Type 4—Learning at home	Involve families with their children in learning activities at home, including homework and other curriculum-linked activities and decisions.
Type 5—Decision making	Include families as participants in school decisions, governance, and advocacy through parent-teacher organizations, school councils, committees, and other parent organizations.
Type 6—Collaborating with community	Identify and integrate community resources and services to enhance school and family community practices and promote student achievement.

Source: Joyce Epstein, Lucretia Coates, Karen C. Salinas, Mavis G. Sanders, and Beth Simon, *School, Family and Community Partnerships: Your Handbook for Action* (Thousand Oaks, CA: Corwin Press, 1997).

U.S. Department of Education reinforced this view in a 1987 publication, *What Works*, outlining practices that promote school success. In it, federal officials asserted that no school can be effective without parental support. The National PTA has since used Epstein's typology as the basis for national parent involvement standards, as has the federal government to a degree.

Despite these new requirements, most schools do not allow parents a deep influence over the core practices or resources of the school. Further, most parents have nowhere to learn about the education system or their rights to participate, except at the school itself. Even when schools are entirely welcoming of parent participation, they are not likely to actively teach parents how to question conventional practices. Perhaps it is too much to ask of any institution that it teach potential critics how to challenge its own practices.

To manage the contradictory goal of encouraging parent participation without disrupting the status quo, schools often draw a clear line between the professional work and expertise of teachers and administrators and the support role that parents are expected to play. As one school administrator told us recently, "Parents are welcome when educators want them there."

Epstein's sixth type of parent involvement suggests that schools can involve communities, as well as individual parents. This sixth type of involvement brings community resources into the school. However, its potential may be limited if the essential relationship between those who have power and those who do not remains the same. In other words, if schools, working together with community agencies, maintain the role of experts diagnosing problems and developing remedies, they are likely to help families "fit in" to existing structures and thereby help cement the status quo. Later in this chapter we consider some opportunities for parents, communities, and schools to consider profound changes in the distribution of power among all those who are needed to make schools socially just.

Teacher Mauro Bautista, whose work with parents we feature throughout this chapter, connects with families and neighborhoods in the six ways Epstein notes (and more). He does so in ways that reflect his sensitivity to community norms. Like all teachers, he doesn't always get it right the first time. But his conviction that parents do care and want to be involved pushes him to try out various methods to engage parents. Here's an example that probably fits into Epstein's second category—communication:

> Recently, I visited the home of one of my students who had missed class six times. I handled the situation poorly at first. I made the student stay after school to do his work and "pay back" the hours he missed. When his mother came to pick him up, she was very upset. She asked me to let her know the punishment in advance, if he ever skipped class again. It was a very awkward conversation.
>
> After he missed again, I handed him a letter that asked his mom to verify his absences. He refused to take the letter and ran out the door. That afternoon, I visited his house.
>
> My student's mom received me very respectfully and offered me something to drink. After I explained why I was there and my strong interest in helping her son receive a good education, she asked him why he had not shown up to class. He answered that he does not like my classes because I give too much work. The mom made it perfectly clear that she did not approve of either his answer or his actions. She emphasized the importance of working hard in school. She thanked me for coming and asked me to keep her informed.
>
> Now, this mother and I frequently talk about her son's progress. And, seeing that his mother and I had formed an alliance, this student has not missed a single day of class since my home visit. The conversations have not only improved his behavior, but also the quality of his academic work. The power of these interactions is evidence of the great care that many parents have about their children's progress in school.
>
> —Mauro Bautista
> Middle-school bilingual education coordinator

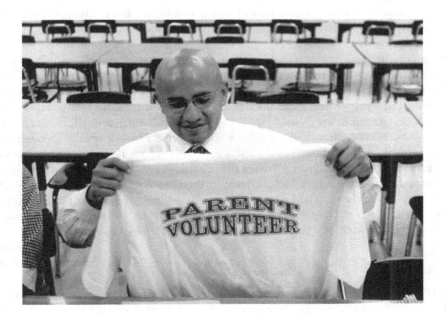

Schools Meeting Families' Needs

One hundred years ago, approximately 2 million American children lived in poverty. Today the number exceeds 15.5 million—about 21 percent of the population, or one in every five children—placing the United States behind most other developed nations.[11] Then and now, educators seek ways to respond to the multiple challenges poor children and their families face.

In the early 1900s, reformers advocated for public schools becoming "social centers" that would provide social and educational services to the broader community. Social reformers appealed to mainstream community interests and established programs that brought some relief to the urban poor, many of whom faced significant oppression. Cities were polluted, unhealthy, dangerous, and congested, and residents had few common spaces to gather. Throughout the Northeast, schools and other public buildings in urban centers began keeping their doors open for recreational and educational activities, sometimes dispensing health information and care, food and clothing, and perhaps job information.

This legacy of service is visible in today's schools. Many schools serving low-income communities offer children, but rarely adults, before- and after-school recreation programs, and perhaps government-subsidized breakfast and lunch, as well. Often, school faculties, public health officials, social workers, and police officers join in helping students in various kinds of trouble or need. Sometimes teachers make home visits or lead activities at community centers to get a better sense of students' lives and to disseminate information and resources in the community.

Such services—even when appreciated—have often reflected problematic perspectives about those being served. At the start of the twentieth century, more affluent members of society saw poor and immigrant city dwellers as helpless, needing charity, and a threat to the health, safety, economy, and morals of established citizens. Schools and social service agencies (such as orphanages and other community relief agencies) acted with a stern compassion that was closely tied to the interests and perspectives of the emerging middle class. One turn-of-the-century reformer declared that "society must, as a measure of self-protection, take upon itself the responsibility of caring for the child."[12]

Middle-class values and perspectives continue to mark many of the services provided by today's schools. Both compassion and self-interest guide the charity that schools and individuals dispense, particularly in socioeconomically diverse communities. For example, the second-grade teacher quoted earlier reported an anecdote reflecting just such a mix of motives.

> One mother approached me a number of times with concern about the cleanliness of a child in our class. It was true that Steven often came to school dirty, wearing the same or ripped clothes. This mother came into our classroom and, while I was occupied with a group of students, put a pair of new shoes on Steven's feet. Steven came up to me and said, "Look! Mrs. Wilson gave me new shoes!" Her behavior was totally unacceptable to me, considering the possible reaction Steven might get from his parents when he walked through the door in these gleaming new shoes. My experience with his parents made me worry about several things: Would his mom get angry when her son told her that another parent had given him the shoes, that other people had meddled in their business? Would she see this action as criticizing her for being a bad parent and provider? Would this action put Steven in a bad position? All kinds of scenarios entered my mind. While Mrs. Wilson might have meant this gesture in the kindest of ways, I saw potential for hurt feelings and conflict.
>
> —Name withheld
> First-year teacher, grade 2

Individual acts of charity are just that: individuals acting on behalf of other individuals—often providing critical, even lifesaving, help, but perhaps also offering only short-range assistance while diminishing others' dignity. When students (or parents) diminish the dignity of another child or family—as Mrs. Wilson might have unintentionally done in this instance—teachers bear some responsibility. In the above example, it would be crucial for the teacher to connect one-on-one with both parents, to help the gift-giving mother understand that she cannot just assume she has the right to give something to a child, publicly and without the parents' permission, and to help Steven's mother understand and exercise agency in relation to the gift. In an ideal situation, a teacher might broker a relationship between these two parents, though that is most likely a longer-range and potentially tricky goal.

Fortunately, an increasing number of schools and civic projects are exploring ways to make schools places where low-income families can access health and social services routinely and with dignity.

Comprehensive Services in Today's Schools

In 1994, researcher Joy Dryfoos published a book that was popular among school reformers: *Full-Service Schools: A Revolution in Health and Social Services for Children, Youth, and Families*.[13] Dryfoos documented a growing interest in formal collaborations among schools, social services, and health agencies to serve the multiple needs of low-income families. She argued that schools should coordinate the resources of families, communities, and social service agencies to meet students' academic, social, emotional, and health needs simultaneously.

Full-service community schools provide services such as child care, health care, nutrition, and counseling—crucial supports for both parents and children. Some full-service schools are part of national projects, like those affiliated with the Children's Aid Society, or city-wide efforts like the Community Schools Initiative in Chicago. Others, like the Molly Stark School in Bennington, Vermont, and Roses in Concrete in Oakland, California, are hyperlocal initiatives. However, all such schools enlist the aid of various community members and groups to provide health and social services for youth and their families, enabling educators to spend more time on teaching. Most are open for extended hours—before school, after school, on weekends, and during summers—and see themselves as family resource centers.

COMER SCHOOLS

One of the most fully developed and longest-running strategies for creating full-service schools is the School Development Program, created by psychiatrist James Comer. Recalling his own childhood experience as an African American growing up in a community that, while poor, surrounded him with a safety net of watchful and caring adults, Comer has sought to re-create aspects of this experience for young people today. Arguing that urban decay over the last few decades has taken a heavy toll on such communities, Comer has given the school the role of the supportive community he remembers.

Comer's School Development Program proceeds from a set of key assumptions. First, given the variety and importance of children's earliest years, many come to school with developmental needs tied to "experience deficits." These experience deficits might derive, for example, from growing up in an environment with few written texts versus a "print-rich" environment, or having little opportunity to watch or practice peaceful problem solving. Second, although the School Development Program recognizes and addresses that *experience* deficits can inhibit development, it does not accept the *academic* deficit ideology that leads to tracking and lowered expectations for learning. Third, the program assumes that students can and are entitled to reach high levels of academic achievement. Fourth, it views academic learning as resting on a foundation in six critical areas of human development: physical, psychological, language, social, ethical, and cognitive. Fifth, following from the prior assumptions, the program shifts the onus of responsibility to schools for the provision of necessary experiences and supports. And, finally, it acknowledges that schools cannot meet this challenge alone and must mobilize other adults, including parents, to help meet students' developmental needs.

Therefore, under Comer's approach, parents, teachers, and administrators are coequal members of a school's Planning and Management Team, which develops a comprehensive school plan; sets academic, social, and community partnership goals; and coordinates school activities, including staff development. This team creates space for dialogue around teaching and learning and monitors progress to identify opportunities to refine and support the plan.

A Student and Staff Support Team, composed of the principal and staff members with expertise in child development and mental health (for example, counselors, social workers, psychologists, or nurses), promotes desirable social conditions and relationships. This team connects all the school's student services, facilitates the sharing of information and advice, addresses individual student needs, accesses resources outside the school, and develops prevention programs.

Finally, a Parent Team helps develop activities to support the school's social and academic programs. Studies of Comer Schools have found significant positive effects of the program on school climate, student attendance, and student achievement.[14]

21ST CENTURY COMMUNITY LEARNING

During the Clinton administration, the full-service community school movement gained considerable momentum because of its compatibility with the national agenda for education reform at the time. Following the examples set by Comer and similar community-school projects, the Clinton administration and private foundations gave support to rural and urban public schools that were working—or agreed to work—in collaboration with other public and nonprofit agencies, local businesses, postsecondary institutions, scientific and cultural agencies, and so on. As of 2017, these federal funds—plus over $1 billion from partnering organizations between 2006 and 2010 alone—have helped to establish 21st Century Community Learning programs for more than 1.6 million children and youth in over 11,500 school-based and community-based centers in all fifty states, the District of Columbia, and most U.S. territories.[15]

Because a central goal of the 21st Century Community Learning Initiative was to provide youth, parents, and community members with engaging and healthy activities in safe community settings, partnering schools typically stay open longer—providing space for homework centers, as well as other after-school and summer programs. Additional components might include a mix of intensive mentoring, academic tutoring and enrichment, violence prevention counseling, services for children and youth with disabilities, and activities such as chorus, band, art, and technology.

Proponents argue that these efforts, reauthorized for continued funding via the Every Student Succeeds Act in 2015, place community involvement where it should be—at the center—when it comes to raising and educating children. Although it is unclear whether 21st Century Community Learning programs are meeting all their goals, parents of participants were more likely to attend parent-teacher organization meetings, after-school events, and open houses and help with homework. These are positive outcomes on top of the by-default value of after-school and summer programs, which help working families keep their jobs *and* avoid exorbitantly high childcare costs. There is some evidence, as well, that students' regular participation helps to diminish achievement gaps, improve grades and behavioral outcomes, reduce school-day absences, and improve rates of homework completion.[16] Benefits like these pose an evidence-based challenge to claims, including those of President Donald Trump, that investments in such programs aren't cost effective and warrant being eliminated from the federal budget.

PROMISE NEIGHBORHOODS

While continuing support for the 21st Century Community Learning Initiative, the Obama administration also took comprehensive, community-based schooling one step further with Promise Neighborhoods. This federal initiative was inspired by the work of Geoffrey Canada. In 1997, Canada, an educator and activist, created the Harlem Children's Zone, a nonprofit, community-based organization that has grown into a comprehensive system of programs that serve 100 blocks of Central Harlem with the goal of keeping all the neighborhood's children on track through college and into jobs. Two principles of the Zone project are to support children's development as early in their lives as possible and to create a critical mass of adults around them who understand what it takes to help children succeed. At the center of the Zone are Promise Academy schools, which have longer school days and years (akin to the Expanded Learning Time reforms mentioned in Chapter 9). The Zone augments the schools' work with Baby College (a series of workshops for parents of children ages 0–3); all-day prekindergarten; health clinics and community centers for children and adults that are open after school, on weekends, and during the summer; youth violence prevention programs; social services to support families; and guidance around college admission and college-going success. Among the Zone's accomplishments is a 96 percent college acceptance rate across its programs in 2016.[17]

Promise Neighborhoods are envisioned as a seamless environment of services created by public schools in partnership with public and nonprofit agencies. The goal is for whole communities to support children from birth through K–12 to college and career. By 2017, more than forty Promise Neighborhood communities in over twenty states and the District of Columbia were using federal grants to begin building "cradle-to-career" educational programs and family and community supports.

The Promise Neighborhood concept is so holistically persuasive that many communities are moving to develop similar projects on their own. Its component features are also being taken up more broadly, as with the emphasis on universal and more intensive prekindergarten for all children. An essential component of Promise Neighborhoods and other community-based approaches, extending access to early learning has a strong research base. Not only do reforms like universal prekindergarten contribute to individual students' well-being and long-term academic success; they also increase the likelihood that every community's children will have the chance to fulfill their inherent promise as learners.[18]

INDIVIDUAL TEACHERS REACHING OUT

Although it's far easier for teachers to support their students' broader set of needs when their schools encourage that support, many teachers make strong contributions on their own. One first-year mathematics teacher, for example, found his teaching role entirely compatible with his care and concern for students and their families. As he brought resources from his own family and personal networks to bear on the needs of his students' and their families, he not only felt fulfilled by the assistance he was able to provide but also recognized how connecting with families around the issues that need addressing in their lives can build the kind of trusting relationships that will also fortify students' learning long-term.

> My wife, a law student, and I visited a student's family to discuss immigration paperwork. They truly appreciate that we are trying to help them gain legal residency in the United States. Our conversation ends with so much appreciation and warmth. After we shake hands or kiss each other on the cheek and exchange genuine words of thanks and love, we walk away with mutual trust, or what Luis Moll more meaningfully calls "confianza." I look

forward to building more of these trusting relationships as I become a more experienced teacher.

—Name withheld
First-year teacher, high school mathematics

Across the country and each day, individual teachers connect with families and communities in myriad ways to support them as they navigate complicated social processes such as obtaining health care and social services, negotiating the juvenile justice system, and grappling with immigration regulations. And as issues like immigration become more contentious, and schools become more explicitly politicized spaces, many teachers are working even more collaboratively with families to protect the rights of all students to an equal education.

Service, Power, and Deficits

Often, service-oriented schools, programs, and individual efforts involve energetic, even heroic attempts to empower families. And yet something is missing or awry in many of these efforts. It has to do with the oxymoron—the contradictory concept—of *empowering others*. This concept of empowerment seems to presume that one party has little or no power until it is bestowed by another. Thus, the concept can communicate the exact opposite of what it supposedly intends, since "giving" power reinforces the idea that the giver is more powerful (and can also take away or *dis*empower).

For these and other reasons, some people associate service-providing models with deficit views of students, families, and communities. Bridge building offers an alternative—and, we think, more productive—metaphor and model.

Bridging the Cultures of Schools and Families

Whereas "service" and "empowerment" are directional—that is, they typically flow from those who *have* to those who *need*—"bridge" implies no such direction. A bridge does not guarantee a two-way flow of respect, of valuing one another's cultures, and of mutual adaptability, but it can allow these processes and dispositions to thrive. Recognizing individuals' and communities' assets, strengths, and beauty does not mean that one is blind to their needs or their flaws. Likewise, recognizing that parents have enormous competence does not mean that they automatically have the resources or power to act on behalf of their children when faced with complicated school structures and bureaucracies in addition to their everyday challenges. This is why "bridging" matters so much.

"Bridging," as we are using it here, emphasizes the mutual respect, collegiality, reciprocity, and sense of belonging that teachers can develop within their school communities.

Learning With and From Communities

This idea that every community, no matter how challenged, has valuable assets that deserve recognition and preservation can be traced in part back to the work of nineteenth- and twentieth-century education activists.

Addams's settlement house, for example, built on and developed the strengths of immigrant cultures. Hull House provided much-needed services, care for children and nursing for the sick. But, simultaneously, it hosted dozens of classes, and clubs met with the goal of maintaining immigrants' home cultures while easing them into knowledge of American ways and language.

The work of Addams and others represents the importance of moving beyond charity to provide services to those "less fortunate." Rather than pitying, fearing, or treating immigrant neighbors with a detached professionalism, Addams worked *with* them—work that strengthened her belief in social equality as an essential foundation for community life and human expression. Hers became a project rooted in a sense of solidarity as much as service. As a result, Hull was a place where community members could strengthen their own lives and the life of the community.

Contemporary educational philosopher Nel Noddings would probably say that Addams's approach embodies an "ethic of care," in contrast to the "ethic of service" that drives many schools' interactions with families, especially in low-income communities. Importantly, an ethic of care expects all participants to understand the conditions that affect them, even if this understanding exposes the faults of local institutions such as schools, law enforcement, social services, and so forth. Caring teachers and administrators, therefore, listen carefully and act respectfully in response to knowledge they acquire about the experiences, meanings, and preferences of community members. This steers educators away from common, deficit-laced judgments about families and communities.

Education scholar Angela Valenzuela has explored care as it relates to the schooling of Mexican immigrant students. She identifies as crucial the concept of *educación*, an education rooted in caring relationships and school content that affirms cultural worth. By not attending to relationships and culture, Valenzuela explains, schools and teachers can end up subtracting students' cultural wealth from them, rather than adding to their already-rich cultural repertoire. This *subtractive* effect, she proposes, diminishes the strength of students' greatest learning assets. Respectful communication between school and home; teachers who are knowledgeable about students' languages, cultures, and communities; and opportunities for authentic interactions among teachers, students, and families can all help dismantle subtractive schooling and establish more "additive" schooling practices.[19]

Learning from families and community members enhances teachers' capacity to care, but care is not only about "knowing"; it requires "doing" as well. W. E. B. Du Bois addresses this crucial element of care. In his landmark 1935 article, "Does the Negro Need Separate Schools?" Du Bois argued:

> The proper education of any people includes sympathetic touch between teacher and pupil; knowledge on the part of the teacher, not simply of the individual taught, but of his surroundings and background, and the history of his class and group; such contact between pupils, and between teacher and pupil, on the basis of perfect social equality, as will increase this sympathy and knowledge.[20]

With his notion of *sympathetic touch*, Du Bois captures three qualities of care that, taken together, bridge schools and communities. First, an empathetic understanding allows educators to know the experiences and aspirations of those for whom they care. Second, because understanding alone is not enough, educators must act in ways that respond to their understanding. Finally, "surroundings and background" and history are not simply artifacts of the past but a scaffold and guide for the future. Caring teachers support students and families to draw on their communities' histories and social circumstances as resources for building their futures.

Few comprehensive school and community engagement projects evoke images of *educación* or establish conditions for teachers to exercise the kind of *sympathetic touch* Du Bois advocated. Schools like Chula Vista Learning Community Charter School, featured in Focal Point 9.7, and El Puente Academy for Peace and Justice, featured in Focal Point 11.1, represent powerful but rare exemplars. Nevertheless, many teachers, on their own and with the support of like-minded colleagues, accomplish much via the relationships they develop and the lessons they teach.

Focal Point 11.1
El Puente Academy for Peace and Justice

Luis Garden Acosta and a group of community activists who were concerned about poverty and violence in one Brooklyn, New York, neighborhood founded the community organization called El Puente in 1982. In 1993, the organization created a small school—El Puente Academy for Peace and Justice—for local youth. El Puente, which means "the bridge" in Spanish, bridges the arts, health, environment, and education; it also bridges school and community. The school serves mostly Latinx students, many of whom qualify for free and reduced lunch. Four-year graduation rates are high, exceeding those of comparable schools in the city, as are indicators of a collaborative school culture and trust among teachers, students, and parents.[21]

The school shares a mission with the community organization that created it: to nurture leadership for peace and justice. Much of this mission is realized through thematic, arts-infused, interdisciplinary, project-based learning. Students take elective arts courses that are based on an overarching school-wide theme. Themes at the academy have included biodiversity, technology, and empowerment. One project, for example, examined the history and role of the Domino Sugar plant, located just four or five blocks away from the school. Another focused on health in the community. Principal Héctor Calderón explains how these projects exemplify the school's mission:

> At one point Domino Sugar distributed 50 percent of the United States' sugar. It was refined right at this plant. Many of the parents of the young people who came here worked at some point or another at Domino Sugar. . . . We looked at the history of sugar and how it came from Europe and the history of slavery—to create something rich and profound as a subject of study.
>
> We looked at the implications of sugar. If I was a chemistry teacher, I was looking at the composition of sugar and the chemical structures that make up sugar. History teachers looked at the history of slavery in the sugar plantations in the Caribbean and throughout the South. The health class looked at the effects of sugar, particularly in the crisis of obesity. The economics teacher was looking at . . . the Domino sugar factory and their use of labor in this country, the wages that people get paid, and who got to work there. Students did a lot of oral history projects with former Domino workers.
>
> All these ideas and projects culminated in an outdoor performance at our community garden where we re-created a lot of these things, the history of sugar, the effects of sugar. It became a carnival-like procession . . . performed through the streets of the community. The whole community came out. . . . It was a great way of bridging the community and the work that we were doing. All the integrated arts projects have that as a final component. . . .
>
> This year the project is health. As part of that we're looking at Radiac Research Corporation . . . a low-level nuclear waste disposal plant, the only one in New York State—a block away from the school. If anything were to ever happen in that place, it would release a toxic cloud that would engulf all of Williamsburg and parts of lower Manhattan. We want to stop the permit this year for Radiac operating the plant on the waterfront.
>
> Williamsburg reads like a "Who's Who of Environmental Hazards." We have the Williamsburg Bridge, we have the Brooklyn-Queens Expressway, where cars are constantly emitting

carbon monoxide into the air. We also have a nuclear plant right here. Every year, one project we do is to measure the level of particulates, and students look at the health effects....Asthma is a huge issue in this community. Through the Community Health and Environment Group, which is an organizing arm of El Puente, our students are doing surveys....We count within a 10-block radius and identify many families as having asthma....We try to provide extra services to those families. Biology takes on another dimension for our students when they're studying the respiratory system and ...asthma and how it affects that population.

One of the things that the health coordinator at El Puente did was help students look at the Dominican and Puerto Rican populations....We found out that there is a higher incidence of asthma in Puerto Ricans. Then we tried to find out why that was. We looked at natural remedies that Dominicans use that may not be as prevalent in the Puerto Rican population. We had a whole presentation....It was the first time that a community-based organization's work was published in a medical journal....

A lot of schools think they've done their mission if they educate kids who go to Harvard and become great at whatever they do. We want our kids to go to the best schools. We want them to have access to a great education. But we also ask the fundamental question:... For the sake of what are we educating our young people? It has to do with this sacred covenant that we have with the world around us. We have a moral and civil obligation to really make the world a better place. To me, the idea of social justice is not some pie-in-the-sky thing: It begins with our students. It begins in daily acts, in understanding the connection between what they learn in school and the community they live in. It begins in practical applications of their knowledge to better the world they live in.

Source: Adapted from Catherine Capellaro, "Bargaining for Better Schools: An Interview With Héctor Calderón," *Rethinking Schools*, 2005, www.rethinkingschools.org/special_reports/quality_teachers/beau194.shtml.

This asset-oriented part of work comes naturally for first-year teacher Martha Guerrero, who teaches in the same community where she was raised, and who takes personal pride in the resources she sees all around her.

> As I pass through my community day and night, I feel proud of the countless strengths and positive characteristics it has. I observe hard workers. I see people who have so much imagination. I see a beautiful culture. I see so much life.
>
> —Martha Guerrero
> First-year teacher, high school social studies

It may require, however, different kinds of hard work—and humility—from those who teach outside their home communities, like Kimberly Min, who became a teacher in a neighborhood quite different from the middle-class one where she grew up. In her view, doing the hard and humbling work to educate herself about the community and to connect authentically with its members has benefited her students, and her own family, too.

> I chose to teach at a school in the heart of South Los Angeles. When I told my friends and family where I was teaching, many were very concerned about my safety. My only response

was that I wanted to be in an area where they needed more credentialed teachers. In fact, this is not the safest place to be.

However, it is my school, and I love to teach here. Once I saw my students for the first time, my full concentration and energies were placed on them. I could set aside my anxiety about the school and focus on teaching. I began to explore the community. As a class, we took a walking field trip to the library and the fire station, which took us past the park, the banks, and stores. This was a part of the community I had never seen, and I felt more empowered by familiarizing myself with the area.

I visited students' homes. . . . My visits strengthened my communication with parents. I understood better how the conditions in their neighborhoods affected both children and parents. Parents explained their concerns about "gang bangers" down the street, the lack of "safe places" for their children to go, and their reasons for "no open windows or doors." . . . In spite of our cultural and ethnic differences we are together in wanting the best for the children that we share. . . .

Many families have lived in the area for generations. Many of my students' parents are graduates of the school. The roots of the community run deep, and the wisdom and love from the parents and grandparents I encounter give me a surge of energy and a sense of inclusion.

The people close to me—family and friends—who once thought so poorly about this community, have changed their perceptions as they see my work and hear my stories about what my students and school mean to me. I am not the only one growing from this experience.

—Kimberly Min
Third-grade teacher

Bridging Students' Multiple Worlds

Bridging the cultures of neighborhood and school is one of the joys of teaching. However, the bridge is not anchored in cement on two sides of a chasm; there are multiple bridges, and they are movable and flexible. Since educators are not necessarily more skilled at connecting with other people's communities than families and students are at connecting with schools, we need one another's help.

The mutual desire to bridge school and family is clear in the relationships that first-year teachers Mariana Pacheco, Zeba Palomino, and Benji Chang developed with parents.

Generally, Latinx parents hesitate to approach or question teachers because teaching is highly respected. I made myself very accessible and expressed my interest in their understanding bilingual education, student learning, and the importance of their voices in public education. I also built personal relationships, made phone calls and home visits. I reinforced their cultural beliefs but made them aware of certain characteristics that they might want to help their children develop. For example, during parent conferences, some parents were concerned with their child's tendency to talk excessively. Many times, I reminded them that in higher education, the willingness to initiate conversations, participation in group projects, and dialogue were required of students and highly valued. I told them about the endless number of oral presentations, speeches, and debates I had to deliver throughout my educational career. I emphasized that they should not discourage their child's talk, but that together we could empower their children by helping them be responsible in [their speech].

—Mariana Pacheco
First-year teacher, grade 2

Most of my immigrant students come from low-income families, with parents who speak little or no English, and who have little or no high school education. . . . This does not mean, however, that parents do not value education. They may simply not know how to get involved. For example, when I called parents to invite them to Back to School Night, quite a few were surprised and pleased to speak with a teacher in Spanish. The school had never contacted them before. They rely on their children to relay information about school, but often the students themselves do not have enough information about how to steer their education or they choose not to talk to their families about it. Therefore, my job is twofold: I must provide students with the support they need to learn math as they develop their English skills, and I must help students connect their home culture with their school culture so that they can understand and succeed.

—Zeba Palomino
First-year teacher, high school mathematics

From day one, I talked with parents and guardians outside of class, and sent home the first of my weekly home letters, explaining and requesting a home visit. . . . I forged stronger home-school connections and uncovered invaluable information that would shape my curriculum and instruction. . . . I communicated to parents and guardians that they were the experts on their child. . . . I used to picture collaboration with families as parents coming to class to help out or at least helping students with their schoolwork every day at home. I now realize that this model was shaped by my middle-class background. My model did not account for working-class families or families at the poverty level, where parents and other family members are always working and cannot "collaborate" with me. My old ideas did not account for families who do have time but do not understand assignments because they were not educated in English. Now I realize that there are many ways to collaborate. Although they may not come in the way that I expected, these collaborative relationships support students in powerful ways.

—Benji Chang
First-year teacher, grade 1

These three teachers, too, have gone beyond typical approaches to parent involvement to bridge their students' multiple worlds. They have gathered important knowledge that they use to design instruction that connects the official curriculum to students' experiences in the world, community, and home. Finding and solving real problems that matter to students—problems like those addressed routinely at a school like El Puente Academy for Peace and Justice (Focal Point 11.1) make schoolwork less abstract and detached. Other examples of bridging through curriculum are included in Chapter 6, where we discuss instructional tasks that are authentic (e.g., when students researched and then redesigned a nearby vacant lot) and that draw on families' "funds of knowledge" (e.g., when students interviewed parents about how to make a living).

Our own experience for nearly a decade with the Futures project in Southern California showed several ways that senior high school students and their families bridge the worlds of home and school to increase students' likelihood of going to college. The Futures project began when our research team joined with Anthony Collatos, then a local high school teacher and now a college professor, in developing a ninth-grade humanities class into a four-year pathway to college. Although the high school was diverse and included lots of middle-class White students, Anthony's class was made up entirely of low-income, underrepresented students, mostly Latino and African American.

Over four years, in addition to completing their college-preparatory coursework, the students joined UCLA researchers in studying issues relevant to their own high school experiences and future plans. They investigated questions of student resistance in high school, hip-hop and popular culture, and the influence of parents on education, as well as the influence of language on educational access. They examined patterns of school success and failure, including how students are tracked into different social and academic groups.

One summer, the students conducted research at the Democratic National Convention. This experience put them in contact with national and local leaders. Students interviewed community, political, and media leaders on topics like access to education, access to the media, the living wage movement, and urban civic engagement. This community-based work was supported by classroom study and research, and vice versa. The student-researchers presented their research numerous times to university faculty, graduate students, administrators, teachers, community members, and teachers in training.

The project also helped bridge the students' worlds of family and school. Monthly meetings, called "Futures and Families," brought families together to increase awareness of college pathways and, at the same time, eased parents' feelings of isolation from the school. These meetings, conducted in English and Spanish, included discussions about college admissions requirements and financial aid options, workshops on deciphering school transcripts, opportunities to research colleges on the Internet, and presentations by students and alumni of color, as well as school and university staff. Through the process, families became more aware of social and political obstacles to college, such as tracking and SATs, as well as useful strategies for addressing such obstacles. Perhaps most important, they learned that they were not alone in their goals and struggles.[22]

Bridging Through Community Liaisons

Projects like Futures would be far less likely to succeed were it not for the labor and love of community members themselves. In the case of Futures specifically, Tere Viramontes, a longtime community member and former parent at the high school, navigated homes, churches, and community organizations, as well as the school, far more deftly than any of us could have.

When schools involve community members in connecting families and schools, they are honoring and leveraging essential knowledge and relationships. Community members like Tere—and Gina Rodriguez and Miriam Rogers, profiled in Focal Point 11.2—have so much to contribute to teacher development, school change, and student learning.

Partnering With Families and Communities in Educational Activism

An activist approach to improving schools draws from the collective power of residents to solve public problems; this power to problem-solve comes from critically examining community issues and acting to address them. Parents and caregivers who are community activists can be especially effective in bringing socially just schooling to all of the neighborhood's children. Such activists are also uniquely well positioned to bridge families and schools. Those who have organized to promote social change do not see themselves as *em*powered by others; their empowerment is derived from their collective actions and "wins," whereby each successful activity informs and emboldens them. By contrast, typical school-controlled support projects may speak of empowering families, but they often place limits on that "power" if parents' goals differ from the school's agenda.

This fourth way of connecting with parents and communities is probably the least mainstream, the least understood, and the most worrisome to traditional educators—but it also has a long tradition in American schooling.

A Tradition of Parent Activism

Parent activism around education is not a recent phenomenon. It began more than a century ago, and its roots are found in what are now some of the most traditional parent organizations.

THE PTA

The forerunner of the PTA—the National Congress of Mothers—can be traced back to 1897. The Congress was founded to act on behalf of children in the home, at school, and in the world. From the beginning, this group's advocacy extended beyond having parents help with school-work or supporting their local schools. The early group voiced public concern over the juvenile justice system, the need for child labor laws, and the importance of federal aid to schools. It promoted cooperation between parents and teachers, advocated for sex education, and lobbied for a national health bureau. By the early 1900s, fathers were also urged to join.

Focal Point 11.2
Bridging Schools and Communities

Gina Rodriguez was born in Tijuana, Mexico. Her family immigrated to the United States when she was five. Gina eventually attended and graduated from college, where she majored in political science and was active in a Chicano political organization called MEChA that focuses on gaining access to quality education and other resources. Gina later became a facilitator and coach for both parents and teachers at her elementary school. There, she aided in strategic planning, goal setting, and gaining access to resources. She also helped bridge the language and cultural gaps between parents and teachers.

Gina helped parents to realize that they had a right to be involved in their children's education and supported them to create on the school's campus a parent center where parents met weekly and organized events and campaigns. In response to safety issues, for example, they organized for school uniforms. The school staff became more appreciative of their involvement both inside and outside the classroom. Parents' concerns and ideas were increasingly welcomed and taken seriously.

Parent leader Miriam Rogers served as a school-community liaison and as president of the African American Parents Group at her local school, which Rogers helped parents and teachers establish. In addition to promoting academic achievement, the group has strengthened relations between teachers and parents, fostered connections between the school's African American and Latinx parents and students, and provided a respectful setting where all voices could be heard.

The group extended the faculty's capacity to go beyond typical classroom curriculum. They provided information about historical and contemporary African American leaders and events. The group circulated a weekly newsletter, including a quote, a profile of an African American leader, and some key vocabulary pertaining to that leader's contribution. In addition, the group has offered students valuable opportunities to perform at events, like a Teacher Appreciation breakfast where youth read poetry and literature by African American writers. Rogers, a parent herself, has helped numerous students who were thought of as "problems" in the classroom to express themselves in a creative, positive light.

Source: Adapted from John Rogers and Carolyn Castelli, "Building Social Justice for New Generation," UCLA IDEA Occasional Paper, 1996.

In the early twentieth century, the PTA and the National Congress of Colored Parents and Teachers (the latter formed to serve children in segregated states) were well known for advocating for reforms in health, safety, and nutrition. By mid-century, they had secured health programs, school lunches, and regulations governing school bus safety. In the second half of the century, the groups (not integrated until the 1970s) addressed drug addiction, the effects of smoking, child protection and toy safety, violence on television, automobile safety belt and child restraint legislation, the circumstances of children and families in the inner cities, and HIV/AIDS education.

Today, the national PTA continues to take progressive stands on many of these issues and tries to have its membership reflect the changing demographics of the country.[23] On the other hand, local PTA groups are often far more conservative in their activities, content to raise money and solicit volunteers to help the school carry out its agenda. They are also susceptible to cliquishness and exclusivity and have been known to represent the interests and needs of some parents' children rather than all students in the community.

COMMUNITY SCHOOLS

A second long-standing activist tradition comes out of the community schools movement described earlier in this chapter. Broadly speaking, community schools began as local efforts to blur the distinction between communities and schools. Only recently has community activism around such schooling coalesced into national groups that support and inform one another's efforts. We discuss these more recent efforts in a later section of this chapter. For the most part, however, community schools have bucked the national century-long trend toward bureaucratic state and national education policies, and away from grassroots control.

It is not surprising that wherever one finds an emphasis on community activism, empowerment, improvement, and local control of schools, there is a good chance of finding political activism as well. In the early 1900s, many of the social centers developed to build community and address community needs also included political activities. Much of this—often to the consternation of the elites who supported these centers—focused on socialist causes and advocacy for minority political views.

During the Depression years, public schools purposefully began taking up social causes. The social reconstructionist curriculum movement, discussed in Chapter 3, argued strongly that schools should develop community-based curricula that engaged schools and students in bettering local conditions. For example, Leonard Covello's tenure as principal of a high school in East Harlem's immigrant community was marked by curricula designed to investigate and shape policies in the neighborhood, including a campaign for public housing.

By the late 1960s, community schools began to focus on local communities' power over the school itself. In the midst of social activism around civil rights and civil unrest in many cities, some local communities—particularly African American communities—sought to wrest control from the education professionals and politicians whom they viewed as part of an oppressive government that had frustrated the quest for equal educational opportunity.

The best-known example of the struggle for local control of schools took place in the Ocean Hill–Brownsville neighborhood of New York City. There, activists employed lessons about civil disobedience and power learned from the civil rights movement. Only direct community participation, these leaders believed, would allow schools to shift from being a source of inequality to being a solution to it. Only if local community members were involved in selecting school personnel and curriculum would the schools be accountable for shaping the next generation in ways that would advance the community itself.

Although the Ocean Hill–Brownsville experiment collapsed in the face of opposition from traditional power bases, including political interests, business, and unions, it sowed the seeds for a new type of parent and community activism. Today, low-income communities increasingly seek to hold schools accountable for providing high-quality education to their children. And while teachers and community members were clearly at odds in New York's struggle over who would control the schools, increasing numbers of teachers today are making common cause with activists in the communities where they teach.[24] In the twenty-first century, this new way of connecting with families and communities offers promise as a strategy for social justice school reform.

Contemporary Organizing for School Reform

Truly transformative teaching must be coupled with activism and resistance in the larger community. I have been involved with an activist organization that fights for equitable school reform. Such organizations represent opportunities to create meaningful alliances with other educators, parents, and students. It is not enough for me to encourage my students to become more active. I must walk the talk myself.

—Matthew Eide
First-year teacher, high school history

Community organizing, generally, can be defined as "the work that occurs in local settings to empower individuals, build relationships, and create action for social change."[25] It entails building relationships that can sustain people through difficult struggles and support political action. In the photo here, Mauro Bautista holds a flier distributed by Inner-City Struggle, a parent

group he supports in his school. The flier advertises a program that includes teachers and students from East Los Angeles advocating for better college preparation in local schools.

Grassroots community organizations are influenced by several traditions. Saul Alinsky's "self-interest"-based model is one of public confrontation between organized "have nots" and powerful, more advantaged "targets" whose concessions can provide solutions to community problems.

Other, less confrontational traditions come from women's work to extend caring into communities beyond the confines of families and home. For example, African American women maintained networks of communication and support during slavery; these were precursors for the courageous work of women like Fannie Jackson Coppin and Anna Julia Cooper and for the broader success of women's groups during the civil rights movement when they could transform those traditions and networks into a political force for social change. At the turn of the twentieth century, Jane Addams and her collaborators saw social networks, social services, and enrichment of community life as key to supplementing the protections afforded by families in low-income and immigrant neighborhoods. These feminist organizing traditions have contemporary counterparts in mobilization efforts for safer neighborhoods, affordable child care, and youth programs.

Despite their great variety, most community organizing efforts share the perspective that power for change exists within networks of people who identify with common ideals and who can engage in collective social action based on those ideals.[26] In the past decade, many local grassroots organizations—focused originally on issues of housing, jobs, and public safety—have turned their attention to school improvement.

Components of Community Organizing

Former civil rights and farmworker organizer Marshall Ganz distills grassroots organizing work into three core components: relationships, common understandings, and action. And, indeed, each of these helps create bridges among schools, families, and communities.

First, any authentic education organizing begins with considerable time spent talking to parents and educators. Within a culture of conversation, people form *relationships* based on common concerns. This might occur through, for example, a survey or "audit" in which community members identify school and community strengths and overlapping areas of interest and frustration. It might occur through "neighborhood walks" or "home visits" meant to extend conversation into the community, including parts that it might not reach on its own. It might occur by tapping into existing networks, such as churches or other community-based groups that already bring people together around common cause.

As relationships develop and deepen, so do norms of reciprocity; people learn that they can count on one another to keep commitments and work on one another's behalf. Individuals draw confidence and knowledge from these networks—resources often described as social capital—and, in turn, contribute to their power. This power can begin to create a counterbalance to that of traditional power brokers, who might include voters, wealthy people, "old boy" networks, and so forth. When families from minoritized communities speak with a unified voice, they often have more success in grabbing and holding the attention of people who exert control over schools, neighborhoods, cities, states, and so on. In this way, an organized community's collective voice becomes its power base, and its power, exercised on behalf of all children, fuels social action.

In addition to reciprocity and collective voice, leadership development is another key aspect of relationship and power building. As networks grow and mature, initial organizers often intentionally yield to others, so the responsibility for solving problems becomes more shared. For this reason, many organizing efforts involve apprenticeship-like experiences intended to grow new leaders from within.

Common understandings—a second key feature of community organizing—develop as people engage in dialogue and generate hopeful alternatives. The dialogic pedagogy developed by Paulo Freire in his work with Brazilian peasants, described in Chapter 3, is probably the best example of such generative dialogue. Participants are not rushed into accepting others' descriptions, analyses, and solutions; instead, they build and rebuild their understandings while adding to the knowledge and insights of others. They construct a shared story of who they are, what they do, and why they do it. Through this collective effort, individual problems are reframed as community, social, or collective problems, which strengthens collective identity and agency. No longer helpless against insurmountable odds, community members often experience a growing sense of power over their futures.

Third, an *activist* community emerges when groups pursue a particular objective—perhaps small at first. The group might act on a grievance long held by individuals but newly articulated as a jointly held claim, and members might strategize together about how to use the group's resources to achieve its goals. These focused campaigns achieve what the community might call tangible "progress," but they also develop the community itself and increase its capacity to take on larger goals.

Together, relationships, common understandings, and collective action enable communities to gain and use new resources. Organizer Ernesto Cortes has seen this happen firsthand in successful education justice organizing efforts:

> When parents and community members are truly engaged, they are organized to act on their own values and visions for their children's future. They do not just volunteer their time for school activities or drop their opinions in the suggestion box. They initiate action, collaborating with educators to implement ideas for reform. This kind of engagement can only happen through community institutions—public schools, churches, civic associations. These institutions provide the public space where people of different backgrounds connect with one another, listen to each other's stories, share concerns; this is where they argue, debate, and deliberate. In these institutions, individuals transcend the boundaries of their private lives to form public relationships. In the context of these public relationships, parents and community members can initiate conversations around their core concerns and values. These conversations go beyond the discussion of surface problems and complaints. Through these conversations, people develop the trust and consensus needed for action.[27]

Parents and community members are not the only ones transformed by such community organizing endeavors; teachers, too, have experienced their transformative power. Education professor Dennis Shirley's book, *Valley Interfaith and School Reform: Organizing for Power in South Texas*, offers some examples. In it, Shirley profiles an elementary school that was able, through organizing, to fuse civic engagement and improved student outcomes. The school's teachers were essential to this effort and were changed by it; they came to see themselves as researchers and intellectuals in partnership with parents and community members. About this transformation, teachers at Sam Houston Elementary wrote:

> No, we have not always taught this way. First, we had many conversations with Valley Interfaith organizers. . . . Those conversations got us to think about relationships and power. We recognized that we did not have relationships to the parents that were meaningful for the overall achievement of the students. The more we thought about it, the more we realized that we needed to change. . . . We started to deal with issues that were important to our parents.

The issues were serious ones—safety and others. . . . Today we find that working in isolation like so many teachers is not for us. We find that collaborating with each other is more effective for student learning. We now believe that education is the responsibility of the teacher, but also administrators, parents, and community members. This belief has encouraged us to involve parents as well as the community in the education of their children. We discovered that parents have so much to contribute. We have learned so much from each other.[28]

Community and parent activism for better schools has been on the rise in recent decades. Community-based organizations working on education reform have improved the safety of school facilities and successfully advocated for increasing the equity of school and district policies and practices. They have supported young people, parents, and community members to win seats on school boards and other local decision-making bodies and to make demands of elected officials at all levels of the system. They have helped increase awareness of educational injustice.[29]

Focal Point 11.3 presents highlights from the successful education organizing efforts of Padres y Jóvenes Unidos, a group that has been working to bring about change in and beyond their local school district. Similar efforts are under way and growing nationwide.

Focal Point 11.3
Padres y Jóvenes Unidos

Padres Unidos was born out of a struggle at Valverde Elementary School in Denver, Colorado, where parents removed a principal for refusing to stop the practice of punishing Mexican children by forcing them to eat their lunches from the cafeteria floor. In 1992, after a year of organizing and successfully replacing the administrative leadership at Valverde, parents determined that it was necessary to build off their experience and work with other parents in dealing with similar issues within Denver Public Schools. Parents from all over the district were calling Valverde parents for guidance, advice, and support. With no office, staff, or money, Padres Unidos was formed by parents willing to organize for educational justice, equity, and excellence in Denver Public Schools.

Padres Unidos has evolved into a multi-issue, statewide organization led by people of color who work for educational excellence, racial justice for youth, immigrant rights, and quality health care for all. Jóvenes Unidos, the youth initiative of Padres Unidos, emerged as young people became active in reforming their schools, ending the school-to-jail track, and organizing for immigrant student rights. Both Padres and Jóvenes Unidos build power to challenge the root cause of discrimination, racism, and inequity by exposing the economic, social, and institutional basis for injustice as well as developing effective strategies to realize meaningful change.

The following are just a few highlights from the group's successful activism over the years:

*   2017—Jóvenes Unidos hosts a rally, partners with other organizations, and offers public comment to encourage the adoption of a "Sanctuary Schools" resolution that will protect the rights of undocumented students in schools citywide and statewide.
*   2014—Jóvenes Unidos present a middle-school improvement plan to the Denver School Board, with a focus on how proposed reforms will impact students of color.
*   2012—Jóvenes Unidos releases a health justice report focused on nutrition, food access, and physical activity in Denver public schools, offering recommendations that will increase equitable access to health citywide.

- 2010–2011—Jóvenes Unidos members educated over 256,000 people through radio, fliers, and face-to-face outreach and presentations on the urgent need to organize and join our legislative campaign to end the School-to-Jail Track in Colorado.
- 2010—Jóvenes Unidos organized a student walkout of over 2,000 to protest Arizona's SB 1070 and demand passage of the DREAM Act and Comprehensive Immigration Reform.
- 2009—Helped bring to Denver a Cesar Chavez Academy, a culturally rich and high-performing school with a proven track record of preparing students for college.
- 2008—Won new district discipline policies that focus on keeping students in school and learning, and won the introduction of a Restorative Justice program.
- 2007—Won new graduation requirements that prepare all students for college by aligning high school graduation requirements to college entrance requirements.
- 2005—Released "Education on Lockdown," a groundbreaking report on the impact of zero-tolerance practices on low-income communities of color, and called for reform.
- 2004—Jóvenes Unidos surveyed over half the student body of North High School and published a groundbreaking report in which students called for drastic change.
- 2002—Participated in a movement to protect bilingual education and immigrant rights in Colorado by defeating Ron Unz's anti-bilingual ballot, Amendment 31.
- 2001—Parents helped create and open Academia Ana Marie Sandoval, a dual-language/Montessori elementary school.
- 1998—After a student was arrested at Lincoln High School and later deported, a practice that is against the law, parents organized for his return and won reforms changing the relationship between INS and the school district.
- 1997—Removed a police substation at Horace Mann Middle School and its principal for telling students what would happen to them when (not if) they went to prison.
- 1996—Helped organize over 5,000 students to walk out of school and protest substandard education for Latino students in Denver Public Schools.

Source: Slightly adapted from Padres y Jóvenes Unidos/Parents and Youth United, *History and Accomplishments*, http://padresunidos.org/history-accomplishments/.

PARENTS PARTICIPATING IN PEDAGOGY AND POLICY

Former math teacher Dr. Laila Hasan, now a teacher educator at the University of Southern California, has implemented an approach to parent organizing that combines the principles of community organizing with helping parents gain an understanding of high-quality teaching and learning.

Hasan worked specifically with parents in low-income neighborhoods where schools were characterized by large numbers of underqualified teachers, high turnover among school administrators, and limited curriculum offerings. Starting with a ten-week seminar, Hasan and twenty-plus parents examined the practices at their children's schools. Teachers played a key role, coming to meetings to model high-quality instruction. Parents had the chance to become "students" during these experiences, many of which were their first with high-quality teaching and learning in academic subjects. In both English and Spanish, teachers guided parents through a writer's workshop, laboratory experiments, algebraic thinking, and historical inquiry. Parents also learned about standardized testing, as well as grading and tracking practices.

Through this process, parents learned what to look for when observing in classrooms. They compared what they learned in the seminar with what was occurring in their children's classrooms. They had the chance to practice asking hard questions of teachers and administrators. As culminating projects, they designed and carried out action research that included other parents at their school sites and then advocated for high-quality teaching and learning in the community's schools.

Throughout this experience, relationship building remains at the fore. Parents construct new identities for themselves, grounded in their knowledgeable analyses of their own children's educational opportunities. Those analyses, in turn, become the engine of their activism. In this sense, the project engages parents as the initiators and core facilitators of their own involvement.

With over 300 program graduates, the project's modest beginnings developed into a significant activist presence. The original group of parents started its own nonprofit, community-based organization. One participating mother soon afterward won an election for a seat on the school board, and many project members now hold influential positions on school leadership committees. Through the efforts of the group and its "ripple effect" out beyond itself, some overcrowded schools that had been operating on alternative schedules returned to traditional academic calendars, adding seventeen days to the school year for students enrolled there.[30]

The theory at work in the project and its offshoots, as in other education organizing efforts, is that parent advocacy must be based on a good understanding of pedagogy and policy. As parents come to know what socially just education looks like for their children and what their rights are as parents, they are likely to set out and succeed in accomplishing much-needed change for their own children and all the children in their community.

PARENTS FOR PUBLIC SCHOOLS

Organizers like Ernesto Cortes and educators like Laila Hasan have worked almost exclusively with parents of color in low-income communities. That's not surprising, since theirs are the neighborhoods where parents often feel most alienated by schools and where activism for school improvement is most desperately needed. There are, however, some notable examples of cross-class and cross-race organizing efforts for school reform. One is Parents for Public Schools (PPS), which began as a local initiative in 1989 in Jackson, Mississippi. A group of twenty parents decided to mobilize parents who reflected the full diversity of their town to build strong public schools and a healthier, more vital community out of their southern city that had been badly torn by school segregation, desegregation, and White flight.

The Jackson group began by recruiting families one by one. Through information sessions in their homes, they began to articulate their belief that a stronger public system was important to their city. Over time, PPS brought racial balance to four primary schools in northeastern Jackson and promoted a $35 million bond issue—the first to pass since desegregation.

Soon after the Jackson victory—which was featured in the national news media—parents in other communities began forming PPS chapters, and the organization now has eighteen chapters in sixteen states. While individual chapter activities and goals vary, all are committed to public school enrollment, meaningful parent and community involvement, and district-wide improvement.

What's particularly striking is that the first PPS chapter brought parents together across race and class lines to combat White, middle-class flight from the public schools and to publicize the economic, social, and business development benefits that come to cities with strong public schools. In other cities—large and small, urban and rural—PPS chapters have addressed school safety, built racial and economic bridges, improved facilities, expanded and strengthened curricula, and increased positive media coverage. The groups believe that parents must become committed owners of, rather than passive consumers in, public schools. Moreover, PPS members commit to advocate for the improvement of public education for every child, not just their own.

Another example is United Opt Out, profiled in Chapter 7, through which parents are working to help educate their counterparts nationwide about the right to opt their children out of mandated standardized testing, and also working to catalyze a broad movement to reduce the role of testing in schools. A third is the Network for Public Education, which brings parents together with representatives from other stakeholder groups strongly committed to preserving public education in the face of increasing corporate intervention in and privatization of schooling. Yet another example is the Alliance to Re-claim Our Schools (AROS), a coalition of parent, youth, community, and labor organizations that together represent over 7 million people nationwide. Its eleven chapters work together on an ambitious national campaign "The Schools All Our Children Deserve." The campaign advocates for the following:

- Billions of dollars for public schools in black and brown communities
- Qualified teachers, relevant curriculum and social and health care services—what we call "Sustainable Community Schools"
- Positive discipline policies and an end to zero-tolerance
- An end to high-stakes tests that are used to punish schools, teachers and students, and more time for teaching and learning
- An end to the expansion of unaccountable charter schools
- A real commitment to parent and educator leadership and democratic process.[31]

THE TRUTH ABOUT PARENT TRIGGER

When it comes to parent and community activism, a few recent policies warrant special mention. In 2010, for example, California passed a law establishing a "parent trigger" option, which allows parents to force major reforms at local, low-performing public schools. To "pull the trigger" on a school, half of the parent population served by the school (or by parents whose children attend feeder schools) must sign a petition in support of the changes. Efforts in California to use this legal provision have generated significant controversy—including claims of misinformation, intimidation, or coercion of local parents. Many have raised concerns about external forces (like pro–charter school organizations) swaying parent input. For example, the organization Parent Revolution, which has been involved in pro-trigger organizing, draws most of its annual budget from contributions it receives via the Gates Foundation, Walton Family Foundation, Broad Foundation, and other philanthropic entities with pro-privatization agendas. Despite the organizing support and funding, California has seen no real track record of successful school turnarounds. Nevertheless, other states—including Louisiana, Mississippi, Connecticut, Indiana, Texas, and Ohio—have shown interest in or implemented similar laws, with mixed results.

Many have concluded that the push to close low-performing public schools takes precedence over supporting school improvement efforts. In Chicago, for example, coalitions of educators and parents have long claimed that the district ignores students, parents, teachers, and community members who oppose school closures and instead listens to corporate investors, charter organizations, and for-profit school management entities.

These local realities—and their resonance with those faced elsewhere, as in New Orleans's Lower Ninth Ward (Focal Point 9.6)—are part of what has led Southside community organizer Jitu Brown to spearhead a nationwide effort, the Journey for Justice (J4J) Alliance, that brings together under one mantle and shared mission pro–public education organizing efforts in twenty-four different cities. J4J's members include community, youth, and parent-led organizations whose members are "not fooled by the illusion of school choice"[32] extended to them in recent years and on the horizon under the current Trump administration. They point to the last two decades of reform—and the disproportionately negative impacts those reforms have had on urban, low-income neighborhoods—as evidence that mainstream corporate interests have been allowed to supersede concern for children and communities, particularly children and communities of color.

J4J is actively working to aggregate the power that grassroots organizations have been building in their respective cities. This, Jitu Brown and others believe, is what holds promise for advancing justice in the face of outsize corporate influence.

TEACHERS AS PARTNERS IN ACTIVISM

Teachers are rarely leaders of these organizing approaches to parent and community involvement in education. Yet, increasingly, teachers like those featured in this book are becoming more involved. They are reaching out to parents and community members and helping to seed education organizing. Likewise, community organizations are reaching out to them and asking them to add their voices and their power to that of parents who are striving to ensure that their children (and *all* children) receive an excellent, socially just education. Many teachers have also discovered that the strategies of community organizing—building relationships, forging common meanings about teaching and learning, and acting together—present powerful methods that they can use in forging alliances with parents and with colleagues, too. First-year teacher Martha Guerrero describes how she integrates such activities into her work as a teacher.

> I am not new to East Los Angeles. I have established a relationship with the community as an organizer. I hope that the relationships that I cultivate with my students and parents will allow me to organize community members in the future. I believe that teachers should develop these genuine relationships with the community to make changes in the educational and political system.
>
> I interact frequently with my students and their families outside of the classroom. I take my students to conferences and work with them on community-related issues. I helped organize [one conference] with the theme "Rights Now Youth Conference: Speaking Truth to Power." At the conference students attended workshops related to education and the criminal justice system. We also attended a Coalition for Educational Justice conference that focused on overcrowding in inner-city schools and high-stakes standardized testing.
>
> —Martha Guerrero
> First-year teacher, high school social studies

Whose Agenda Is It?

When people who are in charge want to preserve existing power relationships, they may use the phrase *getting buy-in*. That means they employ strategies, incentives, arguments, and information to find support for their established agenda. When people who are not in charge of schools want to participate fully in changing school-as-usual, they need to make their voices and their numbers heard. That means they organize.

An organizing approach to parent engagement stems from and leads to recognizing that schools belong to low-income parents and communities of color as much as they do to wealthier, White ones. Such organizing is often an uphill battle. But it is ultimately neither respectful nor effective for educators to ignore the power that families and communities possess as advocates for their children. Community members like Gina Rodriguez, organizers like Ernesto Cortes, educators like Laila Hasan, and coalitions like J4J, along with individual teachers like Martha Guerrero, have all developed strategies for supporting parents to speak with confidence and power about what they want for their own children and for all the community's children, just as the parents of high-status children so often do.

Educators must do more than express their willingness to meet at the same table with parents of different racial groups and socioeconomic positions. Just talking isn't enough. People at the table must learn from one another. And then they must act—together.

None of this means that there is no longer a legitimate role for professional educators. To the contrary, even the most activist parents do not easily develop the knowledge and pedagogical expertise that we've outlined in this book as essential to high-quality and socially just education. That knowledge and expertise is part of what professional educators bring to the table, and it has an essential role to play in making sure that all voices are represented and heard in ways that advance good teaching, a healthy school culture, excellent academic outcomes, a safe community, and other aspects of a socially just education.

Digging Deeper and Tools for Critique

www.routledge.com/cw/teachingtochangetheworld

Notes

1 A 2005 California study found that although efforts by schools to reach out to parents contribute to school success, these activities did not predict higher school achievement scores as strongly as four key school practices: implementing a coherent, standards-based curriculum; analyzing student assessment data from multiple sources; ensuring instructional resources; and prioritizing student achievement—practices we described in earlier chapters. EdSource, *Similar Students, Different Results: Why Do Some Schools Do Better?* (Sacramento, CA: EdSource, 2005), www.edsource.org/pub_abs_simstu05.cfm.

2 For a review of this research, see Joyce Epstein, Lucretia Coates, Karen C. Salinas, Mavis G. Sanders, and Beth S. Simon, *School, Family, and Community Partnerships: Your Handbook for Action* (Thousand Oaks, CA: Corwin Press, 1997); and Ronald F. Ferguson, "Toward Skilled Parenting and Transformed Schools: Inside a National Movement for *Excellence With Equity*," paper prepared for the *First Educational Equity Symposium of the Campaign for Educational Equity, at Teachers College*, Columbia University, New York, October 24 and 25, 2005, www.tc.columbia.edu/centers/EquitySymposium/symposium/resourceDetails. asp?Presid=10.

3 Roberto Suro, "Cavazos Criticizes Hispanics on Schooling," *New York Times*, April 11, 1990, B8.

4 Christopher John Farley, "What Bill Cosby Should Be Talking About," *Time*, June 3, 2004, www.time.com/time/nation/article/0,8599,645801,00.html.

5 "Obama's Father's Day Speech Urges Black Fathers to Be More Engaged in Raising Their Children," *Huffington Post*, June 15, 2008, www.huffingtonpost.com/2008/06/15/obamas-fathers-day-speech_n_107220.html.

6 Guadalupe Valdez, *Con Respecto: Bridging the Distances Between Culturally Diverse Families and Schools* (New York: Teachers College Press, 1996); Angela Valenzuela, *Subtractive Schooling: U.S.-Mexican Youth and the Politics of Caring* (Albany: State University of New York Press, 1999); Ricardo Stanton-Salazar, *Manufacturing Hope and Despair: The School and Kin Support Networks of U.S.-Mexican Youth* (New York: Teachers College Press, 2001).

7 Nancy Gibbs, "Parents Behaving Badly," *Time*, February 21, 2005.

8 For a more complete discussion of this issue, see Amy Wells and Irene Serna, "The Politics of Culture: Understanding Local Political Resistance to Detracking in Racially Mixed Schools," *Harvard Educational Review* 66, no. 1 (1996): 93–118.

9 Jan Nespor, "Networks and Contexts of Reform," *International Journal of Educational Change* 3 (2002): 365–382; Jeannie Oakes and Martin Lipton, "Struggling for Educational Equity in Diverse Communities: School Reform as Social Movement," *International Journal of Educational Change* 3 (2002): 383–406; Joan Talbert, "Professionalism and Politics in High School Teaching Reform," *International Journal of Educational Change* 3 (2002): 277–281; Valerie Strauss, "Why So Many Parents Are Freaking Out About Common Core Math," *The Washington Post*,

November 8, 2014, https://www.washingtonpost.com/news/answer-sheet/wp/2014/11/08/why-so-many-parents-are-freaking-out-about-common-core-math/?utm_term=.15b22d25a6f4.

10 This case is described in Jeannie Oakes, Karen Hunter Quartz, Steve Ryan, and Martin Lipton, *Becoming Good American Schools: The Struggle for Civic Virtue in Education Reform* (San Francisco: Jossey-Bass, 2000).

11 U.S. Census Bureau, *Income and Poverty in the United States*, 2014, www.census.gov/.

12 John Spargo, *The Bitter Cry of Children* (New York: Macmillan, 1906), 119.

13 Joy Dryfoos, *Full-Service Schools: A Revolution in Health and Social Services for Children, Youth and Families* (San Francisco: Jossey-Bass, 1994).

14 See, for example, Geoffrey D. Borman, Gina M. Hewes, Laura T. Overman, and Shelly Brown, "Comprehensive School Reform and Achievement: A Meta-Analysis," *Review of Educational Research* 73, no. 2 (2003): 125–230.

15 Afterschool Alliance, *21st Century Community Learning Centers Providing Locally Designed Afterschool and Summer Learning Programs for Families (Afterschool Supports to Communities Nationwide)*, www.afterschoolalliance.org/documents/21stCCLC-Overview-2017.pdf.

16 Thomas J. Kane, "The Impact of After-School Programs: Interpreting the Results of Four Recent Evaluations," *Working Paper, William T. Grant Foundation*, 2004.

17 Harlem Children's Zone, www.hcz.org/results.

18 Deborah A. Phillips and Jack P. Shonkoff, eds., *From Neurons to Neighborhoods: The Science of Early Childhood Development* (Washington, DC: National Academies Press, 2000).

19 Valenzuela, *Subtractive Schooling*.

20 W. E. B. DuBois, "Does the Negro Need Separate Schools?" *Journal of Negro Education* 4, no. 3 (1935): 328.

21 New York City Department of Education, "2015–16 School Quality Snapshot / HS," http://schools.nyc.gov/OA/SchoolReports/2015-16/School_Quality_Snapshot_2016_HS_K685.pdf.

22 Susan Auerbach, "Engaging Latino Parents in Supporting College Pathways: Lessons From a College Access Program," *Journal of Hispanic Higher Education* 3, no. 2 (2004): 125–145; Susan Auerbach, "Why Do They Give the Good Classes to Some and Not to Others?" Latino Parent Narratives of Struggle in a College Access Program, *Teachers College Record* 104, no. 7 (2002): 1369–1392.

23 Linda Jacobson, "PTA Seeks to Raise Number of Hispanic Members," *Education Week*, June 11, 2003.

24 For a discussion of the community school's movement, see John Rogers, *Community Schools: Lessons From the Past and Present* (Los Angeles: UCLA's IDEA Paper Series #1, 1998); for a discussion of more recent education organizing efforts that bring teachers together in common cause with community members, see Kavitha Mediratta, Seema Shah, and Sara McAlister, *Community Organizing for Stronger Schools: Strategies and Successes* (Cambridge, MA: Harvard University Press, 2009).

25 Susan Stall and Randy Stoecker, "Community Organizing or Organizing Community? Gender and the Crafts of Empowerment," *Working Paper, COMM-ORG*, http://comm-org.wisc.edu.

26 For a fuller discussion of community organizing for school reform, see Jeannie Oakes and John Rogers, *Learning Power: Organizing for Education and Justice* (New York: Teachers College Press, 2006).

27 Ernesto Cortes, Jr., "Making the Public the Leaders in Education Reform," *Teacher Magazine*, November 22, 1995.

28 Dennis Shirley, *Valley Interfaith and School Reform: Organizing for Power in South Texas* (Austin: University of Texas Press, 2002), 92.

29 Mamie Chow, Laurie Olsen, Ruben Lizardo, and Carol Dowell, *School Reform Organizing in the San Francisco Bay Area and Los Angeles, California* (Oakland, CA: California Tomorrow, 2001), 106.

30 See Oakes and Rogers, *Learning Power*.

31 Alliance to Reclaim Our Schools, www.reclaimourschools.org/about.

32 Journey for Justice Alliance, https://www.j4jalliance.com/aboutj4j/.

Chapter 12

Teaching to Change the World
A Profession and a Hopeful Struggle

Teachers entering the profession in the twenty-first century are motivated by all the traditional reasons for teaching—a desire to help, a love of working with young people, memories of one's own schooling, a passion for the knowledge one gets to teach, an opportunity to "give back" what one has received, a paycheck for an honest day's work, the list goes on. But in a nation that is increasingly diverse and increasingly unequal, many new teachers, like the ones cited throughout this book, add another reason—teaching to change the world.

> None of us—as an individual—can save the world as a whole, but . . . each of us must behave as though it were in our power to do so.
>
> —*Vaclav Havel*[1]

> You must do the thing you think you can not do.
>
> —*Eleanor Roosevelt*[2]

These words of the former president of the Czech Republic and playwright Vaclav Havel, and those of former American First Lady and ambassador to the United Nations Eleanor Roosevelt, capture the spirit of many teachers as they begin their careers. Teachers face social, political, and economic challenges that schools, alone, can't overcome, and teachers reach for ambitious goals that they, alone, can't attain. Yet they are determined to use their knowledge and skills to struggle for justice.

> As an educator, I can make a difference in students' lives. I can help them become transformative citizens in our society and liberate their minds to soar above and beyond the constraints of race, ethnicity, and social status. As I continue along my path as an educator, I carry with me the words of Alice Walker, "Keep in mind always the present you are constructing. It should be the future you want."
>
> —Kelly Ganzel
> First-year teacher, high school English

Kelly Ganzel wrote these words at the end of her first year of teaching in a school marked by many of the inequities we described in Chapter 1. Five years later, Kelly was still at that same school, still passionately teaching to make a difference in students' lives.

Kelly and the other teachers like her in this book are idealists, but they are not naive. They know how hard it is to make schools humane and intellectually rich in the face of widening wealth gaps, enduring institutionalized racism, and anti-immigrant sentiments on the rise. To this struggle they bring something more potent and positive than the harmful ideologies of meritocracy, deficit thinking, and White superiority and the limiting metaphors of schools as factories, corporations, or markets. They bring professional knowledge of teaching and learning and a vision of social justice. These teachers have chosen an education *career*; they are not just passing time until something more glamorous or lucrative comes along. Their plans to change the world involve activism in and beyond the classroom.

Chapter Overview

This chapter, a kind of culmination and invitation, looks toward a more socially just future. The early part of the chapter unblinkingly reviews recent history and the status quo in teaching—what teachers for social justice struggle *against*. The latter part of the chapter turns to what teachers struggle *for*—a truly honorable profession, anchored by a commitment to equity and capable of catalyzing social change. We conclude the chapter, and the book, with five philosophical, practical, and personal strategies that teachers use to change the world. They include becoming a part of a learning community, becoming a social justice activist, expanding one's professional influence, making a commitment to a hopeful critique, and finding satisfaction in the everyday.

Teaching: A Powerful and Imperiled Profession

> After nine years in the high-tech industry, I made the leap to high school. It was a conscious decision. But I confess I was unprepared for the fact that teaching would be the hardest job I've ever had. I counted the hours I worked, planned, and graded, and in the end, I realized I was down to the corporate standard of two weeks vacation.
>
> In the high-tech world, I had responsibility—to take care of customers, finish projects on time, train fellow workers on the latest sales application. But as I gain more teaching experience, I realize the enormity of a teacher's responsibility and how different it is from my prior career.

High-tech products are different from "school products." The products we provided did not have feelings, think on their own, or come from a variety of backgrounds. They did not need Kleenex, Band-Aids, tampons, pens, pencils, whiteout, paper, rubber bands (need I go on?). We cannot turn students into excellent readers, writers, thinkers, and, of course, test takers, as easily as we can tighten a screw or correct code.

The challenges students pose are different from the challenge of figuring out a new marketing strategy. My newest clients, ages 14–18, are often very sleepy at 8 A.M. and intolerably boisterous at 2 P.M. They sometimes come to school without having breakfast, getting a ride from a distant relative, and often forgetting materials. They have a keen sense of justice—pouncing on the examples of oppression and injustice in history.

They say funny things, not always appropriate for the classroom. There was also the student who repeated multiple times how much she disliked me. Other students feel I give too much homework. Imagine that!

I love teaching more than any other job, but I do admit to having days when I want to run for higher ground.

—Judy Smith[3]
High school social studies

As we describe in what follows, many teachers do this extraordinarily difficult job with inadequate preparation, limited opportunities to develop their skills on the job, less-than-ideal working conditions, and inadequate pay. These realities are part of what puts the powerful profession of teaching in peril. They're also part of what sets apart Judy and other teachers like her—well prepared, savvy about their own development, and supportive of professionalizing pay—both in terms of what they can accomplish on a daily basis in their own classrooms, and in terms of their staying power in schools and stewardship of the teaching profession.

The Challenge of Learning to Teach

Judy Smith considers herself lucky. She knew that she needed to learn a great deal to be a good teacher, and she thinks her teacher education program served her well.

Before going into teaching, I was certain of three things: I really wanted to be the best teacher I could be (a goal I still work on day in and day out), I needed a teacher education program that would push me and support me, and I really cared about kids and learning. All students deserve the best teachers, and I wanted to help them understand that, too. The combination of academic work and outstanding professors and colleagues in my teacher education program met my needs and set my teaching course. We were asked to love our students; we were required to do rigorous work in our classes; we were taught social justice. In addition, we acquired the mind-set that we teachers must constantly examine our approach, curriculum, and expectations and reach out to other like-minded social justice educators for support and ideas.

Judy expresses a degree of satisfaction and confidence in her preparation that not all beginning teachers feel. This is because there is enormous variation in the experiences preservice teachers receive in their preparation programs.

Some institutions and programs that grant teaching licenses may offer or require so few course hours that there is just enough time to pass along a few bits and pieces of "practical" teacher knowledge, which are then called "professional training." Prospective teachers may get little of the theory about teaching and learning or the foundational knowledge we've discussed in this book. They may have few chances to observe in classrooms and communities, limited contact with knowledgeable mentors, or infrequent supervision by those whose knowledge, experience, and sympathetic touch can help them develop their competence.

The field of teacher education is constrained by public and political perceptions of what it takes to become a teacher and, like any other field, also by its own inertia. That said, there are areas of relative consensus—for example, as reflected in recent efforts to strengthen the connections between teacher preparation and practice in K–12 schools. There are also many exemplary models for teacher education—models that reflect principles explored in this book. Ideally, all prospective teachers would experience optimal preparation; more realistically (since even exemplary models are rarely optimal), teachers and teacher educators must seek out like-minded colleagues and mentors with whom they can collaborate on advancing their own professional growth and, by extension, the growth of the teaching profession.

Professionalism in the Face of Limited Professional Support

Despite the complex work that teaching entails, many novices assume the full scope of teaching responsibility on day one. Other professions (such as law, medicine, accounting, and social work) have multiple levels of induction into full professional responsibility before allowing new practitioners to function independently and unsupervised for long periods of time. But in most schools, first-year novices and twenty-year veterans do exactly the same job. After obtaining an initial license or credential, new teachers may have few opportunities to apprentice with accomplished veterans. In fact, often it's the novices, not the veterans, who work under the most challenging conditions.

Until collegial cultures and scaffolding become the norm, individual teachers must gather and create that support on their own. This is not as daunting as it might seem, though finding collaborators to support one's own goals and development requires trusting relationships—patience and sensitivity—like what's required when *giving* support to students. Veteran teachers, we might say the *best* veteran teachers, are typically generous in offering collegial guidance to novices who are eager to learn.

Why are teacher education and ongoing development often taken so lightly? There are many reasons. First among them is the popular belief that teaching requires little specialized knowledge, experience, support, or expertise. Many people still believe that teachers are "born" and not "made"—that is, that teaching well is mostly a "gift" or a matter of personality, and that everything else can be learned quickly and on the job. Current attitudes largely reflect the days when teaching was strictly women's work, when scientific management reduced complex jobs to simple, prescribed tasks, and when corporate-style hierarchies left decision making to a few managers. Some of these views underlie the proliferation of alternative programs—such as Teach for America and other programs—that give college graduates full responsibility for classrooms after only minimal summer training. They also underlie the proliferation of "scripted" curricula, described in earlier chapters, as well as some of the approaches to teacher evaluation we describe elsewhere and below. These perspectives don't exist in a vacuum, of course. Certainly, in an era when many public-sector services are being targeted by budget cuts, quicker preparation for lower-wage, less skilled teachers represents an attractive policy alternative for many.

Teaching in a Changing America

Since the country's founding, the demographic composition of the United States has always been in flux, and so have beliefs and attitudes about demographic changes. These changes—and what people think and feel about them—make up a central part of the social context in which teachers live and work.[4]

Statistical projections show that the country's student population is growing increasingly diverse, while the teacher population is remaining much as it has been—with a very high representation of White, middle-class females.[5] In 2016, just under 50 percent of public school students were White; marking historic shifts, students of color were the majority, including roughly a quarter Latinx, 15 percent Black, and 5 percent Asian. Meanwhile, three of every four public school teachers were female, and more than eight in ten were White.[6]

This "demographic divide" is long-standing and concerning on multiple counts. Certainly, it places a demand for and burden on teachers of color, who are often expected to draw on their cultural backgrounds and repertoires to build relationships with students, to develop culturally responsive (or sustaining) curricula and learning experiences, and to act as "cultural brokers" who help students, parents, and colleagues bridge their worlds of school, community, and family. Too often in these conversations teachers of color—including bilingual teachers and male elementary school teachers, who are also in demand—are framed as exclusively benefiting students "like them." This is both insulting and short-sighted. A diverse teaching force helps everyone gain perspective and knowledge, and it lessens the burden on teachers of any background to represent any entire group. For these and other reasons, efforts to recruit a diverse teaching corps are thankfully under way. One of them, the fantastic Pathways2Teaching program, is featured in Focal Point 12.1.

Focal Point 12.1
Finding Hope in the Future Generation

Pathways2Teaching is a grow-your-own, concurrent enrollment program designed for high school students of color to explore teaching as potential career choice. Throughout the program, students examine historical and contemporary issues related to social justice and educational equity. Teaching and related fields are presented and promoted as an act of social justice—a way to right the wrongs in and for their communities. Through our curriculum and primary text, *Teaching to Change the World*, students are encouraged to critically examine institutional racism and the policies and practices in schools that label, sort, marginalize, and oppress. This approach engages the political and socioeconomic realities in students' lives and guides them in challenging systemic structures that have shaped their lives and created barriers to a quality education.

Since 2010, the Pathways2Teaching program has served hundreds of students in several Denver metro school districts and through our affiliate programs in other states. Many of our graduates are now enrolled in teacher education programs or in other related areas such as social work.

Through the Pathways2Teaching program, high school students

- engage in a weekly field experience working with elementary students to facilitate their literacy development;
- gain college readiness skills as they learn to navigate the college search and application process;
- earn three college credits upon successful completion of the yearlong course;
- learn to write college essays and research reports;
- acquire public speaking skills as they present their research findings to families and community members;

- interact with college students and faculty during campus visits and guest lectures;
- critically examine educational inequities; and
- understand that teaching is an act of love, a way to engage in social justice, and a way to change the world.

We are indebted to Dr. Margarita Bianco, Pathways2 Teaching's director, for the text of this focal point and to her students for serving as inspiration to us in this fifth edition. There is no more important time than now for young people to interrogate educational inequity and work together to imagine a better future. We are honored that Pathways2 Teaching found this book useful; we're grateful for their contributions to teaching, public education, and social justice; and we look forward to learning about their many accomplishments.

Teacher Shortages and Budget Shortfalls

The start of the twenty-first century ushered in new concerns about teacher shortages. Multiple well-publicized reports predicted that 200,000 new teachers a year would be needed for the next decade plus. Millions of young children were entering school just as teachers of the baby boom generation were retiring. Teaching was also feeling the effects of a more than thirty-year revolution in career opportunities available to women and reductions in job discrimination facing people of color. Members of these groups, who historically had few options other than teaching, were no longer choosing the profession at previous rates now that better-paying careers were available to them. And, to be sure, teaching has not kept pace with salaries or other incentives.

Qualified teachers—particularly special education teachers, bilingual teachers, and science and math teachers—are often in short supply.[7] Not surprisingly, these shortages don't affect all schools equally; they are most acute, consistently, in schools serving low-income communities of color.

Teacher shortages don't mean that students are in classrooms without teachers. The shortages mean that schools often assign teachers to teach subjects for which they are not prepared, particularly for those hard-to-fill positions mentioned above. For example, in 2008, 16 percent of all core academic classes in grades 7–12 were taught by a teacher with neither a major nor a teaching certificate in the subject being taught. The situation was worse in high-poverty schools, where 22 percent of all middle and high school classes were taught by teachers without these qualifications, compared to only half that (11 percent) in schools with more advantaged students. The situation in mathematics is especially dire, with more than one of four math classes in high-poverty secondary schools taught by "out-of-field" teachers.[8]

Even though federal policy stipulates that schools can employ only "highly qualified" teachers, many states have exploited legal loopholes that allow them to hire and keep underqualified and out-of-field teachers. In sum, students of color and students learning English in high-poverty schools are far more likely to be taught by less experienced and lower-paid teachers than those in Whiter and wealthier schools.[9]

In response to economic downturns, many states have made severe cuts to their education budgets. As the cuts hit local communities, districts have increased class sizes, cut salaries, and eliminated programs, services, and positions. Some have laid off large numbers of teachers, beginning with the least experienced. As a result, students have had to say good-bye to teachers who may have had the most up-to-date preparation, as well as enthusiasm for teaching in settings typically considered hard to staff. In many cases, they have lost access to valued school staff, including counselors, librarians, and classroom aides. Seemingly overnight, communities that have struggled with shortages now, at times, report no available jobs or even a surplus of qualified educators. Austere budgets affect all aspects of public education and hit hardest at hiring and keeping well-qualified teachers.

Teacher Retention and Attrition

The biggest challenge to schools keeping a full complement of highly qualified teachers is *not* that too few people are entering the profession. It's that so many new teachers leave the classroom after such a short time. Teacher turnover and attrition are at least as much to blame for shortages (when they occur) as schools' failure to attract qualified candidates. Every year close to 16 percent of teachers leave the schools where they teach; about 7 percent leave teaching altogether, while the rest shift schools. Under a third of those who leave the profession retire, so the majority leave for other reasons. Poor urban and rural schools suffer the effects of this turnover most acutely, often having to fill resulting vacancies with poorly prepared or out-of-field teachers or substitutes.[10]

If teachers were staying in their jobs, there would be plenty of qualified teachers to fill every classroom, even in shortage areas. Not only could schools be more selective about whom they hire, they could also create apprenticeship programs in which new teachers would not immediately have to assume the full responsibilities of teaching. Instead, new teachers could spend their time working side by side with experienced veterans who could help them apply the knowledge and skills they learned in teacher education programs to the particular school and community where they are teaching. We should note that mentors needn't be "old-timers." Partnerships even with recent entrants into the profession—a year or two of experience—can provide valuable scaffolding as *both* work to develop teaching skill and achieve their pedagogical and social justice goals. Of course, this also would be an authentic way for veteran teachers to keep abreast of the latest educational developments and to add to their current knowledge and skills.

Teachers' Salaries and Working Conditions

> No other professional in this country receives the yearly salary a teacher does and the low level of professional respect after completing a bachelor's and master's of education. The results are unqualified applicants, high turnover, and large classroom sizes.
>
> This is a difficult situation for politicians, who will probably not see the benefits [of their actions] over the span of their term. It will take constituents' outrage demonstrated at the polls to force the action. Unfortunately, those most disadvantaged by the current educational system, minorities and low socioeconomic groups, traditionally have the lowest voter turnout.
>
> —Mark Hill
> First-year teacher, high school mathematics

Mark Hill has it right. Teachers do make less than those in jobs requiring comparable education and skills, such as architects, journalists, accountants, and computer programmers. In 2015, public school teachers' weekly wages were 17 percent lower than those of comparable workers, and, in fact, their average weekly salary was $30 less than it was in 1996.[11] Although states vary considerably in absolute salary, teachers typically earn less than other college graduates.[12] In some places, especially those where the cost of living is high, some teachers work second jobs to supplement their income.[13] One of the authors of a book reporting these statistics commented,

> Over time, the wage gap between teachers and their peers becomes a gulf that can sabotage schools' best efforts to recruit the best teachers and to keep them as their skills and

experience grow. This gap puts teachers in an untenable position, where they have to choose between their students and their own families' well-being.[14]

And it's not only teachers who believe that they are underpaid. A recent survey found that 53 percent of parents, in addition to 65 percent of teachers, say that teachers' salaries are not fair for the work they do.[15]

In response to fiscal crises, a growing interest in teacher evaluation (discussed below), and a mix of other motives, some politicians and policymakers are calling on districts to institute merit pay—to tie teachers' pay to their performance, as calculated by students' performance on standardized tests. As explained in Chapter 4, there is no evidence that tying teachers' evaluation to their performance leads to accurate overall insights into teachers' competence or to increases in student test scores.[16] There is also little evidence to suggest that rewarding the highest-performing teachers will encourage more talented individuals to join the profession or to stay in it longer term. According to researchers from the Economic Policy Institute, teacher pay is critical to recruiting and retaining a better teacher workforce, but policies that focus on paying some teachers more than others, through merit or pay-for-performance schemes, won't work unless they also increase teacher salaries across the board.[17]

Although low salaries deter prospective teachers, research findings show that salaries are actually *less* important than other reasons. For example, teachers who leave high-poverty schools, those with the highest rates of turnover and arguably the most acute need to attract and retain high-quality teachers, cite poor working conditions more than anything else. Studies show that salaries and working conditions are more of a factor than student characteristics (although it is students of color and low-income students who typically "lose out" when teachers leave); in fact, some research shows that salaries are near the bottom of teachers' lists of what matters most to them.[18] Teachers point out that deteriorating facilities, overcrowding, inadequate materials, lack of time to meet and plan with colleagues, and the absence of professional autonomy and respect prevent them from doing the job they were prepared to do. Teachers also report consistently that one of their most important working conditions is the support they receive from administrators—specifically that administrators provide the conditions necessary for good teaching and make decisions that are fair and well informed. Increasingly, some teachers are leaving teaching because of the negative discourse surrounding the profession, including teacher bashing in the media.

These factors have had adverse impacts for sure. One recent national survey of teachers showed, for example, that teacher job satisfaction fell by 15 percentage points between 2009 and 2012, from 59 percent responding they are very satisfied to 44 percent; and the years since offer little indication to suggest that morale has improved much.[19] At the same time, the words of teachers like Judy Smith remind us that while the context for teaching is challenging, it need not be our destiny. Judy shares concerns about the longevity of her peers' careers in teaching. She also shares her sense of optimism and her sense of responsibility to work doggedly to make the broader system one that is not just hospitable to good teaching, but encouraging and enabling of it.

I worry about the next generation of teachers. I worry that they face challenges that are beyond their immediate control (example: poor leadership at the administrative level). I worry, too, that we teachers too often resign ourselves to accept our poor working conditions. We almost wear this as a badge of our dedication as teachers.

I hope that the new teachers won't get beaten down and become resigned. We are professionals and should have a system that supports us in educating our children. Teachers, whether it is through unions or other organizations, need to speak up more and educate our oldest students, those persons in the community. It is appalling that we don't have what we need to do our jobs. We can't continue to accept that and then leave after three or four years. We need a serious consciousness-raising effort among ourselves. Then we need the intelligent leadership to educate the public. It is not okay just to be a "dedicated" teacher—one who does all the right things and yet accepts things the way they are.

—Judy Smith
High school social studies

What Is a Good Teacher? A Professional and Political Question

As recently as a few years ago, it was common to equate possessing a credential with being highly qualified, even though credential programs vary widely in their rigor. The No Child Left Behind Act, for example, mandated that districts hire only "highly qualified" teachers, meaning teachers who possessed a bachelor's degree and valid state certification (earned without waiving any requirements) and who demonstrated expertise (usually assessed via state exams) in the subjects they teach.[20] Most states and districts continue to use this as a baseline for hiring.

As interest in teacher quality has increased, however, educators and policymakers alike have begun to question whether credentials and subject area exams are suitable proxies for teacher effectiveness. As mentioned in Chapter 4, many also worry that traditional methods for evaluating teachers—for example, having principals observe teachers and rate their performance using broad categories such as "satisfactory" and "unsatisfactory"—don't provide enough information to determine actual effectiveness or identify teachers' development needs.

In light of these concerns, efforts to create new teacher evaluation systems have proliferated, egged on by federal policy. Of course, when it comes to determining the best way to evaluate teachers, disagreements abound. As discussed at length in Chapter 4, many policymakers and politicians advocate using students' standardized test scores to evaluate or rate teachers in some way. Their rationale goes something like this: by assessing what students learn (using test scores), low- and high-performing teachers can be identified; with high- or low-quality status determined, teachers may be fired, rewarded, or motivated to perform better. In a few extreme cases, this has led to publishing individual teacher ratings for public consumption, despite heated arguments about the data's flaws and the approach's deleterious impacts (not just on teachers themselves).

More recent initiatives keep students' standardized scores in play among "multiple measures" for evaluating teachers. These might include observations, portfolios, performance of leadership roles, lesson plans, and more. Thoughtful policymakers at all levels are coming to understand that test scores alone are insufficient for making high-stakes decisions. Still, in school districts and state houses, legislators are debating *how* and *how much* students' test scores should factor into decisions about ranking schools, closing schools, providing teacher bonuses, dismissing teachers, and so on. And at least some are coming to recognize the complex array of factors that are propelling forward a focus on teacher evaluation as a lynchpin approach for improving education. Among these, for example, is the media's emphasis on (bad) public school teachers—an emphasis that also connects to determined and well-funded efforts to undermine public schools in favor of for-profit school management companies and to correspondingly diminish the influence of teacher unions, mentioned below. Lastly, even when policymakers concede that "multiple measures" are superior to inferring competence from student tests, it is evident that trained teacher observers, portfolio reviewers, collegial supervisors who track improvements, and more all require resources and time, which, once again, are in short supply.

Teachers' Unions

For more than 100 years, teachers have joined unions to advance the profession and to mount a collective voice in education policy. Today, there are two national teachers' unions. The larger, the National Education Association (NEA), with 3 million members, was founded in 1857. Composed initially of higher-education faculty and education administrators, the NEA was formed to influence the nation's rapidly growing education system. Elementary and secondary school teachers were not admitted as members until the 1920s, and it wasn't until the 1960s that the NEA became a strong advocate for teachers.

In contrast to the NEA, the 1.6-million-member American Federation of Teachers (AFT) has been a grassroots teachers' union from the beginning. It began in 1887 when teachers in Chicago began organizing to improve their conditions and prevent schools from turning into the educational factories described in Chapter 4. Leading the organizing effort was Margaret Haley, an elementary school teacher. Focal Point 12.2 tells the story of Haley and what she hoped to achieve. The issues that concerned her are all too familiar to teachers today.

Haley cared both about education for democracy and about teachers' professionalism, and she was determined to protect both. By 1916, the Chicago Teachers' Federation she founded had led to the creation of the AFT, of which John Dewey held membership card number one. Since then, organized teachers have spoken out for teachers' rights as professional workers and have argued that good working conditions for teachers improve education for children. The path has not been easy.

Focal Point 12.2
*Teachers' Unions Organizing for Progressive
Education and Conditions for Teaching*

1904: Margaret Haley Calls for Teachers to Organize

In 1904, Margaret Haley (1861–1939), a schoolteacher from Chicago, spoke at the National Education Association (NEA) convention in St. Louis. In her short but insightful address, "Why Teachers Should Organize," Haley talked about democracy, equity, and citizenship and discussed the importance of teachers' autonomy and professionalism. She criticized state subsidies to corporations, budget cuts to education, the routinization of teaching and learning, the corruption of the press, the deterioration of teachers' salaries, the subservience of elected politicians to lobbies, and the push toward commercialism in public schools. She advocated progressive education, a fairer distribution of wealth, and a strong unionism encompassing mental and manual laborers.

The teachers whom Haley was attempting to organize were primarily young females who were usually forced to resign after marriage. They were supposedly professionals, but were seldom treated or paid as such. Not only were their salaries low, but they were also paid less than their male counterparts. Within their classrooms, they often had the task of educating more than sixty students with little support.

In her speech, Haley expressed deep concern about the increasing deprofessionalization of teachers and listed four major obstacles to efficient teaching: (1) inadequate salaries, clearly inappropriate to meet the increasing cost of living and the demands for higher standards of scholarship and professional attainment; (2) insecurity regarding tenure of office and lack of provision for old age; (3) overwork and overcrowded classrooms, exhausting both mind and body; and (4) lack of recognition for the teacher as an educator, due to pressures to transform schools into factories.

After outlining these and other problems faced by teachers, Haley called for an organized effort of mutual aid and delineated the main tasks for such an organization. She argued that teachers should develop expertise in educational theory and practice, the ability to do scientific teaching, knowledge about the conditions under which good teaching is possible, and skills to reach the public with accurate information. In this speech, Haley raised a concept that would resurface many decades later in the debates on the roles of teachers' unions: professional unionism. She argued that teachers' organizations must promote both professional development and the improvement of working conditions, and that the two functions should be pursued simultaneously.

Haley believed the struggle of public school teachers was part of the struggle carried out by manual workers to improve working and living conditions, to protect human rights, and to achieve a more equitable distribution of the products of their labor. Thus, she brought teachers into an alliance with the labor movement and liberal reformers, and under her leadership, the Chicago Teachers Federation joined the Chicago Federation of Labor. In her view, only through these alliances could teachers become free to save the schools for democracy and to save democracy in the schools. At that time, militant teachers tended to ally with organized labor, and school administrators tended to ally with business interests.

In Haley's perspective, two ideals were contending for hegemony in American life at the beginning of the century: the industrial ideal, which culminates in the supremacy of commercialism, and the ideal of democracy, which places humanity above machines and demands that all activity should be the expression of life. In her address, she cautioned that if educators were unable to carry the ideal of democracy to the industrial world, then the ideal of industrialism would be carried over to the school. Moreover, "if the school cannot bring joy to the work of the world, the joy must go out of its own life, and work in the school as in the factory will become drudgery." Haley thought that public school teachers were the most appropriate social actors to advance this agenda:

> If there is one institution on which the responsibility to perform this service rests most heavily, it is the public school. If there is one body of public servants of whom the public has a right to expect the mental and moral equipment to face the labor question, and other issues vitally affecting the welfare of society and urgently pressing for a rational and scientific solution, it is the public-school teachers, whose special contribution to society is their own power to think, the moral courage to follow their convictions, and the training of citizens to think and to express thought in free and intelligent action.

Source: Margaret Haley, *Battleground: The Autobiography of Margaret Haley*, ed. Robert L. Reid (Chicago: University of Illinois Press, 1982), 285–286.

Following World War I, the Red Scare seized the nation, portraying organized labor as a communist threat. Many school boards pressured teachers to resign from the union. Widespread worker unrest during the Depression in the 1930s made conditions even harder for organized teachers, as some districts required teachers to sign loyalty oaths or fired teachers for joining the union or working on school board elections. "Yellow-dog" contracts required teachers to promise not to join a union as a condition of their employment. During the anticommunist era in the 1950s, shown most dramatically in Senator Joseph McCarthy's House Un-American Activities Committee hearings, McCarthyites labeled members of the teachers' union "subversive."

In fact, the unions did take and continue to take unpopular positions on controversial political issues—often against the mainstream of American culture. One feature on the AFT's website, for example, lists the union's record on social justice and reveals positions that were unpopular at the time:

- Was among the first unions to extend full membership to minorities
- Called for equal pay for African American teachers, the election of African Americans to local school boards, and compulsory school attendance for African American children (1918)
- Demanded equal educational opportunities for African American children (1919)
- Called for the contributions of African Americans to be taught in the public schools (1928)
- Filed an amicus brief in support of the plaintiffs in the *Brown v. Board of Education* case before the Supreme Court (1954)
- Expelled any local unions that refused to admit African Americans (1957)
- Helped organize the March on Washington for Justice and Jobs (1963)
- Traveled south to register new African American voters and to teach in freedom schools (1964–1966)
- Lobbied for passage of the Equal Employment Opportunity Act, the Fair Housing Act, and the Voting Rights Act
- Negotiated unique career ladders and training programs in New York City that enhanced upward career mobility for many minorities (1968)
- Participated as observers for the South African elections (1994)
- Provided organizing assistance and resources to unionists and educators throughout Eastern Europe, for example, in the years leading up to the fall of Communism
- Involved in developing free trade unions and democracy curricula for public education systems in countries around the globe (current)[21]

Although teachers' unions have been part of the country's broader labor organizing tradition, they are different from other unions. Labor unions associated with industry have focused on workers' rights and have not made improving products or increasing profitability a priority. Because demands by organized labor typically increase costs and thereby threaten to decrease profits, unions and industrial leaders are in adversarial positions. In contrast, teachers' unions have made students' interests a priority, and they seek to advance educational goals; in this sense, they and "management" are on the same side.

However, it has been difficult for teachers' unions to develop organizing strategies that stress teachers' professional commitments *and* their rights as workers. Today, teachers' unions continue to advocate for good working (teaching *and* learning) conditions, decent wages, and progressive education policies. They also continue to be portrayed as obstructing education reform and seeking their own gain at the expense of students. For example, one high-profile portrayal occurred in 2004 when Secretary of Education Roderick Paige called the NEA a "terrorist organization" for criticizing the No Child Left Behind Act. Later, Paige said it "was an inappropriate choice of words," even as he continued to accuse the NEA of "obstructionist scare tactics."[22]

In 2005, the *Wall Street Journal* published an opinion piece by professor Terry Moe with a more detailed critique. Moe argued that teachers' unions represented the biggest obstacle to school reform and that they must be curtailed if education is to improve.

The teachers' unions have more influence over the public schools than any other group in American society. . . . They are the 800-pound gorillas of public education. . . .

If we really want to improve schools, something has to be done about the teachers' unions. The idea that an enlightened reform unionism will somehow emerge that voluntarily puts the interests of children first—an idea in vogue among union apologists—is nothing more than a pipe dream. The unions are what they are. They have fundamental, job-related interests that are very real, and are the raison d'être of their organizations. These interests drive their behavior, and this is not going to change. Ever.

If the teachers' unions won't voluntarily give up their power, then it has to be taken away from them.[23]

Attacks such as these have become more widespread and vehement in recent years. In 2010, for example, New Jersey governor Chris Christie told a group of Trenton youth that "greedy" teachers and a union that "cares more about how much they get paid than they care about how well you learn" were to blame for the lack of school supplies, not the $43 million in budget cuts the Trenton district experienced that year.[24] Chester Finn, president of the conservative Fordham Institute, went so far as to blame teachers for their own low salaries and professional status, claiming that teachers' insistence to remain unionized has led others to view and treat them as workers rather than as professionals.[25]

Such attitudes came to a notable head in 2011 when Governor Scott Walker of Wisconsin announced he would address the state budget deficit by limiting public employees', including teachers', collective bargaining rights while also having them contribute more to their pensions and health benefits. Other states were quick to follow suit.[26] In response, thousands of teachers—joining public employees in Wisconsin, Indiana, Iowa, and Florida, among other states—protested en masse. Meanwhile, President Obama and Secretary of Education Arne Duncan responded tepidly, claiming they would encourage the Republican governors to work with, rather than against, unions while at the same time maintaining support for the elimination of tenure and pay-for-performance measures—initiatives that tend to undermine unions' goals. The 2016 presidential campaign, election, and confirmation hearings for Secretary of Education Betsy DeVos all indicate the current administration's tendency to favor policies and approaches that attempt to skirt or undermine teachers' unions and teachers' right to unionize.

Certainly, there is some truth to the claim that teachers' unions are intent on obstructing many proposed reforms, and not all union proposals are in the best interests of students. However, the unions fight hard for increased school funding, safer schools, smaller class sizes, fully qualified teachers, and parent engagement. Undoubtedly, such reforms serve students well.

Furthermore, many of the reforms the unions seek to obstruct are those they consider threats to education quality, not to salaries or working conditions. For example, the unions have fought (and lost) a good many battles against the most destructive elements of high-stakes testing. They have taken strong stands against school closures (and their disproportionate impact on low-income communities of color), as well as the unfettered proliferation of charter schools, where most teachers are not unionized and where research suggests that working conditions and learning outcomes are no better, and in fact oftentimes worse, than those of regular public schools. Organized teachers, too, have been among the most vociferous voices of opposition when it comes to replacing constructivist curricula and pedagogy with scripted teaching. Generally, teachers' groups are the strongest advocates for students' rights.

In sum, poor working conditions dissipate teachers' attention and energies they might otherwise focus on their students. Low salaries send a strong signal that society has little appreciation for teaching. Unions are working to address these and other collective concerns. As Margaret

Haley argued, well-organized teachers are the best hope to "save the schools for democracy and to save democracy in the schools."[27]

Union members or not, some teachers cope with these obstacles on a daily basis by mostly ignoring them; they make the best of difficult situations, or they close their classroom doors and immerse themselves in their work with students. Others, like many quoted in this book, accept as part of their daily work the challenge of improving conditions for teaching and improving the profession writ large. The next sections of this chapter look at promising professionalizing strategies: constructing a learning community, becoming a social justice activist, expanding one's sphere of influence, committing to a hopeful critique, and finding joy in the everyday.

Strategies for Constructing a Career to Change the World

What keeps teachers in teaching? How do teachers continue year after year to teach their own students well, to improve their schools, to change the social conditions that constrain their students' opportunities, and to seek social justice? How can beginning teachers, at the start of a fulfilling career, sustain a sense of agency amid challenges?

There are no sure answers, but there are the experiences and voices of committed teachers to learn from. Some of the teachers we've quoted here began teaching now almost twenty years ago; others were first-year teachers a decade ago. The four teachers featured most prominently in this edition—Mauro Bautista, Mark Hill, Kimberly Min, and Judy Smith—ranged from first- to fifth-year teachers in 2004–2005. Some newer teachers, whom we mention elsewhere and in this chapter, were first- to sixth-year teachers in much more recent years.

Nearly all the teachers quoted in all five editions of this book have remained in education; most are still teaching minoritized students in underfunded schools. Some have taken on other important roles in education, as we describe later.

One of those who have stayed in teaching is kindergarten teacher Cicely Morris Bingener, who was featured in the first edition of this book. Over twenty years ago when Cicely was a student teacher, she was robbed at gunpoint by teenagers when she stopped at a convenience store near her school. The incident crystallized for Cicely "a mission to help children see the range of possibilities for their lives so that they don't see crime or this type of behavior as their only option." Rather than turning away from the community where she was teaching or from teaching altogether, Cicely told us that she was "too angry to leave." Her kindergartners deserved better futures than the young men who robbed her, and she was determined to be a part of ensuring that.

Since then, Cicely has married and become the mother of children herself. Throughout she has remained deeply committed to social justice. Cicely still teaches kindergarten in the community where she began as a student teacher. Her students have included many of the younger siblings of the kindergartners she taught during her first year. She lives near the school and buys her groceries alongside her students' parents. Her school struggles with many of the inequalities we described in Chapter 1, and over the years Cicely has faced frustrations like those of other urban teachers—unsupportive administrators, inadequate facilities, too few community supports, and more.

Why do Cicely and the others remain in teaching? What sustains them? Many things—some philosophical, some professional, and some personal. Cicely combines her determination that students "see the range of possibilities for their lives" with her active struggle against the persistent inequalities that constrain those possibilities. She has continued to build broad and deep knowledge of teaching with a network of like-minded teachers across her city; she has relied on the daily support of, and supports in turn, a partner teacher who shares her passion for teaching and social justice; she has forged connections with parents who join her in making her school caring and just; she has worked as a writer and editor of an online journal focused on teaching for social change; and she has led workshops and mentored new teachers. She pairs her anger with hope, as have many others.

In fact, just this year Cicely appeared in an article about the first-annual "Learning Together: Practitioners and Scholars in Partnership" conference that she attended at her alma mater. After listening to a keynote, "Understanding Student Trauma in the Learning Process," she weighed in: "Are they [students] actually receiving the right services that will help them in the long haul? It makes me very hopeful . . . that the science of brain trauma is being studied."[28] In comments like these, and her ongoing contributions to the profession, are the same threads that ran through writing she did earlier in her career—for example, this excerpt from what she wrote at the end of her sixth year of teaching:

> At a time in my career when many of my teaching peers are making the decision to leave the classroom due to burnout and frustration, I am surprised to report that I am experiencing a new sense of hope and commitment to the teaching profession. Despite the struggles I have faced throughout my first five years of teaching, recent changes in my district, my school site, and myself have offered me a "new lease" on my teaching life. I was, once, merely too angry to leave. Now, I am too hopeful to turn away.
>
> At our school, we are experiencing a major overhaul due, ironically, to our designation as a "low-performing" school. Despite the accuracy or inaccuracy of that dubious distinction, it has afforded us a grant to essentially "rethink" and "reinvent" ourselves as a school. This process has involved representation from teachers, administrators, students, and parents in an in-depth collaboration unprecedented at our school. As a result, there is an overall sense that we stand poised at the edge of a sort of new "promised land" for our school, and it is exciting for all.
>
> I have also grown to see the immense power of parent/teacher partnerships. I believe that so much of the frustration of the social justice–minded educator stems from the mistaken perception that we are "lone freedom fighters" in a sea of oppressive administrators, victimized students, and apathetic parents. In the past year, I have coinitiated a parent/teacher collaborative that has helped connect me with authentic hopes, aspirations, frustrations, and expectations of my students' parents. We now share in the struggle of educating in a way that is explicit as opposed to assumed, and the results have been astonishing and inspiring. The experience is teaching me that learning to struggle involves learning with whom to undertake the struggle, building alliances that make the struggle feasible and fruitful.
>
> By this school year's end, I will have fulfilled my most basic of teaching promises: "I will stay long enough to see my very first class of kindergartners graduate from the fifth grade." However, I see this year not as the end, but the beginning of a new and more powerful commitment: I will stay until we achieve what we are struggling for.
>
> —Cicely Morris Bingener
> Sixth-year teacher

Now, more than a decade later, Cicely is still in the classroom, still inspired every day by what "we are struggling for." Teachers like Cicely have figured out ways to stay connected to their profession, their colleagues, their students, their communities, and their pursuit of social justice. Such teachers are not born. They develop over time, using strategies that nurture their professional expertise, deepen their understanding of students and communities, and fuel their determination to change the world. In the remainder of this chapter, we describe in more detail strategies that Cicely and other teachers use as they forge careers that change the world.

Becoming Part of a Learning Community

> It will probably take me a lifetime to develop into the teacher that I want to be.
>
> —Jasper Hiep Dang Bui
> First-year teacher, English, grade 8

Social convictions alone do not create good teaching. Children in the most vulnerable communities desperately need teachers with a deep knowledge of subject matter, human development, and language acquisition. This commitment and this knowledge are held together with cognitive and sociocultural theories of learning that provide coherence for everyday teaching practice.

Like most new teachers, Michelle Calva discovered that aligning her theory and commitments with the exigencies of everyday school life was an extraordinary challenge.

> Maintaining consistency between theory and practice is the "trick" to good teaching. It's often difficult to consider Vygotsky's theory of the zone of proximal development when you're planning a geography quiz on Wednesday, your principal's coming to observe you on Thursday, and the power goes out for two hours on Friday. It's easy to get caught up in the hectic pace most teachers (including me) keep without stopping to consider the real goals that motivate us. Through personal reflection, reactions from my students, and comments from observers, I seek to keep my classroom practices grounded in the philosophies that I believe.
>
> —Michelle Calva
> First-year teacher, grades 4–6

As we indicated earlier in this chapter, preservice teacher education is only the first step in the career-long process of learning to teach. The range of understandings, skills, and dispositions that teachers need cannot develop fully even in two years of intensive teacher preparation, nor should they. Teacher learning, like student learning, is a fundamentally social and cultural endeavor. As addressed in Chapter 6, such learning requires scaffolding and is best accomplished in a community of learners. Once certified as professionals, teachers must find and create opportunities to deepen their knowledge, skills, and commitments to social justice. We describe some of these opportunities next.

Participating in Induction

Since the 1980s, most states and school districts have had programs specifically designed to help new teachers transition from being students themselves to being professional teachers. The programs typically offer a combination of psychological and instructional support. Mentors provide advice and encouragement to help new teachers feel less isolated as they balance the multiple demands of teaching. They also provide help with the nuts and bolts of navigating the routines at their new schools and finding the resources they need for teaching. The best teacher induction programs also focus on helping teachers deepen their subject knowledge and skills for teaching, and support new teachers to develop their own collaborative communities where they can continue to grow professionally.

In a 1990 survey of new teachers, most reported that their mentors did indeed provide moral support and helped them find teaching resources. Fewer said that their mentors had much influence on curriculum priorities or instructional methods.[29] Despite these somewhat tepid findings, teacher induction programs have, in fact, gained in prominence, alongside recognition of how crucial teachers' early years in the classroom are to their pedagogical development and professional retention. Though they vary considerably by district and even by individual school, some induction programs have shown themselves to be quite valuable for those they serve. For example, responses from 917 new Chicago teachers who participated in a program provided by the New Teacher Center showed that 81 percent believed that their own instructional abilities improved when receiving a year of induction services. That number increased to almost all (99 percent) among teachers with two years of induction support.[30] Thus, when looking for a job, it's certainly worth inquiring about the kinds of induction that will be available to you as a beginning teacher.

Engaging in Professional Development

Most learning opportunities for teachers fall into the broad category of staff development or inservice development. This type of professional development is built into most teachers' work lives, as most states and school systems provide a few paid days each year for teachers' learning as part of broad school and district-wide educational improvement plans. Federal policy also allocates funding for such programs.

Much of this professional development consists of one- or two-day workshop-like sessions with experts brought in to inform teachers about curriculum, instruction, assessment, or classroom management. Teachers sometimes call these "sit-and-get" or "make-and-take" sessions. These workshops seldom have any follow-up that helps teachers integrate what they've learned into their teaching. Most professionals understand that this "training" workshop model has little effect on teaching and learning; about half of the inservice professional development that teachers experience is this type.

Other forms of professional development are more effective. These include regularly scheduled sessions in which teachers plan lessons or study their teaching practices together, ongoing opportunities for teachers to observe and discuss one another's teaching, and "coaches" who work one-on-one with teachers in particular subjects. One large-scale study, for example, found that teachers were more likely to alter their teaching when their professional development lasted a long period of time; brought them together with teachers from the same grade, school, or subject; provided active learning opportunities; matched other reform efforts at their school; and focused on teaching a particular subject, rather than on general teaching skills.[31]

The best professional development helps teachers learn new roles that make up a collaborative learning community. Over time, learning together becomes part of the school culture (as described in Chapter 9), and teachers simply expect to be working together to improve curriculum, teaching, and assessment in their classrooms.

Collaborating With Other Teachers

Many teachers tell us that collaborating with others at their school sites feeds their souls, while also contributing powerfully to their growth as professionals. This was certainly the case for fifth-year teacher John Paul Arellano, sixth-year teacher Catherine Bradshaw, and first-year teacher Scott Lyons, whose school and collaboration were the subject of Chapter 9's Focal Point 9.7. These teachers recount meeting weekly to develop curriculum and compare notes on their fourth graders' progress. Because they participated in a school-wide bilingual/biliteracy program and shared the same students—John Paul and Scott taught language arts and social studies in Spanish and English, respectively; Catherine taught math and science—they worked together to develop coherent instructional goals and to ensure that students were developing deep content knowledge, as well as proficiency in Spanish and English.

Collaboration has helped them home in on two major school-wide goals: (1) putting the principles of critical pedagogy into practice, with an emphasis on Paulo Freire's notion of dialogue, and (2) supporting students' literacy development across the content areas. According to John Paul, they spent several days together at the start of one school year laying the foundation for this work.

> We knew we had to start with the philosophy, and we had to start with dialogue, and we had to start with a non-"banking" approach to education. We pushed ourselves for days to figure out how to get the students to buy in . . . to believe that they had an opinion . . . and to get them to get kind of, well, pissed off. So, how do we get them to do that? In all three of our classes, we were talking about Freire, and we were all showing students what banking education was—teachers delivering information to students, as if they were empty vessels—and the kids were starting to vocalize their ideas about it. And then we had them use iPads and flip cameras, filming each other dialoguing, and then analyzing that. . . . And we [as teachers] got on the same page from that. That was our starting point, and now a few months later we're super-excited about what we're seeing. The collaboration between us is super-strong and the kids know it.
>
> —John Paul Arellano
> Fourth-grade teacher

As Catherine explained, this cohesive thinking around educational philosophy and ideology enabled the team to address with agency and creativity their principal's ideas about implementing an integrated approach to literacy instruction.

> Dr. Ramirez, our principal, doesn't want math to be strictly algorithms and numbers. He wants the kids to recognize that literacy is incorporated in everything. And writing and reading go together; they're not separate entities. And so it's really nice to understand what John Paul and Scott are thinking and doing, because then I can reinforce that. And when students are doing math journal entries, you know, I can specifically say, for example, "Okay, you need a topic sentence and evidence to support that." It's good for the kids to hear that connection across classes. In the past, kids might have thought, "Oh, that's what Mr. Arellano expects from me. But maybe when I go to Ms. Bradshaw's class, I can do things differently." Now they know that we all expect their very best writing, and they know what that is. . . . Whether you're writing about math or social studies, good writing should incorporate these things.
>
> —Catherine Bradshaw
> Fourth-grade teacher

Collaborating with colleagues can be especially helpful for first-year teachers. For Scott, collaborative planning during his first year provided him with much-needed support. It also gave him opportunities to contribute to his more experienced colleagues' learning and practice.

> This year I have great teacher partners, and they have really helped me manage the overwhelming task of making sure that we're all teaching the content standards that we need to cover, as well as incorporating other important elements into our teaching—like how we are focused on the heart, on student voice, and on social justice. The three of us are continually pushing each other's thinking in terms of what we can include in our instruction to ensure we stay true to the curriculum and touch on elements of social justice.
>
> —Scott Lyons
> First-year teacher, grade 4

Finding like-minded teachers with whom to collaborate isn't always easy. John Paul, Catherine, and Scott all chose to work at their school because of its bilingual program and commitment to inquiry and transformative education. They also knew that their principal had the leadership skills to help realize their shared social justice goals.

Many teachers won't find such an ideal situation, but most can find an ally or two with whom to collaborate. Even smaller-scale partnering—like engaging in regular and substantive instructional conversation—can be a foundation on which teachers build the kind of school and work environment they believe in.

Earning National Board Certification

The most recent addition to teachers' formal professional development opportunities is the National Board of Professional Teaching Standards (NBPTS) certification. Created in response to the 1983 *A Nation at Risk* report, the NBPTS hopes to help achieve "world-class" schools by promoting a "world-class" teaching force.

The NBPTS set out to establish a set of high standards for professional teaching. Creating a board that would certify those teachers who could show through performance assessments that they met the standards, NBPTS founders argued, would both raise professional competence *and* recognize and reward teaching excellence. Teachers make up the board's majority; other members include school administrators, school board leaders, governors and state legislators, higher-education officials, teachers' union leaders, and business and community leaders.

Any teacher with three years of classroom experience can volunteer to participate in NBPTS certification. To become certified, teachers must demonstrate through a series of performance-based assessments, teaching portfolios, student work samples, video recordings, and analyses of their own teaching and students' learning that they possess both deep subject matter knowledge and an understanding of how to teach those subjects.

NBPTS certification has become a symbol of professional teaching excellence. A teacher who has met the high standards for certification has been carefully judged by peers to be someone who makes sound professional judgments about students' best interests and acts effectively on those judgments.

Most teachers who have participated in NBPTS say that it is among the most powerful professional development experiences of their careers. Several of the teachers we've quoted in this book now hold NBPTS certification. During the 2004–2005 school year, Kimberly Min spent a great deal of energy preparing for certification.

> The NBPTS process gave me an outlet to reflect and write about my teaching experiences. This self-reflection confirmed my belief that social justice could be incorporated in the curriculum within the state standards. For the past four years, I have tried to engage my students in what Freire calls praxis. Students discuss school and community issues and have turned the dialogue into action by writing letters to administrators, city officials, and their peers regarding issues such as community safety, racial profiling, and sanitary conditions (or lack of) on their school campus. The NBPTS process gave me opportunities to write about this type of teaching.
>
> In the current climate of high-stakes testing, the NBPTS process reconfirmed my belief that it is not only possible to infuse culturally responsive teaching, but necessary. For example, my students participated in cross-curricular projects. They read and researched about important people of color and produced artwork such as murals, dioramas, and portraits. Because the NBPTS process calls for educators to reflect on their practice and

pedagogy, I increased my awareness of my students' needs, and I felt better prepared to teach them.

—Kimberly Min
Third-grade teacher

She has been an NBPTS certified teacher since November 2005.

Joining Teacher Networks

Some of the most powerful sites for teacher learning connect teachers from various schools around a challenge that they all see as important. These networks might depend heavily on the Internet or hold regular face-to-face workshops, meetings, and discussion groups. Through these networks, teachers gain access to expertise that may not be readily available at their schools.

Teacher networks connect members in various ways. Some focus on *subject matter*, such as the National Writing Project (NWP), which began in Berkeley, California, in 1974 and now includes sites in 197 communities. The project's goal is to improve teaching of writing in the nation's schools and to recognize the primary importance of teacher knowledge, expertise, and leadership in achieving this instructional goal. The NWP combines intensive summer institutes for teachers with follow-up opportunities for teachers to meet and learn together. During the summer institutes, teachers demonstrate their most effective practices, study existing research, and improve their knowledge of writing by writing themselves. Teachers quickly become leaders who develop local writing teacher groups in their own districts and schools and work as peer coaches to other teachers. The project also advances the ideal that access to high-quality educational experiences is a basic right of all learners and a cornerstone of equality.

Some of these subject-specific networks have *local chapters* that incubate strong learning communities that are crucial to new teacher development. First-year high school mathematics teacher Samantha Warrick, for example, believes that her "most valuable resource as a teacher" was the support she received from her peers in the Los Angeles chapter of Math for America, a nonprofit organization that seeks to improve mathematics education in public secondary schools.

> I am fortunate enough to be involved in a fellowship group in which I collaborate with fifty other fellows. When I start to feel like my job is impossible or that I am a terrible teacher, I have these people to help keep me focused. Teachers can be their own worst critics so I think that it is important to have people around you that can help you keep your work in perspective. In addition to providing support to one another, we share lesson plans and lesson resources. This has been extremely helpful for me. . . . I would highly suggest to any teacher, especially new teachers, to build a network of colleagues that you can share lesson plans with and turn to when you are feeling discouraged or overwhelmed.
>
> —Samantha Warrick
> First-year teacher, high school mathematics

Professional communities are most helpful when they encourage teachers to learn from one another as well as provide a supportive check on members' perceptions of their own teaching dilemmas—as Math for America does for Samantha. Although many of these networks are organized by universities, state departments of education, or nonprofit organizations, nearly all see their teacher members as the experts and follow a "teachers teaching teachers" model.

Perhaps most helpful for teachers committed to teaching for social justice are activist-oriented networks, whose members assume that good teaching—improved teaching—requires that they

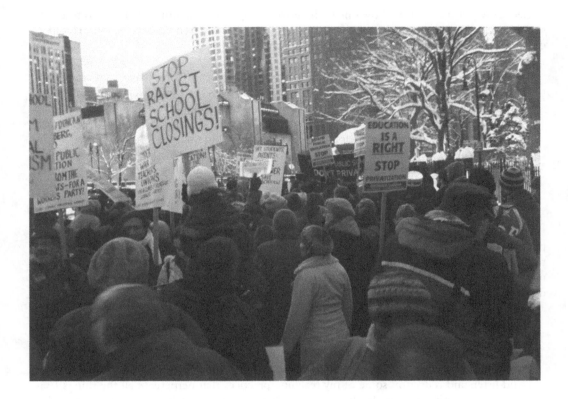

resist practices that disadvantage their students while they pursue changes in curriculum and instruction that will correct the inequalities their students experience.

Resources available through one such network, the New York Collective of Radical Educators (NYCoRE), are featured in other places in this book (see Focal Point 8.6). Another example, Teachers for Social Justice, is a Chicago-based network of teachers, administrators, preservice teachers, and other educators who work toward antiracist and multicultural/multilingual teaching that is grounded in the experiences of the city's students. Members are bound by a core belief: "All agree that all children should have an academically rigorous education that is both caring and critical, an education that helps students pose critical questions about society and 'talk back' to the world."[32] The group shares ideas and curriculum; it also supports activist work among its members and ally organizations. One specific goal is to get the voices of educators into the public discussion of school policies such as those that have led to the closure of some low-performing neighborhood schools. Groups like NYCoRE and Chicago's Teachers for Social Justice exist in many large urban areas, but also host conferences and provide resources with broad reach, even to those in more rural areas.

In networks like these, teachers see their activism as part of their "normal" professional activity. Importantly, such networks emphasize that individual teachers' efforts to bring social justice to their schools do not emerge from a perverse desire to be disruptive, but from well-substantiated conclusions drawn from social science research, critical theory, historical memory, community wisdom, and so on.

Georgene Acosta describes how one such network inspired her continued efforts to teach for social justice. This group met regularly to discuss social justice at their schools, lessons, readings, community actions, and out-of-school teaching activities.

> I considered all the amazing work aimed at promoting peace that I have seen among my colleagues at schools around the city. In her Life Skills class Joy Kraft teaches students to see the damaging effects of racism, sexism, classism, and homophobia and helps students devise nonviolent solutions to these social ills. Chris Morrisey has developed Project Peace, a peer-mediation program that he is helping to establish at his high school. These teachers are my heroes. When I face difficult situations as a teacher, they inspire me to work through those difficulties. They renew my sense of hope and courage by reminding me that I am not alone.
>
> —Georgene Acosta
> First-year teacher, high school English

Third-grade teacher Salina Gray reaped similar benefits from her experience in a collaborative project that brought educators together to develop materials and strategies that they could use to help their students study educational access and equity in their own communities. Teachers met regularly and posted their students' research in an online journal. During the process, Salina described how participating was helping her develop as a teacher.

> I interact with other socially conscious educators, hear their stories, thoughts, opinions, and experiences. This helps me rethink my own experiences . . . [to] question not just my teaching practices, but also the educational system that I grew up in. I like to think that I am dramatically different from those who don't respect their students. But I've had to sit and listen and reflect on some of my teaching practices that perpetuate all the things I say that I am fighting against. In the [project] I have evaluated my beliefs as a teacher, asking what education should be, what it means, and what I actually show my students. Do my actions show my values to my students? So I've become a kinder, more honest Ms. Gray. My students have noticed.
>
> —Salina Gray
> Third-grade teacher

As these examples show, continuous, critical reflection is vital, as are connections to like-minded colleagues. Indeed, the two have gone hand in hand for most accomplished educators. None of us learn to teach well, to teach for social justice, on our own. Although some schools may offer conditions and opportunities for high-quality professional development, committed teachers also do much to create these for themselves.

High school social studies teacher Judy Smith did this informally with some peers and a beloved mentor, Brian Gibbs. For three years, the group met once a month at Brian's house, where they talked about "curriculum, social justice, educational policy, funny students, and more." For Judy, this made all the difference: "That was probably the best three hours I spent a month. We got reenergized and discussed curriculum at the same time."

Becoming a Social Justice Activist

> The following principles guide me as a social justice educator. First, I recognize the experiences and prior knowledge of my students, which inform me about who they are and how they learn. I also engage my students in critical dialogue through the use of culturally responsive teaching, which provides my students opportunities to share their experiences

in their community. Then I try to provide opportunities for my students to be active agents of change, which affirms who they are and what they consider important. I also collaborate with students' families, the community, and other social justice educators. Such teaching can shape, transform, and influence individuals whose everyday decisions, in turn, have an impact on the rest of society.

—Kimberly Min
Third-grade teacher

Kimberly's reflections capture three important ways that teachers can act as social justice activists. One involves treating the cultural knowledge and experiences of their students as a foundation for their intellectual development. Doing so powerfully contrasts with deficit-based views of students, families, and communities. Another involves speaking the unspeakable. Instead of pretending that the problems and inequalities facing communities and schools don't exist, teachers like Kimberly unmask, critique, and engage their students in talking about and understanding them. They also help their students see possibilities—the ways things could, and should, be. A third way that teachers act as agents of social justice is by working in solidarity with students, families, community members, and colleagues to disrupt those problems and inequalities and to make progress toward new possibilities. As teachers do this, they counter the pervasive view that, as terrible as conditions are, there is simply not the knowledge or power to change them.

Like Kimberly, John Paul Arellano connects students' intellectual development with their development of critical consciousness.

I teach in response to the years of processed, mindless, and detached education I received. The self was in no way a part of my education. It isn't fair that I had to wait until the university to connect education with self-discovery. I am a teacher so I can bring relevant issues to the table in the early years of education so that students aren't battling with misconceptions of self and their world around them. There are so many questions in their minds, and they rarely get to hear the truth. When they catch a glimpse of it, they are the best readers, writers, and thinkers around. I teach in the hopes that through the sharing of passion, perspective, and narrative, students will feel as though their questions and doubts are valid. My work is driven by the initial thought that every student is intuitive, knowledgeable, and capable of reason.

—John Paul Arellano
Fourth-grade teacher

Countering Deficit Thinking With Community Strengths

Many teachers have not grown up as members of their students' communities or cultural groups. Bridging the racial, economic, and cultural divide that separates them from their students requires more than simply taking courses in multiculturalism and diversity. As education scholar Lilia Bartolomé contends,

The most pedagogically advanced strategies are sure to be ineffective in the hands of educators who implicitly or explicitly subscribe to a belief system that renders ethnic, racial, and linguistic minority students at best culturally disadvantaged and in need of fixing.[33]

More than sixty years ago, John Dewey argued the importance of connecting curriculum and instruction to community knowledge and resources:

Learning which develops intelligence and character does not come about when only the textbook and the teacher have a say; . . . every individual becomes educated only as he has an opportunity to contribute something from his own experience, no matter how meager or slender that background of experience may be at a given time; and finally . . . enlightenment comes from the give and take, from the exchange of experiences and ideas.[34]

Participating in this "give and take" is part of being a total teacher. Teachers can no more neglect knowledge of and engagement with the community than they can ignore their classroom environment or fail to plan instruction.

To counteract decades of "deficit" approaches to urban education, social justice teachers must discover and build on the strengths of the communities in which they teach. We have detailed many of the strategies for doing this activist curriculum work in Chapter 6 (on instruction), Chapter 8 (on building classroom communities), and Chapter 11 (on connecting with families and neighborhoods).

To summarize here, to build their teaching on the community's strengths, teachers must see and then question common beliefs and practices surrounding ability, race, class, gender, language, difference, and so on. They must sit at the intersection of theory and practice, constantly asking: Why do we do it this way? What assumptions about my students' communities and cultures underlie these practices? Whose interests does this practice serve? How might my students' cultural resources contribute to achieving our educational goals?

As student teachers, Ryan Williams and his classmates spent some time learning about resources and capacity in the neighborhoods surrounding the schools where they would later begin their careers. Among other things, they created an "asset map" of the potential education-related opportunities in the community. To do so, they contacted neighborhood churches, libraries, community groups, and other organizations. Community leaders referred Ryan and his classmates to resources that were not obvious at first glance, such as private homes where neighbors conducted tutorials and held meetings.

> The green building on the corner that I have passed many times is no longer just a stucco structure but a place where community folks come on Tuesdays, Thursdays, and Saturdays to pick up food items from Ms. Rodriquez. The yellow wooden house across from the liquor store is an after-school site for tutoring. The narrow brown and black Evangelist church provides college access information. Each week this community has at least six Neighborhood Watch meetings at which community members discuss a broad range of issues, including quality education and teenage violence. At one of these meetings, Ms. Garcia, a Neighborhood Watch leader, expressed her group's interest in connecting with teachers and the school to discuss how they could work together to provide alternate learning sites for students after school.
>
> —Ryan Williams
> First-year teacher, fourth grade

By the time Ryan began teaching, his knowledge of the community and its assets was strong and specific. The experience opened new possibilities for teaching and for working with parents and community members in support of students.

Engaging in Critical Dialogue About Students' Possible Lives

Deficit thinking may begin with the beliefs and attitudes of people who have power and authority (teachers, parents, the "establishment," etc.), but the greatest damage is done when adults pass on deficit habits of thought and students replicate them. Deficit thinking doesn't end just because justice-minded teachers grasp social theory; students themselves must talk, learn, and construct alternatives to the deficit model.

Through critical dialogue, students can begin to see their personal position as situated in larger economic, social, and political conditions *and* in the particulars of their community and daily experience. To support this, teachers can create or adapt standards-based curricula so they are rigorous and engrossing, develop students' knowledge and problem-solving skills, *and* challenge mainstream thinking about members of minoritized groups, such as people of color, people who are learning English, LGBTQ people, and others.

Judy Smith found ways to have her high school seniors meet the state standards in economics and, at the same time, consider the connections between their own behaviors and injustices that come with global capitalism:

> The international economics unit was the last of the semester. We had already studied basic micro- and macroeconomic concepts. We were ready to move the discussion away from U.S. economic issues to international economics. The California State Standard for this unit was "Economics 12.6: Students analyze issues of international trade and explain how the U.S. economy affects, and is affected by, economic forces beyond the United States' borders."
>
> I broke this down into four themes—free trade, consumerism, sweatshops, and globalization. My goal was to cover and go beyond the standard by teaching students how their individual consumer habits and beliefs have an impact on both the domestic and international environments, other cultures and peoples, and themselves.
>
> "How many of you woke up this morning and thought about what you would wear today? And then how many of you thought about where the clothes were made, how they were made, and how they wound up in your hands?" I asked these questions, and my students gave me strange looks. Ms. Smith, they said in a chorus, of course we thought about what we were going to wear today. And, no, we do not know where our clothes were made and how. In fact, why should we care?
>
> These students were being honest. Why should they care where their clothes are from? They have them, they like them, and they would buy more if they could. Currently the average teenager spends approximately $15 a day. My students claimed that they did, too. They admitted that they buy product after product without thinking about where the product was made, how it was made, or by whom. My challenge: how to get students to think beyond themselves and how their minute decisions impact the global community. Furthermore, how can these students become producers, rather than just consumers?
>
> Using the last unit in the textbook, we weaved the California standards' concepts of free trade, balance of trade, imports, and exports with Bill Bigelow's *Rethinking Globalization* text's concepts of sweatshops, consumerism, child labor, globalization, and personal responsibility. The economics text does not mention the latter concepts, and yet these social injustices and realities exist because of the practice of free trade.
>
> I wanted the students to look at themselves and to understand some of the ethical conflicts and social injustices that exist in business. How do progress and tradition grow together? Is profit more important than human rights? I hoped that after this unit, students would have a better understanding of their role and responsibility in the global marketplace. I wanted them to think about what they buy, for what reasons, and from where. Were there any purchasing habits they could change as a result of what they learned? Furthermore, were there any actions they could take to educate others?
>
> —Judy Smith
> High school social studies

Some teachers also engage students' families in their learning about social justice issues. During her first year teaching fifth grade, for example, Miranda Chavez integrated into her classwork a study of lead and its adverse impacts, especially on young children. Health department officials met with students and their parents multiple times, as did representatives from the local city councilperson's office. Students studied chemistry to understand the nature of lead. They also went out into their community—mostly Spanish-speaking Central American immigrants—to collect paint fragments and soil from spaces in which children played. They then tested these samples for lead content.

As a culminating activity, Miranda invited families to a potluck dinner at which her students presented informational posters they had made—presentations that involved explaining complex chemical processes. The room was packed; almost every parent attended, and the evening was conducted exclusively in Spanish. Some parents joined their children in presenting the lead findings, yet a few felt ill equipped to do so. One parent explained that she "hadn't done anything because she didn't know any English and hadn't attended school herself in her home country."

Feeling the tension in the room, Miranda respectfully addressed all the parents, explaining that they had all played important roles in this project, motivating their children and setting rules to ensure that projects were completed successfully. As these students move on to middle school, she continued, parents will play a crucial role in ensuring their children's future success in school. Knowing English and having a formal education, she assured parents, were not required. Herself a Central American immigrant, Miranda empathized with parents and offered a message of pride, agency, and social change.

Importantly, a social justice approach might begin with attention to inequity and discrimination, but the goal is always to press students—and, in Miranda's case, parents, too—toward a sense of agency within an inequitable system. This approach is evident in so many of the examples offered by teachers and sprinkled throughout this text—teachers at every grade level and in every content area.

It's summed up well by Frank Divinagracia and Salina Gray, whose words bring to life why they work tirelessly—even at peril of being deemed a little "crazy"—to ensure that every student knows their rights, what they're capable of, and how to work toward their goals.

> Since our initial conversations about their rights, and the role of education in their lives, my students place more emphasis on becoming good citizens and leaders. My students look for opportunities to be "teachers." They speak up for themselves now because they realize that their opinions and views are valued and respected. We've had conversations about what makes a "good leader," and reached the consensus that it is more than just getting the grades.
>
> Before I became more explicit about social justice in my classroom, I asked my students, "Why do you go to school?" They said, "to get a job" and "to pass the Stanford 9." Now they say "to be the best that I can be," and "to grow up and change the world."
>
> —Salina Gray
> Third-grade teacher

> I like to tell my students, and sometimes they like to listen, about the lives and experiences and words of various activists. . . . I like telling them how I am like the character in Sandra Cisneros's book *House on Mango Street*. She desperately wanted out of her neighborhood only to discover that the more she learned and grew, the more she knew she had to return home. In returning home she wanted to share with her people all the things that she had learned, and that the shackles that one physically sees are nothing compared with the mental

ones we put on ourselves. I think that my students think I am crazy, but I hope one day that my craziness will infect them.

—Frank Divinagracia
High school mathematics

Acting for Change

Social justice teachers often take their lessons beyond discussing issues in class and find ways to act. In many cases these teachers are themselves activists outside of school and presume that students will learn and gain from participating in similar social change activities. For example, first-year geography teacher Rey Tolteka Cuauhtin had his ninth graders read and analyze an article written by a local university professor called "Dysfunctional Neighborhoods," which characterized students' own community as deficit laden. In the article, the professor described the community as riddled with crime, poverty, laziness, and violence, and added that it provided its members with virtually "no opportunities." This professor also characterized young people in the community as having to endure poor parenting and limited access to positive role models. To develop students' critical analysis skills and sense of agency, Rey asked them to write responses that focused on their community's assets: its "beauty and positivity"; the residents' "hopes, dreams and ambitions"; and the abundance of "hardworking, supportive, and respectful" people. They then made their responses public, too—a counternarrative for all to see.

In the following quote, Kimberly Min describes her third graders taking a similarly critical and constructive look at school administrators, the mayor, and the driver of the neighborhood ice cream truck.

> I incorporate social activism into my teaching in many ways—through history, storytelling, class discussion, writing, artistic expression, performance, and even active protest. . . .
>
> First and foremost, the level of involvement depends on the students and the issues they bring up in class discussion. For example, in a lesson about inequity, my students revealed that the bathrooms closest to our room were the filthiest in the school. After recognizing this as "unfair," students wrote letters to the principal and superintendent, requesting cleaner bathrooms with soap and toilet paper.
>
> In another instance that prompted written protest, my students wrote letters to the mayor, requesting that the police end racial profiling. In return, the mayor's office sent back a letter with his picture, thanking us for our interest. This validated my students' efforts, showing them that their voices mattered. Students learned that they could also protest in other ways than writing.
>
> After learning about nonviolent resistance through movements such as the civil rights bus boycott, students applied this knowledge to their own community. They created picket signs to boycott the ice cream truck that was selling toy guns. This was a response to a second-grade peer being suspended for having a toy gun on campus, which violated the zero-tolerance policy.
>
> I consider these to be the lessons that I am most proud of because students are seen as the change makers.
>
> —Kimberly Min
> Third-grade teacher

Many social justice teachers extend their own activism beyond their schools and classrooms, although their students may be unaware of their teachers' activities. For example, when Noah Lippe-Klein and Ramón Martínez were still relatively new teachers, they were active members of the Coalition for Educational Justice (CEJ). The CEJ, an activist offshoot of their local teachers' union, formed when a group of teachers joined forces with civic, legal, and educational leaders committed to various reforms, including ending the use of high-stakes testing with low-income children of color.

Ramón, Noah, and other CEJ members brought over 300 teachers, parents, and students to a school board meeting to seek support in changing the testing program and related grade retention policies. The coalition organized antitesting actions at several school sites. It won victories when district officials adopted a resolution to seek alternatives to the tests and instructed principals to honor the requests of parents who wanted their children exempted in the meantime.

The CEJ also fought for reducing class sizes, halting the disproportionate expansion of military recruitment on campuses serving predominantly Black and Latino communities ensuring qualified teachers and adequate resources at some of their city's most overcrowded and neglected schools, and preventing private charter companies from taking over schools. In these efforts, the CEJ provided opportunities for student leaders to meet privately with members of their school board about these issues, helping to bring about progress in each area.

Some teachers' activism *is* visible to their students, and it sparks activism among them, too. In fact, this is the very topic of Focal Point 12.3, an essay by Jesse Hagopian, a history teacher and Black Student Union adviser at Garfield High School in Seattle, Washington. Active on multiple fronts, Jesse and his colleagues took a particularly historic stand on behalf of, and alongside, their students, when they held a press conference in 2013 to announce their unanimous decision to not administer a mandated assessment that they believed was "not good for our students, nor . . . an appropriate or useful tool in measuring progress" and that instead "produces specious results, and wreaks havoc on limited school resources." This decision, they announced, was grounded in their collective identity as "professionals who care deeply about our students and cannot continue to participate in a practice that harms our school and our students."[35] The activism that they forged in partnership with teachers, students, parents, and community members city-wide not only yielded successes in the local context but also drew support from public school advocates and stoked other actions nationwide.

Focal Point 12.3
Teachers and Students Taking Action Together

My Greatest Teaching Moment

Seattle high school history teacher Jesse Hagopian's greatest teaching moment came after he was arrested at the state capitol—and his students made their own history. This is Jesse's story.

I achieved the greatest moment in my teaching career this past winter.

I began teaching in an elementary school in Southeast Washington, DC, in 2001. Directly across from the entrance of the school was a decrepit building with vegetation growing out the windows. The library's book collection was more appropriate for an archaeological study than a source for topical information. Police roamed the halls of our elementary school looking for mouthy kids to jack up against the wall. I had one hole in the middle of the chalkboard and another hole in the ceiling that often meant rain flooded my classroom.

. . . The attacks of 9/11 were carried out [that fall], closely followed by the government's launching of the war on Afghanistan. I received a higher degree in education theory that year as I witnessed our nation spend money to bomb children halfway around the world while refusing to care for my students in the shadow of the White House. . . .

My start in education in Washington, DC, public schools taught me that being a social justice educator has to mean two things: provide an antiracist curriculum in the classroom and be an activist in the community—that is, fight to restructure society so education is a priority over war spending and bank bailouts.

My perspective of what it means to be a social justice educator has put me in face-to-face opposition to some of the most powerful people in the education establishment.

When U.S. Secretary of Education Arne Duncan came to a Seattle-area high school in July 2010, I had an opportunity to debate him on his advocacy for teacher "merit pay." When filmmaker David Guggenheim held a special screening of *Waiting for Superman* in Seattle, I got on the invite list. When the film was over, I gave him "two thumbs down," and rigorous debate about charter schools. Recently, I joined the Occupy Education "policy throwdown" with the Gates Foundation and confronted the foundation's PR spokesperson on its advocacy of using standardized testing in teacher evaluations.

These confrontations uncovered more awareness about corporate-driven education reform and helped win over more educators to the mission of the Social Equality Educators (SEE), an organization that I'm part of.

When Washington state announced that it would hold a special legislative session to decide how to further slash the education and health care budgets, SEE headed to Olympia to issue citizen's-arrest warrants to legislators for failing to adhere to the Washington State Constitution that declares education is the state's "Paramount Duty." In the course of delivering arrest warrants to the House Ways and Means Committee, I was arrested.

While I was in jail, unbeknownst to me, my students at Garfield High School set up a Facebook page titled "Free Mr. Hagopian." Hundreds of student Bulldogs joined the page in my support. When I was released that night and appeared for school the next day, the students changed the Facebook page to "Seattle Student Walkout for Education." I have often hoped that my students would one day learn the lessons of history I had taught them—from the struggles of the abolitionists and women's rights advocates in antebellum America, to student movements against the Vietnam War, to the Freedom Riders of the Civil Rights Movement—and use them to start their own revolution.

The moment my students lost their contentedness with studying history and started making their own—that was the most gratifying day of my career.

Epilogue: Only weeks after the student mass walkout, the Washington State Supreme Court ruled that the state legislature was in violation of the Constitution and would need to increase funding to education.

Jesse Hagopian is a founding member of Social Equality Educators, the editor of and contributing author to *More Than a Score: The New Uprising Against High-Stakes Testing* (Haymarket Books, 2014), an editor for *Rethinking Schools*, and recipient of the 2013 "Secondary School Teacher of Year" award from the Academy of Education Arts and Sciences.

Kimberly Min, Ramón Martínez, Jesse Hagopian and his colleagues, and so many more join a venerable American tradition, captured here in the words of escaped slave, abolitionist, and writer Frederick Douglass:

Let me give you a word on the philosophy of reform. The whole history of the progress of human liberty shows that all concessions . . . have been born of earnest struggle. The conflict has been exciting, agitating, all absorbing. . . . It must do this or it does nothing. If there is no struggle there is no progress. Those who profess to favor freedom, yet depreciate agitation, are men who want crops without plowing up the ground. They want rain without thunder and lightning. They want the ocean without the awful roar of the waters. This struggle may be a moral one; or it may be a physical one; or it may be both moral and physical; but it must be a struggle. Power never concedes anything without a demand. It never did and it never will.[36]

When Douglass wrote the words "the awful roar of the waters," *awful* meant something quite different from the present sense of inspiring fear, extreme unpleasantness, or ugliness. To Douglass, the roar of struggle inspired not fear but awe, an overwhelming feeling of reverence—grand, sublime, and powerful. Not for the fainthearted, this struggle lifts the spirits of the hopeful as they take action, make demands, plow up the ground. Career teachers can do just that.

Expanding Your Professional Influence

Not surprisingly, perhaps, as their careers develop, many teachers who are committed to advancing social justice seek to extend their influence within the educational system by taking on new roles within it. Some teachers expand their influence in the ways that have been mentioned earlier—for example, by becoming mentors in teacher induction systems. Judy Smith, for example, has long planned to remain in teaching and shape the profession by supporting others to develop the knowledge, skills, and values to teach all students well.

Others take the route that Kimberly Min followed by becoming one of many NBPTS-certified teachers, who are called on increasingly to serve as teacher leaders in and beyond their school sites. Still others become administrators, who hope that the costs of leaving will be outweighed by the new contributions that different positions enable them to make to the education of the students they care so much about. After four years as a regular classroom teacher, Mauro Bautista took on the role of bilingual coordinator, overseeing all the programming for English Learners at his school site. A few years later, he expressed his desire to eventually become a school leader for social justice.

> My plans for the future are to receive a second master's of education and an administrative credential. My master's program has helped me define social justice educator: "A social justice educator identifies injustices, collaborates with others who are affected by the injustices, and then takes action to disrupt the reproduction of these injustices." My goal is to become an assistant principal and eventually a principal who acts as a social justice educator.
>
> One thing I am discovering is that when you work primarily with adults it is easy to forget that we are here for the students first and foremost. I hope that as I continue my journey through education, I keep students and their families first.
>
> —Mauro Bautista
> Middle-school bilingual education coordinator

Mauro is now a high school principal at the Méndez Learning Center—School of Math and Science, a small learning community, located in Los Angeles.

Mauro's pathway is not altogether unusual. Teacher Jennifer Garcia, quoted in several earlier chapters, is now a high school principal. Jasper Bui became the librarian at his middle school. Javier Espindola became a district literacy coach to other teachers, while Frank Divinagracia became a math coach at his high school. Others are school system content area specialists, educational technology experts, or counselors, or they direct after-school programs. Some, like Ramón Martínez, Benji Chang, Laura Silvina Torres, and Mariana Pacheco, went back to graduate school and became professors and researchers. Others include a museum educator, an educational software developer, a marketing director for an educational media company, and Peace Corps volunteer. All remain committed to changing the world.

Finally, and fittingly, we return to the insights of accomplished career teachers like Cicely Bingener, quoted at the beginning of this chapter. Cicely has had opportunities to move "up" in the educational system, but she chooses to renew her commitment to teaching in her own classroom. Career teaching remains a profoundly powerful pathway, and it presents opportunities to change the world in ways that reside only in the classroom. As Cicely exemplifies, teachers *can* expand their professional influence while also deepening their roots in classroom teaching.

Committing to Critique and Hope

Teaching has the potential to be transformative. It can create positive change in the lives of all—tolerance, awareness, respect, meaning, and fulfillment. But teachers and students must cast a critical eye to make learning reflect their realities and aspirations. As committed, critical, and active agents within schools, students and teachers must create change. By questioning our own views and preconceptions, by critiquing our own practice and pedagogy, and by allowing our reflections to turn into positive action, we create social justice.

—Kimberly Min
Third-grade teacher

Critical and compassionate consciousness is part of what drives me, as well as the deep belief that students should not have to wait until they get to college for critical knowledge to be made available to them. . . . To do my best to offer youth what I was never offered in school, a more meaningful education, that's one reason I'm here. . . . In the current state our world is in, to me, not teaching for social justice is not really teaching.

—Rey Tolteka Cuauhtin
First-year teacher, ninth-grade geography

Kimberly Min and Rey Tolteka Cuauhtin, like most of the other teachers quoted in this book, express optimism about teaching's role in social transformation. They speak of hope and struggle in equal measure. In doing so, their voices join up with those of scholars and activists who argue that advancing democracy and justice, in schools and in society, requires both. Adopting such a stance is one of the most powerful strategies for crafting a career as a social justice educator.

Famed philosopher and public intellectual Cornel West calls this a kind of "prophetic pragmatism"—a view of democracy as a process, rather than a perfect end product. West argues that in diverse cultures like ours, any democratic process must place its faith in "the abilities and capacities of ordinary people to participate in decision making procedures of institutions that regulate their lives." He cautions, however, that participation itself is insufficient. Rather, the democracy must be one that "keeps track of social misery, solicits and channels moral outrage to alleviate it, and projects a future in which the potentialities of ordinary people flourish and flower."[37]

Similarly, Brazilian educator Paulo Freire paired the importance of hope and optimism for better social conditions with an active struggle to attain them. In arguing that hope is a fundamental human need, Freire cautioned against separating it from action. "The idea that hope alone will transform the world . . . is an excellent route to hopelessness, pessimism, and fatalism." Hope, he argues, is what sustains our struggle for a better world:

The attempt to do without hope, in the struggle to improve the world, as if that struggle could be reduced to calculated acts alone, or a purely scientific approach, is a frivolous illusion. . . . Without a minimum of hope, we cannot so much as start the struggle. But without the struggle, hope . . . dissipates, loses its bearings, and turns into hopelessness.[38]

Yes, it is circular. Hope sustains action, and people must act, or hope turns against them—empty. Freire tied all of this specifically to education, making him one of the most provocative, recognized, and influential educators worldwide. For Freire, as for West, hope and struggle are not simply *instruments* that produce improved social conditions, although improved social conditions is a leading goal. Participating in a hopeful struggle is *itself* an improvement. West's prophetic pragmatism and Freire's juxtaposition of hope and struggle provide teachers with a philosophical stance that gives meaning both to the everyday acts of teaching and to the larger efforts teachers make to teach, organize, support, and follow others who join to improve conditions and opportunities for students. This stance makes teaching matter, even in the face of the discouraging realities of their students' lives.

Georgene Acosta, like many of the other teachers in this book, designed her career with these lofty and laudable ideals in mind. And by the end of her first full year of teaching, hope and struggle had merged in her daily actions in her local school. In the face of difficult circumstances, she made a commitment to prophetic pragmatism and to teaching.

> On the morning of May 1, I returned to work after a two-week spring break. I felt rested, reenergized, and ready to begin a fresh week. About ten minutes into my first-period class, the voice of the principal came over the P.A. She began with her usual, "Pardon the interruption . . ." But this would not be one of her pep talks about the importance of literacy, good attendance, and respectful behavior. "Two students at our school, Eddie Marengo and Richard Rivers, were shot and killed over the break."
>
> In the days that followed, I began to gather various bits of information about the circumstances surrounding these two tragic deaths. I learned that the police gunned down Richard, an excellent student in my eleventh-grade class last year, in his own neighborhood, in the early morning hours. Eddie, a freshman whom I did not know personally, was shot in the back of the head while sitting at a bus stop on Easter Sunday.
>
> In the following days and weeks, I experienced a profound sense of despair. I questioned my effectiveness as a social justice educator and wondered, "Am I contributing enough to end violence in my school and in my community?" While pondering the deaths of these two precious young people, I felt myself falling into an abyss of sadness.
>
> As Jean-Paul Sartre said, "Life begins on the other side of despair." I emerged from this abyss with a profound sense of hope. That hope is grounded in my belief that this culture CAN be healed! It CAN be transformed! It CAN nurture and protect its young people. And it CAN give them the tools they need to perpetuate peace!
>
> We must research and analyze the problems that we encounter. We must search for causes and solutions to the problems we find. We must study these solutions and put them to work in our own practices both within and outside of the classroom walls. We must study, we must think, we must ask hard questions, and we must work toward even harder solutions. And we must do these things because we believe, as Vaclav Havel said, that "None of us as an individual can save the world as a whole, but each of us must behave as though it were in our power to do so." We know that there are no quick fixes to the problems that our young people confront on a daily basis. We know that creating meaningful solutions requires commitment, intelligence, dialogue, and, most importantly, patience. We are up for the challenge.
>
> When I think of Eddie and Richard, I feel a deep nameless ache that I know will always be with me. But that nameless feeling helps to sustain my hope. Hope for a world that is

worthy of every one of its precious children. We embrace the idea expressed by Martin Luther King that the universe is on the side of justice and that justice will eventually win. And that is why we teach.

—Georgene Acosta
High school English teacher

Teachers like those cited throughout this book combine their commitment to hope and critique with their professional knowledge and skill to create public schools where children can both forge a common good and enrich their individual lives. Doing so, they experience children's brilliance that defies typical expectations. Such teachers have seen innumerable combinations of students learning together. They have also seen themselves accomplish more than they ever thought they could. They know, in a very grounded way, precisely what *is* possible.

Finding Satisfaction in the Everyday

John Dewey believed that schools should not be thought of as offering *preparation* for democratic life, but that they themselves should be sites of democratic living and seedbeds for social change.[39] Dewey cautioned that teachers' work therefore should not be understood only as a means to some worthwhile end, but as worthwhile in and of itself. In other words, democracy and social justice are not end states, but *ways of being*.

In the following quotes, Mauro Bautista, Mark Hill, Kimberly Min, and Judy Smith, each in his or her own way, describe their satisfaction with the hard work they've chosen to do and with the process of becoming a teacher and learning to teach for social justice.

> Now that I understand the teaching profession, I recognize my understanding will always be a work in progress. The classroom techniques I use depend on my students. I will never be able to look at any one of my classes and say, "Here is the perfect classroom, and now I will have the perfect classroom every year." Each year I will learn what it means to be a social justice educator from my students, their parents, my colleagues, scholars, and myself.
> —Mauro Bautista

> Our school was designated "low performing" several years ago. This was due partly to gaps in the students' K–8 education—long-term subs, poor teachers—as well as to their difficulties outside of school. Minority and low socioeconomic students in areas like ours are the ones who get the short end of the educational stick. Seeking to provide a socially just education for our students, the district and UCLA partnered. Well-prepared and committed students came to do their student teaching and then became permanent staff members. I was one of those teachers.
>
> Each year, the expectations for student behavior and achievement became higher, and our school improved dramatically. . . . This has been largely the result of the school-wide high expectations instituted by well-prepared teachers and a highly supportive school administration.
>
> The students themselves see and feel the change that has taken place. . . . This has become a source of pride for our staff, which continues to help propel our positive momentum.
> —Mark Hill

> During Thanksgiving, my class participated in a "Feast of Resistance." . . . We began by discussing where different fruits come from in the world, as we explored the origin of the banana—a topic in our social studies text. We were able to see how this piece of fruit was

politicized in the global market as we talked about cheap laborers in South America who were exploited. This led to our next discussion about the United Farm Workers and the grape strikes led by Cesar Chavez and Philip Vera Cruz. It was amazing to see the students reenact what they believed to be happening, as students began to role-play the characters of the boss and the exploited fruit pickers. I asked the students, "So what do you think the people did when they asked for a raise and the boss sat in his office and said no?" Darrell responded, "They should have gone on strike." Then I asked, "What's that?" Darrell replied confidently, "Like the bus drivers who went on strike. They just stop working." Then, with no prodding by me, the students began chanting, "Strike, strike, strike."

It was amazing. The students were making huge connections between their prior knowledge and the larger picture and engaged in critical thinking. They showed that they understood inequity in the labor market, and that people of color have the agency to fight back even as they are systematically used for cheap labor. . . . This was a pivotal moment.

—Kimberly Min

There is a specific place on my campus—when I round a corner and catch sight of my portable classroom—where every day I marvel that I am a teacher. . . . Hey, don't get me wrong, there was a cost moving from high tech to high school. In corporate America, luxuries such as fabulous holiday parties and access to the latest technology seduced me for a while. I loved the fast pace, salary, travel, and interesting problem solving. I learned about business, professionalism, and working with others. All valuable. However, that cost, when evaluated in heart-and-soul dollars, changes. In high tech, we did not take much time to examine values, biases, and different cultures. High tech didn't teach me about human suffering and triumph at the same time. High tech didn't expose me to our children and to their critical role in our future and our democracy, or offer intellectual stimulation on history, literacy, and politics. High tech didn't teach me to be a better human being. Teaching high school does.

—Judy Smith

Welcome to the Hopeful Struggle

We conclude in Focal Point 12.4 with a passage from Herbert Kohl, who has been inspiring educators for many decades with sobering and joyful stories of teaching. Kohl's own career began in 1962 in Harlem, where he taught sixth grade, an experience he documented in his classic book, *36 Children*. The excerpt is from an essay Kohl wrote to aspiring teachers about finding satisfaction in the everyday work of teaching for social justice. We don't know if Mauro, Mark, Kimberly, Judy, or the other teachers in this book have read Kohl's essay. We do know that they live his words, as do countless other teachers every day.

Focal Point 12.4
Herbert Kohl Reflects on Teaching for Social Justice

Advice for Those Who Want to Teach "Against the Grain"

The idea that you have to advocate teaching for social justice is a sad statement about the moral sensibility in our schools and society. . . . One cannot simply assume that because an action or sentiment is fair, just, or compassionate that it will be popular or embraced. . . .

So, what are social justice teachers . . . to do in the classroom so that they go against the grain and work in the service of their students?

I have several suggestions, some pedagogical and some personal. First of all, don't teach against your conscience or align yourself with texts, people, and rules that hurt children. Resist in as creative a way as you can, through humor, developing and using narratives, and organizing for social and educational change with others who feel as you do. Don't become isolated or alone in your efforts. . . . Find a school where you can do your work, risk getting fired and stand up for the quality of your work. Don't quit in the face of opposition: make people work hard if they intend to fire you for teaching equity and justice.

However, in order to do this, you must hone your craft as a teacher. . . . This is essential for caring teachers. You have to get it right for your students before presuming to take on larger systems, no matter how terrible they are. As educators, we need to root our struggles for social justice in the work we do on an everyday level in a community with a particular group of students. . . .

Look around at everything other people say is effective with children. Pick and choose, restructure and retool the best of what you can find, make it your own, and most of all watch your students and see what works. Listen to them, observe how they learn, and then, based on your experience and their responses, figure out how to practice social justice in your classroom as you discuss and analyze it. . . .

It is not enough to teach well and create a social justice classroom separate from the larger community. You have to be a community activist as well, a good parent, a decent citizen, and active community member. Is all this possible? Probably not—certainly it isn't easy and often demands sacrifice. . . .

This leads me to my final suggestion. Protect and nurture yourself, have some fun in your life, learn new things that only obliquely relate to issues of social justice. Walk, play ball, play chess, swim, fall in love, give yourself in love to someone else. Don't forget to laugh or feel good about the world. Sing with others, tell stories and listen to other people's stories, have fun so that you can work hard and work hard so that you and your parents and your students can have fun without looking over their shoulders. This is not a question of selfishness but one of survival. Don't turn teaching for social justice into a grim responsibility but take it for the moral and social necessity that it is. And don't be afraid to struggle for what you believe.

Source: Herbert Kohl, "Some Reflections on Teaching for Social Justice," in *Teaching for Social Justice: A Democracy and Education Reader,* eds. William Ayers, Jean Ann Hunt, and Therese Quinn (New York: The New Press and Teachers College Press, 1998), 285–287.

Digging Deeper and Tools for Critique

www.routledge.com/cw/teachingtochangetheworld

Notes

1 Vaclav Havel, *The Art of the Impossible: Politics as Morality in Practice* (New York: Knopf, 1997), 112.
2 Eleanor Roosevelt, *You Learn by Living: Eleven Keys for a More Fulfilling Life* (Louisville, KY: Westminster John Knox Press, 1960), 60. Thanks to Julian Weissglass for reminding us of this quote.
3 Adapted from Judy Smith, "From High Tech to High School," *Forum,* UCLA Graduate School of Education and Information Studies, 2005, 4.
4 Geneva Gay and Tyrone Howard, "Multicultural Teacher Education for the 21st Century," *Teacher Educator* 36, no. 1 (2001): 1–16.
5 *Assessment of Diversity in America's Teaching Force: A Call to Action* (Washington, DC: National Collaborative on Diversity in the Teaching Force, 2004), www.ate1.org/pubs/uploads/diversityreport.pdf.
6 National Center for Education Statistics, *Fast Facts,* https://nces.ed.gov/fastfacts/display.asp?id=28; U.S. Department of Education, *The State of Racial Diversity in the Educator Workforce,* June 2016, https://www2.ed.gov/rschstat/eval/highered/racial-diversity/state-racial-diversity-workforce.pdf.
7 American Association for Employment in Education, *2004 Educator Supply and Demand in the United States,* www.aaee.org/cwt/external/wcpages/fles/2004fullreportforwebsite.pdf.
8 Sarah Almy and Christina Theokas, *Not Prepared for Class: High-Poverty Schools Continue to Have Fewer In-Field Teachers* (Washington, DC: Education Trust, 2010), www.edtrust.org/sites/edtrust.org/fles/publications/fles/Not%20Prepared%20for%20Class.pdf.
9 U.S. Department of Education, Office of Civil Rights, *2009–10 Civil Rights Data Collection (CRDC),* http://ocrdata.ed.gov.
10 A review of the literature on this topic is included in Karen Hunter Quartz, Andrew Thomas, Lauren Anderson, Kimberly Barraza Lyons, Brad Olsen, and Katherine Masyn, *Careers in Motion: A Longitudinal Retention Study of Role Changing Patterns Among Urban Educators* (UCLA: IDEA Technical Report, 2005), http://idea2.gseis.ucla.edu/publications/utec/wp/pdf/04.pdf; Education Trust with Richard Ingersoll, *Core Problems: Out of Field Teaching Persists in Key Academic Courses and High Poverty Schools* (Education Trust, 2008), http://edtrust.org/wp-content/uploads/2013/10/SASSreportCoreProblem.pdf.
11 Sylvia Allgretto and Lawrence Mischel, *The Teacher Pay Gap Is Wider Than Ever* (Economic Policy Institute, August 9, 2016), http://irle.berkeley.edu/files/2016/The-teacher-pay-gap-is-wider-than-ever.pdf.
12 Sylvia Allegretto, Sean Corcoran, and Lawrence Mishel, *The Teaching Penalty: An Update Through 2010* (Washington, DC: Economic Policy Institute, 2011), www.epi.org/publication/the_teaching_penalty_an_update_through_2010/.

13 Andrew Simmons, "The Elusive Teacher Next Door," *San Francisco Chronicle*, June 28, 2017, www.theatlantic.com/education/archive/2017/06/the-elusive-teacher-next-door/531990/.

14 Sylvia Allegretto, Sean Corcoran, and Lawrence Mishel, *How Does Teacher Pay Compare?* (New York: Economic Policy Institute, 2004), www.epinet.org/.

15 *MetLife Survey of the American Teacher: Teachers, Parents and the Economy*, 2012, www.metlife.com/assets/cao/contributions/foundation/american-teacher/2011-Teacher-Survey-Findings.pdf.

16 National Center on Performance Incentives, *Teacher Pay for Performance: Experimental Evidence From the Project on Incentives in Teaching*, September 2010, www.performanceincentives.org/data/fles/gallery/ContentGallery/POINT_REPORT_9.21.10.pdf; Julie Marsh et al., *A Big Apple for Educators: New York City's Experiment With Schoolwide Performance Bonuses* (Rand Corporation), 2011, www.rand.org/content/dam/rand/pubs/monographs/2011/RAND_MG1114.pdf.

17 Allegretto, Corcoran, and Mishel, *The Teaching Penalty*.

18 Susanna Loeb, Linda Darling-Hammond, and John Luczac, "How Teaching Conditions Predict Teacher Turnover in California Schools," *Peabody Journal of Education* 80, no. 3 (2005): 44–70; Eileen Horn, *Recruiting and Retaining Teachers at Hard-to-Staff Schools: Examining the Tradeoffs Teachers Make When Choosing a School* (PhD diss., University of California, Los Angeles, 2005).

19 Metropolitan Life, *Metlife Survey of the American Teacher Finds Decreased Teacher Satisfaction, Increased Parent Engagement Amid Economic Uncertainty*, March 7, 2012, www.metlife.com/about/press-room/index.html?compID=79162.

20 Definition of the Highly Qualified Teacher (HQT), *No Child Left Behind*, Revised, July 1, 2010, www.nj.gov/education/profdev/nclb/hqtcharts.pdf.

21 American Federation of Teachers, *AFT History*, www.aft.org/about/history.

22 Robert Pear, "Education Chief Calls Union 'Terrorist,' Then Recants," *New York Times*, February 24, 2004, www.nytimes.com/2004/02/24/us/education-chief-calls-union-terrorist-then-recants.html.

23 Terry Moe, "No Teacher Left Behind," *Wall Street Journal*, January 13, 2005.

24 Jessica Calefati, "NJEA President Calls Christie 'Irresponsible' After He Blamed Teachers for Lack of School Supplies," *Star-Ledger*, November 9, 2010, www.nj.com/news/index.ssf/2010/11/njea_offcial_calls_christie_i.html.

25 Trip Gabriel, "Teachers Wonder, Why the Scorn?" *New York Times*, March 2, 2011, www.nytimes.com/2011/03/03/education/03teacher.html.

26 "Wisconsin Teachers Union Protests Governor Scott Walker's Bill; Idaho, Florida Follow," *Huffington Post*, February 17, 2011, www.huffingtonpost.com/2011/02/17/teachers-union-wisconsin-scott-walker_n_824888.html; Gabriel, "Teachers Wonder, Why the Scorn?"

27 Margaret Haley, *Battleground: The Autobiography of Margaret Haley*, ed. Robert L. Reid (Chicago: University of Illinois Press, 1982), 285–286.

28 Susanne Ybarra, "UCLA Conference Emphasizes Importance of Partnerships in Education," *Diverse Education*, June 21, 2017, http://diverseeducation.com/article/98081/.

29 Judith Warren Little, "The Mentor Phenomenon and the Social Organization of Teaching," in *Review of Research in Education*, ed. C. B. Cazden (Washington, DC: American Educational Research Association, 1990), 297–351.

30 "Practice," *New Teacher Center*, www.newteachercenter.org/impact/practice/, retrieved on February 24, 2011.

31 Laura M. Desimone, Andrew C. Porter, Michael S. Garet, Kwang Suk Yoon, and Beatrice F. Birman, "Effects of Professional Development on Teachers' Instruction: Results From a Three-Year Longitudinal Study," *Educational Evaluation and Policy Analysis* 24, no. 2 (2002): 81–112.

32 Stephanie Hicks, Teachers for Social Justice, https://www.linkedin.com/in/stephaniedhicks; see also http://www.teachersforjustice.org/.

33 Lilia Bartolomé, "Beyond the Methods Fetish," *Harvard Education Review* 64, no. 2 (1994): 180.

34 John Dewey, "Democracy and Education in the World of Today," *Essays* (first published as a pamphlet by the Society for Ethical Culture, New York, 1938), 296.

35 Development without Limits, http://developmentwithoutlimits.org/episode-34-jesse-hagopian-teacher-co-organizer-of-garfield-high-school-test-boycott/.

36 Frederick Douglass, Speech Celebrating West India Emancipation Day, Canandaigua, New York, August 4, 1857, reproduced in Philip Foner, ed., *The Life and Writings of Frederick Douglass*, Vol. 2 (New York: International Publishers of New York, 1976), 437.

37 Cornel West, "The Limits of Neopragmatism," *Southern California Law Review* 63 (1990): 1747.

38 Paulo Freire, *Pedagogy of Hope* (New York: Continuum, 1995), 9–10.

39 Dewey, "Democracy and Education in the World of Today."

Bibliography

2016 History-Social Science Framework for California. www.cde.ca.gov/ci/hs/cf/sbedrafthssfw.asp.

AAAS. *Science for All Americans.* Washington, DC: Author, 1989.

Academy of Child and Adolescent Psychiatry. *Facts for Families, No. 1: Children and Divorce,* March 2011. www.aacap.org/galleries/FactsForFamilies/01_children_and_divorce.pdf.

Adams, David Wallace. *Education for Extinction: American Indians and the Boarding School Experience 1875–1928.* Lawrence, KS: University Press of Kansas, 1997.

Addams, Jane. "The Public School and the Immigrant Child." In *The Educating of Americans: A Documentary History,* ed. Daniel Calhoun. Boston: Houghton Mifflin, 1969.

The Advancement Project. *Schoolhouse to Jailhouse: On the Ground.* www.advancementproject.org/ our-work/schoolhouse-to-jailhouse/on-the-ground/.

Afterschool Alliance. *21st Century Community Learning Centers Providing Afterschool Supports to Communities Nationwide.* www.afterschoolalliance.org/documents/factsResearch/21stCCLC_ Factsheet.pdf.

Aguinis, Herman, Steven A. Culpepper, and Charles A. Pierce. "Differential Prediction Generalization in College Admissions Testing." *Journal of Education Psychology 108,* no. *7* (October 2016): 1045–1059.

Akinbami, Lara J., Xiang Liu, Patricia N. Pastor, and Cynthia A. Reuben. *Attention Deficit Hyperactivity Disorder Among Children Aged 5–17 Years in the United States, 1998–2009.* Hyatsville, MD: Centers for Disease Control and Prevention, U.S. Department of Health and Human Services, 2011. www.cdc.gov/nchs/data/databriefs/db70.PDF.

Alabama State Legislature. *Beason-Hammon Alabama Taxpayer and Citizen Protection Act (HB56),* 2011. http://immigration.alabama.gov/.

Allegretto, Sylvia, Sean Corcoran, and Lawrence Mishel. *How Does Teacher Pay Compare?* New York: Economic Policy Institute, 2004. www.epinet.org.

Allegretto, Sylvia, Sean Corcoran, and Lawrence Mishel. *The Teaching Penalty: An Update Through 2010.* Washington, DC: Economic Policy Institute, 2011. www.epi.org/publication/ the_teaching_penalty_an_update_through_2010/.

Allen, Brenda A., and A. Wade Boykin. "African-American Children and the Educational Process: Alleviating Cultural Discontinuity Through Prescriptive Pedagogy." *School Psychology Review 21,* no. *4* (1992): 586–596.

Alliance to Reclaim Our Schools. www.reclaimourschools.org/about.

Almy, Sarah, and Christina Theokas. *Not Prepared for Class: High-Poverty Schools Continue to Have Fewer In-Field Teachers.* Washington, DC: Education Trust, 2010. www.edtrust.org/sites/edtrust. org/files/publications/files/Not%20Prepared%20for%20Class.pdf.

American Academy of Religion. *Guidelines for Teaching About Religion in K–12 Public Schools in the United States,*2010.www.aarweb.org/publications/Online_Publications/Curriculum_Guidelines/ AARK-12CurriculumGuidelines.pdf.

American Association for the Advancement of Science. *Science for All Americans.* Washington, DC: Author, 1989.

American Association for Employment in Education. *2004 Educator Supply and Demand Research Report.* www.aaee.org/cwt/external/wcpages/files/2004fullreportforwebsite.pdf.

American Educational Research Association, American Psychological Association, and National Council on Measurement in Education. *Standards for Educational and Psychological Testing.* Washington, DC: American Educational Research Association, 1999.

American Federation of Teachers. *AFT History.* www.aft.org/about/history/.

American Immigration Council. *An Overview of U.S. Refugee Law and Policy,* 2015. www.americanimmigrationcouncil.org/sites/default/files/research/an_overview_of_united_states_refugee_law_and_policy.pdf.

American Social History Project. *Who Built America?* CD-ROM Produced by the City University of New York. www.ashp.cuny.edu.

Anagnostopoulos, Dorothea. "Testing and Student Engagement With Literature in Urban Classrooms: A Multilayered Perspective." *Research in the Teaching of English 38,* no. *2* (2003): 177–212.

Anderson, Jenny. "States Try to Fix Quirks in Teacher Evaluations." *New York Times,* February 19, 2012. www.nytimes.com/2012/02/20/education/states-address-problems-with-teacher-evaluations.html?_r=1&scp=6&sq=teacher%20unions&st=cse.

Anderson, Sarah, and Robert Whitaker. "Prevalence of Obesity Among US Preschool Children in Different Racial and Ethnic Groups." *Archives of Pediatrics and Adolescent Medicine 163,* no. *4* (2009): 344–348.

"A New Mix of Gifted Students." *Washington Post,* July 27, 1997.

"Arizona Ethnic Studies Classes Banned, Teachers With Accents Can No Longer Teach English." June 30, 2010. www.huffingtonpost.com/2010/04/30/arizona-ethnic-studies-cl_n_558731.html.

Armstrong, O. K. "Treason in the Textbooks." *The American Legion Magazine* (September 1940): 8–9, 51, 70–72.

Armstrong, Thomas. *The Myth of the ADD Child.* New York: Dutton, 1985.

Arnold, Felix. *Text-Book of School and Class Management: Theory and Practice.* New York: The Macmillan Company, 1908, 22.

Artiles, Alfredo J., Jeannette Klingner, Annmarie Sullivan, and Edward Fierros. "Shifting Landscapes of Professional Practices: English Learner Special Education Placement in English-Only States." In *Forbidden Language: English Learners and Restrictive Language Policies,* ed. Patricia Gándara and Megan Hopkins. New York: Teachers College Press, 2010, 102–117.

Artiles, Alfredo J., E. Kozleski, S. Trent, D. Osher, and A. Ortiz. "Justifying and Explaining Disproportionality, 1968–2008: A Critique of Underlying Views of Culture." *Exceptional Children 76,* no. *3* (2010): 279–299.

Assessment of Diversity in America's Teaching Force: A Call to Action. Washington, DC: National Collaborative on Diversity in the Teaching Force, 2004. www.ate1.org/pubs/uploads/diversityreport.pdf.

Auerbach, Susan. "Engaging Latino Parents in Supporting College Pathways: Lessons From a College Access Program." *Journal of Hispanic Higher Education 3,* no. *2* (2004): 125–145.

Auerbach, Susan. "Why Do They Give the Good Classes to Some and Not to Others? Latino Parent Narratives of Struggle in a College Access Program." *Teachers College Record 104,* no. *7* (2002): 1369–1392.

Ayers, William. "Democracy and Urban Schooling for Justice and Care." *Journal for a Just and Caring Education 2,* no. *1* (1996): 85–92.

Bagley, William. *Classroom Management.* New York: Macmillan, 1907.

Baker, Bruce D., Danielle Farrie, Monete Johnson, Theresa Luhm, and David G. Sciarra. *Is School Funding Fair? A National Report Card.* Newark, NJ: Education Law Center, 2017. www.schoolfundingfairness.org/National_Report_Card.pdf.

Baker, Bruce D., Danielle Farrie, and David G. Sciarra. "Mind the Gap: 20 Years of Progress and Retrenchment in School Funding and Achievement Gaps." *ETS Research Report Series 2016,* no. *1* (2016): 1–37.

Baker, Bruce D., and Gary Miron. *The Business of Charter Schooling: Understanding the Policies that Charter Operators Use for Financial Benefit.* Boulder, CO: National Education Policy Center, 2015. http://nepc.colorado.edu/publication/charter-revenue, retrieved on July 7, 2017.

Baker, Bruce D., David G. Sciarra, and Danielle Farrie. *Is School Funding Fair? A National Report Card.* Newark, NJ: Education Law Center, 2010. www.schoolfundingfairness.org/National_Report_Card.pdf.

Banks, James A. "African American Scholarship and the Evolution of Multicultural Education." *The Journal of Negro Education 61*, no. *3* (1992): 273–286.

Banks, James A. "Approaches to Multicultural Curriculum Reform." In *Beyond Heroes and Holidays: A Practical Guide to K-12 Anti-Racist, Multicultural Education and Staff Development*, ed. Enid Lee, Deborah Menkart, and Margo Okazawa-Rey. Washington, DC: Teaching for Change, 1998, 37–39.

Banks, James A. "Multicultural Education: Historical Development, Dimension, and Practice." In *Handbook of Research on Multicultural Education*, 2nd ed., ed. James A. Banks and Cherry A. McGee Banks. San Francisco: Jossey Bass, 2004, 3–29.

Banks, James A. "Shaping the Future of Multicultural Education." *The Journal of Negro Education 48*, no. *3* (1979): 237–266.

Bartolomé, Lilia. "Beyond the Methods Fetish." *Harvard Education Review 64* (1994): 180.

Barton, Paul E. *Parsing the Achievement Gap: Baselines for Tracking Progress*. Princeton, NJ: Educational Testing Service, 2003.

Barton, Paul E., and Richard J. Coley. *Parsing the Achievement Gap II*. Princeton, NJ: Educational Testing Service, 2009. www.ets.org/Media/Research/pdf/PICPARSINGII.pdf.

Battistich, Victor, Eric Schaps, and Nance Wilson. "Effects of an Elementary School Intervention on Students Connectedness to School and Social Adjustment During Middle School." *Journal of Primary Prevention 24*, no. *3* (2004): 243–262.

Bauer, Gary L. *National History Standards: Clintonites Miss the Moon*. Washington, DC: Family Research Council, 1995. www.frc.org.

Baum, Susan. "Gifted But Learning Disabled: A Puzzling Paradox." *ERIC Digest #E479*. Reston, VA: Council for Exceptional Children, ERIC Clearinghouse on Disabilities and Gifted Education, 1990.

Beatty, Jack. *The World According to Peter Drucker*. New York: The Free Press, 1998.

Benjamin, Herold. "At Ford Foundation, a Harsh Critique of Urban School Closures." *The Notebook*, March 31, 2011. www.thenotebook.org/blog/113500/ford-foundation-harsh-critique-urban-school-closures/.

Berger, Sandra L. "Differentiating Curriculum for Gifted Students." *ERIC Digest #E510*. Reston, VA: Council for Exceptional Children, ERIC Clearinghouse on Disabilities and Gifted Education, n.d.

Berkman, Michael B., and Eric Plutzer. "Defeating Creationism in the Courtroom, But Not in the Classroom." *Science 331*, no. *6016* (2011): 404–405.

Berliner, David, and Bruce J. Biddle. *The Manufactured Crisis: Myths, Fraud, and the Attack on America's Public Schools*. Reading, MA: Addison-Wesley, 1995.

Biddle, Bruce, and David Berliner. "What Research Says About Unequal Funding for Schools in America." *Education Policy Reports Project (EPRP) From the Arizona State University, Education Policy Studies Laboratory*, 2002. http://wested.org/cs/we/view/rs/694/.

Bigelow, Bill. "Testing, Tracking, and Toeing the Line." In *Rethinking Our Classrooms: Teaching for Equity and Social Justice*, ed. Wayne Au, Bill Bigelow, and Stan Karp. Milwaukee, WI: Rethinking Schools, Ltd., 1994, 133–140.

Bill and Melinda Gates Foundation. *Education and the Workplace*. www.gatesfoundation.org/post-secondaryeducation/Pages/education-and-the-workplace.aspx.

Bill and Melinda Gates Foundation. *Working With Teachers to Develop Fair and Reliable Measures of Effective Teaching*. www.gatesfoundation.org/highschools/Documents/met-framing-paper.pdf.

Blank, Rolf K. "Science Instructional Time Is Declining in Elementary Schools: What Are the Implications for Student Achievement and Closing the Gap?" *Science Education*, October 2013, np.

Blau, Sheridan. "Toward the Separation of School and State." *Inaugural Address, 1997 NCTE Convention, Detroit*, November 20–25, 1997.

Bloomekatz, Ari. "Nine Million U.S. Adults Say They Are Lesbian, Gay, Bisexual or Transgender, Study Finds." *Los Angeles Times*, April 12, 2011. http://articles.latimes.com/2011/apr/12/local/la-me-gay-population-20110412.

Board of Education of Oklahoma City v. Dowell, 498 U.S. 237, 1991.

Borman, Geoffrey D., Gina M. Hewes, Laura T. Overman, and Shelly Brown. "Comprehensive School Reform and Achievement: A Meta-Analysis." *Review of Educational Research 73*, no. *2* (2003): 125–230.

Boston School Documents, no. 7, 1908, p. 53. Cited in Marvin Lazerson. *The Origins of the Urban School.* Cambridge, MA: Harvard University Press, 1971.

Bourdieu, Pierre, and Jean Claude Passeron. *Reproduction in Education, Society and Culture.* Thousand Oaks, CA: Sage, 1990.

Bowles, Samuel, and Herbert Gintis. *Schooling in Capitalist America: Educational Reform and the Contradictions of Economic Life.* New York: Basic Books, 1977.

Bracey, Gerald. *Setting the Record Straight.* Portsmouth, NH: Heinemann, 2004.

Brandt, Ron. "On the High School Curriculum: A Conversation With Ernest Boyer." *Educational Leadership 46,* no. *1* (September 1988): 4–9.

Bransford, John D., Ann L. Brown, and Rodney R. Cocking, eds. *How People Learn: Brain, Mind, Experience, and School.* Washington, DC: National Academy Press, 1999.

Brewer, Dominic J., Daniel I. Rees, and Laura M. Argys. "The Reform Without Cost? A Reply to Our Critics." *Phi Delta Kappan 77,* no. *6* (February 1996): 442–444.

Brookings Institute. *The Suburbanization of Poverty: Trends in Metropolitan Areas, 2000–2008,* January 20, 2010. www.brookings.edu/papers/2010/0120_poverty_kneebone.aspx.

Brophy, Jere, and Thomas Good. *Looking in Classrooms,* 7th ed. New York: Longman, 1997.

Brown, Ann L., and Joseph Campione. "Guided Discovery in a Community of Learners." In *Classroom Lessons: Integrating Cognitive Theory and Classroom Practice,* ed. Kate McGilly. Cambridge, MA: MIT Press, 1994, 229–272.

Brown, Ann L., Kathleen E. Metz, and Joseph C. Campione. "Social Interaction and Individual Understanding in a Community of Learners: The Influence of Piaget and Vygotsky." In *Piaget-Vygotsky: The Social Genesis of Thought,* ed. Anastasia Tryphon and Jacques Voneche. East Sussex, UK: Psychology Press, 1996, 145–170.

Brown, Anthony L., and Kefferlyn D. Brown. "Strange Fruit Indeed: Interrogating Contemporary Textbook Representations of Racial Violence Towards African Americans." *Teachers College Record 112,* no. *1* (2010): 31–67.

Brown, Bryan, and Kihyun Ryoo. "Teaching Science as a Language: A Content-First Approach to Science Teaching." *Journal of Research in Science Teaching 45* (2008): 525–664.

Brown v. Board of Education of Topeka, 347 U.S. 483, 1954.

Bruce, Mary. *Duncan: Katrina Was the "Best Thing" for New Orleans School System,* 2010. http://abcnews.go.com/blogs/politics/2010/01/duncan-katrina-was-the-best-thing-for-new-orleans-schools/.

Bruner, Jerome. *Culture and Education.* Cambridge: Harvard University Press, 1996.

Bruner, Jerome. *The Process of Education.* Cambridge, MA: Harvard University Press, 1960.

Bryk, Anthony. *Trust in Schools: A Core Resource for Improvement.* New York: Russell Sage Foundation, 2004.

Bryk, Anthony, Penny Bender Sebring, Elaine Allensworth, Stuart Luppescu, and John Q. Easton. *Organizing Schools for Improvement: Lessons From Chicago.* Chicago: The University of Chicago Press, 2009.

Bureau of Education. "Bulletin, 1918, No 35." *Cardinal Principles of Secondary Education: A Report of the Commission on the Reorganization of Secondary Education.* Appointed by the National Education Association.

The Bureau of Education: Its History, Activities, and Organization. https://archive.org/stream/bureauofeducatio008925mbp/bureauofeducatio008925mbp_djvu.txt.

Bureau of Labor Statistics. *Occupational Outlook Handbook, 2010–11 Edition, Overview of the 2008–18 Projections.* www.bls.gov/oco/oco2003.htm.

Burke, Kimberly, and Jessica Ashley. *Implementing Restorative Justice: A Guide for Schools.* Springfield, IL: Illinois Criminal Justice Information Authority, 2009.

Burris, Carol C., Jay P. Heubert, and Henry M. Levin. "Accelerating Mathematics Achievement Using Heterogeneous Grouping." *American Educational Research Journal 43,* no. *1* (2006): 105–136.

Burris, Carol C., Kevin D. Welner, and Jennifer Bedoza. "Universal Access to a Quality Education: Research and Recommendations for the Elimination of Curricular Stratification." *National Education Policy Center,* 2016. www.nepc.colorado.edu/publication/universal-access.

Burris, Carol C., Ed Wiley, Kevin G. Welner, and John Murphy. "Accountability, Rigor, and Detracking: Achievement Effects of Embracing a Challenging Curriculum." *Teachers College Record 110,* no. *3* (2008): 571–607.

Cahan, Emily D., and Sheldon H. White. "Proposals for a Second Psychology." *American Psychologist* 47 (1992): 224–235.

"CAIR Asks DOE to Address Bullying of Muslim Students." *Reuters*, June 9, 2011. www.reuters.com/article/2011/06/09/idUS215018+09-Jun-2011+PRN20110609.

Calefati, Jessica. "NJEA President Calls Christie 'Irresponsible'—After He Blamed Teachers for Lack of School Supplies." *The Star-Ledger*, November 9, 2010. www.nj.com/news/index.ssf/2010/11/njea_official_calls_christie_i.html.

California Department of Education. *California Mathematics State Standards—Grade Seven*. California Department of Education, 2000. www.cde.ca.gov/be/st/ss/documents/ccssmathstandardaug 2013.pdf.

California Department of Education. *History-Social Studies Content Standards for California Public Schools: Kindergarten Through Grade Twelve*, 1998. www.cde.ca.gov/be/st/ss/documents/histsocscistnd.pdf.

California State Department of Education. *California's Own History*. Sacramento: Author, 1965.

Campbell, David. "Putting Civics to the Test: The Impact of State-Level Civics Assessments on Civic Knowledge." *American Enterprise Institute*, 2014.

Canter, Lee, and Marlene Canter. *Assertive Discipline: Positive Behavior*. Santa Monica: Lee Canter & Associates, 1997.

Capellaro, Catherine. "Bargaining for Better Schools: An Interview With Héctor Calderón." *Rethinking Schools*, 2005. www.rethinkingschools.org/special_reports/quality_teachers/beau194.shtml.

Carnegie Council on Adolescent Development. *Turning Points: Preparing Youth for the 21st Century*. New York: Carnegie Corporation of New York, 1989.

Carpenter, Thomas P., Megan Loef Franke, and Linda Levi. *Thinking Mathematically: Integrating Arithmetic and Algebra in Elementary School*. Portsmouth, NH: Heinemann, 2003.

Cauley, K. M. "Construction of Local Knowledge: Study of Borrowing in Subtraction." *Journal of Educational Psychology 80* (1988): 202–205.

Cazden, Courtney. *Classroom Discourse*. Portsmouth, NH: Heinemann, 1988.

Center for American Progress. *Gay and Transgender Youth Homelessness by the Numbers*, June 21, 2010. www.americanprogress.org/issues/2010/06/homelessness_numbers.html.

Center for Applied Special Technology (CAST). *Universal Design for Learning Guidelines, 2.0*, Wakefield, MA, 2011. www.udlcenter.org/sites/udlcenter.org/files/updateguidelines2_0.pdf.

Center for Disease Control. *CDC Investigation: Blood Lead Levels Higher After Switch to Flint River Water*, 2016. www.cdc.gov/media/releases/2016/p0624-water-lead.html.

Center for Effective Discipline. *State High School Tests: Changes in State Policies and the Impact of the College and Career Readiness Movement*, December 2011. www.cep-dc.org/displayDocument.cfm?DocumentID=385.

Center for Effective Discipline. *State High School Tests: Exit Exams and Other Assessments*, December 2010. www.cep-dc.org/displayDocument.cfm?DocumentID=34.

Center on Education Policy. *Keeping Informed About School Vouchers: A Review of Major Developments and Research*, July 2011. www.cep-dc.org/index.cfm?DocumentSubTopicID=16.

Center on Education Policy. *State High School Tests: Exit Exams and Other Assessments*, December 2010. www.cep-dc.org/displayDocument.cfm?DocumentID=34.

Cheney, Lynne V. "The End of History." *Wall Street Journal*, October 20, 1994, A26.

Cheney, Lynne V. "The Latest Education Disaster: Whole Math." *Weekly Standard*, August 4, 1997, A22.

Child, Brenda J. *Boarding School Seasons: American Indian Families, 1900–1940*. Lincoln, NE: University of Nebraska Press, 2000.

Child Development Project. *Ways We Want Our Classroom to Be: Class Meetings that Build Commitment to Kindness and Learning*. Oakland, CA: Developmental Studies Center, 1994.

Child Trends Databank. *Food Insecurity*, 2016. www.childtrends.org/?indicators=food-insecurity.

Child Trends Databank. *Neighborhood Safety: Indicators of Child and Youth Well Being*, 2013. www.childtrends.org/wp-content/uploads/2012/08/107_Neighborhood_Safety-1.pdf.

Chow, Mamie, Laurie Olsen, Ruben Lizardo, and Carol Dowell. *School Reform Organizing in the San Francisco Bay Area and Los Angeles, California*. Oakland, CA: California Tomorrow, 2001.

Christian, Donna. *Two-Way Bilingual Education: Students Learning Through Two Languages*. Santa Cruz, CA: National Center for Research on Cultural Diversity and Second Language Learning, 1994.

Clarence Edwards Middle School: Success Through Transformation, National Center on Time and Learning. www.mass2020.org/files/fle/Edwards%20Case%20%Study%20FINAL.pdf.

Clauss, Hunter. "Union Upset by Comments From Emanuel on Schools." *New York Times*, February 4, 2012. www.nytimes.com/2012/02/05/us/rahm-emanuels-comments-in-video-upset-teachers-union.html.

Coalition of Essential Schools. www.essentialschools.org.

Cohen, David, and Heather Hill. *Learning Policy: When State Education Reform Works*. New Haven: Yale University Press, 2001.

Cohen, Elizabeth G. *Designing Groupwork: Strategies for the Heterogeneous Classroom*. New York: Teachers College Press, 1994.

Cohen, Elizabeth G., and Rachel A. Lotan. "Equity in Heterogeneous Classrooms." In *Handbook of Research on Multicultural Education*, 2nd ed., ed. James A. Banks and Cherry A. McGee Banks. San Francisco: Jossey-Bass, 2004, 736–750.

Cohen, Elizabeth G., and Rachel A. Lotan. *Working for Equity in Heterogeneous Classrooms*. New York: Teachers College Press, 1997.

Cohen, Elizabeth G., Rachel A. Lotan, Beth A. Scarloss, and Adele R. Arellano. "Complex Instruction: Equity in Cooperative Learning Classrooms." *Theory Into Practice 38*, no. 2 (1999): 80–86.

Cole, Michael. *Cultural Psychology: A Once and Future Discipline*. Cambridge: Harvard University Press, 1996.

Coleman, James S. *Equality of Educational Opportunity (COLEMAN) Study (EEOS), 1966 (ICPSR06389-v3)*. Ann Arbor, MI: Inter-university Consortium for Political and Social Research [distributor], 2007-04-27. https://doi.org/10.3886/ICPSR06389.v3.

College Board. *Effects of Coaching on SAT Scores*. www.collegeboard.com/prod_downloads/highered/ra/sat/coaching.pdf.

College Board Online. *Test Question of the Day*, March 16, 1998. www.collegeboard.org/practice/sat-question-of-the-day.

Collins, Kevin P., and Sean D. Cleary. "Racial and Ethnic Disparities in Parent-Reported Diagnosis of ADHD: National Survey of Children's Health (2003, 2007, and 2011)." *Journal of Clinical Psychiatry* (2016). www.ncbi.nlm.nih.gov/pubmed/26761486.

Colvin, Richard Lee. "Spurned Nobelists Appeal Science Standards Rejection." *Los Angeles Times*, November 17, 1997, p. A25.

Colvin, Richard Lee. "State Endorses Back-to-Basics Math Standards." *Los Angeles Times*, November 30, 1997, pp. 1, 18, 19, 26.

Committee on a Conceptual Framework for New K-12 Science Standards, Board on Science Education, Division of Behavioral and Social Sciences and Education, and National Research Council of the National Academies. *A Framework for K-12 Science Education: Practices, Crosscutting Concepts and Core Ideas*. www.nap.edu/read/13165/chapter/1.

Common Core State Standards Initiative. www.corestandards.org.

Concerns About the Proposed History-Social Science Framework. www.gtbe.org/blog/wp-content/uploads/2016/06/Concerns-about-the-Proposed-History-Social-Science-Framework.pdf.

Congressional Budget Office. *Supplemental Data to Congressional Budget Office, Trends in the Distribution of Household Income Between 1979 and 2007*, October 2011. http://cbo.gov/publication/42729/.

Congressional Budget Office. *Trends in Family Wealth, 1989 to 2013*, August 2016. www.cbo.gov/sites/default/files/114th-congress-2015-2016/reports/51846-familywealth.pdf.

Cornbleth, Catharine. "An American Curriculum?" *Teachers College Record 99*, no. 4 (1998): 622–646.

Cortes, Ernesto Jr. "Making the Public the Leaders in Education Reform." *Teacher Magazine*, November 22, 1995.

Cortiella, Candace. *The State of Learning Disabilities*. New York: National Center for Learning Disabilities, 2001.

Council of the Great City Schools. *Charting the Right Course: A Report on Urban Student Achievement and Course-Taking*. Washington, DC: Author, 1998.

Council of Great City Schools. *Student Testing in American's Great City Schools: An Inventory and Preliminary Analysis*, October 2015. www.cgcs.org/cms/lib/DC00001581/Centricity/Domain/87/Testing%20Report.pdf.

Crabtree, Charlotte. "A Common Curriculum for the Social Studies." In *Individual Differences and the Common Curriculum*, ed. Gary D. Fenstermacher and John I. Goodlad. Chicago: University of Chicago Press, 1983, 248–281.

Crawford, James. *Language Loyalties: A Sourcebook on the Official English Controversy*. Chicago: University of Chicago Press, 1992.

Crawford, John. "Anatomy of the English-only Movement." In *Language Legislation and Linguistic Rights*, ed. Douglas A. Kibbee. Amsterdam and Philadelphia: John Benjamins, 1998, 96–122.

Cremin, Lawrence. *The Transformation of the School: Progressivism in American Education, 1876–1957*. New York: Vintage Books, 1964.

Cross, Dionne I. "Alignment, Cohesion, and Change: Examining Mathematics Teachers' Beliefs Structures and Their Influence on Instructional Practice." *Journal of Mathematics Teacher Education 12* (2009): 325–346.

Cuban, Larry. *How Teachers Taught: Constancy and Change in American Classrooms, 1890–1990*. New York: Teachers College Press, 1993.

Cubberley, Ellwood. *Changing Conceptions of Education*. Boston: Houghton Mifflin, 1909.

Cummins, James. *Language, Power and Pedagogy: Bilingual Children in the Crossfire*. Clevedon, UK: Multilingual Matters Ltd., 2000.

Cummins, Jim. "From Multicultural to Anti-Racist Education: An Analysis of Programmes and Policies in Ontario." In *Minority Education: From Shame to Struggle*, ed. Tove Skutnabb-Kangas and Jim Cummins. Philadelphia: Multilingual Matters Ltd., 1988, 127–157.

Cutro, Vilsa E., Roland G. Fryer, and Meghan L. Howard. *It May Not Take a Village: Increasing Achievement Among the Poor*. http://citeseerx.ist.psu.edu/viewdoc/download?doi=10.1.1.188.4154&rep=rep1&type=pdf.

Dalton, Ben W., Steven J. Ingels, Jane Downing, Robert Bozick, and Jeffrey Owings. "Advanced Mathematics and Science Coursetaking in the Spring High Schools Senior Classes of 1982, 1992 and 2004." *NCES Publication No. 2007–312*, 2007. http://nces.ed.gov/pubs2007/2007312.pdf.

Darder, Antonia. *Culture and Power in the Classroom: A Critical Foundation for Bicultural Education*. Westport, CT: Bergin & Garvey, 1991.

Darder, Antonia. "Teaching as an Act of Love." In *The Critical Pedagogy Reader*, ed. A. Darder, M. and R. Torres. New York: Routledge Falmer, 2003, 497–510.

Darling-Hammond, Linda. *Overview to Ten Features of Effective Design*. www.schoolredesign.net.

Darling-Hammond, Linda. *The Right to Learn*. San Francisco: Jossey-Bass, 1997.

Darling-Hammond, Linda. "The Right to Learn and the Advancement of Teaching: Research, Policy, and Practice for Democratic Education." *Educational Researcher 26* (August/September 1996): 5.

Darwin, Charles. *On the Origin of Species by Means of Natural Selection, Or, the Preservation of Favoured Races in the Struggle for Life*. London: J. Murray, 1859.

Data Accountability Center. *Individuals With Disabilities Education Act (IDEA) Data*. www.ideadata.org.

DeBray, Elizabeth H. *Politics, Ideology, & Education: Federal Policy During the Clinton and Bush Administrations*. New York: Teachers College Press, 2006.

Dee, Thomas S., and Emily K. Penner. "The Causal Effects of Cultural Relevance Evidence From an Ethnic Studies Curriculum." *American Educational Research Journal XX*, no. *X*, (2016): 1–40. https://doi.org/10.3102/0002831216677002.

Definition of the Highly Qualifed Teacher (HQT). *No Child Left Behind*. Revised, July 1, 2010. www.nj.gov/education/profdev/nclb/hqtcharts.pdf.

DeLany, Brian. "Allocation, Choice, and Stratification Within High Schools: How the Sorting Machine Copes." *American Journal of Education 99*, no. *3* (1991): 191–207.

Delgado, Richard, and Jean Stefancic. *Critical Race Theory: An Introduction*. New York: New York University Press, 2001.

Delgado, Richard, and Jean Stefancic. *Critical White Studies: Looking Behind the Mirror*. Philadelphia: Temple University Press, 1997.

Delpit, Lisa. *Other People's Children: Cultural Conflict in the Classroom.* New York: The New Press, 1995.

Desimone, Laura M., Andrew C. Porter, Michael S. Garet, Kwang Suk Yoon, and Beatrice F. Birman. "Effects of Professional Development on Teachers' Instruction: Results From a Three-Year Longitudinal Study." *Educational Evaluation and Policy Analysis 24,* no. *2* (2002): 81–112.

Dewey, John. "Democracy and Education (1916)." In *John Dewey, the Middle Works,* Vol. *9,* ed. Jo Ann Boydston. Carbondale, IL: Southern Illinois University Press, 1989, 84–85.

Dewey, John. "Democracy and Education in the World of Today." *Essays* [first published as a pamphlet by the Society for Ethical Culture, New York, 1938], p. 296.

Dewey, John. "How We Think." In *John Dewey, the Middle Works,* Vol. *6,* ed. Jo Ann Boydston. Carbondale, IL: Southern Illinois University Press, 1989, 338.

Dewey, John. "My Pedagogic Creed." 1897. In *Early Works,* Vol. *5,* ed. Jo Ann Boydston. Carbondale, IL: Southern Illinois University Press, 1989, 93.

Dewey, John. *School and Society.* Chicago: University of Chicago Press, 1991.

Diegmueller, Karen. "The Best of Both Worlds." *Teacher Magazine,* March 1996.

Diegmueller, Karen. "English Group Loses Funding for Standards." *Education Week,* March 30, 1994.

Diegmueller, Karen. "War of Words." *Education Week,* March 20, 1996.

Dillon, Sam. "Districts Pay Less in Poor Schools, Report Says." *New York Times,* November 30, 2011. www.nytimes.com/2011/12/01/education/us-education-department-finds-salary-gap-in-poor-schools.html?_r=1&partner=rss&emc=rss.

Dillon, Sam. "In Washington, Large Rewards in Teacher Pay." *New York Times,* December 31, 2011. www.nytimes.com/2012/01/01/education/big-pay-days-in-washington-dc-schools-merit-system.html?pagewanted=all.

Dillon, Sam. "Lines Grow Long for Free School Meals, Thanks to Economy." *New York Times,* November 30, 2011. www.nytimes.com/2011/11/30/education/surge-in-free-school-lunches-refects-economic-crisis.html?_r=1&ref=education.

Dillon, Sam. "Obama Turns Some Power of Education Back to States." *New York Times,* September 23, 2011. www.nytimes.com/2011/09/24/education/24educ.html?_r=1.

Dividing Lines. "Technology Counts 2001: The New Divides." *Education Week 20,* no. *35* (2001): 12–13.

Dobbie, Will, and Roland G. Fryer. "Are High-Quality Schools Enough to Increase Achievement Among the Poor? Evidence From the Harlem Children's Zone." *American Economic Journal 3,* no. *3* (2011): 158–187.

Douglass, Frederick. "Speech Celebrating West India Emancipation Day, Canandaigua, New York, August 4, 1857." In *The Life and Writings of Frederick Douglass,* Vol. *2,* ed. Philip Foner. New York: International Publishers of New York, 1976, 437.

Dreifus, Claudia. "The Bilingual Advantage." *New York Times,* May 30, 2011. www.nytimes.com/2011/05/31/science/31conversation.html.

Drucker, Peter. *The Concept of the Corporation.* New York: John Day, 1946.

Dryfoos, Joy. *Full-Service Schools: A Revolution in Health and Social Services for Children, Youth and Families.* San Francisco: Jossey-Bass, 1994.

DuBois, W. E. B. "Does the Negro Need Separate Schools?" *Journal of Negro Education 4,* no. *3* (1935): 328.

DuBois, W. E. B. "The Freedom to Learn." In *W. E. B. DuBois Speaks,* ed. P. S. Foner. New York: Pathfinder, 1970, 230–231.

Duncan, Arne. *Remarks By Secretary Arne Duncan at the Council on Foreign Relations Meeting,* May 5, 2010. www2.ed.gov/news/speeches/2010/05/05262010.html.

Duncan, Arne. *Statement on National Governors Association and State Education Chiefs Common Core Standards,* June 2, 2010. www.ed.gov/news/press-releases/statement-national-governors-association-and-state-education-chiefs-common-core-/.

Duncan-Andrade, Jeffrey M. R. "Note to Educators: Hope Required When Growing Roses in Concrete." *Harvard Educational Review 79,* no. *2* (2009): 181–194.

Durso, Laura E., and Gary J. Gates. *Serving Our Youth: Findings From a National Survey of Service Providers Working With Lesbian, Gay, Bisexual, and Transgender Youth Who Are Homeless or at Risk of Becoming Homeless*. Los Angeles: The Williams Institute With True Colors Fund and The Palette Fund, 2012. http://williamsinstitute.law.ucla.edu/wp-content/uploads/Durso-Gates-LGBT-Homeless-Youth-Survey-July-2012.pdf.

Economic Policy Institute. *The Racial Wealth Gap: How African-Americans Have Been Shortchanged Out of the Materials to Build Wealth*, 2017. www.epi.org/blog/the-racial-wealth-gap-how-african-americans-have-been-shortchanged-out-of-the-materials-to-build-wealth/.

Economic Policy Institute. *Recession Continues to Take Its Toll on American Children*, September 13, 2011. www.epi.org/blog/recession-continues-toll-americas-children/.

Economic Policy Institute. *State of Working America, 2011*. Economic Policy Institute.

Economic Policy Institute. *State of Working America Data Library*, 2017. Economic Policy Institute. www.stateofworkingamerica.org/chart/swa-wages-figure-4f-share-workers-earning/.

Editorial Projects in Education Research Center. "Issues A-Z: The Common Core Explained." *Education Week*, September 28, 2015. www.edweek.org/ew/issues/common-core-state-standards.

EdSource. *Similar Students, Different Results: Why Do Some Schools Do Better?* Sacramento, CA: EdSource, 2005. www.edsource.org/pub_abs_simstu05.cfm.

Education Commission of the States. *ESSA: Mapping Opportunities for Civics Education*, 2017. www.ecs.org/essa-mapping-opportunities-for-civic-education/.

Education Law Center. *Is School Funding Fair? A National Report Card*, 2010. www.educationjustice.org; SchoolFunding.Info.

The Education Trust. *Close the Hidden Funding Gaps in Our Schools*. Washington, DC: Education Trust, 2010. www.edtrust.org/sites/edtrust/files/publications/files/Hidden%20Funding%20Gaps_0.pdf.

The Education Trust. *The Funding Gap 2004*. Washington, DC: Education Trust, 2004. www.edtrust.org/sites/edtrust/files/publications/files/funding2004.pdf.

The Education Trust. *The Funding Gap, 2005*. Washington, DC: Education Trust, 2005. www.edtrust.org/sites/edtrust/files/publications/files/FundingGap2005.pdf.

Education Trust with Richard Ingersoll. *Core Problems: Out of Field Teaching Persists in Key Academic Courses and High Poverty Schools* (Education Trust, 2008). http://edtrust.org/wp-content/uploads/2013/10/SASSreportCoreProblem.pdf.

Education Week. *A Better Balance: Standards, Tests, and the Tools of Reform: Quality Counts 2001*. Washington, DC: Author, 2001.

Education Week. *Quality Counts 2000: Who Should Teach*. Washington, DC: Author, 2000.

Education Week. *Quality Counts 2003: Ensuring a Highly Qualified Teacher for Every Classroom*. Washington, DC: Author, 2003.

Eisenberg, Marla E., and Michael D. Resnick. "Suicidality Among Gay, Lesbian and Bisexual Youth: The Role of Protective Factors." *Journal of Adolescent Health 39*, no. 5 (2006): 662–668.

Epstein, Joyce, Lucretia Coates, Karen C. Salinas, Mavis G. Sanders, and Beth S. Simon. *School, Family, and Community Partnerships: Your Handbook for Action*. Thousand Oaks, CA: Corwin Press, 1997.

ETS. *Guidelines for the Assessment of English Language Learners*, 2009. www.ets.org/s/about/pdf/ell_guidelines.pdf.

Evers, Bill. *Mathematics Content Standards for Grades K–12*, September 15, 1997. www.rahul.net/dehnbase/hold/platinum-standards/altintro.html.

FairTest. *Graduation Test Update: States that Recently Eliminated or Scaled Back High School Exit Exams*, January 24, 2017. www.fairtest.org/graduation-test-update-states-recently-eliminated.

FairTest. *Policy Alternatives to High-Stakes Testing for Grade Promotion*. http://fairtest.org/arn/retenfct/htm.

Faltis, Chris, and Guadalupe Valdés, eds. *Education, Immigrant Students, Refugee Students, and English Learners*. National Society for the Study of Education Yearbook. New York: Teachers College, 2010.

Farley, Christopher John. "What Bill Cosby Should Be Talking About." *Time*, June 3, 2004. www.time.com/time/nation/article/0,8599,645801,00.html.

Fass, Paula. *Outside In: Minorities and the Transformation of American Education.* Oxford and New York: Oxford University Press, 1989.

Federal Communications Commission. www.fcc.gov/general/national-broadband-plan.

Fensterwald, John. "A Great Awakening for History and Social Studies." *EdSource*, April 2015. https://edsource.org/2015/a-great-awakening-for-history-and-social-studies/77748.

Ferguson, Ronald F. "Paying for Public Education: New Evidence on How and Why Money Matters." *Harvard Journal on Legislation 28*, no. *2* (Summer 1991): 465–498.

Ferguson, Ronald F. "Toward Skilled Parenting and Transformed Schools: Inside a National Movement for Excellence With Equity." Paper prepared for the *First Educational Equity Symposium of the Campaign for Educational Equity, at Teachers College*, Columbia University, New York City, October 24 and 25, 2005. www.tc.columbia.edu/centers/EquitySymposium/symposium/resourceDetails.asp?Presid=10.

Fillmore, Lily Wong, and Charles J. Fillmore. "What Does Text Complexity Mean for English Learners and Language Minority Students?" Paper presented at the *Understanding Language Conference*, Stanford University, January 2012. http://ell.stanford.edu/sites/default/files/pdf/academic-papers/06-LWF%20CJF%20Text%20Complexity%20FINAL_0.pdf.

Fine, Michelle, and Sara McClelland. "Sexuality Education and Desire: Still Missing After All These Years." *Harvard Educational Review 76*, no. *3* (2006): 297–337.

Fingerhut, Hannah. *Support Steady for Same-Sex Marriage and Acceptance of Homosexuality*, 2016. www.pewresearch.org/fact-tank/2016/05/12/support-steady-for-same-sex-marriage-and-acceptance-of-homosexuality.

Finn, Jeremy, and Charles M. Achilles. "Answers and Questions About Class Size." *American Educational Research Journal 27* (Fall 1990): 557–577.

Finnan, Christine, Edward St. John, and Jane McCarthy, eds. *Accelerated Schools in Action: Lessons From the Field.* Thousand Oaks, CA: Corwin Press, 1995.

"First Online-Only Candidate Mashup: 2007 Democratic On-line Debate." *Huffington Post*, September 13, 2007. www.huffingtonpost.com/2007/09/12/frst-onlineonly-candidat_n_64221.html.

Fish, Rachel. "The Racialized Construction of Exceptionality." *Social Science Research 61*, no. *1* (2017): 317–334. www.sciencedirect.com/science/article/pii/S0049089X15301642.

Fogel, Alan. *Developing Through Relationships.* Chicago: University of Chicago Press, 1993.

Ford, Donna Y., Terek C. Grantham, and Gilman W. Whiting. "Another Look at the Achievement Gap: Learning From the Experiences of Gifted Black Students." *Urban Education 43*, no. *2* (2008): 216–238.

Forum on Child and Family Statistics. *America's Children: Key National Indicators of Children's Well-Being 2015.* www.childstats.gov/pdf/ac2015/ac_15.pdf.

Forum on Child and Family Statistics. *America's Children: Key National Indicators of Well-Being, 2011, Family Structure and Children's Living Arrangements.* www.childstats.gov/americaschildren/famsoc1.asp.

Freire, Paulo. *Pedagogy of Hope.* New York: Continuum, 1995.

Freire, Paulo. *Pedagogy of Hope: Reliving Pedagogy of the Oppressed.* New York: Continuum, 1997.

Freire, Paulo. *Pedagogy of the Oppressed.* New York: The Continuum International Publishing Group, 1970.

Fry, Richard, D'Vera Cohn, Gretchen Livingston, and Paul Taylor. *The Rising Age Gap in Economic Well-Being: The Old Prosper Relative to the Young.* New York: Pew Foundation, 2011. www.pewsocialtrends.org/2011/11/07/the-rising-age-gap-in-economic-well-being/1/.

Frykholm, Jeffrey A. "The Impact of Reform: Challenges for Mathematics Teacher Preparation." *Journal of Mathematics Teacher Education 2* (1999): 79–105.

Fullan, Michael. *Change Forces: Probing the Depths of Educational Reform.* London: Falmer Press, 1993.

Fullan, Michael. *Successful School Improvement.* Philadelphia: Open University Press, 1992.

Fullan, Michael, and Andy Hargreaves. *What's Worth Fighting for in Your School?* New York: Teachers College Press, 1996.

"Full Text of Obama's Education Speech." *Denver Post*, May 28, 2008. www.denverpost.com/ci_9405199/.

Gabriel, Trip. "Teachers Wonder, Why the Scorn." *New York Times*, March 2, 2011. www.nytimes. com/2011/03/03/education/03teacher.html.

Gallup. *U.S. Adults Estimate that 25% of Americans Are Gay or Lesbian*, May 27, 2011. www.gallup. com/poll/147824/adults-estimate-americans-gay-lesbian.aspx.

Gamoran, Adam. "Alternative Uses of Ability Grouping in Secondary Schools: Can We Bring High-Quality Instruction to Low-Ability Classrooms." *American Journal of Education 102*, no. *1* (1993): 1–22.

Gamoran, Adam. "A Multi-level Analysis of the Effects of Tracking." Paper presented at the *Annual Meeting of the American Sociological Association*, Atlanta, 1988.

Gándara, Patricia, and Megan Hopkins, eds. *Forbidden Language: English Learners and Restrictive Language Policies*. New York: Teachers College Press, 2010.

Gannon, Megan. "Race Is a Social Construct, Scientists Argue." *Scientific American*, February 5, 2016, np. www.scientificamerican.com/article/race-is-a-social-construct-scientists-argue/.

García, Ofelia. "Education, Multilingualism and Translanguaging in the 21st Century." In *Multilingual Education for Social Justice: Globalising the Local*, ed. Ajit Mohanty, Minati Panda, Robert Phillipson, and Tove Skutnabb-Kangas. New Delhi: Orient Blackswan, Former Orient Longman, 2009, 128–145.

García, Ofelia, Jo Anne Kleifgen, and Lorraine Falchi. "From English Language Learners to Emergent Bilinguals." *Equity Matters: Research Review No. 1*. New York: A Research Initiative of the Campaign for Educational Equity, 2008.

Gardner, Howard. *Frames of Mind*. New York: Basic Books, 1983, 1993.

Gardner, Howard. *The Unschooled Mind*. New York: Basic Books, 1991.

Garet, Michael, and Brian DeLany. "Students, Courses, and Stratification." *Sociology of Education 61* (1988): 61–77.

Garfunkel, Sol, and David Mumford. "How to Fix Our Math Education." *New York Times*, August 24, 2011. www.nytimes.com/2011/08/25/opinion/how-to-fx-our-math-education.html?_r=1.

Garland, May, and Uri Treisman. "The Mathematics Workshop Model: An Interview With Uri Treisman." *Journal of Developmental Education 16*, no. *3* (Spring 1993): 14–16, 18, 20, 22.

Garrison, Jim. "Deweyan Pragmatism and the Epistemology of Contemporary Social Constructivism." *American Educational Research Journal 32*, no. *4* (1995): 731.

Gates, Gary J., and Taylor N. T. Brown. *Marriage and Same-Sex Couples After Obergefell*. Los Angeles, CA: Williams Institute, UCLA School of Law, 2015. http://williamsinstitute.law.ucla.edu/wp-content/uploads/Marriage-and-Same-sex-Couples-after-Obergefell-November-2015.pdf.

Gay, Geneva. *Culturally Responsive Teaching: Theory, Research, and Practice*. New York: Teachers College Press, 2000.

Gay, Geneva, and Tyrone Howard. "Multicultural Teacher Education for the 21st Century." *The Teacher Educator 36*, no. *1* (2001): 1–16.

Gay, Lesbian and Straight Education Network. *The 2009 National School Climate Survey*. www.glsen. org/binary-data/GLSEN_ATTACHMENTS/fle/000/001/1675–2.pdf.

Gay, Lesbian and Straight Education Network. *Safe Schools Laws*, 2017. www.lgbtmap.org/equality-maps/safe_school_laws.

Gay, Lesbian and Straight Education Network. *States With Safe Schools Laws*. www.glsen.org/cgi-bin/iowa/all/library/record/2344.html?state=policy&type=policy.

GET City. http://getcity.org.

Gibbs, Nancy. "Parents Behaving Badly." *Time*, February 21, 2005.

Gilreath, James, ed. *Thomas Jefferson and the Education of a Citizen*. Washington, DC: Library of Congress, 1999.

Giroux, Henry A. *Theory and Resistance in Education: A Pedagogy of Opposition*. South Hadley, MA: Bergin & Garvey, 1983.

Glass, Gene, Leonard Cahan, Mary Lee Smith, and Nikola Filby. *School Class Size: Research and Policy*. Beverly Hills: Sage, 1982.

Glasser, William. *The Quality School*. New York: HarperCollins, 1992.

Gleason, Phillip, and Melissa Clark. *Christina Clark Tuttle, and Emily Dwyer. The Evaluation of Charter School Impacts: Final Report*. Washington, DC: National Center for Education Evaluation and Regional Assistance, Institute of Education Sciences, U.S. Department of Education, 2010.

Glick, Joseph, as cited in Barbara Rogoff. *Apprenticeship in Thinking: Cognitive Development in Social Context*. New York: Oxford University Press, 1990, 57.

Glinskis, Emmalina. "Climate Denial in Schools." *Vice News*, April 25, 2017.

GLSEN. *Students Still Face Hostility: Considerable School Improvements Show Progress*. www.glsen. org/article/lgbtq-secondary-students-still-face-hostility-school-considerable-improvements-show-progress.

Goals 2000: Educate America Act (PL 103-227). www2.ed.gov/legislation/GOALS2000/TheAct/sec102.html.

Goleman, Daniel. *Emotional Intelligence: Why It Can Matter More than IQ*. New York: Bantam Books, 1995.

Good, Thomas, and Jere Brophy. *Looking in Classrooms*. New York: Longman, 1997.

Goodlad, John I. *A Place Called School*. New York: McGraw-Hill, 1984.

Gould, Elise, and Hilary Wething. *U.S. Poverty Rates Higher, Safety New Weaker than in Peer Countries*. Washington, DC: Economic Policy Institute, 2015. www.epi.org/publication/ib339-us-poverty-higher-safety-net-weaker/.

Gould, Stephen J. *The Mismeasure of Man*, 2nd ed. New York: Norton, 1996.

Gowen, Annie. "Maryland Schools Remove 2 Black-Authored Books." *Los Angeles Times*, January 11, 1998, p. A6.

Grant, Carl. *The Evolution of Multicultural Education in the United States: A Journey for Civil Rights and Social Justice*. www.iaie.org/download/turin_paper_grant.pdf.

Greene, Jay P. *A Meta-Analysis of the Effectiveness of Bilingual Education*. Claremont, CA: The Tomas Rivera Policy Institute, 1998.

Greenhouse, Jared. *The Complicated Problem of Race and Special Education*, 2015. www. huffingtonpost.com/entry/racism-inherent-in-special-education-leads-to-marginalization_us_55b63c0ae4b0224d8832b8d3.

Gregg, Jeff. "Discipline, Control, and the School Mathematics Tradition." *Teaching and Teacher Education 11*, no. 6 (1995): 579–593.

Grigorenko, Elena L., and Ruby Takaniski, eds. *Immigration, Diversity, and Education*. New York: Routledge, 2009.

Gutiérrez, Kris, Jolynn Asato, Maria Santos, and Neil Gotanda. "Backlash Pedagogy: Language and Culture and the Politics of Reform." *Review of Education, Pedagogy and Cultural Studies 24*, no. 4 (2002): 335–351.

Gutiérrez, Kris, and Lynda Stone. "Hypermediating Literacy Activity: How Learning Contexts Get Reorganized." In *Contemporary Perspectives in Early Childhood Education*, ed. O. Saracho and B. Spodek. Greenwich, CT: Information Age Publishing, 2002, 25–51.

Gutierrez, Rochelle. "Why (Urban) Mathematics Teachers Need Political Knowledge." *Journal of Urban Mathematics 6*, no. 2 (2013): 7–19.

Gutstein, Eric, and Bob Peterson, eds. *Rethinking Mathematics: Teaching Social Justice by the Numbers*. Milwaukee: Rethinking Schools, 2005.

Hagerty, Barbara Bradley. *Evangelical Voters May Be Up for Grabs in '08*, May 16, 2007. www.npr. org/templates/story/story.php?storyId=10215580.

Haggard, Howard W. "Preface." In *Tisn't What You Know, But Are You Intelligent?* ed. Howard W. Haggard. New York: Harper and Brothers, 1927, 1–10.

Haley, Margaret. *Battleground: The Autobiography of Margaret Haley*, ed. Robert L. Reid. Chicago: University of Illinois Press, 1982.

Hallinan, Maureen. "Tracking: From Theory to Practice." *Sociology of Education 67*, no. 2 (1994): 79–84.

Haney, Walt. *Revisiting the Myth of the Texas Miracle in Education: Lessons About Dropout Research and Dropout Prevention*, January 2001. http://civilrightsproject.ucla.edu/research/k-12-education/school-dropouts/revisiting-the-myth-of-the-texas-miracle-in-education-lessons-about-dropout-research-and-dropout-prevention-walt-haney.

Hanson, F. Allan. *Testing Testing: Social Consequences of the Examined Life*. Berkeley: University of California Press, 1993.

Hargreaves, Andy. *Changing Teachers, Changing Times: Teachers' Work and Culture in the Postmodern Age*. New York: Continuum, 1994.

Harmon, Amy. "Climate Science Meets a Stubborn Obstacle: Students." *New York Times*, June 4, 2017. www.nytimes.com/2017/06/04/us/education-climate-change-science-class-students.html?hp&action=click&pgtype=Homepage&clickSource=story-heading&module=second-column-region&region=top-news&WT.nav=top-news&_r=0.

Harrington, Michael. *The Other America: Poverty in the United States* (1962, reprint). New York: Collier Books, 1997.

Hatch, Thomas, Dilruba Ahmed, Ann Lieberman, Deborah Faigenbaum, Melissa Eiler White, and Desiree H. Pointer-Made, eds. *Going Public With Our Teaching: An Anthology of Practice*. New York: Teachers College Press, 2005.

Hattie, John. *Visible Learning: A Synthesis of Over 800 Meta-Analyses Relating to Achievement*. New York: Routledge, 2009.

Havel, Vaclav. *The Art of the Impossible: Politics as Morality in Practice*. New York: Knopf, 1997.

Heath, Shirley Brice. *Ways With Words: Language, Life, and Work in Communities and Classrooms*. New York: Cambridge University Press, 1983.

Hedges, Larry, Richard D. Laine, and Rob Greenwald. "Does Money Matter? A Meta-Analysis of the Effects of Differential School Inputs on Student Outcomes." *Educational Researcher 23*, no. *3* (1994): 5–14.

Hendra, Mary. "In History Class, a Flood of Urgent and Newly Relevant Questions." *Christian Science Monitor 93*, no. *211* (2001): 13.

Herold, Benjamin. "At Ford Foundation, a Harsh Critique of Urban School Closures." *The Notebook*, March 31, 2011. www.thenotebook.org/blog/113500/ford-foundation-harsh-critique-urban-school-closures/.

Herrnstein, Richard, and Charles Murray. *The Bell Curve: Intelligence and Class Structure in American Life*. New York: The Free Press, 1994.

Heubert, Jay P., and Robert M. Hauser, eds. *High Stakes: Testing for Tracking, Promotion, and Graduation*. Washington, DC: National Academy Press, 1999.

Hicks, Stephanie. *Teachers for Social Justice*. www.linkedin.com/in/stephaniedhicks, see also www.teachersforjustice.org/.

Hiebert, Elfrieda H. "The Common Core's Staircase of Text Complexity: Getting the Size of the First Step Right." *Reading Today 29*, no. *3* (2012): 26–27.

Hiebert, James, and Thomas Carpenter. "Teaching and Learning With Understanding." In *Handbook of Research on Mathematics Teaching and Learning*, ed. Douglas A. Grouws. New York: Macmillan, 1992, 65–97.

Higgins, John. "Backlash Against New Math, Reading Tests Ripples Across State." *Seattle Times*, July 9, 2015.

Hirsch, E. D. *Address to California State Board of Education*, April 10, 1997, cited in Common Knowledge (Winter/Spring 1997), p. 4.

Hirsch, E. D. *Cultural Literacy: What Every American Needs to Know*. New York: Houghton Mifflin, 1987.

Hirsch, E. D. *The Schools We Need and Why We Don't Have Them*. New York: Random House, 1996.

Hirsch, E. D. *Toward a Centrist Curriculum: Two Kinds of Multiculturalism in Elementary School*. Charlottesville, VA: Core Knowledge Foundation, 1992. www.coreknowledge.org.

Hispanic Wealth Project. *Annual Report 2016*. http://hispanicwealthproject.org/downloads/2016-HWP-Annual-Report.pdf.

Hoff, David J. "Chapter 1 Aid Failed to Close Learning Gap." *Education Week*, April 2, 1997, pp. 1, 29.

Holden, John P. *America COMPETES Act Keeps America's Leadership on Target*, January 6. 2011. www.whitehouse.gov/blog/2011/01/06/america-competes-act-keeps-americas-leadership-target.

Holdren, John P. "COMPETES Passage Keeps America's Leadership on Target." *The White House Blog*, January 3, 2011. https://obamawhitehouse.archives.gov/blog/2011/01/03/competes-passage-keeps-americas-leadership-target.

Horng, Eileen. *Recruiting and Retaining Teachers at Hard-to-Staff Schools: Examining the Tradeoffs Teachers Make When Choosing a School.* PhD diss., University of California, Los Angeles, 2005.

Howes, Carollee, and Sharon Ritchie. *A Matter of Trust: Connecting Teachers and Learners in the Early Childhood Classroom.* New York: Teachers College Press, 2002.

Howes, Carollee, and Sharon Ritchie. *Teachers and Attachment in Children With Difficult Life Circumstances.* Unpublished manuscript, UCLA, 1997.

Hu, C. T. "The Historical Background: Examinations and Control in Pre-modern China." *Comparative Education 20* (1984): 17, as cited in ed. F. Allan Hanson, *Testing Testing: Social Consequences of the Examined Life.* Berkeley: University of California Press, 1993. http://ark.cdlib.org/ark:/13030/ft4m3nb2h2/.

Human Rights Watch. *Like Walking Through a Hailstorm: Discrimination Against LGBT Youth in Schools,* 2016. www.hrw.org/report/2016/12/07/walking-through-hailstorm/discrimination-against-lgbt-youth-us-schools.

Hurd, Paul DeHart. "Science Needs a 'Lived' Curriculum." *Education Week,* November 12, 1997, p. 48.

Hussar, William J., and Tabitha M. Bailey. *Projections of Education Statistics to 2024* (NCES 2016-013). U.S. Department of Education, National Center for Education Statistics. Washington, DC: U.S. Government Printing Office, 2016.

The Individuals With Disabilities Education Act of 1975. http://idea.ed.gov/explore/view/p/%2Croot%2Cdynamic%2CTopicalBrief%2C23%2C/.

Ingels, Steven J., Ben W. Dalton, and Laura LoGerfo. "Trends Among High School Seniors, 1972–2004." *NCES Publication No. 2008–320.* Washington, DC: National Center for Education Statistics, 2008. http://nces.ed.gov/pubs2008/2008320.pdf.

Institute for Policy Studies. *Income Inequality,* 2011. http://inequality.org/income-inequality/.

Institute for Policy Studies. *The Racial Wealth Gap's Great Recession Surge,* July 29, 2011. http://inequality.org/racial-wealth-gaps-great-recession-surge/.

Institute for Social Policy and Understanding. *American Muslim Poll 2017: Muslims at the Crossroads.* www.ispu.org/wp-content/uploads/2017/03/AMP-2017-Key-Findings_Final.pdf.

International Association for the Evaluation of Educational Achievement (IEA). *Trends in International Mathematics and Science Study (TIMSS),* 2007. www.iea.nl/timss_2007.html.

International Association for the Evaluation of Educational Achievement (IEA). *Trends in International Mathematics and Science Study (TIMSS),* 2015. http://timss2015.org/timss-2015/mathematics/student-achievement/.

International Reading Association. *IRA Calls for Three-Part Initiative to Raise Literacy Achievement Through Common Core State Standards.* www.reading.org/Libraries/Press/pr_Common_Core_Standards.sfb.ashx.

International Reading Association and National Council of Teachers of English. *Standards for the English Language Arts.* Champaign, IL: Author, 1996.

"Internet Helps With Homework." *Los Angeles Times,* September 2, 2001, p. A18.

Jackson, Philip. *The Practice of Teaching.* New York: Teachers College Press, 1987.

Jacobowitz, Robin, and K. T. Tobin. *Time on Test: The Fixed Costs of 3–8 Standardized Testing in New York State.* New Paltz, NY: The Benjamin Center for Public Policy Initiatives, 2015.

Jacobson, Linda. "PTA Seeks to Raise Number of Hispanic Members." *Education Week,* June 11, 2003.

"Japan's High Court Rules Against Rewriting History." *Los Angeles Times,* August 30, 1997.

Jefferson, Thomas. *Notes on the State of Virginia,* quoted in Joel Spring. *The American School.* New York: Longman, 1990, 8–10.

Jenkins, Henry, Katie Clinton, Ravi Purushotma, Alice J. Robison, and Margaret Weigel. *Confronting the Challenges of Participatory Culture: Media Education for the 21st Century.* http://digitallearning.macfound.org/atf/cf/%7B7E45C7E0-A3E0-4B89-AC9C-E807E1B0AE4E%7D/JENKINS_WHITE_PAPER.PDF.

Johnston, Robert C. "System Thwarts Teacher's Bid to Transfer to Needy School." *Education Week,* July 11, 2001.

Joint Center for Housing Studies of Harvard University. *State of the Nation's Housing 2010*, June 2011. www.jchs.harvard.edu/research/publications/state-nations-housing-2010/.

Jones, Beau Fly, Gilbert Valdez, Jeri Nowakowski, and Claudette Rasmussen. *Plugging In*. Oak Brook, IL: North Central Regional Educational Laboratory, 1995.

Jones, Makeba. *Rethinking African American Students' Agency: Meaningful Choices and Negotiating Meaning*. Ph.D. diss., UCLA Graduate School of Education and Information Studies, 1998.

Jordan, Miriam. "Arizona Grades Teachers on Fluency." *Wall Street Journal*, April 30, 2010. http://online.wsj.com/article/SB10001424052748703572504575213883276427528.html.

Journey for Justice Alliance. *Death by a Thousand Cuts: Racism, School Closures, and Public School Sabotage*, 2014. www.issuelab.org/resource/death_by_a_thousand_cuts_racism_school_closures_and_public_school_sabotage.

Kandel, Isaac L. *Examinations and Their Substitutes in the United States*. New York: Carnegie Foundation for the Advancement of Teaching, 1936. Quoted in F. Allan Hanson. *Testing Testing: Social Consequences of the Examined Life*. Berkeley: University of California Press, 1993.

Kane, Thomas J. "The Impact of After-School Programs: Interpreting the Results of Four Recent Evaluations." *Working Paper of the William T. Grant Foundation*, 2004.

Kanpol, Barry, and Peter McLaren. *Critical Multiculturalism: Uncommon Voices in a Common Struggle*. London: Bergen and Garvey, 1995.

Kansas Evolution Hearings Transcripts. www.talkorigins.org/faqs/kansas/kangaroo1.html.

Katz, Michael. *The Undeserving Poor: From War on Poverty to War on the Poor*. New York: Pantheon, 1989.

Kaufman, Leslie. "Darwin Foes Add Warming to Targets." *New York Times*, March 3, 2010. www.nytimes.com/2010/03/04/science/earth/04climate.html.

Keller, Bill. "Asking Candidates Tougher Questions About Faith." *New York Times*, August 25, 2011. www.nytimes.com/2011/08/28/magazine/asking-candidates-tougher-questions-about-faith.html?_r=2.

Kelly, Thomas. "The 4 Percent 'Structural Flaw'." *Education Week*, June 11, 1997, p. 44.

Kemple, James J., Corinne M. Herlihy, and Thomas J. Smith. *Making Progress Toward Graduation: Evidence From the Talent Development High School Model*. Washington, DC: MRDC, 2005.

Key Issues in Children's Health Coverage. www.kff.org/medicaid/issue-brief/key-issues-in-childrens-health-coverage/.

Kids Count Data Center. *2015 American Community Survey*, 2015. http://datacenter.kidscount.org/data/tables/81-children-who-speak-a-language-other-than-english-at-home#detailed/1/any/false/573,869,36,868,867/any/396,397.

Kimmel, Michael S., and Matthew Mahler. "Adolescent Masculinity, Homophobia and Violence: Random School Shootings, 1982–2001." *American Behavioral Scientist 46*, no. *10* (2003): 1439–1458.

King, Joyce Elaine. "Diaspora Literacy and Consciousness in the Struggle Against Miseducation in the Black Community." *Journal of Negro Education 61*, no. *3* (1992): 317–340.

Kleibard, Herbert. *The Struggle for the American Curriculum: 1893–1958*, 2nd ed. New York: Routledge, 1995.

Klein, David, Bastiaan J. Braams, Thomas Parker, William Quirk, Wilfried Schmid, W. Stephen Wilson, Chester E. Finn Jr., Justin Torres, Lawrence Braden, and Ralph A. Raimi. *The State of Math Standards 2005*. Washington, DC: Fordham Institute, 2005.

Kluger, Richard. *Simple Justice*. New York: Vintage, 1977.

Knapp, Michael, Patrick Shields, and Brenda Turnbull. *Teaching for Meaning in High-Poverty Classrooms*. New York: Teachers College Press, 1995.

Knight, Michelle. *Unearthing the Muted Voices of Transformative Professionals*. Ph.D. diss., Los Angeles, UCLA, 1998.

Kohl, Herbert. "The Politics of Children's Literature: What's Wrong With the Rosa Parks Myth." In *Rethinking Our Classrooms: Teaching for Equity and Justice*, Vol. *1*, ed. Bill Bigelow, Linda Christensen, Stan Karp, Barbara Milner, and Bob Peterson. Milwaukee, WI: Rethinking Schools, 1994, 137–140.

Kohl, Herbert. "Some Reflections on Teaching for Social Justice." In *Teaching for Social Justice: A Democracy and Education Reader*, ed. William Ayers, Jean Ann Hunt, and Therese Quinn. New York: The New Press and Teachers College Press, 1998, 285–287.

Kohn, Alfie. *Beyond Discipline: From Compliance to Community*. Alexandria, VA: Association for Supervision and Curriculum Development, 1996.

Kohn, Alfie. *Punished by Rewards*. Boston: Houghton Mifflin, 1993.

Kohn, Alfie. "'Teaching About September 11' in War, Terrorism and Our Classrooms: Teaching in the Aftermath of the September 11th Tragedy." Special issue, *Rethinking Schools 16*, no. *2* (Winter 2001/2002): 5. www.rethinkingschools.org/static/special_reports/sept11/pdf/911insrt.pdf.

Kornrich, Sabino, and Frank F. Furstenberg. "Investing in Children: Changes in Spending on Children, 1972 to 2007." *Demography 49* (2012): 1–23.

Kosciw, Joseph G., Emily A. Greytak, Noreen M. Giga, Christian Villenas, and David J. Danischewski. *The 2015 National School Climate Survey: The Experiences of Lesbian, Gay, Bisexual, Transgender, and Queer Youth in Our Nation's Schools*. New York: GLSEN, 2016. www.glsen.org/sites/default/files/2015%20National%20GLSEN%202015%20National%20School%20Climate%20Survey%20%28NSCS%29%20-%20Full%20Report_0.pdf.

Kounin, Jacob. *Discipline and Group Management in Classrooms*. New York: Holt, Rinehart & Winston, 1970.

Kozol, Jonathan. *Savage Inequalities: Children in America's Schools*. New York: Crown, 1991.

Kozol, Jonathan. *The Shame of the Nation: The Restoration of Apartheid Schooling in America*. New York: Broadway, 2006.

Krashen, Stephen. *Second Language Acquisition and Second Language Learning*, 1981. http://sdkrashen.com/SL_Acquisition_and_Learning/SL_Acquisition_and_Learning.pdf.

Krop, C., D. Brewer, S. Gates, B. Gill, R. Reichardt, M. Sundt, and D. Throgmorton. *Potentially Eligible Students: A Growing Opportunity for the University of California*. Santa Monica, CA: Rand Corporation, 1998.

Krueger, Alan B. "Understanding the Magnitude and Effect of Class Size on Student Achievement." In *The Class Size Debate*, ed. Lawrence Mishel and Richard Rothstein. Washington, DC: Economic Policy Institute, 2002, 7–36.

Kucher, Karen. "Chula Vista School's Turnaround Turns Heads: Elementary Charter Has Gone From Federal Improvement List to Distinguished Status." *San Diego Union Tribune*, November 21, 2011.

La Belle, Thomas J., and Christopher R. Ward. *Multiculturalism and Education: Diversity and Its Impact on Schools and Society*. New York: SUNY Press, 1994.

Ladson-Billings, Gloria. *The Dreamkeepers: Successful Teachers of African American Children*. San Francisco: Jossey-Bass, 1994.

Ladson-Billings, Gloria. "From the Achievement Gap to the Education Debt: Understanding Achievement in U.S. Schools." 2006 American Educational Research Association Presidential Address, *Education Researcher 35*, no. *7* (2006): 3–12.

Langer, Judith, as quoted in Deborah Viadero. "Researchers Flag Six Elements of Good Secondary English Instruction." *Education Week*, June 14, 2000. www.edweek.org.

Lappan, Glenda, as cited in "Revised Mathematics Standards Provide More Guidance." *Education Week*, April 19, 2000. www.edweek.org.

Lareau, Annette. *Home Advantage: Social Class and Parental Intervention in Elementary Education*. London: Falmer, 1989.

Lareau, Annette. *Unequal Childhoods: Class, Race, and Family Life*. Berkeley and Los Angeles: University of California Press, 2003.

Lave, Jean. "Teaching as Learning in Practice." *Mind, Culture, and Activity 3*, no. *3* (1996): 149–164.

Lave, Jean, and Etienne Wenger. *Situated Cognition: Legitimate Peripheral Participation*. Cambridge: Cambridge University Press, 1991.

Lawton, Millicent. "Girls Will Be Girls." *Education Week*, March 30, 1994.

Lee, Carol D. "Is October Brown Chinese? A Cultural Modeling Activity System for Underachieving Students." *American Educational Research Journal 38*, no. *1* (2001): 97–142.

Lee, Carol D. "Literacy in the Academic Disciplines and the Needs of Adolescent Struggling Readers." *Voices in Urban Education* (Special Issue on Adolescent Literacy), no. *3* (Spring 2004): 14–25.

Lee, Enid, Deborah Menkart, and Margo Okazawa-Rey, eds. *Beyond Heroes and Holidays: A Practical Guide to K–12 Anti-Racist, Multicultural Education and Staff Development.* Washington, DC: Network of Educators on the Americas, 1998.

Lee, Seon-Young, Michael S. Matthews, and Paula Olszewski-Kubilius. "A National Picture of Talent Search and Talent Search Educational Programs." *Gifted Child Quarterly 52*, no. *2* (2008): 55–69.

LeMoine, Noma. *English for Your Success: A Language Development Program for African American Children Grades PreK–8.* Saddle Brook, NJ: The Peoples Publishing Group, 1999.

Lenhardt, Amanda, and Mary Madden. *Teen Content Creators and Consumers.* Washington, DC: Pew Internet & American Life Project, 2005. www.pewInternet.org/PPF/r/166/report_display.asp.

Levine, Lawrence W. *Opening of the American Mind: Canons, Culture, and History.* Boston: Beacon Press, 1996.

Levinson, David, Peter W. Cookson, and Alan R. Sadovnik. *Education and Sociology: An Encyclopedia.* New York: Routledge, 2004.

Lewin, Tamar, and Jennifer Medina. "To Cut Failure Rate, Schools Shed Students." *New York Times,* July 31, 2003.

Lewis, Sharon *Improving School Climate: Findings From Schools Implementing Restorative Practices.* Bethlehem, PA: International Institute for Restorative Practices, 2009.

Limbaugh, Rush, as cited in Gary Nash, Charlotte Crabtree, and Ross E. Dunn. *History on Trial.* New York: Knopf, 1997, 5.

Linn, Robert L. "Accountability: Responsibility and Reasonable Expectations (2003 Presidential Address to the American Educational Research Association)." *Educational Researcher 32*, no. *7* (2003): 3–13.

Lionni, Leo. *Tillie and the Wall.* Dragonfly Books; Penguin Random House, Reissue edition (February 20, 1991), np.

Little, Judith Warren. "The Mentor Phenomenon and the Social Organization of Teaching." In *Review of Research in Education,* ed. C. B. Cazden. Washington, DC: American Educational Research Association, 1990, 297–351.

Little, Judith Warren. "Norms of Collegiality and Experimentation: Workplace Conditions of School Success." *American Educational Research Journal 19* (1982): 325–340.

Little, Judith Warren, and Milbery McLaughlin, eds. *Teachers Work: Individuals, Colleagues, and Contexts.* New York: Teachers College Press, 1993.

Loeb, Susanna, Linda Darling-Hammond, and John Luczac. "How Teaching Conditions Predict Teacher Turnover in California Schools." *Peabody Journal of Education 80*, no. *3* (2005): 44–70.

Louis, Karen Seashore, and Sharon D. Kruse. *Professionalism and Community: Perspectives on Reforming Urban Schools.* Newberry Park, CA: Corwin Press, 1995.

MacIver, Douglas, Steven B. Plank, and Robert Balfanz. *Working Together to Become Proficient Readers: Early Impact of the Talent Development Middle School's "Student Team Literature Program".* Report of the Center for Research on the Education of Students Placed at Risk. Baltimore: The Johns Hopkins University, 1998.

MacLeod, Jay. *Ain't No Makin' It.* Boulder, CO: Westview Press, 1995.

MacMillan, Donald L., and Daniel Reschly. "Overrepresentation of Minority Students: The Case for Greater Specificity or Reconsideration of the Variables Examined." *Journal of Special Education 32* (1998): 15–24.

Making Schools Safe for Gay and Lesbian Youth: Breaking the Silence in Schools and in Families. Boston, MA: The Governor's Commission on Gay and Lesbian Youth, 1993.

Manouchehri, Azita, and Terry Goodman. "Implementing Mathematics Reform: The Challenge Within." *Educational Studies in Mathematics 42*, no. *1* (2000): 1–34.

Manzo, Kathleen Kennedy. "Glimmer of History Standards Shows Up in Latest Textbooks." *Education Week,* October 8, 1997.

Margolis, Jane. *Stuck in the Shallow End: Education, Race, and Computing.* Cambridge, MA: MIT Press, 2008.

Margolis, Jane, and Allan Fisher. *Unlocking the Clubhouse: Women and Computing*. Cambridge, MA: MIT Press, 2002.

Marsh, Julie A., Matthew G. Springer, Daniel F. McCaffrey, Kun Yuan, Scott Epstein, Julia Koppich, Nidhi Kalra, Catherine DiMartino, and Art (Xiao) Peng. *A Big Apple for Educators: New York City's Experiment With School-wide Performance Bonuses*. Santa Monica, CA: Rand Corporation, 2011. www.rand.org/content/dam/rand/pubs/monographs/2011/RAND_MG1114.pdf.

Martínez, Ramón Antonio. "Spanglish as a Literacy Tool: Toward an Understanding of the Potential Role of Spanish-English Code-Switching in the Development of Academic Literacy." *Research in the Teaching of English 45*, no. 2 (2010): 124–149.

Marvel, John, Deanna M. Lyter, Pia Peltola, Gregory A. Strizek, and Beth A. Morton. *Teacher Attrition and Mobility: Results From the 2004–05 Teacher Follow-Up Survey*. Washington, DC: Institute of Education Sciences National Center for Educational Statistics, 2007.

Mashup Transcript: Barack Obama, September 13, 2007. www.huffingtonpost.com/2007/09/13/mashup-transcript-barack-_n_64321.html.

MassPartners for Public Schools. *Facing Reality: What Happens When Good Schools Are Labeled "Failures"? Projecting Adequate Yearly Progress in Massachusetts Schools*. Boston: Author, 2005.

Mathematically Correct. http://mathematicallycorrect.com.

Mathematics Content Standards for Grades K-12, Submitted by Bill Evers, Commissioner to California State Academic Standards Commission, September 15, 1997. www.rahul.net/dehnbase/hold/platinum-standards/altintro.html.

Mather, Mark. *Reports on America: Children in Immigrant Families Chart New Path*. Washington, DC: Population Reference Bureau, 2009.

Matthews, Dylan. "Donald Trump Has Tweeted Climate Change Skepticism 115 Times. Here's All of It." *Vox*, June 1, 2017. www.vox.com/policy-and-politics/2017/6/1/15726472/trump-tweets-global-warming-paris-climate-agreement.

Matthews, Jay. "Educators Face Pitfalls of Too Much Success." *Los Angeles Times*, July 25, 2001.

Mayhew, Katherine Camp, and Anna Camp Edwards. *The Dewey School*. New York: Nabu Press, 2011.

McDonnell, Lorraine, and Richard Elmore. "Getting the Job Done: Alternative Policy Instruments." *Educational Evaluation and Policy Analysis 9* (Summer 1987): 133–152.

McFarland, Joel, Bill Hussar, Cristobal de Brey, Tom Snyder, Xiaolei Wang, Sidney Wilkinson-Flicker, Semhar Gebrekristos, Jijun Zhang, Amy Rathbun, Amy Barmer, Farrah Bullock Mann, and Serena Hinz. *The Condition of Education 2017* (NCES 2017-144). U.S. Department of Education. Washington, DC: National Center for Education Statistics, 2017. https://nces.ed.gov/pubsearch/pubsinfo.asp?pubid=2017144.

McGreevy, Patrick, and Anthony York. "Brown Signs California Dream Act." *Los Angeles Times*, October 9, 2011. http://articles.latimes.com/2011/oct/09/local/la-me-brown-dream-act-20111009/.

McIntosh, Peggy. "White Privilege and Male Privilege: A Personal Account of Coming to See Correspondences Through Work in Women's Studies." *Working Paper 189, Center for Research on Women, Wellesley College*, 1988.

McKenna, Phil. "EPA Head Pruitt Denies the Basic Science of Climate Change." *Inside Climate News*, March 9, 2017. https://insideclimatenews.org/news/09032017/scott-pruitt-epa-donald-trump-climate-change-denial-co2-global-warming.

McKinley, James C. "Texas Conservatives Win Curriculum Change." *New York Times*, March 12, 2010. www.nytimes.com/2010/03/13/education/13texas.html.

McKnight, Curtis C., F. Joe Crosswhite, and John A. Dossey. *The Underachieving Curriculum: Assessing U.S. School Mathematics From an International Perspective*. Indianapolis: Stipes, 1987.

McLaren, Peter. *Life in Schools: An Introduction to Critical Pedagogy in the Foundations of Education*. New York: Longman, 1998.

McLaughlin, Clare. "The Homework Gap: The 'Cruelest Part of the Digital Divide'." *NEA Today*, April 20, 2016. http://neatoday.org/2016/04/20/the-homework-gap/.

McTygue, Nancy. "What You Need to Know About California's New History Social Science Framework." *California History-Social Science Project*, Blog post, July 14, 2016. http://chssp.ucdavis.edu/blog/what-you-need-to-know-about-california2019s-new-history-social-science-framework.

Medina, Jennifer. "On New York School Tests, Warning Signs Ignored." *New York Times*, October 10, 2010. www.nytimes.com/2010/10/11/education/11scores.html?pagewanted=all.

Medina, Noe, and Monty Neill. *Fallout From the Testing Explosion: How 100 Million Standardized Exams Undermine Equity and Excellence in Americas Public Schools*, 3rd ed. Cambridge, MA: FairTest, 1990.

Mediratta, Kavitha, Seema Shah, and Sara McAlister. *Community Organizing for Stronger Schools: Strategies and Successes*. Cambridge, MA: Harvard University Press, 2009.

Mehan, Hugh. "Understanding Equality in Schools: The Contribution of Interpretative Studies." *Sociology of Education 65*, no. *1* (January 1992): 1–21.

Mehan, Hugh, Lea Hubbard, Irene Villanueva, and Angela Lintz. *Constructing School Success*. Cambridge: Cambridge University Press, 1996.

Mehan, Hugh, Jane Mercer, and Robert Rueda. "Special Education." In *Education and Sociology*, ed. D. L. Levinson, P. W. Cookson, and A. R. Sadovnik. New York: Routledge Falmer, 2002, 619–624.

Mehan, Hugh, Dina Okamoto, Angela Lintz, and John S. Wills. "Ethnographic Studies of Multicultural Schools and Classrooms." In *Handbook of Research on Multicultural Education*, ed. James A. Banks and Cherry A. McGee Banks. New York: Macmillan, 1995, 129–144.

Meier, Deborah. *The Power of their Ideas: Lessons for America From a Small School in Harlem*. Boston: Beacon Press, 1995.

Meier, Kenneth J., Stewart Joseph Jr., and Robert E. England. *Race, Class and Education: The Politics of Second Generation Discrimination*. Madison: University of Wisconsin Press, 1989.

Menken, Kate. "What Have Been the Benefits and Drawbacks of Testing and Accountability for English Language Learners/Emergent Bilinguals Under No Child Left Behind, and What Are the Implications Under the Common Core State Standards?" In *Common Core Bilingual and English Language Learners: A Resource for Educators*, ed. Guadalupe Valdés, Kate Menken, and Mariana Castro. Philadelphia: Calston Publishing, 2015, 246–247.

"Mental Ability Test, Stanford University, Test 1, Information" (World Book Co, 1920), as reprinted in Bill Bigelow. "Testing, Tracking, and Toeing the Line." In *Rethinking Our Classrooms: Teaching for Equity and Social Justice*, ed. Wayne Au, Bill Bigelow, and Stan Karp. Milwaukee, WI: Rethinking Schools, 1994, 121.

Mesmer, Heidi Anne E., James W. Cunningham, and Elfrieda H. Hiebert. "Toward a Theoretical Model of Text Complexity for the Early Grades: Learning From the Past, Anticipating the Future." *Reading Research Quarterly 47*, no. *3* (2013): 235–258.

MetLife Survey of the American Teacher Finds Decreased Teacher Satisfaction, Increased Parent Engagement Amid Economic Uncertainty, March 7, 2012. www.metlife.com/about/press-room/index.html?compID=79162.

MetLife Survey of the American Teacher: Teachers, Parents and the Economy, 2012. www.metlife.com/assets/cao/contributions/foundation/american-teacher/2011-Teacher-Survey-Findings.pdf.

Mexican American Studies Stats Show Program Works. http://saveethnicstudies.org/proven_results.shtml.

Meyer, Luanna H., Beth Harry, and Mara Sapon-Shevin. "School Inclusion and Multicultural Education." In *Multicultural Education: Issues and Perspectives*, 3rd ed., ed. James A. Banks and Cherry A. McGee Banks. Boston: Allyn & Bacon, 1996, 369–400.

Migration Policy Institute. *Frequently Requested Statistics on Immigrants and Immigration in the United States*, 2017. www.migrationpolicy.org/article/frequently-requested-statistics-immigrants-and-immigration-united-states#Demographic.

Mills vs. Board of Education of District of Columbia, 348 F.Supp. 866 (D.D.C. 1972).

Mishel, Lawrence, Jared Bernstein, and Sylvia Allegretto. *State of Working America, 2004–2005*. Washington, DC: Economic Policy Institute, 2005. www.epinet.org.

Mislevy, Robert J. "Foundations of a New Test Theory." In *Test Theory for a New Generation of Tests*, ed. Norman Frederiksen, Robert J. Mislevy, and Isaac I. Bejar. Hillsdale, NJ: Lawrence Erlbaum, 1993, 19–39.

Moe, Terry. "No Teacher Left Behind." *Wall Street Journal*, January 13, 2005.

Moll, Luis. "Funds of Knowledge for Teaching: Using a Qualitative Approach to Connect Homes and Classrooms." *Theory Into Practice 31*, no. *2* (1992): 132–141.

Morrow, Raymond Allan, and Carlos Alberto Torres. *Social Theory and Education: A Critique of Theories of Social and Cultural Reproduction.* Buffalo: State University of New York Press, 1995.

Moschkovich, Judit. "Mathematics, the Common Core, and Language." *Understanding Language.* Stanford University, 2013. http://ell.stanford.edu/sites/default/files/pdf/academic-papers/02-JMoschkovich%20Math%20FINAL_bound%20with%20appendix.pdf.

Moschkovich, Judit. "Supporting ELLs in Mathematics: CCSS-Aligned Mathematics Tasks With Annotations and Other Resources for Implementing the Common Core State Standards." *Understanding Language.* Stanford University, 2013. http://ell.stanford.edu/sites/default/files/math_archives/Full%20set_UL%20Math%20Resources%2010-28-13%20updated.pdf.

Moyers, Bill. *Going to Bed Hungry.* http://billmoyers.com/2013/04/05/going-to-bed-hungry/.

"Multicultural Book List Proposed in San Francisco." *New York Times*, March 11, 1998.

"Muslim Girl Suspended for Head Scarf." *Reuters*, October 11, 2003. www.cnn.com/2003/EDUCATION/10/11/scarf.reut/index.html.

Myers, Miles. "Where the Debate About English Standards Goes Wrong." *Education Week*, May 15, 1995.

Myrdal, Gunnar. *The American Dilemma: The Negro Problem and Modern Democracy.* New York: Harper & Row, 1944.

Nash, Gary B., Charlotte Crabtree, and Ross E. Dunn. *History on Trial: Culture Wars and the Teaching of the Past.* New York: Knopf, 1997.

Nasir, Na'ilah Suad, Victoria Hand, and Edd Taylor. "Culture and Mathematics in School: Boundaries Between 'Cultural' and 'Domain' Knowledge in the Mathematics Classroom and Beyond." *Review of Research in Education 32*, no. *1* (2008): 187–240.

National Academy Press. *Preventing Reading Difficulties in Young Children.* Washington, DC: The National Research Council, 1998.

National Association of Gifted Children. *2014-2015 State of the States in Gifted Education.* Washington, DC: National Association for Gifted Children, 2015.

National Association of School Psychologists. *Zero Tolerance and Alternative Strategies: A Fact Sheet for Educators and Policymakers*, 2001. www.naspcenter.org/factsheets/zt_fs.html.

National Center for Children in Poverty. *Paid Leave in the States*, 2009. www.paidfamilyleave.org/pdf/PaidLeaveinStates.pdf.

National Center for Education Statistics. *Condition of Education*, 2011. http://nces.ed.gov/programs/coe/indicator_pcp.asp.

National Center for Education Statistics. *Fast Facts.* https://nces.ed.gov/fastfacts/display.asp?id=28.

National Center for Education Statistics. *The Nation's Report Card: Trends in Academic Progress 2012 (NCES 2013 456).* Washington, DC: Institute of Education Sciences, U.S. Department of Education, 2013. https://nces.ed.gov/nationsreportcard/subject/publications/main2012/pdf/2013456.pdf.

National Center for Education Statistics. *Time Spent Teaching Core Academic Subjects in Elementary Schools.* Washington, DC: U.S. Department of Education, 1997.

National Center for History in the Schools. *National Standards for United States History.* Los Angeles: UCLA National Center for History in the Schools, 1994.

National Center on Performance Incentives. *Teacher Pay for Performance: Experimental Evidence From the Project on Incentives in Teaching*, September 2010. www.performanceincentives.org/data/files/gallery/ContentGallery/POINT_REPORT_9.21.10.pdf.

National Coalition for the Homeless. *How Many People Experience Homelessness?* July 2009. www.nationalhomeless.org/factsheets/How_Many.html.

National Commission of Excellence in Education. *A Nation at Risk: The Imperatives for Educational Reform.* Washington, DC: U.S. Department of Education, 1983.

National Commission on Mathematics and Science. *Before It's Too Late: A Report to the Nation From the National Commission on Mathematics and Science Teaching for the 21st Century.* Washington, DC: U.S. Department of Education, 2000.

National Commission on Teaching and America's Future (NCTAF). *No Dream Denied: A Pledge to America's Children.* Washington, DC: Author, 2003.

National Commission on Teaching and America's Future (NCTAF). *What Matters Most: Teaching for America's Future*. New York: Author, 1996.

National Council of Teachers of English (NCTE). *NCTE Common Core State Standards Resources*. www.ncte.org/standards/commoncore.

National Council of Teachers of English (NCTE). "Reading Instruction for *All* Students." National Council of Teachers of English, 2012. www.ncte.org/library/NCTEFiles/Resources/Journals/CC/0221-sep2012/Chron0221PolicyBrief.pdf.

National Council of Teachers of English (NCTE). *Resources for Student-Centered Instruction in a Time of Common Core Standards*. www.ncte.org/standards/common-core.

National Council of Teachers of Mathematics. *Curriculum and Evaluation Standards for School Mathematics*. Reston, VA: Author, 1989.

National Council of Teachers of Mathematics. *NCTM Public Comments on the Common Core Standards for Mathematics*. www.nctm.org/about/content.aspx?id=25186.

National Council of Teachers of Mathematics. *Supporting the Common Core State Standards for Mathematics*. www.nctm.org/uploadedFiles/Standards_and_Positions/Position_Statements/Common%20Core%20State%20Standards.pdf.

National Council on Teacher Quality. *State of the States: Trends and Early Lessons on Teacher Evaluation and Effectiveness Policies*, October 2001. www.nctq.org/p/publications/docs/nctq_stateOfTheStates.pdf.

National Education Association. *Muslims in America: When Bullying Meets Religion*, 2012. www.nea.org/home/42528.htm.

National Education Association. *Truth in Labeling: Disproportionality in Special Education*, 2007. www.nea.org/assets/docs/HE/EW-TruthInLabeling.pdf.

National Forum on Assessment. "Principles and Indicators for Student Assessment Systems." *FairTest, The National Center for Fair and Open Testing*, 1991. www.fairtest.org/princind.htm.

National Public Radio. *Politics and Religion Mix in Presidential Primaries*. www.npr.org/2011/09/16/140533708/politics-and-religion-mix-in-presidential-primaries/.

National Research Council. *America's Lab Report: Investigations in High School Science*. Washington, DC: National Academy Press, 2005.

National Research Council. *Everybody Counts: A Report to the Nation on the Future of Mathematics Education*. Washington, DC: National Academy Press, 1989.

National Research Council. *National Science Education Standards*. Washington, DC: National Academy Press, 1996.

National Research Council. *Taking Science to School: Learning and Teaching Science in Grades K–8*. Washington, DC: The National Academies Press, 2007.

National School Board Association. *Creating and Connecting: Research and Guidelines on Social—And Educational—Networking*, 2007. www.nsba.org/Services/TLN/BenefitsofMembership/Publications/Creating-and-Connecting.pdf.

NCLB Elementary & Secondary Education, Part A—Improving Basic Programs Operated by Local Educational Agencies, State Plans. www2.ed.gov/policy/elsec/leg/esea02/pg2.html#sec1111.

NEA Policy Statement on Charter Schools, Adopted by the 2017 Representative Assembly, July 4, 2017. https://ra.nea.org/nea-policy-statement-charter-schools/.

Neill, A. S. *Summerhill: A Radical Approach to Child Rearing*. New York: St. Martin's Press, 1995, originally published in 1960.

Nespor, Jan. "Networks and Contexts of Reform." *International Journal of Educational Change 3* (2002): 365–382.

Newmann, Fred M. ed. *Student Engagement and Achievement in American Secondary Schools*. New York: Teachers College Press, 1992.

Newmann, Fred M., Walter G. Secada, and Gary Wehlage. *A Guide to Authentic Instruction and Assessment: Vision, Standards, and Scoring*. Madison, WI: Wisconsin Center for Education Research at the University of Wisconsin, 1995.

New York Collective of Radical Educators. *Resources*. www.nycore.org/resources/.

New York Learning Standards and Core Curriculum in Social Studies. www.p12.nysed.gov/ciai/socst/ssrg.html.

Next Generation Science Standards. *HS-ESS3 Earth and Human Activity*. www.nextgenscience.org/dci-arrangement/hs-ess3-earth-and-human-activity.

Ng, Jennifer, and John Rury. "Poverty and Education: A Critical Analysis of the Ruby Payne Phenomenon." *Teachers College Record*, July 18, 2006. www.tcrecord.org/content.asp?contentid=12596.

Nieto, Sonia. *Affirming Diversity: The Sociopolitical Context of Multicultural Education*, 2nd ed. White Plains, NY: Longman, 1996.

Nieto, Sonia. *What Keeps Teachers Going?* New York: Teachers College Press, 2003.

Noblit, George. "In the Meaning: The Possibilities of Caring." *Phi Delta Kappan 77* (May 1995): 682.

No Child Left Behind, Elementary & Secondary Education Act, Part A—Improving Basic Programs Operated by Local Educational Agencies, State Plans. www2.ed.gov/policy/elsec/leg/esea02/pg2.html#sec1111.

Noddings, Nel. *The Challenge to Care in Schools: An Alternative Approach to Education*. New York: Teachers College Press, 1992.

Noddings, Nel. "Teaching Themes of Care." *Phi Delta Kappan 77* (May 1995): 676.

NPR Staff, National Public Radio. *Politics and Religion Mix in Presidential Primaries*. www.npr.org/2011/09/16/140533708/politics-and-religion-mix-in-presidential-primaries.

Oakes, Jeannie. *Keeping Track: How Schools Structure Inequality*. New Haven, CT: Yale University Press, 2005.

Oakes, Jeannie. *Lost Talent: The Underrepresentation of Minorities, Women, and Disabled Persons in Science*. Santa Monica, CA: Rand Corporation, 1990.

Oakes, Jeannie. *Multiplying Inequalities: Race, Social Class and Tracking on Students Opportunities to Learn Mathematics and Science*. Santa Monica: RAND, 1990.

Oakes, Jeannie. *Report to the Court, New Castle County*. Unpublished report submitted to the court, 1995.

Oakes, Jeannie. "Two Cities: Tracking and Within-School Segregation." *Teachers College Record 96*, no. 4 (1995): 681–690.

Oakes, Jeannie, Adam Gamoran, and Reba Page. "Curriculum Differentiation: Opportunities, Outcomes, and Meanings." In *Handbook of Research on Curriculum*, ed. Phillip Jackson. New York: Macmillan, 1992, 570–608.

Oakes, Jeannie, and Gretchen Guiton. "Matchmaking: The Dynamics of High School Tracking Decisions." *American Educational Research Journal 32*, no. 1 (1995): 3–33.

Oakes, Jeannie, and Martin Lipton. "Struggling for Educational Equity in Diverse Communities: School Reform as Social Movement." *International Journal of Educational Change 3* (2002): 383–406.

Oakes, Jeannie, Karen Hunter Quartz, Steve Ryan, and Martin Lipton. *Becoming Good American Schools: The Struggle for Virtue in School Reform*. San Francisco: Jossey-Bass, 2001.

Oakes, Jeannie, and John Rogers. *Learning Power: Organizing for Education and Justice*. New York: Teachers College Press, 2006.

Oakes, Jeannie, John Rogers, David Silver, Siomara Valladares, Veronica Terriquez, Patricia McDonough, Michelle Renée, and Martin Lipton. *Removing the Roadblocks: Fair College Opportunities for All California Students*. University of California All Campus Consortium for Rich Diversity, UCLA, Institute for Democracy, Education, and Access, November 2006, pp. 1–72. http://idea.gseis.ucla.edu/publications/eor-06/RemovingRoadbloacks.pdf.

Oakes, Jeannie, Amy Stuart Wells, Susan Yonezawa, and Karen Ray. "Equity Lessons From Detracking Schools." In *Rethinking Educational Change With Heart and Mind*, ed. Andy Hargreaves. Arlington, VA: Association for Supervision and Curriculum Development, 1997.

Oakes, Jeannie, Amy Stuart Wells, Susan Yonezawa, and Karen Ray. "The Politics of Equity and Change: Lessons From Detracking Schools." In *1997 ASCD Yearbook: Rethinking Educational Change With Heart and Mind*, ed. Andy Hargreaves. Alexandria, VA: Association for Supervision and Curriculum Development, 1997, 43–72.

Obama, Barack. "Full Text of Obama's Education Speech." *Denver Post*, May 28, 2008. www.denverpost.com/ci_9405199/.

"Obama's Father's Day Speech Urges Black Fathers to Be More Engaged in Raising Their Children." *Huffington Post*, June 15, 2008. www.huffingtonpost.com/2008/06/15/obamas-fathers-day-speech_n_107220.html.

"Obama's Remarks on Education." *Wall Street Journal*, March 10, 2009. http://blogs.wsj.com/washwire/2009/03/10/obamas-remarks-on-education-2/.

Offices of Refugee Resettlement. *Unaccompanied Children Released to Sponsors by State*, 2017. www.acf.hhs.gov/orr/programs/ucs/state-by-state-uc-placed-sponsors.

Oh, California. Boston: Houghton Mifflin, 1991.

Olszewski-Kubilius, Paula, and Dana Thomson. "Gifted Programming for Poor or Minority Urban Students: Issues and Lessons Learned." *Gifted Child Today 33*, no. *4* (2010): 58–64. www.davidsongifted.org/db/Articles_id_10670.aspx.

Opinion Research Corporation's Pre-Teen Caravan and Teen Caravan Omnibus Surveys, as reported on www.prnewswire.com.

"Opt-outs From Common Core Test on English 2017." *Newsday*, March 31, 2017.

Orellana, Marjorie Faulstich *Translating Childhoods: Immigrant Youth, Language, and Culture*. New Brunswick, NJ: Rutgers University Press, 2009.

Orfield, Gary, Mark Bachmeier, David James, and Tamela Eitle. *Deepening Segregation in American Public Schools*. Cambridge, MA: Civil Rights Project, Harvard University, 1997.

Orfield, Gary, and Susan Eaton. *Dismantling Desegregation: The Quiet Reversal of Brown v. Board of Education*. Boston: New Press, 1996.

Orfield, Gary, Jongyeon Ee, Erica Frankenberg, and Genevieve Siegel-Hawley. *"Brown" at 62: School Segregation by Race, Poverty and State*. Los Angeles: UCLA Civil Rights Project-Proyecto Derechos Civiles, 2016.

Orfield, Gary, and Mindy L. Kornhaber, eds. *Raising Standards or Raising Barriers? Inequality and High-Stakes Testing in Public Education*. New York: Century Foundation Press, 2001.

Orfield, Gary, and Chungmei Lee. *Brown at 50: King's Dream or Plessy's Nightmare?* Cambridge, MA: Civil Rights Project, Harvard University, 2004.

Orfield, Gary, and Chungmei Lee. *Historic Reversals, Accelerating Resegregation, and the Need for New Integration Strategies*. Los Angeles: UCLA Civil Rights Project/Proyecto Derechos Civiles, 2007.

Organisation for Economic Co-operation and Development (OECD). *How's Life? 2015: Measuring Well-being*. www.oecd.org/statistics/Better-Life-Initiative-2016-country-notes-data.xlsx.

Organisation for Economic Co-operation and Development (OECD). *International Outcomes of Learning in Mathematics Literacy and Problem Solving: Programme for International Student Assessment PISA 2012 Results*. www.oecd.org/pisa/keyfindings/pisa-2012-results.htm.

Otto, Roland, as quoted in Richard Lee Colvin. "Spurned Nobelists Appeal Science Standards Rejection." *Los Angeles Times*, November 17, 1997, p. A25.

"Over 2,000 Occupy Arrests (Map)." *Mother Jones*, October 26, 2011. http://motherjones.com/politics/2011/10/occupy-wall-street-protest-map.

Owens, Ann. "Racial Residential Segregation of School-Age Children and Adults: The Role of Schooling as a Segregating Force." *RSF: The Russell Sage Foundation Journal of the Social Sciences 3*, no. *2* (2017): 63–80. doi:10.7758/RSF.2017.3.2.03.

Padres y Jóvenes Unidos/Parents and Youth United. *History and Accomplishments*. http://padresunidos.org/history-accomplishments/.

Paley, Vivian Gussin. *Kawanzaa and Me: A Teacher's Story*. Cambridge, MA: Harvard University Press, 1996.

Paley, Vivian Gussin. *You Can't Say You Can't Play*. Cambridge, MA: Harvard University Press, 1993.

Palmer, Lisa. "Public Schools' Global Warming Teachings: A Rich Field for Mining for News Stories." *The Yale Forum on Climate Change and the Media*, June 24, 2010. www.yaleclimatemediaforum.org/2010/06/teaching-climate-change-as-edu-news-beat/.

Parker, Francis. *Talks on Pedagogies*. New York: E. L. Kellogg, 1894.

Passow, Harry, Miriam Goldberg, and Abraham J. Tannenbaum, eds. *Education of the Disadvantaged*. New York: Holt, Rinehart & Winston, 1967.

Peace Builders. Tucson, AZ: Heartsprings, 1995.

Pear, Robert. "Education Chief Calls Union 'Terrorist,' then Recants." *New York Times*, February 24, 2004. www.nytimes.com/2004/02/23/us/education-chief-calls-union-terrorist-then-recants.html.

Pearson, P. David. "The Politics of Reading Research and Practice." *Conference Presentation*, May 15, 1997 (Houston). http://ed-web3.educ.msu.edu.cdpds/pdpaper.politics.html.

Pearson, P. David. *Reclaiming the Center: The Search for Common Ground in Teaching Reading.* http://ed-web3.educ.msu.edu.cdpds/pdpaper.rtc21197.htm.

Pearson, P. David. "Reclaiming the Center: The Search for Common Ground in Teaching Reading." In *The First R: Every Child's Right to Read*, ed. M. F. Graves, O. van den Broek, and B. M. Taylor. New York: Teachers College Press, 1996, 259–274. http://ed-web3.educ.msu.edu.cdpds/pdpaper.rtc21197.htm.

Pearson, P. David. "Research Foundations of the Common Core State Standards in English Language Arts." In *Quality Reading Instruction in the Age of Common Core State Standards*, ed. Susan B. Neuman and Linda Gambrell. Newark, DE: International Reading Association, 2013, 237–262.

Pew Forum on Religion and Public Life. *2007 Religious Landscape Survey.* http://religions.pewforum.org.

Pew Forum on Religion and Public Life. *Many Americans Mix Multiple Faiths*, December 9, 2009. www.pewforum.org/Other-Beliefsand-Practices/Many-Americans-Mix-Multiple-Faiths.aspx.

Pew Forum on Religion and Public Life. *Religion Among the Millennials*, February 10, 2010. www.pewforum.org/Age/Religion-Amongthe-Millennials.aspx.

Pew Research Center. *America's Changing Religious Landscape*, May 12, 2015. www.pewforum.org/2015/05/12/americas-changing-religious-landscape/.

Pew Research Center. *Multiracial in America: Proud, Diverse and Growing in Numbers.* Washington, DC, June 2015. www.pewsocialtrends.org/2015/06/11/multiracial-in-america/.

Pew Research Center. *Parenting in America: Outlook, Worries, Aspirations Are Strongly Linked to Financial Situation*, 2015. www.pewsocialtrends.org/2015/12/17/1-the-american-family-today/.

Pew Research Center. *Spring 2016 Global Attitudes Survey.* www.pewglobal.org/.

Pew Research Center. *U.S. Public Becoming Less Religious*, November 3, 2015. www.pewforum.org/2015/11/03/chapter-1-importance-of-religion-and-religious-beliefs/.

Pflaum, Nadia. "Trump: U.S. Spends More than 'Almost Any Other Major Country' on Education." *Politico Fact Ohio*, September 21, 2016. www.politifact.com/ohio/statements/2016/sep/21/donald-trump/trump-us-spends-more-almost-any-other-major-country/.

Phi Delta Kappan Special Issue on Tracking and Detracking 77, no. 3 (1995).

Philip, Thomas, and Flávio S. Azevedo. "Everyday Science Learning and Equity: Mapping the Contested Terrain." *Science Education 101* (2017): 526–532.

Phillips, Deborah A., and Jack P. Shonkoff, eds. *From Neurons to Neighborhoods: The Science of Early Childhood Development.* Washington, DC: National Academies Press, 2000.

Phillips, Denis C., and Harvey Siegel. "Philosophy of Education." In *The Stanford Encyclopedia of Philosophy* (Winter 2015 Edition), ed. Edward N. Zalta. https://plato.stanford.edu/archives/win2015/entries/education-philosophy.

Phillips, Rich. "Toy Gun Leads to Florida Boy's Expulsion." *CNN.com*, October 6, 2010. www.cnn.com/2010/US/10/06/toy.gun.expelled/index.html.

Picower, Bree. "6 Elements of SJE." *Using Their Words.* www.usingtheirwords.org/?page_id=180/.

Plessy v. Ferguson, 163 U.S. 537, 1896.

Plyler v. Doe, 457 U.S. 202, 1982.

Popham, W. James. *F Is for Assessment*, 2005. www.edutopia.org/assessment/.

Population Reference Bureau, analysis of data from the U.S. Census Bureau. *2008–2015 American Community Survey.* http://datacenter.kidscount.org/data/tables/5064-children-living-in-families-where-no-parent-has-full-time-year-round-employment-by-race?loc=1&loct=1#detailed/1/any/false/573,869,36,868,867/10,11,9,12,1,185,13/11486,11487.

Powell, Michael. "Pa. Case Is Newest Round in Evolution Debate: 'Intelligent Design' Teaching Challenged." *Washington Post*, September 27, 2005, p. A03.

"Practice." *New Teacher Center.* www.newteachercenter.org/impact/practice/, retrieved on February 24, 2011.

Press Briefing By Press Secretary Jay Carney, Domestic Policy Council Director Melody Barnes, and Secretary of Education Arne Duncan, August 8, 2011. www.whitehouse.gov/the-press-office/2011/08/08/press-briefing-press-secretary-jay-carney-domestic-policy-council-direct.

Public Broadcasting Systems 2011 Survey on Media and Technology Use. *Deepening Connections: Teachers Increasingly Rely on Media and Technology.* www.grunwald.com/pdfs/PBS-Grunwald_2011_Annual_Ed_Tech_Study.pdf.

Public Education Network. *Open to the Public: Speaking Out on "No Child Left Behind"*, 2004. www.publiceducation.org/portals/nclb/hearings/national/Open_to_the_Public.pdf.

Public Education Network. *Open to the Public: Speaking Out on "No Child Left Behind"*, 2005. www.publiceducation.org/portals/nclb/hearings/national/Open_to_the_Public.pdf.

Pyle, Amy. "Attacking the Textbook Crisis." *Los Angeles Times*, September 29, 1997.

Quartz, Karen Hunter, Andrew Thomas, Lauren Anderson, Kimberly Barraza Lyons, Brad Olsen, and Katherine Masyn. "Careers in Motion: A Longitudinal Retention Study of Role Changing Patterns Among Urban Educators." *IDEA Technical Report*, UCLA, 2005. http://idea2.gseis.ucla.edu/publications/utec/wp/pdf/04.pdf.

Quinn, Helen, Okhee Lee, and Guadalupe Valdés. "Language Demands and Opportunities in Relation to Next Generation Science Standards for English Language Learners: What Teachers Need to Know." *Understanding Language*. Stanford University, 2013. http://ell.stanford.edu/sites/default/files/pdf/academic-papers/03-Quinn%20Lee%20Valdes%20Language%20and%20Opportunities%20in%20Science%20FINAL.pdf.

Rampey, Bobby D., Gloria S. Dion, and Patricia L. Donahue. *NAEP 2008 Trends in Academic Progress*. Washington, DC: National Center for Education Statistics, Institute of Education Sciences, U.S. Department of Education, April 2009. http://nces.ed.gov/nationsreportcard/pdf/main2008/2009479.pdf.

Ravitch, Diane. *The Death and Life of the Great American School System*. New York: Basic Books, 2011.

Ravitch, Diane. "Diversity and Democracy: Multicultural Education in America." *American Educator* *14*, no. *1* (Spring 1990): 18.

Ravitch, Diane. "In Need of a Renaissance: Real Reform Will Renew Not Abandon Our Neighborhood Schools." *American Educator* (Spring 2010): 10–22. www.aft.org/pdfs/americaneducator/summer2010/Ravitch.pdf.

Ravitch, Diane. "The South's New Re-segregation Plan: The Koch Brothers, ALEC and the Sneaky Scheme to Undo Brown v Board of Education." *Salon*, April 14, 2016. www.salon.com/2016/04/14/the_souths_new_re_segregation_plan_the_koch_brothers_alec_and_the_sneaky_scheme_to_undo_brown_v_board_of_education/.

Ray, Nicholas. *Lesbian, Gay, Bisexual and Transgender Youth: An Epidemic of Homelessness*. New York: National Gay and Lesbian Task Force Policy Institute and the National Coalition for the Homeless, 2006.

Redford, Jeremy, Danielle Battle, and Stacey Bielick. *Homeschooling in the United States: 2012 (NCES 2016-096.REV)*. Washington, DC: National Center for Education Statistics, Institute of Education Sciences, U.S. Department of Education, 2017.

Regents Exam Study Guides: The Complete Series. www.studyworld.com/books/study_guides/regents_exam_study_guides_.htm.

Reich, Robert. *The Work of Nations: Preparing Ourselves for 21st Century Capitalism*. New York: Knopf, 1991.

Renzulli, Joseph S., in an interview with Anne Turnbaugh Lockwood. "Beyond the Golden Chromosome." *Focus in Change*, a publication of the National Center for Effective Schools at the University of Wisconsin, Madison (no. 11, Fall 1993), p. 3.

Renzulli, Joseph S., and Sally Reis. "The Reform Movement and the Quiet Crisis in Gifted Education." *Gifted Child Quarterly 35* (1991): 26–35.

Renzulli, Joseph S., and Sally Reis. *The Schoolwide Enrichment Model: A Comprehensive Plan for Educational Excellence*. Mansfield Center, CT: Creative Learning Press, 1985.

Resnick, Lauren. *Education and Learning to Think*. Washington, DC: National Academy Press, 1983.

"Resolution: NCTE Will Oppose Common Core Standards and National Tests." *Schools Matter*, October 11, 2011. www.schoolsmatter.info/2011/10/resolution-ncte-will-oppose-common-core.html.

Reuters. *CAIR Asks DOE to Address Bullying of Muslim Students*, June 9, 2011. www.reuters.com/article/2011/06/09/idUS215018+09-Jun-2011+PRN20110609/.

Rible, Daniela. "First School in Lower 9th Ward Reopened." *New America Media*, August 30, 2007.

Rice, Jacob Mayer. *The Public School System of the United States* (1893), as quoted in Herbert Kliebard. *The Struggle for the American Curriculum: 1893–1958*. New York: Routledge, 1995, 34.

Richardson, John G. "Common Delinquent, and Special: On the Formalization of Common Schooling in the American States." *American Educational Research Journal 31*, no. 4 (1994): 695–723.

Richardson, Valerie. "School Head Fights 'Ethnic Chauvinism' in Arizona." *Washington Times*, July 28, 2009. www.washingtontimes.com/news/2009/jul/28/school-head-fights-ethnic-chauvinism-in-arizona/?page=all.

Riessman, Frank. *The Culturally Deprived Child*. New York: Harper & Row, 1962.

Rist, Ray. "Student Social Class and Teacher Expectations: The Self-Fulfilling Prophecy of Ghetto Education." In *Challenging the Myths: The Schools, the Blacks, and the Poor*. Reprint Series No. 5. Cambridge, MA: Harvard Educational Review, 1971.

Robelen, Eric W. "Majority of States' Standards Don't Mention 9/11." *Education Week*, 2011, www.edweek.org/ew/articles/2011/08/31/02sept11_ep.h31.html.

Robelen, Eric W. "Work Begins on 'Next Generation' of Science Standards." *Education Week*, February 9, 2010. www.edweek.org/ew/articles/2010/02/10/21science.h29.html?tkn=SPOFfprCmajnEL%2BWkFfxsr9%2B4xsDsmoxNteC.

Rogers, John S. "Community Schools: Lessons From the Past and Present." *UCLA IDEA Paper Series #1*, 1998.

Rogers, John S., and Carolyn Castelli. "Building Social Justice for a New Generation." *UCLA IDEA Occasional Paper*, 1996.

Rogers, John S., and Carolyn Castelli, eds. *Building Social Justice for a New Generation: Profiles of Social Justice Fellows From UCLA's Teacher Education Program, 1997*. Los Angeles: UCLA, 1997.

Rogers, John S., Jennifer Jellison Holme, and David Silver. "More Questions than Answers: CAHSEE Results, Opportunity to Learn, and the Class of 2006." *UCLA's IDEA*, 2005.

Rogers, John S., Jeannie Oakes, Sophie Fanelli, David Medina, Siomara Valladres, and Veronica Terriquez. "California Educational Opportunity Report." *University of California All Campus Consortium for Rich Diversity*. University of California Los Angeles, Institute for Democracy, Education, and Access, November 2007, pp. 1–28. http://idea.gseis.ucla.edu/publications/eor-07/2007-educational-opportunity-report-the-racialopportunity-gap/.

Rogers, John S., and Robert Polkinghorn. "The Inquiry Process in the Accelerated School: A Deweyan Approach to School Renewal." Paper presented at the *Annual Meeting of the American Educational Research Association*, Boston, 1990.

Rogoff, Barbara. *Apprenticeship in Thinking: Cognitive Development in Social Context*. New York: Oxford University Press, 1990.

Roosevelt, Eleanor. *You Learn by Living: Eleven Keys for a More Fulfilling Life*. Louisville, KY: Westminster John Knox Press, 1960, 60.

Rosenthal, Robert, and Lenore Jacobson. *Pygmalion in the Classroom*. New York: Holt, Rinehart & Winston, 1968.

Rosser, J. Martin. "The Decline of Literacy." *Education Week*, May 15, 1996.

Rothstein, Richard. *The Color of Law: A Forgotten History of How Our Government Segregated America*. New York: Liveright, 2017.

RSF Russell Sage Foundation—Chartbook of Social Inequality. www.russellsage.org/sites/all/files/chartbook/Income%20and%20Earnings.pdf.

Ruiz Soto, Ariel G., Sarah Hooker, and Jeanne Batalova. *ELL Information Center Fact Sheet Series*. Migration Policy Institute, 2015. www.migrationpolicy.org/research/states-and-districts-highest-number-and-share-english-language-learners.

Ryan, Alan. *John Dewey and the High Tide of American Liberalism*. New York: W.W. Norton, 1995.

Sadker, Myra, and David Sadker. *Failing at Fairness: How America's Schools Cheat Girls*. New York: Macmillan, 1994.

Santos, Fernanda, and Sharon Otterman. "City Teacher Data Reports Are Released." *New York Times*, February 24, 2012. www.nytimes.com/schoolbook/2012/02/24/teacher-data-reports-are-released.

Sapon-Shevin, Mara. "Building a Safe Community for Learning." In *To Become a Teacher: Making a Difference in Children's Lives*, ed. William Ayers. New York: Teachers College Press, 1995.

Saracho, Olivia N., and Bernard Spodek. *Contemporary Perspectives on Language Policy and Literacy Instruction in Early Childhood Education*. Charlotte, NC: Information Age Publishing, 2004.

Sarason, Seymour. *The Culture of the School and the Problem of Change*, 3rd ed. Boston: Allyn & Bacon, 1996.

Saulny, Susan. "Black? White? Asian? More Young Americans Choose All of the Above." *New York Times*, January 29, 2011. www.nytimes.com/2011/01/30/us/30mixed.html?_r=1&ref=raceremixed.

Saulny, Susan. "Census Data Presents Rise in Multiracial Population of Youths." *New York Times*, March 24, 2011. www.nytimes.com/2011/03/25/us/25race.html.

Saxe, Geoffrey. *Culture and Cognitive Development: Studies in Mathematical Understanding*. New York: Erlbaum, 1990.

Schieble, Melissa. "Reframing Equity Under Common Core: A Commentary on the Text Exemplar List for Grades 9–12." *English Teaching 13* no. *1* (2014): 155–168 (p. 158).

Schmidt, William. "Are There Surprises in the TIMSS Twelfth Grade Results?" *TIMSS United States*, Report No. 8. East Lansing, MI: TIMSS U.S. National Research Center, Michigan State University, April 1998.

Schmidt, William. *Facing the Consequences: Using TIMSS for a Closer Look at U.S. Mathematics and Science Education*. Dordrecht, The Netherlands: Kluwer Academic, 1999.

Schmidt, William, Curtis McKnight, and Senta Raizen. *A Splintered Vision: An Investigation of U.S. Mathematics and Science Education*. Boston: Kluwer Academic, 1997.

Schofield, Janet Ward. *Computers and Classroom Culture*. New York: Cambridge University Press, 1995.

"Scientifically Based Research." *ERIC Digest #167*. Clearinghouse on Educational Policy and Management, College of Education, University of Oregon, 2003. http://cepm.uoregon.edu/publications/digests/digest167.html.

Scribner, Sylvia, and Michael Cole. *The Psychology of Literacy*. Cambridge, MA: Harvard University Press, 1981.

Scull, Janie, and Amber M. Winkler. *Shifting Trends in Special Education*. Washington, DC: Thomas B. Fordham Institute, 2011.

Seashore Louis, Karen, and Sharon D. Kruse. *Professionalism and Community: Perspectives on Reforming Urban Schools*. Newberry Park, CA: Corwin Press, 1995.

"SEL Facts." *Collaborative for Academic, Social, and Emotional Learning*. http://casel.org/why-it-matters/sel-faqs/.

Senge, Peter M. *The Fifth Discipline: The Art and Practice of the Learning Organization*. London: Random House, 1990.

"September 11 and Our Classrooms." *Rethinking Schools 16*, no. *2* (Winter 2001/2002).

Severson, Kim. "Systematic Cheating Is Found in Atlanta School System." *New York Times*, July 5, 2011. www.nytimes.com/2011/07/06/education/06atlanta.html.

"S.F. Board OKs Reading of Works by Nonwhites." *Los Angeles Times*, March 21, 1998, p. 1.

Shappee, Rudolph T. "Serving the City's Children: San Diego City Schools, the First Fifty Years." *The Journal of San Diego History 37*, no. *2* (Spring 1991). www.sandiegohistory.org/journal/91spring/schools.htm.

Shavelson, Richard. "The Splintered Curriculum." *Education Week*, May 7, 1997, p. 38.

Shirley, Dennis. *Valley Interfaith and School Reform: Organizing for Power in South Texas*. Austin: University of Texas Press, 2002.

Sholz, John K., and Kara Levine. "U.S. Black-White Wealth Inequality." In *Social Inequality*, ed. Kathryn M. Neckerman. New York: Russell Sage Foundation, 2004, 895–929.

Shor, Ira. *Empowering Education: Critical Teaching for Social Change*. Chicago: University of Chicago Press, 1992.

Simmons, Andrew. "The Elusive Teacher Next Door." *San Francisco Chronicle*, June 28, 2017. www.theatlantic.com/education/archive/2017/06/the-elusive-teacher-next-door/531990/.

Sirotnik, Kenneth. "Equal Access to Quality in Public Schooling: Issues in the Assessment of Equity and Excellence." In *Access to Knowledge: The Continuing Agenda for Our Nation's Schools*, rev. ed., ed. John I. Goodlad and Pamela Keating. New York: The College Board, 1994, 159–185.

Sizer, Theodore. *Horace's Hope: What Works for the American High School.* Boston: Houghton Mifflin, 1996.

Slavin, Robert. *Cooperative Learning: Theory, Research, and Practice.* Englewood Cliffs, NJ: Prentice Hall, 1995.

Slavin, Robert. "How Title I Can (Still) Save America's Children." *Education Week,* May 21, 1997, p. 52.

Sleeter, Christine E. *The Academic and Social Value of Ethnic Studies: A Research Review.* Washington, DC: National Education Association Research Department, 2011.

Sleeter, Christine E. "Becoming White: Reinterpreting a Family Story by Putting Race Back Into the Picture." *Race, Ethnicity and Education 14,* no. 4 (2011): 421–433.

Sleeter, Christine E. *Critical Family History: Placing History in a Sociocultural Historical Context.*   https://sites.google.com/a/christinesleeter.org/critical-family-history/Home/critical-family-history-theory/.

Sleeter, Christine E. "Learning Disabilities: The Social Construction of a Special Education Category." *Exceptional Children 53,* no. 1 (1986): 46–54.

Sleeter, Christine E. "Reform and Control: An Analysis of SB 2042." *Teacher Education Quarterly 30,* no. 1 (2003): 19–30.

Sleeter, Christine E. "Standardizing Imperialism." *Rethinking Schools Online 19,* no. 1 (2004): 1–6.

Sleeter, Christine E. *Un-standardizing the Curriculum: Multicultural Teaching in the Standards-based Classroom.* New York: Teachers College Press, 2005.

Sleeter, Christine E. "Why Is There Learning Disabilities? A Critical Analysis of the Birth of the Field in Its Social Context." In *The Formation of the School Subject Matter: The Struggle for Creating an American Institution,* ed. T. S. Popkewitz. New York: Falmer Press, 1987, 210–237.

Smith, Judy. "From High Tech to High School." *Forum,* UCLA Graduate School of Education and Information Studies, 2005.

Smith, Marshall S., and Jennifer O'Day. "Systemic School Reform." In *The Politics of Curriculum and Testing (Politics of Education Association Yearbook),* ed. Susan H. Fuhrman and Betty Malen. London: Taylor & Francis, 1991, 233–267.

Snider, William. "Schools Are Reopened in Selma Amid Continuing Racial Tension." *Education Week,* February 21, 1990.

Sobol, Thomas. "Revising the New York State Social Studies Curriculum." *Teachers College Record 95,* no. 2 (2003): 258–272.

Social Issues. *In US, More Adults Identifying as LGBT,* January 11, 2017. www.gallup.com/poll/201731/lgbt-identification-rises.aspx.

Soltero, Carlos R. "Plyler v. Doe (1982) and Educating Children of Illegal Aliens." In *Latinos and American Law: Landmark Supreme Court Cases.* Austin, TX: University of Texas Press, 2006, 118–132.

Southern Education Foundation. *Race and Ethnicity in a New Era of Public Funding for Private Schools: Private School Enrollment in the South and the Nation,* 2016. www.southerneducation.org/getattachment/be785c57-6ce7-4682-b80d-04d89994a0b6/Race-and-Ethnicity-in-a-New-Era-of-Public-Funding.aspx.

Southern Poverty Law Center. *SPLC Testifes About Increase in Anti-Muslim Bias,* March 29, 2011. www.splcenter.org/get-informed/news/splc-testifes-about-increase-in-anti-muslim-bias/.

Spargo, John. *The Bitter Cry of Children.* New York: Macmillan, 1906.

Spear-Swerling, Louise, and Robert J. Sternberg. *Off Track: When Poor Readers Become Learning Disabled.* Boulder, CO: Westview Press, 1996.

Sperling, Melanie, and Sarah W. Freedman. "Research on Writing." In *Handbook of Research on Teaching,* ed. V. Richardson. Washington, DC: American Educational Research Association, 2001, 370–389.

Spring, Joel. *American Education.* Boston: McGraw-Hill, 1996.

Spring, Joel. *The American School, 1642–1990.* New York: Longman, 1990.

Springer, Matthew, Lam Pham, and Tuan Nguyen. *Teacher Merit Pay and Student Test Scores: A Meta-Analysis,* Unpublished paper, 2017. https://my.vanderbilt.edu/matthewspringer/working-papers/.

Stall, Susan, and Randy Stoecker. "Community Organizing or Organizing Community? Gender and the Crafts of Empowerment." *Working Paper.* http://comm-org.wisc.edu.

Stanford School ReDesign Network. *Ten Features of Effective Design.* www.srnleads.org/data/pdfs/10_features.pdf.

Stanton-Salazar, Ricardo. *Manufacturing Hope and Despair: The School and Kin Support Networks of U.S.-Mexican Youth.* New York: Teachers College Press, 2001.

Starnes, Bobby, and Eliot Wigginton, eds. *A Foxfire Christmas: Appalachian Memories and Traditions.* Chapel Hill: University of North Carolina Press, 1996.

Statement Regarding the NAACP's Resolution on a Moratorium on Charter Schools, October 15, 2016. www.NAACP.org/latest/statement-regardingNAACPs-Resolution-Moratorium-charter-schools/.

"State Testing: An Interactive Breakdown of 2015–2016 Plans." *Education Week,* April 1, 2016. www.edweek.org/ew/section/multimedia/state-testing-an-interactive-breakdown-of-2015-16. html.

Steele, Claude. "Race and the Schooling of Black Americans." *The Atlantic Monthly,* April 1992, pp. 68–78.

Steele, Claude. "A Threat in the Air: How Stereotypes Shape the Intellectual Identities and Performance of Women and African-Americans." *American Psychologist 52* (1997): 613–629.

Steele, Claude. *Whistling Vivaldi: And Other Clues to How Stereotypes Affect Us.* New York: W. W. Norton & Company, Inc., 2010.

Steinberg, Laurence. *Beyond the Classroom.* New York: Simon & Schuster, 1996.

Sternberg, Robert. "Myths, Countermyths, and Truths About Intelligence." *Education Researcher 25* (March 1996): 11–16, 13.

Sternberg, Robert. "A Waste of Talent: Why We Should (and Can) Teach to All Our Students Abilities." *Education Week,* December 3, 1997, p. 56.

Stevenson, Harold, and James Stigler. *The Learning Gap: Why Our Schools Are Failing and What We Can Learn From Japanese and Chinese Education.* New York: Simon & Schuster, 1994.

Stigler, James, and James Hiebert. "Cameras in the Classroom: International Video Survey Examines Mathematics Teaching Practices in Three Countries." *Connections.* UCLA Graduate School of Education, Spring 1977, 1–5; also included on the website of the Third International Mathematics and Science Study at www.ed.gov/NCES/timss/video/.

Stille, Alexander. "The Paradox of the New Elite." *New York Times,* October 22, 2011, p. SR1.

Stillman, Jamy, and Lauren Anderson. *Teaching for Equity in Complex Times.* New York: Teachers College Press, 2017.

Straughn, Jeremy B., and Scott L. Feld. "America as a 'Christian Nation'? Understanding Religious Boundaries of National Identity in the United States." *Sociology of Religion 71,* no. 3 (2010): 280–306.

Strauss, Valerie. "Three Big Problems With School 'Choice' that Supporters Don't Like to Talk About." *Washington Post,* May 3, 2017. www.washingtonpost.com/news/answer-sheet/wp/2017/05/03/three-big-problems-with-school-choice-that-supporters-dont-like-to-talk-about/?utm_term=.06f47fefd308.

Strauss, Valerie. "Why So Many Parents Are Freaking Out About Common Core Math?" *The Washington Post,* November 8, 2014. www.washingtonpost.com/news/answer-sheet/wp/2014/11/08/why-so-many-parents-are-freaking-out-about-common-core-math/?utm_term=. 15b22d25a6f4.

"Study: Hard Courses Help Urban ACT's." *New York Times,* January 15, 1998.

Summers, Lawrence H. *Remarks at NBER Conference on Diversifying the Science and Engineering Workforce.* Cambridge, MA: Harvard Office of the President, June 14, 2005.

Suro, Roberto. "Cavazos Criticizes Hispanics on Schooling." *New York Times,* April 11, 1990, p. B8.

Talbert, Joan. "Professionalism and Politics in High School Teaching Reform." *International Journal of Educational Change 3* (2002): 277–281.

Taylor, Kate. "A Manhattan School District Where School Choice Amounts to Segregation." *New York Times,* June 7, 2017. www.nytimes.com/2017/06/07/nyregion/a-manhattan-district-where-school-choice-amounts-to-segregation.html.

"Technology Counts 2017: Where Schools Stand." *Education Week.* www.edweek.org/ew/toc/2017/06/14/index.html.

Tharp, Roland. *Transforming Teaching: Achieving Excellence, Fairness, Inclusion, and Harmony.* Boulder, CO: Westview Press, 2000.

Thernstrom, Stephan, and Abigail Thernstrom. *No Excuses: Closing the Racial Gap in Learning.* New York: Simon and Schuster, 2003.

Thomas B. Fordham Institute. *Our Review of the Common Core State Standards.* http://standards.educationgadfly.net/commoncore/math/.

Title I of the Elementary and Secondary Education Act of 1965.

Title IX of the Education Amendments of 1972, 20 U.S.C.A. §§ 1681–1688.

Tomlinson, Carol Ann. "Differentiated Instruction in the Regular Classroom: What Does It Mean? How Does It Look?" *Understanding Our Gifted 14,* no. *1* (2001): 3–6.

Tomlinson, Carol Ann. *How to Differentiate Instruction for Mixed-Ability Classrooms.* Alexandria, VA: Association for Supervision and Curriculum Development, 1995.

Tomlinson, Carol Ann, and Jay McTighe. *Integrating Differentiated Instruction & Understanding by Design.* Alexandria, VA: Association for Supervision and Instruction, 2006.

"Toy Gun Leads to Florida Boy's Expulsion." *CNN,* October 6, 2010.

"Tragic Side of Mission Era Being Told." *Los Angeles Times,* September 2, 1997.

Trump, Donald. 2017. www.facebook.com/DonaldTrump/videos/10156570856100725/, retrieved on June 15, 2017.

Tyack, David. *The One Best System: A History of American Urban Education.* Cambridge, MA: Harvard University Press, 1974.

Tyack, David, and Elisabeth Hansot. *Managers of Virtue: Public School Leadership in America, 1820–1980.* New York: Basic Books, 1982.

UCLA Community School. *Research, Practice and Policy Brief,* Spring 2017. http://cs.gseis.ucla.edu/assets/CS17-PolicyBrief-Web.pdf.

United Nations. *Convention on the Rights of the Child,* 2001. www.unicef.org/crc/.

United States Department of Labor, Bureau of Labor Statistics. *Labor Force Statistics From the Current Population Survey,* 2017. www.bls.gov/cps/cpsaat07.htm.

University of Wisconsin-Madison, Institute for Research on Poverty. *Reducing Health Disparities by Poverty Status,* 2015. www.irp.wisc.edu/publications/policybriefs/pdfs/PB4-ProvenPolicies ToReduceHealthDisparities.pdf.

Urbina, Ina. "It's a Fork, It's a Spoon, It's a . . . Weapon?" *New York Times,* October 11, 2009. www.nytimes.com/2009/10/12/education/12discipline.html?ref=education.

The Urban Institute. *Children of the Undocumented: Growing Up Under a Cloud.* www.urban.org/events/Children-of-the-undocumented.cfm.

The Urban Institute. *Investor-Owners in the Boom and Bust,* 2011. www.metrotrends.org/commentary/mortgage-lending.cfm.

The Urban Institute. *Issues in Focus: Immigration.* www.urban.org/content/IssuesInFocus/immigrationstudies/immigration.htm.

U.S. Bureau of Labor Statistics. *2010 American Community Survey.* http://factfinder2.census.gov/faces/tableservices/jsf/pages/productview.xhtml?pid=ACS_10_1YR_B01001G&prodType=table.

U.S. Bureau of Labor Statistics. *Child Poverty in the United States 2009 and 2010: Selected Race Groups and Hispanic Origin.* www.census.gov/prod/2011pubs/acsbr10-05.pdf.

U.S. Bureau of Labor Statistics. *Current Population Survey.* Annual Social and Economic Supplements. www.census.gov/cps/.

U.S. Bureau of Labor Statistics. *Educational Attainment in the United States: 2010,* April 2011. www.census.gov/hhes/socdemo/education/data/cps/2010/tables.html.

U.S. Bureau of Labor Statistics. *How We're Changing, Demographic State of the Nation: 1997.* Washington, DC: U.S. Department of Commerce, 1997.

U.S. Bureau of Labor Statistics. *Income, Poverty, and Health Insurance Coverage in the United States: 2010,* September 2011. www.census.gov/prod/2011pubs/p60-239.pdf.

U.S. Bureau of Labor Statistics. *Living Arrangements of Children, 2009.* www.census.gov/prod/2011pubs/p70-126.pdf.

U.S. Bureau of Labor Statistics. *Occupational Outlook Handbook, 2010–11 Edition, Overview of the 2008–18 Projections*. www.bls.gov/oco/oco2003.htm.

U.S. Census Bureau. *Income and Poverty in the United States*, 2014. www.census.gov/.

U.S. Census Bureau. *Income and Poverty in the United States*, 2015. www.census.gov/content/dam/Census/library/publications/2016/demo/p60-256.pdf.

U.S. Census Bureau. *Living Arrangements of Children: 2009*, 2011. www.census.gov/prod/2011pubs/p70-126.pdf.

U.S. Commission on Civil Rights. *Minorities in Special Education (2007 Briefing)*, 2009. www.usccr.gov/pubs/MinoritiesinSpecialEducation.pdf.

U.S. Department of Agriculture. *USDA National School Lunch Program*. www.fns.usda.gov/cnd/lunch/.

U.S. Department of Education. *29th Annual Report to Congress on the Implementation of the Individuals With Disabilities Education Act*, 2007. www2.ed.gov/about/reports/annual/osep/2007/parts-b-c/29th-vol-2.pdf.

U.S. Department of Education. *Comparability of State and Local Expenditure Among Schools Within Districts*, November 2011. www2.ed.gov/rschstat/eval/title-i/school-level-expenditures/school-level-expenditures.pdf.

U.S. Department of Education. *The Condition of Education*, 2011. http://nces.ed.gov/programs/coe/.

U.S. Department of Education. *The Condition of Education*, 2017. http://nces.ed.gov/programs/coe/.

U.S. Department of Education. *Digest of Education Statistics*, 2010. http://nces.ed.gov/fastfacts/display.asp?id=65.

U.S. Department of Education. *Overview: The Federal Role in Education*. www2.ed.gov/about/overview/fed/role.html.

U.S. Department of Education. *Reading First*. www2.ed.gov/programs/readingfrst/index.html.

U.S. Department of Education. *The State of Racial Diversity in the Educator Workforce*, June 2016. www2.ed.gov/rschstat/eval/highered/racial-diversity/state-racial-diversity-workforce.pdf.

U.S. Department of Education, National Center for Education Statistics. *Digest of Education Statistics, 2010*, 2011. http://nces.ed.gov/fastfacts/display.asp?id=64.

U.S. Department of Education, National Center for Education Statistics. *Educational Technology in U.S. Public Schools: Fall 2008 (NCES 2010–034)*. Washington, DC: U.S. Government Printing Office, 2010. http://nces.ed.gov/fastfacts/display.asp?id=46.

U.S. Department of Education, National Center for Education Statistics. *International Outcomes of Learning in Mathematics Literacy and Problem Solving: PISA 2003 Results From the U.S. Perspective (NCES 2005–003)*. Washington, DC: U.S. Government Printing Office, 2004.

U.S. Department of Education and Office for Civil Rights. *Civil Rights Data Collection (CRDC)*, 2013–14, 2016. http://ocrdata.ed.gov.

U.S. Department of Education and Office for Civil Rights. *A First Look: Key Data Highlights on Equity and Opportunity Gaps in Our Nation's Public Schools*, October 2016.

U.S. Department of Education, Office of Elementary and Secondary Education. *State Plans to Ensure Equitable Access to Excellent Teachers*, 1915. www2.ed.gov/programs/titleiparta/equitable/titleiiequityanalysis1031.pdf.

U.S. Department of Education, Office of Planning, Evaluation and Policy Development, Performance Information Management Service. *Free and Reduced-Price Lunch Eligibility Data in EDFacts: A White Paper on Current Status and Potential Changes*, Washington, DC, 2012.

U.S. Department of Education, Office of Special Education Programs. *Individuals With Disabilities Education Act (IDEA) Database*. www2.ed.gov/programs/osepidea/618-data/state-level-data-files/index.html#bcc, retrieved on September 25, 2015.

U.S. Department of Health and Human Services, Administration for Children and Families. *Trends in Foster Care and Adoption*, June 2011. www.acf.hhs.gov/programs/cb/stats_research/afcars/tar/report18.htm.

U.S. Department of Health and Human Services, Administration for Children and Families. *Trends in Foster Care and Adoption: FY 2006-FY 2015*, 2015. www.acf.hhs.gov/sites/default/files/cb/trends_fostercare_adoption2015.pdf.

U.S. Department of Housing and Urban Development. *The 2008 Annual Homeless Assessment Report to Congress: A Summary of Findings*, July 2009. www.hmis.info/ClassicAsp/documents/2008AHARSummary.pdf.

U.S. Department of Housing and Urban Development. 1997 report. Cited in Ronald Brownstein. "Cities Still Carry Poverty Burden, HUD Study Says." *Los Angeles Times*, June 23, 1997, pp. A1, A12.

Useem, Elizabeth. "Student Selection Into Course Sequences in Mathematics: The Impact of Parental Involvement and School Policies." *Journal of Research on Adolescence 1*, no. *3* (1991): 231–250.

U.S. House of Representatives. H.R. 236. *Student Bill of Rights.*

U.S. Surgeon General. *Youth Violence: A Report of the Surgeon General*, 2001. www.surgeongeneral. gov/library/youthviolence/report.html.

Valdez, Guadalupe. *Con Respecto: Bridging the Distances Between Culturally Diverse Families and Schools*. New York: Teachers College Press, 1996.

Valencia, Richard, ed. *The Origins of Deficit Thinking: Educational Thought and Practice*. London: Falmer Press, 1997.

Valenzuela, Angela. *Leaving Children Behind: How "Texas-Style" Accountability Fails Latino Youth.* Albany: State University of New York Press, 2005.

Valenzuela, Angela. *Subtractive Schooling: U.S.-Mexican Youth and the Politics of Caring*. Albany: State University of New York Press, 1999.

van Geel, Mitch, Paul Vedder, and Jenny Tanilon. "Bullying and Weapon Carrying a Meta-analysis." *JAMA Pediatrics 168*, no. *8* (2014): 714–720. doi:10.1001/jamapediatrics.2014.213. http://jamanetwork.com/journals/jamapediatrics/fullarticle/1879724.

Vedantam, Shankar. "Bilingualism's Brain Benefits." *Washington Post*, June 14, 2004, p. A07.

Vevea, Rebecca. "Emanuel's Point Man on School Closings." *Chicago News Cooperative*, November 22, 2011. www.chicagonewscoop.org/emanuels-point-man-on-school-closings-prepares-to-release-list/.

Villegas, Anamaria M., and Susan M. Watts. "Life in the Classroom: The Influence of Class Placement and Student Race/Ethnicity." Paper presented at the *Annual Meeting of the American Educational Research Association*, Chicago, IL, April 1991.

Waugh, Janet, as quoted in *Kansas Restores Evolution Standards for Science Classes*, February 14, 2001. http://articles.cnn.com/2001-02-14/us/kansas.evolution.02_1_science-standards-kansas-board-sue-gamble?_s=PM:US.

Webb, James T., and Diane Latimer. "ADHD and Children Who Are Gifted." *ERIC Digest #E522*. Reston, VA: Council for Exceptional Children, ERIC Clearinghouse on Disabilities and Gifted Education, 1993.

Webster's Encyclopedic Unabridged Dictionary of the English Language. New York: Gramercy Books, 1989.

Weller, Christian E., and Jaryn Fields. *The Black and White Labor Gap in America: Why African Americans Struggle to Find Jobs and Remain Employed Compared to Whites*. Washington, DC: Center for American Progress, 2011. www.americanprogress.org/issues/2011/07/pdf/black_unemployment.pdf.

Wells, Amy Stuart. *Time to Choose: America at the Crossroads of School Choice Policy*. New York: Hill & Wang, 1993.

Wells, Amy Stuart, and Robert L. Crain. "Perpetuation Theory and the Long-Term Effects of School Desegregation." *Review of Educational Research 64*, no. *4* (1994): 531–555.

Wells, Amy Stuart, and Irene Serna. "The Politics of Culture: Understanding Local Political Resistance to Detrack-ing in Racially Mixed Schools." *Harvard Educational Review 66*, no. *1* (1996): 93–118.

Welner, Kevin G. "The Dirty Dozen: How Charter Schools Influence Student Enrollment." *Teachers College Record*, April 2013. www.tcrecord.org ID Number: 17104.

Welner, Kevin G. *Legal Rights, Local Wrongs: When Community Control Collides With Educational Equity*. Buffalo: State University of New York Press, 2001.

Welner, Kevin G., Jeannie Oakes, and Gilbert FitzGerald. *Report to the Woodland Hills School District*. Los Angeles: UCLA Graduate School of Education and Information Studies, 1998.

Wenger, Etienne. *Communities of Practice: Learning, Meaning, and Identity*. Cambridge, UK: Cambridge University Press, 1999.

West, Cornel. "The Limits of Neopragmatism." *Southern California Law Review 63* (1990): 1747, 1749.

"What Is Authentic Assessment?" *Authentic Assessment Toolbox*. http://jfmueller.faculty.noctrl.edu/toolbox/whatisit.htm.

What Works Clearinghouse. http://ies.ed.gov/ncee/wwc/.

Whitehurst, Grover J. *Statement of Grover J. Whitehurst, Assistant Secretary for Research and Improvement, Before the Senate Committee on Health, Education, Labor and Pensions*. Washington, DC: U.S. Department of Education, 2002. www2.ed.gov/offces/OERI/speeches/06252002.html.

Whitman, David. *The Surprising Roots of the Common Core: How Conservatives Gave Rise to "Obamacore"*. Washington, DC: The Brookings Institution, Brown Center on Education Policy, 2015, 4.

Whitman, Walt. "Song of Myself." In *Leaves of Grass*. New York: Rome Brothers, 1855.

Who Built America? CD-ROM produced by the American Social History Project, City University of New York, as cited in *Rethinking Schools*, Summer 1996. www.ashp.cuny.edu.

Wiener, Jon. "Why Did Harvard Give a PhD for a Discredited Approach to Race and IQ?" *The Nation*, May 11, 2013.

Wiggins, Grant. "Common Core Standards Don't Add Up." *Education Week*, September 27, 2011. www.edweek.org/ew/articles/2011/09/28/05wiggins.h31.html.

Wiley, Edward W., William J. Mathis, and David R. Garcia. *The Impact of the Adequate Yearly Progress Requirement of the Federal "No Child Left Behind" Act on Schools in the Great Lakes Region*. Tempe, AZ: Education Policy Studies Laboratory, 2005.

Wiley, Terrence G. "In What Ways Are the Common Core State Standards De Facto Language Education Policy?" In *Common Core Bilingual and English Language Learners: A Resource for Educators*, ed. Guadalupe Valdés, Kate Menken, and Mariana Castro. Philadelphia: Calston Publishing, 2015, 10–11.

Wilgoren, Jodi. "Kansas Approves Challenges to Evolution." *New York Times*, November 9, 2005. www.nytimes.com/2005/11/09/national/09kansas.html?scp=1&sq=Evolution%20of%20Kansas%20science%20standards%20continues%20as%20Darwin&st=cse.

Williams v. State of California, complaint filed May 17, 2000. www.decentschools.org.

The Williams Institute. *United States Census Snapshot: 2010*. http://williamsinstitute.law.ucla.edu/research/census-lgbt-demographics-studies/us-census-snapshot-2010/.

Williams, Luther S. *Letter to the California State Board of Education*, December 11, 1997.

Willis, Paul *Learning to Labour: How Working Class Kids Get Working Class Jobs*. Farnborough, Hants: Saxon House, 1977.

Wills, John S. "The Situation of African Americans in American History: Using History as a Resource for Understanding the Experiences of Contemporary African Americans," as quoted in Hugh Mehan, Dina Oka-moto, Angela Lintz, and John S. Wills, "Ethnographic Studies of Multicultural Schools and Classrooms." In *Handbook of Research on Multicultural Education*, ed. James A. Banks and Cherry A. McGee Banks. New York: Macmillan, 1995, 129–144.

Wilson, Valerie, and William M. Rodgers III. *Black-White Wage Gaps Expand With Rising Wage Inequality*. Economic Policy Institute, 2016. www.epi.org/files/pdf/101972.pdf.

Wiltz, Teresa. *Why More Grandparents Are Raising Children*. Washington, DC: Pew Charitable Trust, 2016. www.pewtrusts.org/en/research-and-analysis/blogs/stateline/2016/11/02/why-more-grandparents-are-raising-children.

Wineburg, Sam. *Historical Thinking and Other Unnatural Acts: Charting the Future of Teaching the Past*. Philadelphia: Temple University Press, 2001.

"Wisconsin Teachers Union Protests Governor Scott Walker's Bill; Idaho, Florida Follow." *Huffington Post*, February 17, 2011. www.huffingtonpost.com/2011/02/17/teachers-union-wisconsin-scott-walker_n_824888.html.

WNYC News. *Allegations of Islam Indoctrination in Public Schools Spread to New Jersey*, April 2017. www.wnyc.org/story/allegations-islam-indoctrination-public-schools-spread-nj/.

Woodson, Carter Godwin. *The Education of the Negro Prior to 1861: A History of the Education of the Colored People of the United States From the Beginning of Slavery to the Civil War*, 1919. Project Gutenberg, 2004. www.gutenberg.org/etext/11089/.

Woodson, Carter Godwin. *The Mis-Education of the Negro*. Washington, DC: Associated Publishers, 1933.

Worrell, Frank C. "Why Are There so Few African Americans in Gifted Programs?" In *Surmounting All Odds: Education, Opportunity, and Society in the New Millennium*, ed. C. C. Yeakey and R. D. Henderson. Greenwich, CT: Information Age, 2003, 423–454.

Ybarra, Susanne. "UCLA Conference Emphasizes Importance of Partnerships in Education." *Diverse Education*, June 21, 2017. http://diverseeducation.com/article/98081/.

Yonezawa, Susan. *Making Decisions About Students' Lives*. PhD diss., University of California, Los Angeles, 1997.

Yonezawa, Susan, and Jeannie Oakes. "Making All Parents Partners in the Placement Process." *Education Leadership 56*, no. 7 (April 1999): 33–36.

Yosso, Tara. *Critical Race Counterstories Along the Chicana/Chicano Educational Pipeline*. New York: Routledge, 2005.

Yosso, Tara. "Whose Cultural Has Capital? A Critical Race Theory Discussion of Community Cultural Wealth." *Race, Ethnicity, & Education 8*, no. 1 (March 2005): 69–91.

"Young Black Men Faced Highest Rate of US Police Killings in 2016." *The Guardian*, January 8, 2017. www.theguardian.com/us-news/2017/jan/08/the-counted-police-killings-2016-young-black-men.

Zangwill, Israel. *The Melting Pot: The Great American Drama* (Play). Washington, DC, 1908. www.gutenberg.org/ebooks/23893.

Zerubavel, Eviatar. *The Fine Line: Making Distinctions in Everyday Life*. Chicago: University of Chicago Press, 1993.

Zinn, Howard. *Teaching a People's History*. http://zinnedfuproject.org.

Zong, Jie, and Jeanne Batalova. *Frequently Requested Statistics on Immigrants and Immigration in the United States*. Migration Policy Institute, 2017. www.migrationpolicy.org/article/frequently-requested-statistics-immigrants-and-immigration-united-states.

Photo Credits

Index

Page numbers in italic indicate a figure and in bold indicate a table on the corresponding page.